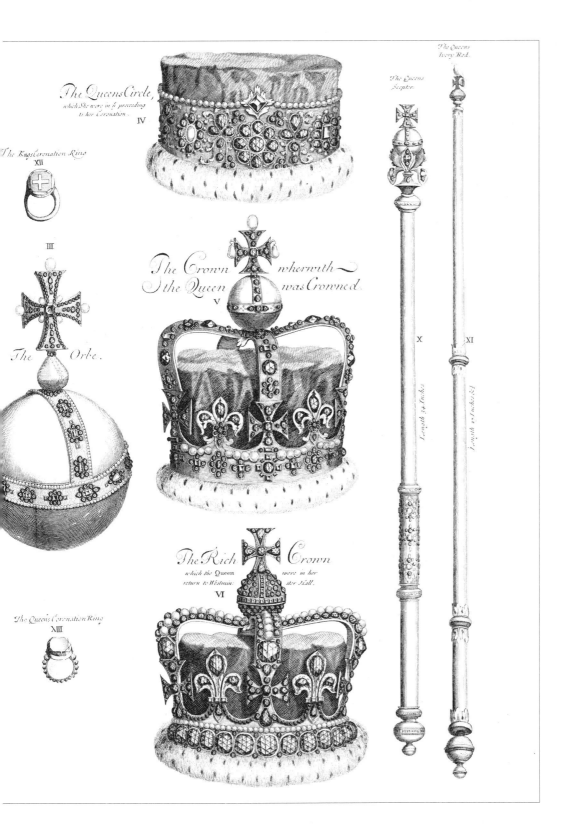

The Queens Circle, *which She wore in ye proceeding to her Coronation.* IV

The Kings Coronation Ring XII

III

The Orbe.

The Crown *wherwith* the Queen *was Crowned.* V

The Queens Scepter.

The Queens Ivory Rod.

Length 54 Inches

Length 42 Inches

X

XI

The Rich Crown *which the Queen wore in her return to Westmin: ster Hall.* VI

The Queens Coronation Ring XIII

Also by Roy Strong

The Anointing of David from a manuscript related to the Winchester Bible,
illumination, English, *c*.1160–80

CORONATION

A HISTORY OF KINGSHIP AND
THE BRITISH MONARCHY

ROY STRONG

HarperCollins*Publishers*

HarperCollins*Publishers*
77–85 Fulham Palace Road
Hammersmith, London w6 8jb

www.harpercollins.co.uk

Published by HarperCollins*Publishers* 2005
9 8 7 6 5 4 3 2 1

A catalogue record for this book
is available from the British Library

ISBN: 0–00–716054–2

Typeset in Postscript Linotype Minion
with Castellar and Spectrum display
by Rowland Phototypesetting Ltd,
Bury St Edmunds, Suffolk

Printed and bound in Italy by
Lego Spa, Italy

TO

THE DEAN AND CHAPTER

OF

WESTMINSTER

FROM

THEIR

HIGH BAILIFF

AND

SEARCHER OF THE SANCTUARY

2005

CONTENTS

PREFACE

This book is a direct consequence of having the honour of holding the post of High Bailiff and Searcher of the Sanctuary at Westminster Abbey. It is a position lost in the mists of the medieval past when its orbit of activity was practical. Today the post, along with that of High Steward, is purely an honorary one – but not without purpose, for it enables the Dean and Chapter to draw into the Abbey's service those who might bear witness to the faith it upholds and the ideals of the nation that it has come to epitomise. This book is my contribution.

It is a remarkable fact that the history of the English Coronation, particularly in the modern period, remains such a neglected field of study. The pioneer work remains Percy Schramm's still magisterial study published in English in 1937. To that we must add the recent monumental and definitive catalogue of the Crown Jewels in two vast volumes in a limited edition and hence inaccessible to the general public. The present book sets out to remedy that lack by providing both for the general and more specialised reader the first overall documented history of the Coronation in a single volume.

The need for such a publication is an urgent one as another Coronation will sooner or later take place. In researching and writing this book I have been struck by the widespread ignorance as to the nature of this ancient rite, *au fond* a foundation stone of the British state and a bulwark against its total secularisation. It is no empty pageant but one that, like so many other historic customs and institutions under attack today which some wish cheerfully to sweep away, has proved itself amazingly flexible over the centuries. Any nation calls for rites of passage and the Coronation, with its central concept of setting a single human being apart by dint of anointing with holy oil as the embodiment of both crown and nation, is the greatest of them all.

I began my scholarly life almost half a century ago working under the late Dame Frances Yates on Elizabethan court pageantry. At the time I confess to finding Coronations dull and, I thought, merely repetitious. How wrong I was! Researching this book has been one long revelation as the ceremonial inaugurating a new reign gradually revealed its ability to respond to and reflect every theological, political, social and cultural nuance over the centuries.

I do not claim to have written the last word on this subject. Who could? But I have opened up a topic that in some areas has already attracted fine scholarly contributions. My debt to those scholars, particularly those working on the early and medieval periods, I acknowledge with gratitude. One of the problems of working on this subject is the sheer quantity of the manuscript and printed material, so much that inevitably at some point a line firmly had to be drawn or else the book would never have been finished and the result would have been unwieldly. What is new is the attempt throughout to draw the camera's lens back and place what can all too easily become an antiquarian account of a series of isolated pageants into the wider perspective of what those involved at the time were setting out to achieve.

Coronation could not have been written without recourse to manuscript material. In the case of the early, medieval and Tudor periods that has been fairly fully explored. It is the material for the modern period which has largely gone without investigation and it is that which in the main has preoccupied me. I cannot express my gratitude enough for the graciousness extended to me at all the archives explored to write this book: the College of Arms, the British Library, Westminster Abbey Muniments, Lambeth Palace Library, St John's College, Cambridge and the Public Record Office. In the case of the last I am grateful to R. W. O'Hara who, under my direction, worked through the material there. From the outset, thanks to the enthusiastic support of Garter King of Arms, I was given unfettered access to the huge collections in the College. Robert Yorke, their librarian, saw that, each time I went, everything I asked for was to hand. Equally Dr Richard Mortimer and Dr Tony Trowles saw that I was fed with the plethora which exists in the Abbey. At St John's College, Cambridge, I was looked after by Jonathan Harrison, the Special Collections Librarian.

The advent of the information technology revolution truly also facilitates far speedier research. The ability to consult the British Library catalogue online and so much of its manuscript holdings remains a constant source of wonder to me. What has also speeded research is that splendid British Library resource, Articles Direct, from their supply centre at Boston Spa.

I cannot list nor remember now everyone who has helped me on my way but I record my gratitude to the Lord Chamberlain, Lord Luce, who welcomed this project which meant that, with the gracious permission of Her Majesty The Queen, I was given free access to all the material at the College of Arms, in particularly that connected with 1953. Amongst others who have assisted I record: Dr Andrew Hughes (University of Toronto), Dr Simon Thurley (English Heritage), John M. Burton (Surveyor of the Fabric of Westminster Abbey), Professor David Sturdy (University of Ulster), Dr Pamela Tudor-Craig, Clare Browne (Victoria & Albert Museum), Dr Richard Barber, Daniel McDowell, The Hon. Lady Roberts (Royal Archives, Windsor Castle), and Anna Keay (English Heritage). Particular gratitude is owed to the Very Revd Dr Wesley Carr, Dean of Westminster, for reading the closing chapters and making several pertinent suggestions.

I am one of those authors who rather depends on an inspired and committed editor who is prepared, which is unusual, to read what I write as I go along. In Arabella Pike I had just that. Once finished a book passes into the hands of the publication team whom I would like also to thank, in particular the designer Vera Brice. She has had to cope with the decision, a welcome one, that this book should incorporate what in effect is the largest visual archive on the topic.

ROY STRONG
The Laskett
June 2005

ILLUSTRATIONS

Overleaf The Coronation of Queen Victoria, painting, 1838

THE MONARCHY AD 871 TO THE PRESENT

Dynasty	Reign	Monarch	Coronation date in Westminster Abbey (with other locations as applicable)	Coronation of Queen or consort, date as Monarch's unless otherwise stated
Anglo-Saxons	871–899	ALFRED THE GREAT	(not known if crowned)	Ealswith (not known if crowned)
	899–959	EDWARD THE ELDER ÆLFWARD ATHELSTAN EDMUND I, EDRED, EADWIG	8 June 901, Kingston upon Thames 4 September 925, Kingston upon Thames 940, 946, 955 or 956, Kingston upon Thames	
	959–975	EDGAR	Whit Sunday 973, Bath	👑 Emma ? Whit Sunday 973
	975–1016	EDMUND THE MARTYR ÆTHELRED II		
	1016–1035	CANUTE	(not known if crowned)	1. Ælfgifu; 2. Emma (not known if crowned)
	1037–1042	HAROLD I, HARTHACNUT		
	1042–1066	EDWARD THE CONFESSOR	Easter Sunday, 1043, Winchester	👑 Emma
	1066	HAROLD II	6 January 1066	
Normans	1066–1087	WILLIAM I (The Conqueror)	Christmas Day, 1066	👑 Matilda
	1087–1100	WILLIAM II (Rufus)	26 September 1087	
	1100–1135	HENRY I	5 August 1100	1. Edith; 2. Adeliza (not known if crowned)
	1135–1154	STEPHEN	22 December 1135	
Angevins & Plantagenets	1154–1189	HENRY II	19 December 1154	👑 Eleanor of Aquitaine
	1189–1199	RICHARD I (Lionheart)	3 September 1189	👑 Berengaria of Navarre (Coronation date unknown)
	1199–1216	JOHN	Ascension Day, 29 May 1199	👑 2. Isabella of Angoulême (Coronation date unknown)
	1216–1272	HENRY III	1. 28 October 1216, Gloucester 2. 17 May 1220, Westminster	👑 Eleanor of Provence 1236
	1272–1307	EDWARD I	19 August 1274	👑 1. Eleanor of Castile 👑 2. Margaret of France (Coronation date unknown)
	1307–1327	EDWARD II	25 February 1308	👑 Isabella of France
	1327–1377	EDWARD III	1 February 1327	👑 Philippa of Hainault
	1377–1399	RICHARD II	16 June 1377	👑 1. Anne of Bohemia 22 January 1382 👑 2. Isabella of France 5 January 1397
Yorkists & Lancastrians	1399–1413	HENRY IV	13 October 1399	👑 Joan of Navarre 26 February 1403
	1413–1422	HENRY V	9 April 1413	👑 Catherine of France 2 February 1421
	1422–1461 1470–1471	HENRY VI	1. 6 November 1429, Notre Dame, Paris 2. 16 December 1431, Westminster	👑 Margaret of Anjou 30 May 1445

	Reign	Monarch	Coronation date in Westminster Abbey (with other locations as applicable)	Coronation of Queen or consort, date as Monarch's unless otherwise stated
Yorkists & Lancastrians	1461–1470 1471–1483	EDWARD IV	28 June 1461	👑 Elizabeth Woodville 26 May 1465
	1483	EDWARD V	6 July 1483	
	1483–1485	RICHARD III	30 October 1485	👑 Anne Neville
Tudors	1485–1509	HENRY VII	24 June 1509	👑 Elizabeth of York 25 November 1487
	1509–1547	HENRY VIII	20 February 1547	👑 1. Catherine of Aragon 👑 2. Anne Boleyn 1 June 1553
	1547–1553	EDWARD VI	1 October 1553	
	1553–1558	MARY I (Tudor)	15 January 1559	👑 Philip of Spain
	1558–1603	ELIZABETH I		
Stuarts	1603–1625	JAMES I and VI	1. 29 July 1567, Stirling 2. 25 July 1603, Westminster	👑 Anne of Denmark
	1625–1649	CHARLES I	1. 2 February 1626, Westminster 2. 8 June 1633, Edinburgh, Holyrood	Henrietta Maria of France (*acknowledged queen but not crowned with Charles in Abbey*)
	Commonwealth			
	1660–1685	CHARLES II	1. 1 January 1651, Scone Abbey 2. 23 April 1661, Westminster	👑 Catherine of Braganza
Stuarts	1685–1688	JAMES II	23 April 1685	👑 2. Mary of Modena
	1689–1702	WILLIAM III & MARY II	11 April 1689	👑 Joint Monarchs
	1702–1714	ANNE	23 April 1702	George, Prince of Denmark
Hanoverians	1714–1727	GEORGE I	20 October 1714	
	1727–1760	GEORGE II	11 October 1727	👑 Caroline of Ansbach
	1760–1820	GEORGE III	22 September 1761	👑 Charlotte of Mecklenburg-Strelitz
	1820–1830	GEORGE IV	19 July 1821	Caroline of Brunswick (*excluded from Coronation*)
	1830–1837	WILLIAM IV	8 September 1831	👑 Adelaide of Saxe-Coburg Meiningen
	1837–1901	VICTORIA	28 June 1838	Prince Albert of Saxe-Coburg-Gotha
	1901–1910	EDWARD VII	9 August 1902	👑 Alexandra of Denmark
House of Windsor	1910–1936	GEORGE V	22 June 1911	👑 Mary of Teck
	1936	EDWARD VIII		
	1936–1952	GEORGE VI	12 May 1937	👑 Elizabeth Bowes-Lyon
	1952–	ELIZABETH II	2 June 1953	Prince Philip of Greece

PROLOGUE

1953

On my dressing table rests a small leather box with a lid embossed in gold with a stylised crown and below it the date 1953. The graphics are unmistakably of the period we associate with the Festival of Britain, which indeed opened only two years before. At the time I was coming up to being seventeen and in the sixth form of Edmonton County Grammar School sited on the fastnesses of the North Circular Road. The box was a gift to every boy in the school on the occasion of the Coronation of Queen Elizabeth II. In it we were to keep our shirt studs, a fact which immediately dates the object to a now vanished sartorial era. The object is as fresh as the day on which I received it and I keep it to hand to remind me of my earliest memory of real spectacle, as I was one of the two young people from my school selected to be bussed into central London on the great day to stand on the Victoria Embankment and watch the great procession make its way to Westminster Abbey. The date was 2 June 1953.

The fact that it was the forward and not the return procession that I saw turned out to be a stroke of luck, for it enabled me to return home in time to watch most of the coronation on television. The arrival of that in the sitting room of the north London terraced house in which I grew up was another major event. But to return to the morning. That I recall as being a grey one, but then at that age just about everything I could remember had been grey, for the coronation was just eight years on from the end of the war, one which had reduced the country to penury. The capital still visibly wore the monochrome robes of that conflict, enlivened on the day by the splashes of colour of the street decorations and by the tiny red, white and blue Union flags which we clutched and waved.

It was a long wait and, as I was not tall, my chances of seeing anything were not that great. Nonetheless, there was the thrill of anticipation as a military band was heard from afar and then the great procession unfolded. I do not think that I ever saw more than the top half of a horse and rider. No matter, for two images stick in mind, ones shared at the time by millions of others. The first was an open carriage over which the capacious figure of Queen Salote of Tonga presided, beaming and waving to everyone in a manner which won all hearts. The second, of course, was the encrusted golden coach in which the Queen rode with the Duke of Edinburgh. It must have been lit from within for the Queen's smiling features and the glitter of her diamonds remain firmly fixed in my memory.

Subsequent to that there were the pictures on the tiny television screen, hypnotic, like some dream or apparition, certainly images enough to haunt a stage-struck and historically inclined youth for the rest of his life. But I add to that the subsequent film of the coronation, for there it was on the large screen in colour, never to be forgotten, glittering, glamorous, effulgent. This was the England I fell in love with, a country proud of its great traditions and springing to life again in a pageant that seemed to inaugurate a second Elizabethan age. This was a masque of hope, a vision to uplift the mind after years of drear deprivation.

In retrospect I had seen part of what is now recognised to have been the greatest public spectacle of the twentieth century. What I was not to know was that this impoverished child in his dreary navy-blue blazer, cheap grey flannel trousers and black and gold school tie was to stand, half a century on, resplendent in scarlet and black in my role as High Bailiff and Searcher of the Sanctuary of Westminster Abbey, along with the whole college, to welcome the Queen at the great service which commemorated her coronation.

It is now all so long ago that most readers may well ask what is a coronation? Where did such an extraordinary ceremonial come from? What formed and shaped it over the centuries? And how can such a pageant ever have any relevance to the Britain of the twenty-first century? When I last visited the crown jewels in the Tower of London, part of that display was a projection of the film of the coronation. Looking at it, I could not believe that such a thing had been staged in the second half of the twentieth century and, equally, I could not help wondering whether one would ever be staged again. But then that was a viewpoint which sprang from ignorance, unaware of the rich resonances of the ritual or its deep significance in terms of the committal of the monarch to the people. It was questions like these that prompted me to write this book, launching me on a voyage that proved to be one of constant surprise. Amongst many other things it was to reveal the coronation as the perfect microcosm of a country that has always opted for evolution and not revolution. But I must begin at the beginning, and that takes us back not just centuries but no less than a thousand years.

1

The Lord's Anointed

THE EARLIEST ACCOUNT of an English Coronation comes in a life of St Oswald, Archbishop of York, by a monk of Ramsay, written about the year 1000.[1] He describes how, in the year 973, Edgar (959–75) 'convoked all the archbishops, bishops, all great abbots and religious abbesses, all dukes, prefects and judges, and all who had claim to rank and dignity from east to west and north to south over wide lands' to assemble in Bath. They gathered, we are told, not to expel or plot against the king 'as the wretched Jews had once treated the kind Jesus', but rather 'that the most reverent bishops might bless, anoint, consecrate him, by Christ's leave, from whom and by whom the blessed unction of highest blessing and holy religion has proceeded'. The text refers to the King as *imperator*, emperor, for by that date he was not only ruler of Mercia but also of Northumbria and of the West Saxons. Edgar had assumed the imperial style by 964, by which time his several kingdoms also included parts of Scandinavia and Ireland. This was a king who had come to the throne at the age of sixteen and was to die at 32. His reign was Anglo-Saxon England at its zenith, an age of peace and an era when, under the aegis of great churchmen, headed by Dunstan, Archbishop of Canterbury, a radical reform of the Church was achieved. Bath, the Roman Aquae Sulis, the place chosen for the King's Coronation, even in the tenth century and in spite of all the barbarian depredations, would still have been a city which retained overtones of its past imperial grandeur, a setting fit for its revival by a great Saxon King.

The day chosen for the event was Pentecost, the feast of the Holy Spirit. Edgar, crowned with a rich diadem and holding a sceptre,

Previous page St Edward's Crown as re-recreated for the Coronation of Charles II, 1661

Opposite The Coronation of Harold, the last Saxon king, as depicted in the Bayeux Tapestry, *c.*1075

awaited the arrival of a huge ecclesiastical procession, all in white vestments: clergy, bishops, abbots, abbesses and nuns, along with those described as aged and reverend priests. The King was led by hand to the church by two bishops, probably ones representing the northern and southern extremities of his realm, the bishops of Chester-le-Street (later to become the mighty palatine see of Durham) and of Wells. In the church the great lay magnates were already assembled. As the splendid procession wound its way from exterior secular and into interior sacred space the anthem *Firmetur manus tua* was sung: 'Let thy hand be strengthened, and thy right hand be exalted, Let justice and judgement be the preparation of thy seat, and mercy and truth go before thy face.' Here in the open air had already begun that great series of incantations to the heavens to endue this man with the virtues necessary for the right exercise of kingship.

On entering the church Edgar doffed his crown and prostrated himself before the altar while the Archbishop of Canterbury, St Dunstan, perhaps the greatest figure in the history of the Anglo-Saxon church, intoned the Te Deum, that majestic hymn of praise to God in which 'all angels cry aloud, the heavens and all the powers therein' and in which petition is made to 'save thy people and bless thine heritage. Govern them and lift them up for ever.' That prostration was an act of self-obliteration, for what was enacted before those assembled was the 'death' and 'rebirth' of a man who was to leave the church fully sanctified and endowed with grace by Holy Church as a king fit to rule. St Dunstan was so moved by the king's action that he wept tears of joy at his humility. But such a rebirth is not bestowed without conditions, and so the great ceremonial opened with an action which was to set the English Coronation apart from any other and also account for its extraordinary longevity.

The *promissio regis*, the Coronation oath, consisted of what were known as the *tria praecepta*, three pledges by the King to God. First, 'that the Church of God and all Christian people preserve peace at all times', secondly, 'that he forbid rapacity and all iniquities to all degrees' and, finally, 'that in all judgments he enjoin equity and mercy . . .'. These came in the form of a written document, whether in Latin or the vernacular is unknown, which was delivered to the King by Dunstan and then placed on the altar. The archbishop then administered the oath to the King seated. We do not know whether the oath was sworn aloud by the King to the assembled clergy and lay magnates. Logic would suggest that this happened. The placing of the *tria praecepta* at the opening of the Coronation service remained through the centuries one of the defining documents as to the nature of the monarchy. Monarchy in England never became, as it did in France, absolute. It always remained conditional upon being faithful to the three pledges given in the oath, to maintain peace, administer justice and exercise equity and mercy.[2]

That done, the action moved on to the bestowal of unction, the anointing of the King's head by the bishops (whose identities are not given, but presumably were the Archbishops of Canterbury and York) with holy oil, chrism, a fragrant mixture of oil and balsam, poured from an animal's horn. In this ritual occurred the sacred moment of rebirth, one accompanied by a succession of prayers invoking the Kings of the Old Testament as exemplars of the virtues to be granted through this action, recalling also those kings, prophets and priests who had been similarly anointed and calling upon the Holy Spirit to descend and sanctify Edgar in the same way. Following this, the most solemn moment of the whole Coronation service, came the anthem *Unxerunt Solomonem*: 'Zadok the Priest and Nathan the Prophet anointed Solomon King; and they blew the trumpets, and piped the pipes, and rejoiced with great joy, so that the earth rent with the sound of them; and they said, "God save King Solomon. Long live the King, may the King live for ever." ' All of this, for over a thousand years, has been re-enacted at every Coronation, although ennobled since the eighteenth century by Handel's radiant and triumphant music. It is extraordinary to grasp that its roots lie as far back as the last quarter of the tenth century. Nor has the ritual of investiture which followed changed that much. Upon Edgar were bestowed the following regalia: the ring, 'the seal of holy faith'; the sword by which to vanquish his enemies, the foes of Holy Church, and protect the realm; the 'crown of glory and righteousness'; the sceptre, 'the sign of kingly power, the rod of the kingdom, the rod of virtue'; and the staff or *baculus* 'of virtue and equity'. A Mass followed and, after the whole ceremony was over, those assembled moved again from sacred to secular space where a great feast was held. Edgar, wearing a crown of laurel entwined with roses, sat enthroned, flanked by the two archbishops, presiding over a banquet of the great magnates. Elsewhere his Queen held court over a parallel one for abbots and abbesses. This description in the life of St Oswald is detailed enough to establish that the text or ordo used was

Zadok the Priest anoints
Solomon, illumination,
French XVth century

that known as the Second Recension, a consideration of which I will
come to later in this chapter. That scholars have established this to be
the case means that we can deduce that Edgar's Queen must also have
been crowned, although the Monk of Ramsay does not refer to the fact,
for the ordo includes prayers for this which permit her to be anointed
like her husband but only allow for investiture with two ornaments, a
ring and a crown.

So much for what we do know about the 973 Coronation, but there is
much that we do not. We do not know where the action was staged or
anything about the gestures used, the vestments worn, the appearance
of the regalia or the music sung. There is also the puzzling fact that,
although Edgar had been a king since 957, he waited until 973 for his
Coronation. Some scholars argue that he had undergone an earlier cer-

emony of blessing and unction and that this one was to mark his ascendancy to imperial status, while others maintain that his humility was such that he deliberately waited until he reached thirty, the canonical age a man could be made a bishop and also about the age when Christ was baptised and began his ministry (Luke 3: 23).

What is in no doubt, however, is that this spectacle was the apogee of his reign, designed to mark Edgar's imperial status and blaze it abroad both in his own country and on the Continent. Shortly after that he received the homage of his subject kings, who symbolically rowed him from his palace to the church at Chester while he tended the prow. The Coronation was also an outward manifestation of Edgar's commitment to the reform movement associated with Archbishop Dunstan, which introduced new rules to govern monastic life based on those used on the Continent at the great abbey of Cluny. So the Coronation ordo enshrined a vision of the English monarchy which reflected that role, one which owed its debt to continental exemplars, the king cast as *rector et defensor ecclesiae*. Time and again this

The Anointing of David from the Glasgow Psalter, illumination, English, early XIIth century

ordo, the Second Recension, draws out, by means of symbolism and doxology, the parallel between kingship and episcopacy. This was emphasised in the choice of the day for the ceremony, one on which the Holy Spirit descended giving the Apostles the grace to carry out their task. What is astonishing to a modern reader is that here already at such a very early date are virtually all the elements of our present Coronation ceremony as it was last enacted in 1953 for Elizabeth II. The fact that these same elements could be used again and again through the centuries and continue to be responsive to the ideas and aspirations of far different eras is a gigantic index as to just how flexible the English Coronation ceremony continues to be. As a consequence, apart from the papacy, no other inauguration ritual can boast such longevity. Such rituals should not be lightly dismissed as so much insubstantial pageantry. They are powerful icons in which a society enshrines its identity and its continuity. The importance of them has been admirably summed up by Meyer Fortes:

> The mysterious quality of continuity through time in its organisation and values, which is basic to the self-image of every society, modern, archaic, or primitive, is in some ways congealed in these installation ceremonies . . . Politics and law, rank and kinship, religious and philosophical concepts and values, the economics of display and hospitality, the aesthetics and symbolism of institutional representation, and last but not least the social psychology of popular participation, all are concentrated in them.[3]

When Edgar was crowned, such a rite of inauguration in some form had been in existence in Anglo-Saxon England for over a century. How did such a thing come about and whence did it come? To answer that I must widen our camera's lens to take in the fate of Western Europe in the aftermath of the collapse of the Roman Empire, the rise in its place of the barbarian kingdoms and the establishment as a consequence of the role of the Church as the bestower of legitimacy on dynasties by dint of the rite of unction.

What is unction and how did it come to occupy such a central position in king-making?[4] The first question is a relatively simple one to answer, the second far more complex. Unction was the application to a modern ruler of a ritual recorded in the Old Testament, the anointing of a chosen leader with holy oil. In the First Book of Samuel the elders ask the prophet to choose a king for them who will act both as their judge and their leader in war. Samuel chose Saul. 'Then Samuel took a vial of oil, and poured it upon his head, and kissed him, and said, Is it not because the Lord hath anointed thee to be captain over his inheritance?' (I Samuel 10: 1).

Later in the same book Samuel is led to choose Saul's successor and the ritual is re-enacted: 'Then Samuel took the horn of oil, and anointed him in the midst of his brethren: and the Spirit of the Lord came upon David from that day forward' (I Samuel 16: 13).

Even more important was the precedent set by David's son, Solomon, always cast as the ideal king. In the First Book of Kings David summons Zadok the priest, Nathan the prophet and Benaiah, the son of the chief priest, and orders them to mount his son, Solomon, on David's own mule and bring him down to Gihon: 'And let Zadok the priest and Nathan the prophet anoint him there King over Israel: and blow ye with the trumpet, and say, God save King Solomon. Then ye shall come up after him, that he may come and sit upon my throne; for he shall be king in my stead' (I Kings 1: 34–5).

They did what was commanded of them: 'And Zadok the priest took an horn of oil out of the tabernacle, and anointed Solomon. And they blew the trumpet; and all the people said, God save King Solomon' (I Kings 1: 39; I Chronicles 29: 22–3).

In these biblical passages virtually all the elements which were to constitute the early Coronation ceremonies are already there: the selection of a king, his anointing with holy oil by a priest, his acclamation by the people and his enthronement. The Old Testament was equally specific as to the effects of anointing. In the case of Saul, 'And the Spirit of the Lord will come upon thee, and thou shalt prophesy with them, and shalt be turned into another man' (I Samuel 10: 6).

Detail of an initial letter from the Winchester Bible with, at the top, the Anointing of David, illumination, English, *c.*1155-60 and *c.*1170-85

The Elevation on a Shield
and Coronation of an
Eastern Emperor,
illumination, Byzantine,
XIVth century

In New Testament terms it was an outward action representing an
inward descent upon the King of the Holy Spirit. Collectively it was
from the application of these texts to the task of king-making in the
seventh and eighth centuries that the earliest ordines were to emerge.

But there is a huge time lapse between those Old Testament rulers
and the earliest application of unction to the barbarian kings. That
bridge can be crossed by the continuing role played by sacred oils in the
life of the Early Church. The Old Testament did not only provide precedents for the anointing of kings, it also gave ones for the anointing of
priests as well as artefacts connected with worship. God commanded
Moses to prepare the holy oil of anointing for hallowing the tabernacle,
ark, table, vessels and altar for the ritual of worship and also for anointing Aaron and his sons as priests (Exodus 29: 7–8; Leviticus 8: 10–12). As
a consequence holy oil was used at the consecration of churches and
altars and in the ordination of both bishops and priests.

The most important of all the holy oils was chrism, a mixture of
olive oil and balsam which was used in the Early Church in the rite of
baptism and confirmation.[5] The word chrism itself was a Greek
rendering of the Hebrew word for the holy oil of anointing. The exotic fragrance and richness of chrism opened it up to early writers bestowing on it an allegorical significance as embodying the fullness of

sacramental grace and the gifts of the Holy Spirit with the sweetness of Christian virtue. Only the pope and the bishops could consecrate holy oils, an event which took place annually at the solemn Mass on Maundy Thursday from at least as early as the fifth century. One oil was without the addition of balsam. This was used for anointing the sick, for extreme unction and for other uses by the faithful. The other was chrism, used at baptism and confirmation. Both forms of oil are integral to the history of the Coronation, for although initially kings were to be anointed with chrism, gradually that right was withheld as the Schoolmen were to argue that chrism was a purely ecclesiastical institution whose use should be confined to the ordination of bishops and priests and not for royal unction.

One final fact. Although oil was native to the Mediterranean cultures, to the Northern barbarian tribes it was a luxury item, rare, costly and exotic. Within this context it is hardly surprising that oil became viewed as a potent substance capable of solving every difficuty. When the pope bestowed unction on the first Carolingian King Pepin in 751 it was done not only in the context of Old Testament exemplars, but also in the light of people's knowledge of and confidence in the efficacy of holy oil in relation both to the sacraments and to bodily healing.

That a rite of anointing kings with holy oil emerged between the seventh and eighth centuries came directly out of the Christianisation of the barbarian kingdoms.[6] With the final dissolution of the Roman Empire in the West in 476 there evolved in its place the *imperium christianum* presided over by the pope. That spiritual empire was to assume a temporal dimension thanks to the Donation of Constantine, a forgery datable to 752–7, a document which purported to declare Pope Sylvester I (314–5) and his successors rulers not only of Italy but of all the provinces which had once made up the Roman Empire in the West. This, in effect, cast the popes into the role of king-makers, one which they were able to exercise through the introduction of the rite of unction as barbarian kings converted and sought divine sanction for their kingship. As pagans they had claimed descent from the gods. Now they were endowed with a new kind of divinity as 'the Lord's anointed' (I Samuel 26: 11), a phrase which was rendered in the Vulgate version of the Bible as Christus Domini, employing the Greek word 'christos' meaning anointed, which, in the Middle Ages, was seen as the origin of the name of Christ.

The bestowal of unction was the prerogative of the Church which, although through its role it established a ruler as being sacred and set apart from ordinary mortals, simultaneously demonstrated that that could only be done thanks to their access to supernatural forces. In this way regnum was to be subject to sacerdotium in the medieval scheme of things. It was the pope and bishops who controlled and compiled the anointing rituals or ordines, filling them with prayers framing a vision of monarchy as they conceived it. That is vividly caught in the anointing prayer composed by Hincmar, Archbishop of Reims (c.806–82), *Omnipotens sempiterne Deus*, for the Coronation of Louis the Stammerer in 877, one which was to be incorporated into virtually every Coronation ordo thereafter: 'Almighty eternal God . . . we ask thee to attend to the prayers of our humility and to establish this thy servant in the high rulership of the kingdom, and anoint him with the oil of the grace of thy Holy Spirit wherewith thou hast anointed those priests, kings, prophets, and martyrs who through faith conquered kingdoms, worked justice, and obtained thy promises.'[7]

In this Holy Church invoked the descent of the Holy Spirit on to the candidate for kingship, making him a new man, transmitting through anointing the divine grace by which alone he would be able to fulfil his royal ministerium as defender of the Church. In this manner kingship became an office within the Church without bestowing on it any priestly status, or at least not at the outset. Only as the rite of Coronation developed and spread would the theocratic priestly view of kingship threaten to shatter this relationship of Church and State.

All of this could be grafted with ease on to any secular ceremony of installation which already existed within the pagan tradition. So the earliest ordines progress without difficulty from unction to the handing over to the King of royal insignia, initially jointly by both principes and pontifices, but soon after by the latter only. These could include items which may well have been part of any pre-Christian installation ceremony, ones like a sceptre or a long rod or *baculus*. One certain link with the pagan past was the placing of a galea or helmet on the King's head, which was only replaced by a crown in the tenth century. But the falling into place of all these elements into a common pattern was a gradual process involving several areas of Western Europe: Visigothic Spain, early Capetian France, Anglo-Saxon England and Celtic Ireland. It is to a consideration as to how these various strands eventually came together that we must now turn.

The advent of coronations

One of the earliest references to royal unction comes in a life of the Celtic saint, Columba, written by Abbot Adoman of Iona (679–704).[8] The monastery of Iona was the great centre of Celtic Christianity, a major seat of learning with daughter houses in Scotland and the north of England, so its influence spread wide. In his life of the saint the abbot recounts the story of Columba's anointing of Aidan mac Gabrain as King of Dalriada in the late sixth century:

> Concerning an angel of the Lord, who appeared in a vision to Saint Columba, then living in the island of Hinba; and who was sent to bid him ordain Aidan as king.
>
> At one time, while the memorable man was living in the island of Hinba, he saw one night, in a trance of the mind, an angel of the Lord, who had been sent to him, and who had in his hand a glass book of the ordination of kings. And when the venerable man had received it from the hand of the angel, by the angel's command he began to read it. But when he refused to ordain Aidan as king, according to what was commanded him in the book, because he loved Iogenan, Aidan's brother, more, the angel suddenly stretched out his hand and struck the holy man with a scourge, the livid scar from which remained on his side all the days of his life. And the angel added these words, saying: 'Know surely that I am sent to you by God, with the book of glass, in order that, according to what you have read in it, you shall ordain Aidan to the king-ship. But if you refuse to obey this command, I shall strike you again.'
>
> So when this angel of the Lord had appeared on three successive nights with the same book of glass in his hand, and had charged him with the same commands of the Lord, for the ordaining of the same king, the holy man submitted to the word of the Lord. He sailed over to the island of Io, and there, as he had been bidden, he ordained as King Aidan, who arrived about that time. And among the words of the ordination he

prophesied future things of Aidan's sons, and grandsons, and great-grandsons. And laying his hand upon Aidan's head he ordained and blessed him.[9]

Scholarly debate concludes that such an anointing never actually took place, but, on the other hand, the text can be taken as sure evidence of a strong desire by the abbots of Iona that they should consecrate the Dalriada kings. And in order to achieve that St Columba was cast in retrospect as the reincarnation of the Old Testament prophet Samuel. The text would also indicate that by the close of the seventh century such a book with a rite for unction actually existed. As a whole the episode worked, too, from an important premise: the assertion that the Church had a key role to play in king-making.

Within the Celtic world the next appearance of royal unction is in the *Collectio Canonum Hibernensis* (*c.* 690–725), in which there is a chapter headed 'De ordinatione regis' with a text which implies that anointing was part of the action. The world of seventh- and eighth-century Ireland was a turbulent one with up to one hundred and fifty kings at any one time and no automatic right of succession. The introduction of unction fulfilled the twofold purpose of increasing the influence of the Church and, at the same time, stabilising disputes over succession.

Much the same motives prompted its introduction in Visigothic Spain in 672. In this case it was the further legitimisation of an elected ruler, Wamba, who received unction in the royal city of Toledo as a sign that his kingdom had been bestowed by God. But by far the most important anointing was that of Pepin, the first Carolingian king of West Francia, in 751. Pepin brought to an end the rule of the Merovingian kings, seeking sanction for his action from the pope. This was a step in terms of power politics both in the interests of the new dynasty and of the papacy during precisely the years when the Donation of Constantine was forged. Unction under the aegis of the pope not only enhanced the mystique of the new dynasty but, by implication, cast the Franks as Israel reborn, the chosen people of God.[10]

As a consequence the second half of the eighth century saw an ever-escalating interplay between the papacy and the Carolingians. In the winter of 753 Pope Stephen II (752–7) crossed the Alps to reanoint Pepin and anoint his two sons. Charlemagne's sons were anointed in Rome in 781 and 800. In the former year Pope Adrian I (772–95) made two of Charlemagne's sons, Carloman King of Italy and Louis King of Aquitaine. But more important than any of these was what took place in Rome on Christmas Day 800 when Pope Leo III crowned Charlemagne as Holy Roman Emperor by placing a crown on his head. With that act arrived the second central symbolic action of any Coronation, the bestowal of a crown.[11]

Arguments about that Coronation and what it signified continue, but no one demurs from the fact that by crowning Charlemagne the pope was introducing a rite which was associated with the Byzantine emperors. It was also one, like anointing, with a firm biblical basis. In

Pope Leo III crowns Charlemagne Holy Roman Emperor in 800, illumination, French, XIVth century

16   CORONATION

the Second Book of Samuel an Amalekite brings David the crown and bracelet of Saul: 'and I took the crown that was upon his head, and the bracelet that was on his arm, and have brought them hither unto my lord' (II Samuel 1: 10). Even more graphic is the account of the crowning of Joash by the chief priest: 'And he brought forth the king's son, and put the crown upon him, and gave him the testimony; and they made him king, and anointed him; and they clapped their hands, and said, God save the King' (II Kings 11: 12).

Crowns had no role in barbarian installation ceremonies which could involve instead, as did the Anglo-Saxon ritual, the placing of a galea or helmet on the elected ruler's head. In the Eastern Empire, however, the crown had been adopted as early as the Emperor Constantine in the fourth century as a symbol of his regality and vice-regency of Christ on earth. The first Byzantine emperor to be crowned by a patriarch was Leo I in 457 and the first to be crowned in a church was Phocas (602–10), but only from the second half of the seventh century did all this come to rest in the great church of Hagia Sophia.[12] In 800, therefore, the pope did what had become the norm for the patriarch, crown an emperor, only this time one of the West. The people present all acclaimed Charlemagne as 'Augustus, crowned by God, Emperor of the Romans'. Thereafter crowns, in the case of the Holy Roman Emperors as often as not donated by the popes themselves, ousted helmets as Kings in the West opted for the style *a Deo coronatus*. In 816 yet another pope crossed the Alps, this time to crown Charlemagne's son, Louis the Pious, emperor in a ceremony which, for the very first time, brought together unction and crowning within a single ritual.

All of this represented the redefinition in the West of kingship as an office, one whose remit was defined by the Christian Church and its clergy. It was they who composed the rituals which turned king-making into a liturgical rite in which the central act was anointing, preceded by an agreement of conditions formulated in an oath and followed by investiture with regalia and enthronement. That this development gained momentum was due to two factors. One was that primogeniture was unknown at that date. The most suitable candidate for ruler was chosen from within a royal family by a process of election by the principes. This secular side of king-making did not suddenly vanish with the advent of Coronation rites. Each Coronation was always prefaced by certain rituals which took place in secular space,

Opposite Charlemagne enthroned as Holy Roman Emperor, illumination, Carolingian, IXth century

OVERLEAF
Left The Coronation of Charles the Bald as King of the Franks, illumination, Ottonian, IXth century

Right Otto II enthroned as Holy Roman Emperor, illumination, Ottonian, c.985

18   CORONATION

generally in the palace. It usually involved election and an enthrone-ment. We know little about such happenings because, unlike the Coronation in church, there was no tradition of compiling an ordo. The second reason why clerics came to play such a key role was that it was precisely during this period that they began to occupy a major part in the running of any state. In England, for instance, from as early as the reign of Athelstan (924–39) the king's council had at its core a group of bishops who were in constant attendance on the king and were crucial players in both the legislative and administrative process.

It was inevitable that sooner or later these new king-making cere-monies would call for being codified in written form. Special ordines first emerge during the eighth century in West Francia, the result of two personalities, Charles the Bald (823–77), King of West Francia and subsequently Holy Roman Emperor, and Hincmar, Archbishop of Reims (845–82), his principal councillor. The latter is generally acknowledged as being responsible for the compilation of the four earliest ordines, including those for the 13-year-old Judith on her mar-riage to Æthelwulf, King of Wessex, in 856 and for Charles's son Louis the Stammerer as King of Lotharingia in 869. These Frankish ordines were to be heavily drawn upon by those who compiled the ones for the Anglo-Saxon kings.

ANGLO-SAXON CORONATIONS

The Anglo-Saxons were made up of a mixture of tribes who came from an area of the Continent stretching from between the mouths of the rivers Rhine and Elbe. They began first to attack England from the third century on and then, by the middle of the fifth, decided to settle. By the close of the following century they had carved the country up into a series of petty kingdoms, each with its own royal family. The Anglo-Saxons were pagan, but during the seventh century were Christianised in the aftermath of Pope Gregory the Great's mission of 597 to Kent. A golden age of Christian civilisation followed, which was only disrupted by a fresh wave of invasions in the form of the Vikings. It was those which precipitated the rise to dominance of the royal house of Wessex, first under Alfred and then under his descendants throughout the tenth century. They were the first kings of a united England and it is with Alfred's descendants that we arrive for the first

time on firmer ground that they inaugurated their reigns with the rite of unction.

In common with the other Germanic tribes, kingship was central to the Anglo-Saxons. A ruler was elected from among the members of a royal race or dynasty, the *stirps regia*, who were descendants of the god, Woden. The making of a new king involved some kind of enthronement, investiture with weapons or regalia, the mounting of an ancestral burial mound, even a symbolic marriage with the earth-goddess. Such installation rites would certainly have included a feast and conceivably also, after the election but before any form of enthronement, some kind of ancestor of the Coronation oath. Insignia included a pagan spear or long staff (*baculus*), a helmet (galea) and a standard or banner, all three items connected with leadership in battle. To these customs the Vikings were to add, in the ninth century, an early form of throne, a stone or high seat, to which the king was conducted to the acclamation of the people.[13]

None of these presented any problems when the ceremony was Christianised, the only victim being the standard or banner. Otherwise everything was taken over into the Christian rite, even the helmet which only gave way to a crown in the tenth century. The earliest representation of a King of England wearing a crown is on the charter of the New Minster at Winchester, dated 966, which depicts Edgar wearing one adorned with fleurons. In 1052 Edward the Confessor was to order an imperial crown and he is depicted, as indeed is Harold, the last Saxon King, wearing one with fleurons in the Bayeux Tapestry. The spear or long staff was easily accommodated within the Christian scheme of things by references to the Rod of Aaron and that of Moses, descendants of the wooden staffs borne by kings and judges in ancient civilisations.[14]

All of these items from the pagan past were redeployed in what was a Christian liturgy. What little we know about early Coronation ceremonies stems in the main from the surviving liturgical texts known as ordines or recensions. There are four major ones in the history of the English Coronation. The first two pre-date the Norman Conquest in 1066 and together form perhaps the most complicated documents in the entire history of the ceremony. Amongst both medievalists and liturgical scholars they have been and still remain subjects of lively debate, often of a highly complex and technical nature. In what follows I have attempted to superimpose some degree of clarity and, inevitably, simplification upon what is a highly contentious field of study, bearing

ENIT:AD:EDVVARDV: REGE

in mind, too, that most people's knowledge of liturgy in the twenty-first century tends to be minimal. An ordo comprises a liturgical sequence of prayers and blessings by which various actions are given sacramental significance, in particular by invoking divine sanction, blessings and the descent of the gifts of the Holy Spirit upon the person chosen as king. The fact that such rituals could only be performed by clergy, bishops in fact, means that the ordines for them came to appear in the service books of cathedrals, especially in what are called pontificals, that is a body of texts for ceremonies which can only be performed by a bishop. In many ways what these texts provide the reader with is something akin to the words of a Shakespeare play minus any stage directions or, to use ecclesiastical parlance, rubrics. If the latter existed at all – and it is likely that they did – they would have been in a separate book which would have told those involved what they should do. As a consequence of their absence we know nothing of the arrangement of the setting, the

Edward the Confessor, enthroned and clasping a baculus or rod, as he appears in the Bayeux Tapestry, *c.*1075 form taken by symbolic gestures like prostration and genuflection, the details of the dress worn or the music sung.

None of the surviving texts of these first two recensions can be dated as having been written before the year 900. What is certain is that, although they were written down much later, they record the format of rituals as they were performed at much earlier dates. Much scholarly attention has been focused upon the interconnexion of these texts and, although everyone agrees that they go back to earlier lost texts, there is little agreement as to exactly how much earlier. The issue is further clouded by the fact that what does survive can only be a fragment of what once existed, items which have defied the hand of time and wanton destruction. Nonetheless as documents they tell us a great deal about the nature of kingship in pre-Conquest England and about the relationship of Church and State.[15]

The First Recension exists in three manuscripts, of which the earliest is the Leofric Missal, written about the year 900 at the Abbey of St Vaast near Arras and brought to England about 1042 by Bishop Leofric of Exeter. Views at to what this text is range from it never having actually been used at all to being the normal rite used for the inauguration of the Kings of West Sussex from before 856, perhaps for the Coronation of Egbert in 839 or even earlier, at the close of the eighth century. In the academic argument over that, much hangs upon whether the ordo drawn up by Hincmar, Archbishop of Reims, in 856 for the marriage of the West Frankish princess, Judith, to the Anglo-Saxon King Æthelwulf was a wholly West Frankish compilation of his own or whether Hincmar was merely adapting his rite from what was an ancient Anglo-Saxon norm. If the latter is the case then the First Recension is a very old rite indeed.[16]

The two other manuscripts of the First Recension contain rubrics pointing to a date not earlier than the tenth century. The texts they contain are identical to the one in the Leofric Missal, except for the addition of two prayers from the ordo for Judith. The two manuscripts are the Pontifical of Egbert, Archbishop of York, datable to around 1000, and the 'Lanalet' Pontifical, which has been variously dated from the late tenth century to the 1030s.

Putting all of these together we emerge with a Coronation service which was in use a long time before 900, but, as I indicated, just how long before and for whom it was used is open to debate. The texts are headed 'Blessings on a newly elected king' and 'The Mass for kings on the day of their hallowing'. In the case of the various recensions I propose to present them in list form with the intention of giving the reader a clear idea of each ceremony's exact structure and sequence:

1. The service opens with an anthem: 'Righteous art thou, O Lord, and true is thy judgement' (Psalm 119: 137) and a psalm: 'Blessed are those that are undefiled in the way' (Psalm 119: 1).

2. A prayer that the King 'may with wisdom foster his power and might . . .'

3. An Old Testament reading from Leviticus (26: 6–9) with God's promise of peace, the defeat of enemies and the multiplication of people.

4. The gradual from Psalm 86: 2: 'Save thy servant' and the versicle 'Ponder my words, O Lord' (Psalm 5: 1). The Alleluia. 'The King shall rejoice in thy strength, O Lord)' (Psalm 21: 1) or 'Thou has set a crown of pure gold' (Psalm 21: 3).

5. Gospel reading from Matthew (22: 15–22) with the passage in which Christ calls for them to show him the tribute money and says: 'Render therefore unto Caesar the things which are Caesar's; and unto God the things that are God's.'

6. Three prayers invoking the attributes God should bestow on the King: the grace of truth, goodness, the spirit of wisdom and government and, finally: 'In his days let justice and equity arise . . . that . . . he may show to the whole people a pattern of life well-pleasing to thee . . . And so joining prudence with counsel, may he find with peace and wisdom means to rule his people . . .'

7. 'Here shall the bishop pour oil from the horn over the King's head with this anthem: 'Zadok the priest and Nathan the prophet . . .' (I Kings 1: 45) and the psalm 'The King shall rejoice in thy strength, O Lord' (Psalm 21: 1). Unction is accompanied by a collect recalling 'thy servant Aaron a priest, by the anointing of oil and afterwards by the effusion of oil, didst make the Kings and prophets to govern thy people Israel . . .'

8. The investiture: 'Here all the bishops, with the nobles give the sceptre into his hand', an action followed by a long series of short prayers calling down blessings and regal attributes. Then, 'Here shall the staff [*baculus*] be given into his hand', followed by a further prayer invoking the descent of blessings. Finally, 'Here all the bishops shall take the helmet and put it on the King's head' with a last invocation of blessings. After this 'All the

people shall say three times with the bishops and priests, May King N. live for ever. Amen. Amen. Amen. Then shall the whole people come to kiss the prince and be strengthened with a blessing.'

9. The Mass.

10. At the conclusion comes the *promissio regis* in the form of the *tria prae-cepta*: 'that the Church of God and all Christian people preserve the peace at all times', 'that he forbid rapacity and all iniquities to all degrees' and, lastly, 'that in all judgements he enjoin equity and mercy . . .'

We have no idea when and for whom this ordo was used. The earliest reference to unction being administered is recorded in the *Anglo-Saxon Chronicle* quite suddenly under the year 787 when it states that Ecgferth, the son of Offa, King of Mercia, was 'consecrated king'.[17] Presumably this was a means to ensure his succession to the throne. Then follows a complete silence until 4 September 925 when Athelstan was anointed by the Archbishop of Canterbury. Athelstan, along with Edward the Elder and Edgar, was one of the three great tenth-century Anglo-Saxon kings. In 937, he would rout an alliance of the Danes and rebel subject princes at the battle of Brunanburh. The location for his Coronation was Kingston upon Thames and it was followed by a great feast:

> *With festive treat the court abounds;*
> *Foams the brisk wine, the hall resounds:*
> *The pages run, the servants haste,*
> *And food and verse regale the taste.*
> *The minstrels sing, the guests commend,*
> *While in praise to Christ contend.*[18]

Kingston first appears in 835 or 836 as a meeting place for Egbert and Coelnorth, Archbishop of Canterbury. Edward the Elder, son of Alfred, and likewise a warrior who laid low the Danes, was crowned there in 901. Athelstan's brother, Edmund, was also crowned at Kingston in 940 and his brother, Eadred, in 946 and Edmund's son, Eadwig, in 955 or 956.[19] Once again we get an unexpected glimpse of what could be the reality of such an occasion. Eadwig is recorded as getting up during the Coronation feast and going to his chamber. Dunstan, the future Archbishop of Canterbury, and the Bishop of

Pages from the Leofric Missal, illumination, English, *c.*900

Lichfield were sent to fetch him back. What they saw was the unedifying sight of the new King with two women, Athelgifu and her daughter, Elfgifu, to whom the King was uncanonically married, and the crown, 'which shone with the various glitter of gold, silver and precious stones', tossed on to the floor. Unsavoury though the episode was it provides the earliest evidence that we have that the Kings now wore crowns.[20]

With the mention of Dunstan we can move on to a consideration of that other vexed document, the Second Recension. Everyone agrees that it was used under Dunstan's aegis for the great Coronation of Edgar in 973 and also that it was still in use in 1101. As it refers to a king crowned 'of the Angles and the Saxons' and to the person concerned as a successor to a glorious father, that could only mean Edward the Elder crowned on 8 June 901 or Athelstan, his son, crowned on 4 September 925. That at least provides some options for possible dating. What is also certain is that this ordo represents a revision of the First

Recension, bringing it into line with developments on the Continent.[21]

There are at least five versions of this text, of which the most important is that known as the Claudius Pontifical, which evidence indicates was written for and at Christ Church, Canterbury. The ordo is a fusion of insular with continental elements drawing on the Leofric and Egbert versions of the First Recension and marrying into them items drawn from Hincmar of Reims' ordo of Metz (869), the West Frankish ordo of *c.*900 (the Erdmann ordo) and what was called the ordo of Stavelot (the ordo of the Seven Forms). The resulting recension surpasses all of those upon which it was based in terms of clarity, structure and power of expression and language.

Although there are variations between the surviving manuscripts, once again I present the recension as a list, pointing up what had changed. The Second Recension, thanks to the inclusion of rubrics, paints a far fuller picture of the action than the first:

1. The ordo opens with the King discovered amidst his seniores, the ealdormen who have elected him.

2. Two bishops lead the King to the church while the choir chants the anthem, *Firmetur manus tua*: 'Let thy hand be strengthened, and thy right hand be exulted . . .', invoking the regal qualities of strength, justice, mercy and truth.

3. 'When the King is come to the church, he shall lie prostrate before the altar: and then shall the hymn *Te Deum laudamus* be sung to the end.'

4. 'After which he shall arise from the ground: and the King chosen by the bishops and people shall promise to observe these three things.' Then follow the *tria praecepta* as in the First Recension.

5. Prayers follow, including a long one invoking in plenitude biblical precedents, Abraham, Moses, Joshua, David and Solomon, as exemplars of truth, mildness, courage, humility and wisdom. It petitions that the King may serve God, walk in the way of justice, and cherish the Church and his people, protecting both from their enemies. It calls for him to triumph over his enemies protected by the helmet of God's protection and His invincible shield. It asks that the King reign with honour and be anointed with the grace of the Holy Spirit.

6. The anointing, during which is sung in some versions *Unxerunt Salomonem* ('Zadok the Priest') as the anthem and in others a special anthem with the text: 'O people of England, thou hast not been for-

gotten in the sight of the Lord: for in thee may the King that rules the English people of God be exulted, may he be anointed with the oil of gladness and confirmed by God's strength.'

7. Investiture by the bishops with a multiplication of regalia: the ring, the sword, the crown, the sceptre and the rod. Each item is presented with prayers outlining their symbolic significance as I have already described at Edgar's Coronation. Some versions add to these a red regal mantle, 'the garment of chiefest honour, the mantle of royal dignity'.

8. A series of blessings calls upon God, the Virgin Mary, the saints and angels to guard and watch over the King.

9. He is then enthroned with the prayer *Sta et retine*: 'Stand and hold fast from henceforth that place whereof hitherto thou hast been heir, by the succession of thy forefathers, being now delivered unto thee by the authority of Almighty God, and by the hand of us, and all the bishops and servants of God . . .'

10. A series of further blessings.

11. The Queen is then consecrated and anointed and 'she must be adorned with the ring for the integrity of her faith, and with a crown for the glory of eternity'.

12. The Mass.

In what way does this ordo differ from its predecessor? In the first place it is the first one with clear sections: election, oath, consecration, unction, investiture and blessing. In the second, the role of the laity is reduced, the delivery of the regalia no longer being at the hands of both principes and pontifices but of the pontifices only. In short, anything which suggests that power might have been conferred from below has been eliminated. There is no act of allegiance or indeed of acclamation. This is an ordo whose fundamental driving force is theological, represented in the opening act of prostration by the candidate on entering the church. Prostration in early liturgies was an expression beyond that of mere humility, contrition and supplication. What it signalled was an annihilation of the initiate's former self in preparation for a 'rebirth' into a new status. That rebirth was, however, to be conditional upon the *promissio regis*, now significantly moved to the front from its place in the First Recension at the very end. This new siting had huge constitutional repercussions. In it were spelt out the obligations of late Anglo-Saxon kingship: 'The duty of a hallowed king is that he judge no man unrighteously, and that he defend and protect widows and orphans and strangers, that he forbid thefts . . . feed the needy with alms, and have old and wise men for counsellors, and set righteous men for stewards . . .'[22]

The Second Recension recast the nature, context and function of kingship. Much of that is caught in the new items of regalia. The ring, which makes its first appearance in the ordination of bishops, is given as a symbol of faith. The sword, for which there is also no pagan precedent, is girded upon the king for the defence of both the Church and his own people.[23] The recension also integrates the Queen into the Coronation ritual, casting her in the role of a virtuous helpmate. She, too, was anointed with chrism, an index of high status and that her role was seen as important and not subsidiary to that of the king.[24]

Apart from the unusually full account of the Second Recension in action for Edgar in 973 little if anything is known about the Coronations of later kings. Indeed, it is not known whether Canute, the Danish king who succeeded to England by conquest, was even crowned at all. Chaos followed his demise in 1035 until, seven years later in 1042, Canute's stepson, Edward the Confessor, succeeded. By that date the place of crowning was still not fixed, for Edward's took place at Winchester in 1043. The *Anglo-Saxon Chronicle* provides us with a crumb about that event, one which shows that the importance of the *promissio regis* was fully understood, for we are told that Eadsige, Archbishop of Canterbury, 'gave him [Edward] good instruction before all the people, and admonished him well for his own sake and for the sake of all the people'.[25] If the Second Recension was a perfect mirror of ideal Anglo-Saxon kingship, what replaced it after the Norman Conquest was to reflect a far more assertive and controversial vision of the monarchy in what was to be an age of conflict between Church and State. There is a striking representation of the last Saxon Coronation in the Bayeux Tapestry. On 6 January 1066 Harold was crowned King in Edward the Confessor's new Abbey Church of Westminster, which had been consecrated only nine days before. His claim to the throne was tenuous, his mother being a Norse princess and his sister, the Confessor's Queen. The Coronation took place the day after the Confessor's death, so that any preparations must have been minimal. The tapestry is accepted as having been made

Opposite Canute and his wife Ælfgyfu crowned by angels, illumination, English, after 1020

The return of Edward the
Confessor to England and
his Coronation, illumina-
tion, English, mid-XIIIth
century

in England in about 1075 and its English origins mean that the scene is
as it would have been envisaged by those within the native tradition.
But the story line is that of the Norman conquerors, for what is depicted is what, in their eyes, was a usurpation and, although no doubt both
the archbishops of Canterbury and York took part following the
Second Recension ordo, York is omitted in favour of including the
tainted Stigand of Canterbury, already under a cloud and deposed
from the see in 1070.

Such an image is, of course, not reportage but symbolic.
Nonetheless it evokes more vividly than the dead texts of the ordines
something of the atmosphere of such an event as well as giving an
indication of the visual spectacle. It suggests that the royal throne had
advanced from the primitive bench on which Edward the Confessor
sits in the tapestry to being something more akin to an elevated seat or
chair with an approach by way of steps. Harold wears the familiar late
Anglo-Saxon crown with fleurons on his head and also sports a royal
mantle, suggesting, perhaps, as some versions of the ordines say, that
this may have been part of the regalia by 1066. To his right there are
two principes, one of whom lifts high what may be the sword with

which the king was girded during the ceremony. In his right hand he supports a long foliated rod, a *baculus*, and, in his left, something new, an orb surmounted by a cross. The orb is an imperial attribute, first certainly adopted by the Holy Roman Emperors very early in the eleventh century and appropriated shortly after by the Dane Canute (1016–35). An orb and sceptre appear on Edward the Confessor's seal, lifted unchanged from the Ottonian rulers of Germany. Perhaps an orb also, by the year of the Conquest, had become part of the coronation regalia. In this tableau we have brought together for the first time a coronation and what was to become its immemorial setting, Westminster Abbey, along with the potent memory of its founder, the man who was to further sanctify the royal family, this time as heirs and descendants of a saint.[26]

no dñi. c̄ı. lxvij. Dux normannie
Wiłłs urbem londoniarum adiens. ...

2

King and Priest

IN THE AFTERMATH of the battle of Hastings the defeated Anglo-Saxon magnates came to make their submission to Duke William of Normandy at Berkhamsted. This was succession not by election but by force of arms, for William was only Edward the Confessor's second cousin once removed. Although he was later to embroider on to the train of events that Edward had promised him the crown, the truth of the matter is that England was the victim of the explosive vitality of the Normans, a vitality which was also to conquer southern Italy and Sicily and, during the First Crusade, much of the Holy Land.

The Anglo-Saxon magnates had little choice in the autumn of 1066, therefore, other than to petition him to accept the crown of England on the grounds that they were accustomed to a king as their lord. Many of the Normans spoke against William accepting, fully conscious of the duke's consequent elevation in status that such an acceptance would bestow and the implication of it for them. But the duke was not slow to realise the advantage of being seen to be the rightful heir of Edward the Confessor claiming his kingdom. In this manner what was conquest could be dressed up in the robes of legitimacy. And, although William had wished to wait for the arrival of his wife, the urgency was such, after this decision, that the Coronation took place on Christmas Day 1066.[1]

Over this Coronation more academic ink has been spilt than almost any other, excepting that of Edward II in 1308. And, as in the case of Anglo-Saxon Coronations, we are up against paucity of material and the fact that what evidence we do have is patchy and not always compatible. With the Conquest we also enter the age of the chronicles,

Opposite The Coronation of William I as depicted in Matthew Paris, *Flores Historiarum*, illumination, English, 1250–52

but what they produced can range from eyewitness accounts to something secondhand or, even worse, fabricated. What can be pieced together about Christmas Day 1066, therefore, is a synthesis of the evidence from the chroniclers together with the one unique eyewitness account by a Norman cleric, Guy, Bishop of Amiens. He wrote a Latin poem on the battle of Hastings, the *Carmen de Hastingae proelio*, which culminates with the Coronation. The poem was written almost certainly to celebrate William's triumphant home-coming to Normandy in Lent 1067, literally weeks after the event.

Everyone agrees that the 1066 Coronation was different, but the problem centres around the degree of difference. In recent years it has been argued that this was the occasion on which a new ordo was introduced, the one we know as the Third Recension. It was probably composed, they argue, by Ealdred, the Anglo-Saxon Archbishop of York, in response to the quite unique set of circumstances which surrounded 1066. It has also been suggested that it was composed even earlier at the behest of Edward the Confessor and had been already used for Harold II. There is no way of settling that debate. What this new ordo does reflect are imperial aspirations of a kind that we know both the Confessor and equally William I had. Ealdred was uniquely qualified to provide an ordo with imperial overtones, for he had been present at the Coronation of the German King Henry IV in 1056 and would have known the continental ordines upon which the Third Recension drew. Edward the Confessor's vision of imperial status for the kings of England is reflected in the imagery of his coinage, his use of the Byzantine imperial style of basileus and, even more spectacularly, in the construction of Westminster Abbey, which was a building of European status designed to rival the great imperial churches of the Rhineland at Mainz and Speyer. There are equally imperial echoes around the Conqueror, whose crown at the Coronation Guy of Amiens records was 'Greece inspired', that is, it was modelled on that of the Byzantine Emperors which had pendologues, detachable strings of pearls alongside the cheeks. It was also studded with twelve precious or semi-precious stones. These related, in terms of biblical symbolism, to the breastplate of the High Priest and appear also as the foundation stones of the Heavenly City in the Book of Revelation. And his choice of Christmas Day for his Coronation would have been made in the full knowledge that both the Byzantine Emperors and the Western Holy Roman Emperors had also chosen it for theirs.[2]

A Byzantine crown with pendologues, mosaic, Byzantine, *c*.1028–50

ΡΟΓΕΡΙΟC ΡΗΞ ΙC

Roger II, King of Sicily, crowned by Christ with a diadem of the Byzantine type, mosaic, Sicily, XIIth century

An opposing case, however, continues to be maintained for the use of the Second Recension, albeit with revisions and additions, on the grounds that it was still in use and that William would not have wished to introduce something new but, rather, use an existing rite to emphasise continuity in his role as the rightful heir to Anglo-Saxon England. That argument depends, of course, on what was used at the Coronation of Harold II. None of this, as I have said, seems to be solvable and it is impossible to do more than piece together what can be gleaned to have happened, highlighting innovations, and leave the reader to draw his own conclusions. Those who opt for the use of the Second Recension in 1066 favour the introduction of the Third Recension during the second quarter of the twelfth century. What is certain is that Harold II's Coronation was a rushed affair following immediately after Edward the Confessor's death, allowing no time for preparation, but William I's had a lead of three months allowing ample time to prepare what was a formidable spectacle.

Both Harold II's and William I's Coronations mark the advent of a spacial configuration for royal ceremonial which has lasted down until today, that of the Palace of Westminster and the adjacent Abbey. It is likely that we owe that to Edward the Confessor. Both the economic expansion of the eleventh century and the growing mercantile traffic across the North Sea rendered a royal presence in London highly desirable. Such political and economic practicalities went hand in hand with a dynastic one, a desire to emulate the example of the French monarchy which already had its royal Coronation church of St

Westminster Abbey endowed with a mythical past. St Peter himself consecrates the building, illumination, English, mid-XIIIth century

Denis. Up until Edward the Confessor the royal palace had been in the City of London. Now a new residence was built on the island of Thorney close to a Benedictine Abbey dedicated to St Peter, the guardian of the keys of heaven, for whom the king had a special devotion. Nothing is known about Edward's palace, but a great deal is known about the Abbey which he embarked on to replace the one he found there.[3]

This was built to the east of the existing foundation and, by 1066, thanks to his benefactions, Westminster was to be among the richest religious houses in the country. What arose was grander than any church in England and in a new style, the Romanesque as it was practised in Normandy, but far exceeding both in size and splendour any church there. When complete it was to be 320 feet long. By 1066 the east end and transepts must have been up, although the nave and the twin west towers were not to be completed before the middle of the 1080s at the earliest. This was one of the great buildings of early medieval Europe. William's decision to be crowned there must have been conditioned by a desire to cancel out Harold II's Coronation and also to be seen to be crowned in the burial church of the Confessor as

Reconstruction of the Abbey and Palace of Westminster at the close of the XIth century his rightful heir. It was a precedent which, once established, proved permanent.

There is much in William's Coronation with which we will be familiar as well as much which could be innovative. It opened, as in the case of Edgar's at Bath, with a great procession. However, this time it was not only of monks and other clergy headed by a crucifer, but went on to include the great magnates of the realm and the future king led by the two archbishops. That was different from 973 when Edgar was led by the bishops of Durham and of Bath and Wells, an arrangement which was to reappear later. 'In this manner,' runs the *Carmen*, 'to the chanting of the Laudes, the king sought the church and was conducted to the royal chair.' What were the Laudes?

The Laudes are a set of jubilant acclamations which invoke God as an all-conquering and victorious commander.[4] They open with the resounding salute 'Christus vincit, Christus regnat, Christus imperat', and continue in a splendid descent through the celestial and thence through the terrestrial hierarchy. In these chants the serried ranks of heaven and earth are presented as mirror images of each other, each terrestrial rank being linked to a heavenly intercessor. The ruler, as Christus Domini, the anointed of the Lord, has as his intercessor a group of angelic and archangelic powers. To the queen is assigned a choir of virgins who intercede on her behalf. In sum the Laudes were a unique form of litany addressed solely and triumphantly to the victorious Christ in his divinity as the king of heaven and earth, and the prime exemplar and guarantor of power and prosperity to all rulers who safeguarded the fabric of Christian society. The act of unction, which was shortly to follow this procession, was to turn the Duke of Normandy into a type of Christ on earth and the embodiment of theocratic kingship.

It was customary to chant the Laudes at the great festivals of the Church, including Christmas (which it was), but here, in this procession, we already have a potent statement as to the nature of post-Conquest kingship. They were also to be sung at the solemn Mass which marked the ceremonial crown-wearings that were to become a feature of Norman and Angevin court life, when the magnates of the realm gathered at Christmas, Easter and Pentecost to attend on the king and queen and take part in the service and also in the great feast which followed it. As in the case of the debate over which ordo was used, so it has been argued that crown-wearings pre-date the

Conquest. Whether they did or not, the evidence shows a sharp elevation of the monarch to almost semi-divine status.

In this manner William I was conducted to the new Abbey. On entering it there was yet a further deviation from the Second Recension. That opened with the king in the midst of the magnates of the realm who had acclaimed him. This action was now moved into the sacred precincts of the Abbey church, taking place on what the *Carmen* refers to as a pulpitum. This would appear to mark the first appearance of some kind of stage or elevated dais which lifted some of the action aloft and apart from the assembled dignitaries. If we turn to the reconstructed ground plan of the Abbey, it must have been erected at the crossing beneath the central tower. Its advent in 1066 would surely have been prompted by the need to give emphasis and prominence to an action in which the duke was seen to be 'elected' by both the indigenous Anglo-Saxons and the occupying Normans. It began with Geoffrey, Bishop of Coutances, addressing the latter in French, asking them: 'If the king presented please you, declare it to us, for it is fitting that this be done by your free choice.' In response came applause. The action was repeated for the Anglo-Saxons in their own language by Ealdred of York.

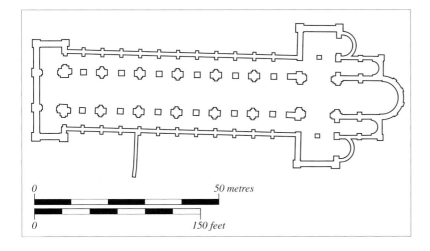

0   50 metres

0   150 feet

Groundplan of Edward the Confessor's church

The rite which followed took place in an arena which was to remain unchanged until the Coronation of Edward I. The high altar stood where the present one does. It was sited in an apse which was 26 feet 8 inches wide and with an approach to the altar measuring 14 feet 9 inches. The flanking north and south aisles had upper and lower chapels to which access was had by way of turret staircases. Such staircases may have led up to viewing points for the ceremonial, a feature which was to be repeated in Henry III's rebuilding in the thirteenth century. The monks' choir stalls were beneath the tower, so presumably the purpose of the pulpitum was also to lift part of the proceedings above them so that they could be seen.

This innovatory but politically necessary acclamation was to have an unfortunate consequence, for the roar of approval was such that one chronicler records: 'the armed and mounted men who had been stationed around the Abbey to guard it hearing the tremendous shouting in a language they could not understand, thought that something had gone wrong, and under this misapprehension they set fire to the environs of the city'.[5]

While events outside the Abbey had taken a nasty turn, those within it went on with the accustomed opening prostration before the altar and thence to the administration of unction with chrism by the Archbishop of York (Canterbury, although present, was tainted and under an ecclesiastical cloud). There was, however, yet another major departure from the Edgar ordo. William took the Coronation oath after and not before he had been anointed. One version of the *Anglo-Saxon Chronicle* records: 'And he [William] promised Ealdred on Christ's book and swore moreover (before Ealdred would place the crown on his head) that he would rule all this people as well as the best of kings before him, if they would be loyal to him.'[6]

The changed placing must have been designed to reinforce the sanctity of the king's oath, for it was made by William as a man who had just been sanctified and endowed with the gifts of the Holy Spirit. Thereafter the ceremony follows what has been argued to be compatible with either the Second or the Third Recensions: investiture with the regalia, enthronement and the Mass.

THE THIRD RECENSION

The Conqueror's Coronation has provided material for a lively and unresolved academic debate as to when the Third Recension came into use. That debate equally hovers around any consideration of the seven Coronations between 1066 and 1200. The best approach to these is a collective one. The Coronations are:

William I	Christmas Day 1066
William II	Sunday, 26 September 1087
Henry I	Sunday, 5 August 1100
Stephen	Sunday, 22 December 1135
Henry II	Sunday, 19 December 1154
Richard I	Sunday, 3 September 1189
John	Ascension Day, 27 May 1199

To these we can add the Coronation of Henry II's son, Henry the Younger, on 14 June 1170. That is a salutary reminder that the monarchy was still in theory an elective one, albeit from members of the ruling dynasty. The Coronation of Henry the Younger, who was to die before his father, was an attempt to settle the succession in terms of primogeniture during his father's lifetime.[7]

The century and a half during which these Coronations happened witnessed huge changes as the Norman Conquest created a new ruling class of those who came over with the Conqueror. That was structured in what we know as the feudal system, a mode of land tenure stretching downwards from the king via the great lay and ecclesiastical magnates who held their estates in return for knight service to the crown. This restructuring of society, in which the oath of fealty of one man was to another as his liege lord, was to have repercussions on the Coronation, moving, as we shall see, the Coronation oath centre stage. In the case of the ecclesiastical tenants-in-chief it would have even greater repercussions, for the papacy was to assert the superiority of clerical over lay authority and forbid a ceremony in which a priest was seen to be subservient to royal authority. That, too, would affect the Coronation.

At some date, either before or after 1066 and almost certainly by the Coronation of Stephen in 1135, the Third Recension came into use.[8] What this represented was a rejection of all but the most important Anglo-Saxon forms in favour of the parallel parts of the great continental Coronation ordo. This was the German one used for the consecration of the Holy Roman Emperor, the *Pontificale romano-germanicum*, which was compiled at the Abbey of St Alban's, Mainz, about the year 961. The introduction of the Third Recension brought insular Anglo-Saxon traditions in line with continental custom, a development typical of the years after 1066. It has been, as I have indicated, attributed to Ealdred, Archbishop of York (d. 1069). It has equally been seen as the work of William's great reforming Archbishop of Canterbury, Lanfranc (1070–93), and also of Gilbert Crispin, Abbot of Westminster (1085–1117), the friend and ally of Lanfranc's successor, Anselm. One certain fact is that this ordo was to remain in use until the Coronation of Edward II in 1308.

The Third Recension is found in seven manuscripts, one of which is French, all the others being English. Out of the six English manuscripts three derive from a pontifical compiled in the great monastery at Christ Church, Canterbury. Some of these manuscripts can be at least approximately dated. The earliest versions cut out the anointing of the king's head with chrism, indicating a date after the initial clash of Church and State between Henry I and Archbishop Anselm in the years 1100 to 1107, one which included the withdrawal of the use of chrism. Another indicator is the preoccupation with crowns. That probably goes back to Henry I's daughter, the Empress Matilda, wife of the Emperor Henry V, who was widowed in 1125 and who returned to England bearing the imperial crown of her husband. Henry II was crowned with it in 1154.

There are variations between these manuscripts but, as in the case of the previous two recensions, I present the reader with the overall contents in simple list form:

---

1. The king is led by two bishops 'from the assembly of faithful elders' to the church while the choir sings *Firmetur manus tua*.

2. The king prostrates himself with the bishops alongside him in front of the altar before which have been spread carpets and cloths.

3. The litany is then sung, after which the bishops arise and raise the king.

4. The king takes the triple oath, to preserve both Church and people in true peace, to forbid all rapacity and iniquity to men of every degree and to ordain the practice of justice and mercy in all matters of judgement.

5. The *recognitio*. A bishop asks the assembled people whether they are willing 'to submit themselves to this man as their prince and ruler, and obey his command'. Both clergy and people reply affirming their willingness.

6. The consecration. This opens with prayers recalling exemplars from the

Old Testament and calling down blessings. The Archbishop of Canterbury begins by anointing the king's hands with holy oil 'that thou mayest be blessed and set up as king in this kingdom over our people that the Lord thy God hath given thee to rule and govern'. Then he anoints his head, breast, shoulders and elbows, with further prayers while the choir sings: 'Fear God.'

7. The delivery of the regalia. The king is invested by the bishops with the sword, bracelets (armils) and mantle, each with a prayer. The crown is then blessed and placed on the king's head. Then follows investiture with the ring, sceptre and rod.

8. The king is blessed, after which he kisses the bishops, who lead him to his throne while the choir sings the Te Deum.

9. That finished, the archbishop says the prayer *Sta et retine*.

10. Then follows the consecration and Coronation of the queen. On entering the church she is greeted by a prayer asking that she 'may obtain the crown that is next unto virginity'. The consecration opens with a blessing after which, with appropriate prayers, she is anointed with holy oil and then invested with a ring. Her crown is then blessed and she is crowned.

11. The Mass follows.

What does this new Recension mean and why was it necessary? The possible political circumstances that prompted it have already been touched upon, but they need to be placed within a far broader ideological perspective. In one respect there is no doubt that the Third Recension embodies a reaction to the eleventh-century reform movement which found its test case in the rejection of the lay investiture of ecclesiastical dignitaries. On their appointment they were presented by the king with a staff or crozier and a ring, symbols of their office. This act was followed by one of homage in which they received their lands as one of the king's tenants-in-chief. Although this practice of the lay investiture of clerics had gone unchallenged under William I, it was not to do so under his immediate successors. From the last years of the eleventh century onwards there was a fierce struggle between Church and State, known as the Investiture Contest, during which archbishops of Canterbury were sent into exile and England was laid under interdict by the pope. It was only to be resolved when, on 29 December 1170, Henry II's Archbishop of

Canterbury was murdered in his own cathedral. The Church emerged as victor.

What the reformed papacy was attempting to achieve was a reversal of what the introduction of the rite of unction had led to, a race of priest-kings who were viewed as being somehow almost semi-divine. The Christianisation of the barbarian monarchies which had followed the conversion of the pagan tribes of Northern Europe had exalted rulers, through the bestowal of unction, into beings akin to priest-kings. The use of chrism to consecrate the ruler, which was also used in the ordination of a priest, meant that the two were increasingly viewed as variants of something very similar. The biblical precedent was Melchizedek, who was both priest and king, and rulers were cast as Christus Domini, representatives of God on earth, and mediators, because of their apparent dual nature, between clergy and people.

The papacy, realising the threat this embodied, in the eleventh century began to draw back from the endorsement of theocratic kingship. The sacraments were codified and reduced to being seven in number, with royal unction not among them. The whole pressure was to downgrade the very idea of the priest-king, and early versions of the Third Recension record the withdrawal of the use of chrism for the anointing of the king's head, replacing it with the anointing of several parts of his body with ordinary holy oil. Chrism was in fact to creep back into use later, but its removal for a period was significant.[9]

The Third Recension is, therefore, a crucial document in which the Church redrew the boundaries that differentiated the laity from the clergy. The battle which ensued centred, as I have said, on the removal of the king's right to invest his ecclesiastical dignitaries with office and was to dominate the twelfth century. Under Henry I, one of the most powerful of the Angevin kings, Archbishop Anselm was driven into exile and so, even more famously, was Thomas Becket under the first Plantagenet, Henry II. The struggle between him and the king was to produce the most extreme claims for theocratic kingship, ones which based the royal control of the Church on the anointment of the king with chrism. The significance of that was caught in the royal style. Before the Coronation the king was only Dominus. After, at least from the reign of William II, he was 'King by the Grace of God'.

The author known as Anonymous of York but probably William Bonne-Ame, later Archbishop of Rouen, who wrote what is referred to

The Coronation of Henry I
as depicted in Matthew
Paris, *Flores Historiarum*,
illumination, English,
1250–52

as Tract 24a, succinctly sums up how the supporters of the king as Christus Domini saw the monarchy:

> kings are consecrated in God's church before the sacred altar and are anointed with holy oil [he means chrism here] and sacred benediction to exercise ruling power over Christians, the Lord's people . . . the Holy Church of God . . . as one who has been made God and Christ through grace . . . wherefore he is not called a layman, since he is the anointed of the Lord [Christus Domini] and through grace he is God. He is the supreme-ruler, the chief shepherd, master, defender and instructor of the Holy Church, lord over his brethren and worthy to be 'adored' by all, since he is the chief and supreme prelate.[10]

Such were the breathtaking claims made on behalf of Henry II, stemming from what was enacted at his Coronation as performed according to the Second Recension. This was an appeal back to the mystique and magic of the old pre-Conquest Anglo-Saxon monarchy. By the time that this tract was being written theocratic kingship was, in fact, in retreat and Becket's murder had dealt the final blow.

The investiture controversy and the redefinition of the lay and clerical spheres provide the backcloth prompting the Third Recension. That incorporated several other changes. One was the enhanced status accorded the crown, which was blessed, a ritual derived from one used at the Coronation of the Byzantine emperors. There was also a multiplication of robes and regalia. Armils or bracelets, which had an Old Testament precedent, appear together with a royal mantle whose four corners signify the four corners of the world subject to God. The mantle does appear, in fact, in a late manuscript of the Second Recension but it is universal in the third. In the latter the investiture with the ring and crown is reversed and there are some notable enhancements to the ritual, with the king being blessed after crowning and then solemnly enthroned in state to the splendour of the Te Deum being sung.

There is also a notable enhancement of the status of the queen, delineating clearly the nature of medieval queenship.[11] This is the first ordo which works from the premise that her Coronation is an action directly parallel with that of her husband. The queen is twice blessed, first on entering the church and again at the altar. The prayer said over her was taken almost word for word from that said over a newly ordained abbess. Here she is cast as an exemplar of female chastity, as the mistress of the royal household and, as signified in her investiture with a ring as a symbol of faith, a support to the Church, a patron of missionaries and a leader of her household's spirituality.

The only full account of a Coronation definitely using this ordo before 1200 is that of Richard I in 1189. Of the seven others, including that of Henry the Younger, we know little, although it is clear that the twelfth century saw enormous change and development. When, at last, we do get a full-length eyewitness account it is of a major spectacle of state, which leaves one wondering how far what is described happened earlier during that century. The twelfth century, after all, was one of the greatest eras in the history of the country, and the increasing power and grandeur which surrounded the monarchy is likely to have been reflected in the rite of Coronation. The brilliant if hot-headed Henry II ruled over a vast continental empire, the greatest in Western Europe since Charlemagne. And even though his two sons, Richard I, the crusading troubadour king who was only in England five months out of a ten-year reign, and the feckless John, who opened a chasm between himself and the magnates, threw this inheritance away, there is no doubt that the English monarchy was still regarded as one of the grandest in Western Europe.

The Great Seals of Henry II and Richard I, images of English monarchs enthroned in majesty clasping regalia, the latter flanked by the moon and sun

We can trace that progressive rise in grandeur in several different ways. One is in the development of Westminster as a royal enclosure or preserve. The elements of this were already in place in 1066 but they were to be consolidated during the century and a half which followed.[12] Although nothing is known of Edward the Confessor's palace, in 1097 work was underway on a new great hall for William II, who was to hold his first court there in 1099. That vast hall is still there, exactly the same in size as it was when first built, 240 feet long and 67 feet 6 inches wide, by far the largest hall in England and, probably, in Western Europe at the time. If the Abbey was seen to reflect imperial aspirations surely this was its secular counterpart. It was built deliberately to house the great feasts which followed the Coronation and as the setting for the ritual crown-wearings which punctuated the court year, in which the ruler displayed himself as the image of Christ on earth to his magnates.

Recent research has pointed out that one of the ordo's prayers of blessing, opening with the word *Prospice*, includes the following words: 'Grant that the glorious dignity of the royal hall [*palatium*] may shine before the eyes of all with greatest splendour of kingly power and that it may seem to glow with the brightest rays and to glitter as if suffused by illumination of the utmost brilliance.'

From the outset this was not a hall of the usual Norman type, for the main entrance was placed at the northern end in order to establish a processional route which was directly to the enthroned monarch at the opposite side. The upper walls were lighted by Romanesque windows set into an arcaded wall gallery. The vast size of this structure demonstrated at a stroke that this was to be the secular ceremonial centre of the Anglo-Norman kingdom. The palace itself continued to expand. In 1167 there is reference to a 'new hall', a small one for domestic purposes sited roughly in line with the great one but further east. Jutting out at right angles from that was the great chamber which already, by the twelfth century, was for the king's private use. The Norman and the Angevin kings contrived to be migratory through their vast English and French domains and it was only gradually that their Westminster palace began to establish its primacy. All through the reign of Henry II the various organs of government, as they became ever more complex, began to find a permanent home amidst this ever-expanding palace. The Court of Audit held its biennial sessions here, and under John the royal treasury ceased to be at Winchester. For over four centuries the palace was to combine the demands of a royal residence with those of the major offices of state. Only in 1512 was this to change when Henry VIII left Westminster eventually for Whitehall.

The Abbey's rise was to be far slower.[13] Although kings were crowned there, royal interest thereafter ceased, preferring to favour their own foundations and choosing also to be buried elsewhere. In the years immediately after 1066 there was no attempt by the monks to exploit their connexion with the vanquished Anglo-Saxon royal house. That only came to be of advantage at the turn of the eleventh to the twelfth century. Henry I's Coronation charter placed voluntary restraints on his use of the royal prerogative, citing in three clauses the laws of Edward the Confessor, by which was meant the whole body of Anglo-Saxon law before the Conquest. In doing this Henry was exploiting what the monks of Westminster Abbey had already embarked upon, capitalising on its role as the resting place of a king on his way to beatification. That can be traced in the series of lives of Edward the Confessor which record the steady upward curve to canon-isation: the *Vita Ædwardi Regis* by an anonymous writer about 1067; the Prior Osbert de Clare's *Vita Beati Eadwardi Regis Anglorum*, com-pleted by 1138 to accompany the first petition to the pope for his canonisation; and, finally, Ailred de Rievaulx's *Vita Sancti Edwardi Regis*, written after the king's canonisation in 1161 and in time for the translation of his body to a new shrine in 1163.

The driving force behind this came not initially from the crown but the Abbey, setting out to defend its territorial rights by upping its royal associations. In this they were helped by Abbot Baldwin of Bury St Edmunds (1065–97), a monk from St Denis, who was all too famil-iar with how to exploit such a royal foundation. That was achieved through a whole series of forged charters by a monk, Guerno of St Augustine's, Canterbury. St Augustine's had remained a bulwark of pre-Conquest Anglo-Saxon Christianity and is the most likely source of the design of the Bayeux Tapestry in which Edward the Confessor is depicted as a saintly bearded patriarch.

The first opening of the tomb of Edward the Confessor in 1163 as depicted in a mid-XIIIth century life of the saint, illumination, English, mid-XIIIth century

Opposite Pilgrims flocking to the shrine of St Edward, illumination, English, mid-XIIIth century

The key figure in the canonisation campaign was Prior Osbert de Clare during whose time a whole series of forged charters was produced, including ones in the names of Popes Nicholas II and Paschal II confirming the Abbey's claim to be both the permanent setting for the Coronation and also the place where St Edward's regalia (to which I will come) were kept. By the twelfth century the papacy claimed the sole right to proclaim saints, and in 1139 Innocent II declined Westminster's petition to canonise the king on the grounds of insufficient support within the realm. Otherwise the moment was propitious, the prior being the king's illegitimate kinsman and having the endorsement of the king, Stephen, and his brother, Henry of Blois, Bishop of Winchester. The real reason for the pope's refusal was probably the king's arrest of the Bishop of Salisbury in the same year. After this failure royal interest in the Abbey went into abeyance until

Henry II, who made much of his Anglo-Saxon ancestry, saw the potential of having a royal saint in his battle with the Church. On this occasion it worked. Edward was canonised and his remains translated amidst splendour on 13 October 1163 in a ceremony designed to impress the pope, just as the battle against Becket was about to reach its zenith. For Henry II, St Edward the Confessor enhanced the charismatic character of his kingly rule and the sacred nature of English kingship. Neither of his successors, Richard I or John, were to take any interest in the new royal saint and his cult was not to go into the ascendant again until the reign of Henry III.

The fact that the Abbey cast itself as the custodian of St Edward's regalia means that items recognised as constituting them must have existed. The early history of the regalia is shrouded in mystery, not helped by the fact that they were all deliberately destroyed under the

Commonwealth. Recent scholarship, however, has come down in favour of a nucleus of royal ornaments which can be argued to have been deposited by Edward the Confessor either for safekeeping or indeed as regalia to be used by the future kings of England.[14] If the latter was, indeed, the case they constituted what was the earliest set of royal regalia in Western Europe. These items were always royal property and the Abbey's role was never other than as custodian.

By about 1200, of what did these regalia consist? There was St Edward's Crown, which evidence indicates is likely to have been the work of a Byzantine craftsman working in England. It was a circlet with four fleurons and possibly four crosses arising from it, above which rose a double arch, on the crossing of which there was a cross with bells that tinkled when the wearer moved. The indications are that Edward, with his pretensions as *Basileus Anglorum*, abandoned the earlier open crown of the late Anglo-Saxon kings in favour of one modelled on that worn by Eastern Emperors. To the crown can be added two sceptres and what was known as St Edward's staff. One of the sceptres again betrayed Byzantine influence, having four pendant pearls and a gold cross at the top. The second one was made of iron with a fleur-de-lys at the summit. The use of iron was probably due to a biblical precedent, Psalm 2, which speaks of the awaited Messiah as coming to rule with a rod of iron (*virga ferrea*). Sceptres such as these were symbols of command, but St Edward's staff was topped with a dove, the emblem of peace, and spoke of a king's pastoral care for his people. It had a spike at the other end. Finally come liturgical items. One was the *crux natans*, said to have been rescued by the Confessor from the sea on what would have been his return journey to England in 1041, and therefore likely to have been acquired by him in Normandy. The descriptions indicate a wooden cross covered at the front with gold plate set with jewels in mounts on which there was a figure of the crucified Christ, probably in ivory. Inventory descriptions of St Edward's chalice, later known as the regal, indicate that it was a large and richly carved late antique cup, of a type eagerly sought after in the tenth and eleventh centuries, to which gold mounts had been added. The gold paten which accompanied it was of enamelled Anglo-Saxon work. An ivory comb, also assigned to St Edward, could be Anglo-Saxon, but its use is uncertain. When it came to vestments everything is far more problematic, although it is possible that a mantle and possibly a supertunic could have been part of the original

regalia. The mantle was adorned with golden eagles and was of a type worn by the Eastern emperors.

William of Sudbury, a learned monk of Westminster, wrote a tract for Richard II on the regalia arguing that they were even older, that they had been the gift of Pope Leo to Alfred the Great on the occasion of his 'Coronation' in Rome. That at least can be dismissed as later embroidery, but it is likely that these items do go back to the Confessor. Indeed, the earliest reference to what could be items of regalia comes in 1138 when the monks threatened to sell off his ornaments. None of them as described by later medieval inventories are likely to be items removed from the saint's grave at any of successive openings. The only occasion when that happened was in 1163 at the translation. The prior recorded as having taken from the tomb cloth to be made into embroidered copes along with the ring which, according to legend, was the one recovered from John the Evangelist in paradise.

In the tenth and eleventh centuries kingly robes, in response to the role of Christus Domini, were deliberately priestly in character, although not Mass vestments. Royal robes looked to those worn by bishops, and both in turn looked to those recorded in the Old Testament as having been worn by priests and kings. In this way the tunicle, the dalmatic and the cope became regal robes.[15] In such robes and vestments, especially those in which a king received unction, monarchs began to be buried. Henry the Younger was buried at Rouen in 1183 and both Matthew Paris and Ralph de Diceto record that he lay upon the bier attired in the linen vestments in which he was anointed and still showing traces of chrism. It was during this period that the custom arose of putting a linen coif on the anointed's head which was only removed at a later date (the details we learn from later Coronations). Such interment in the Coronation robes was probably a twelfth-century innovation, fully reflective of claims to theocratic kingship. It was certainly done in the case of Richard I, and the fact that tomb effigies of both Henry II and John depict them in their Coronation robes suggest that they too were buried wearing them. The tradition continued into the first quarter of the fourteenth century.[16]

In the twelfth century the items called for by the Coronation ritual were not only housed in the Abbey but also in the king's Jewel House. Each king had his own items of personal regalia quite separate from what became regarded as sacred relics in the Abbey. Such personal regalia included crowns and sceptres and ceremonial swords. By

Edward the Confessor holding the legendary ring of St John the Evangelist, illumination in the Lytlington Missal, English, 1383–84

1200 the number of swords used in the ceremony had multiplied and the king was also invested with golden spurs. All of this indicates that we have arrived at the age of chivalry, the spurs being an artefact which formed an integral part of the ritual of knighthood. From the mid-twelfth century onwards the ceremony of knighting became the pivotal moment in a knight's life. It could be a relatively simple affair and it could equally be staged as a grand spectacle. The girding on of a sword was already part of the action in the Second Recension, one which would have had far greater resonances in the era of chivalry. The Church during this period attempted to adopt knighthood as an order of a quasi-religious nature, assigning it a role as the secular arm of Holy Church, for its protection and for the defence of the weak. The addition of spurs to the regalia emphasised the knightly ideal of kingship even more forcefully in a period enlivened by the Crusades. It is to be recalled that Richard I was England's crusading king.[17]

The sword was an intensely personal item of equipment, one which symbolised a man's ability to demonstrate his physical strength and skill. In the Coronation ceremony, to the king as defender of the Church and the country's leader in war was now added the vision of him as the personification of ideal knighthood. The sword quite early on came to symbolise the royal presence, and sword-bearing before the monarch became a mark of signal honour. As early as 1099 the King of Scotland carried the sword before William Rufus when he held court in London. At the Coronation of Richard I in 1189 no fewer than three swords were borne before him suggesting that by that date chivalrous romance was impinging upon reality. The twelfth century was the golden age of Arthurian legend for which the Angevin kings had a passion. King Arthur's grave was even 'discovered' at Glastonbury in 1190 and swords believed to have been used by the Knights of the Round Table became collector's items. The swords in the *chansons de geste* became almost personalities in their own right, bearing names and being endowed with quasi-magical powers. King John, for instance, had the sword of Tristram. This had been Ogier's sword which had been shortened in his fight with Morhaut, champion of Ireland. In Geoffrey of Monmouth's *Historia Regum Britanniae*, a myth-laden history of Britain written in the reign of Stephen, four swords were carried before King Arthur, each one representing one of his kingdoms. Could the three which preceded Richard I in 1189 have stood for England, Anjou and Normandy over which he ruled?

While the historic *mise-en-scène* as well as the ornaments became increasingly grander and more complex, other aspects of the Coronation at the same time began to assume a pattern which we would recognise today. It was, for example, only in the twelfth century that the Archbishop of Canterbury finally attained his role as the chief officiant.[18] That, too, was an offshoot of the investiture struggle. Although

King Arthur as the heroic
king, illumination, English,
XVth century

the archbishops of Canterbury had crowned the Anglo-Saxon kings,
the situation was a far from immutable one. Stigand did not crown
William I, and Henry I was crowned by the Bishop of London (albeit
as the Archbishop of Canterbury's 'vicar'). The resolution in favour of
Canterbury only came in 1170 when Henry II wanted his son crowned
within his own lifetime.

A letter had been sent from Pope Alexander III to the king as long
ago as 1161 saying that the young prince could be crowned by any of the
bishops. Five years later the pope, under pressure from the exiled
Becket, rescinded his decision. In two letters the claim of Canterbury
was spelt out, the first stating 'it has come to our hearing that the

Coronation and anointing of the kings of the English belongs to the Archbishop of Canterbury by the ancient custom and dignity of his church . . .' The second reiterates 'this dignity and privilege of old'. To add to the king's difficulties, the Archbishop of York was specifically forbidden by the pope to crown anyone.

All of this worked in the long run in favour of Canterbury, but in the meantime it had a fatal flaw as the pope failed to inform Henry II that he had revoked his letter of 1161. In Becket's eyes Canterbury's right of bestowing unction gave any archbishop control over who succeeded to the throne. The result was that in spite of the existence of the pope's letters of revocation Henry II went ahead and had his son crowned by the Archbishop of York. In retaliation Becket got the pope not only to excommunicate the bishops who had taken part but to lay England under an interdict. However, before news of the papal actions had reached England Henry II offered to make peace with his troublesome archbishop. That happened on 22 July 1170, a settlement which included provision for the younger Henry and his wife to be recrowned by Becket. In this way the six-year exile of the archbishop was brought to its end.

Just before Becket set sail for England he excommunicated, on apostolic authority, the Archbishop of York together with the bishops of London and Salisbury, who had taken part in the Coronation. The bishops bitterly protested and Becket offered to absolve them, but added that only the pope could exculpate the Archbishop of York. The bishops complained to the king who, in his anger, is said to have cried, 'Will no one rid me of this turbulent priest?' Four knights responded to Henry's plea and murdered Becket in his own cathedral. The supremacy of Canterbury was now sealed by the shedding of a martyr's blood in the cause of Holy Church.

Becket was right in that the role of the archbishop in the king-making process was an important one. In the period before primogeniture he took a leading part in the formal election of a new king by the assembled magnates. William I had nominated his second son, William Rufus. On his death the crown passed to his younger brother, Henry I, and from thence to his cousin, Stephen of Blois, after which it descended to Henry II, son of Henry I's daughter, the Empress Matilda, by Geoffrey of Anjou. By Henry's death primogeniture was taking over, reflected in the king's crowning of his eldest son, who was, in fact, to predecease him. In the event, the crown was to pass to the younger brothers, first Richard I and then John. Few of these successions were entirely automatic, involving anything from a *coup d'état* to a civil war.

The Archbishop of Canterbury played a crucial role not only as one of the greatest magnates in the realm but also as the man who could bestow unction, transforming a candidate from being merely Dominus to being Rex Dei Gratia. He also played a crucial role in the *recognitio* which remained of importance even as late as 1199. Matthew Paris provides a vivid picture of what happened on that occasion. Before the archbishop, Hubert Walter, proceeded to the anointing of John he addressed the assembled bishops, earls and barons: 'Hear, all of you, and be it known that no one has an antecedent right to succeed another in the kingdom, unless he shall have been unanimously elected, under the guidance of the Holy Spirit.'

The archbishop went on to remind them of the example of Saul, 'the first anointed king', pointing out that if anyone else of the royal dynasty excelled John 'in merit' he should be elected instead. Later in the reign Hubert Walter was asked why he had acted in such a manner: 'he replied that he knew John would one day or other bring the kingdom into great confusion, wherefore he determined that he should owe his elevation to election and not to hereditary right'.[19]

In this episode we also catch something else, that it is one thing to follow a recension as it appears on the page of a pontifical and quite another to square it with what could happen on the day.

The archbishop was also the person who administered to the new king the Coronation oath, and that was to assume a place of major importance in defining the role and duties of the medieval English king.[20] The oath was not an empty ritual to be gone through, for its contents were studied both by the clerics and by the great magnates involved in the king-making process. The oath was a sacred contract administered by the archbishop with the assistance of the clergy in the presence of the lay magnates of the kingdom. In feudal society it formed the linchpin by which that society was held together. It assumed a place of even greater significance after 1066 than before it.

Although our information about the actual wording of the oaths taken by eleventh- and twelfth-century kings is scanty, there is no doubting their importance, as we have already seen in the Coronation of 1066. An account of the Coronation of Henry the Younger in 1170 describes him swearing with both his hands on the altar, on which lay not only the Gospels but relics of the saints. On that occasion, in the light of the struggle with Becket, he swore to maintain the liberty and the dignity of the Church. The oath which had begun its life under the Anglo-Saxon kings as the *promissio regis*, under the Normans and Angevins developed into a sacred pledge. Oaths in a feudal society were inviolate.

So the oath moved centre stage, its centrality reflected in the custom of issuing, after the Coronation, what were in effect its contents in the form of a charter.[20] The first of these came from Henry I, who had added to the second of his three promises a vow to rectify the injustices perpetrated during the reign of his brother, William Rufus. That charter, which took out to the country the pledge made in the Coronation oath, was to be evoked by successive generations as a guarantee of the rights of English men and women in respect of the crown. It was confirmed and reissued by Stephen in 1135 or 1136, by Henry II in 1154 and, most famously, in 1215 when Archbishop Stephen Langton cited it as the precedent and model for Magna Carta. The charter's message was 'I restore to you the law of King Edward', that is, the Norman and Angevin kings confirmed the validity of the totality of Anglo-Saxon law as it was in the time of Edward the Confessor.[21]

That oath was the obverse side of which the reverse was the act of fealty by both clerical and lay magnates. As yet it formed no part of the proceedings in church but, at this period, was a separate event enacted in the great hall of the palace when prelates and nobles rendered homage and fealty to the new ruler. Only in the case of Richard I and John do we know when this was done, in the instance of the former on the second day following the Coronation, and of the latter on the next day.[22] Much the same in terms of information applies to the Coronation feast, of which we only gain some kind of picture for that of Richard I.

During this period the Coronation was not the only occasion on which the monarch appeared crowned.[23] Circumstances could precipitate second Coronations (but not unctions), particularly on the occasion of a king marrying. In 1141 Stephen was crowned a second time at Canterbury with his wife, Matilda of Boulogne. In 1194 Richard I was crowned again on returning from the Crusade and from his years of imprisonment in Austria. In both those cases a special form of service was drawn up, initially for the crowning of 1141. The king attended by his nobles waited in his chamber for the arrival of the ecclesiastical procession. He then knelt and had the crown placed on his head by the Archbishop of Canterbury while a prayer was said. After this there was a procession to the church, during which an anthem was sung. Prayers were said and the king was led to his throne, after which a Mass was sung and the king communicated. There was a second procession back, in which the magnates carried candles, and a banquet followed.

To these rare events can be added the more regular crown-wearings at Christmas, Easter and Pentecost when the king held court. On those occasions the king and queen were escorted in a great procession to the church, where they sat crowned and enthroned. An elaborate votive Mass was sung by the archbishop during which the Laudes were chanted. Afterwards there was the usual feast, with the magnates assuming the roles of servants such as the butler or pantler or steward.

By the year 1200 the Coronation had become an essential rite of passage whereby someone was made king. That person remained Dominus Anglorum and his queen Domina Anglorum until unction was bestowed, after which they became Rex et Regina Anglorum. The transition was emphasised in the development of the procession in which the royal regalia was now carried to the church by the great nobles. That solemn transportation of crown, sceptre, orb, vestments, chalice and paten was an emphatic statement that he who walked behind them was not yet king. He became so only by a sacred initiation to be gone through at the hands of the clergy in the presence of the magnates. No document captures more vividly this huge transformation since 1066 than the description of the Coronation of Richard I in 1189.

THE CORONATION AND CHIVALRY: RICHARD I

The chronicler Roger of Wendover provides us with what is the fullest description yet of a Coronation, so much so that I quote it in full:

> Then the Duke came to London, where had assembled the Archbishops, Bishops, earls and barons, and a large number of knights to meet him; and by whose advice and consent the Duke was consecrated and crowned king of England, at Westminster, on the third of September, being Sunday, the feast of the ordination of Pope St Gregory . . .
>
> First came the bishops and abbots and many clerks vested

A magna g̃ mentis amaritudine mortu
o piissimo ac sapientissimo Henrico An
glorum rege: Ricardus filius eius coro

in silken copes, with the cross, torch bearers, censers, and holy water going before them, up to the door of the king's inner chamber; and there they received the said Duke Richard, who was to be crowned, and led him to the high altar of the church of Westminster with an ordered procession and triumphal chanting: and the whole way by which they went, from the door of the king's chamber to the altar, was covered with woollen cloths.

Now the order of the procession was as follows: at the head came the clerks in vestments carrying holy water, crosses, torches and censers. Then came the priors, then the abbots; next came the bishops and in the midst of them went four barons carrying four golden candlesticks. Then came Godfrey de Lucy carrying the king's coif, and John Marshal by him carrying two great and weighty golden spurs. Next came William Marshal, Earl of Strigul, carrying the royal sceptre, on the top of which was a golden cross, and William de Patyrick, Earl of Salisbury, by his side, bearing a golden rod with a golden dove on the top. Then came David, brother to the king of Scotland, Earl of Huntingdon, and John, Earl of Moreton, brother of the Duke, and Robert, Earl of Leicester, carrying three royal swords taken from the king's treasury, and their scabbards were wholly covered with gold: and the Earl of Moreton went in the midst. Then came six earls and barons carrying on their shoulders a very large board on which were placed the royal ensigns and vestments. Then came William de Mandeville, Earl of Albemarle, carrying a golden crown great and heavy, and adorned on all sides with precious stones. Then came Richard, Duke of Normandy, and Hugh, Bishop of Durham, went on his right hand, and Reginald, Bishop of Bath, on his left: and four barons carried over them a silken canopy on four tall lances: and the whole crowd of earls, barons, knights and others, clerk and lay, followed up to the door of the church, and they came and were brought with the Duke into the choir.

Now when the Duke came to the altar he swore in the presence of the Archbishops, Bishops, clergy and people, on his knees before the altar, and the most holy gospels laid thereon, and the relics of any saints, that he would keep peace, honour and duty towards God and holy church and her customs all the

Opposite The Anointing of Richard I from Matthew Paris, *Flores Historiarum*, illumination, English, 1250–52

days of his life. Secondly, he swore that he would exercise right justice and equity among the people committed to his charge. Thirdly, he swore that he would annul any evil laws and customs that might have been introduced into the realm and make good laws and keep them without fraud or evil intent. Then they stripped him altogether, except his shirt and breeches, and his shirt was torn apart at the shoulders. Then they shod him with buskins worked with gold. Then Baldwin, Archbishop of Canterbury, poured the holy oil on his head and, with prayers appointed for this purpose, anointed him king in three places, to wit, his head, his breast, and his arms, which signifies glory, courage and knowledge.

Next the Archbishops placed on his consecrated head a linen cloth, and above it the coif which Godfrey de Lucy had carried. Then they clothed him with the royal vestments: first, that is, with the tunic, then with the dalmatic; then the Archbishop gave him the sword of the realm wherewith he was to repress the evildoers against the church. Then two earls put upon him the spurs which John Marshal had carried. Then he was vested with the mantle. After that he was led to the altar, and there the said Archbishop forbad him by Almighty God to take this great office upon him, unless he intended to keep inviolate the oaths above mentioned and the vows he had made. And he replied that by the help of God he would keep all the above without deceit.

Then he himself took the crown from the altar, and gave it to the Archbishop, and the Archbishop set it on his head, and two earls held it up on account of its weight.

Then the Archbishop put the royal sceptre into his right hand and the royal rod into his left, and thus crowned the king was led to his seat, by the aforesaid Bishops of Durham and Bath, preceded by torch bearers and the said three swords.

Then was the Mass of Sunday begun; and when they came to the offertory the aforesaid Bishops led him to the altar, and he offered a mark of the purest gold (for this is the offering which a king must make at every one of his Coronations) and the same Bishops led him back again to his seat.

Now when the Mass had been celebrated and everything duly finished the same two Bishops, one on the right and the other on the left, led him back crowned and carrying the sceptre in his right hand and the rod in his left, from the church to his chamber, with the ordered procession going before them as above.

Then the procession returned to the choir, and the lord king laid aside his royal crown and royal vestments, and put on lighter crowns and vestments, and so crowned he came to breakfast. And the Archbishops and Bishops sat with him at table each according to his degree and rank; and the earls and barons served in the king's house as their ranks demanded. And the citizens of London served in the butlery, and the citizens of Winchester in the kitchen . . . Now the second day after his Coronation, Richard, King of England, received the homage and fealty of the Bishops, earls and barons of England . . .[24]

What can be added? Other sources tell us that the Coronation was followed by three days of festival and that the king bestowed lavish gifts on the magnates. It was also the occasion when there were Jews in the crowd, some of whom tried to enter the Abbey, triggering a riot during which houses were set on fire. When the king was told about this at the feast he sent Ranulf de Glanville to quell it. But so far out of hand had it got that he was driven back into the feast by threats.[25] This is also the first feast about which we know any details. It called for at least 5,050 dishes, 1,770 pitchers and 900 cups on and in which to serve the food and drink. To this can be added the first piece of music likely to have been composed for the occasion in honour of a monarch. The words are in Latin but in translation they read:

> *The age of gold returns*
> *The world's reform draws nigh*
> *The rich man new cast down*
> *The pauper raised on high.*[26]

The chronicle account catches to the full the magnificence of a Coronation by that date, its sense of unfolding spectacle, its choreography, its richness in terms of robes and artefacts, its use of contrasting passages of speech with chant. Much is already familiar but there is also so much that is new. The ecclesiastical procession now fetches the king-elect, or duke as he is resolutely referred to, from his royal chamber. In the procession various dignitaries are assigned roles bearing everything from items of regalia to candlesticks (these never reappear). The royal robes are carried on the board used in the exchequer and the king now proceeds beneath a canopy. Later, after his crowning, he doffs his regalian robes and ornaments, putting on lighter ones along with a lighter crown. As another chronicler so rightly put it, all was done 'cum pompa magnifica'. Everything was firmly in place for the major transformation which was to occur under the aegis of Henry III.

But there is a wider context to which this Coronation belongs, for it was the prelude to the king's departure on the Third Crusade. It was staged in the midst of all the fervour leading up to such an event, when the chivalry of Christendom rallied to rescue and preserve the Holy Land and the Holy Places from the Infidel. When Richard at last set sail a few months later in December he took with him King Arthur's sword, Excalibur, which he was later to present to Tancred, King of Sicily.[27] But the fact that he took it at all indicates some notion of self-identification with the king of legend whose court was the pattern of chivalry. Can it at least be suggested that the Coronation of Richard was in a sense that of Arthur revived? The suggestion, although unprovable, is at least worth the making and a number of factors suggest that this could well have been in the mind of whoever put together the secular ceremonial in 1189.

I have already referred earlier to the account of the Coronation of King Arthur in Geoffrey of Monmouth's seminal *Historia Regum Britanniae*, compiled during the first half of the twelfth century. The two chapters on Arthur's Coronation festivities would have been incentive enough to escalate regal spectacle.[28] Arthur is conducted to the church by two archbishops with four knights bearing golden swords before him. We are told that there was wonderful music during the procession and at the actual church service, which is not recounted. As they leave for the banquet both Arthur and his queen take off their heavy crowns and put on 'lighter ornaments', just as Richard did before the feast. There were, in fact, two banquets, one for the men and the other for the ladies. The English Coronation banquet was also a male preserve like the Arthurian. 'For the Britons,' writes Geoffrey, 'still observed the ancient custom of Troy by which men and women used to celebrate their festivals apart.' There followed three days of festival with tournaments, archery and other competitive sports and, after this, on the fourth day, 'all who, upon account of their titles, bore any kind of office at this solemnity, were called upon to receive honours and preferments . . .' The scenario for 1189 was exactly the same. Was this an attempt to emulate King Arthur? This was a Coronation staged at precisely the period when the Arthurian romances of chivalry under the aegis of that great innovator of the genre, Chrétien de Troyes, took off as a new ideal of courtly life. Indeed Chrétien's greatest patron was Richard I's brother-in-law, Henry of Champagne.[29] Was the Coronation of 1189 an attempt to revive the world of Arthur, 'For at that time Britain had arrived at such a pitch of grandeur, luxury of ornaments, and politeness of inhabitants, it far surpassed all other kingdoms'? It is an hypothesis that is worth the making. What is clear is that we have travelled already a vast distance from the feudal testimony of 1066 and entered the new world of Camelot.

liqui munu rionuat r naue r ts noo icmgita iar q oatt r nat
laratc sunt o aic q cuint iiscuo r tis quam totum tanp q unimus
clamalat noce magna dicctcs bu ti cua. bi ago qm cuco duit dic bca
dicunus te rpr bu dci unu q dignat qm npi hebirt prte ai scis i scla sclor.

3

Kingship and Consent

IN THE SAME YEAR 'the lord king, inspired by his devotion to St Edward, ordered the church of St Peter at Westminster to be enlarged.' With these words the chronicler, Matthew Paris, records Henry III's decision not so much to 'enlarge' as to demolish and rebuild the Coronation church.[1] This was a building project on a scale unparalleled anywhere else in Western Europe at the time. It was not only, however, driven on by the king's commitment to the cult of his saintly forebear, but equally by a desire to outshine the French king, Louis IX, the builder of the Sainte-Chapelle. In St Edward the Confessor Henry III saw an ideal pattern for his own kingship, one which he set out to imitate and emulate.[2] The very fact that he was to eclipse the saint by rebuilding his church on an even grander scale is evidence enough of that. Although its role as a royal valhalla and as a meeting place for both the King's Council and the nascent House of Commons has long since gone, it still retains its place at the heart of the nation as a royal church, what is called a royal peculiar, one which is exempt from episcopal jurisdiction, and as the setting for a proliferation of royal events, of which over seven centuries later the Coronation still remains the greatest.

The contribution of Henry III to the history of the Coronation, therefore, cannot be overestimated. He was to provide it with its *mise-en-scène*, a supremely graceful, soaring, many-pinnacled glasshouse, rivalling, if not surpassing, the greatest of the French Gothic cathedrals, which indeed inspired it. In Henry III's mind Westminster Abbey had above all to eclipse in splendour the French Coronation church of Reims. To achieve that the king employed for the task a man well

Opposite Coronation of a King, probably Edward II or III, as depicted in the ordo for Edward II, illumination, English, *c.* 1325–50

The second Coronation of Henry III, 1220, illumination, English, XIIIth century

versed about all that was happening in France, Henry de Reyns. The Gothic style was still relatively new to England when the Abbey arose with a speed which must have astonished contemporaries. Twenty-five years before, the monks had also, it seems likely, taken the decision to rebuild. They began with a Lady chapel sited beyond the existing east end, a project to which Henry III contributed the golden spurs with which he was invested at his Coronation there in 1220. Lack of funds meant that the scheme stagnated until the king suddenly embarked on his own massive project, lavishing on it the equivalent of the crown's total revenues for two years. In just twenty-four years the east end, transepts, choir and part of the nave were already up, enough for the church to be formally dedicated on 13 October 1269. This was a church built by a man who had a highly elevated concept of the office of kingship. By 1245 the Abbey had established itself as the immutable setting for the crowning of the kings of England. It was, therefore, custom-built from the outset with that ceremony in mind. Henry III had been crowned in haste as a child of nine in Gloucester cathedral with a gold circlet because London was in the hands of the French. But the central role of the Abbey in his eyes is reflected in the fact that he obtained a papal dispensation to be not only crowned but also anointed a second time in the Abbey in 1220. Both Coronations would have been according to the Third Recension.[3] But the new dynastic church by its very scale and concept would seem to call for a ceremony to match (although it has been equally argued that it prompted no such development). And, indeed, that is precisely what happened, for sometime towards the end of the thirteenth century a new ordo was compiled, the Fourth Recension. This, we know, was certainly used for the Coronation of Edward II in 1308, but there is no way of proving one way or the other that it was used for his father, Edward I, in 1274. As a document (to which I will come shortly), it is difficult not to believe that Henry III had some hand in it. Why else the grand ceremonial north entrance through which the great processions passed, the pushing back of the choir westwards to leave a large clear space at the crossing on which to erect a stage, or the deeply symbolic cosmic pavement in the sacrarium? And that is to name but a few of the features which must have been conceived with the action of the Coronation in mind.

Henry III left an indelible legacy in this church. He lies buried on the site of the former tomb of the Confessor, hard by the new shrine which he built, on which he lavished gold and precious stones and

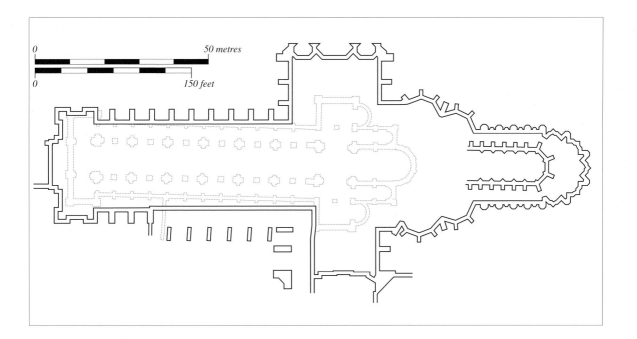

around which he accumulated relics of the Holy Blood, a nail from the Cross, the Virgin's girdle and the stone on which Christ had stood at his Ascension.[4] To these his son, Edward I, was to add more, and one in particular to which we must turn our attention and which was to play a major role in the history of the Coronation, the Stone of Scone. Although Edward was overlord of both the Welsh princes and the kings of Scotland, his ambition was to totally subjugate them and bring the entire island under his rule. In the case of Wales and the erection of a network of castles he would be successful. In that of Scotland he would fail.

The Stone of Scone upon which Alexander III, King of Scotland, had sat in 1249 when he was crowned, was taken by Edward I in 1296 during his Scottish campaign and presented, along with the Scottish crown and sceptre, to the shrine of the Confessor. It remained in the Abbey ever since until a Labour prime minister, Tony Blair, at the very close of the twentieth century returned it by diktat to Scotland on the back of devolution. By this act a unique medieval artefact was vandalised.

What in fact is the Coronation chair and when did it enter the Coronation story? Modern scholarship has shed a mass of new light on this intriguing object.[5] We know that the Stone was acquired in the

The groundplan of Henry III's Abbey superimposed onto that of Edward the Confessor

summer of 1296 and that Edward I had decreed that a chair cast in bronze was to be made to receive it and that it was to be placed next to the altar at the west end of the shrine of St Edward. To make that bronze chair a wooden mould or pattern had to be made. That is likely to have been designed by the king's master-mason, Michael of Canterbury, who was used to designing thrones, and carried out by the king's painter, Walter of Durham. In the summer of 1297 all of that was abandoned due to the expense of the war in Flanders. Instead, a wooden chair was made and installed on a low painted step or dais next to the shrine's altar. This had a canopy or cover over it, which Richard II was later to restore or repair. The existing chair is, therefore, not earlier than the summer of 1297 and not later than March 1300. Its initial decoration was not very complex, with only gilding over a lead white base.

There is no connexion with the Coronation, explicable in the sense that for the next thirty years any reference to the Stone is always to it as a sign of victory. It is significant that the Coronations of both Edward II and Edward III pass by with no reference to its use, nor, which is more to the point, is there any reference in the two sets of negotiations for the Stone's return to Scotland in 1324 and 1328. If it had been used for the Coronation of an English king it would certainly have been pointed out on one or both of those occasions, but then the kings of England never officially styled themselves as kings of Scotland. It is from 1300 onwards, after the Stone had come to England, that the earliest legendary histories of the Stone surface, different in both countries. According to Scottish myth the Stone was brought to Scotland by Pharaoh's daughter Scota and it arrived via Ireland. In the English version it was the stone on which the patriarch Jacob had laid his head at Bethel and dreamt of a ladder of angels stretching from earth to heaven (Genesis 28: 10–22). In both sets of negotiations it figured as an artefact attached to the shrine of St Edward and as a sign to the English of a great victory. Nothing came of the 1324 request for its return, but in 1328 Edward III actually ordered the Abbey to send it north. The abbot, in fact, refused. It is precisely around this time that the Jacob legend appears, and it would seem likely that a far more elaborate programme of gilded and pounced decoration was applied to the chair in its newly enhanced status. Although in an inventory of 1300 it is referred to 'in order that the Kings of England and Scotland might sit on it on the day of their

Opposite The Coronation Chair inset with the Stone of Scone, English, *c.*1297–1300

Coronation' the line is, in fact, crossed. Its earliest certain use was to be in 1399 for Henry IV, but little is known about it for most of the fourteenth century, although its use at Coronations during this period cannot be ruled out. Thomas of Walsingham, when describing the form and manner of an English Coronation, writes that details are to be found in books in the Abbey and with the Archbishop of Canterbury, including the enthronement of the king upon the royal seat above the Stone.[6]

Westminster Palace also underwent a building programme under the aegis of Henry III, particularly in terms of interior decoration and elaborate wallpainting.[7] It, too, both internally and externally, was the setting for much of the Coronation, providing the secular space through which the processions moved and where the feast was staged. With the loss of the continental empire under John the monarchy ceased even more to be migratory, and Westminster became the administrative centre of Plantagenet government. To the exchequer and treasury, which had arrived in the twelfth century, were to be added the Court of Common Pleas in the thirteenth and the Court of the King's Bench in the fourteenth. But it was the palace as a royal residence which was to expand and develop in regal splendour, reflecting accurately all the aspirations of Henry III. Of these developments the most significant was the Painted Chamber.

In all probability this existed in the twelfth century before Henry III's radical transformation of it into one of the most splendid rooms in the palace.[8] The Painted Chamber, which was the king's own principal apartment and bed chamber, was 26 feet wide, over 80 feet long and 30 feet high. It was in this room that the kings of England, according to the Fourth Recension, passed their Coronation vigil. During the second half of the thirteenth century it was redecorated with a series of wallpaintings of Old Testament scenes, representations of Triumphant Virtues and, above the royal bed, the Coronation of St Edward with attendant scenes telling the story of the Confessor, St John and the ring. This story first appears in the life written by St Ailred of Rievaulx in 1163. It tells how the king was approached by St John the Evangelist in disguise as a beggar, and the Confessor, his purse empty, gave him as alms a ring. Several years later two English pilgrims encountered St John in the Holy Land, this time disguised as a handsome old man. He gave them the ring with the instruction that they should deliver it back to the king and tell him that he, too, would shortly join the company of saints.

What we are witnessing here is the king's identification of himself with the Confessor, manifested in a programme of decoration in the inner sanctum of royal secular power. Palace and Abbey were linked by the same imagery, but it is striking that the main scene chosen to be depicted in the wallpainting was not the moment of unction, when the Holy Spirit descended, but instead the king enthroned, holding in his right hand the rod with the dove and with his crown supported by the archbishops of Canterbury and York. I shall return to the significance of that, along with other early representations of Coronations, at the close of this chapter.

Henry III's obsession with St Edward gradually permeates outwards to sanctify virtually anything of any age connected with the rite of Coronation. The king inherited his crown from his father and we have no notion as to its age or appearance, but Henry III saw it as the crown of St Edward. In 1267, when there was a great sale of royal jewels, it was exempted on the grounds of it being the 'diadem of the most sainted King Edward'. So it attained the status of a hallowed relic and was left as such by Henry III to be used at the Coronations of successive kings of England. The ancient chalice or regal together with its paten are referred to at the Coronation of Henry's queen, Eleanor of

The Coronation of Edward the Confessor. Copy of the lost wall painting of *c.*1267 above Henry III's bed in the Painted Chamber of Westminster Palace

The Coronation Spoon, late XIIth century

Provence, in 1236, as those of St Edward and, in the words of Matthew Paris, as being 'from the regalia of the kings of old'. He, on that occasion, equally describes the sword Curtana as being the saint's, and six years later St Edward's sceptre makes its appearance. To all of these we can add a ring which had been taken from the tomb when the saint's body was translated.[9]

Sometime about 1245 the queen was presented with *La Estoire de Seint Aedward le Rei*, a highly mythologising account of the Confessor's life and miracles which has as its subtext a parallel between Edward and her husband. In it the Saxon king has a vision of a royal Coronation church:

> *And then let the king be consecrated*
> *Enthroned and crowned,*
> *And there be the regalia preserved*
> *In sure and certain protection.*[10]

This life epitomised what was to be the courtly cult of the royal saint, for it never took off in terms of popular appeal. And what happens during the thirteenth century is a wish fulfilment of precisely these verses. The Fourth Recension works from the premise of the existence of sacred saintly relics in the safe keeping of the Abbey, the 'royal ornaments of St Edward', relics so precious that the king must be divested of most of them before he leaves the church after his Coronation. If he retains some of the items at his feast then they must be returned immediately after to the abbot who holds them 'as of right'. The result of this was that by the middle of the fourteenth century a motley and confusing collection of crowns, sceptres, rods and assorted royal vestments was assigned to St Edward. These were to be deliberately destroyed by the Parliamentarians in the middle of the seventeenth century. All later antiquarians have been able to do since is to try to make sense out of what the various inventories list, and match the descriptions to any surviving pictorial evidence. The results of this exercise so far cannot be described as anything other than unsatisfactory.

What adds to the confused history of the old regalia is that there would always have been two sets, one the royal ornaments of St Edward and the other personal to the king. Out of the former the only item to survive today is a late twelfth-century spoon, silver gilt with four pearls, later additions, inset into the broadest part of its handle, its bowl engraved with elegant arabesques. This is listed among the secular regalia in 1349 as 'Item i coclear antique forme' (Item, one spoon of ancient form). It has the unique feature of a double-lobed bowl and is probably the work of a major late Romanesque goldsmith working in London. Such a spoon was made for a specific ceremonial purpose, the double bowl sustaining the notion that it was used for the holy oil during unction, the archbishop dipping two of his fingers into it. Medieval depictions of regal unction, however, cannot support its use in this way, for spoons only appear either in connexion with incense boats or as chalice spoons for mixing a little water with the communion wine. If it was used for either of these purposes, that had been forgotten by the middle of the fourteenth century when it was listed with the secular plate as not for liturgical use. Nonetheless what has survived is an object made for Henry II, Richard I or even John and the only piece of goldsmith's work executed for an English royal patron to come down to us from the twelfth century.[11]

The personal regalia of both the king and the queen were kept in the Tower and only add to the complications. Edward II, for example, had no fewer than ten crowns, and we might well puzzle over the origin and exact status of another crown which appears in the wardrobe accounts of his father, Edward I, in 1279: 'a great crown of gold with square balas-rubies (or spinels), emeralds, eastern sapphires, rubies and great eastern pearls . . . which is appointed to be carried over the head of the Kings of England when they go from the church to the banquet on the day of their Coronation'.[12]

All of this is deeply reflective of a new richness, an expansiveness of a kind we have already seen anticipated in the description of Richard I's Coronation. The symbolic overtones implicit in that were to develop and flourish in the two centuries that followed. But in order to do so it demanded a new ordo in tune with what were in effect new concepts of kingship and new notions as to the relationship of a ruler to his people. To accommodate the changed nuances called for a vastly expanded ceremonial, one which simultaneously elevated the wearer of the crown and, at the same time, spelt out his new obligations. The success of the Fourth Recension in meeting these demands can be measured by the fact that it has provided a framework for every Coronation since.

THE FOURTH RECENSION

What is extraordinary about the Fourth Recension is that no one seems able exactly to pinpoint the date of its compilation.[13] In that respect it shares an attribute of its predecessors over whose dating and first use generations of scholars have argued and still argue. What everyone does accept is that it was used in 1308 for Edward II and that, although it was certainly modified for the event, the ordo was already in existence. So it pre-dates 1308, but by how much? The discovery of a mid-thirteenth-century fragmentary rubric for a Coronation related to the Fourth Recension texts in a manuscript by one William de Hasele (d. 1283) is a strong pointer that the fourth ordo may go back quite a way.[14] What the rubric spells out is not a particular Coronation but one in abstract, describing but not naming the various officers present and their role at some future event. This memorandum is likely to have been inserted into this manuscript shortly after 1266, which should mean that some version of the Fourth Recension was in existence by that date.

It is difficult surely to accept that Henry III could have rebuilt Westminster Abbey without having something in his mind concerning the Coronation, particularly when one is aware of his keen interest in the activities of the French monarchy, and that so much of the fourth ordo echoes what was done at the French Coronation. The king was now to be anointed in five places like his French counterpart, and two anthems and three benedictions of the sword and ring were inserted, these last lifted virtually verbatim from the French Coronation ordo. In both we see the ruler cast as hero undergoing a rite of passage in which there is a careful balance struck between the actions of the monarch and those of the clergy, of royal as against ecclesiastical power.[15] There is moreover in the English ordo a carefully observed balance between the parts played by the monarch and the magnates as embodiments of royal power and of its limitations. In that there is a parting of the ways, for the focus of the French Coronation was always to be on the *sacre*, the basis of absolutist rule and one which was to end in disaster in 1789. In sharp contrast, in England, where checks and limitations on the power of the crown were emerging fast during the thirteenth and

The second Coronation of
Henry III, 1259, illumination, English, XIVth century

fourteenth centuries, the focus was on the oath which spelt out the
boundaries of royal power. In this way the Coronation was already by
the mid-fourteenth century flexible enough to be accommodated
within the terms of a constitutional monarchy. In the Fourth Recension
there is this enhancement of the monarchy in terms of its splendour
and magnificence simultaneously with the ruler swearing an oath in
which his power is limited. That curtailment is also vividly reflected in
the pre-Coronation meeting of the king-to-be with the magnates in
order to discuss the Coronation, and also in the reintroduction of the
formal acclamation of the ruler from the earlier ordines.

Although the age of the theocratic priest-kings had long gone, unction was still seen to bestow the quasi-magical power on the king of being able to touch for the King's Evil, the healing of scrofula.[16] That Henry I was the first king of England to exercise this power is hardly surprising, locked as he was into a battle with the Church. He based his powers to heal on the cure of a scrofulous woman recorded in ancient lives of St Edward. The Plantagenets enjoyed huge prestige for their healing powers. Edward I, for example, touched 1,736 individuals during the eighteenth year of his reign. A chaplain of Edward III and a future Archbishop of Canterbury, Thomas Bradwardine, writes of the 'miracles' performed by the king which could be testified to 'by sick persons who had been cured, by those present when the cures took place, or who had seen the results of them, by the people of many nations, and by their universal renown'.[17] In its very early days, when the Gregorian reform was at its height, the royal claim to heal was denounced as a falsehood, but thereafter a silence fell upon ecclesiastical writers, who were content not to refer to something of which they disapproved but not to openly attack it. But this did not erode in any way its popular appeal.

Whoever compiled the Fourth Recension (one scholar suggests Walter of Wenlock, Abbot of Westminster) must have been acutely aware of all these irreconcilabilities. Only when the monarch was enthroned aloft on a raised stage, kissed by the officiating clergy and rendered fealty to by the supporting magnates was he seen as having sovereignty over both. The peers stretched forth their hands to touch the crown, offering it both loyalty and support. In that dramatic moment both lay and ecclesiastical representatives came together in what was a rebuttal of Pope Boniface VIII's bull, *Unam Sanctam* (1302), which relegated the secular power of princes to a lower order subject to the universal pontiff.

In what way does the Fourth Recension differ from its predecessors? In the first place, items which had been part of the First and Second Recensions but which had been dropped in the Third reappear. Fifteen texts in all have been added, hugely increasing its length. The longest addition was the special order of the Mass, for which were provided the introit, two collects, the epistle, gradual, tract, gospel, gospel offertory verse, two special orations, two secrets, a preface, a special benediction and two post-communion prayers. This is the first time, also, when an ordo has substantial rubrics with precise directions.

These can vary quite considerably from one manuscript to another. Indeed, an indication as to just how complicated the ceremony had become is reflected in a description of the action at the Coronation of Edward III in 1327, the *Corounement du Nouel Rei*, which only includes the incipits for the prayers. This account enabled an onlooker to follow the action at which they were present.[18]

There are a considerable number of manuscript copies of this ordo and, as in the case of its predecessors, they vary. Some, in addition, provide notation for the chants, enabling us for the first time to recreate the music. The manuscripts fall into three groups. One pre-dates 1308, of which one, written in a large clear script, may have been used at the Coronation of Edward II, possibly carried by the king's monk. A second group, it has been suggested, pre-dates Edward III's Coronation and yet a third, and by far the largest group,

Coronation of a king from the Lytlington Missal, illumination, English, *c*.1382–84

has a text which may precede or follow the Coronation of Richard II in 1377.

Two of the key manuscripts are fortunately virtually identical and both are in the muniment room of Westminster Abbey. One is the Lytlington or Westminster Missal, compiled by Abbot Lytlington (1362–86), which can be dated to 1383–4, and the other is the *Liber Regalis*, which recent art historical research dates to the 1390s. As the *Liber Regalis* was to be the text which those putting together the Coronation of James I in 1603 turned to, I give a synopsis of the action as it appears in that manuscript.[19]

1. A stage is to be erected at the crossing in Westminster Abbey with a flight of steps from the west side for the king to ascend and a further flight on the eastern side for him to descend and approach the high altar.

2. On the stage a 'lofty throne' is to be sited so that the king may 'be clearly seen by all the people'.

3. If the Archbishop of Canterbury be incapacitated he shall choose one of his suffragans to perform the ceremony.

4. On the day before his coronation the king is to ride bare-headed to the Palace of Westminster 'to be seen by the people'.

5. The Coronation is to be on a Sunday or a holy day.

6. The king is to spend the night before in prayer and contemplation, seeking the virtues needful for a ruler.

7. The Abbot of Westminster is to instruct the king about the Coronation. If he for some reason is unavailable, the prior and convent shall choose another.

8. On the day of the Coronation the prelates and nobles of the realm should assemble at the palace 'to consider about the consecration and election of the new king, and also about confirming and surely establishing the laws and customs of the realm'.

9. The king is bathed 'as is the custom' and attired in 'spotless apparel', not wearing shoes but socks only. The effect must be that his body 'glistens by the actual washing and the beauty of the vestments'. In the great hall he is lifted 'with all gentleness and reverence' on to a throne covered with cloth of gold.

10. From the Abbey a clerical procession consisting of members of the episcopacy and of the convent shall make its way to the great hall. They

return in procession with the king to the Abbey chanting and singing anthems.

11. The royal almoner supervises a path laid with ray (striped) cloth from the palace to the Abbey. After the event the cloth within the Abbey is the perquisite of the sacrist and that outside is distributed by the almoner to the poor.

12. The stage and steps within the Abbey are to be covered with carpets by the royal ushers and cloth of gold is to be hung around the top of the stage.

13. Royal chamberlains must see that the throne is adorned 'with silken and most precious coverings'.

14. There then follow details of the procession. The king is to be preceded by the prelates and monks and himself led by the hand by the bishops of Durham and Bath 'in accordance with ancient custom'. Immediately before the king the chancellor, if he be a bishop, with the chalice of St Edward. Before him also the treasurer, again if he be a bishop or abbot, bearing the paten. Both are to be *in pontificalibus*. After the chalice and paten follow dukes or earls, 'especially who by kinship are nearly related to the king', who bear the sceptre with the cross and the golden rod with the dove. All of these items of regalia should be delivered from the Abbey to the palace by the abbot. After the regalia come three earls bearing swords, Curtana carried by the Earl of Chester and the two others by the earls of Huntingdon and Warwick. Then follows a noble appointed by the king carrying the spurs. The king and the queen (if there be one) are each under canopies of purple silk carried on four silver lances topped with silver-gilt bells. Each canopy is carried by sixteen Barons of the Cinque Ports, four to a lance supporting it in rota. The fabric afterwards is a perquisite of the barons, the lances and bells of the Abbey, as, in addition, are all the carpets, silken cloths and cushions placed in the church. This was 'in accordance with ancient custom'.

15. When the king is seated on the stage the Archbishop of Canterbury, who is to consecrate him, addresses the assembled people at each of the four sides, 'inquiring their will and consent'. As he does this the king stands and turns to face each side in turn. The people give their assent shouting 'So be it' and 'Long live the king' and 'uttering with great joy' his name.

16. The choir sings the anthem *Firmetur manus tua*.

17. The archbishop who is to celebrate Mass revests himself at the altar 'on account of the crowd that is come together, lest he should be hindered by it'.

18. The bishops of Durham and Bath shall support the king on either side

86   CORONATION

and together with the other bishops shall lead him down the steps to the high altar. The abbot is always to be in attendance acting as a prompt to the king 'so that everything may be done right'.

19. The king makes an offering of a pound of gold and then prostrates himself upon the carpets and cushions which have been laid by the ushers. The archbishop says a prayer over him.

20. One of the bishops makes a short sermon to the people while the archbishop sits in a chair before the altar, the king sitting opposite him.

21. Then the archbishop administers the Coronation oath followed by an admonition on behalf of the bishops, to which the king also responds. He then confirms all that he has agreed to by swearing at the altar.

22. The king prostrates himself again before the altar while the archbishop kneels and intones the *Veni creator spiritus*. A prayer follows and then two bishops or singers intone the litany. While this is sung the archbishop and all the other bishops prostrate themselves alongside the king and privately recite the seven penitential psalms.

25. More prayers and responses follow, after which the king sits again in his chair and then goes to the altar and divests himself of his robes, except his tunic and shirt 'which are open at the breast, and between the shoulders, and on the shoulders, and also at the elbow . . .' The silver loops sealing the openings are undone by the archbishop, the king kneeling beneath a canopy. The archbishop anoints the king with holy oil on his hands, breast, between the shoulders, on the shoulders, on both elbows and on the head in the form of a cross. Then his head is anointed a second time with chrism. The holy oil is to be in a silver phial and the chrism in one of gilt. After this the silver loops are fastened. During this action the anthem *Unxerunt Salomonem* is sung.

26. The first phase of vesting then follows, opening with a linen coif for the head, then the *colobium sindonis* cut like a dalmatic. The coif the king is to wear for seven days and on the eighth a bishop is to say a Mass of the Trinity in the Chapel Royal, after which he is to wash the king's hair in hot water, dry it and 'reverently arrange' it and put on it a golden circlet which the king shall wear the whole day.

27. The archbishop blesses the royal ornaments and the king is vested in them by the abbot; first a long tunic reaching to his feet 'wrought with golden figures before and behind', then buskins, sandals and spurs. The sword is blessed and delivered by the bishops. The king is girded with it and then vested with the armils which 'shall hang like a stole round his neck, from both shoulders to the elbows, and shall be bound to the elbows by silken knots . . .' Then comes the mantle, 'which is square and

Opposite Coronation of a king from the Lytlington Missal, illumination, English, *c*.1382–84

worked all over with golden eagles'. The crown is blessed and placed on the king's head, after which follows a blessing and the delivery of the ring. The king takes off the sword and offers it at the altar, from which it is redeemed by the earl 'who is the greatest of those present'. Gloves are put on the king's hands and then the sceptre with the cross put into his right hand and the gold rod with the dove in his left. All of these actions are accompanied by prayers. The regalia, it stipulates, must be laid ready on the altar by the sacrist from the outset, 'that everything may be done without hindrance from the very great concourse of people'.

28. The king then kisses the bishops and, together with 'the nobles of the realm', he is led back up the steps to the throne on the stage while the Te Deum is sung. When ended, the archbishop says the prayer *Sta et retine* and the king is enthroned, and 'the peers of the realm shall stand around the king and stretch forth their hands as a sign of fealty, and offer themselves to support the king and the crown'.

29. The Mass then follows. The gospel is carried to the king to kiss and he then descends to present to the archbishop the bread and wine and also an offering of a mark of gold. When the archbishop has given the kiss of peace to the bishop who took the gospel to the king, the same bishop takes the pax to him. When the peace has been given the king descends and receives communion in both kinds.

30. The Mass ended, the king descends to the high altar and a procession of clergy and nobles forms to the shrine of St Edward. The Great Chamberlain divests the king of his regalia and vestments, which are laid on the altar by the abbot. The Great Chamberlain then revests the king in robes of state and the archbishop puts on him another crown but returns to him the regalia sceptres. Then follows a procession back through the church 'with great glory'.

31. The Abbey of Westminster is to receive on the day a hundred bushels of corn and a 'modius' of wine and of fish.

32. The sceptres are to be returned to the Abbey immediately after the feast to join the rest of the regalia there, 'the repository of the royal ensigns for ever, by papal bulls, kings' charters, and old custom always observed'. A list then follows of the principal officers at the feast.

The text also contains provision for the Coronation of a queen either with a king or on her own. It stipulates that she is to be attired

Coronation of a king and
queen from the Lytlington
Missal, illumination,
English, c.1382–84

in crimson devoid of embroidery and that her hair should be worn
loose and held by a jewelled circlet. When she is crowned on her own
she is anointed only on the head and given a sceptre in addition to a
ring and a crown. When she is crowned with her husband she is

anointed also on the breast and receives in addition a rod. All these indicate that the crowning on her own of a queen is an earlier rite elaborated in the joint Coronation ordo, which elevates queenship on to a level comparable to that of the king.[20]

Even the full text, of which I have given only a synopsis, does not provide for every contingency as any attempt to restage even in the mind's eye a Coronation quickly reveals. Full though the rubrics are, they are still not full enough and the ordo remains a play text awaiting its director and designer. Anyone who has been involved with elaborate royal ceremonial knows (I speak from experience) that much can be improvised for a particular event and not even written down, so that the gap between the text of the Fourth Recension and what actually happened on the day could well have been substantial. Between 1216 and 1327 there are only six Coronations: Henry III (1216 and 1220), Eleanor of Provence (1236), Edward I (1274), Edward II (1308) and Edward III (1327).[21] Our knowledge of these is fuller for some than for others, but it is a fragmentary story rather like a jigsaw puzzle from which some of the most important pieces are missing and, moreover, are likely to remain so. Collectively, however, they take the story forward. In particular, they mirror the power struggles at the heart of this century and a half of Plantagenet rule.

Kingship under siege

In order to understand the change in focus in the Coronation during the thirteenth and fourteenth centuries we need to reconnoitre back in time to the disastrous reign of Henry III's father, John, when relationships between the king and his magnates totally collapsed. John had not only broken rules of conduct which feudal society had regarded as sacrosanct, but lost England's continental empire to France and been locked into a seven-year struggle with the pope over the appointment of a new Archbishop of Canterbury, leading to the country being laid under an interdict. Peace was made with the pope, by which the kingdom was received as a papal fief, only to be followed by a disastrous war with France. In May 1215 the king was forced to put his seal to the Great Charter or Magna Carta.

This document set the agenda for the centuries to follow, a foundation stone which saw the king as someone no longer answerable to

God alone but also to the law. No fewer than sixty clauses put into writing an agreed body of laws covering every aspect of government and of the relationship of the king to his subjects. The importance of Magna Carta only grew with time, but in a single document we see embodied a change of focus which was to radically affect the Coronation.

The fifty-six-year rule of Henry III was about the maintenance of some constraints on a king who still sought a continental empire, who was arrogant, extravagant and obstinate and whose aim was to be absolute. Both the new Abbey and the transformation of Westminster Palace were visual manifestations of his mania for majesty on the grand scale. His reign was punctuated by conflicts with the barons. For almost a decade, between 1257 and 1265, king and barons were locked in a power struggle over the control of central government. The magnates attempted to force the king to rule according to a Council of Fifteen of their own choosing. Civil war resulted, the king winning when the barons were defeated at the battle of Evesham and their leader, Simon de Montfort, was slain. During this strife the vehicle for reconciliation became the Great Council to which, as the reign progressed, came not only the magnates but knights of the shires and burgesses representing the towns. These began to be called 'parliaments', parleys between the king and his subjects about affairs of state. Parliament was an emergent institution which was destined to play a major role in the Coronation's history. By the fourteenth century Parliament invariably followed every Coronation.

Although there were periodic clashes between the king and the barons, for the majority of the time they worked together in harmony governing the state. That depended, however, on the king observing the rules, the key one of which was to keep a check on patronage, his distribution of rewards and benefits. Neither Henry III nor his warrior son, Edward I, the conqueror of Wales, could be faulted on that score, but in 1307 there came to the throne a king who ushered on to the scene a new phenomenon, the royal favourite. The wayward Edward II's passion for Piers Gaveston upset the balance dramatically, so much so that it was to precipitate a major change in the Coronation oath.

As in so much about the early history of the Coronation we are hampered in the case of the oath by uneven evidence.[22] It is generally accepted that Richard I's oath was different from the standard *tria praecepta*. What had been the second promise was replaced by the third one and a new third promise was introduced, in which the monarch guaranteed the observation of good laws and customs and the abolition of evil. The old clause two, which prohibited rapacities and iniquities, was dropped. According to the chronicler Matthew Paris, John swore a different oath again and the young Henry III made that taken by Richard I. Nothing is known about the oath taken at the Coronation of Edward I, although we do know that he swore an additional fourth clause prohibiting the alienation of the rights of the Crown. This we discover through papal letters, and it certainly went back to Henry III, although whether it was tacked on to the king's Coronation oath or to an oath of fealty whereby he recognised papal overlordship is unknown. What this embodied was the development of the notion of the crown in connexion with the idea of the inalienability of royal rights and possessions by whoever temporarily might be wearing it. The concept of the crown as an abstract entity was common in England since the twelfth century, but in the course of the thirteenth century the impersonal crown also gained constitutional importance.

None of all this could ever have anticipated the revolutionary oath which the wayward Edward II was forced to accept in 1308. This time the whole format was recast. The third promise was turned into an introduction, the two promises which followed it remained the same, but the fourth was dramatically new. In it the king bound himself to observe the future laws made by the community of the realm. The fact that so many copies of this oath exist is an index as to just how significant it was regarded in retrospect. Both the Latin and the Anglo-Norman text (which was the one the king used) therefore survive. In the former, Edward swore to keep the just laws *quas vulgus elegerit*. In the latter, 'les quels la communaute de vostre roialme aura eslu'. The word *vulgus* is not exactly the same as *la communaute de vostre roialme*, though at the time they must have regarded it as equivalent. By 1308 the magnates were increasingly calling upon the *populus*, *vulgus* or the 'people' in support of their opposition to the king. What the oath brought centre stage at the Coronation was the king's relationship with his own people and the rules which should circumscribe it.

What precipitated this? When the king met the magnates to discuss the Coronation the subject of Piers Gaveston came up. He had just been created Earl of Cornwall. In the Coronation he eclipsed everyone by wearing purple velvet embroidered with pearls; he was assigned the place of greatest honour in the procession, carrying the crown. In the service itself it was Gaveston who redeemed the sword and carried it before the king. Worse, he flaunted himself at the feast afterwards as marshal. No fewer than nine chroniclers record the quarrel between Edward and the magnates on this occasion. The *Annales Paulini* record that he was forced to promise 'that he would do whatever they demanded in the next parliament, so long as the Coronation was not put off'. It was, in fact, delayed from 18 to 25 February, and in the 'parliamentum' which immediately followed Gaveston was sent into exile.

What began its life as a mechanism to get rid of a royal favourite was to become the ideological linchpin from which flowed the events of the reign. It forced Edward to accept the Ordinances of 1311, submitting himself to the dictates of the magnates. His attempt to reverse this eleven years later and destroy clause four ended in failure. The Statute of York moved from the premise that a king could not alienate part of his sovereignty to the barons. The governance of the realm was the joint task of the king and the *communitas regni*, redefining parliament as not merely consisting of the barons acting on behalf of the *communitas* but actually including them in their own right. In the end, in 1327, Edward was deposed and subsequently murdered. Every king since has sworn that oath.

The catastrophic reign of Edward neatly demonstrates that the ideological bargains struck at Coronations belong to the heart of medieval history. They also explain what happened at the Coronation of the young Edward III, which, as a consequence of his father's behaviour, was to represent a high tide of radicalism. Two manuscripts record that at this Coronation the Anglo-Saxon election was revived. In one version four earls *ex parte populi* report the election of the king to those assembled in the Abbey.[23] They ask that the prince, thus elected *ab omni populo*, be received and consecrated by the clergy. The Archbishop of Canterbury then selects four bishops and four abbots to inquire *ad populum* in the church if the latter will testify to the truth of the earls' report. If the answer from those assembled is positive, both envoys and clergy give thanks to God and the elected king is led into the Abbey. What all this means is that Edward III was not presented as king by hereditary right, but because he was elected by the magnates and the 'people'. The Fourth Recension in its final form is not so extreme as here, but it does preserve the presentation to the people at the opening of the action, 'inquiring their will and consent'.

Although all of this would seem to lead to some diminution in regal status, everything, in fact, was pushed very much in the opposite direction. Thirty years after his Coronation Henry III asked the great theologian, Robert Grosseteste, in what way was he different as a consequence of unction.[24] The bishop replied circumspectly, making a clear distinction between the sacerdotal and royal offices. He stated that the king receives through this act the spiritual benefits and graces necessary for the virtues he requires to meet his royal obligations. The reply cannot have pleased the king. Other thirteenth-century theologians, however, are far less cautious and speak of the effect of anointing with chrism as meaning the reception by the king of the sevenfold gifts of the Holy Spirit. It is not known at which Coronation chrism was reintroduced. The chroniclers refer to it being used in 1170 for Henry the Younger and it is also noted as having been used for Edward I, who had a golden eagle made for the event, the earliest reference to an object that could be the ampulla for the holy oil which became part of the regalia. One thing is certain: the Fourth Recension is absolutely specific that the king is anointed in all in eight places with holy oil and on the head with chrism.[25]

The question which Henry III addressed to Grosseteste, and its answer, had their effect, for the king decided not to be buried in the apparel he wore when he was anointed but in his robes of majesty. For his burial in 1272 there was delivered: 'one royal rod, one dalmatic of red samite with orphreys and stones, one mantle of red samite most splendidly adorned with orphreys and precious stones, a gold brooch, a pair of stockings of red samite with orphreys, one pair of shoes of red samite . . .' When the tomb of Edward I was opened in 1774 he was found to be similarly clothed in 'a dalmatic . . . of red silk damask' over which there was 'the royal mantle, or pall, of rich crimson satin, fastened on the left shoulder [i.e. his right] with a magnificent fibula of metal gilt with gold'. In his left hand he held a rod topped with a white enamelled dove and in his left a sceptre. Only Edward II was buried wearing the tunic, shirt, cap, coif and gloves 'in which the king was anointed on the day of his Coronation', although for the funeral the body was further dressed in royal robes including a mantle, a dalmatic, hose, shoes and spurs, all items which had been worn at his Coronation, but which were returned after the event to the Royal Wardrobe.[26]

What we catch here is that henceforth emphasis was to be placed on the elaboration of the secular presentation of the monarchy in what

Second Great Seal of Henry III, 1259, with an innovatory throne and the introduction of Edward the Confessor's sceptre with the dove from his forged Great Seal (*see page 55*)

was a highly symbolic age accustomed to think and look in terms of signs and symbols. In its new setting and with this in mind the Coronation was to fully respond to the opportunities offered to enhance the magnificence of the wearer of the crown. Every aspect was to be explored: ceremonial, dress, gesture, music, poetry and decoration together with the lavishness of the entertainments which gradually began to frame such an event.

SYMBOLIC SHOW

So much connected with a Coronation depended on moveables. The Abbey with its soaring architecture, its army of statuary, its wall-paintings, stained glass and bejewelled shrine was, when it came to staging a late medieval Coronation, like a theatre awaiting the arrival of the scenery, props and costumes, not to mention the actors and musicians. Only at the beginning of the fourteenth century do we begin to learn something about items like the great stage which was erected at the crossing and just how extraordinary it was. An entry in the accounts of the royal Office of Works for 1307–11 reads as follows: 'Concerning the royal seat ordained and made in the monks' church in the midst of the choir in which the king and queen were crowned: note these seats were wainscoted all round and so high that men at arms, namely earls, barons, knights and other nobles could ride beneath them.'[27]

This matter-of-fact entry conjures up an astonishing picture, that the stage occupying the crossing must have been at least thirteen feet high and probably more to enable those on horseback to ride beneath it as though it were some kind of bridge. The arrangement was the reverse of that of a modern Coronation where tiered seats are erected in the transepts to look down on the action at the crossing.

The medieval Coronation stage was one both looked up to and down upon. Those at floor level gazed up, glimpsing the king as he was presented to each side at the opening of the ceremony. Later in the proceedings they could surely see the king enthroned above them as the throne, at least later, was approached by a flight of steps and therefore must have been very high. But onlookers could also look down on the action. In the corners of each terminal wall of the transepts there are newel staircases leading to the galleries in the triforium. The *Liber Regalis* constantly refers to the great concourse of people who could hinder the action and, indeed, these events could be densely crowded, so much so that in 1308 the king was forced to enter the Abbey another way and a wall was pushed over, killing a knight.[28] These must have been occasions when the whole medieval establishment came together, producing a crush, which made it essential for the regalia to be already on the high altar at the opening or otherwise there was no way of getting it there.

Once the stage was established as a feature the Royal Works would have stuck more or less to a formula. We have, in fact, to wait until the Household Ordinances of Henry VII (1494) to get a far fuller description of one of these Coronation stages, a structure which had to support one if not two thrones, plus a throng of officiating clergy and nobility. Then it is described as being railed and covered in red cloth with, at ground level, part if not all of it walled in, creating a room beneath which housed drink for the king and to which access could only be had by doors guarded by the royal ushers. This would suggest

Opposite Photograph of Henry III's Westminster Abbey, the view from the choir towards the sacrarium and high altar

that by the late fifteenth century it had ceased to be a bridge-like construction. We learn far more, too, about the staircase approaches, both of which seem to have been as wide as the stage itself, approaching from the west and descending towards the high altar from the east.[29] Considerable improvisation as to the decoration of these stages must have occurred for on to them could be bestowed the riches of the Royal Wardrobe. Even though barely a week elapsed between Edward II's deposition and his son's Coronation, the stage was not only erected but hung around with 21 tapestries, 6 pieces of cloth of gold having diaper work of silk and 22 pieces of cloth of gold on linen, and the whole floor covered with lawn cloth on to which was laid the same ray cloth as lined the path from the palace. The throne on this occasion was covered in cloth of gold, with five cushions acting as a footrest, and above it there was a canopy.[30]

Much of the drama of the ritual must have lain in the choreographed descent and ascent of the king with attendants both down and up the great staircase leading to the sanctuary and the high altar. There, too, in 1327 both the king's chair and that for the archbishop were covered with cloth of gold. These stood on the celebrated Cosmati pavement which was probably the gift of the pope and for which Abbot Richard de Ware had brought from Rome both the craftsmen and some of the materials. It is an abstract spelt out in Purbeck marble, porphry, onyx, various limestones, alabaster and opaque glasses in a kaleidoscope of sophisticated colours: purple, green, golden yellow, blue, turquoise, white and red. What is depicted is an image of the cosmos in terms of the Greek Platonic tradition in which geometry and pure number linked the tangible world of the senses and the divine world approached through the intellect.[31]

The inscription on it ends with these words: 'Here is the perfectly rounded sphere which reveals the eternal pattern of the universe.' In it are mapped out the three levels of existence ascending up and through the sensible and intelligible worlds to the spiritual sphere symbolised in the single round stone at the centre as the eternal archetype. It is difficult not to believe that this sacred space with its complex cosmic imagery on which the kings of England were henceforth to be anointed was laid out with the Coronation in mind. For that of Edward I it was covered with a rich cloth, and yet the pavement's schema in one sense is only completed when the king has been anointed and crowned as an image of the ninth sphere, the boundary between the created

Opposite The cosmati pavement of the Abbey's sacrarium, 1260s

universe and the divine reality beyond. Indeed, every argument for kingship through into the seventeenth century works from this premise, that a king rules over the hierarchy of his subjects as God rules over the hierarchy of the universe. The one is a mirror-image of the other.

Such an image would conjure up, too, the music of the spheres, for in that scheme of things the cosmos was constructed according to the proportions of the musical scale. Terrestrial music was but an earthly counterpart of the celestial music of the spheres. Music played a major part in the Coronation rite which moved from speech to chant, not forgetting the important part which silence could play in such great rituals. For the first time, in 1308, we are able to shed some light on the role played by music in Coronations. On that occasion there were significant changes to what was used. The antiphon *Confortare*, for instance, was deliberately moved in order to highlight the act of crowning, but even more significant was the alteration of the antiphon *Unxerunt Salomonem* which traditionally accompanied the anointing. For that there was composed a totally new tune which borrowed part of the melody of the Magnificat antiphon for the feast of St Edmund, king and martyr. In doing this those present would have been reminded of Edward II's descent from a second Anglo-Saxon royal saint. The new composition drew on pre-Advent antiphons in which Christ is described as ascending his throne and which also celebrated his baptism. The parallel offered is between Christ's baptism and the king's reception of unction. To further elevate the monarchy the Coronation Mass borrowed music from that used for the Coronation of a pope.[32]

If the Abbey's interior was transformed for the occasion so, too, was the palace. The Coronation of Edward II had a six-month lead time and the palace, which was in a run-down state, was completely cleaned and put in order. As winter drew on and the evenings darkened candles were supplied so that the work would not be impeded. There is mention also of the construction of a temporary second great hall, the duplicate of the one in stone. This was over five hundred feet long and in it was staged the prefatory secular enthronement of the king. Above the throne, in an arch, stood a gilded copper statue of a king. The first occasion on which such a temporary hall went up that we know about was in 1274 for Edward I. In addition, in 1308, there was a fountain in the lesser domestic hall which spouted red and white wine and a spiced drink called pimento.[33]

There was a similar rush to spruce up things in 1327. This time the great chamber was hung with tapestries adorned with shields with the royal arms, the bench coverings were patterned with coats of arms and the royal seat was covered with cloth of gold and provided with cushions. Westminster Hall itself was adorned with hangings and its floor covered with linen cloth. The king's seat glittered with the usual cloth of gold and Turkey silk.[34]

What all of this tells us is that the guest list must have run into thousands, and inevitably not all of the guests had London residences. In 1308 there were fourteen lesser halls built parallel to the temporary great hall. The Coronation now consisted not only of the rite itself and the feast which followed, but went on to include several days of tilts, tourneys and further feasting. Edward I's festivities lasted for fourteen days in emulation of Solomon. In the case of Edward II we know that 40 ovens had to be built, calling for a small army of cooks, not to mention vast quantities of fuel.[35] In the case of Edward I we get a glimpse of the huge quantities of provisions sent for from all over the kingdom. In February 1274 orders went out to the county of Gloucestershire alone to provide 60 oxen and cows, 60 swine, 2 fat boars, 40 pigs and 3,000 capons and hens. Bishops, abbots and priors were asked to procure as many swans, peacocks, cranes, rabbits and kids as they could.[36]

In these fragmentary pieces of information we witness the Coronation expanding as an event far beyond what happened in the Abbey. In fact, a Coronation had become the greatest festivity of any reign. While in the Abbey the Church might reign triumphant as lay deferred to clerical power, outside a deliberate riposte was staged in which the whole pyramid of medieval feudal society was displayed in witness to a revival of royal power. By the middle of the fourteenth century the secular aspect had developed into a massive display of rank and power, one which inevitably, as happened in 1308 over Piers Gaveston, led to clashes of interest and conflicting claims among the king and his assembled magnates.

CORONATION OFFICES

The Red Book of the Exchequer suddenly records in 1236 the Coronation of Henry III's queen, Eleanor of Provence.[37] The reason for this was that 'Great disputes arose about the services of the officers of the king's household, and about the rights belonging to their offices.'

This was eventually to lead to the establishment at each Coronation of a Court of Claims whose role was to sort out and pronounce upon the bids by rival contenders to perform this or that service for the king on the day. The earliest records that we have for one of these courts in action are for the Coronation of Richard II in 1377, but it is possible that they existed earlier.

The emergence of such a court must have been the eventual consequence of the clashes and claims which caused someone to put pen to paper in 1236. On that occasion Earl Warenne claimed the right to carry the sword 'Curtana'. The Earl of Chester and Huntingdon claimed that right as his own on the grounds that it was a service which descended with the earldom of Chester. In that case the king intervened and we are told 'the strife subsided'. The two sceptres were carried by two knights 'because that service does not fall to any one by right, but only those to whom the king is pleased to entrust it'. The list runs through claims as varied as the right to be steward at the feast for the day to being the person who presented the king with his napkin. In every instance those who petitioned did so on the basis that it was 'his of old', 'comes from old time' or 'by old-established right'.

The truth of the matter was that the grounds for these claims were often flimsy, and 'old' could mean little more than a generation back.[38] The links argued on precedent and from association with land tenure could be dubious in the extreme, but they were fought hard and often became fact. For those who won there was not only the glamour of the occasion and the opportunity to be in proximity to the king, but perks to be had ranging from pieces of plate to cloths of estate. Some, like the queen's chamberlain in 1236, could do extremely well out of such an event, for he left the richer by the queen's bed as well as basins and other items. Most of this had begun to be systematised by the middle of the thirteenth century, when the grant of a particular piece of land was made in return for a certain Coronation service, a transaction known as serjeanty. The earliest traceable instance of this comes in 1212 and was for holding the queen's towel at her Coronation. Already by the twelfth century many of the nobles acted on state occasions such as Coronations and crown-wearings as almoner, steward, marshal, seneschal, butler and chamberlain. Some of these posts were less onerous than others. The almoner, for example, distributed the leftovers from the feast to the poor and exercised jurisdiction over all comers, settling the disputes which could arise at such distributions. The marshal had to maintain order within the palace and also arrange hostelry for the small army of guests. In return he claimed a saddled palfrey from every earl and baron knighted on the day. Bearing in mind the hordes of guests, he will have earned them.

Such services drew in not only the aristocratic and knightly classes but also townspeople. The Cinque Ports sent canopy bearers for the king and queen, sixteen in all, four to each stave.[39] They first appear in 1189 at the Coronation of Richard I *quod de consuetudine antiqua in coronationis regis habuerunt*. The ports involved were Hastings, Romney, Hythe, Dover and Sandwich, to which were later added Winchelsea and Rye. Together they occupied a crucial geographical position in terms of the defence of the realm, as well as in those of trade and commerce. Each year they supplied the crown with 57 ships. The canopy bearers were barons for the day and their perquisite was the fabric of the canopy itself, which was generally sold off and the money divided between the towns involved. Although the Cinque Ports had already ceased to be of any importance by 1500, they were to continue to render this service until the reign of George IV. It was William IV who, disgusted at the extravagance of his predecessor, abolished it. Nevertheless, the barons were to resurface in 1901 before a Court of Claims and attain a place as standard bearers at the Coronation of Edward VII.

Of all of these offices the most legendary is that of King's Champion. That office was certainly in existence by 1327 and was attached to the manor of Scrivelsby, Lincolnshire. The terms of the land tenure or serjeanty specified that the tenant should at each Coronation proffer: 'to defend with his body against any man who may assert that the king is not rightful king, that he speak not good nor truth, and for the execution of this proffer our Lord the King shall give him the best charger he has save one and his best armour save one'.[40]

This office may well have originally been held by the Marmion family, lords of Tamworth Castle and Scrivelsby, whose last co-heir died about 1292, after which Scrivelsby passed to the Dymokes. In 1377 this office was further defined. The Champion was to ride ahead of the procession and if anyone actually challenged him he would get both the horse and the armour which the king provided, otherwise not. On that occasion he turned up at the north door of the Abbey and was sent away and told to perform his challenge at the feast, which he did.

Challenges were a feature of late medieval feasts, and so there it stayed until the last occasion when this was enacted, the Coronation of George IV. Under William IV the Champion went the same way as the Cinque Ports canopy bearers, but also returned in a banner-bearing guise in 1902.[41]

The rivalry over Coronation services is a keen index of a highly stratified society where rank was measured in both the duty performed and proximity to the monarch. In spite of so many posts being assigned by descent, either through land tenure or title, there was always at any Coronation a large pool of patronage at the king's disposal. The choice of this or that person to bear a sceptre or a crown or to fasten on the spurs or redeem the sword was looked upon as a benchmark in terms of royal favour. In 1308 Edward II's decision that the crown, in the words of the *Annales Paulini*, was 'to be carried in the filthy hands of Piers Gaveston' added fuel to fires already burning brightly enough in the minds of the assembled magnates.[42] In the make-up of the chivalrous mind such marks of favour were of signal importance. In a feudal society such events should be public manifestations of the immutable *ordo* of society, and not be soiled by upstarts.

Thirteen hundred and eight is interesting for another reason in this context, for the magnates made a bid to carry articles of the regalia of St Edward, items which, in the words of the same chronicler, 'they ought not to have touched, for they are relics; only the king's own [i.e. personal] Coronation regalia, in which he will return to the palace after the mass and then sit at the feast do they have the right to bear'.[43] The magnates, in fact, got their way on that occasion, for only the chalice and paten were borne by clerics.

These great processions, increasingly spectacular to watch, took the Coronation out to a wider public. They moved in and out of the great internal spaces of both the Abbey and the palace but, more importantly, made their way in the open along the ray-cloth path linking the one building to the other. Those who lined the route would have seen their future ruler, bare-headed, devoid of his robes of state and walking in his stockinged feet, a bishop guiding him by either hand. He would be framed by the silver staves of the canopy borne by the Barons of the Cinque Ports, and the onlookers would have been alerted to his imminence by the tinkling of the silver-gilt bells and the chant of the monks. Several hours later they would have seen the same figure re-emerge transformed, dazzling in his robes of state, no longer led but triumphant, clasping orb and sceptre, and on his head a crown of gold and precious jewels. For an age whose mental premise was the image rather than the word the impact must have been overwhelming.

PICTURING THE CORONATION

It is only at this period that for the first time we begin to get some impression of what these events must have looked like. England, however, produces nothing comparable to the magnificent Coronation Book of Charles V of France prompted by his Coronation on 19 May 1364. This contains no less than 38 miniatures closely related to the text ordo but expanding it in terms of showing setting, dress, gesture and action.[44] As a reflection of its English equivalent it must be discounted, although it does include a record, albeit a diagrammatic one, of a Coronation stage. A narrow flight of steps leads down to the high altar. The enclosure floats on narrow wooden pillars painted with golden fleur de lys and the rails of the stage have been draped with rich fabrics as we know happened at Westminster. That at least provides an impression of what went up in the abbey, although reduced in the miniature to toy-town proportions.

In the case of England we are confronted from the mid-thirteenth century onwards with a series of illuminations seemingly depicting Coronations. Some, like those in the Lytlington Missal and the *Liber Regalis*, are actually set into copies of the Coronation ordo. Most, however, were occasioned by another circumstance, for their recurrence in chronicles reflects the fact that the accession of a new ruler measured time. Royal bureaucracy actually measured time by regnal years. The richest sequence of these Coronation scenes occurs in a *Flores Historiarum* on loan to the British Library. Illuminated in Westminster in the 1250s while the new church was arising, it includes no fewer than ten Coronation tableaux, starting with King Arthur. Even though they emanate from a scriptorium in the Coronation church, they cannot be relied upon in any way as accurate depictions of a late medieval Coronation.[45]

The grandest of the sequence, in tune with its origin, shows that of Edward the Confessor. He is seated on a regal seat with a footstool, while one bishop pours oil from a vessel on to the already crowned

OVERLEAF
Scenes from the Coronation Book of Charles V of France, illuminations, French, *c*.1364
(a) The king takes the oath
(b) Investiture with the spurs
(c) The archbishop crowns the king
(d) The king enthroned on the scaffold

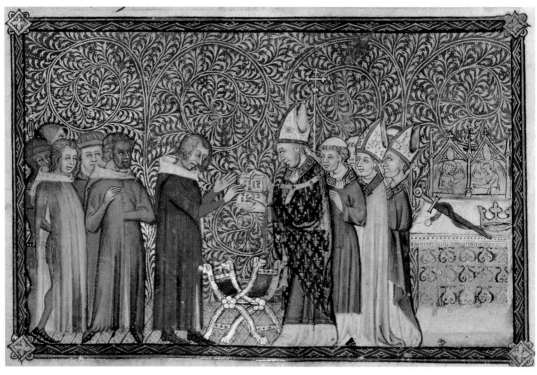

a

b

c

d

head of the royal saint, a reversal of the actual sequence, and the other bishop places the rod with the dove in the king's left hand, just as prescribed in the Fourth Recension. To one side there is a throng of clerics while, on the other, a complementary assembly of magnates lifts their swords in salute, much in the way we saw done in the Coronation of Harold in the Bayeux Tapestry. This image is very similar to the one which was in the Painted Chamber at Westminster, executed probably during the 1260s. In this version, however, the laity are entirely excluded in favour of seventeen bishops and mitred abbots. The rod with the dove is placed this time in the king's right hand in accordance with how it appears on the great seal of Henry III. Nor do the illuminations which accompany the ordines in the *Liber Regalis* or Lytlington Missal take us any further, beyond an incidental detail in the *Liber* which has a scene of a double Coronation, with the queen's throne shown correctly as lower than the king's.[46]

The most arresting of all these Coronation images is that which prefaces the ordo in Anglo-French for Edward II. It dates from about 1325–30 and the owner has been tentatively identified as Henry de Cobham.[47] Lord Cobham probably participated in the Coronation of Edward II or Edward III in his role as a Baron of the Cinque Ports. It is difficult otherwise to account for the Coronation ordo appearing in a book whose main text is the Apocalypse. Opinions vary as to whether the king depicted in the illumination is Edward II or Edward III, but what we see does seem to reflect some knowledge of the Coronation. The king is seated on a chair whose back is adorned with fleurons and which resembles the Coronation chair. Although what the king wears in no way accords with the vestments listed in the regalia, it does show some semblance of knowledge as to what was actually worn. There is a white ankle-length undergarment over which comes a bright red tunic, then a dalmatic with broad yellow and golden horizontal bands, and finally a pallium in gold and peach-coloured brocade fastened in the manner of a cope with a morse. In his right hand the king holds a rod topped by a fleuron and in his left an orb arising from a series of fleurons. The king is surrounded by six bishops, two of whom support the crown, and two others, in the foreground, who proffer containers whose purpose has so far defied identification. This without doubt is some kind of composite image of the king at his enthronement.

These miniatures show that king-making was by the fourteenth century a consensual process.[48] The king is no longer an isolated figure upon whose head a crown is bestowed by an angel or the hand of God. The throne in every instance is surrounded by people, the rapidly emerging estates of the realm. These miniatures spell out the great shift in climate which has taken place as we move through the thirteenth and into the fourteenth century. This is a period which witnesses the emergence of a new thinking about political systems, about the involvement of citizens and how they should participate. The monarchy is recast into a greater vision which includes the notion of consent by drawing in an enlarged constituency of those ruled. Although still in our terms narrow, in medieval understanding it was very wide. This huge change in the concept of kingship and the structure of the state was the result of the reception of Aristotelianism, a philosophy in which sense experience was established as the origin of universal knowledge. The consequence of that was that those capable of responding to reason should be brought into the consensus of kingship: males, the secular nobility and bourgeoisie, the intelligentsia and lawyers. Aristotelianism and the recognition of the powers of reason also meant a cultivation of the arts of persuasion. In the case of the coronation those arts would embrace music, visual spectacle, rhetoric and ceremonial, all aimed no longer at an ecclesiastical audience but at a lay one. In its final form the English Coronation utilised all those powers in a gigantic festival whose aim was to reconcile divine election with popular consent.

4

Sacred Monarchy

IN SHAKESPEARE'S *Richard II* the Earl of Salisbury encounters a captain at a camp in Wales. The fate of the king is already sealed and the captain repeats a rumour that he is in fact dead. He then says:

> *The bay-trees in our country are all wither'd*
> *And meteors fright the fixed stars of heaven;*
> *The pale-fac'd moon looks bloody on the earth*
> *And lean-look'd prophets whisper fearful change;*
> *Rich men look sad and ruffians dance and leap,*
> *The one in fear to lose what they enjoy,*
> *The other to enjoy by rage and war;*
> *These signs forerun the death or fall of kings.*
>
> (II, iv, ll. 8–15)

Such a passage is a window into the minds of those who lived in the pre-Newtonian age. Belief in the occult and what, to a post-Enlightenment mind, would seem to be the irrational was the norm. The monarch in his kingdom was a mirror of the divine order reflecting God's rule over the hierarchies of heaven. Thus the fate of kings signalled cosmic consequences as the God-ordained natural order of things had been violated.

MYSTICAL MONARCHY

The three centuries which take us to the collapse of the monarchy in 1649 are those of sacred monarchy, an apotheosis which spirals ever

Opposite Richard II enthroned, painting, English, *c.*1390–1400

upwards until James I actually enunciates the Divine Right of Kings, informing his eldest son 'you are a little GOD to sit on his Throne, and rule over other men'.[1] This escalation in the mystique of monarchy was to have profound repercussions on the Coronation, first in the phase which runs down to the Reformation, the subject of this chapter, and second in that which was to end with a royal head being severed on a scaffold.

Although the notion of the priest-king had long gone, that did not destroy the fervent belief that he who had received unction was different from ordinary mortals. That was reinforced by the emergence of the theory known as the king's two bodies, his mortal one which made up the transitory aspect of monarchy, and the immortal one which was his fictive entity, the undying legal 'body' of the crown, of which the sovereign was but the temporary representative. On the theory that the king never dies the state depended for continuity in the administration of government. In this way we begin to witness what might be described as a new secular mysticism surrounding the monarchy, one which was based not so much on holy unction but on the precepts of law.[2]

All of this was to happen during the century preceding the triumph of the Tudors, in fact precisely in a period when it would be thought that exactly the opposite would occur. For most of the fifteenth century the monarchy was in crisis. Richard II was deposed. Henry IV, his successor, was little more than a usurper. His son, Henry V, was to revive successfully for a short period the war with France, but disastrously left a baby as heir to the new dual monarchy of France and England. Built up as the descendant of two royal saints, St Edward and St Louis, it was unfortunate that Henry VI grew up to be a pious simpleton, precipitating a major crisis as to what should be done with a man unfit to be king. The sanctity of kingship was such, however, that it was to take two decades before he was finally removed and replaced by Edward IV, a descendant of the second and fourth sons of Edward III. Unfortunately, Edward IV's premature death left the country for a second time with a child king, Edward V. The mysterious disappearance of both him and his brother in the Tower opened the way for the brief usurpation of their uncle, Richard III, who, in his turn, was defeated by what was in effect yet another usurper, albeit a successful one, Henry VII, the first of the Tudors.

The turbulence of the period we know as the Wars of the Roses, indeed, was from time to time challenged as the contending parties

Mary I touching for
scrofula, illumination,
English, c.1553–58

tried to discredit each other. Sir John Fortescue, chief justice of the
King's Bench and a partisan of the Lancastrian Henry VI, for example,
denied the Yorkist Edward IV any of the wonder-working powers
which, he argued, could only be exercised by the deposed king: 'Those
who witness these deeds [royal healing of scrofula by touch] are
strengthened in their loyalty to the king, and this monarch's undoubted title to the throne is thus confirmed by divine approval.'[3]

For whoever wore the crown, it was of supreme importance that he
was seen to possess the healing attribute, so much so that in the case of

114   CORONATION

touching for scrofula the coin bestowed by the monarch on the sufferer was increased in value as an added attraction. At some date it ceased to be the lowly silver penny and became the gold angel. This was first coined under Edward IV, but whether it was Edward or Henry VII who made the change is unknown. What it reveals is the desire that the mysterious powers bestowed by unction at Coronation were seen to be effective.[4]

Royal healing powers were, in fact, extended during the fourteenth century when rings made from coins presented by the king and laid at the foot of the cross during the Good Friday liturgy in the Chapel Royal were considered to be capable of relieving muscular pains or spasms, and more especially epilepsy. It was for that reason they were known as cramp rings.[5] The practice is first certainly identifiable in the reign of Edward II, and every monarch up until the death of Mary Tudor in 1558 took part in what became a ritual. As in the case of royal healing for scrofula, which would never have taken off but for Henry II's battle with the Church, so in the case of cramp rings there is a connexion between the development of this new healing power and the fate of the monarchy. It is, therefore, no surprise that it first emerges during the reign of a king under siege or that it enters its most significant phase during the reign of another beleaguered monarch, Henry VI. During precisely the period when the child monarch was being built up as the dual ruler of both France and England the ritual in the Chapel Royal was changed. Instead of coins being offered, taken away and made into rings, on Good Friday a bowl of rings was presented which the king fingered. This new ritual is described as follows: 'the king's highness rubbeth the rings between his hands, saying: "Sanctify, O Lord, these rings ... and consecrate them by the rubbing of our hands, which thou hast been pleased according to our ministry to sanctify by an external effusion of holy oil upon them" '.[6]

Fortescue argues that the king's hands have this magical power through the unction bestowed at Coronation. So what had begun as a simple offering of coins at the foot of the cross on Good Friday was transformed into a rite for a miracle-working king. By the beginning of the sixteenth century attempts were made to link this new royal miracle with the legendary ring bestowed by St John on Edward the Confessor and preserved in Westminster Abbey. If the Reformation had not intervened it is interesting to speculate as to where that association would have led.

Opposite Richard II attended by St John the Evangelist and two English royal saints, Edward the Confessor and Edmund, in the Wilton Diptych, painting, English, probably *c.*1395

Unction for kings from Henry IV onwards was further sanctified by the use for the first time of what was proclaimed to be the Holy Oil of St Thomas.[7] As in the case of the cramp rings the saga has its turning point in the reign of Edward II, but it was built on the fulfilment of a much earlier legend. In any consideration of the Holy Oil of St Thomas it is essential to grasp the primacy attached to prophecy during the Middle Ages. In the case of the Oil this had its origins in a legend circulating at the beginning of the thirteenth century. In it the Virgin appeared to St Thomas in a vision while he was praying in the church of St Columba in Sens during his exile. She presented him with a gold eagle which contained a stone flask filled with the Oil, and informed him that this was to be used at the Coronation of unspecified kings of England at some future date. As the story was elaborated, her prophecy was that the first king to be anointed with it would recover Normandy and Aquitaine and go on to build many churches in the Holy Land, drive the pagans from Babylon and build churches there, too.

In its full-blown fifteenth-century version the Holy Oil was entrusted by St Thomas to a monk of the monastery of St Cyprian of Poitiers, with the message that it would be revealed at an opportune moment and that that signal would come from the King of the Pagans. Now when the latter discovered the existence of the Oil through his demons, realising the threat which it posed to him he sent a pagan knight and a Christian and his son to find the ampulla. The pagan knight died on the journey, but the Christian and his son discovered the Holy Oil, taking it first to the German king and then to Jean II, Duke of Brabant. He brought it to England and presented it to his brother-in-law, Edward II, with the idea that it should be used at his Coronation. The Council, however, declined to do so. Nine years later the king began to have second thoughts about the Oil and sent an emissary to Pope John XXII at Avignon seeking permission to be anointed. The pope wisely prevaricated, saying that the king could be anointed but only in secret. Edward did not pursue the matter and the ampulla seems to have been placed in the Royal Treasury in the Tower.

There it remained until 1399, when Richard II alighted upon it while rummaging through the royal jewels. The ampulla was a small stone phial containing the Oil set, by that date, into a gold eagle. In form it would have resembled a late medieval brooch which could be worn, as many relics were, suspended from a chain around the neck.

Vem archeuelque de Vams ·

Es luc lamr vem fut tour maintenaur les

The baptism of Clovis, 496, at which an angel descended from heaven with holy oil for his anointing, illumination, French, XIVth century

He asked the then Archbishop of Canterbury to anoint him, but he refused on the grounds that the unction received at Coronation was unique and unrepeatable. The king's faith in the ampulla was such that he took it with him to Ireland, suspending it around his neck. On his return Archbishop Arundel, now his sworn enemy, gained possession of it: 'it was not the divine will that he [Richard II] should be anointed with it, so noble a sacrament was another's due'. So Arundel kept it 'until the Coronation of this new king [Henry IV], who was the first of English kings to be anointed with so precious a liquid'.

There is no doubt that the Lancastrian adoption of the Holy Oil was in emulation of the French Sainte Ampoulle, oil delivered from heaven during the baptism of Clovis, the first Christian king of France. Hence the French king's style of *Rex Christianissimus*. Buried amidst the legend of the Holy Oil of St Thomas there is a substructure of truth. We know that it existed in the reign of Edward II and that it resurfaced in 1399. We also know that it was certainly used at the Coronations of Henry IV and Henry VI and quite possibly that of

Henry V. It is to be recalled that part of the prophecy predicted the reconquest of Normandy and Aquitaine, and this must connect with the appearance during the fifteenth century for the first time of two squires clothed to represent Normandy and Guyenne (Aquitaine) in the Coronation procession. Moreover, by the middle of the century the Holy Oil of St Thomas had acquired a solemn ceremony of delivery from the palace to the Abbey for the Coronation. It was borne in procession by a bishop in pontificals attended by a cross and candles to the high altar. As it passed the waiting king he rose from his chair. All of this is recorded in the *Liber Regie Capelle* compiled about 1445–8 and recording what happened in the Chapel Royal. By then it was certainly housed in a gold eagle, the ampulla, and in 1483 Richard III made it over to the Abbot of Westminster with the stipulation that after his death it should become part of the Coronation regalia 'for evermore'. And by re-creation it has.

In the context of the Lancastrian pursuit of the santification of their dynasty, we might add Henry VII's campaign for the canonisation of Henry VI.[8] As early as 1473 an effigy of the king had appeared on the choir screen of York Minster and the cult could not be suppressed. In the context of the new Tudor dynasty a royal saint to add to the Confessor was a desideratum, and negotiations were begun with Rome. They came to nothing, but Henry VII's intention, when work began on what we know as his chapel in Westminster Abbey, was that its focal point was to be the shrine of 'St' Henry VI, his body being translated from Windsor. The fact that Henry VIII never pursued the project any further should not detract from what was initially to be a second dynastic valhalla, this time of the Tudors gathered around the shrine of a second royal saint in the same way that the Plantagenets encircled St Edward in what was the Coronation church.

All through this century when the crown was beleaguered there was an augmentation and elaboration of anything which would exalt its mystery. Crown-wearings, for example, increased in number. Originally confined to Christmas, Easter and Whitsun, there were now added Epiphany, All Saints and the two feasts of Edward the Confessor. In addition, there was the innovation of the queen wearing her crown on the anniversary of her Coronation.[9]

To all of this we can add the increasing mystique attached to the regalia in Westminster Abbey and to other artefacts which were deployed at the Coronation. About 1450 a monk called Richard Sporley compiled an inventory of the Abbey's relics in which the regalia figure. It is worth quoting in full, if only because in the ensuing century these relics alone survived the purge of the Reformation:

Relics of Holy Confessors

Saint Edward, king and confessor, for the memory of posterity and for the dignity of the royal Coronation, caused to be preserved in this church all the royal ornaments with which he was crowned; namely his tunicle, supertunica, armil, girdle, and embroidered pall; a pair of buskins, a pair of gloves, a golden sceptre, one wooden rod gilt, another of iron.

Also an excellent golden crown, a golden comb, and a spoon.

Also for the Coronation of the queen, a crown and two rods.

Also for the communion of the lord king, on the day of his Coronation, one chalice of onyx stone with a foot, rivets, and a paten of the best gold; all of which are to be considered precious relics.[10]

About 1387–9 Richard II had asked a monk at the Abbey, Walter of Sudbury, 'whether the regalia of [his] reign are the regalia of King Alfred and take their origin from him'. In the resulting treatise, *De Primis Regalibus Ornamentis Regni Angliae*, Walter describes the Abbey as a royal seat, *sedes regia*, one deliberately chosen by Edward the Confessor as the repository for the regalia. The latter he defines as insignia, 'signs' of the sacrament of Coronation and the means whereby the king takes on 'the royal dignity, which among and above all the riches, pleasures, and honours of this world takes first place, supereminently at the very highest point'. In Walter's mind the royal prerogative and the privileges of the Abbey are indissolubly intertwined thanks to its role as the custodian of the regalia and of the shrine of St Edward.[11]

Richard II, like Henry III, had a mystical cult of the crown jewels. Indeed, so much so that in 1390, much to the consternation of the populace, he began to carry them around with him and in 1399 even took them to Ireland, suspending, as we have seen, the Holy Oil of St Thomas around his neck. All of this runs side by side during the 1390s with changes in forms of address to him, the period when 'highness' and 'majesty' entered, terms of the kind which, up until then, were reserved for the Deity. The word 'prince' was also rarely used until the same period, implying recognition of Richard's role as the supreme lawgiver in a sovereign realm, while 'your majesty' paid tribute to his sacral character. More than any other monarch he created a new mystique of monarchy which was to be taken up and developed, one which used language, ceremony and symbolic artefacts.[12]

Like Henry III, too, he had a cult of St Edward and through that of the Abbey, to the extent that in 1397 he adopted new arms, those of England being impaled with those of the Confessor. In times of crisis throughout the reign his first recourse was to the shrine.[13] Perhaps that cult went back to his Coronation in 1377 when the following incident occurred:

> It is generally accepted that immediately after his Coronation the king should go into the vestry, where he should take off the regalia and put on other garments laid out ready for him by his chamberlains before returning by the shortest route to his palace, but at the Coronation of the present king the contrary was done, with deplorable results; for when the coronation was over, a certain knight, Sir Simon Burley, took the king up in his arms, attired as he was, in his regalia, and went into the palace by the royal gate with crowds milling all round him and pressing upon him, so that on the way he lost one of the consecrated shoes through his thoughtlessness.[14]

That loss was made good thirteen years later on 10 March 1390 when he sent to the Abbey a pair of red velvet shoes embroidered with fleur-de-lys in pearls, which had been blessed by Pope Urban VI, with the instruction that they were to be deposited with the rest of the regalia.[15]

That desire to elevate the monarchy finds reflection, too, during the fifteenth century in the adoption of a form of crown which was imperial, that is, it had a high narrow diadem arising above the circlet in the shape of a mitre. Up until that date such a form of crown was the prerogative of the Holy Roman Emperors. It has been reasonably postulated that we may owe this innovation to Richard II whose wife, Anne of Bohemia, was a daughter of Emperor Charles IV. Froissart's description of the crowning of Henry IV in 1399 refers to an arched or closed crown, and one was certainly worn by Henry V. One of the earliest representations of an English crown incorporating what are

Henry V wearing an imperial arched crown in a sculpture in his chantrey in Westminster Abbey, mid-XVth century

called 'imperial arches' is to be found in his chantry in Westminster Abbey, constructed about 1438–52, where the king is depicted twice, once being crowned with what is meant to be St Edward's crown, and once enthroned wearing an imperial crown with high arches. Under Henry VI the closed imperial crown becomes general and its most spectacular migration occurred in 1471 when Edward IV used it on his second Great Seal. That was not to be followed by Henry VII who used an open crown, although he was to introduce an imperial crown on to the coinage and make use of it elsewhere, typified by his bequest to Westminster Abbey of 29 copes of cloth of gold and crimson silk richly emblazoned with the crown imperial over the Beaufort portcullis. In the series of drawings known as *The Pageant of Richard Beauchamp, Earl of Warwick*, made c.1485–90, Henry IV, Henry V and Henry VI and their queens are all depicted with closed crowns. Although the fifteenth-century English preoccupation with an imperial crown was probably directed towards English claims to France, it was to be repeated throughout Europe by rulers in response to the late medieval legal notion that *rex in regno suo est imperator*, every king within his own kingdom is an emperor. In 1517 Cuthbert Tunstall, then Master of the Rolls, wrote to Henry VIII: 'But the Crown of England is an Empire of hitselff, mych bettyr then now the Empire of Rome: for which cause your Grace werith a close crown . . .' All of this, however, was to take a very different direction after 1529 and the break with Rome.[16]

The orb as we know it today also makes its first appearance in this century. Initially orbs, too, were imperial attributes, one being used first at the Coronation of Emperor Henry II in 1014. This orb was a sphere with a horizontal band of precious stones and a cross on its summit, a form which surfaces in an English context on the first seal of Edward the Confessor in use from 1053 to 1065. Under the Normans and later it was combined with the Anglo-Saxon long rod or verge, resulting in a curious form of attribute, a ball from which arose a foliated stem topped by a cross. This is what we see on the Great Seals. Modern scholarship concludes that it was Richard II who was responsible for the emergence of the orb to prominence. At his Coronation in 1377 he is described as being invested not with St Edward's sceptre (likely to have been in need of repair) but an orb with a long stem and a cross at the top, which must have formed part of his personal regalia. It, or an approximation to it, appears in the portrait of Richard II in Westminster Abbey. His successors, the Lancastrian kings, took up the orb, changing it to the imperial form of a ball with a cross on its summit. The earliest appearance of it in this guise is in an illumination of Edward IV, and it first appears carried in the Coronation procession of Richard III where it is referred to as the 'ball with the cross' and as signifying 'monarchie'. The king was not, however, invested with it. Although orbs now became part of a king's personal regalia there is no mention of one for the Coronations of either Henry VII or Henry VIII, although, as we shall see, it resurfaces in response to particular circumstances in 1547 for Edward VI.[17]

Side by side with the arrival of an imperial crown and an orb, the swords, which already by 1400 played such a significant role in the various processions as well as in the investiture in the Abbey, assume their final form. The association of ceremonial swords with royal authority

OPPOSITE
Orbs and Sceptres.
Orbs and sceptres varied in shape and there is no way of knowing whether any is an accurate record of one which actually existed
Top left Harold in the Bayeux Tapestry, *c.*1075
Top right Second Great Seal of Edward IV, 1461
Bottom left Richard II, painting, *c.*1390–1400
Bottom right Henry VI, drawing, *c.*1485–90

Edward IV with orb and sceptre wearing an arched imperial crown, illumination, English, XVth century

goes back to the eighth century. An official royal sword is first recorded in England in the ninth century, while courtiers holding what must
be the royal sword appear in the Bayeux Tapestry. The sword first surfaces as an item in the investiture in the Second Recension, and there
is the record that three swords were carried in the Coronation procession of Richard I in 1189. The investiture sword, which eventually
became known as 'The Sword of Offering', was at an early date symbolised by the use of a second sword which was called 'The Sword of
Estate' (later reduced to State). The earliest reference to this ceremonial
duplicate being used comes in 1380, significantly in connexion with a
king obsessed by status and regal dignity, Richard II: 'one sword for
Parliament, set with gold, with diamonds, balasses, "balesets", small
sapphires, and pearls'. Thenceforth the sword of state, the visible
symbol of the royal presence, recurs.[18]

References to the various ceremonial swords increase during the
fifteenth century and the texts begin to provide a symbolic gloss as to
their meaning. From the Coronation of Henry IV in 1399 onwards they
were multiplied to four in number, the fourth, symbolising Lancaster

(of which he was duke), being the one which the king had worn at his landing at Ravenspur.[19] Swords were new made for each Coronation, but in 1399 the chronicler Adam of Usk gives for the first time meaning to them: 'one was sheathed as a token of the augmentation of military honour, two were wreathed in red and bound round with golden bands to represent two-fold mercy, and the fourth naked and without a point, the emblem of justice without rancour'.[20]

The next text which invests the swords with meaning comes in a poem on the Coronation of Henry VI. The verses list three swords, although four were actually carried:

> *Thre swerdis there were borne, oon poyntlees, and two poyntid;*
> *The toon was a swerde of mercy, the oothir of astate,*
> *The thrid was of the empier the which ert our gate.*[21]

In this scenario they represented mercy (the sword Curtana), estate (state) and empire (perhaps the dual monarchy of France and England). Four were borne at Richard II's Coronation and again they were given a gloss: a naked pointless one for mercy, two swords representing justice to the temporality and to the clergy, and the fourth, the sword of state.[22] The meanings may shift, but what they reflect is an increasing desire to see these ceremonial objects as the embodiments of abstract concepts.

During the fifteenth century the Abbey and its abbots strengthen their hold on the Coronation and any artefacts connected with it. The abbot now goes to the incoming monarch to instruct him in the mysteries of the rite. It is he, too, who is the custodian of the regalia around which ever more legend accrues. He and his monks bear these sacred relics to Westminster Hall on the Coronation day, and to them they must be returned. Throughout the whole ceremony the abbot is to be there guiding the king in the action and it is he, too, who now invests the king with the buskins, sandals, spurs, *colobium sindonis* and supertunica.

This empire-building by the Abbey, it has been suggested, explains one of the more weird transmutations in the regalia which occurs sometime during the fourteenth into the fifteenth centuries. The armils began their life as bracelets with which the king was invested, a fact which is likely to have been lost sight of by the fourteenth century when bracelets were no longer part of men's attire. But the Fourth Recension calls for armils, and the monks of Westminster must have searched in vain through what they called the St Edward's regalia try-ing to identify them, deciding that a cloth-of-gold stole adorned with 'ancient work' in the form of shields bearing leopards' heads (the leop-ard as an emblem of England is not earlier than *c*.1200) and vines together with jewels in gold mounts was indeed the armils. By 1483, in the Little Device drawn up for Richard III's Coronation, an 'armyll' is described as 'made in the manner of a stole woven with gold and sett with stones to be putt . . . abowte the Kinges nek and comyng from both shulders to the Kinges bothe elbowes wher they shalbe fastened by the seyde Abbott . . .' What the monks of Westminster did not know was that the armils never had been part of the regalia but were sup-plied from the Royal Jewel House. Richard II was invested with both them and the stole, according to Thomas of Walsingham, and bejewelled bracelets were worn by both Lancastrian and early Tudor kings as part of their robes of estate. Along with the orb they were to surface in 1547 at Edward VI's Coronation.[23]

So during a period which was at times one of acute dislocation the aura surrounding the monarchy increased rather than decreased. Indeed kings, whether of Lancastrian or Yorkist descent, availed them-selves of any opportunity to gain back some of what had been lost in terms of regal status through the coronation oath of 1308. To that development we can add another powerful force which again was dra-matically to affect the Coronation. That was the rise of the laity. Up until the late Middle Ages the clergy who performed the rite of unction and Coronation were not only priests but, being educated and literate, were also the people who ran the government and held the great administrative offices of state like the treasurer and chancellor. The fall of Henry VIII's minister, Cardinal Wolsey, in 1529 marked the end of the clerical dominance of these offices of state. In the sixteenth centu-ry royal power drew upon an ever widening spectrum of society, reaching out through and often across the aristocracy, which had threatened its stability, to the gentry and to townspeople. This, of course, affected the Coronation.

The Abbey ritual was more or less fixed, but what happened on the days either side of it was open to accommodate every kind of innova-tion, resulting in a long series of accretions, each with a purpose. The Coronation became the occasion when peerages were bestowed and knights created, both designed to draw new allegiances to the crown and vividly demonstrating its role as the fount of honour. The event itself began to be prefaced by a state entry into London of increasing complexity, a vehicle which recognised the importance of the support to the regime of the City as represented by the Lord Mayor and Aldermen as well as the craft companies. It equally exhibited the monarch to the populace as he rode in triumph. As the sixteenth century progressed that became the occasion for pageantry, in which the City was able both to laud the ruler and to present its own view as to the role of the crown in society. The feast which followed the Coronation also burgeoned. It already drew in an elaborate hierarchy of those whose loyalty to the state needed to be cultivated, but to that was now added even greater splendour and the deployment of allegory. Add to all of this even further days of festivity, during which what were called 'justes of peace' were held. Honoured guests could be given places from which to watch the sport as the chivalry of England demonstrated its prowess in the royal tiltyard in tribute to the crown. By the time of the last pre-Reformation Coronation in 1533 it had expanded to an event which could at times spread over almost a whole week.

The period 1377 to 1533, which begins with the Coronation of Richard II and closes with that of Anne Boleyn, is a dynamic one as the occasion explodes in all directions. There were fifteen Coronations in all. Of some we know a great deal and of others practically nothing. What can be said is that they all reflect the same impulses and can therefore be treated as a group. For convenience I list them:

Richard II	17 July 1377
Anne of Bohemia	22 January 1382
Isabella of France	5 January 1397
Henry IV	13 October 1399
Joan of Navarre	26 February 1403
Henry V	9 April 1413
Catherine of France	2 February 1421
Henry VI	6 November 1429
Margaret of Anjou	30 May 1445
Edward IV	28 June 1461
Elizabeth Woodville	26 May 1465

128   CORONATION

Richard III and Ann Neville	6 July 1483
Henry VII	30 October 1485
Elizabeth of York	25 November 1487
Henry VIII	24 June 1509
Anne Boleyn	1 June 1533[24]

To these should be added the abortive Coronation of Henry VIII's third queen, Jane Seymour, delayed on account of plague and eventually abandoned owing to her death.

The days chosen included feast days. Henry IV, for example, was crowned on the feast of the translation of St Edward and his son on Passion Sunday. Such a litany of Coronations is an indication of their indispensability for anyone who wished to wield power. But the fact that the crown was seized first by this claimant and then by that for a time threatened to undermine the Coronation's centrality as the key rite of passage. Indeed, if it had not been for the return to stability after 1485, it was in danger of being marginalised.

THE CORONATION UNDER THREAT

Between 1377 and 1533 four monarchs came to the throne other than as direct heirs apparent. Each needed to be recognised as king virtually instantly, certainly before the increasingly elaborate ceremony of a Coronation in the Abbey could be mounted. As a consequence of this it was inevitable that some kind of secular enthronement began to be evolved to bridge the gap until the mystery of unction could be bestowed.

The occasion arose first in 1399 when Richard II was deposed. On 29 September Henry of Lancaster, accompanied by a great train of prelates and lords, made his way to the Tower, where the king was held prisoner. The chronicler Froissart describes how Richard was brought into the hall 'aparelled lyke a kyng in his robes of estate, his scepter in his hande, and his crowne on his head'.[25] He then formally renounced the crown, assigning it to Henry of Lancaster, taking it from his head and handing it to him. He, in turn, passed it to the Archbishop of Canterbury, and both it and the sceptre were placed in a coffer and carried to Westminster Abbey. This cannot have been anything other than a piece of invented ceremonial.[26]

Opposite The Coronation of Joan of Navarre, 1403, drawing, *c.*1485–90

Richard II resigns his crown, illumination, Flemish, XVth century

On the following day Parliament renounced its allegiance to Richard. From the chronicler Adam of Usk we learn that Richard's ring had been taken from him and, in the presence of Parliament, was presented to Henry. The Archbishop of York then read, as though in the person of the deposed king, his surrender of the crown. That was followed by a sermon by the Archbishop of Canterbury on the evils of Richard, extolling the virtues of Henry, after which what amounted to some kind of secular enthronement and oath-taking under the aegis of both archbishops took place: 'the throne being vacant . . . the said duke of Lancaster, being raised up to be king, forthwith had enthronement at the hands of the said archbishops, and, thus seated on the king's throne, he there straightway openly and publicly read a certain declaration in writing . . .'.[27]

That pledge stated his lawful right of succession and that he affirmed the legal status quo. This event established a precedent whereby someone became king at once. It was one which was to be built on in such a way, as the fifteenth century progressed, that it threatened to undermine the rite of Coronation.

It is significant that Henry IV did not resort to what is prescribed for the morning of the Coronation in both the Westminster Missal and the *Liber Regalis*, that the prelates and nobles of the realm should assemble at the palace 'to consider about the consecration and election of the new king, and also about confirming and surely establishing the laws and customs of the realm'.[28] That had been done in 1308 and 1327, but kings thereafter did all they could to pull the monarchy back from any hint of election. Henry IV and his successors worked from the premise that the crown was theirs by right.

Ironically, the precedent set by Henry IV was to be revived not by a Lancastrian king but by two Yorkist ones, Edward IV and Richard III.[29] As in 1399, both kings needed to be seen to ascend the throne immediately as the result of popular acclamation. In 1461, the sequence of events began with a proclamation calling upon all men to meet at St Paul's the following day, 4 March. On that occasion Edward made a solemn offering at the high altar, the Te Deum was sung and George Neville, Bishop of Exeter, preached at Paul's Cross setting forth the Yorkist claim to the crown. Edward then rode to Westminster, entered the hall and went into that part of it which since the fourteenth century had housed the Court of Chancery. There before the primate, Thomas Bourchier, the chancellor, George Neville, and the lords he put on the royal parliament robes and a cap of maintenance (not a crown) and took what was in effect a version of the Coronation oath: 'that he sholde truly and justly kepe the realme and the lawes thereof maynteyne as a true and juste kyng'. Some sources add that this was taken after an acclamation by the populace gathered in the hall. Edward IV then took possession of the marble King's Bench, that place from which the law-giving virtues of the crown were held to emanate. There he sat in majesty holding a sceptre.

After this he proceeded to Westminster Abbey, where he was met in procession by the abbot and his monks bearing the sceptre of St Edward, which was presented to him. He was then conducted to the high altar and to the Confessor's shrine, at each of which he made an offering. After this he descended into the choir and sat on a throne while the choir sang the Te Deum, which was followed by the rendering of homage by the peers. Then something akin to the old *Laudes regiae* was sung. Edward IV was not crowned until three months later, after his defeat of the Lancastrians at Towton, a fact which, although unintentional, gave an impression that Coronation was an additional rather than an essential rite of passage for a king.

Over twenty years later, in 1483, the whole sequence was repeated with variations for Richard III. On 26 June he rode to Westminster Hall, put on the royal robes and, bearing a sceptre in his hand, took possession of the royal estate by an act of enthronement on the marble chair of the Court of the King's Bench. Richard also took an oath and, like Edward, dated his reign from that day. He also went to the Abbey, received the sceptre, made offerings and heard the Te Deum, but homage was not rendered, the king preferring to return in procession to the City to St Paul's.[30]

What are we to make of all this? Richard was crowned only ten days later (much must have been in hand already for the Coronation of Edward V), but Edward IV put off his Coronation until as late as 28 June. These happenings reflect a keen awareness of where the ability to king-make now resided, and that it was no longer solely with the clergy and their rites within the Abbey. Securing London with its vast commercial riches and teeming populace was seen to be crucial to anyone who aspired to be king. That is caught in the fact that two days after his Coronation Edward IV returned to the City and wore his crown to St Paul's, where an angel descended and censed him. Under the Yorkists crown-wearings, too, were revived and Richard III even wore his into battle. On 22 August 1485 that crown was taken from his body at the battle of Bosworth and set on the head of an obscure Welsh magnate, Henry of Richmond. It was, as the king's official historian, Polydore Vergil, was to write, as if he had been 'already by commandment of the people proclamyd king after the maner of his auncestors, and that was the first signe of prosperytie'.[31] In this way Henry VII was king *de facto*, by conquest, if not yet *de jure*.

If it were not for the necessity of securing the mysterious powers bestowed by unction and the Tudor succession, the secular ceremony might well have grown in importance. Edward IV's delay in being crowned is an indication that, if other affairs were more pressing, that could wait. What this does capture is the centrality of London, which throughout the period of the Wars of the Roses was to remain economically prosperous and which could literally make or break kings. Those who seized the crown needed the wealth, power and influence of the great City merchants to survive. In order to meet these new challenges it is hardly surprising to find the role of London in the Coronation dramatically magnified.[32]

THE NEW JERUSALEM

Richard II's Coronation was the first to respond in any very substantial way to this shift in the balance of political power, for on that occasion the vigil procession was invented. This established a sequence of events which was to remain immutable until 1661, the last occasion when there was a state entry into London. That sequence involved the Lord Mayor and Aldermen together with representatives of the great craft companies meeting the new ruler outside the City and conducting him to the Tower. On the morrow they would return to take their places in a great procession on horseback through the City to the Palace of Westminster. First in 1377, and then intermittently, that entry was to be elaborated by the introduction of symbolic pageantry. The involvement of the City on such a scale was an innovation of the first magnitude, fully recognising its crucial importance to the crown. The emergence of pageantry occurred virtually simultaneously on both sides of the Channel, reflecting the dilemma of both monarchies as they tried to free themselves from the juridical restraints which had been imposed on them by institutions and customs earlier in the Middle Ages. The result was an explosion of spectacle and display which was to be repeated in the twentieth century. On both occasions they were profound acknowledgements of where in society the monarchy now had to look for its support.

That change began in 1377 when the boy king was welcomed into what was billed as *camera vestra*, your chamber. The sudden and innovative appearance of pageantry is likely to have been triggered by the real fears that attended the accession of a child of ten and the need to build him up in the eyes of the populace. It was equally an act of reconciliation by the City with the king's uncle, John of Gaunt. On 15 July, at some time after 9 a.m., the magnates together with the Lord Mayor and Aldermen went to the Tower. They were all attired in white, the colour of innocency, in tribute to the ten-year-old boy king who was also clothed in the same colour. A great procession was then formed, led by men of Bayeux, in which also took part the citizens of London representing the different wards, some of them making music, the Lord Mayor and Aldermen, with the king himself surrounded by the great magnates. Ahead of him rode John of Gaunt and the earls of Cambridge and Hertford and, immediately before them, Simon Burley, the young king's guardian, who carried the Sword of State. The king himself rode bareheaded as if to emphasise that his Coronation had yet to come and that this exhibition of him to the populace was a public version of the *recognitio* in the Abbey.

The procession made its way through Cheapside and along Fleet Street and, via the Strand, to Westminster Hall. En route the great conduits were made to run with red and white wine. At the one in Cheapside there stood a castle with four towers, on each turret of which there was a virgin of the king's age who blew golden leaves on to him and offered him a cup of wine from the conduit. In the centre of the castle there was a spire, on the summit of which floated an angel who descended and offered the king a crown of gold. On reaching Westminster Hall there was enacted what was known as a voidee. The king went up to the marble table and requested wine, after which all drank and retired.[33]

We already know some of the underlying reasons for such an innovation, but what in the case of the young Richard did it signify? The key figure in the 1377 Coronation was the king's uncle, John of Gaunt, who presided over the Court of Claims. The accession, in fact, occurred at a period when there was trouble both at home and abroad. The government itself was split between the great magnates, hereditary custodians of power, and the new men, like Simon Burley, who increasingly began to figure in the administration. The whole Coronation was stage-managed to present a public face of unity in which various contending parties were equally balanced in the ceremonial roles assigned to them. But the most arresting feature of 1377 was the castle with its maidens and crown-bestowing angel. Pageantry of this kind was a late-fourteenth-century phenomenon; the rapid development of the entrance of a ruler into his capital city was a major occasion for symbolic theatre on the grand scale.[34] England led the way in this development in an era which saw the emergence of the miracle play. It followed shortly after in France, but with a crucial difference. There the solemn entry into Paris occurred after and not before the *sacre* at Reims.[35] In England the processional entry preceded the Coronation. This meant that the ruler was not yet king in the fullest sense of the word. So the London reception becomes that of a ruler-to-

The New Jerusalem coming
down from Heaven,
illumination, English,
XIIIth century

be, one who can be appealed to, and instructed through the language
of pageantry in the art of monarchy as cast by the citizens of London.

What was this castle? It was a materialisation in paint and canvas
of the Heavenly Jerusalem brought down to earth, a realisation of the
text of the Apocalypse (Revelation 21: 2–3); 'And I saw the holy city, the
new Jerusalem, coming down from God out of heaven, prepared as a
bride adorned for her husband.' The Heavenly City is 'like unto a stone
most precious, even like a jasper stone, clear as crystal' (21: 11). These
castles, which were to become a recurring feature of London royal
entries, were indeed painted jasper green. But why was such a feature
thought apposite to greet a royal personage? The medieval entry has
liturgical roots.[36] In the *Rituale Romanum*, amidst prayers concerning
the Office of the Dying, are also ones concerned with the soul's arrival
in paradise. This arrival is described as an *entrée joyeuse* with the heavenly host gathered to receive the soul into the celestial Jerusalem. The
medieval reception of a ruler was modelled on this, combined with
Christ's entry into Jerusalem on Palm Sunday. So, when the King of
England entered London, the City took on the guise of the New
Jerusalem with the ruler as the Anointed One. Any pre-Reformation

London royal entry was not only a secular but also an ecclesiastical event. Along the route from time to time there would be gatherings of clergy arrayed in rich copes, bearing crosses and candles, who would cense the king as he passed. So the royal entry was a combination of a re-enactment of Palm Sunday, with its cries of *Benedictus qui venit*, with the apocalyptic vision of the end of things, Christ's Second Coming back to earth as envisioned in the Book of Revelation. Already by 1236 the City had adorned its streets for a royal welcome on the occasion of Henry III's marriage to Eleanor of Provence and her Coronation:

> The whole city was ornamented with flags and banners, chaplets and hangings, candles and lamps, and wonderful devices and extraordinary representations . . . The citizens, too, went out to meet the king and queen, dressed out in their ornaments . . . On the same day, when they left the city for Westminster, to perform the duty of butler to the king (which office belonged to them by right of old, at the Coronation), they proceeded thither dressed in silk garments, with mantles worked in gold, and with costly changes of raiment, mounted on valuable horses, glittering with new bits and saddles, and riding in troops arranged in order. They carried with them three hundred and sixty gold and silver cups, preceded by the king's trumpeters and with horns sounding, so that such a wonderful novelty struck all who beheld it with astonishment.[37]

In 1308, something very similar was staged when Edward II and Isabella of France rode through London before their Coronation, but this time the celestial connexion was made: 'then was London ornamented with jewels like New Jerusalem'.[38] The Heavenly Jerusalem was to reappear later in Richard II's reign, in 1392, when the City staged a pageant entry as a token of submission to the king, with angels descending with golden crowns;[39] in 1432, when Henry VI entered London as king of both France and England; in 1445 to greet his wife, Margaret of Anjou, prior to her Coronation (appropriate also because her father claimed to be King of Jerusalem);[40] and even as late as 1547 to welcome the Protestant Edward VI.[41]

Not every king or queen was accorded a Coronation pageant entry. Indeed, they were irregular events, and it was not until the sixteenth century that a pageant entry was to become mandatory. When, however, they did occur they presented material of great importance on the concept of king- and queenship and its duties. In the case of a king, time and again what the citizens staged in the streets was an allegorical representation of the Coronation and its significance as they viewed it. Although there is mention of a tower full of angels, presumably the Heavenly City, at the north end of London Bridge for Henry VI in 1429, what can be argued to have been Henry VI's delayed Coronation entry proper took place in February 1432, three years on from his actual Coronation at the age of eight as King of England but only two months after his Coronation as King of France. In the London entry the king is cast as the Christ-figure on whom the Holy Spirit descends, that is, a pageant re-enactment of the unction in the Abbey. In one pageant seven angelic virgins appear and stage an allegorical version of the Coronation. On the young king each bestowed a piece of spiritual armour, partly drawing on St Paul's text defining the 'whole armour of God' (Ephesians 6: 11–17), but equally based on the ceremony of investiture in the actual Coronation: the crown of glory, the sceptre of clemency, the sword of justice and the pallium (cloak) of prudence. From that pageant the king proceeded to one in which his capital city was transformed by his sacred presence into the earthly paradise, and from thence he rode on to a vision of the New Jerusalem, with himself cast as the Solomonic king. How much of this programme stemmed from the City and how much from the court is open to question, but the desire to present the boy ruler as the embodiment of theocratic kingship was strong at a period when being king of two countries was under severe strain and moving to collapse.[42] That these equations were not lost in the wider context of the whole country can be demonstrated by moving out of London and turning to the city of York's reception of Henry VII in 1486, where a similar re-enactment of the Coronation for the populace took place. At the city gate the king was greeted with a wilderness from which, at his approach, red and white roses sprang, while above the heavens opened, filled with 'Anglicall armony', as the inevitable golden crown descended. Ebrank, the city's mythical founder, appeared and knelt to present Henry not with the city's keys but a crown. Next he was greeted by a council of his ancestors, the six Henrys, presided over by Solomon who delivered to the king a 'septour of sapience'. Later David surrendered the 'swerd of victorie' in token of Henry's 'power imperiall', and the citizens of York

erupted from their city, cast as the New Jerusalem, all attired in the Tudor colours of white and green. In both these royal entries the tendency to give a symbolic meaning to any royal attribute marries in exactly with what we have seen happen to the processional swords.[43]

By the close of the fifteenth century much of this pageantry came to be codified. The Household Ordinances of 1494 laid down how a queen was to be received at her Coronation:

> At the Tour gate the merye [i.e. mayor] & the worschipfulle men of the cete of London to mete hir in their best arraye, goinge on ffoot ij and ij togedure, till they came to Westminster: And at the condit in Cornylle [i.e. Cornhill] ther must be ordined a sight with angelles singinge, and freche balettes theron in latene, engliche, and ffrenche, mad by the wyseste docturs of this realme; and the condyt in Chepe in the same wyse; and the condit must ryn both red wyn and whitwyne; and the crosse in Chepe must be araied in the most rialle wyse that myght be thought; and the condit next Poules in the same wyse . . .[44]

This records more or less what happened both for Elizabeth of York in 1487 and Anne Boleyn in 1533. In 1487 the queen arrived from Greenwich by water and was met by the Lord Mayor and the City companies in barges and 'a great red dragon spowting fflamys of fyers into tenmys [Thames]'. Although there were no pageants, the route had children attired as angels and virgins singing 'swete songes' as she passed by.[45] Thirty-six years later the City sent fifty barges to escort Anne Boleyn, and there was much music-making, and the fire-spouting dragon made a second appearance. This was in response to what amounted to a three-line whip from government, Henry VIII requesting that the City authorities prepare for the reception of his 'moste deare and welbeloued wyfe . . . with pageauntes in places accustomed, for the honor of her grace'. She rode along a route whose theme was that common for queens, in which a new queen was presented as a parallel to the Virgin Mary, culminating in her Assumption and Coronation, along with biblical analogies of those who were fruitful in progeny, dwelling on 'the fruitfulnes of saint Anne and of her generacion, trustyng that like fruite should come of her'. But the most spectacular pageant provides us with a rarity, a drawing for one of the arches straddling the street (a design only, for the pageant ended up at

Opposite The Dual Monarchy of France and England descending to Henry VI, illumination, English, *c.*1445

ground level and not over an arch), designed by Holbein and representing Mount Parnassus from which the Muses, amidst much music-making and song, harangued the queen-to-be repeatedly on the need for her to produce a male child. She was, in fact, already pregnant with the future Elizabeth I.[46]

Anne Boleyn's entry sheds some rare light on how the subject-matter of these vigil entries was controlled. That was already true in 1501 when an entry was staged for Henry VIII's first queen, Katherine of Aragon, as bride of Prince Arthur, when eight City dignitaries were appointed to deal 'from tyme to tyme with the kynges commyssioners touchyng preparacion to be made for receyvyng the prynces'.[47] Thirty-two years later the City was left with only a fortnight in which to meet the king's demands. They submitted their proposals for three pageants only to the Privy Council's representatives, the Duke of Norfolk and Thomas Cromwell, the king's chief minister. These cannot have been well received, and more must have been demanded, for in the final show there were no fewer than six scenic pageants and six more platforms en route that provided music and song. That they were able to achieve this in such a short space of time was due to government support. Their queries ran as follows. Should the clergy attend? No. Should the Merchants of the German Steelyard provide a pageant? Yes. Could they have assistance in terms of labour from the King's Office of Works? Yes. Could they borrow royal musicians and singers? Yes. More than that, the Privy Councillors seem to have gone on to provide them with the two men who would write the scenario, John Leland and Nicholas Udall, both loyal supporters of the king over his divorce and the break with Rome. So, under their aegis, the City was able to add a new-fangled Renaissance courtly classical gloss to the time-honoured civic theme of a new queen as the Virgin Mary and mother-to-be of a future messianic ruler. In this Anne was cast as something very different, as the Just Virgin Astraea of Virgil's celebrated Fourth Eclogue, whose return to earth heralded a new Golden Age. By 1533 England had broken with the Universal Church and, as we shall see in the next chapter, the monarchy's obsession with control of its own public image was to be absolute.[48]

This sudden efflorescence of pageantry added a totally new dimension to the Coronation. So, too, did two other phenomena occasioned by the City. The first was the emergence of a tradition of the City dignitaries meeting the new king or queen at its boundaries

Pageant Arch by Hans
Holbein for the entry of
Anne Boleyn into London,
drawing, 1533

and conducting him or her to the Tower. As we have seen, Elizabeth of
York and Anne Boleyn made their entry by water amidst a flotilla of
City company barges come to escort them en fête. But the custom went
back much further in date to Henry VI in 1429 who, on 4 November,
rode from Kingston-on-Thames to the Tower via Fenchurch Street,
joined en route by the Lord Mayor and Aldermen as an escort attired
in scarlet. By 1445 that had become far more spectacular. The bride and
queen-to-be of Henry VI, Margaret of Anjou, was escorted through
London by 'lordys of the realme, whythe nobylle and grete and
costelowe araye, the Mayre of London and the aldyrmen in scharlet,
whythe alle the craftys of London in blewe, wythe dyvers dyvysyngys,
every crafte to be knowe from othyr . . .'[49] What this catches is the gradual emergence of a London hierarchy expressed through costume, one

in which there was a sharp division between the Lord Mayor and Aldermen and the attendant citizens, representatives of the various companies. That enhancement in the appearance of the members of the governing body first occurs in the 1432 entry of Henry VI, who had not long before entered Paris to be greeted by the First President and members of the Parlement of Paris. In direct response to their grandeur the Lord Mayor of London set himself apart 'in rede crymsyn velwett, a grete velwet hatte furred royally, a girdell of gold aboute his neck, trillyng doun behynde hym'. What was more, a ceremonial sword was borne before him. The sheriffs and aldermen attended in scarlet with fur collars, and the guilds all wore white embroidered with the devices of their craft.[50]

The latter were to line the route during the state entry through the City, ranked in order of precedence and standing along streets which were gravelled and railed on either side. The Lord Mayor, sheriffs and aldermen, however, took part in the actual entry procession itself and that, too, during the fifteenth century blossomed as never before into what can only be described as mobile magnificence dazzling every beholder with the glory of the crown. Henry IV's entry in 1399 ran to 600 persons, including 6 dukes, 6 earls, 18 barons, numberless knights and squires and the king himself, bareheaded in a jacket of cloth of gold with the Garter on his leg. Henry VI similarly was 'in riall araye, with all hys lordys ryally arayed in cloth of gold for the most part'.[51] By 1509 royal attire was even richer, Henry VIII wearing: 'a robe of Crimosyn velvet, furred with armyns, his iacket or cote of raised gold, the Placard embrowdered with Diamondes, Rubies, Emeraudes, greate Pearles, and other riche Stones, a greate Bauderike aboute his necke, of greate Balasses'.[52]

Edward Hall, the king's chronicler and eulogist, then goes on to comment on the clothes of those in the great procession as a whole: 'what payn, labour, and diligence, the Taylors, Embrouderours, and Golde Smithes tooke, bothe to make and devise garementes, for Lordes, Ladies, Knightes, and Esquiers, and also for deckyng, trappyng, and adornyng of Coursers, Jenetes, and Palffries'.[53]

By the third quarter of the fifteenth century that procession became codified. What is known as the Little Device was drawn up for the Coronation of Richard III and reused for that of Henry VII and Henry VIII.[54] It describes the action of the Coronation in the Abbey according to the Fourth Recension, but gives very full instructions about the state entry. The king was to wear a white or green satin doublet with a long gown furred with ermine and to be astride a richly caparisoned horse. Behind him there was to be a spare horse and then seven henchmen in crimson satin doublets and gowns of white cloth of gold riding richly caparisoned horses. The king rode bareheaded beneath a canopy borne by four knights who were to change in rota. Before him there was to be his swordbearer flanked to the right by the Lord Great Chamberlain and to the left by the Earl Marshal. Ahead of them were to be two squires attired to represent the duchies of Guyenne and Normandy. The Constable was to be in charge of marshalling the procession, which was to include lords, Knights of the Bath (of whom more later), the Lord Mayor and City dignitaries, knights, esquires in livery and yeomen of the crown and of the chamber.

The instructions in respect of the queen are as exact. She was to be carried in a litter and attired in a kirtle of white damask cloth of gold trimmed with miniver, over which she was to wear a mantle of the same fabric trimmed with ermine. Her hair was to be worn loose and held by a circlet of gold and precious stones. Over her, four knights were to carry a canopy of white damask on silver staves with bells at the top. Behind the queen there were to be five henchmen on horseback in crimson satin doublets and blue velvet gowns. The Yeoman of

The Coronation of Henry VIII, 1509, woodcut

the Queen's Horses was to lead the palfrey of estate trapped in crimson cloth of gold, and there were to be three chariots filled with ladies, the first of which would be lined with crimson cloth of gold, the second with crimson velvet and the third with crimson damask. Then were to come seven ladies on horseback in blue velvet bordered with crimson satin. Both ahead of the queen and around her were to be lords, knights, squires, ushers and yeomen of her chamber.

Everything was based on precedent, and the Little Device records what may have been at least in part the norm at earlier London entries. What is indisputable is that the display side of the monarchy multiplied through the fifteenth century in the same way as its mystical aspects. Magnificence was to be a major attribute of monarchy and its effulgence was made possible by the emergence of what was to become a key department of the Royal Household. The Great Wardrobe began as a subdepartment of the Wardrobe and was originally a large storehouse for bulk purchases and a site where armour, tents and liveries were made. In 1360 a permanent home was found for it north of Barnard's Castle, close to the Thames. The Great Wardrobe during the fourteenth century developed into a world of its own as the main court repository for jewels, plate, armour, tapestries, tents and every kind of portable trapping. In the fifteenth century it evolved still further, the armour passing to the King's Armoury in the Tower and the jewels to the Keeper of the King's Jewels at the Palace of Westminster. Falling under the control of the Lord Chamberlain, the Great Wardrobe became the crown's *domus magnificencie*, the crucial department in charge of the display side of the monarchy and hence an increasingly important player in any Coronation.[55]

The published accounts for Wardrobe work for the Coronations of both Richard III and Henry VII give an astounding insight into the ever-expanding complexity of such an event, which now called not only for the necessary robes and decoration for the Abbey and Westminster Hall, but for horse trappings, canopies, liveries, banners, saddlery, cushions and a plethora of other items needed for the processional entry through London. For Richard III there was a huge issue of liveries to the various participants and a long list of banners: 1 with white lions, 2 of the Trinity, 3 of Our Lady, 1 with the arms of St George, 4 with the king's arms and 3 with those of St Edward.[56] For Henry VII the long list includes purchases of red velvet for dragons and red roses on a trapper, payments for twelve coats of arms for heralds 'beten and wrought in oyle colers with fyne gold', and also to an unnamed draughtsman 'for devising of xij trappours of the kinges Armes portred on papir with divers colours for the brauderers and the henxmen Jakettes'. The trapper designs included one with the arms of St Edward, a second with those of St Edmund, a third with falcons and a fourth with the arms of the mythical Welsh ancestor of the first Tudor king, Cadwallader.[57] Such accounts conjure up a frenzy of activity as supplies were bought and delivered and a small army of tailors, embroiderers, goldsmiths, saddlers and others set to work. All of this is reflected in the ever-spiralling cost of a Coronation. For the first time we have the totals: for Richard III and Anne Neville (including the creation of their short-lived son as Prince of Wales) £3,124 12s ¾d; Henry VII £1,506 18s 10¾d; and Henry VIII £4,748 6s 3d.

By 1533 the Coronation was clearly something very different from what it had been in the fourteenth century. Although the London end of the event was certainly the greatest change, it was by no means the only one, and it is to a consideration of the others that I must now turn the reader's attention.

CHANGING INSTITUTIONS AND SETTINGS

On the surface it would seem that there is no lack of information about Coronations during this period. In one sense this is true, but in another not. The evidence is, in fact, extremely uneven. There is a plethora for Henry IV and Henry VI and even more for Richard III, whose Coronation, being the first double one of a king and queen since 1308, spawned no fewer than twenty descriptions. But very little is known about those of Henry V, Edward IV, Henry VII or Henry VIII. To that we must add a cautionary note, one sounded before, that such descriptions, either single or embedded in chronicles, often contradict one another. Even taking all of this into consideration it can still be said that we know more than ever before.

Why is this? In the first instance, the increasing complexity of the ceremony simply demanded written accounts to assist those caught up in it, either as officiants or onlookers. To that we can add a growing literate lay audience who wanted to know about Coronations, both the form of the ceremony and what it meant. The turning point for this came with Henry VI's Coronation, for which accounts in the vernacular exist. The largest single group of this type of manuscript is known as the *Forma et Modus*. This provides a description in paragraphs of the whole ceremony and lists the principal officers and their duties. The text they incorporate is an abridged version of the Fourth Recension with only the incipits. The *Forma et Modus* proliferated both in the original Latin and in an English translation and the text, scholars agree, cannot be earlier than the fifteenth century.[58] Other sources, which no longer survive, must certainly have existed.

The account of Henry VII's Coronation abridges the ceremony 'because they be sufficiently recorded at Westminster . . .'.[59] In the case of his wife, Elizabeth of York, when it came to details about creating the Knights of the Bath, the author states that this was done 'in Maner and Forme as the Picture therof made, shewethe'.[60] Indeed, we have such a book, probably made for John Writhe, Garter King of Arms from 1478 to 1504, which depicts in strip cartoon fashion the making of such a knight.[61] Later in the account of her Coronation there is a further reference to a pictorial record having been made. And there are other surviving instances of this desire to pictorially record ceremonial, this time from the opening of the sixteenth century. The Great Tournament Roll depicts the event which was staged on the birth of an heir to Henry VIII in 1511 and a similar roll illustrates the king's procession to the Parliament of that year. All of this indicates that the ceremonies of state and their exact execution were, by the turn of the fifteenth to the sixteenth century, of great importance.

Both the rolls are attributable to someone within the orbit of the then Garter King of Arms, Sir Thomas Wriothesley. What that fact pinpoints is the emergence of the heralds as key personnel when it came to details of secular ritual.[62] The heralds first take on shape in the thirteenth century when they acted as officers controlling the etiquette of tournaments. Until the middle of the next century they remained interchangeable with minstrels, but, by 1400, their status had dramatically changed in response to an increasing elaboration in tournament ceremonial. Kings of Arms appear and, in 1415, Henry V appointed a chief of heralds in Garter King of Arms, who took his place at the head of a hierarchy which included other Kings of Arms and, below them, Pursuivants, who were probationary heralds. As tournaments were ritualistic and also called for a knowledge of the heraldry of the combatants, there was a gradual extension of their sphere of activity throughout the fifteenth century. It was written by one

William Bruges, first Garter King of Arms wearing his crown, illumination, English, *c.*1430

Nicholas Upton about 1440 that 'heralds wear their masters' coats of arms at their feasts and weddings, at King's and Queen's Coronations and at ceremonies of princes, dukes and other great lords'.

At the accession or Coronation of a new monarch it became the custom to create new Kings of Arms. Richard II created Chandos, Henry IV Lancaster and Leicester, Edward IV probably March, Richard III Gloucester and Henry VII Richmond. In 1420 the heralds held their

first chapter, marking their transformation into some kind of official organisation, and in 1483/4 Richard III granted them a house, albeit it was soon taken away from them. Nonetheless we are witnessing the nascent College of Arms whose role was to become crucial in later centuries in the staging of the Coronation.

Just as heralds gradually became institutionalised, so did the Court

of Claims. It was inevitable that, as the ceremony developed, contrary claims would multiply and there would be a need for some kind of adjudicating mechanism. In 1377 John of Gaunt, Duke of Lancaster, who was in charge of Richard II's Coronation, issued a proclamation directing claimants to appear before him and his deputies on a certain day, thereby in effect constituting the first Court of Claims, a body

Tournament on the birth of a son to Henry VIII, 1511, but utilising the pavilion used for the Coronation Tournament, 1509, illumination, English, c.1511 which became a norm for every subsequent Coronation. The resulting *Processus* which records its proceedings provides us with the earliest record of those who contended to perform services, and what the decision of the court was, thereby becoming a point of reference for all future cases. On that occasion eighteen claims in all were heard. In most there was no choice because the service stemmed from the tenure of a particular piece of land. Only if that estate was in the hands of the king, or the owner was a minor, could the king select someone of his own choosing. Although there was not a lot of room for manoeuvre in 1377, John of Gaunt did manage to go some way towards balancing the contending parties in awarding these honorary but highly coveted ceremonial roles. In this way Henry Percy, who was one of the Lancaster faction, was made Earl Marshal, while Edmund, Earl of March, member of another magnate grouping, was awarded the task of carrying the king's second sword and train. What the 1377 court proceedings made clear was that where there was no hereditary right or where it was ambiguous, it was in the king's power to appoint serjeanties at his own pleasure.[63]

Although we know that subsequent courts were held on the eve of Coronations (Henry VI's was held on 28 October 1429), no records have survived. That the same mechanism operated in the case of a queen can be gathered from what was recorded in 1533 about that of Anne Boleyn: 'Dyvers other put in petie claimes which wer not allowed because they seemed only to be done at the kynges coronacion.'[64]

Thanks to the multiplication of material we gain a far clearer notion as to the key organisational players. The most important single officer was the man appointed by the king to be Lord Great Chamberlain. He remained with him throughout the occasion, assisting him to dress when he arose, carrying his train, having the necessary offerings to hand in the Abbey and supervising the feast. His fee was the king's bed. Next came the Constable and the Marshal, both originally military officers. Of these the more important was the Constable whose task it was literally to marshal everyone according to status throughout the ceremonial. The Coronation feast produced the greatest roll call of officers, including a Chief Butler, Panterer, Carver, Sewer and Cupbearer. Of far greater significance was the Almoner, an office held by the Beauchamps of Bedford, who was responsible for laying the ray cloth from Westminster Hall to the west door of the Abbey and up the nave to the scaffold.[65] That the task was not devoid of its prob-

Opposite Tudor badges and devices reflecting the escalation of heraldic and other imagery during the XVth century, illumination, *c.*1500

comfort Et Lyesse

SACRED MONARCHY   151

lems we gather from what occurred at the Coronation of Elizabeth of York in 1487 when the cloth was fought over so violently before even the procession had barely been able to walk along it 'that in the Presence certeyne Persones wer slayne' and the close of the procession was thrown into chaos.[66]

In the case of the Abbey, the fifteenth century witnesses the abbot finally assuming an unassailable hold on the ecclesiastical side of the proceedings, one which was to descend to his successor after the Reformation, the dean. It was the Abbot who organised the ecclesiastical procession from the Abbey to Westminster Hall, who saw that the items of the regalia were sent to the palace and who assisted in the king's investiture. It was his task, too, to see that the regalia were safely returned to the custody of the Abbey.

The Abbey's fortunes, however, fluctuated throughout the fifteenth century. As Richard II had such a cult of St Edward and indeed of the Abbey, it inevitably went under a cloud during the following reign. Its fortunes revived a little under Henry V, whose chantry chapel put the monks to more trouble than it was worth, but in the middle of the century the institution was in a bad way and attempts at reform failed. Add to that the fact that Henry VI's energies were directed towards his own foundations at Windsor and Eton. It was not until 1500, with the arrival of Abbot Islip and the project for a new regal shrine, which we know as Henry VII's chapel, that its fortunes fully revived. But whatever its woes, no one challenged its right to house the regalia and to be the historic setting for the Coronation of the kings of England.[67]

For the first time in this period we have a drawing which records the appearance of a part of the Abbey's interior, the high altar as it features in the Obituary Roll of Abbot Islip from 1532. That is the only depiction we have of any part of the interior as it appeared before the Dissolution. It is a sharp reminder that from the close of the fourteenth century, after a long period of stagnation, work was resumed on building the nave and, by the deposition of Richard II, the perimeter walls, the arcade piers and the lowest parts of the west front had been built. The withdrawal of royal favour after 1399, together with what seems to have been a fall in income, slowed up work throughout the first half of the fifteenth century. Then, in 1441, the screen behind the high altar, visible in the Islip Roll drawing, was begun; under Edward IV work was resumed on the nave and, between 1500 and 1528, the two west towers arose to roof level. In this way the Abbey, as the architec-

The only record of the
appearance of the high altar
of Westminster Abbey
before the Reformation,
drawing, 1532

tural framework into which the Coronation was set, became more complete than at any time since the demolition of its Romanesque predecessor.

The most recent isometric realisation of the Abbey's interior as it stood on the eve of the Dissolution shows the crossing, the site on which arose the Coronation scaffold or stage, blocked off from the north and south transepts by wooden screens with doors in the middle of them.[68] These presumably remained in place and the Coronation stage floated above, fully consonant with the 'hyghe scaffolde' of Henry IV and 'the hyghe scaffold' referred to for Henry VI, not that a single image survives recording what a medieval Coronation stage must have looked like. The images we have never arise above visualising from a chronicle text, as can be seen in the illumination of the Coronation of Henry IV in Froissart, or they are formulaic along the lines of the sculpture referred to earlier in the chantry of Henry V. In the case of the latter there is also the representation of the Coronation of Henry VI in *The Pageant of the Birth, Life and Death of Richard Beauchamp, Earl of Warwick* (c.1485–90), and of Henry VIII in the Islip Roll (1532). All that can be said is that these images are atmospheric.

More important than the changes within the Abbey was the transformation of Westminster Hall into one of the most spectacular festival venues in Western Europe. The floor space of the old Romanesque hall had always been encumbered by a double row of wooden posts supporting the roof. In the autumn of 1393 Richard II took the decision, fully in accord with his exalted notion of kingship and driven on by a desire to eclipse the Grand'Salle of the Valois kings, to rebuild the hall, sweeping away the columns. The work was entrusted to Henry Yevele and Hugh Herland, and the result was the greatest masterpiece of English medieval architectural carpentry, with soaring wooden vaulting spanning no less than 69 feet. The hall is likely to have been used, albeit in an unfinished state, for the Coronation feast of Isabella of France in 1397, and it was certainly utilised for that of Henry IV.[69]

This provided the late medieval monarchy with a setting for the increased secular ceremonial which surrounded it, matching that of the Abbey. And, indeed, that thought must have been in Richard II's mind, for the north front was rebuilt to resemble a church façade, a secular counterpoint of the west front of the Abbey. On this façade at ground level there were niches for a series of twenty-seven large statues of the kings and queens of England, presumably running from Edward the Confessor and Edith to Richard II himself and Isabella of France. At the upper level there were to be four 'great kings', two of which must have been Richard and St Edward, and the other pair possibly St Edmund and William II or Edward II. The grand schema was never fully realised.

Within, the relationship to a church was further emphasised in the

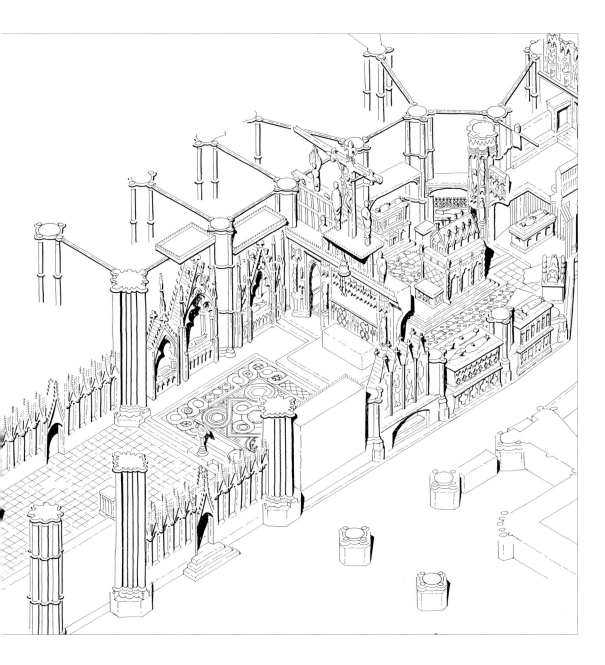

shield-bearing angels which still terminate every hammer-beam, heaven come to earth and hovering over the enthroned king. The south wall, now occupied by a broad nineteenth-century staircase, was once the site of the royal dais, approached by a flight of five or six steps and bearing the marble table and chair at which the king presided at

Diagram of the choir, presbytery and shrine area of Westminster Abbey on the eve of the Reformation the Coronation feast. Above it was a window and, flanking the royal seat, six over-life-size polychrome statues of kings of England, reinforcing the authority of the present wearer of the crown. When Richard was enthroned in state the effect of this innovatory tableau of exalted majesty must have been overwhelming. And it should never be forgotten that the long-vanished marble chair, the work of Henry III, was the true throne of the English kings, far eclipsing in importance the chair in the Abbey.

All of this has vanished, and we owe what little we do know about these arrangements to the seventeenth-century antiquarian, Sir William Dugdale, who writes of the marble seat, or King's Bench as it was known, being 'fixed in the wall there against the middle of the Marble Table'. The latter measured 19 feet in length by 3 in width. No

The Coronation of Henry VIII, 1509, drawing, 1532

visual record exists showing this arrangement, which also related to the hall's use between Coronations, something we have already encountered in accounts of inaugurations. By the fourteenth century the Court of Common Pleas had been joined by those of Chancery and the King's Bench, named literally because both were sited on the dais at the south end. The Court of Chancery was, indeed, dignified by its association with the marble chair and table and the chancellor was installed on its seat. Nor must we forget that the hall between times was the hawking ground of stalls and shoppers.[70]

A reconstructed view of Westminster about 1532 shows a very different configuration of buildings from the early Middle Ages. Both Palace and Abbey, held in to the south by the Thames and to east, north and west by what amounted to a moat, had filled almost every vacant space with buildings of one kind or another. To the north and west there was the Abbey and St Margaret's, surrounded by a myriad of gardens, farm buildings and offices for works connected with the running of the monastery. To the south and east, the riverside palace had developed into an imposing complex embracing Westminster

Westminster Hall as rebuilt by Richard II, the site of the secular enthronement and the Coronation Banquet

Reconstruction of the Palace and Abbey of Westminster at the close of the Middle Ages

Hall, the White Hall, the Painted Chamber and St Stephen's Chapel. But if one considers the balance overall, it is less the expansion of the ecclesiastical than of the monarchical area which is the most striking and a harbinger of what was to come as we move into the sixteenth century.

HIERARCHY MADE VISIBLE

The Fourth Recension was to be the last. On the surface it would appear that the history of the Coronation, as it were, should stop here. But in another sense it starts again because this basic liturgical text, seemingly unchanging, was to prove adaptable to every political, constitutional and social circumstance down until the present day. From the very outset it proved amazingly flexible and accommodating, not only as to what was performed in the Abbey but equally to whatever accrued around it, for, as we have already seen, the Coronation had expanded into a multiple event involving all sorts and conditions of people. And, as I have indicated, the accretions in the fifteenth century were of a particular kind, bred of the political situation of the monarchy, ones which set out to strengthen its authority and magnify it visibly to the public.

So it was that Richard II created four earls and nine knights at his Coronation, and a similar distribution of honours occurred at those, for instance, of Edward IV and Henry VII. Such creations established from the outset of a reign the role of the crown as the fount of honour. The fifteenth century was in a sense a golden age of aristocratic power when successive kings struggled to lift themselves above being *primus inter pares*. Equally the aristocracy felt threatened from below by what the old families would have regarded as new parvenu creations and also by the increasing wealth and power of the urban merchant classes. As a consequence of this, all over Europe in the fifteenth century there was an escalation in the outward trappings of rank, of the signs and symbols which set people apart on the ladder of hierarchy. And the same was true of England. In the case of the Coronation of the king, from 1399 onwards, he no longer walked from Westminster Hall in a simple white garment, but in splendid red robes. By 1483 in the Little Device the king swept from Palace to Abbey arrayed in layers of crimson with a great mantle of crimson satin furred with miniver, and with a crimson satin cap of maintenance trimmed with gold ribbon on his head. That change must have been prompted by the emergence of a robed House of Lords, although even the use of that term is to anticipate, for the expression appears first in 1544. Until the fourteenth century there were only earls and barons. Then dukes and marquesses were added, making the hierarchy more elaborate. What was to become the Lords, in fact, took time to develop as an institution. Its clerical component consisted of the two archbishops, the bishops and some, but not all, of the heads of the religious houses. What set the secular peers apart from the Commons was that they were not elected but summoned individually by writ. In addition, by the reign of Edward III, they had secured the privilege of being tried by one another and not in the common law courts. The practice of summoning peers' heirs to Parliament, on the death of the previous holder of the title, also gave the peerage yet further definition and exclusivity. In this way what had begun as an individual summons evolved into an hereditary right and the peerage became a caste.[71]

That process had already advanced far by the Coronation of Henry IV in 1399, when the chronicler Froissart records that the lords wore

The Coronation of Henry
IV, 1399, illumination,
Flemish, c.1460–80

'robes of scarlet, furred with menyver, barred at their shulders, accord-ynge to their degrees'. The emergence of a hierarchy defined in terms of dress had occurred by the close of the fourteenth century, during which there emerged a ceremony for creating a new title. A procession headed by heralds, including Garter King of Arms, entered the royal presence bearing the patent of creation. Behind them followed a peer carrying the robe in which the new one was to be invested. In the case of the highest ranks of the peerage these ceremonies could be far more elaborate, involving sword-bearing and the carrying in of a cap of estate. Dukes in the middle of the fourteenth century were invested with a cap of estate and circlet of gold and precious stones, the beginning of the Coronation coronet which would progressively spread and be codified according to aristocratic rank.[72]

The effect of this was to frame the monarchy with a group of people identifiable by their dress. The upper echelons had robes of estate but all ranks had parliament robes of scarlet in which rank was delineated by

bars of miniver: a duke 5, a marquess 4, an earl 3 and a baron 2. One of the earliest records of such robes appears on the charter of Henry VI's foundation of King's College, Cambridge. We lack detailed evidence telling us exactly what was worn by peers and their wives at Coronations throughout this period, but it was clearly not yet finally codified as it became later. The description of Elizabeth of York's Coronation gives us a fair idea of how far things had got by 1487. The Earl of Oxford in his capacity as Lord Great Chamberlain was described as being 'in his Parliament Roobees', but the Duke of Bedford, who carried the crown, wore 'his Roobees of Astate'. The description of 1487 continues: 'Next her folowd the Duchesse of Bedeford, and another Duchesse and contesse apparelled in Mantells and Sircoots of Scarlet, furred and powderde, the Duchesses having on ther Heds Coronatts of Golde richely garnyshed with Perle and precious Stones, and the Comtesse on her Hed Serkeletts of Golde in like wyse garnyshed, as dooth apper in the Bok of Picture therof made.'[73]

Foundation charter of King's College, Cambridge, 1441, showing peers wearing their robes

Would that this had survived. From this text we learn not only that by then peers' wives were in livery robes, but that they wore coronets defining their rank and that these were worn in the procession to the Abbey. By then marquesses certainly had coronets, and if we move on to the Coronation of Anne Boleyn in 1533 we can see these developments go a step further. At the conclusion of the ceremony Anne had gone to the shrine of St Edward to change, before issuing forth to process back to Westminster Hall: 'Now in the meane season every duches had put on their bonettes a coronet of gold wrought with flowers, and every Marquess put on a demy Coronal of golde, every counties a plaine circlet of gold without flowers, and every king of armes put on a croune of Coper and gilte all whiche were worne till nyght.'[74] The formula had not yet been extended across all the ranks of the peerage, but by the third decade of the sixteenth century it was well on the way. Nor was there as yet any mention of the putting on of coronets immediately after the crowning.

From 1399 every Coronation was marked by something else which was new, the making of what became known as Knights of the Bath. The first reference to them under that name occurs at the Coronation of Henry VI. The available numbers are as follows: 46 for Henry IV, 50 for Henry VI, 46 for Margaret of Anjou, 28 for Edward IV, 37 for Elizabeth Woodville, 17 for Richard III, 7 for Henry VII, 26 for Henry VIII and 18 for Anne Boleyn. By the time the Little Device was compiled, the process of making them was referred to as 'after the forme of the auncient custom of the Kinges of Englande'. By 1533 the costumes of the knights were already being looked upon as an anachronism. Thomas Cranmer, who crowned Anne Bolyen and described the whole event, wrote of the Knights of the Bath: 'so strange . . . as also their garmentes stranger to beholde or loke on . . .'. Although the ceremony certainly drew on ancient precedent, the Knights of the Bath were, in fact, an innovation only a century old.[75]

The account of those created at the Coronation of Richard III in 1483 can fortunately be matched with the pictorial record in Writhe's manuscript.[76] The action took place in the Tower the day before the state entry into London. This opened with the knights-to-be serving the first course of dinner to the king, after which they were led away by their 'governors' to be shaved by the king's barber and undergo a ritual bath. The arrangements were of a kind which had already been formalised in the twelfth century, and which marked the coming of age of a warrior and the completion of his military apprenticeship.[77] Once the baths were ready, this was reported to the king who commanded his chamberlain to conduct the wisest knights to the esquires' chamber, where they were to instruct the candidates in the duties of knighthood. The candidates, attired in black hooded gowns, were then led by their governors to the Chapel of St John for the vigil, praying all night before a lighted candle. At dawn they confessed, heard matins and Mass and were put to bed for a few hours. Later that day the governors reappeared before the king saying, 'Most victorious prince, when it liken unto your majesty, my masters shall awake.' The king then commanded the knights to be awakened, and they arrived, this time astride horses, preceded by their spurs and sword, arrayed in red gowns, black hose with leather soles, white girdles and red tartarin mantles fastened with a white lace from which a pair of white gloves was suspended. Within the great hall the king sat enthroned. One by one they were summoned to be invested, two lords affixing the spurs and the king himself dubbing and girding the knight with the invocation 'Be ye a good knight' and kissing him. After this they went to the chapel again to give thanks and, as they came out, the master cook appeared claiming as his fee their spurs, a reminder to them that if ever they offended against the tenets of knighthood it would be his task to hack off their spurs with a cook's knife. Finally, for the procession into London they donned a blue straight-sleeved robe with a knot of white silk lace on the left shoulder.[78]

The Knights of the Bath were the institutionalisation of an old tradition, the dubbing of knights on the occasion of a great feast, and what could be greater than a Coronation? It was an exercise in chivalrous kingship, with the king as the supreme knight and sovereign lord. Through it he honoured chivalry and its virtues as a bond of the aristocratic elite. Those chosen were, first, royal and therefore entitled to the honour by birth, second, young aristocrats who again merited it through lineage but in addition to which loyalty to the crown was taken into account. But the net spread wider down the social scale to the likes of judges or sheriffs in the shires. Here it was loyalty and service to the crown which was rewarded, spelt out to the aspiring knight in the bath, who was told he should 'above all other erthly thynges love the Kyng thy Sovrayn Lord, hym, and his right defende unto they power, And before all worldly thyngis put him in worshippe'.[79]

The making of Knights of
the Bath as recorded in
Writhe's Garter Book,
1484–88

The knight-to-be arrives at the Tower
The knight-to-be is bathed
The knight-to-be keeps vigil
The king girds the new knight with a
sword
The master cook threatens to dock the
knight's spurs

A lady removes a cordon of wh[ite]
silk from a knight who has
performed a deed of prowess

Opposite The knight-to-be arri[ves]
at the king's hall attended by
trumpeters

Without labouring the point, all this concern with status symbols is equally reflected in the great processions, not only for the entry through the City but even more in the one which went from Westminster Hall to the Abbey. There was always a balance between those, like the Barons of the Cinque Ports who bore the regal canopy, claiming their task as a right, and those appointed as a mark of signal favour by the king to carry this or that item of the regalia. For virtually every Coronation we have detailed lists recording who carried the swords, the spurs, the orb, the various rods and sceptres and the crown. To the bishops were naturally assigned the chalice of St Edward and the paten, and only at the Coronation of Henry VI did the clerics extend radically beyond that remit, for on that occasion the procession to the Abbey was of prelates, each of whom carried a relic, the prior of Westminster bearing St Edward's staff and the abbot the sceptre. But this was the exception.

The Coronation revisited

In spite of the Fourth Recension no Coronation was, in fact, exactly like another.[80] When it came to staging one all kinds of other factors and pressures could come into play. They could be of a practical nature. The vigil was omitted for Richard II, who was considered far too young for such an ordeal, as indeed was the eight-year-old Henry VI. The rendering of fealty likewise responded to the practical political needs of the moment. In the Fourth Recension it follows directly after the investiture, but no one demurred from rendering it a movable feast. According to Adam of Usk, certain lords did homage the day after the Coronation of Henry IV. In the case of Henry V it took place three days after his father's death, and the same was to occur on his own demise, his heir being a nine-month-old child.

It could be affected by a need to build up a new ruler. All the evidence points to a series of deliberate changes made in 1399 to enhance the usurper Henry IV. Instead of walking to the Abbey in white as a humble suppliant he donned ceremonial robes and, within the Abbey, the Coronation chair was removed from the shrine and lifted up on to the scaffold for the enthronement. Also for the first time, the Holy Oil of St Thomas was used. That deliberate deployment of the Coronation as a means to enhance someone in the eyes of the public is more often traceable in the case of queens. The Coronations of both Elizabeth Woodville and Anne Boleyn were calculated attempts to present queens who were not princesses of royal blood as worthy of their new-found status.

Practicalities must have dictated all sorts of decisions. In the case of Henry VI the actual investiture was split in two. The first phase was enacted before the high altar when the king after unction was vested in a gown of scarlet, probably the *colobium sindonis*, an ermine mantle, St Edward's spurs and a sceptre together with the *virga regia*. The bishops girded him with the sword, saying to him thrice 'Accipe gladium super femur tuum potentissimum', to which the child replied 'Observabo.' The sword was then taken from him, laid on the altar and then redeemed for a hundred shillings 'in signe and tokyn that the vertue and power shuld come first from holy Church'. He was then crowned, following which he arose, prostrated himself and then had all these garments removed, after which 'they rayed hym lyke as a bisshop should say masse with a dalmatyke and a stole aboute his nek, but not Crossed and sandalles'. The crown was placed back on his head and he was led up the steps back to the stage at the crossing and solemnly enthroned. Two bishops supported the crown, 'for hyt was ovyr hevy for hym, for he was of a tender age'. The pathetic nature of the occasion was caught earlier in the proceedings when this solitary figure on high sat 'there beholding the Peple All aboute sadly and wysely'.

Henry VI's Coronation was remarkable for other things. His father had made good by conquest the Plantagenet claim to France, and Henry VI was king of both countries. The French claim was there at Henry IV's Coronation when, in the procession to the Abbey, he walked beneath a canopy of dark blue silk, the French royal colour, and wore the broomscod device of the French king, Charles VI. In 1429 the fragile political situation, in which the English hold on France was already slipping, led to an emphasis on anything which would bolster up the dual monarchy.

Only six years before, when the French royal library was dispersed, the king's uncle, the Duke of Bedford, brought to England the illuminated ordo of Charles V. The impact of that as a source book can be followed in what is recorded in the *Liber Regie Capelle*. Borrowing directly from that ordo, on the morning of the Coronation the king was met by a procession of prelates, the convent of Westminster and members of the Chapel Royal 'chanting those anthems which are

168　　CORONATION

usually sung at the reception of kings', the imperial *Ecce mitto angelum meum*. The Bishop of Durham recited over the king enthroned in Westminster Hall the prayer *Omnipotens sempiterne Deus, qui famulum tuum*, also taken from the same source, where it appears at the raising of the French king from his bed. There was another prayer added when the king made his entry into the Abbey and the anthem *Domine virtute* was sung by the Chapel Royal as the king made his way to the stage. Both were also taken from the ordo of Charles V.[81]

All of this must have been done to lift the English rite on to a level with the French as part of a major propaganda exercise. This was carried through even into the symbolic dishes known as subtleties served at the banquet. With the first course came one which depicted the young king flanked by St Louis and St Edward the Confessor with the injunction:

> *Holy seyntes, Edwarde and seynt Lowyce*
> *Concerue this braunche, borne of your blessyd bloode.*

As a finale the kneeling Henry VI, flanked by St Denis and St George, received a crown from the hands of the Christ Child:

> *Borne by dyscent and tytylle of ryght*
> *Justely to raygne in Ingelonde and yn Fraunce.*[82]

The Coronation of Henry VI is the only one which has this wider political perspective. In the main the focus is a narrower one and the preoccupation was with pulling the monarchy back from where it had found itself in 1308 in terms of the oath and election. Nothing could quite obliterate these (they had been abolished in France), but there were ways of mitigating or sidelining their implications. The imperial anthems with which the ecclesiastical procession greeted the king worked from the premise that he was already king in his full regality. Up until these introductions from the French ordo the ruler was only hailed in such a way after the *recognitio*, the oath and unction. Everything was done to reduce the ritual of the *recognitio*, the last lingering trace of elective monarchy, to a mere formality. What those present were asked, where we know it, varied considerably. Henry IV was presented as a man from God, Henry V as 'by ryght and dyscent of heritage' and, in the case of Henry VI, they were asked 'Yf ye holde you welle plesyd with alle and wylle be plesyd with hym, say you nowe, ye! and holde uppe youre handys.'

Opposite Henry VI crowned as King of France, 1431, drawing, 1485–90

The oath was equally downplayed, although the actual text for nearly all of them is unknown. It is to be assumed that it continued in the form that it had taken in 1308; in fact, a severe curtailment to any theocratic pretensions. Through clause four the community of the realm had been accorded a place in the Coronation, because through Parliament it had a role in law-making and therefore also had the right of restraining any ruler if he failed to keep the laws and customs which they had jointly made. The oath was taken on the sacrament. Only in 1377, amidst a high tide of reaction, was there a definite attempt to downgrade the oath, moving it to before the *recognitio* to emphasise that Richard II was king by right and not by election.

Richard II's Coronation had another variation. After his initial prostration on arrival in the Abbey, there was a procession to the high altar of lay magnates bearing various items of the regalia: the Earl of Arundel the crown, William, Earl of Suffolk, the sceptre with the cross together with a 'certain precious vestment' and, finally, William, Earl of Salisbury, with another vestment. To each of these items there must have accrued a considerable mystique by the fifteenth century. They were truly holy relics. Indeed, the chronicler Grafton specifically refers to St Edward's cope at Richard III's Coronation as 'an holy relique'.

The late Middle Ages witnesses an intensification of religious experience through the use of a new religious art, whose aim was realism, and also through theatre. Coronations in the century and a half before the Reformation should, perhaps, be viewed in that context, certainly one in which contemporaries would have seen such events. For those who saw them they must have been extraordinary visual and aural experiences, ones akin to pictures of Christ descending into Limbo and reappearing in the full glory of Resurrection. The monarch arrived, ascended to the pulpitum in his robes of state and sat on high in the literal sense, for the stage or scaffold was at least thirteen feet high. He then descended down the other side to the sacrarium next to the altar, was partially stripped and then, hidden from the gaze of the onlookers by a pall, anointed. After this he was vested in robes which were virtually all ancient holy relics, seated in the Coronation chair (first certainly used in 1399) and crowned. He then 'ascended' in full magnificence, like a glittering icon, and was led up the great flight of steps to be enthroned on a chair which was up a further flight. The effect of his epiphany on those groundlings in the transepts seeing this figure from afar almost floating twenty-five feet above them must have been electrifying. What is striking about the post-unction descriptions is how the ruler was seen as some kind of cleric. Henry IV appeared 'aparelled lyke a prelate of the churche', and we have already encountered the young Henry VI arrayed 'lyke as a bisshop shuld say masse with a dalmatyke and a stole aboute his nek'. Few things are more confusing than the vestments used at the Coronation. They are first described in an inventory of 1359 as consisting of a crimson tunic or tunicle, a supertunica of embroidered black samite with a pectoral (probably a fastening of some kind), a stole, a mantle of black samite interwoven with gold with golden borders encrusted with pearls, precious stones and other ornament, silk gloves with borders of cloth of gold and buskins of striped cloth of gold. Further information about these comes from the *Liber Regalis* and the Westminster Missal, both from the 1380s, which describe the supertunica as being 'interwoven before and behind with great figures of gold', and the four-cornered mantle as 'interwoven with eagles all over'. The description of the garments as black could be explained by colour change through age from dark red. It has also been suggested that both these garments could have been of Byzantine origin and part of the imperial regalia which the Empress brought to England in 1125.

As these robes assumed iconic status, the habit of divesting from them and revesting in a personal set of Coronation robes and crown grew up. That was already the case in 1327, for an inventory of 1356 is the earliest description we have of such robes. After he had laid aside the vestments of St Edward Edward III put on: two tunicles of red samite, a mantle of red samite garnished with emeralds and orient pearls, possibly a gorget of red samite worked with gold, a jewelled stole of red samite with gold lappets and two rochets of white silk, one likely to have been the garment in which he walked to the Abbey and the other the *colobium sindonis*, put on immediately after unction to prevent oil seeping through and damaging the historic vestments. These by a patent under his privy seal dated 24 February 1357 he 'ordained for the Coronation of the kings'.[83]

By 1483 and the Little Device, the Lord Great Chamberlain was to re-dress the king in his traverse in the shrine of St Edward for the return procession 'with hosen, sandallis, and other robes of estate, that is to say, a surcote of purpill velvet close or open, furred with mynever pure, bordered with armyns, and ribbanded with gold at the color, hands, and speris; a hode of estate furred with armyns poudred with armyns, with a greit lace of silke, and ij tarcellis purpill . . .'. To that ensemble the archbishop would add one of the king's personal crowns.

It might well be asked, who was at a Coronation? Who was actually present in the Abbey and where? They are not questions upon which the available sources shed much, if any, light. We can begin with the presence of the participants, and to them we can add the rest of the aristocratic caste who needed to render homage either at the event or just after. Often a Coronation was followed almost immediately by a Parliament to which the aristocratic community, both lay and clerical, would have been summoned by writ, and members of what was to become the Commons, the knights of the shires and burgesses, would have arrived by way of election. In 1399 Parliament met the day after the Coronation. Henry V was crowned on 9 April 1413 and Parliament assembled on 15 May. Henry VI was crowned while Parliament was in session and, in the case of Henry VII, the Coronation was on 30 October 1485 and Parliament met on 7 November. But that relationship does not apply in every instance. Edward IV was crowned on 28 June 1461 and Parliament was summoned for 4 November. Richard III was crowned on 6 July 1483 and Parliament was summoned this time for 6 November. In both cases they began their work by confirming the king's right to the throne. The distancing of the meeting of Parliament from the Coronation would suggest that both monarchs were keen to emphasise that they had come to the crown by hereditary right and owed nothing to parliamentary sanction. However, Henry VII was an exception to that rule, for Parliament confirmed him in his right a week after his Coronation.

The presence or imminent presence of virtually the whole medieval establishment for Parliament would fit well with a Coronation. But one is left asking who got in and whether it could have included the knights and burgesses. Could, in fact, anyone push their way into the Abbey? And what parts of the building accommodated them? The transepts must have been full, so, too, the clerestory, but was it crammed at ground level along the nave? There is no way of knowing. A chance reference at the Coronation of Henry VII to a scaffold collapsing, 'with muche people, and none slayne, blessid be god', indicates a packed concourse but gives no clue as to its composition. Outside, the fate of Elizabeth of York's procession provides a glimpse of the hurly-burly in which people were actually killed squabbling over the ray cloth. That certainly would explain why by 1533 the processional route was railed.

Another great change was the feast. For the first time we know much more about these great occasions, with long descriptions and surviving menus. The completion of the new hall seems to have triggered a new theatrical splendour. From Henry IV onwards the royal table, at the head of a flight of steps, became subject to deliberate stage-management. On that occasion Henry sat with the two arch-bishops and seventeen other bishops, with the Prince of Wales to his right holding the sword Curtana and Henry Percy to his left holding the sword Lancaster, while some sources record there were other lords holding sceptres. At the 1377 feast in the old hall Richard II only had the Earl of Derby holding the sword of state. In the next century all of that was elaborated. Catherine of France sat with the Archbishop of Canterbury and Henry, Cardinal of Winchester, to her right with the King of Scots to her left and, further along that side, the Duchess of York and the Countess of Huntingdon. The Earl of March knelt holding a sceptre to the queen's right and the Earl Marshal was placed holding a second to her left, while a countess sat under the table at each end. Queens always had ladies in attendance. Elizabeth of York had the Countess of Oxford and Countess Rivers kneeling either side of her who 'at certeyne tymys helde a Kerchief byfor her Grace', an arrangement repeated for Anne Boleyn, for 'when she list to spet or do other-wyse at her pleasure'.

The feast was a vehicle whereby the king exhibited his largesse and displayed the dignity of the monarchy through the ceremonial and order of his household and servants, and through the display of food and plate. The intense interest in seating arrangements is linked to the wider awareness in the later Middle Ages that all-pervading notions of social hierarchy could be articulated in the organisation of space. A stage or scaffold was erected either to one side or at the north end of the hall for the minstrels and the heralds, who wore their crowns. In a rare reference we are told that at Henry VII's banquet the minstrels struck up a song at the second course. There were, in addition, when called for, special viewing boxes for onlookers. In 1377 the king's mother, Princess Joan, and her ladies, sat 'in a fair closet made in the upper way'. Later we are given glimpses of Henry VII and his mother, the Lady Margaret Beaufort, thus accommodated 'that they might prevely at ther pleasur see that noble Feste and Service', an arrangement repeated for Henry VIII in 1533.

The tables and their occupants remained more or less pre-ordained by custom, although accounts for feasts often give conflicting evidence as to who sat where. Invariably the two tables immediately below the royal dais had, to the right, the Barons of the Cinque Ports who had carried the canopies, with the Lord Mayor, Aldermen and eminent London citizens to the left. A drawing exists of Anne Boleyn presiding over her banquet seated beneath a vast canopy with a diminutive Archbishop of Canterbury to her right and, behind her, the 'kinges closett'. In front four tables stretch away labelled: 'at this table the maire of London & his brethren the aldermen', 'duchesses mar-quesses & countesses at this table and ladys on the oone syde &c.', 'lorde chancellor erles & barons', 'busshoppes at this table' and 'the barons of the cincq portes & maisters of the chauncery'. The Lord Mayor contin-ued, at the close of the meal, to go through the ritual of presenting the king with a cup of spiced wine, for which he gained the cup as the reward for his service.

Three courses were served, and they were only reduced to two by Henry VII, not out of parsimony but because of the lengthiness of the proceedings. According to the Little Device, the king was expected to enter Westminster Hall at seven in the morning. It was a very long day which called for tremendous stamina. Such courses were grandly served, arriving in procession to the sound of trumpets under the supervision of the Earl Marshal who rode about the hall on horseback with a small retinue of assistants carrying staves which they did not hesitate to use in order to maintain good order. After the second course the hereditary Champion, a member of the Dymock family, entered on horseback and approached the dais. Throwing down his gauntlet in several different places in the hall (three, four and six are mentioned in accounts), the heralds proclaimed his challenge. This over, he approached the dais, a lord proffered him a cup from which he drank, tossing what remained in it to the ground, and he left the hall taking it with him. The heralds then proclaimed largesse and the king's style, again in more than one place. And it was over.

The late medieval feast was a distinct phase in the history of eat-ing.[84] Exact etiquette and ceremonial were paramount, added to which there was an ever-rising commitment to luxurious display. That took

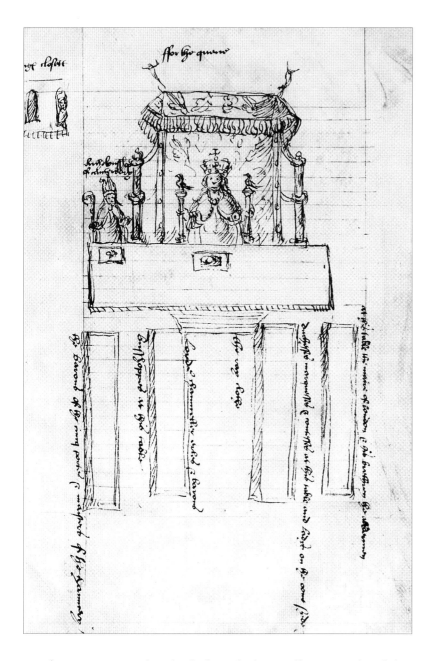

The seating plan for Anne Boleyn's Coronation feast in Westminster Hall

two forms. One was plate, both that which actually was used and that which was there for no other purpose than to register to the guests the riches of the monarchy. At Richard III's Coronation there is mention that he ate alternately from gold and silver plate, his wife from silver gilt and the bishops from plain silver. But this above all was the century of the buffet, those monumental exhibitions of gold and silver plate on a tiered dresser designed to impress by their sheer splendour. That mushroomed throughout the fifteenth century, so that by 1509 the buffet had as many as nine tiers 'garnyshid with weightie & many flagones, pottes and cuppes of golde, sylver and gilte'.

Display took a second guise in the advent of figurative food. That also could take two forms. The first was in the dishes actually consumed, where an heraldic overlay begins to be everywhere apparent. At Henry VI's banquet there was a red leche with a white lion armed, a royal custard adorned with a golden leopard holding a fleur-de-lys and fritters like suns, again holding fleur-de-lys. The heraldic message they gave was of a king who ruled over both France and England. But the tours de force of such feasts were the subtleties, food sculptures, generally it seems not for consumption but for admiration and instruction. These, too, began on an heraldic theme but quickly developed far more complex subject-matter. We have already encountered those at the Coronation of Henry VI, but his mother had an equally interesting series in 1421: a pelican in its piety, a group featuring her namesake, St Catherine of Alexandria, cast as a royal Romano-British saint, disputing with learned doctors and, finally, a tiger holding a mirror and a man (symbolising Henry V) riding away from it carrying a tiger's whelp and throwing down more mirrors as he sped away. It was believed that a tiger could not resist looking at its own reflection, a useful piece of folklore but a somewhat backhanded compliment to the queen's father. Information on these subtleties is patchy, but Henry VIII and Anne Boleyn had them, not described, although in 1533 the chronicler also adds 'shippes made of waxe mervailous gorgious to behold'. And even though the feast was over, that was not to be the end of the Coronation celebrations.

JUSTES OF PEACE

In 1377, after the great feast, Richard II retired to the king's chamber and 'spent the rest of that day up until dinner time in dancing, leaping, and solemn minstrelsy for joy at that solemnity'. Dinner followed, after which, 'wearied with extreme toil', the ten-year-old king finally went to bed. That is a rare glimpse of what could happen after the feast, but, in

Opposite Tournament on the occasion of the coronation of Joan of Navarre, 1403, drawing, English, 1485–90

Here shewes howe atte Coronacion of Quene Jane Erle Richard
kepte iuste for the Quenes part ayenst all other comers Where
he so notably and so knyghtly behaved hym self: as redounded
to his noble fame and perpetuell worshyp

general, further festivities were staged on subsequent days. A tournament was already an established feature at fourteenth-century Coronations, although details are lacking. Any Coronation entailed a gathering of a large number of knights, and the opportunity to stage a tournament was not to be passed over.[85]

The evidence about these Coronation tournaments is slightly fuller for the fifteenth century. The Rois Roll depicts the tournament staged for the Coronation of Joan of Navarre in 1403. Although drawn later in the century, it captures the splendour and panoply of such an event. On the occasion of the Coronation of Margaret of Anjou in May 1445 there was a three-day tournament held in the abbey's sanctuary. One was also held for the Coronation of Elizabeth Woodville twenty years later, at which Lord Stanley was awarded the honours and a ring with rubies. There are references to others for Henry VII and Anne Boleyn, but the only Coronation tilt for which we have a full description is that described by Edward Hall for Henry VIII. Indeed, the description of the two-day tilt exceeds in space and detail what he accords the Coronation.

By 1509, the Tudor court was set on its course to emulate that of Burgundy in display and magnificence as expressed through exercises of arms framed by dramatic pageantry. Hall gives a graphic description of the decor erected in the tiltyard at the Palace of Westminster on this occasion:

> In the saied Palaice, was made a curious Fountain, and ouer it a Castle: on the toppe thereof, a great Croune Emperiall [that is, with arches as introduced during the fifteenth century], all the imbatelling with Roses, and Pomegranetes gilded: and under and aboute the saied Castle, a curious Vine, the leaues and grapes thereof, gilded with fine Golde, the walles of the same Castle coloured White and Grene losengis [the Tudor colours]. And in euery losenge, either a Rose or a Pomegranet [heraldic emblems of the Tudors and of Aragon], or a Sheffe of Arrowes [emblem of Katherine of Aragon], or else H. [for Henry VIII] and K. [for Katherine] gilded with fine Gold, with certain Arches or Turrettes gilded, to support the same Castle.[86]

On the castle were hung the shields of the defendants and from the mouths of gargoyles spouted red and white wine. What is likely to be this structure was re-erected in 1511 for a tilt on the occasion of the birth of a male heir who soon died.

The tournament lasted two days. On the first, the defendants entered heralded by trumpeters, followed by 'fresh young galantes & noble menne gorgeously appareled, with curious deuices, of cuttes and embrouderies, aswell in their coates, as in trappers for their horses, some of golde, some in siluer, some in Tynsels, and diuerse other in goldesmithes worke, goodly to beholde . . '.[87] Following them came a castle covered in cloth of gold, from the top of which roses and pomegranates cascaded downwards, and in the middle of which stood Pallas holding a crystal shield. The defendants followed with their horses caparisoned in green velvet embroidered in gold with yet more roses and pomegranates. Escorted by a hundred scholars of Pallas, they petitioned the king to fight. Against them came challengers disguised as the knights of Diana, equally richly attired, who this time petitioned the queen. The decision on the first day was to run at tilt and the prize was to be the crystal shield or a sphere of gold carried in by the challengers.

It was only on the second day that the challengers actually revealed their identity as followers of the goddess of chastity and the hunt. Men attired as huntsmen and attended by greyhounds bounded into the arena blowing their horns, followed by 'a Pagent like a Parke, paled with pales of White and Grene [the Tudor colours again], wherein wer certain Fallowe Dere, and in the same Parke curious Trees made by crafte, with Busshes, Fernes, and other thynges in likewise, goodly to beholde . . '.[88] This was brought to rest before the queen and the palings opened, letting loose the deer who were slain and presented to her and her ladies. There then followed a tourney after which prizes were distributed.

The tournament was a peacetime exercise designed to train knights in the martial arts. It was to continue to fulfil that function all through the sixteenth century. The equivalent of this spectacle today is Trooping the Colour. Both, in effect, were rituals displaying the monarch as the apex of the country's fighting force. In the elaborately choreographed spectacles of the late Middle Ages and Renaissance they paid homage to the crown as the centre of courtly chivalry, to the king in his role as liege lord able, as he did in the case of the Knights of the Bath, to make knights and to present both his queen and her ladies as chivalrous heroines to whom such knights paid tribute. In their way these rituals of courtly chivalry were as crucial for loyalty to the monarchy as the state entry into London was for securing the commitment of a wider constituency. No extra event at a Coronation was devoid of a purpose.

END OF AN ERA

When Anne Boleyn was crowned it was only a few weeks from the passing of the famous Act in Restraint of Appeals which formally severed England from the Universal Church. We are already into the period of the greatest change to overtake the country since 1066. It also marks the end of an era for the monarchy, whose role after the Reformation was to be a radically different one from what it had been before. Just how different is less easy to grasp, for the fifteenth century was a period during which, apart from the writings of Sir John Fortescue, there were no discussions on the theory and nature of kingship. What happened to the Coronation, however, sheds some light on what can be defined as the idea of monarchy. One fact is clear: the right to the throne depended on the descent of the claimant, but there was a complete absence of fixed rules whereby to adjudicate the primacy of the contending hereditary claims. That lack of clarity meant that whoever laid claim had to look to other means by which to validate it, and that involved making a greater appeal to popular support in a way not seen before. As a consequence, the Coronation became parade and pageant, appealing above all to the teeming populace of the City of London. Although the inauguration ceremonies seemed, at times, almost to challenge the necessity of the rite of Coronation, no king went without unction and crowning. The Coronation ceremony's longevity rests precisely on its ability to legitimate anyone and thus ensure a façade of continuity and stability to the country. To that we can add other themes which tempered these events, such as the presentation of Henry VI as a king of a dual monarchy or Henry IV's use of the various honorary roles as pay-offs for his supporters. Even a queen's Coronation could be motivated by a particular reason, for both Edward IV and Henry VIII used them to bolster the public image of women, who were viewed with condescension if not downright hostility by the magnates.

Coronations have always embodied hope and renewal, and that was true, too, in the late Middle Ages. Of Richard II's Coronation Thomas of Walsingham wrote: 'It was a day of joy and gladness . . . the

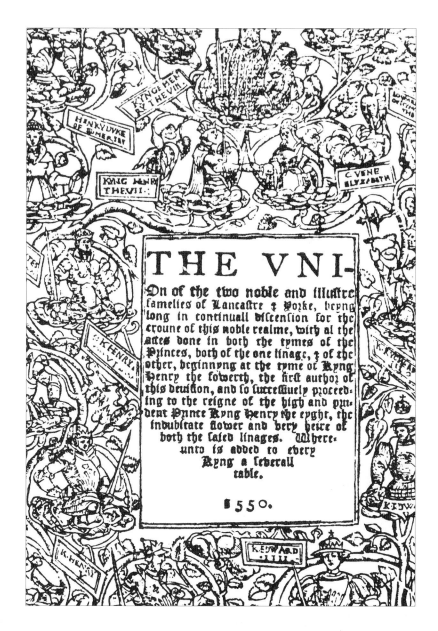

Rose tree of the Tudor family of a type which figured in Elizabeth I's Coronation entry, 1559, woodcut, 1550

long awaited day of the renewal of peace and of the laws of the land, long exiled by the weakness of an aged king and the greed of his courtiers and servants.'[89] But, as was so often the case, Coronations in retrospect become monuments also to hopes forever betrayed.

5

Crown Imperial

ONE PAGEANT which greeted Anne Boleyn in 1533 can act as our bridge leading us out of the old world of pre-Reformation England and into the new Protestant era. It sharply reminded those who saw it, and even more those who understood its verbal content, that indeed Anne's coronation marked less the golden age returned than the sharp dawn of a new political reality. The pageant concerned stood at Leadenhall:

> where was built a sumptuous and costly pageant in a manner
> of a castle wherein was fashioned a heavenly roof and under it
> upon a green was a root or stock, whereout sprang a multitude
> of white and red roses curiously wrought. So from the heaven-
> ly roof descended a white falcon [Anne's cognisance], and
> lighted upon the said stock and root: and incontinent [i.e. at
> once] descended an angel with goodly harmony, having a close
> crown between his hands, and set it on the falcon's head.[1]

This was accompanied by a song, one verse of which ran as follows:

> *Honour and grace be to our Queen ANNE!*
> *For whose cause an Angel celestial*
> *Descendeth, the Falcon as white as swan,*
> *To crown with a Diadem Imperial!*[2]

Another of Nicholas Udall's excruciating verses refers to 'an Angell descending crowned the empire-worthy bird . . .'. Empire indeed. For those that followed current events the reference could only be to the most celebrated piece of all the legislation which marked the advent of

Opposite Elizabeth I in her Coronation robes, 1559, painting, *c.*1603

the Reformation in England, the Act in Restraint of Appeals (1533: 24 Henry VIII, c. 12). The break with Rome, together with the dramatic events of the middle years of the sixteenth century, were to have a profound effect on both the reality and the idea of the monarchy, one which inevitably affected also the rite of Coronation.

TUDOR IMPERIALISM

The Act opened with the oft-quoted but seminal line: 'Where by divers sundry old authentic histories and chronicles it is manifestly declared and expressed that this realm of England is an empire, and so hath been accepted in the world, governed by one supreme head and king having the dignity and royal estate of the imperial crown of the same . . .'[3]

No attempt is made to spell out what these 'old authentic histories and chronicles' were, but, even if their contents were already under attack by the critical, the mythical imperial origins of the country, as spelt out by Geoffrey of Monmouth in his famous *Historia Regum Britanniae*, were still firmly in place in the early Tudor period. In it he records the arrival in the island of the grandson of the Trojan Aeneas, founder of the Roman Empire. Brutus conquered the giants then in possession of the land and went on to found New Troy, the later London. Thus, however tenuously, the rulers of England could claim kinship with the ancient imperial stock. To Brutus could be added King Arthur, a direct descendant of Constantine, who not only defeated the Saxons, Picts and Scots and the armies of Ireland, Iceland, Sweden, the Orkneys, Norway and Denmark, but went on to conquer Gaul and lay siege to Rome itself. Civil war in Britain forced him to withdraw, and he was eventually killed himself. Henry VII called his eldest son Arthur and, although much of this mythical history came under attack, it lingered on through the sixteenth into the seventeenth century, providing poets, if not legislators, with a rich fund of mythology with which to endow the rulers of Tudor England.

What in fact did Henry VIII mean in his claim to imperial status? From quite early on in his reign the king harboured imperial aspirations, naming two ships *Henry Imperial* and *Mary Imperial* as early as 1519. But it was only from 1529 onwards, when the divorce proceedings got underway, that his exploration of history to justify his imperial status and eventually his right to supremacy over the Church took on meaning. The two key figures in his view of history were the early Christian Emperor Constantine and King Arthur, but there was a particular emphasis on the former as the model for secular rulership in ecclesiastical matters. In 1534, the year of the Act of Supremacy which designated Henry as Supreme Head of the Church of England, the king was instrumental in publishing the humanist Polydore Vergil's *Anglica Historia*. In that book the claims to an imperial crown and its association with the half-British Constantine were spelt out. The whole basis of the Tudor Reformation was, indeed, built around this return to the Church as it had been in his reign. All of this was to have huge long-term implications, but these were sidestepped or not realised at the time. The situation was aided by the fact that there was no change of style by the king. He remained King and not Emperor of England.[4]

The early phase of Tudor imperialism was by no means expansive, but insular, in fact merely taking to a logical legalistic and administrative conclusion what had already been claimed by many late medieval European monarchs, that every king was *rex in regno suo imperator*, emperor within his own domain. In the Act in Restraint of Appeals England broke away from the Universal Church by severing the judicial links between the country and Rome. The following year came a series of momentous Acts which completed the destruction of papal power in England and redefined the monarchy. The most important of these was the Act of Supremacy, which claimed for the crown all those powers over the Church in England once exercised by the pope, not only its laws, courts and appointments, but its doctrine too. The centuries of papal rule were described as ones of usurpation and the king's actions cast as a resumption of the powers exercised over the Church by early Christian emperors. Of these Constantine, born of a British mother, was to be the touchstone.

Already at the close of the 1520s, when the divorce proceedings against Katherine of Aragon had got underway, Henry VIII had begun to examine the historical basis of the relationship of the monarchy to the Church. That role was, of course, defined in the Coronation: a duty to watch over the orthodoxy of the faith of his subjects and to be a guardian, custodian and transmitter of the faith. With this in mind the king began to revise the Coronation oath.[5] The draft, with his alterations, still survives, although there is no evidence that this new form was ever administered to a Tudor monarch. What is striking is that Henry VIII recognised the crucial nature of the Coronation as defining the role of the monarchy in respect of the Church. We can trace his thoughts by printing in sequence a draft and then its revision: 'that he shall kepe and mayntene the rights and the libertees of holie churche of old tyme graunted by the righteous cristen kinges of England'. And the revision with the additions in italics: 'mayntene the *lawfull* right and libertees of old tyme graunted by the righteous cristen kinges of Englond *to the holy chirche of inglond nott preiudyciall to his jurysdiccion and dignite ryall*'.

This spelt out the absolute control of the Church, advertised as 'of England' and not 'in England', that every late medieval king aspired to, which, through the Reformation, Henry VIII achieved. He could not, of course, reswear his Coronation oath, but his desire to revise that oath in the interests of the royal prerogative was not lost on those who were to frame the oaths of his successors.[6]

The break with Rome was in effect a return to theocratic kingship, as Henry VIII was both king and pope within his own realm. Such a titanic change demanded a new imagery for the monarchy, one which visibly spelt out the subjection of sacerdotium to regnum.[7] The printing press and the arrival of both the woodcut and then line engraving were to place in the hands of royal apologists powerful visual weapons with which to project a new image of monarchy to the populace. The definitive one for the Tudor Reformation monarchy is Holbein's title-page to Miles Coverdale's translation of the Bible into English (1535). Here Henry sits enthroned, wearing his imperial crown and robes of state. In one hand he holds the sword of justice, while with the other he presents the Bible to the kneeling clergy. Beneath his feet we see the royal arms encircled by a Garter surmounted by a large imperial crown. To the king's right stands David, a marker as to the emphasis which was now to be given in presenting the Tudor monarchy as Old Testament kingship revived. Henry VIII is portrayed both as David and as Solomon, Edward VI as Josiah, and Elizabeth as Deborah. To the king's left stands St Paul holding a sword, no longer as a symbol of his martyrdom but, as in the revised iconography of Protestantism, as the author of the New Testament epistles. This is the evangelical symbol for the Bible or 'the sworde of the Spirit, which is the worde of God' (Ephesians 6: 17). In this tableau Henry VIII is portrayed as the apostolic successor to Christ.

This is a seminal image in which the tenets of the Reformation and the crown imperial become inextricably intertwined, so that sword and crown run as a leitmotif throughout the sixteenth century in visual representations of the ruler. Swords which had already gained quite complicated symbolic resonances throughout the fifteenth century now took on an additional meaning as one of the prime symbols of the king as the guardian of the reformed faith. Indeed, accounts of Edward VI's coronation gloss the sword of state as signifying 'the kinges titill of the defender of the faith', an ironic use if ever there was one of the title bestowed on Henry VIII by the pope for his defence of Catholic orthodoxy.[8]

In the aftermath of the Reformation Acts there were three Coronations within 25 years, in fact three almost within a decade counting from the year of Henry VIII's death in 1547. They were staged during a period of tumultuous and violent change as England became first Protestant under Edward VI, then Catholic under Mary Tudor and finally Protestant again under Elizabeth I, albeit the Elizabethan settlement of 1559 reduced the role of the monarch from Supreme Head to Governor. As regards the idea of monarchy, these Coronations coincide with the early phase of Tudor imperialism. From 1570 onwards

Henry VIII with the sword and the Bible, symbols of Tudor Protestant kingship, 1536 the idea began to develop in other directions, turning what was an insular vision into a global one.

The attitudes engendered by that early phase can conveniently be summed up in one book which was in virtually every parish church, John Foxe's *Actes and Monuments*. It first appeared in 1563, but the more profusely illustrated edition of 1570 spells out in strip cartoon fashion universal history as recast in the interests of the Tudor imperial reform. The leitmotif was the struggle of the imperial crown against the papal tiara. Woodcuts trace the gradual usurpation by the popes of the powers once exercised by the emperors, and how the mighty acts of Henry VIII had reversed this, turning the clock back to the virtuous age of the early Christian Emperors, above all to the age of the British Constantine. Two images succinctly encapsulate the general drift, one in which Pope Alexander III treads upon the neck of the Emperor Frederick Barbarossa, and a final tableau in which Henry VIII, sword in hand and with the imperial crown perched on his hat, presents the Bible to Thomas Cranmer as he plants his feet on Pope Clement VII, whose tiara topples from his head. The motif is worked in the dedication to Elizabeth I in a woodcut which appeared in the first edition. There, within the letter C, the first letter of Constantine, Elizabeth sits

Tudor anti-papal propaganda from John Foxe's *Actes and Monuments*: the pope treads on the neck of a Holy Roman Emperor, wood engraving, 1570

Opposite The triumph of the crown over the tiara from Foxe's *Actes and Monuments*: Henry VIII treads the pope underfoot, wood engraving, 1570

Elizabeth I as the Protestant Queen on the frontispiece to the Bishops' Bible, wood engraving, 1569

enthroned, her feet on a cushion, while below evil snakes are vanquished and a pope clutches a pair of broken keys.

Everywhere we look, thanks to the new mass medium of printing, we see the crown imperial proliferating. Another famous and widely seen example is the title-page of the Bishops' Bible (1568). On it the figures of Justice and Mercy support an enormous imperial crown over the head of the enthroned queen. Nor should it be forgotten that the royal arms surmounted by the crown replaced the rood, the images of the crucified Christ flanked by Mary and John, over the chancel arch of every parish church. Never before had the imperial crown, an invention of the fifteenth century, been so universally seen. All of this must have had an effect on the object itself, if indeed such an object existed. It can be no coincidence that it is during this period precisely that the imperial state crown as an object moves to prominence. Indeed, the Reformation legislation with its perpetual reference to the imperial crown called for such an object. It first appears in an inventory of 1521 in a group of items making up the personal regalia of a king and his consort: two crowns, two sceptres and one orb, plus the mysterious bracelets or armils. All of these were kept in the Jewel House in the Tower and remained sacrosanct and nearly untouched until destroyed in 1649.

That fact indicates a very different attitude to the personal regalia from what prevailed in the medieval period. Kings then usually had several crowns, one of which was generally his *magna corona*, but they came and went, remodelled in the interest of fashion or pawned or sold to meet financial needs. The items of personal regalia listed in the inventory of 1521 appear in every successive one.[9] In the two earliest, of 1521 and 1522, the imperial state crown is depleted of some stones, removed by the king in order to make other jewels for his wearing. What is unclear is when this crown was made and when was it worn. The fact that it had been pillaged for gems indicates surely that it was rarely if ever worn. What we do know is that it was used in the actual crowning ceremony for all three Coronations from 1547. This was a revolutionary innovation which must have affected the status of the object, for it is never after referred to again as being depleted of stones.

The change in status is reflected in its appearance, along with both the sceptre and orb, in Daniel Mytens's portrait of Charles I dated 1631. There they are placed on a table to the king's right as objects defining sacred monarchy, ones by then seen to be of venerable antiquity. The crown consisted of a circlet set with 8 balas rubies, 8 sapphires, 5 pointed diamonds, 20 rubies and 19 pearls. From this arose 5 crosses alternating with 5 fleur-de-lys, all decorated with precious stones, and each of the fleur-de-lys bearing a figure. In the Mytens painting we see the figure of the Virgin and Child, and inventories refer to St George (patron saint of England) as being another. These appeared on the third and second fleur-de-lys respectively, leaving three which are

In the aftermath of the Reformation the Imperial Crown was emphasised as never before.
Top left On Coverdale's Bible, 1536
Top right Henry VIII's Golden Bulla, 1527
Bottom left Elizabeth I's coronation portrait, 1559
Bottom right Elizabeth I's Armada Portrait, c.1588

variously described as having the figures of Christ or a king. It has reasonably been suggested that these three figures are likely to have been of Christ and of two royal saints, St Edward the Confessor and St Edmund, the martyred king of East Anglia.

This was a hugely impressive crown weighing some 7lbs 6oz and, therefore, was very heavy to wear. The accompanying regalia, which also figure in Mytens's canvas, are 'a septer of golde with a Dove ther vpon' and 'a rounde Baule of gold with a Crosse ther vpon'. But when was this set of regalia made? The crown, which is arched, gives the only clue as to date, for it cannot be earlier than the middle of the fifteenth century. It has been attributed to both Henry VII and Henry VIII, but it could equally have been made for Edward IV on whose second Great Seal an imperial arched crown appears for the first time.

As we shall see, a triple crowning was introduced in 1547, which

The unique depiction of the old Tudor Crown of State, orb and sceptre which were destroyed in 1649, painting, 1631

was repeated in 1553 and 1559. That involved the crown of St Edward, the imperial state crown and a personal crown. Both Edward VI and Mary had to have personal crowns made and Elizabeth is likely to have used her sister's. In 1547 a personal crown was a necessity, for the king was only nine years old. That crown, made by the king's goldsmith, is recorded in an early Jacobean inventory as follows: 'a Crown Imperial of gold set about the nether border with 9 great pointed diamonds and between every diamond a knot of pearle set with five pearls in a knot. In the upper border 8 rock rubies and 20 round pearls. The four arches being set each of them with a table ruby, an emerald and vpon two of the arches 17 pearls, and between every arch a great balas ruby set in a collet of gold and upon the top a very great balas ruby pierced.'[10]

In the case of the personal crown of Elizabeth, we again for the first time have a visual record, albeit a confusing one in the form of two portraits of her in her Coronation robes which are likely to go back to a single lost portrait of 1559.[11] One is the panel painting formerly at Warwick Castle but now in the National Portrait Gallery. The other is a miniature by Nicholas Hilliard in a private collection. The former was painted around 1600 and the latter sometime during the 1590s. Nonetheless, they depict faithfully what the queen wore on her return from the Abbey on 15 January 1559 as recorded in the accounts for the occasion and also in the inventory of her wardrobe in 1600:

1. First one Mantle of Clothe of golde tissued with golde and silver furred with powdered Armyons with a Mantle lace of silke and golde with buttons and Tassells.

2. Item one kirtle of the same tissue the traine and skirts furred with powdered Armyons the rest lyned with Sarceonet with a paire of bodies and sleeves to the same.[12]

An Italian who saw her records her appearance in this way: 'her majesty carrying in her hands the sceptre and orb and wearing the ample royal robe of cloth of gold'.[13] The accounts record how those robes were her sister's altered. If they can be demonstrated to be accurate in the portrait, it follows that the regalia depicted must have existed, although they match nothing in the inventories.

These revolutionary changes in the whole status and power of the monarchy were not the only ones to affect the Coronation. The whole physical setting of the occasion was also to undergo a radical transformation as the Reformation altered the face of the political, religious and cultural landscape of the nation.

THE FATE OF THE PALACE AND THE ABBEY

For five hundred years Westminster had been the nerve centre of the kingdom, with the palace housing the court as well as the administrative and legal institutions of the realm, the Exchequer, the Chancery, the law courts and Parliament itself. Across the way was the Abbey, the monastery which housed the regalia, in which the rite of Coronation was enacted and in which there was the dynastic valhalla of England's kings fanning out in a series of tombs from the shrine of St Edward. Within a decade all of this would irrevocably alter as the Reformation took its toll and the whole historic enclave was replaced more or less with the Westminster we know today.

In 1529, on the fall of Cardinal Wolsey, Henry VIII had confiscated his London residence, York Place, literally a few hundred yards north of the old medieval palace. That acquisition sealed the fate of Westminster Palace. The king had already ceased to use it as a royal residence thanks to two fires, the latter in 1512. Its status had also been eroded by the new Tudor palaces of Richmond and Greenwich, but its death blow was to be York Place in its new guise as Whitehall Palace, which was to remain the official London seat of the court until its destruction by fire in 1697. Under Henry's aegis and egged on by Anne Boleyn, York Place was transformed into what is likely to have been the largest royal palace in Western Europe. It was finished enough to receive Anne Boleyn after her Coronation in 1533. Initially it was called the Palace of Westminster, and the old palace was used as a quarry to build the new one, the former declared to be 'only a member and parcell of the said new Palace'. What this achieved for the first time was a division between the court and royal household and the organs of government. The Chancery, Exchequer, Common Law and Prerogative Courts, the High Court of Parliament as well as the four new financial courts added by Henry VIII still operated from the old palace.[14]

The hall retained its status, for after the 1512 fire John Stow, the chronicler, records it was repaired: '. . . the great Hall, with the offices neare adioyning . . . for feastes at Coronations, Arraignments of great persons . . . keeping of the Courts of iustice, &c.'. From 1538 to 1540 it underwent further restoration, this time the roof being releaded with material stripped from dissolved monastic houses. And, over forty years later, in 1584 it was refloored with a mixture of loam, clay and 'sope and ashes'. Nothing, in fact, was to impair the association of the palace and the hall with the rite of Coronation, for on the morning of the event the king took boat from Whitehall. No Tudor Coronation was to start at Whitehall.[15]

If Westminster Palace changed its status, the Abbey's fate was far more dramatic. Already, in 1538, the shrine of St Edward along with all its relics had been demolished and transported to the treasury. The bones of the royal saint were interred elsewhere. What happened to the Coronation chair can only be conjectured, but by the sixteenth century it had assumed a life of its own far removed from being a relic placed in tribute near the shrine. All three mid-Tudor Coronations were to use what was now referred to as St Edward's chair. Also, although the regalia were relics of the saint, no one attempted to remove or destroy them. Even if they were not used they remained undisturbed.

An inventory taken in 1606 demonstrates that they must have quietly lain in store for almost half a century, 'being jewells and ornaments for the coronacion'.[16] The list opens with 'ij. Books concerning the Order of the King's and Queen's coronacion', conceivably the Lytlington Missal and the *Liber Regalis*. Their follows a list of 21 items, amongst them what must be St Edward's crown, the regal, the spurs, the *crux nutans*, the 'Eagle of golde called the Ampull', 'a Scepter with a Crosse of Gold and precious stones', 'a Long Scepter with a Pike of Steele in the bottom' and 'a Longe Scepter for the King with a Dove vpon the top'. By that date they made an extraordinary survival into post-Reformation England which was to have implications for the Coronations of the first two Stuart kings.

The regalia may have survived, but in an Abbey transformed as the monasteries were dissolved.[17] On 16 January 1540 the abbot, William Boston, a placeman of the architect of Reformation, Thomas Cromwell, and 24 monks signed the Deed of Surrender. For nearly a year the building stood empty and abandoned. Then, on 17 December 1540, Henry VIII by Letters Patent elevated the Abbey into a cathedral consisting of a bishop, a dean and twelve prebendaries. The area of Westminster itself was accorded city status. Thereafter the Abbey fell victim to the religious wheel of fortune of three successive reigns. The first bishop only lasted six months before being sent to the Tower. He was succeeded by the conservative Thomas Thirlby, with the last abbot, Boston, in his new persona as dean. Both these were in office for the Coronation of Edward VI. In 1549 there was a new dean, Richard Cox, a radical reformer who set about destroying every image in the place, a task which extended to the destruction of most of the monastic library. Again one notices that items which related to the Coronation somehow survived, otherwise we would not still have the Lytlington Missal or the *Liber Regalis*. Thirlby, viewed with extreme hostility by the rabidly reforming government of Edward VI, was removed from office, and what had been the independent bishopric of Westminister was joined to the see of London in the person of Nicholas Ridley. In May 1553 what little was left in the Abbey was carted away by the king's commissioners. All that remained were two gilt cups, a silver pot, three hearse cloths, twelve cushions, a carpet and two cloths for the communion table, eight cloths for stalls, three for the pulpit and a small carpet for the dean's stall. Virtually everything we see of the kind recorded in the drawing of the high altar in the Islip Roll would have vanished in destruction and greed.

Two months after that, everything went in reverse with the accession of Mary Tudor. The dean was arrested, imprisoned, and subsequently fled the country. Nine out of the twelve prebendaries were also deprived of office and likewise fled. Mary put in her own chaplain, Hugh Weston, as dean, and the building was spruced up enough for her Coronation in October. Three years later, on 7 September 1556, the Abbey was refounded as the Benedictine monastery of St Peter, Westminster, with John de Feckenham as its mitred abbot. He set about at once restoring the shrine of St Edward, and on 5 July 1557 the saint's body was returned to it. A year later Feckenham was to preach at the queen's funeral and to be in office still for Elizabeth I's Coronation. Indeed, the queen is said to have tried to persuade Feckenham to go along with her proposed religious settlement, but he was not to be won over. On 10 July 1559 the monastery was once again dissolved. A year later it was reconstituted as what we know as a royal peculiar, that is, a church answerable directly to the crown and not to any bishop, presided over by a dean and chapter and with the foundation of a school. That period of the Abbey's history lies beyond the boundaries of the mid-Tudor Coronations. But what is important is the beginning of the radical transformation of the urban landscape around the actual building, as the advent of a great new palace led to the gentrification of Whitehall as an arena for secular display and entertainment. When the Abbey next impinged on a Coronation, in 1603, the religious situation was also a very different one.

This is an extraordinarily complex period which is reflected in changes to the Coronation and also in a war of ideas waged in the pageantry staged by the City for the vigil entry. In the interests of clarity I intend to deal with what happened to the Coronation first.

Three Tudor Coronations[18]

Henry VIII died on 28 January 1547. As he lay on his deathbed the vultures were already gathering for any pickings which might be had when the crown passed to a child of nine. Foremost amongst them was Edward Seymour, Earl of Hertford, soon, in violation of the late king's will, to assume the role of Lord Protector with the title of Duke of Somerset. Henry VIII's death was concealed from the public until 31 January while Hertford made his way north to secure the person of the king. The day of the announcement of the king's death was the day on which Edward reached the Tower of London where Thomas Cranmer, the Archbishop of Canterbury, and Wriothesley, Earl of Southampton, stood at the head of the Privy Council on the drawbridge to welcome him with elaborate deference. And there for three weeks he stayed while those who had seized power apportioned offices and conferred titles upon themselves in the new king's name. And it was there, too, that on 13 February the Privy Council met to discuss what form the Coronation should take, the date for which was fixed for Shrove Sunday, 20 February. The entry in the Acts of the Privy Council opens by stating that the Lord Protector and the other members of the Council:

> did finally resolve, that forasmuche as divers of the old observ-
> vaunces and ceremonies toforetymes used at the coronacions
> of the Kinges of this realme were by them thought meate for
> sundry respectes to be correctid, and namely for the tedious
> length of the same which shuld weary and be hartsome perad-
> venture to the Kinges Majeste being yet of tendre age fully to
> endure and bide owte; and also for that many poinctes of the
> same were suche as by the lawes of the realme att this present
> were nat allowable . . .[19]

The entry then goes on to rewrite the Coronation. What follows implies that someone, almost certainly Cranmer, had before him a text of the Fourth Recension which was gone through, decisions being taken piecemeal as to what was to be done. It is a frustrating fact that for none of these three Tudor Coronations does there exist a text with rubrics as to what was actually enacted. All we have are accounts by heralds, eyewitnesses and foreign correspondents. In the case of Edward, there are discrepancies between what was decided at this council meeting in the Tower and what was actually performed on the day. That alterations to the ceremony could be made for minors we know from the example of Henry VI. Add to that the fact that the rite as outlined in the Little Device had expanded into an incredibly demanding ceremonial for anyone, let alone a child of nine, so to contract it was eminently reasonable. But contraction was only one aspect, for by far the most significant phrase was the one which read 'for that many poinctes of the same were suche as by the lawes of the realme att this present were nat allowable . . .'. In short, in 1547 the Coronation was to be recast to accord with the great Acts of the English Reformation and to give out signals that something even more sweeping was in the pipeline from the Protestant radicals now in charge of government.

There is no indication, however, that at any juncture thought was ever given to abandoning the rite of Coronation altogether as incompatible with the post-Reformation status of the crown. Protestant rulers abroad had already undergone Coronations: Gustavus Vasa of Sweden in 1528 and Christian III of Denmark in 1537. The need to establish in the eyes both of the Tudor establishment and the London populace, not to mention the foreign ambassadors who, for the first time, were asked to the event and who would write home, that the advent of a child-king did not mean any diminution in royal power or authority, was paramount. So the procedure of the Little Device was adhered to, but with significant modifications to accord with the crown's new imperial status.[20] And, as Dale Hoak has demonstrated, that included a radical alteration of the oath, recasting the relationship of the monarch to Parliament, one which was also to be used for Elizabeth I.

What must have struck potently those present was the shift in emphasis away from the clergy in favour of the laity. So, for example, the young king was no longer escorted by the two customary bishops but by a single bishop and a lord, in this instance the Earl of Shrewsbury. The *recognitio* remained, but any hint of election was eliminated. When the young king was carried in a chair to the four sides of the scaffold, with Cranmer at his side, it was not for a ritual which could be regarded in any way as election, but for the recognition of Edward as the 'rightfull and undoubted enheritour by the lawes of

God and man to the Royal Dignitie and Crowne Imperiall of this realme . . .', and they were gathered to agree to Edward's 'Consecracion, Enunction and Coronacion'. All that they were called upon to reply was: 'Yea, yea, yea, God save King Edwarde, King Edwarde, King Edwarde.' Any hint of election had already been disposed of before the event, for Edward was the first king to issue a proclamation declaring that he had come to the throne 'fully invested and established in the crown imperial of this realm'.

The same revisionism was applied to the oath, which Edward was described as having taken on the sacrament placed on the altar as was usual, although Cranmer's revised form went on to add that the king was then to lay his hands on the Gospels and say 'The thinges which I have before promysed I shall observe and kepe; so God helpe me and theis Holy Evangelistes by me bodily towched upon this Holy Awltare.' Accounts of the mid-Tudor Coronations tend not to be overdetailed, so it is perfectly possible that this happened, and it was certainly fully in accord with all the other changes.

As Cranmer said in his sermon which followed the oath-taking: 'Your Majesty is God's Viceregent, and Christ's Vicar within your own Dominion.' The monarchy was thus rendered seemingly absolute. Edward swore to confirm the laws and liberties granted by his progenitors, but it was left to the crown to decide what those were. Peace and concord were pledged to Church and people, but any mention of the clergy being included was eliminated. The clause that gave protection to the clergy's liberties and privileges vanished and a new clause read: 'Do ye grawnte to make no newe lawes but such as shalbe to thonour and glory of God and to the good of the Commen Wealth, and that the same shlbe made by the cionsent of your people as hath been accustomed.' What that, in fact, meant was the consent of Parliament. Now it was parliamentary consent and not the royal prerogative which had carried through the Reformation and given it its veneer of popular support. Now we have that fact ensconced in the Coronation oath, for everyone from Cranmer downwards involved in the Coronation of 1547 knew that it was to be followed by even more radical religious reform, which would be carried through by statute. This situation was repeated in 1559 when again a Parliament following the Coronation was made the vehicle re-establishing Protestantism. Hoak finds the source for this configuration in the writings of the reformers, John Aylmer and John Hales, and in those of Sir Thomas Smith, later author of *De Republica Anglorum*, in which he assigns a central place to Parliament in the governance of the realm. All of these articulated a vision of the new Protestant polity based on the crown in Parliament, one which first emerged in the circle surrounding Edward VI's Lord Protector, the Duke of Somerset.

So in this way the oath was rewritten as a bulwark of the recently assumed royal supremacy over Church and State based on an alliance of ruler and ruled in Parliament. This was further emphasised in Cranmer's sermon, which reminded those present of Pope Paul III's threat to depose Henry VIII because he had fallen into heresy and thus broken his Coronation oath. In the name of the people of England Cranmer rejected this and declared 'that this promise reacheth not at your highness's sword, spiritual or temporal, or in the least at your highness' swaying the sceptre of this your dominion, as you and your predecessors have had them from God'.[21]

Unction was administered, but the gloss to it utterly removed any notion that it bestowed something on the child king that he had not already got. As the king was Supreme Head of the Church of England unction could add nothing to his status. In his sermon Cranmer once again spelt out the role of unction in the new scheme of things for, in his eyes, kings were 'God's anointed' by birth and not by the action of unction:

> not in respect of the oil which the bishop useth, but in consideration of their power which is ordained; of the sword which is authorized; of their persons which are elected of God, and endued with gifts of his Spirit, for the better ruling and guiding of his people. The oil, if added, is but a ceremony; if it be wanting, that the king is yet a perfect monarch notwithstanding, and God's anointed, as well as if he was inoiled. Now for the person or bishop that doth anoint a king, it is proper to be done by the chiefest; but if they cannot, or will not, any bishop may perform this ceremony.

And so they did in the case of both Mary and Elizabeth. But in this Protestant gloss on an ancient Catholic ritual Cranmer brings the whole house of cards tumbling down. The monarchy was desacralised, although that fact seems not to have been taken in in 1547. And so a ritual, which had just been described as adding nothing, proceeded.

When a comparison is made between those parts of the royal anatomy which the Privy Council wished to have anointed and those which Cranmer actually anointed, Edward was more fully endowed with unction than any medieval king. The Privy Council had listed the palms, breast, middle of the back, two elbows and his head with a cross in holy oil. The head was to have a second cross in chrism. Cranmer, however, is recorded as having used both holy oil and chrism on the soles of the king's feet, his breast, wrists, elbows and head.

This submission of sacerdotium to regnum was to be emphasised further as the ceremony unfolded. After unction Edward had retired to a traverse close to the altar and re-emerged 'cloathed in rich robes', but there is no mention of the vestments of St Edward, banished no doubt, too, as superstitious relics, a rejection which was not extended to the actual ornaments. There then followed one of the most inexplicable innovations in the whole event: a triple crowning, first, with the historic crown of St Edward, secondly, with 'the Emperiall Crowne of this Realme of England' and, thirdly, with the new personal crown made for the occasion. It seems that the first and very probably the second and third crownings were performed jointly by Cranmer and Somerset, each one prefaced by a fanfare of trumpets from the battlements of the Abbey. None of this appears amongst the action as laid down by the Privy Council, which only refers to the crown of St Edward. This was something quite unprecedented. Only the Holy Roman Emperor was crowned with three crowns, a silver one for Germany, an iron one for Italy and a gold one for the Empire. These involved three separate Coronations at Aix, at Monza or Milan and finally in Rome with the pope officiating.[22] The only other ruler with a triple crown was, in fact, the pope. The tiara as we know it today first evolved with its jewelled circlets during the pontificate of that most assertive of medieval popes, Boniface VIII (1294–1303). By the close of his pontificate it had two circlets of precious stones, and by 1315 had acquired a third. By 1400 the tapering helmet-like headdress with its three encircling diadems had become a papal leitmotif. To it was applied a variety of allegorical interpretations from the Trinity to the three Theological Virtues, from the three Churches, militant, suffering and triumphant, to the three powers, sacerdotal, royal and imperial. But the most likely source of this papal innovation was the triple crown of the Holy Roman Empire which the popes claimed alone as being in their bestowal.[23]

Turning to what happened in 1547, it is difficult not to conclude that something along these lines must have been in the minds of those who put together Edward VI's Coronation. The Acts which had carried through the Henrician Reformation moved from the premise of the imperial status of the monarchy, and that called for some kind of visual signification. It called again for emphasis in 1547, for the Council under Somerset had already decided that it would move in the direction of radical reformation, and the right to take that action depended on the imperial crown and its rights within the realm. That must have prompted this astonishing piece of theatre whose true focus was neither the crown of St Edward, nor the new personal crown, but 'the Emperiall Crowne of this Realm of England'. While the choir sang the Te Deum a ring was placed on the king's marriage finger.

Having omitted the vestments, the investiture, whose procedure was not laid down in the Council minute, became a somewhat motley affair which opened with the Master of the Jewel House delivering the bracelets or armils. The regalia on the altar were hallowed but, apart from one piece from the Archbishop of Canterbury, these were delivered by the great magnates of the realm who had carried them in the procession, a further dramatic secularisation of the rite. The king, crowned with 'the Emperiall Crowne' and holding a sceptre and orb, was carried up the steps of the scaffold and enthroned in St Edward's chair. Somerset rendered homage, then the Archbishop of Canterbury and the Lord Chancellor, and finally the lords and clergy collectively: 'Because that Time would not serve for every of them to declare their Homage particularly . . .'

There was one final novelty, the proclamation of a general pardon during the homage, a feature which was to be repeated at subsequent Coronations. That topic had been discussed by the Privy Council, who remained undecided as to whether the pardon should be issued in the name of the late king or that of his successor. Somewhat cynically the decision was made in favour of the latter as Henry VIII was already in heaven and no longer in need of present gratitude from the populace!

Cranmer's sermon on this occasion provides us with a unique insight into what those involved in 1547 had set out to achieve by the changes. One other aim was to impress, and that is caught in the fact that, for the first time that we know, ambassadors were admitted and given a special place both in the various processions and from which to watch the proceedings in the Abbey. They, of course, would have written home giving an account of what they had seen. Odet de Selve, the French ambassador, was certainly impressed by what he regarded as 'le plus grand triumphe et solennité qu'il est possible'.

Cranmer's sermon was also important because it set the agenda for the reign. Already on the new king's accession iconoclasm had broken out in London and, although the culprits had been brought to book by the Privy Council, it was clear that this was the direction in which the new Protestant administration would go. In his sermon the archbishop cast Edward as King Josiah returned, the Old Testament king celebrated both for his fidelity to divine law and for wiping out idolatry: 'to see, with your predecessor Josias, God truly worshipped; and idolatry, the tyranny of the Bishops of Rome banished from your subjects, and images removed. These be the signs of a second Josias, who reformed the Church of God.' And this was precisely the role Edward VI fulfilled as the destruction was set in motion three days after the Coronation when Cranmer began for the first time publicly to attack images.[24]

What occurred during the next six years was a tide of reform which left every church unrecognisable, the interiors stripped bare, the walls

Tudor anti-papalism: Henry VIII designates Edward VI his heir, the attack on religious images gets underway and the Pope is vanquished, painting, mid-XVIth century

whitewashed and then painted with biblical texts and the stone altars demolished, replaced by wooden communion tables in the body of the church. The Latin Mass vanished, to be replaced first by the Prayer Book of 1549 and then by that of 1552, which was more extreme. Both were in the vernacular. All of this and more had happened by 1553, the year in which Edward's Catholic sister Mary succeeded on a tide of dynastic loyalty for the House of Tudor, which was disastrously misread by her as a yearning for a return to the Church of Rome.

Mary was proclaimed queen in London on 19 July, she entered the City in triumph on 3 August, and her Coronation was to be on 1 October.[25] She had already made up her mind by September to put the religious clock back to before 1529, but she was made to realise that she could not do this without the sanction of Parliament, which according to custom met only after the Coronation. What upset her was that without Parliament meeting her own bastardy could not be reversed. For a time the Council was divided as to whether it should meet before or after the event, but in the end the traditional sequence of Coronation followed by Parliament prevailed. That was not Mary's only misgiving, as she feared that the oath which she wished to take in 'the old form' would be tampered with and that she would be called upon in some way to condone 'the new religion'. She would, she said, have added to the oath as a cover the words 'just and licit laws'. We have no copy of the oath Mary took but it would not have been that of Edward or Elizabeth. The dilemma in which Mary found herself gives her Coronation a curious poignancy, for at the feast the heralds included in the proclamation of her style the title of Supreme Head of the Church of England.

It was, therefore, with profound unease that Mary approached the event. Cranmer, still archbishop, who should have performed the ceremony, was dispatched to the Tower for his part in the attempt to put Jane Grey on the throne and Stephen Gardiner, the conservative Bishop of Winchester, was released from the Marshalsea and chosen by Mary to perform the rite in his stead. At this juncture there was no option other than to follow what had been done in 1547, although eliminating as much as possible of what the queen would have regarded as offensive. But this time we have no scenario by the Privy Council, nor a detailed text with rubrics. Her profound anxiety is reflected in the fact that she wrote to her cousin, Cardinal Pole, petitioning him to send an express absolution not only for her but all loyal Catholics who would take part in the ceremony. The queen also wrote to the Bishop of Arras in Brussels for an uncontaminated supply of holy oil, which he was able to supply just in time. In this way, the Coronation of 1553 cannot be viewed as a putting back of the clock so much as an exercise in damage limitation, for when it took place the official position was one of religious toleration, even though the incoming government was already rounding up reformers and imprisoning them.

So in what way was 1553 different from 1547? Stow in his *Annales* states that it was performed 'according to the olde custome', and the imperial ambassador, Simon Renard, wrote that Mary was crowned 'according to the rites of the old religion'. It was certainly far more extended than Edward VI's Coronation, the queen setting out for the Abbey some time between ten and eleven o'clock in the morning and not returning to Westminster Hall until four, between five and six hours in all. The alterations which she was able to achieve were, in fact, quite minor, but enough to make those present realise that what they took part in was an effort to return to the past. She followed the 1547 rite in being led by a bishop and a nobleman, and the same ornaments were carried, leaving out any which might be seen as relics, also as before by great aristocrats. She was not vested in the robes of St Edward, and she also underwent the same triple crowning. But in this instance there was a crucial difference, for Gardiner alone placed them upon her head, being handed them from the altar by the Duke of Norfolk. The ornaments, too, were presented, bar one, by the great magnates as in 1547, the Marquess of Winchester the orb, the Earl of Arundel the sceptre, the Earl of Bath St Edward's staff and the Earl of Pembroke the spurs. The homage was again rendered collectively with a general pardon being issued. The French ambassador describes her as kneeling throughout the Mass with the king's sceptre in her right hand and the queen's with the dove in her right and that she only appeared carrying the orb as she left the Abbey after revesting. This was certainly a departure from the norm, and as he was present on the scaffold this is likely to have been correct.

Stow is not alone in his belief that the Coronation was a return to some older format, for a contemporary chronicler also writes that it had 'so many and sondery cerymonyes in anoynting, crowning, and other olde customes . . .'. But it could be argued, bearing in mind the sweeping away of all forms of liturgical visual spectacle which had taken place under Edward VI, that Mary's Coronation must have

Great Seal of Mary I and Philip II, 1554, with an imperial crown surmounting the arms of the vast territories over which they ruled

appeared like something from a world which had gone, and that would have prompted the belief that they were witnessing the revival of 'olde customes'.

As with Edward VI, accounts of Mary's Coronation are somewhat unsatisfactory, but from them emerge some minor points. One is a note by a herald that neither duke, nor marquess, nor earl put on their coronets until the queen was crowned, carrying them in their hands in the procession. They had worn them in 1547, which makes it strange that the herald notes that in 1553 it was 'according to the ancyente', although, perhaps, they may have been carried in 1509. The peeresses wore theirs on their heads from the outset. Peers were to continue wearing their coronets until the end of the Coronation feast. To that might be added the explanation in an Italian published account of the event which gives the triple crowning a different and highly unlikely meaning: 'one for England, one for France, and one for Ireland'.

Elizabeth I had taken part in the Coronations of her brother and sister. She was, therefore, familiar with the rite in its more reformist and also in its re-Catholicised mode. Few Coronations, however, are as poorly documented as this one, so much so that scholars have suggested that the irregularities which occurred led to a reluctance to record what happened.[26] Certainly Elizabeth was as sure in her religious views as Mary had been, when she came to the throne on 17 November 1558. She, too, had to wait for Parliament to assemble before a re-Reformation could be achieved, so, like Mary, she had to undergo a Coronation at the hands of those with whom she had little or no religious affinity. Nonetheless, it was clear what was going to happen, for from the outset she initiated changes in the Chapel Royal of the kind she was to demand for her Coronation. The result was that all Mary's Catholic hierarchy refused to perform the rite save one, the bishop of the minor see of Carlisle, Owen Oglethorpe. Even he refused to con-

Diagram of the arrangements in Westminster Abbey for the Coronation of Elizabeth I, 1559

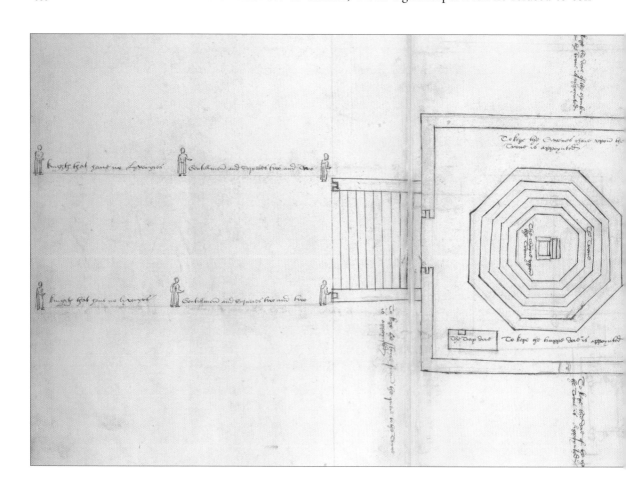

form to all her demands, one of which was to omit the elevation of the Host in the Mass. He had declined to do this in the Chapel Royal at Christmas, with the result that the queen left after the Gospel. That problem was solved by a compliant dean of the chapel, George Carew, who sang the Coronation Mass and omitted the elevation. During the Mass both the Epistle and Gospel were read not only in Latin but also in the vernacular. What happened at the moment of consecration no one has ever been able certainly to establish, nor is it helped by the three known accounts, one at second hand by an Italian who was not present in the Abbey and two others that are both pretty contracted and unclear. One reads 'Her Grace retorned into her Closett hearing the consecration of the Masse', and the other that she withdrew 'to her traverse'.

For the first time in the history of the Coronation we have a plan of the Abbey arrangements, but it was drawn up before and not after

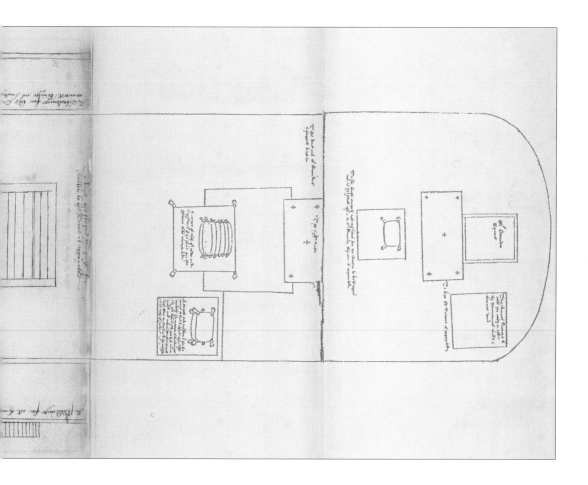

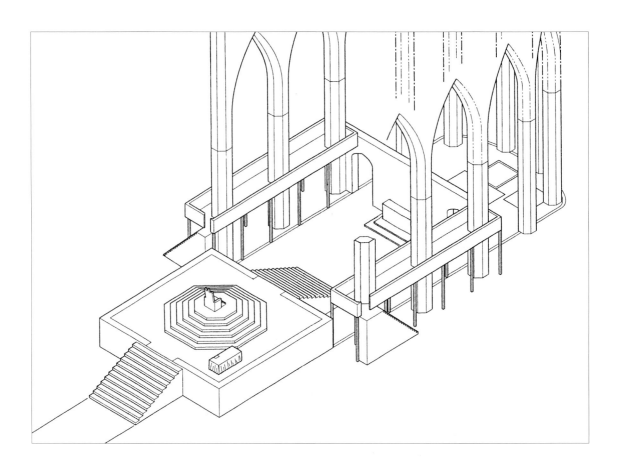

Realisation of the arrangement of Westminster Abbey
for the Coronation of
Elizabeth I, 1559

the event. The only traverse it shows is one behind the high Altar next
to St Edward's shrine labelled 'The Quenes Travers to make her reydy
in after the Ceremonyes and Service don.' That arrangement follows
the Fourth Recension. It has been argued that on the day there was a
second traverse to the left of the high altar. This had certainly been so
in the Coronations of Edward and Mary, who had resorted to one for
devesting before unction and revesting after. It must surely have been
the same in 1559. What was unusual this time was that Elizabeth went
into it after having descended to make the offertory instead of returning to the scaffold. Accounts tell us that she was back again enthroned
on high in St Edward's chair about the time of the Agnus and received
and kissed the pax. Elizabeth was, therefore, probably accurate when
she said in 1571 to the French ambassador that 'she had been crowned
and anointed according to the ceremonies of the Catholic church, and
by Catholic bishops without, however, attending mass'. All this would

indicate that she did not communicate, giving out yet another signal to those present of her impending religious changes.

The same ground plan which provides us with all these details goes on to give something even more exciting, a plan of the structure which straddled the crossing. This is a quite astonishing construction, for the Coronation chair is not merely approached by a single flight of steps but is set at the apex of an octagon of five steps. Was this an innovation? Mary's is described by a foreign observer as even more elevated: 'Her Majesty ascended upon a great platform, so high that it was mounted by twenty steps, and upon this another smaller one with ten steps to the chair where she seated herself.' The effect of this as the ceremonial unfolded must have been electrifying, with the monarch transmuted into some distant deity floating above the groundlings below. The same manuscript goes on to give a drawing of the layout of the Coronation feast. The queen sits beneath a cloth of estate at a table set upon a dais approached by steps. The walls are hung with arras and before stretch four tables the length of the hall with, to one side, an indication of a tiered buffet for the display of plate.

Elizabeth's view of the Catholic clergy was already apparent in the opening procession to the Abbey. Both Edward and Mary had been escorted by a bishop and a lay magnate. Elizabeth dropped the bishop altogether and was led by the earls of Pembroke and Shrewsbury. The bishops, too, for the first time did homage after the lay magnates and not before. Her attitude was equally mirrored in the fact that Oglethorpe alone of the bishops was sent the customary yardage of scarlet cloth. We can add to that the elimination of the clergy from the London streets, whose role in the past had been to cense and sprinkle the monarch with holy water as he passed.

All in all Elizabeth's Coronation was a muddled affair before the Anglican Settlement, which could only come with Parliament after the event. That change, Dale Hoak argues, was anticipated in her Coronation oath which reverted to that of 1547 but with an addition likely to have been the work of the secretary of state, William Cecil, that the sovereign would conduct his rule 'according to the Laws of God, [and] the true profession of the Gospel established in this Kingdom'. The phraseology could never be anything other than Protestant, and by 'established' he would have meant through Parliament by statute. In fact, it very much reflected her own religious preferences which were far more for a return to 1549 than to 1553, although on that score she was to lose. In the Chapel Royal the altar remained where it always had been with a cross upon it, and services were conducted with quite a high degree of ceremonial. Indeed, what went on there was to be viewed with considerable misgivings by reforming clerics until well into the reign.[27]

Elizabeth was nothing if not astute. The Coronation, she knew, was a necessity which had to be gone through, but it was seen by very few. In fact, from what we know it is significant that she only sprang to life when she left the Abbey. The Italian observer, Il Schifanoya, writes: 'She returned very cheerfully with a most smiling countenance for everyone, giving them all a thousand greetings, so that in my opinion she exceeded the bounds of gravity and decorum.' In this Il Schifanoya catches at once what 1559 was really about, a realisation by the queen that the future of the monarchy lay no longer with the Church. Rulership was God-ordained, but it needed the support of the people. The truth was that her real Coronation had happened the previous day in the most stage-managed state entry into London of any Tudor monarch. On that occasion the curtain had gone up on an arena of pageantry in which she was cast as the people's heroine and which, supreme actress as she was, Elizabeth was to play for all it was worth for 45 years. Looked at in this context the Coronation to her was a necessary irrelevance, and it is significant that when it came to choosing the day for it there was no thumbing through the pages of a missal for a suitable saint's day. Instead, she turned to her court astrologer and magus, the celebrated Dr John Dee, who selected a date upon which the constellations would rain down upon her their most benign influences.[28] Set into this context the reader will now understand why I have reversed the normal order and placed a consideration of the entry vigil procession after that of the Coronation.

THREE ROYAL ENTRIES

The Reformation witnessed the suppression of the ecclesiastical processions. They were abolished as part of the Edwardian reform, restored by the Marian counter-reform and abolished again in 1559. The diarist, Henry Machyn, pinpoints the exact moment of their short-lived revival. On 25 November 1553, on St Katherine's Day, her image was borne around St Paul's attended by 500 people carrying

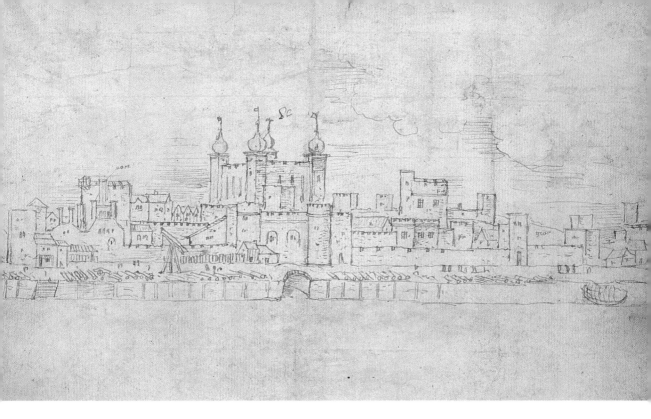

candles. The day after, a sermon was preached at Paul's Cross in defence of processions.[29] Their fate was to be sealed finally at the opening of Parliament in 1559 when the Abbot of Westminster came, as was traditional, to greet the queen. At the sight of the conventual procession Elizabeth cried 'Away with those candles, for we can see well enough.'[30] The consequence of this was that the only processions which the public witnessed by the close of the sixteenth century were secular ones, and of these the most magnificent were royal: the entry into London of Elizabeth after her summer progress, the procession of the Knights of the Garter on St George's Day and the regular procession in which the queen went to the Chapel Royal in each of her palaces. This may seem tangential to the history of the Coronation, but the wiping out of ecclesiastical pageantry only heightened the importance of the secular ceremonial surrounding the monarchy.

The Coronation began with the removal of the monarch to the Tower. Edward VI had arrived from Enfield, being greeted with salvoes of artillery both from the Tower itself and from the ships moored in the Thames. Both Mary and Elizabeth went by water. Il Schifanoya, the Italian observer, records the splendour of 12 January 1559:

The Tower of London, the point of departure for the state entry into London, drawing, *c*.1557–62

The necessary ships, galleys, brigantines, &c. were prepared as sumptuously as possible to accompany her Majesty and her Court thither by the Thames, which reminded one of Ascension Day in Venice ... her Majesty, accompanied by many knights, barons, ladies, and by the whole Court ... embarked in her barge, which was covered with its usual tapestries, both externally and internally, and was towed by a long galley rowed by 40 men in their shirts, with a band of music, as usual when the Queen goes by water.[31]

In 1553 Mary had been greeted by a flotilla of bedecked boats filled with the lord mayor and aldermen. The Tower discharged its ordinance as she arrived.

All three vigil processions follow the Little Device and reflect an acute awareness that this was the first occasion when any great concourse of the populace saw their new ruler. That first impression was of huge importance, and the contribution of the Tudor Great Wardrobe to this initial display of the monarch through the crowded London streets cannot be overestimated. Clothes had to reflect the office. Edward VI, a child who needed building up in the public eye, was arrayed in a gown of cloth of silver embroidered with gold, beneath which he wore white velvet braided with Venice silver and scattered with rubies, diamonds and pearls. The colour scheme remained as initiated in 1377 by Richard II: essentially white, the colour of innocence, and the king was bareheaded, but his appearance can hardly be described as an understatement. He sat on a horse with a caparison of pearl-bedecked crimson satin and he was stage-managed to ride 'a little before his Canape, because the People might the better see his Grace'.[32] For an appreciation of the role of the Great Wardrobe in orchestrating these displays we might take the 1559 entry.[33] The queen's litter was of white cloth of gold raised with silver and cloth of tissue with silver and gold on a ground of gold. It was lined with pink satin, and the queen sat on eight cushions of yellow cloth of gold. At its four corners there were gilded knobs in the form of lions, and the litter was carried by two elaborately caparisoned mules. Over it knights carried a canopy of purple cloth of gold, a fabric which was re-echoed in the costumes of the henchmen and ladies attendant on her. She was immediately flanked on either side by footmen in crimson velvet running coats, with scarlet cloaks guarded with black velvet and doublets of yellow cloth of gold, one of the fabrics of the litter. Behind her came Sir Robert Dudley in purple cloth of gold matching the canopy, his horse trapped in crimson cloth of gold, followed by three carriages for ladies, essays in crimson and gold, including what was worn. Nothing was arbitrary about this configuration. The Great Wardrobe on these occasions resembled a theatrical wardrobe of today working under the direction of a designer, who had conceived a *mise-en-scène* in which purple, crimson and gold framed white and gold, with the queen herself bejewelled and wearing a circlet glittering with precious stones.

There happen to be three sets of drawings of this procession to conjure up something of its presence. None is eyewitness but working records by heralds either before or after the event, reflect a concern with recording the niceties of processional hierarchical order. What they do capture is the growth in the procession, so that our Italian observer in 1559 reckoned that it included a thousand horses. Processional order was an obsession and the manuscripts recording it are innumerable. To grasp the full impact of a mid-Tudor entry procession it seems apposite to print one full listing of everyone who took part. College of Arms MS. M 6 has one particular set of drawings which is more graphic than any of the others, so it is appropriate that the listing there should be given:[34]

ELIZABETH I's PROCESSION

Messengers of the Chamber
The Gentleman Harbinger and the Sergeant Porter
Strangers' and ambassadors' servants
Gentlemen and Esquires
Sewers of the Chamber
Gentlemen Ushers extraordinary
Gentlemen Ushers ordinary
Chaplains having no dignity
Aldermen of London
Esquires of the Body
The six Clerks of the Chancery
The Clerks of the Signet
The Clerks of the Privy Seal
The Clerks of the Privy Council

Chaplains having dignities

Masters of the Chancery

Knights Bachelor

Knights Baronets

Serjeants-at-law

The Queen's Attorney and the Queen's Solicitor

The Barons of the Exchequer

The Judges of the Law

The Lord Chief Baron and the Lord Chief Justice of England

The trumpeters

The new Knights of the Bath

Knights of the Privy Council

Knights of the Order of the Garter

Noblemen's sons

Lords Barons

Bishops

Earls' sons

Marquesses' sons

Lords Viscounts

The Earls

The Queen's Almoner and the Prelate of the Garter

Mr Secretary

The Treasurer of the Household and the Comptroller of the Household

Lord Clinton, Lord Admiral of England, and Lord William Howard, Lord
    Chamberlain

The Lord Privy Seal and the Lord Steward of the Household

The Archbishop of York and the Archbishop of Canterbury

Norroy and Clarenceux Kings of Arms

The Lord Chancellor and the Lord Treasurer

Ambassadors

Those representing the Duchies of Guyenne and Normandy

The Lord Mayor of London bareheaded and Garter King of Arms bare-
    headed and the Gentleman Usher of the Privy Chamber bareheaded (A
    note that from the Archbisops to here was flanked by Serjeants-at-arms)

The Duke of Norfolk bareheaded and Garter King of Arms bareheaded
    and the Earl of Oxford, Lord Great Chamberlain, bareheaded

Lord Giles Paulet leading the first litter horse

The Queen in her litter

Lord Ambrose Dudley leading the second litter horse

Opposite Elizabeth I enters
London, drawing, *c.*1559

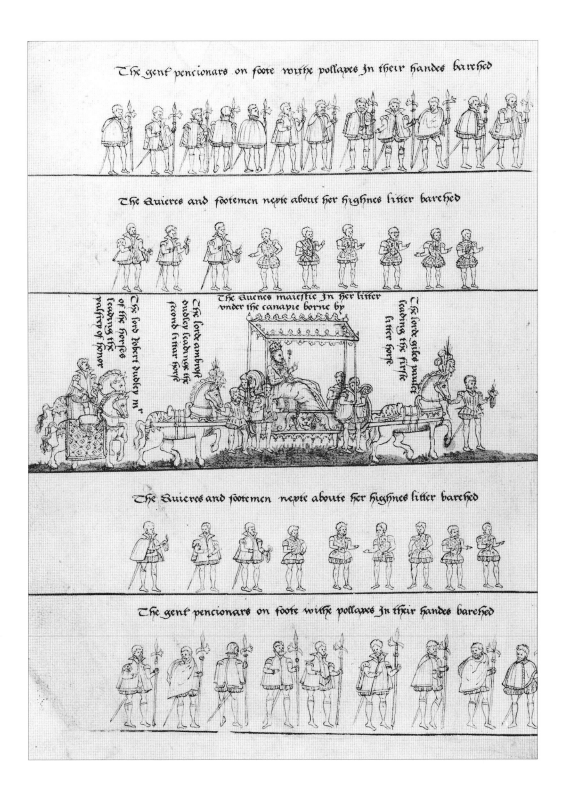

The gent pencionars on foote withe pollaxes In their handes barehed

The Auieres and footemen nexte about her highnes litter barehed

The Auenes maiestie In her litter vnder the canapie borne by

The lord robert dudley m^r of the horses leadinge the palfrey of honor

The lorde ambrose dudley leadinge the second litter horse

The lorde giles pawlet leadinge the firste litter horse

The Auieres and footemen nexte aboute her highnes litter barehed

The gent pencionars on foote withe pollaxes In their handes barehed

Lord Robert Dudley, Master of the Horse, leading the Palfrey of Honour
  (A note that this part of the procession was flanked by squires and foot-
  men and outside of them the Gentlemen Pensioners, all bareheaded)
Six ladies riding upon palfreys
Six horses drawing the first chariot filled with ladies
Six ladies riding upon palfreys following the first chariot
Six horses drawing the second chariot filled with ladies
Six ladies upon palfreys following the second chariot
Six horses drawing the third chariot filled with ladies
Six ladies riding upon palfreys following the third chariot
All other ladies
The henchmen
The Captain of the Guard
The Yeomen of the Guard

Only a listing of this kind can capture the enormity of such a procession which, for those in the London streets, must have seemed never
ending. Witnessing such a cavalcade was to see the whole of the
nation's establishment pass by, ranked in correct pecking order. It set
out to present the ruler in visual and ceremonial terms as the greatest
lord of all, but more than that it represented a coming together of two
hierarchies, the neo-feudal one of the Court and the great families, and
the other which was based on the wealth created by the London crafts.
The Lord Mayor and Aldermen actually rode in the procession but the
urban elite, those who were members of the great City companies,
lined the route. The populace stood behind them. The monarch was
the apex of both these hierarchies.[35]

A further impression of such a procession can be had from the lost
wallpainting of Edward VI's entry which was destroyed by fire at
Cowdray Park. Now it is only known through an eighteenth-century
engraving. Once again it is not an accurate record and its value is
purely atmospheric, but in it we can see Edward VI, beneath and not
in front of his canopy, just about to pass the cross in Cheapside. What
it does capture is the appearance of the houses decked in rich cloths
and tapestries let down from windows and balconies, and also the
members of the craft companies lining the route. This is a retrospec-
tive view of 1547 which totally omits the pageants and also the clergy,

who were certainly present along the way, and dresses the clerics in the procession in the Protestant garb of rochet and chimere.[36]

Anne Boleyn's entry had set a final precedent that a Coronation went hand-in-hand with the staging of pageants. There had been none for Edward IV, Henry VII, Elizabeth of York or Henry VIII and Katherine of Aragon. Why did they now become mandatory? The clue lies in 1533 when there had been such pressure for them from government that the City was offered help by the King's Works and the use of the royal musicians and singers. Something of the sort was repeated in 1547 and again in 1559 when the royal Office of the Revels assisted the City with the loan of costumes. That crumb of information indicates that those in power must have known what was to be staged before the event.

Edward VI's entry was a confused affair, the City worthies resorting largely to recycling what they had staged for the boy king Henry VI in 1429. Nonetheless it has the distinction of being the first post-Reformation entry.[37] The Great Conduit in Cheapside may have had 'a Crowne Emperiall of Gold, garnished as it stood, with rich Pearle and Stones' on its summit, but otherwise it was a virtual rerun of what had appeared as part of the earlier series summed up by the speech of Charity listing a kind of royal investiture: 'God give unto thee a Crowne of Glory, and the Scepter of Piety, with a Sword mighty of Victory, a Mantle of Prudence to cloath thee, a Shield of Faith to defend thee, with a Helme of Health to thine Encrease, and gird thee with a Girdle of Love and perfect Peace.'

Further on, the imperial theme was reiterated in what was an updated version of what had been staged in 1533. From heaven a phoenix (Jane Seymour) descended to a mount, which sprouted red and white roses, to be approached by a golden lion (Henry VIII) 'makeing Semblance of Amyty unto the Bird'. A young lion (Edward VI) appeared, the phoenix and the golden lion vanishing, and an angel promptly descended to place a 'Crowne Imperial' on his head.

Those in the procession were restless and pushed on in places, not even bothering to listen to the speeches which had been prepared. One bypassed pageant featured an enthroned St Edward the Confessor, all the stranger as his shrine had been demolished a decade before, The only time the king and great ones lingered was at St Paul's when an acrobat whizzed down a rope from the cathedral's battlements, kissed the king's foot and then performed tricks, 'which staied the king's

Majesty with all the Trayne a good space of Time'. At the conduit in Fleet Street Faith and Justice attended on Truth in celebration of the Reformation:

> *I ancient Truth, which long Time was suppressed*
> *With heathen Rites and detestable Idolatrye,*
> *Have in thy Realme been in great Part refreshed*
> *By God's Servant my Defender King Henry.*

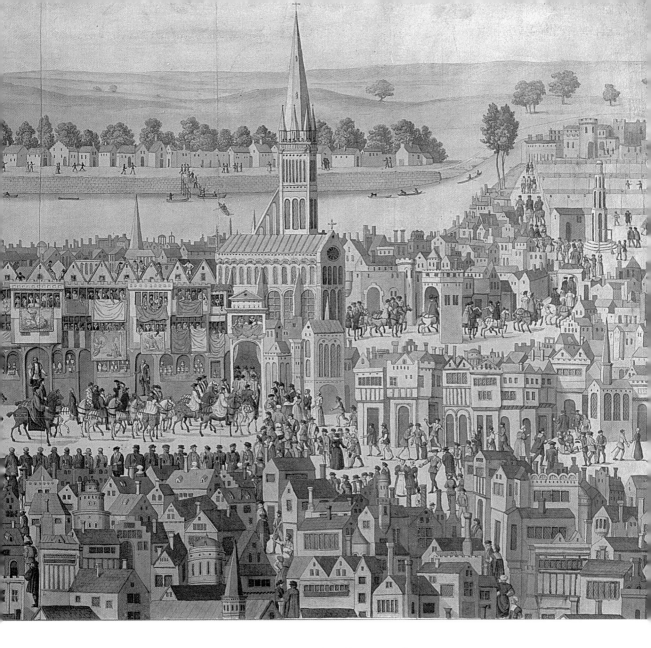

Perhaps the Spanish ambassador was accurate when he wrote that there was 'no very memorable show of triumph or magnificence'.[38] Feeble though this entry was, at least we have fairly full descriptions along with transcripts of the execrable verse. In the case of Mary we have virtually nothing and extremely inadequate descriptions.[39] What they make clear is that the most impressive of the pageants were all by foreign resident communities in London: the Hansa, the Florentines and the Genoese. They included personifications of the virtues and in

The Coronation entry of Edward VI, 1547, as depicted in retrospect and omitting the pageants, copy of a lost mid-XVIth century wall-painting one an angel blowing a trumpet descended, but any details are lacking. About the indigenous contribution there is a blank, almost as though people in retrospect wished to wipe the memory from their minds or, equally, that those on the government side failed to see any potential in the manipulation of street theatre. Some insight into what may have been wrong with this occasion is, perhaps, caught in an anecdote about the stage set up near Aldgate on which stood Christ's Hospital for poor children, a post-Reformation foundation out of the dissolution of the monasteries. One of the children made an oration, but it was noted that 'when she came near unto them she cast her eye another way, and never staied nor gave any countenance to them'.[40]

That observation is important for another reason, for here for the first time we have chroniclers and others noting the behaviour of the incoming ruler as he or she made their first public appearance. There is no record of Edward VI reacting to the crowds in any way, and what little we know of Mary's behaviour indicates elements of a public relations disaster. The contrast with what happened on 14 January 1559 could not have been greater.

No other royal entry has attracted so much scholarly attention as that of Elizabeth I.[41] More and more it has been realised to have been a meticulously planned propaganda exercise on behalf of what was expected of the incoming regime. Those who organised and wrote the pageants were Protestants, and government must have known what was planned. The queen's responses were such that what she saw cannot have come as a surprise, and that knowledge meant that her responses were ready with all the finesse of a great actress. Unlike her brother and sister, Elizabeth did not lack the common touch. As early as a week before her expected accession the Spanish Count de Feria had written: 'She is very attached to the people and very confident that they take her part, which is true.' As in the case of the Coronation there must have been directives from her, for why else the absence of the clergy along the route and the elimination of pageants by resident foreigners? This was to be a purely English occasion, one which was to be capitalised on to the full extent by the publication of no less than two editions describing it published before 25 March 1559. *The Quene's Majestie's passage through the citie of London to westminster the day before her coronacion* is a landmark. It ensured that those who had not been in the streets could relive the experience. Even those who were could wander around both on the day and for several days after and understand what the pageants had said, for the other great innovation was to inscribe on each of them verses and titles, not only in Latin but also in the vernacular, so that when the actors had departed the message could still be understood.

The pamphlet almost goes over the top in its adulation of the young queen's rapport with her subjects:

> as appeared by the assemblie, prayers, wisshes, welcomminges, cryes, tender wordes, and all other signes, whiche argue a wonderfull earnest love of most obedient subjectes towarde theyr soveraygne. And on the other syde her grace by holding up her handes, and merie countenance to such as stoode farre of, and most tender and gentle language to those that stode nigh to her grace ... To all that wished her grace wel, she gave heartie thankes, and to suche as bade god save her grace, she sayd agayne god save them all, and thanked them with all heart.[42]

She took into her litter the posies of flowers proffered, stayed it to listen to requests, bade silence so that she might hear the words of the speeches and in Cheapside 'smyled ... for that she had heard one say, Remember old king Henry the eight'. And, at the sight of the Christ's Hospital children, she cast her eyes to heaven in remembrance of the poor. On 14 January 1559 a great star was born. But, it should be added, the inclusion of so many references to the reactions and exchanges with the ordinary people who were lining the streets was in itself a calculated decision, presenting a new queen whose rule demanded the support not just of the establishment but also of loving subjects.

Set within the context of all the Coronations already discussed, this one more than anything which we have encountered so far sees the birth of modern popular monarchy in an anticipation of the late-twentieth-century royal walkabout. Here, too, was a pageant series which launched a politico-religious programme for the reign, fiercely Protestant and patriotic. The first arch at the end of Gracechurch Street was firmly labelled 'The vniting of the two houses of Lancastre and York'. Up it grew a vast rose tree with Henry VII and Elizabeth of York at the bottom, Henry VIII and Anne Boleyn over them and, at the summit, Elizabeth herself enthroned. Both Henry and his daughter wore arched imperial crowns. Words not minced: here was come a new peace after the 'warre' of the previous reign. On the procession moved to 'The seate of worthie governance', where again the queen encountered herself enthroned, borne up by the virtues of Pure Religion, Love of Subjects, Wisdom and Justice. As everything was labelled no one could miss the message about Pure Religion which trod underfoot Superstition and Ignorance. What was celebrated here were the queen's necessary public virtues. Next came her private ones, and so at Cornhill sat the Eight Beatitudes according to St Matthew. These, a child informed her, she had acquired when 'iustice couldst none gette', yet another indictment of Mary's reign.

Then came an encounter between the queen and the Lord Mayor and Aldermen who stood en tableau at the end of Cheapside. That had been the custom since 1547, when a short speech was made by the recorder and a gift of money made. There is no indication of any reaction to this by either Edward or Mary, but Elizabeth seized the chance saying, on receipt of the gift: 'I will be as good unto you, as ever quene was to her people . . . And perswade yourselves, that for the safetie and quietnes of you all, I will not spare, if nede be to spend my blood, God thanke you all.'[43]

Not for nothing had the dignitaries placed themselves within sight of the most important pageant of the entry and greatest indictment of the previous reign, depicted as 'A decayed commonweal', a barren mount on which a youth sat depressed beneath a dead tree. Opposed to that was 'A flourishing commonweale', a flower-bedecked mount with a sprightly youth beneath a laurel tree. This had the most dramatic denouement of them all. Mary Tudor's motto was *Veritas Temporis Filia*, Truth the Daughter of Time, in her case Catholic truth. With a bitter sense of irony this was taken and turned upside down, for out of a cave between the mounts came Time leading his daughter Truth clutching a book. Those who remembered 1547 would have recalled Truth's appearance on that occasion. The queen must have known what was to happen next: 'Tyme? sayth she, and Tyme hath brought me hether . . . when her grace understoode that the Byble in Englishe shoulde be delivered unto her by Truth . . . she thanked the citie for that gift . . . as soone as she had received the booke, kyssed it, and with both her handes held up the same, and so laid it upon her brest . . .'[44]

One final tableau awaited her, this time herself again, arrayed in parliament robes as 'Debora the iudge and restorer of the house of Israel'. Here, for the first time, Parliament makes its debut presenting Elizabeth as a new Deborah, wife, prophetess and mother, attended by the three

Time brings forth his daughter Truth, a motif in the 1559 entry, wood engraving, 1535

estates of the realm, a visible statement of what the returning Protestant exiles, John Aylmer and John Hales, saw as central to the new polity, the crown in Parliament as being at the heart of the governance of the realm. This was post-Reformation Tudor Old Testament kingship returned in feminist guise, but with the reminder 'to consult for the worthie government of her people'. This could only refer to the coming Parliament, writs for which had been issued on 5 December, which would pass the Act of Uniformity and return England to Protestantism.

Elizabeth I crowned and
bearing orb and sceptre,
painting, 1569

Set within this astonishing perspective the Coronation seems almost an irrelevance. The state entry of 1559 demonstrates forcefully that the history of the Coronation cannot be narrowed down to what happens within the walls of the Abbey. The inauguration of a new reign must embrace every aspect, and what happened on 14 January, although no one could guess it, defined the nation's future. Only one action at the Coronation itself can be said to belong within the orbit of what had happened on the previous day. Elizabeth prized her Coronation ring as symbolising her marriage to her kingdom. Early in September 1561 she would say to William Maitland of Lethington, Mary Queen of Scots' ambassador: 'I am already married to the realm of England when I was crowned with this ring which I wear continually in token thereof.' And never was a truer word spoken.

ELIZABETHAN IMPERIALISM AND THE HOLLOW CROWN

Elizabeth reigned for 45 years. During that period there was a huge development in the people's perception of the monarchy and equally how the monarchy presented itself to the people. The opening of the reign was hesitant, but after the Northern Rebellion of 1569 and the papal bull of excommunication in 1570 we see stirrings of a mythology which was to develop and expand over three decades in such a way that by 1595 the poet George Peele could hail her on her Accession Day, 17 November, as:

> Elizabeth great Empresse of the world,
> Britanias Atlas, Star of Englands globe,
> That swaies the massie scepter of her land,
> And holds the royall raynes of Albion . . .[45]

Five years earlier Edmund Spenser had produced the first three books of his epic *The Faerie Queene* which he dedicated 'To the most high, mightie, and magnificent Empresse, renowned for pietie, vertue, and all gratious government, Elizabeth, Queene of England, Fraunce, and Ireland, and of Virginia, Defender of the Faith, &c.' Poetic fiction this may be, but it is a very different kind of imperial vision from that which existed in the immediate post-Reformation era. Suddenly there are global aspirations for the imperial crown.[46]

That dramatic change we owe to the man who chose the day of

Elizabeth's Coronation, Dr John Dee. His *General and Rare Memorials Pertayning to the Perfect Arte of Navigation* (1577) is an encouragement to the queen to found a mighty navy and make good her claim 'to this Imperial Brytish Monarchy . . .'. To justify this, Dee turns to themes which, although they had appeared spasmodically earlier in the century, were never turned to serious practical use. These drew on the myth of Aeneas, of the queen as a descendant of the Trojan Brutus, and also on King Arthur, whose conquests justified her claims to an overseas empire which was to be established by sea power. For her 'Title Royall to . . . foreyn Regions' he includes much of America as well as Iceland, Greenland and all the northern islands as far as Russia.

The impact of all of this was a revolutionary vision of empire, one not insular but maritime and expansive. With the establishment of Virginia as a colony in the 1580s it began to have fragile, if transitory, substance. This extraordinary transmutation of what had begun as an insular myth into one which was global is neatly captured in the famous 'Sieve' portrait of Elizabeth at Siena in which the crown of the Holy Roman Empire lurks near her right arm and in the background can be glimpsed the globe of the world, with Britain suffused in a halo and the motto: 'I see all and much is missing.' With the defeat of the Spanish Armada in 1588, the prognostications were seemingly fulfilled as Elizabeth is depicted with her hand on the globe, above which hovers an imperial diadem.[47]

Such images may seem tangential but they monitor how items like crowns, sceptres and orbs, which, for any ruler, start as items with which they are invested, take on a life of their own in the world of secular ceremonial. And that touches the most important shift of all. The queen's success lay in her ability to marry the common touch with the invented ritual of a post-Reformation desacralised monarchy. That was to find its greatest vehicle for her in the celebration of her Accession Day each 17 November. From the pageantry of the tiltyard at Whitehall to frolics on the village green, this was built up over the decades into a day of national rejoicing celebrating the achievement of the programme laid out in the 1559 entry. So remote had the Coronation itself become that later in the reign Accession Day often came to be referred to as the Coronation Day.

There was a fatal flaw in this scenario. The secular sanction of kingship had none of the power of the old sacred unction of Coronation. Mary's passionate Catholicism would have made her view even her

flawed Coronation in a pre-Reformation light. But for both Edward and Elizabeth the problems posed by the rite of Coronation in a Protestant context had not been confronted, only postponed.

All of this remained in abeyance as long as Elizabeth was on the throne, although it did not go undiscussed as the reign drew to its close. The Elizabethan theatre, that great populist innovation, put royalty on stage together with its ceremonial, and in so doing began to question its very premises.[48] Shakespeare's history plays, the product of the last decade of Elizabeth's reign, brought a penetrating spotlight to bear on the fragility of kingship.

> *Not all the water in the rough rude sea*
> *Can wash the balm off from an anointed king;*
> *The breath of worldly men cannot depose*
> *The deputy elected by the Lord;*
> *For every man that Bullingbrook hath press'd*

Elizabethan imperialism. The crown of the Holy Roman Emperors can be glimpsed above the Queen's right arm and an aureole is bestowed on her kingdom right, painting, *c*.1580

The defeat of the Armada unleashed wild prognostications of empire. Here the Queen rests her hand on the globe of the world with the imperial crown above, painting, c.1588

To lift shrewd steel against our golden crown,
God for his Richard hath in heavenly pay
A glorious angel; then if angels fight,
Weak men must fall, for heaven still guards the right.

(*Richard II*, III, ii, ll. 54–62)

But this is seen to be a delusion as Richard II is deposed and realises what he wears is but a 'hollow crown'.

This is taken even further in Henry V, where the king dismisses all that the ritual and regalia of Coronation stand for as a 'proud dream'.

> *I know*
> *'Tis not the balm, the sceptre, and the ball,*
> *The sword, the mace, the crown imperial,*
> *The intertissued robe of gold and pearl,*
> *The farced title running 'fore the king,*
> *The throne he sits on, nor the tide of pomp*
> *That beats upon the high shore of this world,*
> *No, not all these, thrice-gorgeous ceremony,*
> *Not all these, laid in bed majestical,*
> *Can sleep so soundly as the wretched slave.*
> (*Henry V*, IV, i, ll. 279–88)

In lines like these the demystification of monarchy is taken to an almost puritan extreme of the rejection of the fabricated image and its ritual, so that it is little wonder that in contemporary printed versions these lines and, in the case of *Richard II*, the deposition scene, were omitted. The history plays were written and performed as the cult of 'our gracious empresse', based on secular and no longer on sacred ceremonial, was drifting towards eclipse. It was her successors who had to face head on all the questions which had been left unanswered about the significance of the Coronation in relation to kingship after 1603.

6

From Divinity to Destruction

O N 2 J U N E 1643 Parliament rejected a motion enjoining the Dean and Chapter of Westminster to deliver the keys to the treasury where the St Edward's regalia were kept. The following day a second motion on the same topic was actually passed, but only by a majority of one vote. This time Parliament agreed that the treasury if necessary might be broken open so that its contents might be inventoried, after which new locks were to be affixed to the door. Those entrusted with this task were Sir Henry Mildmay, Master of the Jewel House, a man who, in spite of his household appointment, had sided with Parliament in the Civil War, and Henry Marten, MP for Berkshire and future regicide. They, together with two others, were to draw up the new inventory, but nothing was to be removed.[1]

What happened when they undertook this exercise forms one of the more colourful scenes of the Civil War or, at least, as it was narrated about thirty years later by Peter Heylyn, chaplain to the king and a prebendary of the abbey. As the sub-dean refused point-blank to hand over the keys, the treasury was indeed broken into, and here is how Heylyn describes the ensuing scene, in which the regicide-to-be:

> . . . made himself Master of the Spoil. And having forced open a great Iron Chest, took out the Crowns, the Robes, the Swords, and Scepter, belonging antiently to K. EDWARD the Confessor and used by all our Kings at their inaugurations. With a scorn greater than his Lusts, and the rest of his Vices, he openly declares, That there would be no further use for these Toys and Trifles. And in the jollity of that humour, invests

James I in robes of state, painting, *c.*1620

George Wither (an old Puritan Satyrist) in the Royal Habiliments. Who being thus crown'd, and Royally array'd, (as right well became him) first marcht about the Room with a stately Garb, and afterwards with a thousand Apish and Ridiculous actions exposed those Sacred Ornaments to contempt and laughter.[2]

There is, in fact, no evidence that the poet George Wither was ever there or indeed that such a scene took place.[3] This is history written in retrospect by a member of the victorious party anxious to blacken any aspect of the previous republican regime. But what is so striking is that anything of the kind could be conceived as happening in the first place, that the regalia of St Edward, 'those Sacred Ornaments', could actually be derided as 'Toys and Trifles'. In 1643 we are six years from the execution of the king, Charles I, whose own coronation was for a time to be described as the last. The royalist newsletter, *Mercurius Aulicus*, reporting on this inventory, went on prophetically to write: 'I doubt the king himself will be taken shortly to be some superstitious monument of decayed divinity and so thought fit to be removed.'[4] That the whole edifice of the monarchy, as built up for over a century by the Tudors, could be reduced to dust in less than half that time by their successors is some indictment of Stuart rule. And a large part of that blame can be laid at the door of the very precise concept of monarchy which James VI of Scotland brought south with him in 1603.

DIVINE KINGSHIP AND DISTANCE

Although Elizabeth I certainly had an exalted view of her office, what may be described as its doctrinal details were never fully spelt out, and her ability to hold the affections of the populace softened what was, in fact, Tudor absolutism. All of that changed with the arrival of James VI of Scotland as James I of England. The new king wrote extensively on the nature of kingship, so that no one could be under any illusion about what he claimed to be his rights.[5] For him, the sovereign had a personal and an individual right, derived directly from God, to his throne. James's views were nothing if not extreme, for his powers were his not only by divine but also by hereditary right. This meant that he claimed powers of complete disposal over his subjects' persons and

Rubens celebrates the Union of the crowns of England and Scotland in his ceiling painting for Whitehall Palace, *c.*1630

property. The royal prerogative was also deemed to be in his eyes above the ordinary course of the law. In a scheme of things where the monarch was, in the king's own words, 'a little God', there was no place for either the law of the land or any authority of an estate of the realm, should such a body conflict with the king's will. Such an ideological premise, if not handled with delicacy, was a recipe sooner or later for disaster, given the major role accorded by the Tudors to Parliament in carrying through the Reformation. And that is precisely what happened.

James wrote much about what we categorise as the Divine Right of Kings, and in doing so discussed the significance of Coronations.[6] In *A Paterne for a Kings Inauguration*, written after the death of his eldest son Prince Henry in 1612 for the future Charles I, he states: 'Kings therefore, as GODS Deputie-iudges vpon earth, sit in thrones, clad with long robes, not as laikes [i.e. laymen] and simply *togati* (as inferior secular Iudges are) but as *mixtae personae* . . . being bound to make a reckoning to GOD for their subiects soules as well as their bodies.'[7]

This throwback to theocratic kingship was not lost on contemporaries. A young lawyer watching the investiture of James I at his Coronation with the robes of St Edward wrote that they signified 'that *Rex est persona mixta cum sacerdote*'.[8] That view resurfaced also at the Coronation of Charles I when the historic prayer *Deus ineffabilis* had restored to it passages making a plea that the king might obtain God's favour for his people like Aaron in the tabernacle, Elisha in the waters and Zacharias in the Temple, and also be a Peter with the keys of discipline and a Paul in matters of doctrine.[9] An observer at the event, the distinguished biblical scholar, Joseph Mead, wrote: 'It understands the king not to be merely laic, but a mixed person.'[10] Inevitably such a passage in a prayer was seized upon in the trial of Charles's Archbishop of Canterbury, William Laud, in 1644. Laud was the key figure in the compilation of the 1626 rite. Thomas Fuller, the historian of the Church of England, wrote of this prayer in the middle of the 1650s: 'This I may call a Protestant passage, though anciently used in popish times, as fixing more spiritual power in the king than the pope will willingly allow, jealous that any will willingly allow Peter's keys save himself.'[11]

As far as the Stuart dynasty was concerned, the monarchy was divine. In excess of the Tudors such an institution owed nothing at all to the people's will. In the context of the Coronation this meant that the *recognitio* could only be a formal presentation of a ruler to his people, not for their approval but to call them to render fealty. Drafts for the Coronation rite of 1603 include three different speeches to be addressed to the onlookers at the *recognitio*. The third, which retained some hint of election or approval by those present, beginning 'Will you take this worthie Prince James . . ', was inevitably not the one chosen. Following the Tudors, the *recognitio* was seen as merely a presentation of someone who was already monarch in the fullest sense of the word. Here was 'the rightfull inheritour of the Crowne' to whom all present are bidden to render 'homage, service and bounden dutie'. Those present signified their willingness by crying out 'Yea yea God saue Kinge James.' It was repeated at Charles I's Coronation, although the archbishop had difficulty in eliciting any response from the crowd.[12]

In his *Paterne for a Kings Inauguration* James bids his son in respect of his Coronation 'to have that action performed in publike, and in a publike place, that the love of his people may appear in that solemne action'. He then provides an explanation of the meaning of the various items of investiture: the purple robe should remind the wearer that he should prove worthy of his throne, the crown was to call to mind that his strength resided in the love of his people, the sceptre symbolised royal authority, and the sword that his role was to punish the wicked and defend the good.[13] In his *Trew Law of Free Monarchies* James has a few more things to say about the Coronation. 'By the Law of Nature,' he writes, 'the King becomes a naturall Father to all his Lieges at the Coronation', and that entailed caring for their 'nourishing, education, and vertuous government . . '.[14] No other ruler of England had written so much in the public domain about what he understood the Coronation to embody.

Such views would have impinged on those present in the Abbey thanks to the Coronation sermon. That, in the context of Protestantism, achieved an importance during the seventeenth century in an age in which the sermon was a central means of public expression and debate. Up until now all we have had is Thomas Cranmer's revolutionary exposition of the rite of Coronation in 1547, but from 1603 onwards every Coronation sermon was to be published, meaning that the views of kingship enshrined in them had a wide audience amongst the literate laity. It also represented a shift in the balance of the actual rite, for within a Protestant context the Word was all important.

D. J. Sturdy, in his study of Coronation sermons from James I to

William III and Mary II, demonstrates their importance as indexes to the Anglican view of kingship during a period of turbulence which saw the extinction of the monarchy.[15] The clerics chosen to preach on such an occasion were inevitably high in royal favour. At the Coronation of James I the honour fell to Thomas Bilson, Bishop of Winchester, and at that of Charles I to Richard Senhouse, Bishop of Carlisle.[16]

Bilson, in the words of Anthony Wood, was 'a principal maintainer of the church of England' in the face of the Puritan onslaught and was equally a stout defender of the rights of kings against the claims of the papacy. The latter conviction would have endeared him to James I and indeed formed the core of his 1603 sermon:

> It is a Romish Error Repugnant to the word of God . . . to restraine Princes from protecting and promoting the true Worship of God within their Realmes. Neither hath the Man of sinne [i.e. the pope] more grossely betrayed his Pride and Rage in any thing, than in his abasing the honor and abusing the power, and impugning the Right of Princes; by deposing them from their Seats, and translating their Kingdomes to others, by absolving their Subjects from all allegiance, and giving them leave to rebell, by setting his feete in Emperors' necks, and spurning off their Crownes with his Shooe . . .[17]

In this way the Foxian view of English history was enunciated in the presence of Catholic emissaries, for representatives of the Catholic kings were present in 1603! And, of course, Bilson was an unequivocal believer in Divine Right: 'the Princes function in generall is established by God, but more specially . . . their power, their honour, and their service are ordained and confirmed of God. To express them more distinctly; Their Authoritie is derived from God, resembling his image; Their dignities is allowed of God, to partake with his homage: Their Duetie is enjoyned them by God, to preserve his heritage . . .'.[18] James I could almost have written it himself.

For England the real crunch came with the Coronation oath. How could that ever fit with James's magisterial concept of kingship? To James, the oath, in fact, presented no problems at all, for he argued that it was taken not as in any way a pledge to those over whom he ruled but as one to God. In the oath, he writes, a king 'makes not his Crowne stoupe by this meanes to any power in the Pope, or in the Church, or in the People'.[19] Such an interpretation, of course, was diametrically opposed to how virtually all common lawyers and most parliamentarians saw it. It only called for the right circumstances to set both parties on a pathway to collision.

The oath in James's view was 'the clearest, civill, and fundamentall Law, whereby the Kings office is properly defined'. In it a ruler promises 'to maintaine the Religion presently professed within that countrie . . . And next to maintaine all the lowable and good Laws made by their predecessours . . . And lastly, to maintaine the whole countrey, and euery state therein, in all their ancient Priviledges and Liberties, as well as against all forreine enemies, as among themselves . . .'.[20] Later he goes on to reiterate that although the Coronation oath is between a king and his subjects, the latter have no right, if he violates the oath, to resist or overthrow him. Such an act pertains to God alone. And, in a final reiteration of the people's powerlessness in the face of a monarch by Divine Right, he states: 'For, as he [the king] is their [the people's] heritable over-lord, and so by birth, not by any right in the Coronation, commeth his crowne, it is like vnlawful . . . to displace him.'[21]

From that viewpoint the Coronation in James's scheme of things was unnecessary, as the king was king from the moment of his predecessor's demise. Indeed, his viewpoint was endorsed by the judges in 1608 in Calvin's case, who resolved that the 'Coronation is but a royal ornament and solemnization of the royal title', and that 'by the laws of England there can be no interregnum in the same'.[22]

James I was enunciating a theory of monarchy which Elizabeth I may well also have believed but certainly never articulated. As time passed and crisis succeeded crisis, there was an increasing realisation of what such a theory of rulership meant, and by the time of Charles I's Coronation in 1626 the oath was cause for considerable unease. At the end of May 1625, two months after James I's death, the Venetian secretary wrote: 'Men talk of the possibility of his Majesty not being crowned, so as to remain more absolute, avoiding the obligation to swear to the laws and without the discontent of his subjects. The parliament men would wish for this observance, as without it they would consider their laws at the discretion of the king and not dependent on the general public authority . . .'.[23]

At his trial in 1644 Laud was charged with altering the oath. He, in fact, decisively proved that what Charles I swore was exactly the same as that which his father had sworn in 1603. He went on to state that 'there is a latitude left for them that are trusted to add to these Interrogations . . .'.[24] In that turn of phrase he alluded to the various forms the Oath could take, which we know to have been true for the Tudor Coronations, and there can be no doubt that in 1603 the same thing occurred, a revision of the oath being in accord with James's view of monarchical power.

As we have no texts for the oaths of the post-Reformation Tudors, it is difficult to measure just how dramatic was the change under James. Edward VI only promised 'to keep to the people . . . the laws and liberties of the this realm . . .'. What those were it was left to the crown to decide. The fourth question, which asked the king to observe the laws of the people's choice, was abandoned and rewritten to reverse such an arrangement. Virtually nothing is known of Mary's oath but, in the case of Elizabeth I, Dale Hoak has argued an addition to the effect that in respect of the law, the sovereign was to act 'according to the Laws of God, [and] the true profession of the Gospel established in this Kingdom'. In effect, the oath was Protestantised before the country was.

What occurred in 1603 was to build on these foundations with what was a new translation of the 1308 French oath, revising the term in respect of laws from *aura esleu* 'will have chosen' to 'the laws and customs which the commonalty . . . have chosen'. This meant that the king in no way pledged to abide by any future laws but only those already in existence, but even that constraint was negated by the addition of the phrase 'agreeing to the prerogative of the kinge and the auncient Customes of this Realm'.[25] Poor Archbishop Laud had this phrase laid at his door at his trial: 'After this day's work was ended, it instantly spread over all the City, that I had altered the King's Oath at his Coronation, and from thence to all parts of the kingdome . . .'.[26]

In this way the contents of the Coronation oath touch the heart of the constitutional conflict of the seventeenth century. The republican viewpoint was to be unequivocally in the opposite direction and during the 1640s there was to be a lively debate about the exact meaning of the crucial phrase, which in Latin read *quas vulgus elegerit*, as to whether it meant 'which the people have chosen' or 'which the people shall choose'. For parliamentarians the Coronation oath was first and foremost taken to the people, an oath which, once broken, dissolved the obligation between the two parties. Milton in his *Eikonoklastes* (1649), a response to the *Eikon Basilike* (to which I will come shortly), writes: 'the Oathe then were interchang'd, and mutual; stood or fell together'.[27]

The doctrinal position taken up by the Stuarts was compounded by a complete absence of the common touch and an aversion to public ceremonial. Within weeks of James's accession the Earl of Worcester, Master of the Horse, was to write of him: 'The King . . . utterly mislykethe of multitudes, and by his wyll would have none at all . . .'[28] James I made a state entry into London but, as Arthur Wilson, albeit a hostile source, records: 'He endured this days brunt with patience, being assured he should never have such another . . .'[29] As a result, most of the speeches went undelivered as the king hurried past them, his brusqueness and disinterest only saved by his queen, Anne of Denmark, who 'did all the way so humbly and with mildenes, salute her subjects', and Prince Henry who 'smiling . . . saluted them all with many a bende'.[30] His successor did not even make a Coronation entry, indeed worse, an entry was prepared which he cancelled.

As far as the public was concerned, the ruler for the first time became a remote and rarely seen presence, a man cast as an emperor enthroned in the solitude of his palace precincts.[31] Mercifully James had one saving grace, the hurly-burly of his court. There he remained accessible to all who made up the established classes. With the accession of his son that, too, was severely curtailed. Charles set out to remodel his court to resemble what he had seen in Madrid. The stately ceremonial and etiquette he introduced kept at a distance even the established classes upon whose support he depended.[32]

What made all of this worse was that, for the first time, the royal image could no longer be controlled as it had been in the Tudor era. As the reign of Charles I progressed, this alienation from the populace created an opposition which set about desacralising and demystifying the monarchy. As the divisions widened still further in the 1640s these attacks drove those who supported the crown, in their turn, to adopt an even more extreme position. It was then that terms like 'his Sacred Person' and the 'anoynted King' gained currency as verbal expressions of his divinity.[33]

In the long run, ironically, it was the monarchists who won thanks, in part, to the publication simultaneously with Charles I's execution of the famous *Eikon Basilike*. This book ran into innumerable editions and bore within it a very different image of Charles I, one which did not work from absolutist but from humanitarian principles. The king

Right Charles I with the
old Tudor State Regalia,
painting, 1631 and *above*,
Henrietta Maria with her
small crown, painting, *c.*1636

presented himself, by means of a series of meditations on events of his own reign, as a benign ruler, a Christian, a sensitive human being and a father. The contents of the book worked from a premise that both James and Charles had in reality ignored, namely, that it was the people who, in fact, made and sustained kings. In doing so the book acknowledged belatedly that for kingship to flourish it had to return to the foundation stone of Tudor rule, popular support.[34]

ANTIQUARIANISM AND THE RETURN OF RITUAL

The Divine Right of Kings and the sanctity of the royal prerogative were not the only things to affect the Coronation. As early as 15 May 1603 the Venetian ambassador was writing: 'For the Coronation, the Heralds – whose office it is to arrange the pageant – are examining precedents, even remote ones.'[35] This is one of a number of hints that there was some debate about what form the ceremony should take, for a month later he returned to the topic, saying that anointing was a Catholic rite and 'as anointing is a function by God to mark the pre-eminence of kings it cannot well be omitted, and they cannot make up their minds what they should adopt'. James, he adds, was antipathetic to all of it, denying the traditional power to heal scrofula by touch, 'for the age of miracles is past . . . However he will have the full ceremony, so as not to lose his prerogative, which belongs to the kings of England as kings of France.'[36]

Whatever went on, the upshot was a decision to translate into English the *Liber Regalis*, expurgating from it anything which might be construed as popish. This was an astonishing decision, because logic would suggest building on the Tudor Coronations with their triple crowning. That this happened calls for explanation, for a number of converging factors contributed to it.

The political and religious situation was very different in 1603 from what it had been in 1559. The country, and along with it the Church of England, had acquired an identity and an ideological basis which had evolved during the 45 years of the rule of Elizabeth Tudor. To the creation of a new national mythology (of a kind we see fully fledged in Shakespeare's histories) much was contributed by the rise of antiquarianism, a movement which explored and constructed a national past. Its arrival as a phenomenon was epitomised by the foundation of the Elizabethan Society of Antiquaries sometime around 1586, the year in which William Camden's landmark *Britannia* appeared.[37] Camden was a major figure, along with his pupil, the future Sir Robert Cotton, whose famous library is still largely intact as part of the manuscript holdings of the present British Library. Those involved in this movement were men of affairs strongly motivated by the new patriotism of the post-Armada years, anxious to demonstrate and establish the antiquity and independence of English institutions, which included the monarchy, Church and Parliament. Cotton, as Camden's pupil, wrote papers, for example, on the offices of Constable, Earl Marshal and Steward, all central to the rite of Coronation. John Selden, friend of both Camden and Cotton, was later to write about the history of anointing in his *Titles of Honor* (1614). His discussion of the topic cites the biblical precedents, quotes Thomas Becket on its symbolism and also Robert Grosseteste's letter to Henry III. He traces the rite back to the Anglo-Saxon kings and asserts that the holy oil in the Abbey was 'as good as that of the holy Viol at Rheims'.[38] This quest into the English past went along with a new pride in the English language, seeing it as a native pre-Conquest inheritance which had been marred by the introduction of Latin after the Norman Conquest.[39] It is into this context of ideas that we can place the decision both to use and to translate the *Liber Regalis*.

To this we must add the fact that the ideological position of the Church of England was also very different in 1603 from what it had been during the shifting sands of the middle years of the previous century. There, too, a sustained effort had been made to establish the credentials of the Church of England not as new institution, nor as any branch of one of the other Reformist Churches, but as something idiosyncratic and true to itself, the ancient Ecclesia Anglicana, a continuation of an institution whose roots stretched back to the Ancient British Church which flourished before the arrival of the popish Augustine. Archbishop Matthew Parker's *De Antiquitate Ecclesiae . . .* (1572) presented the Anglican Church as a revival of the ancient pure Christian faith practised in this country before its pollution at the hands of the popes. Under Archbishop Whitgift's aegis came Richard Hooker's *The Laws of Ecclesiastical Polity* (1593–7) which provided a sound basis for the Church of England's position as one with a venerable past, independent of both Rome and the Reformist Churches. Into this resurgent confidence the decision to translate the *Liber Regalis* can be said to fit neatly.

The antiquarians in 1603 were all men close to government and Camden more than any other was in a pre-eminent position vis-à-vis any Coronation. He had been patronised by Gabriel Goodman, Dean of Westminster, in the 1570s and, in 1575, was appointed to the second mastership at Westminster School, of which he was to become headmaster eighteen years later. Early in 1587 Camden had also been made keeper of the Abbey library, and a decade later Clarenceux King of Arms. Although the plague had led to his removal to Robert Cotton's house in Huntingdonshire for most of the summer and autumn of 1603, he is certainly recorded as having walked in the Coronation procession. Here was a herald who held office in the institution in which resided the *Liber Regalis*. It is difficult not to conclude that Camden played a key role in determining what happened in 1603.

Camden was fiercely Anglican and a prime defender of the ancient dignity of the Church, but the ultimate decision to use the *Liber Regalis* would not have lain with him but with the archbishop, Whitgift, and men like Sir Robert Cecil, Secretary of State and a key figure on the Coronation Commission. Seven years after the Coronation Thomas Milles, in his *The Catalogue of Honor* (1610), printed an account of the ceremony which had been presented to the king by the archbishop. It was noted that he had 'faithfully observed the forme, set downe in the ancient Booke kept among the Regalia at Westminster'.[40]

One more person who may well have also been influential was the Dean of Westminster. In 1603 he was Lancelot Andrewes, the prime fount of the Anglican tradition of 'the beauty of holiness', which was labelled Arminianism and involved such things as the resiting of the communion table back where the altar had stood, the use of ceremonial such as bowing to the altar, and incense. And just to round off the circle, Andrewes was also close to Cecil who was the Abbey's high steward.

No text survives which we know was actually used in the Abbey on the occasion, but the most important draft is the manuscript at Lambeth Palace headed 'A brief as well out of the rites of Coronation called Liber Regalis, as allso other bookes of good recorde', indicating that other sources must have been looked at. The Lambeth manuscript offers alternatives in places and also has corrections, although the fact that the dean throughout is referred to as the abbot is not one of them.

What have been struck through are phrases like the one describing the king being anointed on the head *faciendo signum crucis*, or a phrase like 'at the intercession of all thy Saintes' in the prayer *Deus ineffabilis*.[41] There must have been an awareness that 1603 was a rushed job, because Charles I appointed a committee to review the Coronation.[42] Its first meeting was on 4 January 1626, less than a month before the Coronation which took place on Candlemas Day, 2 February. On that committee sat both lords and bishops, but there can be no doubt that William Laud, then Bishop of St David's, was the key player in the preparation of the rite. Equally, it is clear that the king himself took a keen personal interest. Laud wrote: 'The Truth is, when we met in the Committee, we were fain to mend slips of the Pen, to make sense in some places and good English in other . . .'[43] On 18 January Charles's favourite, the Duke of Buckingham, took Laud to see the king in order to go over the text with him in case 'he disliked anything therein'. That personal interest is also reflected in the fact that thirteen days later, on 31 January, there took place something unprecedented, what amounted to a dress rehearsal. In this Laud read the rubrics and the king tried on the various items of the regalia which had been brought from the Abbey. As in 1603, the antiquarian urge in 1626 was strong: 'to consult of the Ceremonies of the Coronation, that the ancient Manner might be observed'.[44]

Concern with antiquity is noticeable also in the fact that Charles I was meant to have taken his oath on what was believed to be the Gospel Book on which the Anglo-Saxon kings had taken theirs and which in 1626 was in the library of Sir Robert Cotton: 'vpon which for divers hundred yeares together the Kinges of England had solemnlie taken ther Coronation oath'.[45] An arrangement was made that this precious manuscript should be collected en route from Whitehall Palace, but the king's barge overshot the landing. In the event the oath was sworn instead on the Great Bible from the Chapel Royal.[46] At the rehearsal Charles I noticed that one of the wings of the dove atop one of the sceptres of St Edward was missing. He sent for the royal goldsmith and demanded its immediate repair, and fell into a fury when he was told that it could not be done in time. However, the sceptre was taken away and an entirely new dove was instead manufactured.[47] The fact that the king wanted to see the regalia before the event must reflect a new awareness of their antiquity. They were on the way to becoming Heylyn's 'Sacred Ornaments'. Thomas Fuller's account of the regalia in the middle of the 1650s captures this crossing of the line into regal hagiography:

> Posterity conceived so great an opinion of King Edward's Piety, that his Cloaths were deposited amongst the Regalia, and solemnly worn by our English Kings on their Coronation never counting themselves so fine, as when invested with his Robes; the Sanctity of Edward the first Wearer, excusing, yea adorning the modern Antiquenesse of his Apparell . . . But now Edward's Staffe is broken, Chair Overturned, Cloaths rent, and Crown melted; our present Ages esteeming them the Reliques of Superstition . . .'[48]

All of this registers a change of mental attitude to such things, a shift of a reverence once accorded to relics in pre-Reformation days to those things hallowed by antiquity and association. Sir William Segar, Garter King of Arms at the Coronation of Charles I, also reflects this when he refers to 'the pretious sanctified Oyle for the anoynting being in an ancient Cruett of stone placed in the back of a golden Eagle garnished with precious stones'.[49] Such mystique accounts for the fact surely that Charles I was moved to add items to the regalia, the first additions, since Richard III had, in fact, deposited the ampulla. Laud records how, in the aftermath of the 1626 Coronation, three of the swords used, including Curtana, the king ordered 'to be kept in Church'. The future archbishop records that he offered them 'Solemnly at the Altar in the Name of the King, and laid them up with the rest'.[50] By 1649, the year when they began the voyage to destruction, their antiquity had increased and the crown of St Edward had become that of Alfred. Hand in hand with this veneration of things deemed ancient went an ever greater interest in well-ordered ritual. We have no way of knowing what earlier Coronations were like from that viewpoint. Were they unrehearsed chaos or were they well conducted? What is certain is that by the Coronation of Charles I there was a genuine concern about the rite being well ordered, and more than one source records that 1626 was an immaculately choreographed event. That that was so we find confirmed, for example, in the Earl Marshal's order laying down that no one except those he called for should be on the scaffold, that all the peers must appear wearing their Coronation robes and that, although the dictates of fashion were conceded, in the case of peeresses, nonetheless, what they wore, too, was to be of 'one manner'.[51]

The return of ceremonial and ritual to church services was another index of the strength of the Church of England at the opening of the seventeenth century, reflecting a keen desire that it should not be mistaken for either one of the Reformist Churches or for the Church of Rome. So we see the spread of a High Anglican way of doing things in terms of the dressing of the altar and of the gesture and posture of participants of a kind which fanned out from the Chapel Royal (Elizabeth had always favoured a return to 1549 rather than 1552 and her chapel was a rule unto itself) and from the example of Lancelot Andrewes. How much this new movement had affected the Abbey under Andrewes's incumbency is unclear, but his successor, Richard Neile, was certainly one of this school and moved the communion table out of the main body of the church and placed it where the old high altar had stood.[52] But even in 1603, what the Venetian secretary dismissed as 'a common moveable table' was described by another Italian onlooker as being dressed with gold brocade and yellow flowered silk and adorned with an arrangement of flagons, basins and cups while, 'in the middle, was a cup covered with a plain cloth of cambric, in which was a vessel wherein was the oil with which the King was to be anointed'.[53] This, unbelievably in the context of post-Reformation England, was the ampulla containing the oil which the Virgin had delivered to St Thomas! If anything is evidence of the deep desire to emphasise continuity, this decision to use an accidental survival of a miraculous relic is it.

Although Mass vestments had gone, the cope, a choir vestment, took on that kind of role for the Church of England. Both in 1603 and in 1626 much is made of the rich copes worn, not necessarily survivors from the pre-Reformation era but newly made. The Stuart Coronations were liturgical spectacles in the grand manner, to the extent that more than one foreign observer in 1603 saw no difference from what would have happened in a Catholic church.

We can add to this sense of strength and continuity the decision to consecrate new holy oil for the Coronation of Charles I. In doing this the new ritualists may have had in mind the practice of the Eastern Church, for the hallowing of inanimate things had otherwise been swept away at the Reformation. For the oil the royal physicians had prepared a compound of orange and jasmine, distilled roses, distilled cinnamon, oil of ben with extract of flowers of bensoint with ambergris, musk and civet. It was consecrated by Laud in his chapel. Not only

Imaginary view of the
Coronation of James I, 1603,
engraving, c.1603

was there new oil, but Laud noted that 'all the vncion was now performed in forma Crucij + and the old Crucifixe among the Regalia
stood on the Altar'. That means that, in excess of what the *Liber Regalis*
prescribed, the oil was applied in the form of a cross not only on the
head but, in addition, on the other specified parts of the body.[54]

Simultaneously with the burgeoning of 'the beauty of holiness'
came the heralds' desire to record the exact movements of everyone
involved in a Coronation. Indeed, a special box was constructed in 1626
so that they had a clear view of the action and could note it down for
future reference. Sir William Segar's notes amongst the Anstis papers
in the College of Arms form what must be the earliest surviving documents in which there is an attempt to record every single movement
that was made.[55] He notes the precise position of the various partici-

pants, describing how Charles I descended from the scaffold preceded by a flotilla of the great officers of state bearing the various items of the historic regalia. He then goes on to record how the Constable sat between the Lord Great Chamberlain and the Earl Marshal opposite the king. On either side of the latter stood the escorting bishops of Durham and Wells with the acting dean (Laud) behind. To the king's left stood the Earl of Essex holding Curtana, while to the right stood those personating Normandy and Guyenne along with the Master of the Jewel House. Both archbishops, he notes, sat to the west of the north end of the high altar with the prebends, while at the opposite end sat two more bishops. Segar carefully puts down a mass of detail, including when the king took off his ruff and put it on again. But even he could not take it all in, and when it came to the investiture with the ring Charles had 'All the lords about the king all this time', which made Segar miss who actually placed the ring on the king's finger. In the margin is the despairing note 'by whom'.

We take for granted the immaculately choreographed and fully rehearsed ceremonial of today, the foundation stone of so much of which is modern technology. But there was none of this in earlier centuries. It is astonishing to reach the second quarter of the seventeenth century before we get any kind of reference to a rehearsal. It is hardly surprising, therefore, that 1626 goes down as something of a landmark, which was precisely how a more than satisfied Laud saw it: 'In so great a ceremony, and amidst an incredible concourse of People, nothing was lost, or broke, or disordered . . . and I heard some of the Nobility saying to the King in their return, that they never had seen any Solemnity, although much less, performed with so little Noise, and so great Order.'[56]

For 1626 we have for the first time a text which was actually used at the event. At St John's College, Cambridge, there is William Laud's annotated copy, the text probably in the hand of John Cosin, later Bishop of Durham. It includes the prayer used by Laud to consecrate the new holy oil, and amongst the annotations comes this summing up of the event: 'The daye was verye faire and the ceremonye was performed without any interruption and in verye good order.'

Two Coronations Considered[57]

James I's and Charles I's Coronations can, as we have already demonstrated, be seen as a single manifestation, for both embodied a return to the *Liber Regalis* and were equally responses to the impulses of the new century. But there were other things, some of which they shared and others which set them apart. They certainly shared an obsession with the cost of it all, for royal finances were on an ever downward spiral. Indeed, the commission to supervise the Coronation in 1603 had as its opening mandate on 20 May to consider what was 'accordable to honour without superfluity of charge'.[58] It was pointed out to James that although he could be crowned on his own, a joint Coronation with his queen, Anne of Denmark, would reduce the costs by a third. By the accession of his son in 1625 the royal finances were in an even worse state, a major contributing factor in the cancellation of the Coronation entry into London, for which the king had to bear the cost of dressing the entire retinue of several hundred. Even without the cost of the entry, Sir John Fortescue's account for the Great Wardrobe for the Coronation of 1603 itself came to nearly £20,000. The two royal robes for James alone, one of purple and the other of crimson velvet, came to over £2,000. The barges which bore them to Westminster Palace cost nearly £700. One is struck by the vast list of robes and other apparel along with horse furniture which had to be supplied at the expense of the crown to the bishops, the heralds and pursuivants, the ministers of the Chapel Royal and the Closet, the trumpeters and other musicians, the Abbey prebends and choristers as well as the children of the Chapel Royal.[59]

What separates the Coronations is the sense of urgency, which is there in 1603 and which is totally absent 23 years later. Elizabeth died on 24 March and her funeral took place a month later, on 28 April. Sir Robert Cecil's political masterpiece was the unquestioned, smooth succession of the King of Scots. That the Coronation was not devoid of significance we can gather from the plea made by those involved in the Bye Plot, who argued that 'their Practise against the King could not be Treason, because done against him before he had been crowned'.[60] James, sticking to ancient usage, was crowned on a saint's day, that of his namesake, the apostle James, 25 July.

There were no such pressures around in 1625 and, indeed, virtually a year elapsed between James's death on 27 March and 2 February the following year when his son was crowned. By then Charles had married Henrietta Maria and conducted his bride to London. But such a delay must be set within the claims of Stuart kingship which rendered the Coronation an additional but by no means essential rite for king-making.

Both events not only shared lack of money, but also visitations by the plague which severely curtailed public spectacle. This meant in the case of James moving the Coronation entry back a year and in that of Charles its eventual abandonment. The plague also radically affected the creation of the Knights of the Bath. In 1603 the ceremony was relocated away from the Tower to St James's Palace and the knights paraded around the Whitehall tiltyard attended by their squires and pages before returning to St James's where the king dubbed them in the gallery. In 1626 the ceremony was curtailed even more, the king merely dubbing the knights in the hall of Whitehall, their oaths having been taken previously in Henry VII's chapel in Westminster Abbey by the Earl Marshal, the Earl of Arundel, and the Lord Chamberlain, the Earl of Pembroke.[61]

By 1603 both the ritual and dress of the Knights of the Bath had become a curiosity. No wonder that they had to parade around the tiltyard to be seen! The handsome Lord Herbert of Cherbury provides a long account of his creation in 1603. Vain as the proverbial peacock, he wrote: 'I cou'd tell how much my person was commended by the Lords and Ladies that came to see the Solemnity then used, but I shall flatter myself too much if I believed it.' So proud was he that he had his portrait painted wearing the robes he wore on the second day. It was created to hang in his study and is now at Powys Castle.[62]

Lord Herbert was not the only one to be recorded in his robes, for Sir William Pope, the future Earl of Downe, commemorated this honour in the same way.[63] So, too, did the thirteen-year-old William Lord Russell in 1626. Attended by his dwarf, he wears the purple robes donned on the third day of the ritual, with the badge of the order with its triple crown introduced by James I during the course of his reign. Russell was to live long enough to see the return of the monarchy in 1660 and, as Duke of Bedford, carry the new St Edward's sceptre at the Coronation of Charles II.[64]

Two Knights of the Bath, 1603
Above Sir William Pope, later 1st Earl of Downe, painting, *c.*1603
Left Edward Herbert, 1st Baron Herbert of Cherbury, painting, *c.*1603

William Russell, later 1st
Duke of Bedford, made
Knight of the Bath at the
Coronation of Charles I,
painting, 1627

For both Coronations there was the customary Court of Claims with its litany of people who claimed this, that or the other service on grounds of historic land tenure. Perhaps the oddest in 1603 was Sir Christopher Leigh's claim to make a mess of 'herout or pigernout'.[65] No great change there. But in the case of Westminster Abbey it was very different. That had physically altered since 1559. A payment 'for taking doune the great partition crosse over the Quier in the Abbey and vj weynescot pewes there and other seats and setting them all vp againe . . .' indicates that the interior had been turned into a preaching arena.[66] At Charles I's Coronation there is an even more interesting reference to 'the description of the stage and the Throne and Seates in the Church with a Modell'.[67] The Surveyor of Works in 1626 was Inigo Jones, and the sudden appearance of an architectural model would accord with the practice of Italian Renaissance architects. The very name of Jones suggests that the scaffold and its balustrading would have looked very different from 1603, a classical dressing perhaps superimposed on to the Gothic interior.[68]

For both Coronations the physical arrangement of the temporary decor repeated much of what had gone before. There was, however, one major change. St Edward's chair, which was always reupholstered in a rich fabric, now stood in the centre of the sacrarium, with chairs either side of the altar hidden by traverse curtains. The earliest reference to the use of St Edward's chair was for Henry IV when it was used for the enthronement on the scaffold. For the Tudor Coronations, too, the chair had been up on the scaffold at the summit of a flight of steps. It is difficult to explain what prompted this shift of location. All that the *Liber Regalis* refers to as being in the sacrarium area is 'a suitable chair' and, for the scaffold, a 'royal throne'. Perhaps it was also a response to the antiquarian urges which underlay so much of 1603. What is certain is that once it had migrated there it was to stay.

The sacrarium floor and up and over and down the scaffold were decked with red cloth. The scaffold itself had the usual arrangement of thrones, both on an octagonal dais as in 1559, approached by flights of steps before which, at ground level, stood chairs. What increased in 1626 was the number of special areas for various groups of people, for special scaffolds were built for the Knights of the Bath, the heralds, the judges, the ambassadors and musicians. In addition there were what were known as degrees built on either side for 'the great ladies'. This is the first reference I can find to any kind of seating being provided for onlookers. Up until then they must have stood on the ground and looked up or climbed to the clerestory and looked down. Degrees refer to gradated seating of a kind Inigo Jones was accustomed to erect for court performances of plays and masques. This innovation could explain why in 1626 a model was called for.

What remains opaque is who gained access to the Abbey. The Venetian ambassador in 1603 refers to admission tickets for the first time. We know that in the religious thaw which marks the opening years of the century Catholic ambassadors attended the ceremony, even though they absented themselves when it came to the communion. The fact that a young lawyer like Humphrey Repington gained access indicates that the possibility must have been there for quite a wide constituency of people to get in. For anyone set on invading the Abbey it was clearly possible to worm one's way in, as Symondes D'Ewes recounts in 1626 when, having failed to get in earlier, he writes: 'In my passage, spying a doore guarded by one and thronged by a few, I went, and with a little trouble found an easie entrance . . . Being in, I instantlie setled myselfe at the Stage on which stood the roiall seate.'[69]

What this means from the standpoint of the historian is that for the first time we begin to have several accounts by different onlookers of the same event. These bring to life the dead text and rubrics. They suggest that Anglican grand liturgy did not seem that much different from its Catholic counterpart. A French observer, probably an ambassador, in 1603 wrote that the two archbishops and the bishops were 'vested as are the archbishops and bishops of the Roman Catholic Church. The service was held as solemnly as in the Roman Catholic Church.'[70]

Our eyewitnesses really drive home the fact that they were looking at the making of a priest-king. Giovanni degli Effetti writes of the investiture of James I that he wore 'a vestment of crimson velvet lined with white, with light sleeves, and over this a royal surplice [cotta] with the tunicle of a deacon, embroidered, I think, with the arms of England'. Repington puts it even more succinctly: 'A priest's cap of black velvet, a priest's coat of cloth of gold.'

Inevitably the return to the *Liber Regalis* accorded the clergy a major status in this procedure. Once again the bishops of Durham and Bath escorted the king in the procession to the Abbey. Drafts refer to two more bishops carrying the regal and the paten as they did in the Middle Ages, but in fact they were carried by an earl. That honour only returned to the bishops in 1626. By the time Charles travelled north to

be crowned King of Scotland in 1633 the High Anglican tide had risen far higher. The Scottish presbyters looked on in horror at the communion table dressed 'in the manner of an altar' with a tapestry of the crucifixion behind it, bishops attired in blue silk with rochets with loops of gold, not to mention the bowing. It 'bred gryt feir of inbringinge of poperie'.[71]

The fear of popery was endemic, and made worse by both queens. Anne of Denmark, James I's queen, had become Catholic by 1603, and although she took part in the Coronation there is no evidence that she

Peers in their robes graduated according to rank, engraving, 1608 communicated. In the case of Henrietta Maria, prepared texts work from the premise that it, too, was going to be a double Coronation. But that never happened. Her resident bishop made claim to crowning her outside the Abbey, but in the end the Sorbonne pronounced against the whole thing. Instead she watched the procession from a window.[72]

What of the ceremony itself? Clearly the codification of dress and rank had now fully evolved, along with the various forms of coronet. We know exactly what the peers of the realm looked like from the series of full-length engravings in Robert Glover's *Nobilitas Politica et Civilis* (1608), which were reused in Milles's *Catalogue of Honor* (1610). Degli Effetti says that in 1603 the peers wore their caps of maintenance but not their coronets in the procession. More memorable must have been the dozen countesses who followed Anne of Denmark, 'with gowns of crimson velvet lined with ermine, and the hair done up, and plain little crowns of gold'. That these dresses were uniform in material but not in style we know, for a few of the countesses sat for their portraits.

The sequence of both Coronations is identical, a pre-Reformation ritual performed in the vernacular and with all the blessing, censing and prayers to the saints deleted. It is interesting when in accounts of either 1603 or 1626 there is information or a comment which enlarges our perception of these early Stuart Coronations. In 1626, for example, the *recognitio* has a gloss relating to the four directions in which the king turns to the three estates of the realm: to the east and the altar for the clergy, to the north and south transepts to the third estate and to the west towards the scaffold to the nobility.

Degli Effetti describes the mantle as being 'like a cope, of violet brocade with a large orphrey of white cloth of silver'. Whether that can be identified as the one which was 'square and worked all over with eagles' seems doubtful. He also saw the actual crowning as making James 'Emperor of his kingdoms, and Head of the Church'. That imperial theme which he caught we find reflected also in another innovation, the striking of a Coronation medal in which James appears in profile *à l'antique*, a practice which was to be repeated in 1626.[73] And degli Effetti goes on to record that the homage-rendering could be a somewhat slap-happy affair, with the king laughing and chatting to the peers as they swore fealty, kissed his right hand and kissed or touched the crown. One of James's favourites, Lord Pembroke, kissed James instead of the crown 'and the King, laughing, gave him a slap, but it was

Lucy, Countess of Bedford
in her robes for the
Coronation of 1603,
painting, *c*.1603

in joke'. No such indecorum marred 1626. The Duke of Buckingham held the text for the homage which each peer read, having also to make three obeisances to the throne and kiss the king's left cheek.

And, for the first time, we begin to know something about the music. Up until 1603, there would have been the Mass of the day, with the three special anthems marking the entrance and reception of the monarch into the Abbey, the anointing and the crowning. The first was the anthem *Firmetur*, 'Let thy hand be strengthened', the second *Unxerunt Salomonem*, 'Zadok the Priest', and the last *Confortare*, 'Be strong and play the man'. Only in 1626 do we get a reference that the last was said by the archbishop 'but formerly the Quire sung it'. In 1603 we know that trumpeters were stationed in different parts of the Abbey, indicating that there must have been quite complex effects, but the rubrics do not even refer to the trumpets, let alone any of the other music. It is the ambassador of the Duke of Württemberg who tells us that during the homage-rendering – which would have been quite a lengthy process – 'the whole time the organs, voices and other music resounded at intervals'. This is a reminder that both Coronations must have been major musical events in which all the resources of both the Abbey and the Chapel Royal would have been called upon. In 1603 the great William Byrd contributed, but it is only in 1626 that we get a clearer idea of the music, for Thomas Tomkins was paid 25 shillings 'for composing of many songes againste the Coronation of Kinge Charles'. Tomkins became organist at the Chapel Royal in 1621, and settings exist for the anthems 'The King shall rejoice' and 'Zadok the Priest' as well as for 'Be strong and of a good courage' which was printed in 1668 in his *Musica Deo Sacra* as 'one of his Coronation Songs'. Things could go wrong, and in 1626 the Gloria ended up being said 'because they could not take the ArchBishops voice soe farre of . . .'.

In terms of the music, the procession from Westminster Palace to the Abbey was far more important, for that was where the major music-making took place. The musical component of that grand procession, which the public witnessed, had become far more complex from the middle of the fifteenth century onwards. In 1483, Richard III had 40 trumpeters and 19 minstrels. By 1547 there were some hundred musicians taking part, not counting the Abbey choir, but we know nothing of the actual music until 1603 when it is likely that Thomas Weelkes's seven-part setting of 'O Lord grant the King a long life' was sung. Tomkins set the same words for the 1626 procession, about which a great deal more is known. The musicians were divided up into three sections. At the head went a fife and drum band, later a separate group of trumpets and kettle drums and, finally, 'three windy musicians', as they were designated, listed as two sackbuts and a double curtal (in fact a cornet and two slide trumpets) supporting the singers.[74]

How are we to sum up these two Coronations? In a sense they were failures, and the blame can be squarely laid at the door of the kings themselves. Neither recognised what their predecessor had understood from the moment of her accession, that royal power henceforth needed the support of a far broader segment of society. And that demanded being visible to the populace in grand ceremonies. The demand was there, for, in 1603, in spite of James's proclamation that crowds should not gather, the route leading to the Abbey was jammed with people and the river covered with boats to see the king and queen arrive in their barge, 'in the shape of a gilded Bucentaur'. The Londoners got their entry in 1604, although James clearly would have avoided it if he could; but not in 1626, and it is to that political blunder that we must now turn our attention.

CROWN AND CITY

By the opening of the seventeenth century the population of London had risen to about a quarter of a million. This was matched by a corresponding rise in urban self-consciousness as its citizens took pride in its role as an ever-expanding centre of international trade and finance, and as the setting for a new social phenomenon, the Season. The latter was when the nobility and gentry came to town to attend the court and Parliament, precipitating a new arena for social intercourse which involved luxury shopping, theatre-going and rides in the park.[75] Thomas Dekker took as one of the central threads in his pageant series to welcome James I the exalted status of the City portrayed as the *camera regis*, the king's chamber. The Recorder in his speech bade James: 'Come, therefore, O worthyest of Kings, as a glorious bridegroome through your Royall Chamber.'[76] In his two further pageants entitled *Nova Fœlix Arabia* and *Hortus Euporiae* he went on to cast it also as the King Presence Chamber and Privy Chamber. Ben Jonson, who provided additional arches for the occasion, topped his opening one with a

The first arch in James I's
state entry, 1604, engraving,
1604

cut-out panorama of the City's skyline. For him London was Nova
Roma, the seat of empire: 'the state and magnificence (as proper to a
triumphall Arch) but the very site, fabricke, strength, policie, dignitie
and affections of the Citie'.[77] Here was the City casting itself as a major
prop of the monarchy, a role which Elizabeth had assiduously cultivated for it throughout her reign, making a ceremonial entry annually on
her return from her summer progress. This carefully nurtured support
was to be as dust by 1641, which saw the London mob advancing on
Whitehall Palace.

That is not to say that it did not all start optimistically enough. In
the last week of March 1603, a few days after the queen's death, the
Common Council had set up a committee to call 'unto them all suche
persons and men of learninge quallitie and experience and for suche

auncient precedentes and recordes as they shall thinke fitt'.[78] By mid-July we learn that no fewer than six arches had been constructed, deemed 'superb' by the Venetian secretary, but as 'such small-timbered gentlemen that they cannot last long' by the letter-writer John Chamberlain. In his view they would rot and fall down by the time the plague had abated.[79]

Although there was mention of the king making his solemn entry in the autumn, it was in the end delayed until the following March.[80] That it had been transposed until after the Coronation eroded an essential point of the festivity, for normally the man who rode through the streets was seen at least by those who thronged them as not as yet fully king. Their acclamation was part of the king-making. Now James I rode through not as an aspirant to the crown, but as a fully fledged monarch. What also contributed to the erosion of the significance of the event was that by the spring of 1604 the political circumstances had changed, for not only had the terms of a peace with Spain been agreed in February, but the embassy to conclude the treaty was on its way. So when work was restarted on the arches at the beginning of February their content needed to be updated. The initial series had been the work of Thomas Dekker, but now Ben Jonson was brought in to add two more, plus an extra pageant for the City of Westminster. James I could hardly personally have influenced what was proposed in 1603, but the hand of the court is certainly visible in Jonson's work. He had already caught the eye of the new regime when he staged a delightful progress fête for Anne of Denmark en route south from Scotland. It was unfortunate that Jonson and Dekker loathed each other, and both pretended that the other's contribution did not exist.

For the first time there is a plethora of printed matter about this entry, as London joined the other great cities of Europe in commemorating the auspicious event with the publication of the text and also engravings of the arches (a drawing for one has recently come to light).[81] Both poets had to contend with the king's dislike of the whole affair. Dekker handled it as tactfully as he could: 'you must understand that a regard being had that his Majestie should not be wearied with tedious Speeches, a greater part of those which are in this book set downe here were left unspoken . . .'.[82] Unlike 1559, there was no pausing en route to listen intently, nor lively exchange with the crowd.

But then what was put together in 1604 was very different from the populism of 1559. Inevitably all Catholic imagery had gone, but

Arches for the state entry
of James I, 1604,
engravings, 1604
Left to right
The Italian Pageant
The Dutch Pageant
The Temple of Janus
The New World

along with it went both biblical and folk elements comprehensible
to the largely illiterate crowd. Instead, they were confronted with an
explosion of pillars, obelisks, domes, statues, arbours, cartouches
and strapwork designed in the main to one end: to delight, to use
Jonson's snobbish phrase, 'the sharpe and learned'. 'Neither was it
becomming,' he wrote from his Olympian heights, 'or could it stand
with the dignitie of these shewes (after the most miserable and desper-
ate shift of the Puppits) to require a Truch-man [i.e. someone who
explained it], or (with the ignorant Painter) one to write, This is a Dog;
or, This is a Hare: but so presented, as vpon the view, they might, without cloud, or obscuritie, declare themselves to the sharpe and learned:
And for the multitude, no doubt but their grounded ivdgements did
gaze, said it was fine, and were satisfied.'[83]

In Jonson's hijacking of popular pageantry we see the seeds
planted for what was to contribute to the fall of the monarchy. For
the Stuart kings spectacle did not take on the public face it had

under Elizabeth, but was enacted in the closed, private world of the
court whose members were recast as awestruck onlookers to the
arcane mysteries of the Jonson masques.

In this entry James was invested with the iconography of
Gloriana married to a new and assertive classical imperialism.
London is Nova Roma welcoming the emperor of a reunited Britain,
a king who was descended from the imperial stock in the form of the
Trojan Brutus, the first ruler of Britain. The symbolism of the old
reign was re-enacted in the evocation of a flower-bedecked spring in
winter or the descent to earth of Astraea, the maiden Justice, bringing the golden age. Not everything about Elizabeth's reign was given
this gilded gloss, for recent scholarship has suggested that buried
within the eulogies were a few swipes at it in references to 'old mali-
cious arts' and 'vile spies', for, in truth, the last years of her reign
had been far from golden. To that was added an even more intense
imperialism, one which had reached fulfilment:

Arch for the state entry of
James I, 1604: Nova Faelix
Arabia, engraving, 1604

And then so rich an Empyre, whose fayre brest,
Contaynes foure kingdomes by your entrance blest,
By Brute divided, but by you alone,
All one againe united and made One . . .[84]

'HIC VIR, HIC EST' ran the Virgilian tag on the Italian arch on
which James appeared like a Roman emperor on horseback riding
towards an enthroned Henry VII. In one pageant the figure of 'Arabia

Britannica' wore 'an Imperiall Crowne on her head' and at Temple Bar this was rounded off with another Virgilian tag: 'REDEVNT SATURNIA REGNA', 'to shew that now those golden times were returned againe, wherein Peace was with us so advanced, Rest received, Libertie restored, Safetie assured, and all Blessednesse appearing'.

James I at least endured this passage through the London streets. Charles I cancelled his.[85] This time the City had erected only two arches and the foreign residents three. As in 1603, the Venetian secretary deemed them superb. The scenario had been written by Thomas Middleton and it is greatly to be regretted that his text has not survived. In it we would have had a glimpse into the minds of the London authorities as to what they hoped for from the new reign. What strikes one most is Charles I's complete indifference to his cancellation. Plague as in 1603 dictated postponement, but in January 1626 the entry was scheduled to take place in May. Then on 26 May the Earl of Pembroke, the Lord Chamberlain, informed the Lord Mayor and Aldermen that 'His Majesty had altered his purpose', ordering the demolition of the arches as they got in the way of coaches passing through the city streets. Such an entry was of course, hugely expensive for the crown, as also for the City. It is hardly surprising that this blunt message was ill-received, and the Venetian ambassador records the 'murmurs of the people and the disgust of those who spent the money'. This was no way to begin a reign, denying the City its traditional act of loyalty to the crown. The hope that Charles would relent and actually make an entry was to linger on into the 1630s, but it never happened. This was the beginning of what was to lead to the total isolation of the king and court from the City. Although in this respect Charles I was anticipating what Louis XIV did in withdrawing from Paris to Versailles, the result was that when war broke out, London fought for Parliament.

THE DESTRUCTION OF DIVINITY

Although Parliament had already inventoried St Edward's regalia in 1644, it was not until after Charles I's execution on 30 January 1649 that the Council of State and Parliament felt that they were in a position to disperse the royal possessions.[86] On 4 July an Act was passed to trace, inventory and value all the late king's goods. The task of disposal for the vast majority of items fell to the Council of State. It is clear that the new form of governance, the Commonwealth, was bent on destroying both St Edward's and the personal regalia of the crown. A new list was made of the former in which the ancient vestments formed one category and anything which was gold or contained jewels formed another. The descriptions of the textile items remain opaque.[87] There was a robe of crimson taffeta 'very old' and another laced with gold, which were both valued at ten shillings. A third robe, liver-coloured, was not only 'very old' but 'worth nothing', and a fourth, again of crimson taffeta, was put down at five shillings. A pair of silver buskins with silver stockings, again 'very old', were priced at twelve shillings and sixpence, a pair of gold shoes at two shillings, a pair of embroidered gloves at a shilling, three swords (given by Charles I) valued at three pounds and a horn comb (actually used by Charles I to comb his hair after anointing) 'worth nothing'.

Virtually everything must have been destroyed except, it seems, the 'Three swords with scabbards of Cloth of Gould'. The recent catalogue of the crown jewels establishes that these, in fact, survived. They were sold to one Roger Humphreys for five pounds in November 1649 and must have been recovered at the Restoration. Claude Blair in his study of these remarkable artefacts demonstrates that they must have been made as a set between about 1610 and 1620 and were certainly those used in 1626 and presented by Charles I to the Abbey as part of the regalia.[88] The maker is likely to have been one Robert South, a member of the London Cutlers' Company, and their apperance is first recorded among the engravings illustrating Francis Sandford's account of the Coronation of James II. Thus it is that the three swords, of Mercy (Curtana), of Spiritual and of Temporal Justice, are those which Laud offered on the high altar in 1626.

The items which contained precious metals and jewels were removed to the Tower. This list included the crown of St Edward (by then King Alfred's), that known as Queen Edith's, the gold chalice and paten, the ampulla, all the various rods and sceptres, the spurs, spoon and any jewels taken off the vestments. The inventory and valuations make interesting reading. As St Edward's regalia are about to pass into oblivion it is worth listing what went to the Tower:

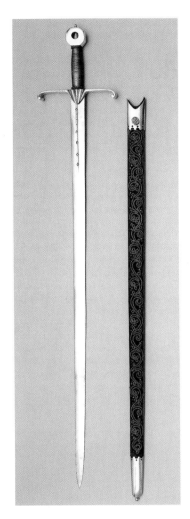

1. Queen Edith's crown found to be only silver-gilt and set with garnets and 'foule pearle' £16

2. 'King Alfred's crown (i.e. St Edward's) of gold wirework set with precious stones and with little bells £248

3. The gold paten set with semi-precious stones £77 11s

4. The regal described as a glass cup 'wrought in figures and sett in gould with some stones and pearles formerly Calld an Aggatt Cup' £102 15s

5. A golden dove set with precious stones and pearls in a box, presumably the ampulla £26

The three ceremonial swords used at the Coronation of Charles I, 1626
Left to right
Curtana or the Sword of Mercy
The Sword of Temporal Justice
The Sword of Spiritual Justice

Antique vessel used as a chalice once part of the French royal regalia. St Edward's chalice was similar

6. Gold and stones taken from the armils £18 15s

7. A sceptre of black and white ivory bound and with a foot of gold with a dove on the top £4 10s

8. A large sceptre of wood covered with silver gilt with a dove on the top £35

9. A small sceptre of iron cased in silver gilt with a fleur-de-lys at the top £2 10s

10. Two sceptres, one with the upper end gold and the lower silver set with precious stones, the other silver-gilt with a dove £65 16s 10½d

11. A silver-gilt spoon 16s

12. Gold from the tassels of the liver-coloured robe together with a gold neck button from a coat and some pearls £13

13. A pair of silver-gilt spurs set with 'slight stones' £1 13s 4d[89]

On 9 August 1649 all these items were ordered to be delivered to the trustees who had care of the fate of the royal goods, 'who are to cause the same to be totally broken, and that they melt down the Gold and silver there, and to sell the Jewels for the best Advantage of the Commonwealth, and to take the like care of those that are in the Tower'. Virtually everything on this list was sent to the Mint and the jewels sold. The ivory sceptre was sold to one of the royal creditors, Philip Lavender, the regal to one Edward Miller or Milner and the spoon to Clement Kynnersley, Yeoman of the Removing Wardrobe to Charles I and Wardrobe Keeper under Parliament and the Protector. The last was the solitary object to resurface at the Restoration.

The phrase 'to take the like care of those that are in the Tower' refers to the personal regalia and those again are worth listing as they vanish:

1. The imperial crown as recorded in Mytens's portrait of Charles I £1,110
2. The queen's gold crown set with jewels £338 3s 4d
3. A small crown, found in an iron chest, set with jewels £431 16s 8d
4. The orb £57 10s
5. The two Coronation bracelets set with rubies and pearls totalling £36
6. Two sceptres £60[90]

Order following order had been sent to the Clerk of the Jewel House to surrender what was in his charge, but they were 'not obeyed'. Eventually in the autumn of 1649 the 'Trustees of Parl. broake into the Jewel-house and took away these three crowns, 2 Scept[res], bracelets, globe, &c., and secured all other things'. The order was that they should be 'totallie broken and defaced' at the Mint and the gold and silver from them turned into coin. The instruction to mint them reflected a real fear that if made into anything else identifiable they were in danger of becoming royalist relics.

In retrospect royalist apologists were able to cast Charles I's Coronation in a prophetic light. The text chosen by the Bishop of Carlisle, 'Be faithful unto death and I will give you the crown of life' (Revelation 2: 10), was seen as such. So too was the king's decision to wear white – the colour of innocency – for the anointing deemed equally anticipatory of the martyrdom to come. It was forgotten that this was no innovation, for his father had worn the same.[91] After his execution, what need had Charles of an earthly crown when a heavenly one now beckoned? And in the *Eikon Basilike*, William Marshall's celebrated engraving of Charles as the Martyr King presents us with a visual ascent through three crowns:

A royal saint. The ultimate apotheosis in an ascent for the martyred Charles I from the earthly crown at his feet to one of stars, engraving, 1649

The Explanation of the EMBLEME.

Ponderibus *genus omne mali, probriq; gravatus,*
Vixq; *ferenda ferens,* Palma ut Depressa, *resurgo.*

Ac, *velut undarum* Fluctús Ventiq;, *furorem*
Irati Populi Rupes immota repello.
Clarior è tenebris, *cœlestis stella, corusco.*
(Victor et æternùm-felici pace *triumpho.*

Auro Fulgentem *rutilo gemmisq; micantem,*
At curis Gravidam *spernendo* calco Coronam.

pinosam, *at ferri facilem, quo Spes mea,* Christi
Auxilio, Nobis *non est* tractare *molestum.*

Eternam, *fixis fidei, sempérq;-*beatam
In Cœlos *oculis* Specto, Nobisq; *paratam.*

uod Vanum est, *sperno; quod* Christi Gratia *præbet*
Amplecti *studium est:* Virtutis Gloria *merces.*

Though clogg'd with weights of miseries
Palm-like Depress'd, I higher rise.

And as th'unmoved Rock out-brave's
The boistrous Windes and rageing waves:
So triumph I. And shine more bright
In sad Affliction's Darksom night.

That Splendid, but yet toilsom Crown
Regardlessly I trample down.

With joie I take this Crown of thorn,
Though sharp, yet easie to be born.

That heav'nlie Crown, already mine,
I View with eies of Faith divine.

I slight vain things; and do embrace
Glorie, the just reward of Grace.

Τὸ Χρῖ ὀδὲν ἠδίκησε τὴν πόλιν, ὀδὲ τὸ Κάτωσα.

G.D.

That Splendid, but yet toilsom Crown
Regardlessly I trample down:
With joie I take this Crown of thorn,
Though sharp, yet easie to be born.
That heav'nlie Crown, already mine,
I view with eies of Faith divine.

Let the historian of the seemingly vanquished Church of England have the last word. Thomas Fuller in 1655 published a very full account of Charles I's Coronation and gave his readers the reason why: 'I have insisted the longer on this subject moved thereunto by this consideration, that if it be the last solemnity performed on an English king in this kind, posterity will conceive my pains well bestowed, because on the last. But if hereafter divine providence shall assign England another king, though the transactions herein be not wholly providential, something of state may be chosen out grateful for imitation.'[92] And so it proved to be.

7

From Reaction to Revolution

A T ABOUT TEN O CLOCK on the morning of 13 February 1689, which happened to be Ash Wednesday, a great procession made its way from the Palace of Westminster to the Whitehall Banqueting House. Some rode in carriages, others were on horseback, some even arrived on foot. What united them, whether they were lords spiritual or temporal or members of the Commons, was that they were all part of what is known as a Convention Parliament, that is, one not summoned by the crown but of the kind which had voted to bring back the king in 1660. The work of this one, however, was very different, for it was to get rid of a king and bring in another of its own choosing. And this was achieved by means of an act of invented ceremony, in fact, the single event which transformed the coronation as radically as had the Reformation a century before. It can, indeed, be argued that it gave the ancient rite new purpose and relevance.

On entering the Banqueting House the delegation was confronted at the far end with a dais and canopy beneath which sat the Dutch Stadtholder, William of Orange, side by side with his English wife, James II's daughter, Mary. The delegates parted on arrival, the Lords to the right and the Commons to the left, thus forming an avenue up which advanced a procession, headed by the Usher of the Black Rod and the Speakers of both Houses, which paused en route to make three deep obeisances to the enthroned couple. The Speaker of the Lords requested permission to present the declaration of both Houses, which was read by the Deputy Clerk of Parliament. What was read out combined what is known as the Declaration of Rights with the offer of the crown to William and Mary, although the executive power was to

Opposite Charles II enthroned wearing the re-created Regalia, painting 1660s or 1670s

De Afhaalinge van de Coninglyke Cieraden uyt d...

haer Maÿ.t gaen met de Barge na Wesmin.r hall B. their Maÿ.tis King Barge to Westminster hall

De Salvinge D ÿe Anoitment

Koninglyke festyn in Westminster holl G. Kingly Banquet in Westminster hall

Romyn de Hooghe fecit. Hók delin. Adsiviun...

Scenes from the Coronation
of William III and Mary II,
1689, Dutch engraving,
c.1689

reside only in the former. Mary signified her acceptance of what was offered with a little curtsy while William rose and briefly spoke, accepting both the crown and implicitly those things which were contained in the Declaration that were not as yet an Act of Parliament. Immediately there were shouts of joy both within the Banqueting House and also without, and the heralds left forthwith to proclaim William III and Mary II.

This ceremony was almost certainly devised by the same men who had composed the Declaration. It was designed to cast the occasion as a joyous one expressive of the will of the nation. That was far from the truth. The House of Lords had, in fact, usurped the role of the non-existent Privy Council, ordering a proclamation 'in the usual manner and at the usual places accustomed on like occasions'. In reality only 35 out of a potential 153 peers and only three out of 35 bishops actually took part in the event.[1]

It was one of huge importance, for it signalled the demise of prerogative kingship and the acceptance by the monarchy that henceforth the crown would be subject to the laws as made by Parliament. In effect it was the end of mystic kingship by Divine Right. Not that that fact was exactly spelt out, but the curtain was slowly descending on the attempt in 1660 and after to put the clock back to 1642. It is fascinating how such an archaic ritual as the Coronation was able to accommodate so radical a change, one which seemingly eroded its very purpose as envisaged by a king like Charles I. In 1689 the Coronation took up the role it was to play so often, of papering over the cracks of a dramatic political change with the myth of continuity.

What is so striking about the last four Stuart Coronations is that on the surface they would seem to be clones of each other. Certainly that is true, as we shall see, of much of the ritual, the robes and decorations of both Palace and Abbey. But beneath this surface things were very different, for in them we make a voyage from kingship as construed in the world of Divine Right, with its relationship to late Renaissance hermetic and magical cosmology, to a form of kingship constructed as part of a constitution in which Parliament and not the king was sovereign (albeit much of the royal prerogative power was left intact), a schema more fully in accord with the new mechanistic universe of the post-Newtonian age into which we are now about to enter.

There was virtually a twenty-year gulf between 1642, when civil war broke out, and 1661, when Charles II was crowned. The war had been horrendous, ending in the king's execution, followed first by the years of the Commonwealth and then by those of the Protectorship of Oliver Cromwell. As the Protectorate disintegrated after Cromwell's death there began a steady flow of literature presenting republicanism as an un-English activity and its adoption as the major source of the country's woes. The sigh of relief at the restoration of Charles Stuart was an audible one. But nothing could obliterate what had been done and said during those years, which meant that in the long run the clock could never actually fully be put back. Viewed in retrospect, the Restoration monarchy was as failed a concept as the republic and the Protectorship that had preceded it. But in its initial phases that was by no means apparent amidst a spontaneous surge of popular acclaim which heralded what on the surface was a return to mystic kingship.[2]

Those who looked on at the series of great spectacles which unfolded during those opening years did not see a swarthy six-footer with brown eyes and a sensuous lip, but a martyr's son, the living embodiment of some spiritual, historical or mythological analogue. Charles to them was Jove, Neptune, the Sun, Moses, Aeneas, Apollo, Christ, St Paul; and every single event in his life, from the star which had appeared at his birth to his hiding in an oak tree to escape after the battle of Worcester, was charged with significance and expressive of divine intervention.[3] But in reality, the Restoration came at a pivotal point in the make-up of the educated mind. The old world of correspondences between the celestial and sublunar worlds was still in place for the vast majority of the population. Natural phenomena, like the violent thunderstorm which immediately followed Charles II's Coronation feast, were seen as cosmic messages. But the Restoration, in fact, signalled the arrival of the empiricists, those inquirers into the natural world who looked back to Francis Bacon and who, within a few years, would be members of the Royal Society. These were the men who in the long term were to blast away the world of hermetic mystery and replace it, under Newton's aegis, with the mechanistic universe of the Enlightenment age. People who had that kind of mind-set were already in evidence in 1661. Samuel Pepys, the diarist, was one of them. No mystical haze pervades his perception of the world around him. He saw the Coronation first and foremost as a dazzling spectacle and no more than that, and as for the storm: 'Strange it is, to think that those two days have held up fair till now that all is done and the King gone out of the hall; and then it fell a-raining and thundering and lightening as I have not seen it do for some years – which people did take great notice of God's blessing of the work of those two days – which is a foolery, to take much notice of such things.'[4] George Morley, the bishop who preached on that occasion, certainly did not subscribe to Pepys's dismissal. For Morley, the shouts of acclamation and joy which punctuated the Coronation culminated in those which came 'even from Heaven itself'.[5] Men like Pepys would have been in a minority in 1661. John Evelyn's view was very different, casting the Restoration as an event cosmic in its magnitude. 'Let it be a new year, a new Aera to all future Generations, as it is the beginning of this, and of that immense Platonick Revolution.'[6] Charles II was universally portrayed as the wandering Aeneas of Virgil's epic, the *Aeneid*, who returned to a London identified as Nova Roma to reign over an expanding empire. Everything on his arrival was done to put the clock back. Touching for scrofula was revived. This ritual provides us with a measure of the rise and fall of magical monarchy during the last decades of the seventeenth century. From May 1660, when it was officially revived, till September 1664, Charles touched 23,000 persons. At the close of the reign he was touching just over six thousand annually, a reflection of the fact that he was the most successful miracle-working king ever to sit on the English throne. His brother also continued to attract large numbers but, being Catholic, made the mistake of reinstating the ancient pre-Reformation liturgy with the prayers in Latin, invocations to the Virgin and saints and signing the sufferer with the sign of the cross. This began to discredit the rite within the eyes of his Protestant subjects. The accession of a Dutch Calvinist in 1688/9 further eroded the tradition, because William III refused point-blank to do it. In 1703 it was revived in simplified form for Anne who performed it last on 27 April 1714. The Hanoverians were never to claim the magical powers to heal.

Marc Bloch in his magisterial history of this phenomenon explains how the exiled Stuarts continued the rite and, indeed, how people came over from England to the Jacobite court in order to be touched. The practice was to continue in the Stuart line until the death of the Cardinal of York, 'Henry IX', in 1807. This shows that in England it was one thing not to perform the rite, but quite another to lose faith in it. Although Enlightenment rationalists like Hume could dismiss it as being 'attended by ridicule in the eyes of all men of understanding', the populace did not lose its belief in the therapeutic powers of the monarchy for many a long day. Although touching had ceased, its healing power was now transferred to the coinage and regal relics, a superstition which lasted into the Victorian period.[7]

All of this is important to grasp as a background to the survival and reinvigoration of the Coronation, which was after all a mega magical rite. Why in fact did this happen? There was no violent attack on the rite, nor did William III refuse to take part in it. The key resides in the Revolution of 1688/9 when Charles II's brother, James II, was disposed of and replaced by his daughter and son-in-law. That event precipitated the rewriting of the Coronation oath in which the joint sovereigns acknowledged that they were below and not above the law as made by Parliament, and also declared their allegiance to the Established Church. In this way the Coronation, an archaic rite, was to become one of the foundation stones of the modern state.

How did this come about? In spite of the return of mystical kingship, the Stuarts were in the long run to fail in their bid, in the person of James II, to become absolute, with the royal prerogative power as the sovereign one in the state (Divine Right and absolutism are two separate concepts, the one not necessarily implying the other). That failure in effect nullified their theory of divine hereditary right. On the Continent during the sixteenth and seventeenth centuries, other crowns were successful in making themselves absolute and the embodiment of the state, as in Louis XIV's *L'état c'est moi*. In the medieval period both continental and English monarchs had sworn an oath administered by the Church, but in the case of continental rulers that oath had gradually been reduced to only a moral and religious dimension. In sharp contrast, in England, owing to the rise of Parliament, something very different occurred, for Parliament gave a new vigour to the idea that the crown was subject to the law and that the king owed duties to his subjects. What happened in 1688/9 was to spell all of this out first in the Bill of Rights (1689) and, later, in the Act of Settlement (1701).

Charles II touching for scrofula, engraving, 1684

That this would happen could not have been forecast during the reign of Charles II, apart from the crisis of the early 1680s when attempts were made to exclude his Catholic brother from succession to the throne. Nonetheless, the Exclusion controversy not only established that the crown was hereditary and not elective, but it also established that Parliament potentially had the power to determine to whom the crown could descend if events went in a wrong direction. In that way Parliament was extending its powers from the basis it had in the fourteenth and fifteenth centuries when it had legalised the accession of rulers such as Henry VII who had won the crown on the battlefield.[8] This issue arose once again after the accession of James II, for he managed to alienate a substantial proportion of both emergent political parties, Whig and Tory. To them his actions indicated an intention to Catholicise the country (an embassy was sent to the pope), destroy Parliament, violate ancient law and custom, weaken local government in both the shires and boroughs and create a centralised absolutist state with the aid of a standing army. As early as 1686 his son-in-law, William of Orange, had been urged to invade but it was only in December 1687, after James's queen, Mary of Modena, was known to be pregnant, that the need for action was seen as urgent. In May 1688 William agreed to come with an army and a month later the Old Pretender was born. On 5 November William landed at Torbay and the king fled, was captured, and then was allowed to flee again.[9]

This was not the first occasion in the country's history when what was a far from straightforward political scene had to be endowed with some kind of legitimacy. But in 1688/9 this could not be achieved by the kind of out-and-out usurpation of 1399. At the Restoration, Parliament was the only mechanism by which the conflicting groups could reach some kind of accommodation. What happened is best described as being the work of reluctant revolutionaries. On 22 January 1689 a Convention Parliament convened and six days later embarked on the great debate which squared the circle of one king being got rid of and another brought in. The fiction that carried the day was that James II had 'abdicated' and therefore the throne was 'vacant'.

On the following day, 29 January, came the debate which led to the Declaration of Rights. A motion was carried that it was 'inconsistent with the safety and welfare of the Protestant kingdom, to be governed by a Popish Prince'. But it did not end with the prompt offering of the crown to William and Mary. Thanks to a small group within the Commons, the offer of the crown was to be contingent upon certain conditions. These were compiled by a committee of 39 who were to list 'such things as are absolutely necessary for securing the laws and liberties of the realm'. The result was a written declaration in which certain rights were claimed, several of which, far from being ancient, were quite new. The Declaration of Rights framed what were in essence the principles of constitutional monarchy in a combination of the settlement of the crown with a statement of rights. It was a victory for those who wanted to change not merely the king but kingship itself. The event was a watershed in the political and constitutional history not only of England but also of Europe.[10]

THE CORONATION OATH REWRITTEN

In essence, 1688/9 threw up previously unresolved constitutional issues which had gone into abeyance in 1660, in particular those surrounding the meaning of the Coronation oath which bound the ruler to observe the laws of St Edward and those which Parliament in the future would make (this was the radical interpretation of *quas vulgus elegerit*). The interpretation of the oath had resurfaced in the 1680s as a consequence of the Exclusion crisis when the Whig position was neatly encapsulated in the striking image which prefaced Edward Cooke's *Argumentum Antinormannicum* (1682). In the background William the Conqueror can be seen winning the battle of Hastings, while in the foreground Britannia bestows upon him a sceptre and a document inscribed 'St Edward's Laws'. The text explains that after William had consented to observe the ancient constitution he took the Coronation oath by which he vowed to rule with justice and avoid 'Absolute or Despotical Power' and 'to observe and keep the Sacred Laws of St Edward'.

Most chroniclers followed this account of the aftermath of 1066, stating that one of the king's first acts had been to codify and confirm the laws of Edward the Confessor. In and after the twelfth century several men set out to give some kind of text to these laws. In 1688 John Petyt, who looked after the Tower records, assisted the House of Lords to define what was happening in terms of an historical perspective. Petyt made out a case for the people's right to depose and to elect a new sovereign based on his assertion that the original contract between the king and his subjects was in the Coronation oath, and that James II had violated this by failing to keep faith with St Edward's laws and therefore with the sacrosanct ancient constitution. In this way he managed to cast the events of 1688/9 as another defining moment in the country's history comparable to 1066 when the nation's ancient constitution, traceable in its eyes back to Saxon times, was challenged but triumphantly reasserted.

The irony is that when it actually came to rewriting the Coronation oath, any reference to the laws of St Edward vanished. In this again we witness the intellectual tensions between two different worlds of thought. The oath was to jettison any reference to history in favour of following John Locke's view that the ultimate guarantee of protection against any sovereign no longer lay in appeals to ancient custom but to the principles of nature and reason, both of which were eternal as they stood outside the confines of history. So the historical mythology central to earlier ages was moulded into the thought context of the new age. And yet more remarkable, it was to be embedded in a medieval ritual.[11]

In 1689 this essentially Whig reading of the Coronation oath provided a way out of a major political crisis. It offered to Parliament a way to get rid of James II, arguing that as he had violated his Coronation oath he had therefore ceased to be king, although the government as such had not been dissolved. What James had done had precipitated an 'abdication and vacancy' which Parliament was free to fill. On 25 February 1689 a committee of 39 was set up to examine the oath. Only nine were Tories, the rest being Whigs, so that it was inevitable that the Whigs' interpretation of the oath was the premise from which the committee moved. What was transacted, far from reducing the Coronation to an insubstantial pageant from another age long since gone, put at its heart that which was to be the foundation stone of the post-1688/9 state. Those involved in the revision of the oath were most concerned that there should never be a repetition of recent events. One of them, indeed, categorised the oath as the 'very touch-stone and symbol of your Government', and in its revised form that was to be true. The committee went on to rewrite two sections of the traditional oath, one relating to law and the other to religion. Both were embodied in a statute which signalled the demise of all the old forms of the oath, spelling out that the king was now definitely subject

William I receives the
ancient laws from Britannia
from Edward Cooke's
*Argumentum
Antinormannicum,*
engraving, 1682

to the law of Parliament. He was to swear to govern 'the people of England and the dominions thereunto belonging, according to the statutes in parliament agreed on, and the laws and customs of the same'. In this turn of phrase the American colonies ('the dominions') were gathered in simultaneously with the laws of St Edward vanishing. It also simplified the primacy of statute law over custom or common law and made it clear that in this sphere the royal prerogative was abrogated, no longer having power either to grant or rescind it. The royal powers of pardon were left intact.

In spite of the preponderance of Whigs on the committee, the result was a happy consensus. It was equally to be so in the matter of religion where the existing oath remained even in translation essentially pre-Reformation, with terms like 'Holy Church'. At last it was Protestantised: 'Will you to the utmost of Your Power Maintain . . . the Protestant Reformed Religion Established by Law.' Those last three words signified a victory for the Tories, making a clear reference to the Church of England, but not at the expense of alienating the Dissenting communities. It also sent a firm message that the anointing and crowning of a Dutch Calvinist prince as King of England would open no doors to the toleration of Dissent.

On 25 March this recasting of the Coronation oath was carried by 188 votes to 149, not so very far off a split down the middle. Those who were opposed were fully cognisant of its implications for kingship. Across country, too, there was widespread unease at a lawful king being displaced and also at the violation of the oath of allegiance taken to James II and the hereditary succession. None of this was in fact to go away, as the Jacobite cause was to live on well into the Enlightenment century.[12]

We can wind up the story with the Act of Settlement (1701). By it the succession to the throne, after the deaths of William and his sister-in-law and of any children they might have, was to be the Protestant Hanoverian line in the form of the descendants of James I's daughter, Elizabeth, Queen of Bohemia. In that year the crown would have passed to her daughter, Sophia, Electress of Hanover, but, by 1714, it was to go to her son, the future George I. Whoever inherited the English crown was now required 'to joyn in communion with the Church of England as by Law established', and further was called upon to make a declaration during the Coronation against the doctrine of transubstantiation. The first occasion when that actually was inserted into the ceremony was in 1702. It was introduced immediately after the sermon and before the oath. It was so violently anti-Catholic that it ought to be quoted at least in part.

> I, Anne, by the Grace of God, Queen of England, Scotland, France, and Ireland, Defender of the Faith, &c, do solemnly and sincerely in the presence of God profess, testifie, and declare, that I do believe that in the sacrament of the Lord's Supper there is not any Transubstantiation of the elements of bread and wine into the body and blood of Christ, at or after the consecration thereof by any person whatsoever. 2 That the invocation or adoration of the Virgin Mary, or any other saint, and the sacrifice of the mass, as they are now used in the Church of Rome, are superstitious and idolatrous . . .

Nor did the Act end there, for there were provisions 'for the further limitation of the Crown and better securing the Rights and Liberties of the Subject'. These provisions, seemingly intrusive, actually turned out to have little if any effect.[13]

So it was that even with the clipping of regal power in 1688/9 the powers of the crown, in fact, remained very considerable, even if the old magic was progressively discounted. The Hanoverians when they came had little upon which to build. George I ascended the throne in 1714 neither by Divine Right, nor even by popular choice, but as a consequence of the Act of Settlement. In the long run, however, this worked in favour of the survival of the monarchy into a new age.

PUTTING BACK THE CLOCK

The Coronation of Charles II was a monument to one man, Sir Edward Walker.[14] He was 48 in 1660, and had begun his career in the service of the Earl Marshal, Thomas Howard, Earl of Arundel, in the 1630s. It was through Arundel that Walker gained entry to the College of Arms, first as a pursuivant and later as Chester Herald. From there he graduated to royal service and in 1642, on the outbreak of civil war, became secretary-at-war to the king. Indeed, we have a portrait of him in this role with his royal master in the National Portrait Gallery. Walker was close to Charles I and followed his son into exile. Not everyone, however, was so enamoured of him. Edward Hyde, soon to be ennobled as Earl of Clarendon, and Sir Edward Nicholas, secretary of state, had a very different opinion of him. 'Sir Edward Walker,' the latter wrote, 'is a very importunate, ambitious, and foolish man, that studies nothing but his own ends . . .'

In 1660 Walker was made one of the clerks of the Council and given the task of organising the Coronation. Walker, it is to be remembered, had never actually seen one as he was only fourteen in 1626. Add to that the fact that there had been no state entry since 1604 and no Coronation feast since 1559. What we witness is a man putting together something from manuscripts and other texts to which he had access. They at least in some instances were pretty full, but the problem of the destroyed regalia and vestments was a serious one, for no visual records existed of what the items in Westminster Abbey actually looked like. All Walker seemingly worked from was the 1605 indenture which listed the items handed over by Lancelot Andrewes to his successor as dean.[15] What is certain is that the overall drive to put the clock back ensured that from the outset 1661 was to be a rerun of 1626. That desire is caught in a manuscript copy of Charles I's Coronation annotated by Walker for Charles II with the names of those who should perform this or that service in 1661.[16] It is also caught in his delivery of another copy of the formulary for 1626, 'as it was vsed at his late Majesties Coronation', listing the various clerics required for the present one and what they did.[17] From the outset, therefore, the ceremony was to be an essay in antiquarian endeavour. We are fortunate in that Walker wrote an account of all of this in *The Preparations for His Majesties Coronation*. It is a document which exists in a number of copies and was eventually, in 1820, printed.[18] In it Walker writes how he had examined accounts of previous Coronations, 'And by Comparing them together . . .' he had been able to decide what should be done at this one, the regalia that would be required and all the other preparations, including those for staging the feast as it was 'anciently disposed'. The report he presented to the committee set up to deal with the Coronation represents one long litany of decisions which had to be made: whether Charles was to make a state entry into London or not, 'for much depends hereupon', whether, if he had a state entry, he was to ride hatted or bareheaded, what was to be the route to Westminster Palace, what was and was not to be carried in the procession to the Abbey, whether peers were to wear their coronets in the king's presence or not. And so it runs on. This is an essay in looking backwards. Walker writes of the robes being 'according to antient presidents', and this is echoed in other sources. The Wardrobe Accounts, for example, refer to the making of four copes in January 1661 'embroydered according to the Antient Manner',[19] and Rugg in his *Diurnal* describes the arrival of the Champion at the feast as 'according to the old custome'.[20]

The crucial meeting of the Coronation Committee occurred on 22 October 1660. It was the one at which all the major decisions were taken. Yes, there was to be a state entry, the king would go from Whitehall to Westminster by water, the ceremony was to be in the vernacular and approval was given to the designs presented for the regalia.[21] The keen interest of Charles II in all of this is caught in payments for calico to 'cutt out Patterns of severall things for his Majestie to view'.[22] This means that the various vestments must have been tried on in what, in the terms of a modern couture house, was a series of toiles. What we do not know is what Charles thought of them or indeed whether he altered anything.

The regalia presented a really major problem.[23] Walker begins his account of their recreation with this memorable passage: 'And because through the Rapine of the late vnhappy times, all the Royall Ornaments & Regalia ... were taken away, sold & destroyed, the Committee mett divers times, not only to direct the makeing such Royall Ornaments & Regalia, but even to settle the forme and fashion of each particular . . .'[24]

Walker's *Preparations* includes drawings of both the regalia and vestments,[25] although whether any of them resembled anything worn in 1626 must remain speculative. Much clearly puzzled him. Even when the king decided in favour of a garment through which he could be anointed, Walker was to write: 'quere the lyning, length, & how to be fastened, & by whom those Ornaments to be provided'.[26] The answer to that was the Jewel House for metalwork and the Great Wardrobe for the vestments. In the case of the crowns he lists: 'Two crownes the one called St Edwards Crowne, & another Imperiall Crowne to be putt on after the Coronacion, One wherof is already made.' The one already made must have been the imperial crown, which still exists today but bears no resemblance to the old imperial crown which we have already glimpsed in Mytens's portrait of Charles II's father. Walker goes on to list the sceptre with the dove, a long sceptre with a spike at the bottom (St Edward's staff), the ball with a cross (the orb), the spurs, the ring with a ruby, the bracelets, the chalice and paten, the eagle of gold (the

Ampulla), the long gilt spoon, two pointed swords and a third, Curtana. There is no indication that the last four items, in fact, existed and had survived. Having listed all this on the basis of the 1605 indenture, he concludes that two crowns were definitely needed, and the sceptre with the steel spike 'which is that which (I conceive) is called St Edwards Staffe', and also the one with the dove. Over the sceptre with the ball and cross at its summit and the orb, he keeps wondering whether they were not variants of the same thing. Of the sceptre with the cross he writes: 'whether it be the Ball with the Crosse is the question, for I finde great variety in severall Coronations'. He then describes what he has discovered had been held by various monarchs from Henry VI onwards. No conclusion, however, was reached from this mound of material: 'So the question will be whether there shall be 2 or 3 Scepters besides the Ball and Crosse'[27] He was still fretting about this early in February 1661 when he wrote: 'most of them [i.e. the regalia] are provided, Onely the question of whether the Scepter with the Crosse, or St Edwards Staffe should be omitted, in reguard in all late Coronations there is no mention but of 2 Scepters & the Orbe or Ball with Crosse.'[28] In the end the lot was made, posing appalling difficulties about the purpose to which they should be put in the actual ceremony.

Although the majority of the decisions were reached at that October 1660 meeting, certain items were put in hand as early as May. On the twenty-eighth of that month the Venetian resident recorded the making of a crown and sceptre and also ermine-lined robes for the Coronation.[29] If this was what acted as the imperial crown it would explain why it bore no resemblance to the pre-Civil War one. Suddenly also for the first time we have visual records which record the regalia. That is less important for the items which still survive, but more for the vestments which do not. Francis Sandford's richly illustrated account of James II's Coronation is one source, a publication to which I will refer throughout this chapter. As that Coronation was a clone of 1661 its engravings record in effect what was made for Charles II. To those we must add the evidence of the drawings which appear in Walker's *Preparations*. In 1685 the great mantle should have been covered with a rich embroidery of gold eagles, but in the event there was no time and, as in 1661, it was made only of 'a Rich Gold stuff'. The same thing occurred when it came to the armils. We should bear in mind when looking at these pages depicting both the vestments and

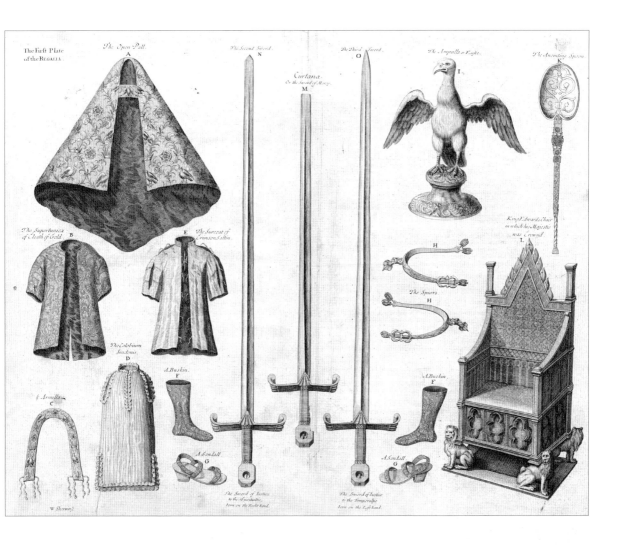

the regalia that the Coronation Committee headed by the king studied every detail 'even to settle the form and fashion of each particular . . .'. When it came to choosing between antiquarian evidence and the demands of contemporary style, the latter always won. What we see could never be anything other than items reflecting the rhythms of the European Baroque.[30]

Money was also tight. Charles II had to have an imperial crown which was worn on occasions like the state opening of Parliament. The result was an impressive diadem set with 890 diamonds, 10 rubies, 18 sapphires, 20 emeralds and 549 pearls. As the crown of St Edward was only ever used once, for the actual crowning, the decision was made to

Opposite St Edward's Staff, 1661

Above The Coronation Chair, vestments and other items of regalia as used in 1685, engraving, 1687

Items from the re-created
Regalia, 1660–1
Top left The Ampulla,
1660–61
Top right The Sceptre with
the Dove, 1661
Centre The Armills, 1660–61
Bottom The Spurs, 1660–61

Opposite The Regalia used at
the Coronation of James II
and Mary of Modena, 1686,
engraving, 1687

The Second Plate of the REGALIA.

St Edward's Crown
with which the
King was Crown'd.
I

The Queens Circle,
which She wore in ye proceeding
to her Coronation.
IV

The Kings Coronation Ring
XII

III

The Crown wherwith
the Queen was Crown'd.
V

The Orbe.

The Crown of State
which the King wore in his
Return to Westminster Hall.
II

The Queens Coronation Ring
XIII

The Rich Crown
which the Queen wore in her
return to Westminster Hall.
VI

fill a frame with hired gem stones, and this continued until 1821. We are fortunate, for not only do most of the items still survive, but we have two stunning visual records of them. One is a still life painted in the 1670s by an unknown artist, now in the Museum of London. The other is John Michael Wright's icon of the king which was painted for the man who provided the regalia, Sir Robert Vyner.[31] Recent scholarship dates the portrait to the 1670s, and in it we can see St Edward's crown along with the orb in the king's left hand and the sceptre with the ball and cross in his right.

Little more was to be added in the seventeenth century, apart from a corresponding set of regalia for a queen prompted by the Coronation

FROM REACTION TO REVOLUTION   293

Above St Edward's Crown,
1661, but with later additions
Right The Orb, 1661

Opposite Detail of St
Edward's Crown

The 1661 Regalia, painting 1670s

of Mary of Modena in 1685, which was reused four years later for Mary II. The Coronation of James II's queen called for two crowns and two sceptres, one crown being the traditional jewelled circlet worn in the procession to the Abbey, and the other that used for the actual crowning. John Evelyn records seeing a drawing of this in May 1685 when he dined with Hyde, Earl of Clarendon: 'There was shew'd a dragt of the exact shape and dimensions of the Crowne the Queen had been crown'd withall, together with the Jewells and Pearles, their weight and value, which amounted to 10065 pounds sterling, an immense summ ...'[32] The crown actually cost £35,000 and the stones were all hired ones.[33]

In this way the crown jewels which we know today were recreated.

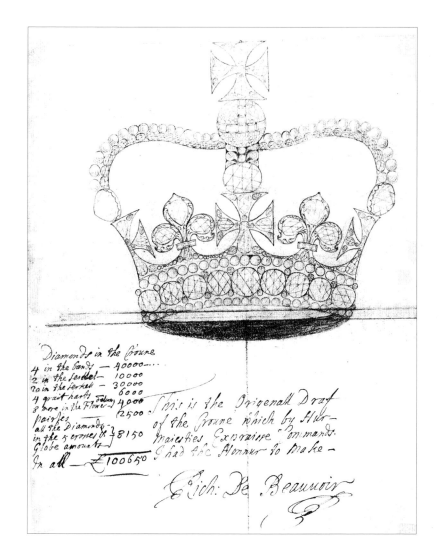

Diamonds in the Croune
4 in the bands — 40000...·
2 in the settell — 10000
20 in the terkell — 30000
4 great harts   — 6000
8 more in the Flower} 4000
pairses ———— 12500
all the Diamonds
in the 5 crones & 8150
Globe amounts—
In all —— £100650

This is the Origenall Draf
of the Croune which by Her—
Maiesties Exppraisse Commands
I had the Honnur to Make —

Rich: De Beauuoir

Design for Mary of
Modena's crown, drawing,
1685

Looking at them it is difficult to believe that they bear any resemblance
in style to those which existed before the Civil War, although certainly
there were attempts to recapture their iconography. In this sense 1661
was, in effect, a fresh start. Nor was the Abbey to reassert its ancient
right to be custodian of the regalia. The usual division between the
Coronation regalia and the king's personal regalia in the matter of
where they were kept, ceased, and both were housed within the Jewel
House in the Tower of London. Apart from their evacuation during the
Second World War they have remained there ever since.

Mary of Modena's Diadem,
1685

One of the most celebrated documents marking the Restoration is
the paper generally known as the 'Advice' given by William
Cavendish, Duke of Newcastle, to Charles II shortly before his
Restoration. Newcastle had been born in the reign of Elizabeth and
was, therefore, fully cognisant of court life before the great cata-
clysm. For a time also he had been governor to the infant Charles II.
In his 'Advice' there is a twofold thrust, one stressing the importance
of maintaining and restoring order in a state where it had been violated, the other endeavouring to hold up Gloriana's court to the
restored king as a paradigm to emulate. As regards the first,
Newcastle has a great deal to say about the importance of ceremony
in respect of the monarchy. He had realised that fact at an even earlier date, writing to the young prince at the close of the 1630s about
the importance of ceremonial as a weapon of state: 'for what preserves you kings more than ceremony'.

In 1659 when he wrote his words of advice, the topic was forcefully to resurface: 'Seremoney though itt is nothing in itt Self, yett it doth Every thing – for what is a king, more than a subiecte, Butt for seremoney, & order, when that fayles him, hees Ruiened, – therefore your Majestie willbee pleased to keepe itt upp strickly, in your owne, person, & Courte . . . when you appeare, to shew your Selfe Gloryously, to your People; Like a God, for the Holly writt sayes, wee have Calld you Gods . . .'

It is not known whether Charles II even read this document, but it reads for all the world like a text upon which the last state entry into London (although no one in 1661 could have foretold that) was to be based.[34]

This solemn entry with its procession a mile and a half long made visible to its onlookers the reinstatement of the whole regal hierarchy. It set out to dazzle, and to obliterate, if it could, all memory either of the Commonwealth or of the Protectorship. The royalist Sir John Reresby wrote later in his memoirs: 'The triomphall arches, pagiants, musick, made to receive and entertain him and the whole Court and other attendants as he passed were fairer or richer than was ever known upon the like occasion in England . . .'[35]

There had been no royal entry in 1626. In James I's case it had come after the Coronation, which to a great degree muted its impact. It is difficult not think (bearing in mind Newcastle's cult of Gloriana) that those around Charles II would have had in mind the most famous entry of them all, Elizabeth I's in 1559. That saw the birth of a new kind of popular monarchy lived out through street theatre.

Although the decision to make a state entry was taken much earlier, it was not until 19 February that the City was told that there was to be an entry.[36] That was two days after the date for the Coronation had been postponed to 23 April. The City's reaction was that Charles should be received 'with such magnificence as was due and becoming the Majesty of so great a King . . .'. A contribution of £6,000 apiece was levied on the various livery companies, with a further £3,000 apiece being extracted on 1 April.

The entry excited European interest, and there were to be no less than three German and one Italian accounts published. For insular publishing, too, the 1661 entry was a landmark, for it was the only occasion when a festival book equal to any produced on the Continent was published. That this happened was partly the consequence of choosing

John Ogilby to write the scenario.[37] Ogilby had begun his life as a dancing master and teacher and graduated to being Deputy Master of the Revels in Ireland before the Civil War. The outbreak of war left him destitute, but at the Restoration he became the king's cosmographer and printer. In this capacity he was to become a great pioneer of lavishly illustrated books of which *The Entertainment of His Most Excellent Majestie Charles II* . . . was one of the most splendid. In English terms it was a rare instance of the complete text for the entry being printed alongside engravings of the triumphal arches.

Ogilby had secured a patent granting him the exclusive publishing rights on 11 April.[38] Never one to miss a money-making opportunity, he issued his account of the entry in several different guises. The earliest account was rushed through in ten days, an unillustrated guide to the pageants which were already standing in the London streets. His remit was limited to the London entry, which he wrote, and information on what the City of Westminster provided is cursory. When it

Charles II's state entry into London, 1661, painting, c.1661

came to the Coronation itself, he procured the services of Elias Ashmole, Windsor Herald. There was a catch to all of this, as everything had to be submitted to Sir Edward Walker in his role as Garter King of Arms to be approved for publication.[39] Walker was not best pleased that Ogilby had cornered the market because it rendered his own account redundant, so he exercised his powers to the full, deleting his colleague Ashmole's description of the punch-up that had occurred at the Coronation feast, when the royal footmen had attempted to seize the canopy which was the prerogative of the Barons of the Cinque Ports. That this was originally in Ashmole's narrative can be gauged by its appearance in the various manuscript versions.

These were not the only tensions around the 1661 entry, for there were others which involved its designers. Ogilby states somewhat darkly that the arches were 'by Mr Peter Mills, surveyor of the city, and another person, who desirest to have his name concealed'. The drawings for those arches exist in the Royal Institute of British Architects, and there can be no doubt as to the mysterious person's identity. It was Sir Balthasar Gerbier, coloniser, traitor, engineer, projector, secret agent, ambassador, picture collector, miniaturist and one time master of ceremonies to Charles I.[40] That appointment was in 1641, but Gerbier lasted no time at all, disgracing himself. During the Interregnum he further tarnished himself in royalists' eyes because of his proposals for works of art to celebrate the glories of the republic. In 1660 he popped up again, claiming the mastership of ceremonies, only to be suspended from the office at once. To Charles II Gerbier was *persona non grata*, hence the need for concealment.

Nonetheless, he was about the only person capable of undertaking such a project, having designed masques for Charles I's favourite, the Duke of Buckingham. To that can be added the fact that he had been in Antwerp during the period of the preparations for the great entry of the Archduke Ferdinand in 1634. The famous *Pompa Introitus Ferdinandi* designed by Rubens was certainly the visual inspiration of much that was to appear straddling the streets of London in 1661.

As the great day approached, these arches excited huge interest. On 12 April Samuel Pepys wrote: 'then into the City and saw in what forwardness all things are for the Coronacion, which will be very magnificent'.[41] Evelyn similarly wrote of them that they were 'of good invention & architecture'.[42] Such arches and the messages they bore were not so transitory, for they were stand for nearly a year, not being demolished until March 1662.[43] We catch a rare glimpse of how someone at the time read them, in a letter by a certain William Smith: 'The first His Majesty shall encounter is in Leadenhall Street, and it presenteth Anarchy and the confusion which that government brings: the second is erected at the Royal Exchange, and it holds forth Presbytery, and with it the decay of Trade; the third, which is the most sumptuous, stands in Cheapside, relating the Honours due to Hierarchy, and sheweth the restoration of Episcopacy.'[44] The striking thing about this account is that some of the interpretations he places on the arches are difficult to reconcile with what Ogilby says they meant in his published text. But the general drift is clear, a celebration of the restoration of hierarchy. In those terms perhaps the greatest monument of all was to be the enormous procession.

On 22 April the king and his brother, the Duke of York, arrived at the Tower of London by 7 a.m., where there assembled also the peerage, privy councillors and gentlemen together with their servants. By 8 a.m.

everyone else who was to be part of the procession had to be on Tower Hill 'where they shall be placed and disposed by his Majesties Officers of Armes . . . and placed according to their degrees'.[45] Those who took part in it outvied each other in the ostentation of their dress and equipage. Lord Wharton it was who 'exceeded all for dimonds; his horse was set with dimons and pearles and other costly ornements'.[46] Even as an onlooker Pepys was moved to put on his new velvet coat! The route through the streets was railed, and gravelled to prevent the horses slipping. On one side it was lined with members of the livery companies and on the other with the trained bands. There was a strong military presence in 1661, fully reflecting unease about the City's sudden muchvaunted loyalty. The houses along the way were swagged with carpets and tapestries, and the onlookers, Walker records, 'came from all parts of England, & also from fforraigne parts . . .'.[47] Pepys ensconced himself in a house close to the Royal Exchange, 'a good room to ourselfs, with wine and good cake'. His eye was caught by the ladies leaning out of the window opposite: 'One of which, over against us, I took much notice of and spoke of her, which made good sport among us.'[48]

The great procession set off at about 10 a.m. It comprised a thousand people on horseback and an even greater number on foot. The footmen in attendance on the king and the Duke of York alone numbered 600. Walker catches the overwhelming impact it had on those who saw it pass: 'The magnificence of which proceeding, for the richnesse & beauty of the Habitts of his Majestie, the Nobility, & all others, with their Horses & furniture, being so great, as no age hath seene the like in this, or any other Kingdome . . .'.[49] It left Pepys exhausted: 'So glorious was the show with gold and silver, that we were not able to look at it – our eyes at last being so much overcome with it.' Thanks to a painting by Dirk Stoop and the engravings in Ogilby we can recapture some of its splendour.

But what was the City's homage to its sovereign? First, as well it might, it stressed the loyalty to the crown of its citizens. One aspect of the Civil War had been the breakdown of the relationship between the crown and the City, and during the Interregnum London had been a hotbed of subversion, turbulence and political and religious dissent. Now all of this had to be consigned to oblivion as history was rewritten in favour of 'the glorious Restauration of our Sovereign to his Throne, and of us his Subjects to our Laws, Liberties, and Religion, after a dismal Night of Usurpation and oppression'.[50] The fact that the

City was still full of people who were far from happy at the turn of events was adroitly papered over.

The Charles of the entry was the wandering Aeneas, the founder of the Roman Empire, making his entry into his imperial capital of Nova Roma. The legend S.P.Q.L., Senatus populusque Londiniensis, appears no less than four times. Recent history is adjusted to accord with the king as the messianic hero of Virgil's famous Fourth Eclogue, whose birth augurs the return of the golden age. This is late Stuart Augustanism in all its plenitude: 'The City of London ... took the occasion of His Majesties Coronation to express their Joy with greatest Magnificence imagineable ... imitating therein the antient Romanes, who, at the return of their Emperours, created Arches of Marble, which though we, by reason of the shortness of the Time, could not equal in

The entry procession, 1661, engraving, 1662

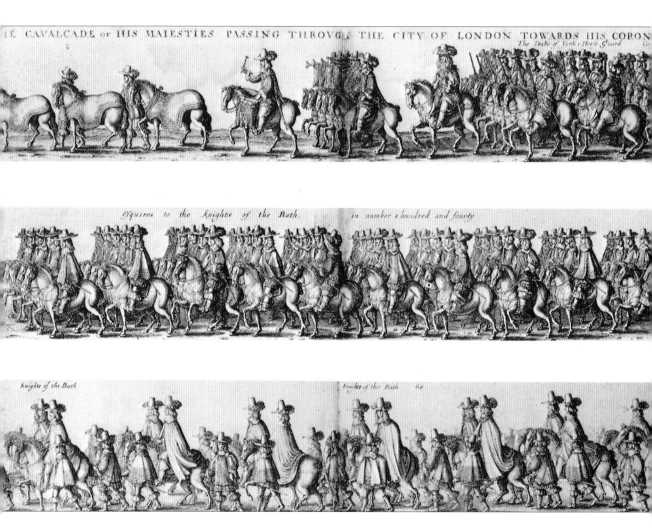

Materials, yet do ours far exceed theirs in Number, and stupendous Proportions.'[51]

There were four arches in all. The first and second acclaimed Charles as the English Augustus whose return had brought golden-age peace both on land and sea. More, both prognosticated further territorial and maritime empire. The third and fourth arches wound up the story with the consequences of this, concord and plenty. The format echoed less that of earlier royal entries and more that of the masques at his father's court, in which the royal presence effected miraculous resolutions and vanquished all evil opposition merely by appearing. Ogilby, like Gerbier, was familiar with the masques, as we know he had actually danced in one. We catch this in action at the first Leadenhall arch. Music struck up the sound of battle and the menacing figure of

Designs for the first and
fourth arches for Charles II's
state entry, 1661, drawings,
*c.*1660–61

Rebellion riding a hydra appeared and challenged the king: 'Stand! Stand! Who'ere You are! this Stage is ours . . .' The figures of Monarchy and Loyalty promptly appear to the sound of an English march accompanying a figure personating Charles II himself on horseback. We are told Usurpation flew at the very sight of him, one of whose hydra heads was a portrait of Oliver Cromwell. Further along the route the River Thames greeted the king with promises of an ever-expanding maritime empire bringing both trade and prosperity, but perhaps the nub of it all was summed up in the verse:

> *Comes not here the King of Peace,*
> *Who, the Stars so long fore-told,*
> *From all Woes should us release,*
> *Converting Iron-times to Gold?*

In these words the Restoration is cast in an apocalyptic light in which Charles becomes both Christ entering Jerusalem and the promised world-ruler, the imperator, of Virgil's Fourth Eclogue ushering in the golden age. Beneath the Augustan glory we can still catch the ethos of an era which had imagined itself to be living through the events of the Book of Revelation.

Sixteen sixty-one was the apogee of the royal entry for sheer extravagance and eulogy. It was also a great musical event, for it included no less than 28 instrumental and two vocal groups totalling over two hundred performers. Much of that involved singers and musicians doubling up and rushing from one part of the route to another further on. The most revolutionary feature were the famous *vingt-quatre violons du Roi* formed in imitation of the same ensemble at the court of Louis XIV. This would have been the first occasion when such an instrumental group had been heard, and it was placed to effect in the Temple of Concord.[52]

There is no record of the king's reaction to the event. Did he have any dialogue with his new subjects? In that matter the young Elizabeth had been as successful and forthcoming as Charles II's grandfather had been stony and indifferent. But we need to turn our attention to why 1661 was the last occasion when there was a ceremonial entry into the City, for James II in 1685 was not to demand one, but in order, so it was written, to appear 'frugal and cautious, and no great Admirer of outward Pomp and Popularity thought it best to save a Charge of at least threescore Thousand Pounds.'[53] Pomp he certainly loved, for the

Coronation is a monument to that, but, when it came to popularity, he may well have been nervous of riding through a City whose Protestantism was evident in its notorious pope-burning processions in the era of the Popish Plot and the Exclusion Crisis. The entry never reappears as a topic. In the case of William and Mary, the rush to crown them would have precluded any possibility of an entry, and in 1702 there is silence on the matter. But then we need to place this into a wider intellectual context. By 1700 the seeing is believing principle, based on the old pre-Newtonian cosmology of correspondences, was going into eclipse. The procession through the London streets, however, was to be rediscovered in the twentieth century in response to a very different socio-political climate.

FOUR CORONATIONS CONSIDERED

Each of these four late Stuart Coronations was an expressions in seemingly immutable historic pageantry of a very different agenda.[54] In 1661 it was the culminating event of a programme designed to re-establish mystical monarchy. That programme had been ongoing from the moment of the king's return in May 1660. It ranged through the reconstruction of court life, both in its secular as well as its religious context, embracing such things as touching for the King's Evil, the re-establishment of the Chapels Royal and their musical tradition, the staging of royal eating in public and the revival of the ceremonies of the Order of the Garter which took place only a few days before the Coronation. Indeed, the Garter was to be central to the apotheosis of the Restoration monarchy, for St George's Day, 23 April, had long been the occasion for popular patriotic celebration. The late Stuarts drew on this, three of them, Charles II, James II and Anne, all choosing to be crowned on that day.

In the case of James II's Coronation, according to Francis Sandford, it was the king's command to do 'All, that Art, Ornament, and Expence could do to the making of the Spectacle Dazzling and Stupendious . . .' Sandford's lavish book celebrating the event, along with a similar publication depicting Lord Castlemaine's embassy to the pope, sit more easily within the context of le Roi Soleil and the absolutism of the court of Versailles than they do in the insular tradition. This time there was a royal consort, Mary of Modena, and the model

for her Coronation went back to Anne of Denmark in 1603. But no amount of dazzle could conceal the major fault-line in this event, the fact that a Catholic king was being crowned by a Protestant archbishop. James naturally had qualms of conscience and, therefore, he asked to have eliminated from the service anything which might compromise him. So the Archbishop of York 'was desired to review the Forms of Divine Service used at former Coronations, and (keeping to the Essentials) to abridge, as much as might be, the extream length thereof . . .'.[55] That was a euphemism for axing the communion service which had been part of every Coronation since time immemorial.

It was promptly to be put back in 1689 for William and Mary as part of what might be described as a Protestantisation of the whole ceremony, which was not even performed on a saint's day or Sunday but midweek. Mary II's view of the Coronation was that it was 'all vanity' and it was Henry Compton, Bishop of London, who had to impress on her its seriousness.[56] In fact, its swift staging made a crucial contribution towards publicly legitimising a new regime and naturalising a Dutch Calvinist prince into the English dynastic tradition. Every effort, however, was made to present the queen as her husband's equal, although politically she was a mere cipher. A second throne, for example, was made for her 'like unto St Edwards Chaire', and she was drawn into as much of the ceremonial as was thought fit, being anointed and crowned simultaneously with her husband and walking as equals together under a single canopy both to and from the Abbey. In spite of

A. The QUEENS Majestie.
B. The Bishop of London.
C. The Bishop of Winchester.
D. The Dutchess of Norfolk.
E. Four Earls Daughters.

F. Sixteen Barons of the Cinque ports.
G. a Lady of the Bed chamber.
H. Two of her Maᵗⁱᵉ women.
I. Gentlemen Pensioners.

the fact that there was what amounted to a three-line whip on all those who had letters calling for their presence by 'reason of their Offices or tenures or otherwise . . . to do any service', only 10 bishops were present and 81 out of a potential 153 lords. Despite all the propaganda around the occasion, including engravings depicting various moments during the service (set in a building which bore no relation to the Abbey), 1689 remains an awkward, untidy affair. This was pageantry in the service of *raison d'état*, and the gaps in the ranks must have been all too apparent at the time. No such haste clouded Anne's Coronation in 1702, which celebrated the accession of an English queen noted for her devotion to the Church of England.

James II and Mary of Modena process to Westminster Abbey, 1685, engraving, 1687

THE GREAT THEATRE

The 1661 Coronation became the template for every one which followed it in terms of the physical arrangements and also of what was worn or the artefacts needed. No alteration, however radical to the rite itself, in fact affected the repetition by the Office of the King's Works or the Great Wardrobe of what was to be done. That was aided throughout this period in terms of continuity by the fact that Sir Christopher Wren was Surveyor for the last three Stuart Coronations and, indeed, also for the first Hanoverian. So they can with ease be considered collectively, thus avoiding pointless repetition.

We are also fortunate that one publication provides us with a hitherto unknown richness of information on practicalities. Details which we have known so little about up until now suddenly spring to life thanks to Lancaster Herald Francis Sandford's *The History of the Coronation of the Most High Most Mighty and Most Excellent Monarch, James II* (1687). That work was commissioned by the king himself at the very first meeting of the Coronation Committee when Sandford was asked along with Gregory King, Rouge Dragon Pursuivant, to compile it. It was to be an exact record and indeed it is, for here, for the very first time, are ground plans and cross-sections

James II and Mary of Modena enthroned, 1685, engraving, 1687

covering both the temporary structures in Westminster Hall and also those in the Abbey, as well as lavish and detailed engravings of the procession, the Coronation itself at crucial moments and the feast, including one of the entrance of the Champion. The book even goes on to include a plate of the great firework display which brought the festival to its close. This volume has already crossed our path in connexion with both the regalia and the vestments. What is astonishing is the king's instruction that the figures should be portraits and, indeed, they are. The order was to 'Express the faces or likeness of such Persons in the Proceeding, particularly Represented . . .'. So we are able to spot Samuel Pepys, in his guise as a Baron of the Cinque Ports, supporting a stave of the royal canopy with its tinkling bells. In this way Sandford's book is a mine of information telling us virtually all that we need to know about the mechanics of a Coronation in the late seventeenth century. To it, however, we should add the two plates which appear in Ogilby's *Entertainment*, one a not altogether satisfactory engraving of the procession in 1661, the second a synoptic view of the Abbey with a simultaneous record of both the crowning and the enthronisation of the king. But as Sandford specifically says that James II's Coronation was a repeat of the arrangements for Charles II, to all intents and purposes the volume also tells us what had been done in 1661.

Everything, of course, began with the proclamation by the heralds and other officers of the new monarch, a procedure which calls for no comment except in the case of what occurred in 1689. William and Mary only became king and queen after the ceremonial in the Whitehall Banqueting House, after which they were proclaimed at four different places in the vicinity of the court and in the City. At Temple Bar a quite bizarre piece of invented pageantry took place. The gate was firmly shut. An officer within inquired, 'Where is King James II?', to which someone without replied, 'He is dead, he is dead, he is dead', which others heard as 'He has abdicated the government.' In such a curious way the reign of William and Mary began.[57]

Every Coronation started with the establishment of a committee in which it was essential to involve the key officers of the household in charge of implementing its practicalities. The heralds as custodians of ceremonial had to be present. The committee for Charles II's Coronation was set up on 26 September 1660, seven months before the event, although the Coronation was originally to have been early in

February.[58] The committee included officers like the Lord High Treasurer on account of cost, the Lord Great Chamberlain who was crucial to so much of the ceremonial, the Master of the Wardrobe on account of the robes and furnishings and the Lord Steward in charge of the royal kitchens and hence the feast. Several more were involved, but any four of them could form a quorum.

We get a vivid picture of these meetings in progress in 1685 from Sandford who describes how the Clerk of the Great Wardrobe had brought with him 'the Books of Record of the said Office, an Account of the Necessaries to be provided out of the Great Wardrobe for the day of the Coronation . . .'. This he read aloud to the committee. The heralds, too, arrived armed 'with their Books and Records of former Coronations'.[59] And in their case, too, the accounts of those of James I, Charles I and Charles II were read to the committee. The hereditary Earl Marshal, the Duke of Norfolk, was also crucial to any planning, for he was not only the man in charge of the heralds but the person who presented the scheme for the whole occasion. Any Coronation called for several household departments to work in unison, often against the clock, as was certainly the case for the Coronation of Queen Anne when Wardrobe workmen were forced to labour day and night to meet the deadline.[60]

The heralds, as custodians and record-keepers of previous Coronations, bitterly resented being passed over. But this is what happened in 1689, and it evoked the following somewhat acerbic record:

> If there be any thing in the aforesaid Ceremonials omitted, or not performed according to former Precedents, the officers of Arms are not to be blamed, since the Lords of the Committee for the Coronation conferred with Mr. Negus Secretary to his Grace the Duke of Norfolke Earle Marshal of England, and very little with them, the said Mr. Negus pretending they were to receive their Orders from the Earle Marshall, whereas at other Coronations, they constantly attended the Lords of Committee till all matters relating to the Coronation were settled and approved . . .'[61]

The result of this is a considerable variation between the heralds' and other accounts of the event. The heralds repeat in their version what happened in 1685, and where variations occurred, as with the presentation of the Bible, they misplace them in the sequence. A milestone though 1689 was, as a Coronation it appears in many ways to have been a botched job.

Another task of the Coronation Committee was to set up the Court of Claims. That for Charles II was headed by Lord Hyde, the Lord Chancellor, and convened on 26 March in the Painted Chamber of the Palace of Westminster.[62] James II's sat on 24 March and wound up its work on 9 April. Sandford includes a very full record of all the claims and decisions made.[63] There appear such old favourites as the presentation to the king of 'a Mess of Gerout or Grout' by the owner of the manor of Bardolf in Addington in Surrey, or 'To find the King a Right Hand Glove, and to support the Kings Right Arm, while he holds the Scepter' by the lord of the manor of Worksop in Nottinghamshire. The court was an archaic survival, although it could still, as in the past, offer opportunities for useful acts of patronage. In 1689, for instance, the Lord Mayor petitioned to act as chief butler both to William and Mary. It was granted, thus doubling his fee of a gold cup.

Far more opportunities, in fact, existed in what became an institutionalised distribution of Coronation honours. Much was made of that in 1661 when six earls and the same number of barons were created by the king in the Banqueting House. This was staged as a great spectacle, with each person to be ennobled accompanied by other peers bearing their robes and insignia. They made three obeisances en route to the king enthroned in state, then the patent of nobility was presented by the Garter King of Arms to the Lord Chamberlain, by him to the king, and by the king to the secretary of state who read it aloud and returned it to the king, who gave it to the person created. Evelyn catches the scene: '. . . then were they robed, their Coronets & Collers put on by his Majestie, then were they placed in rank on both sides of the State & Throne: but the Barons put of their caps & circles and held them in their hands, The Earles keeping on their Coronets as Cousins to the King.'[64]

Such a distribution of honours bolstered the incoming regime. In 1689 Anne's difficult husband, Prince George of Denmark, was placated by being made a duke along with ten others to whom titles were also given.

One honour ceased abruptly: the Order of the Bath. It had been revived in 1661 when 68 knights were created, although Evelyn records that he declined the offer. Following the arrangements of 1626 the ritual was transferred from the Tower, this time to the Palace of

Overleaf Groundplan and side elevation of the Abbey prepared for the Coronation in 1685, engraving, 1687

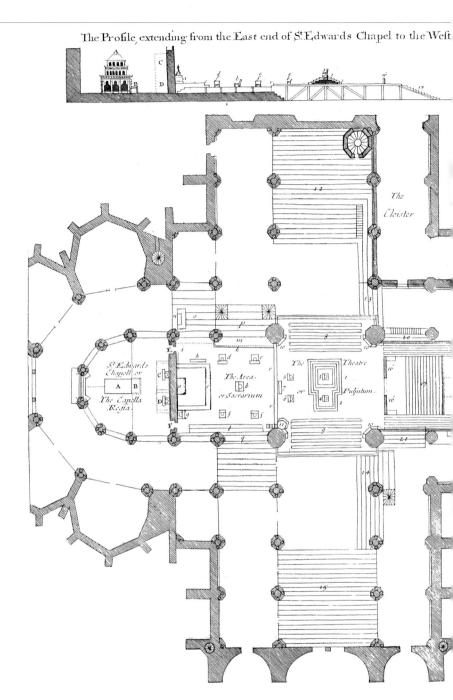

The Profile, extending from the East end of S.ᵗ Edwards Chapel to the Weſt

The Cleiſter

The Theatre or Pulpitum

The Area or Sacrarium

S.ᵗ Edwards Chapell or The Capella Regia

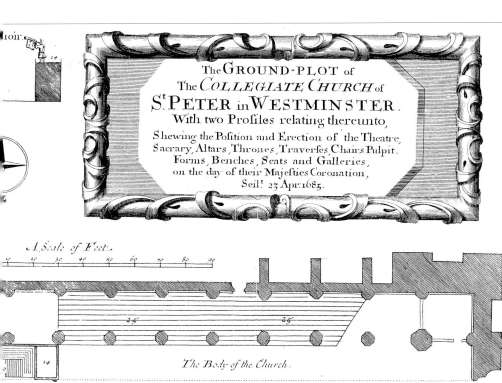

The GROUND-PLOT of
The COLLEGIATE CHURCH of
St. PETER in WESTMINSTER.

With two Profiles relating thereunto,

Shewing the Position and Erection of the Theatre,
Sacrary, Altars, Thrones, Traverses, Chairs Pulpit.
Forms, Benches, Seats and Galleries,
on the day of their Majesties Coronation,
Scil! 23 Apr: 1685.

A Scale of Feet.

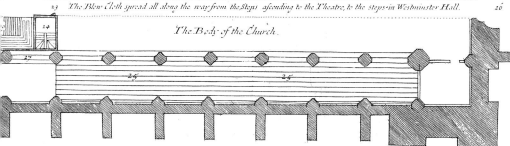

The Body of the Church.

23 The Blew Cloth spread all along the way from the Steps ascending to the Theatre, to the steps in Westminster Hall.   26

The Body of the Church.

re the Prebends of Westminster stood.

hich sate the Dukes of Normandie and Aquitain, and the

n which sate the Bishops.

in which sate Prince George and the Princess Anne of
some other persons of the Chiefest quality.

for the Kings Choir.

which sate the Kings Choir of Vocall Musick.

ry in which sate Ambassadors, Forreign Ministers and
quality.

Gallery in which sate the Master and Kings Choir of
Musick.

scat from the Area to the Theatre.

rene, being an ascent of 4 Steps above the Theatre.

rone adjoyning thereto being an ascent of 3 steps.

state in which the King was inthroned.

state in which the Queen was inthroned.

d Faldstool where the King first kneeled and sate and
t during the Recognition.

d Faldstool where the Queen first kneeled and sate.

which the Litanie was sung.

where the Peers sate.

where Peeresses sate.

10 Seats railed in, on the Inside of the 4 great Pillars for the Kings, Heralds
and Pursuivants at Arms.

11 The Pulpit.

12 Galleries or Seats in the South Cross for Spectators.

13 A Gallery for the Princess Anne of D. Maids & Serv.ts and over it another Gallery.

14 A Gallery where sate severall of the Nobility of Scotland and Ireland others
of the best quality and over it another Gallery for the Queen Dowagers Servants.

15 Galleries or seats in the North Cross for Spectators.

16 The Rail where the Serieants at Arms stood, both within and without.

17 The 12 steps ascending from the Choir to the Theatre.

18 The Benches or seats on each side, and west end of the Choir, where sate the
six Clerks, Kings Chaplains, Aldermen, Masters in Chancery, Serieants at Law,
Esquires of the body, Gentlemen of the Privy Chamber and Iudges.

19 19 The stairs whereby the former part of the Preceeding descend into the
Choir, in order to their return to West.r Hall.

20 A Gallery for the Queens Maids and Servants.

21 The Gallery in which the Choir of West.r sate.

22 The Great Organ and Organ Loft in which sate severall spectators.

23 The dore at the entrance into the Choir.

24 24 The Gallery over the Choir dore for the Serieants Trumpeter and the
other Trumpets and Kettle Drums

25 25 Galleries for Spectators in the North and South Iles of the Church

26 The great West dore of the Church.

27 The Gallery where the Kings Scholars of Westminster sate in number 40.

Westminster and the Abbey.⁶⁵ It included the usual tour of the knights in their picturesque robes on horseback up Charing Cross and then back to Whitehall, where they circled the courtyard and were dubbed in the Banqueting House, after which there was a service in the Chapel Royal. In 1685 there was not even a passing reference to the order and it was never to re-emerge in the context of a Coronation. When it was revived at the close of the reign of George I its purpose was a very different one.

The structural adaptation of both the palace and the Abbey fell to the King's Works. Sandford's views, and more particularly his ground plans and elevations, provide us with the information denied us for earlier periods. By the last quarter of the seventeenth century, too, the Public Record Office begins to to be repository of a large collection of plans recording the arrangements in the Abbey for each Coronation.⁶⁶ One of the most revealing records is the cross-section of the interior of the Abbey at the crossing running north–south, showing what Sandford calls the theatre together with flanking scaffolds of tiered seats in the transepts. This was quite obviously not a repetition of 1626. In 1661 there were sixteen steps up from the west side to the theatre and only two down to the sacrarium which, as can clearly be seen from the east–west cross-section, was boarded over with a false floor which was unlikely to have been a feature of earlier Coronations.

Why was this? The stage or theatre must have evolved considerably through the centuries, for the Works accounts for 1307–11, we may recall, state that it was so high that people could ride on horseback under it. That presupposes that it must have been at least thirteen feet in height and that it must have been open at the sides to the north and south. That certainly was not true by the close of the fifteenth century when the sides were boarded in, thus creating a below-stage room to which access could be had by doors guarded by the royal ushers. The evidence would suggest that the theatre was gradually lowered with the consequence that it was no longer so much to be looked up to, as in the Middle Ages, but looked down upon. We can also recall the observer who describes Mary I's stage as having twenty steps up and a further ten up to her throne on top of it. The ground plan of Elizabeth's shows twelve steps up and also down to the sacrarium, with a further five up to the throne.

How can we explain this? With the Reformation there must have been changes to the building of the kind we have already encountered

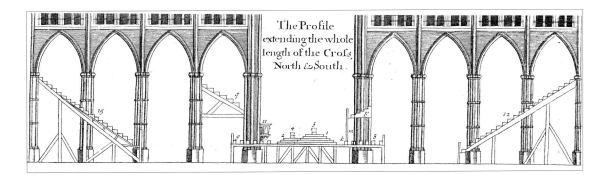

at the Coronation of James I, when things had to be demolished and put back afterwards. But it might be suggested that the real cause of the lowering of the theatre was the introduction of tiered seating in the transepts in 1661. Walker writes that in the north transept there 'were scaffolds for persons of all Conditions to sitt and behold this great & Sacred Solemnity'. This is where Pepys sat, although complaining bitterly that he could not see much and that he was forced to leave before the end because he 'had so great a list to pisse'.[67] We can see these tiered seats in Hollar's engraving on both sides in a way which is architecturally impossible, for they were a long way back in the transepts. In the engraving they have been moved forwards as though to throw up a signal that now 'persons of all Conditions' might see the Coronation. What happened in 1661 was the reversal of the traditional visual experience of the Coronation. The theatre was lowered and the sacrarium lifted. In this way the theatre with the enthronisation could be looked down upon and so, to a degree, could the anointing and crowning which instead of being hidden was elevated, and the difference in height between the sacrarium and the theatre was minimised.

Sandford's ground plan gives us the exact size of the theatre, 40 feet long by 50 wide and about 8 feet high, giving about 8-inch risers to the steps up from the west side. Nonetheless, even at 8 feet there was still room, if not for a horse and rider, at least enough to meet Sir Edward Walker's citation: 'Vnder the floore of the stage are Certaine Roomes and Partitions to be made where the kings officers must have wine and other necessaries as occasion shall require.'[68]

Seats to see the Coronation, even if only the procession passing up the nave from the west door, became for the first time that we know a money-spinner for those in the Abbey. The earliest evidence of this as an activity comes in a petition dated 30 May 1661 from the verger and

Cross-section of the Abbey showing the tiers of seating and the theatre, 1685, engraving, 1687

The Coronation of
Charles II, 1661, engraving,
1662

Altar dish of the type used
at coronations, 1664

others to the Dean and Chapter asking for the division among the staff
of the proceeds which had been taken at the Coronation and the opening of Parliament.[69] It is at this period that we come across the earliest
records of the sharing out of the takings between the various interested parties. We learn most about this from a document written on the
occasion of the Coronation of George I:

At the Coronations of King James [II], King William and Queen Mary, and Queen Anne, the Dean and Chap[ter] of Westminster had scaffolds built for their families and friends on the south side of the choir from the pulpit to the place where the trumpets and drums are seated.

The Chanter, the minor canons, Gentlemen of the Choir and other officers of the same church by the Dean's leave did at those solemnities build scaffolds in all the aisles westward from the Choir to the South Cross of the Abbey . . .[70]

In 1661 a warrant was granted to the Dean and Chapter to erect a scaffold in the churchyard with again a division of the takings. In 1689, for example, the amounts distributed varied from £35 to Henry Purcell to £5 to each bellringer, from £24 to the chanter and sacrist to £2 to the college butler and gardener. After all the payouts £24 14s 11d was left for the fabric fund.[71] One need hardly add that this would in no way have compensated for the enormous damage done to the medieval fabric every time these scaffolds were erected.

In 1689 the Commons requested that they also be in the Abbey so that they could witness the Coronation of the couple they had placed on the throne. The Privy Council instructed Wren to build a special gallery on the north side facing the throne to accommodate them. This apparently affected the Coronation's choreography, for after the oath and the *Veni creator* the king and queen moved to the east side of the theatre 'that they might be more Conspicuous to the Members of the House of Commons, (who, with their Speaker, were seated in the North Cross,) . . .'[72] All of this is ample evidence of the growing public interest in the ceremony. Celia Fiennes in 1702 records vast numbers of spectators watching Queen Anne leaving the Abbey, describing the 'prodigious numbers in scaffolds built in the Abbey and all the Streetes on each side to Westminster Hall'.[73]

This early democratisation of the ceremonial sees a massive increase of accommodation for all sorts of people, which we can see in the ground plan of the Abbey in Sandford. In 1661 two galleries were built at the west end of the choir, the one to the north filled with aldermen, judges and the legal profession, not to mention the Abbey choir and the Gentlemen and Children of the Chapel Royal. The one to the south had the Knights of the Bath and Gentlemen of the Privy Chamber. Benches either side of the stage accommodated the peers and peeresses, while to the south side of the sacrarium there was a two-tiered box for the

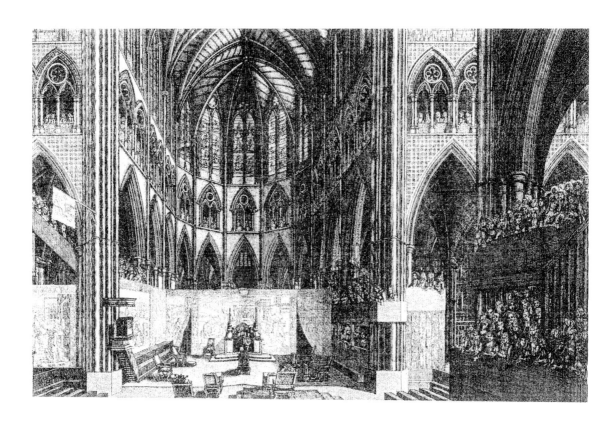

Duchess of York and for foreign dignitaries. Opposite there was
another tiered gallery for the musicians. At James II's there was a lower
gallery 'behind the Opposit pillar North [which] was for the Scots and
Irish Nobility', evidence of the need to draw in representatives of the
other kingdoms before the Act of Union in 1707.[74]

What we are witnessing is an ever spiralling colonisation of every
nook and cranny in the Abbey which could afford any kind of viewpoint. In Hollar's engraving of 1661 we see no faces peering down from
the east end, but in 1685 there are rows of people along the triforium.
This development is admirably summed up in the Earl Marshal's warrant to Wren for the Coronation of Anne, in which he states each peer
is to be granted eight tickets: 'these are to signifie to you that care must
be taken to make Galleries and Seats for as many as possible on each
side of the Quire & Great Theatre (and elsewhere Convenient). And
you may make use of the Crown Arches over the Upper Galleries
between the Great Pillars of the Musick Gallery as you did the last
Coronation.'[75]

This does not reflect a diminishing interest in the Coronation as some primeval rite living on into what was shortly to be the Age of Enlightenment, but, on the contrary, a wider interest and desire to see the inauguration of the monarch. But the sight lines must often have been appalling, reduced at times to transitory glimpses of not much more than the procession coming and going. Pepys opined in 1661 that everything went on in the sacrarium 'which, to my great grief, I and most in the Abbey could not see'.[76] The accoustics, too, must have been highly questionable. Few can have heard the sermon, but even if the words of the clerics were barely audible, devoid as they were of modern technical amplification, the substantial array of musicians and choristers must have been heard. Indeed, the considerable development of the musical aspects might be a reflection of the need for the service to have some elements which a very large congregation could actually hear and share as an experience, wherever they were in the Abbey.

Charles II's Wardrobe accounts provide us with the template for the furnishing of the great theatre.[77] The whole area was covered in red say, elaborated by Turkey carpets laid on the steps from the west side, while those on the east were covered in silk. Cloth of gold and its variants predominated for the royal thrones, chairs and faldstools and their cushions. The Archbishop of Canterbury's chair was covered in purple velvet, and Juxon's case actually survives in the Victoria & Albert Museum. St Edward's chair moved to far greater prominence, covered, as it had been at previous Coronations, with cloth of gold. Charles II was crowned in it but not anointed. In 1685 that changed, and James II was both anointed and crowned in it, an action which has been repeated ever since.

The chairs of state used for the enthronement could be very elaborate indeed. In 1689 they were 'carved all over very rich with Scrowles and leaves and figures in the forepart and Crownes and Scepters in the fore rayles and Crownes and Scepters on the top of the backs and all gilt with gold'.[78] Anne similarly had for her throne 'a Rich Chaire of State the Top of the back Carved with a Lyon and a Vnicorne and Sheilds Cyphers & Crownes and Scepters, the Lower part Carved and Richly Guilt all over . . .'. It survives at Hatfield House. Looking forward in time, others survive for George I, George III, George IV, William IV and Queen Victoria. How Anne's got to Hatfield is unknown, but the migration of the others to various country houses can be explained because the thrones became perquisites of

Archbishop Juxon's chair and footstool for the Coronation of Charles II, 1661

Opposite Queen Anne's Coronation chair, 1702

the office of Lord Great Chamberlain or Lord Chamberlain.[79] Sandford records those for James II and Mary of Modena.

The sacrarium itself was hung with tapestries from the royal collection and the altar banked with ecclesiastical plate. Celia Fiennes records it in 1702 when it was 'finely deck'd with gold tissue carpet and fine linnen, on the top all the plaite of the Abby set . . .'.[80] This typically Anglican arrangement is recorded in both the Ogilby and Sandford engravings. Tapestries formed an important part of the *mise-en-scène* both in the Palace of Westminster and in the Abbey. In 1685 the order was for all the various rooms of the palace to be hung with exactly the same tapestries as had been used in 1661, except for the Abbey 'for which there was a particular Direction'. This must mean that they were chosen by the king and there were two sets, one with the story of

Abraham and the other with that of Josiah. Putting all of this together, the overall palette was red and gold, colours which would have been amplified when those who took part arrived on stage. Westminster Hall was also dressed overall as the setting for both the opening ceremony and the feast. This is how it was described in 1661: 'The hall against that day was repreared [on] the outside of it, but within it was most nobly trimed vp, newly washed, all the shops [sic] taken doune and the courts of justice likewise. The hall was most richly hanged on both sides and a place made most desently, a desent by 3 or four staires higher then the other place where on stood the King's table . . .'[81]

As 1685 was a repetition of 1661 we can turn to Sandford for the ground plan, the only difference being that in 1685 there were two canopies for a king and a queen. The perspective view gives again evidence of the enormous interest in seeing such an event, each side of the hall being filled with a gallery for onlookers. As in the case of all the scaffolds, these galleries must have been an innovation in 1661.

At the south end of the hall the royal dais is approached by two flights of steps set within a galleried and tapestried enclosure with buffets either side from which to administer. At the north door there was an innovation which only began in 1685, a classical arch superimposed in pasteboard and *trompe l'oeil* over the existing Gothic architecture. The engraving in Sandford records this simple piece of scene painting for which Robert Streeter, the son of the man who painted the ceiling of the Sheldonian Theatre, was paid £15 2s 8d.[82] This was a feature which was to take on a life of its own during the eighteenth century.

THE PROCESSION REVISITED

Westminster Hall was, of course, where it all began on the great day. Those who were to take part assembled there, robing in the various rooms of the palace, like the Court of Requests or the House of Lords. There, too, the monarch came by river from Whitehall and was similarly dressed before making his ceremonial entry into the hall, where he seated himself beneath the stage with a table close to hand on which lay the various royal regalia delivered by the Dean and Chapter of Westminster, who still came in procession from the Abbey. The

James II's Coronation
Banquet, 1685, engraving, 1687

regalia were then delivered to those who were to carry the various items in the procession. The route from the throne the entire way to the steps leading up to the great theatre was covered with the traditional blue cloth, in 1685 1,220 yards of it. In the open it was railed and lined by soldiers who, in 1685, were guards and grenadiers, in places as many as six deep. Their presence is some indication that the monarchy was dependent on the military. What the ground plan in Sandford does not record is what must have been an explosion of specially built scaffolds all the way for spectators, as Pepys observes.[83] Sir Edward Walker wrote: 'all the windowes, streetes, & Scaffolds being full of Spectators who with loud Acclamations exprest their height of joy and satisfaction'.[84]

James II's Coronation was the first occasion that a printed directive appeared, to be distributed to those who took part. Entitled *Form of the proceeding to the Coronation of their Majesties*, it was 'To be observed by all Persons concerned'.[85] Although such processions were meant to be the epitome of stately ceremonial, they could quickly descend into chaos. In 1689 (as one would have expected), things went wrong: 'they passed by the mistake of those who led the Proceeding, from the Court of Requests through the Court of Wards, they should have gone downe the stairs into the Hall, which occasioned some disorder, and a long stay . . .'. Worse was to follow, for the Earl Marshal had forgotten to summon the dean and the procession from the Abbey bearing the regalia.[86] In 1702, Wren had failed to allow enough room for the procession, with consequent 'great disorders'.[87]

Engravings of the procession now appear, and exist for Charles II, for James II and for William and Mary. Of these none can surpass the lesiurely account in Sandford of James II's procession, running to nineteen plates crammed with every kind of delightful detail, like the herb women who head the procession scattering flowers from baskets. The procession was also a musical event with trumpeters sounding and the choirs singing anthems. From these visual sources we can see that by the late seventeeth century what was worn was becoming increasingly mummified, and a strict control was exercised, particularly over the peeresses. In 1685 it was laid down that their petticoats could only be white or cloth of silver. In that year baronets petitioned that they might have velvet robes, which was granted. As a measure of how much such details mattered, James II also decided that the Gentlemen Pensioners should be allowed to wear their hats.

The proliferation of portraits of peers in their robes makes it easy to envisage what such a procession looked like, but it must have been the women who stood out. Celia Fiennes catches this in her description of those at Anne's Coronation: 'Their heads were dress'd with much haire and long locks full of diamonds – some perfect peakes of

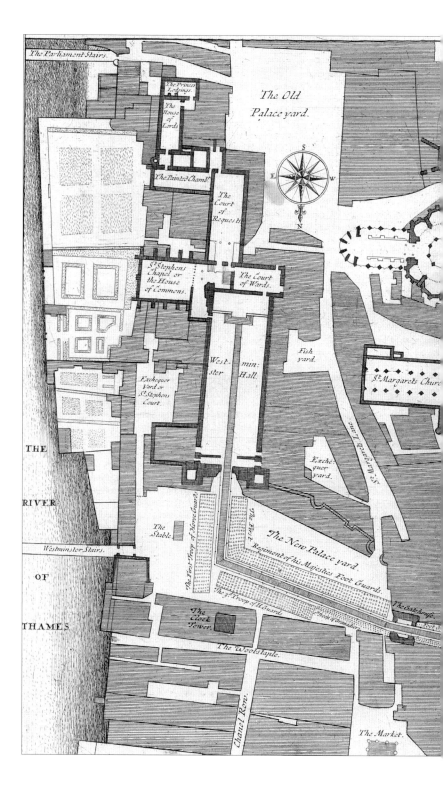

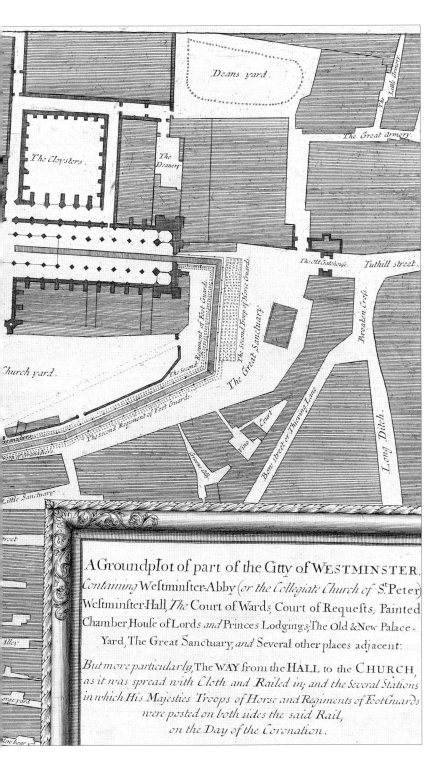

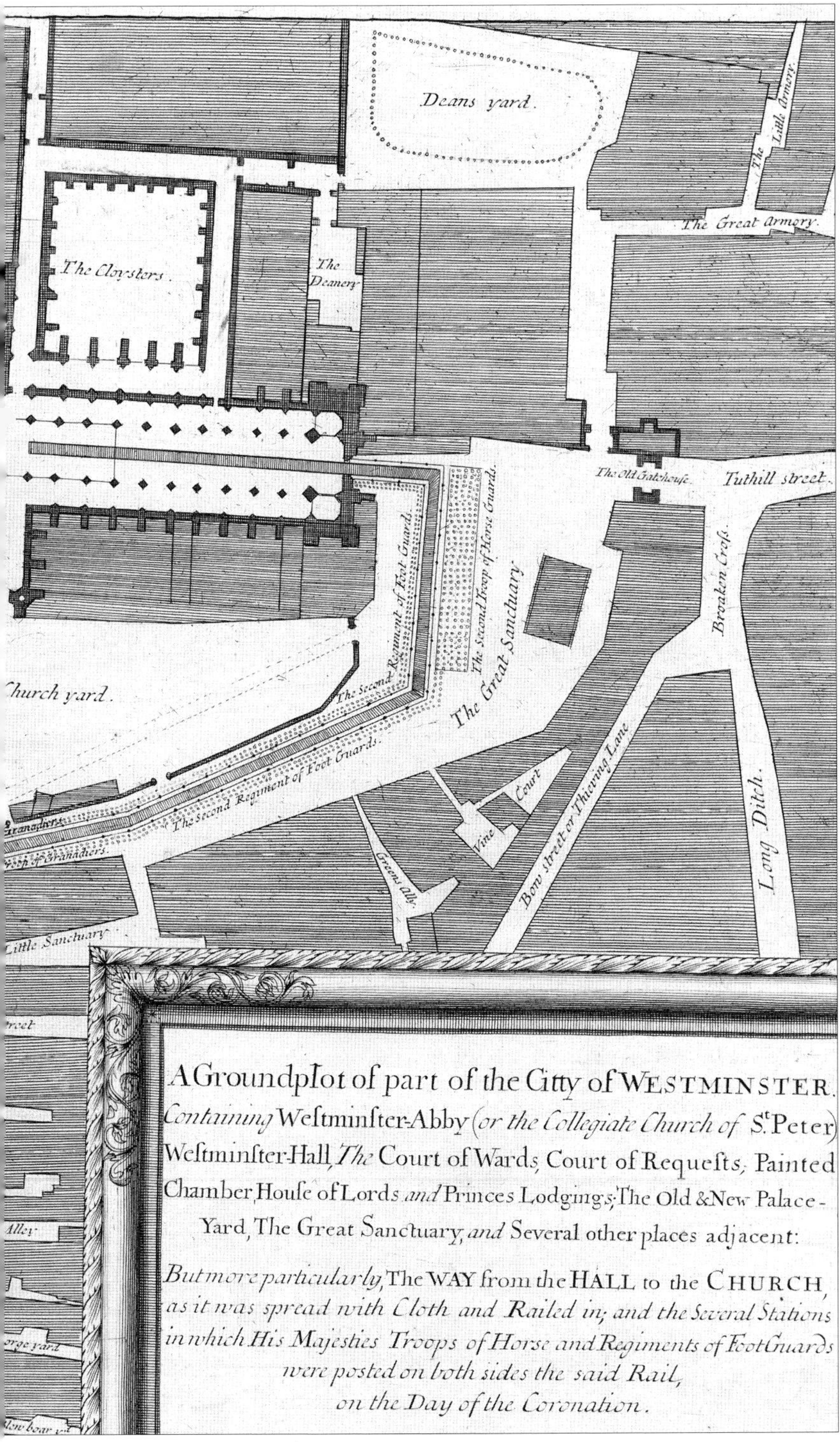
Deans yard.
The Little Armory.
The Great Armory.
The Cloysters.
The Deanery
The Old Gatehouse.
Tuthill street.
The Second Regiment of Foot Guards.
The Second Troop of Horse Guards.
The Great Sanctuary
Breaken Cross.
The Second Regiment of Foot Guards.
Court
Vine
Green Ally
Bow street or Thieving Lane
Long Ditch.
A Groundplot of part of the City of WESTMINSTER.
Containing Westminster-Abby (or the Collegiate Church of St. Peter)
Westminster-Hall, The Court of Wards, Court of Requests, Painted
Chamber, House of Lords and Princes Lodgings; The Old & New Palace-
Yard, The Great Sanctuary, and Several other places adjacent:
But more particularly, The WAY from the HALL to the CHURCH,
as it was spread with Cloth and Railed in; and the Several Stations
in which His Majesties Troops of Horse and Regiments of Foot Guards
were posted on both sides the said Rail,
on the Day of the Coronation.

Plan of the processional route for James II's Coronation, 1685, engraving, 1687

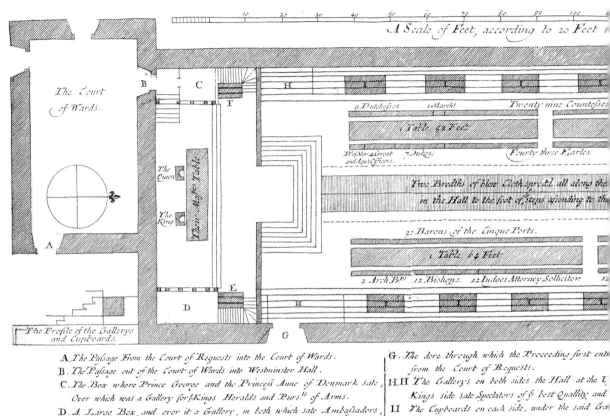

A Ground Plott of WESTMINSTER HALL, shewing the P...
Cupboards, Galleries &c. on the day of their M...

A Scale of Feet, according to 20 Feet ...

The Court
of Wards.

The
Queen

The
King

Their Majesties Table

9 Dutcheßes   1 Marchß   Twenty nine Countesses

Table 54 Feet.

D.ß of Nor. 4 Great   7 Dukes.   Fourty three Earles.
and Aqußs Officers.

Two Bredths of Blew Cloth spredd all along the ...
in the Hall to the foot of steps afcending to the ...

32 Barons of the Cinque Ports.

Table 64 Feet

2 Arch Bßs   12 Bishops.   12 Iudges Attorney Solliciter   1...

The Profile of the Galleries
and Cupboards.

A. The Paßage From the Court of Requests into the Court of Wards.
B. The Paßage out of the Court of Wards into Westminster Hall.
C. The Box where Prince George and the Princeß Anne of Denmark sate,
    Over which was a Gallery for ye Kings Heralds and Purs.ts of Arms.
D. A Large Box, and over it a Gallery, in both which sate Ambaßadors,
    Forrein Ministers, and Strangers of Quallity.
E. The Kings Cupboard.   F The Queens Cupboard.

G. The dore through which the Proceeding first ent...
    from the Court of Requests.
H.H. The Gallerys on both sides the Hall at the U...
    Kings side sate Spectators of ye best Quallity and ...
II The Cupboards on each side, under the said Ga...
K. The door through which the Meat was brought ...
L. The Paßage into the Hall from the Cellars.

bows of diamonds as was the Countess of Pembrook – their heads so
dress'd as a space left for their coronets [which they carried] to be set,
all the rest filled with haire, jewells and gold, and white small ribbon,
or gold thin lace, in forme of a peake, and gold gauze on their rowles;
they also have diamond necklaces and jewels on their habitts.'[88]

Frances, Duchess of Richmond, died on 15 October 1702, six months
after Anne's Coronation. In a codicil to her will dated 7 October she
ordered her executors: 'to have my Effigie as well done in Wax as can bee

332   CORONATION

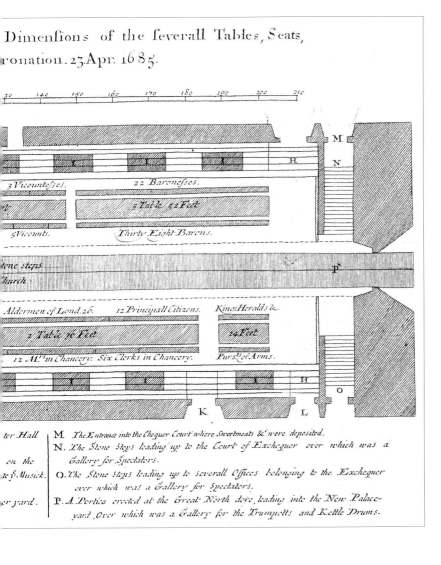

Plan of a table at the
Coronation Banquet of
James II, 1685, engraving,
1687

and set up near the old Duke Ludowick and Dutchess Frances of
Richmond and Lennox, put in a presse by itselfe distinct from the other
with cleare crowne glasse before it and dressed in my Coronation Robes
and coronette'. That figure with its robes and diamond (now paste) jewellery can still be seen in the Undercroft museum of the Abbey.[89] All one
needs is to multiply that figure in the mind's eye to get some notion of
the splendour of the peeresses and their diamonds, which, of course,
shimmered and caught the light, flashing as they moved.

Celia Fiennes gives a rare description of what the dean and prebends wore: 'very rich copes and mitres, black velvet embroydered with gold starrs, or else tissue of gold and silver'.[90] Three such copes survive, two still in the Abbey and the third now in the Victoria & Albert Museum.

Other elements were pretty unchanging. The regalia remained the same bar the addition of a Bible in 1689 which was borne between the

Above The King's Herb Woman and her Maids, 1685, engraving, 1687
Right Wax funeral effigy of Frances, Duchess of Richmond wearing her robes for the Coronation of Queen Anne, 1702

OPPOSITE
Above Two Pursuivants, Baronesses and Barons in James II's Coronation procession, 1685, engraving, 1687
Below Officers of Mary of Modena's Household together with peers bearing her regalia in the Coronation procession, 1685, engraving, 1687

chalice and the paten. So what strikes the casual onlooker is how immutable it all was, which was certainly true on a cursory glance at the procession. But it was far from true when it came to the actual service. With that in mind, it is now time to turn our attention to the service and set the dramatic innovations of James II, William and Mary and Anne into the wider perspective of the successive reworkings of the whole rite.

THE CORONATION SERVICE REVISITED

By the second half of the seventeenth century, even if we take account of all the antiquarian stirrings, the Middle Ages were a long way away. Although we have seen how the earlier rites were studied, what they recorded was used as a quarry to justify present needs. Scholarly studies of the early Coronation rites hardly existed, so it is scarcely sur-prising that ancient prayers were thrown out and various actions

altered. When the history of the Coronation began to be the subject of serious study at the close of the Victorian period, scholars like Wickham Legg threw up their hands in horror at the apparent butchering that went on in the late Stuart period. But, it can be argued, that butchering ensured the survival of the rite. It could be adapted to any circumstance.

Of the four late Stuart Coronations, by far the most radical was that of the Catholic James II who, as we have already heard, not only wanted it shortened but wanted the communion service eliminated. That task was assigned to William Sancroft, Archbishop of Canterbury who, with the assistance of six other bishops, had the job of axing the communion service and abridging the remainder. Ironically that request would have brought the service into line with other Protestant Coronation rites on the European mainland. A manuscript in Sancroft's hand exists in St John's College, Cambridge. It is a heavily revised version with spaces left for yet further alterations and includes a draft for a communion service which was not used. From this it is clear that Sancroft and his colleagues rifled through a mass of material including the *Liber Regalis*, a number of early Coronation rolls, the orders for that of James I, the one drafted for the joint Coronations of Charles I and Henrietta Maria, which never took place, as well that for Charles II. In addition, material by Elias Ashmole, Thomas Fuller, William Prynne and Peter Heylyn was gone through. The result of all this was the dropping of a great number of the historic prayers, the moving of the litany from after the oath to before it, and of the *Veni creator* to before the sermon.[91]

The text, ironically enough, was Protestantised, with any blessings of material artefacts transformed into a blessing on the king. A single example will suffice. The blessing of the sword in 1626 read as follows: 'Hear our prayers, we beseech thee O Lord, and vouchsafe by the right hand of thy Majesty to bless and sanctify this sword . . .' This becomes in 1685: 'Hear our prayers we beseech thee O Lord, and by the right hand of thy Majesty, vouchsafe to bless and sanctify this thy servant James our King . . .'[92] This brought the Coronation into line with Anglican theology, in which the blessing of material artefacts had no place. Sixteen eighty-five was also the first occasion when the king was invested with the orb and anointed as well as crowned in St Edward's chair. There was also a musical innovation, the introduction of a verse anthem, an adaptation of part of Psalm 89, which was sung during the homage. Evelyn, who did not go to the Coronation, possibly out of disapproval, wrote: '(to the greate sorrow of the people) no Sacrament, as ought to have ben'.[93] More importantly, a detailed study of his emendations reveals that the text enshrined a refutation of kingship by Divine Right. The alterations in phraseology spell it out that James was king by divine authority not thanks to birth, but to the Church's bestowal of unction upon him at the Coronation.

Sancroft could never bring himself to accept William and Mary as king and queen, becoming what was known as a non-juror, one of those bishops and clergy who remained loyal to the old Stuart line even though it was now Catholic. Sancroft having declined, Henry Compton, Bishop of London, was co-opted on to the Coronation Committee. He had been one of Sancroft's six assistants in 1685 and, indeed, worked from that revision, this time putting back the communion service as the frame into which the Coronation itself was set. This in its turn repeated the irony of 1685 in reverse. Then the eucharist had been axed to meet the demands of a Roman Catholic. In 1689 it

was restored in the interests of a Protestant settlement, thus in a sense remedievalising the ceremony. The Bible, a specially printed and richly decorated volume, joined the regalia, being carried in the procession, used for the oath, and used again in the new ceremonial presentation which happened immediately after the crowning. William and Mary were admonished to make it 'the Rule of [their] whole life and Government' as it was 'the most valuable thing that this world affords'. The action was explained in the accompanying prayer: 'And accordingly . . . when they made Jehoash King, they not only anointed and Crowned him; but they gave him a Testimony also, that is the Book of the Law of God, to be the Rule of his whole life and Government.'[94] It is difficult not conclude that the source for this piece of invented ceremonial was none other than Cromwell's investiture in 1657 as Lord Protector, in which he too was presented with the Bible as 'the grounds of the true Protestant Religion', as it contained the precepts of good government.[95]

In general, in 1689 the service was subject to further Protestantisation, the anointing and crowning being inserted in exactly the same place as when a bishop is consecrated in the Book of Common Prayer, where a Bible was also presented. The new consecratory prayer for the holy oil, the only item left which was still blessed (an action never repeated at any subsequent Coronation until oil was blessed in the chapel of St Edward in 1902), was made up for the most part of sections lifted from the baptism and confirmation services from the same source. There were even further changes. The places anointed were now reduced to three (accounts, however, are confused on this point), and the order was reversed, the head now being the first instead of last. In the investiture, the order of the delivery of the ring and two sceptres was reversed to before and not after the crowning.

All in all, with its expurgation of yet more ancient prayers, the Coronation service by the second half of the seventeenth century had begun to take on a life of its own. Further links with its historic antecedents went with Anne in 1702 when the prayer blessing the oil was dropped (it is unclear what happened to the oil used), along with another historic prayer: 'Let thy hand by strengthened'. The buskins and sandals vanished, too. At that Coronation also the declaration against the doctrine of transubstantiation, the cult of the Virgin Mary, the invocation of the saints and the sacrifice of the Mass was introduced in accordance with the Act of Settlement.

By 1702 the Coronation service had been mangled and amputated in such a way it had become one of the supreme instances of the invention of tradition. A Protestantised medieval Catholic liturgical rite was now a vehicle whereby the incoming monarch subscribed to the established post-Revolution hierarchy of Church and State, the ruler of an island which cast itself as the inviolate citadel of the reformed faith. Sixteen eighty-nine and 1702 had transformed the Coronation service into an anti-Catholic festival and that, bearing in mind its history, was some testament to its flexibility. It was to remain virtually unchanged until 1902.

There are two further indexes as to the meaning of late Stuart Coronations. One is the sermon. Communion was a rare event in an age when the emphasis was on the Word as expounded by pulpit oratory.[96] D. J. Sturdy in his study of these sermons has written: 'the Coronation sermon was taken with great seriousness by the individual preacher as an occasion when the church, addressing the king and the political nation gathered together, could seek to influence their mutual relationship'. These sermons would have been listened to intently on their delivery, but all of them were also published, some running into more than one edition. Three out of the four, those for the Coronations of Charles II, James II and William and Mary, came at critical junctures in the nation's history, and the chosen cleric did not flinch from touching on the central constitutional issues of the day, discoursing on the nature of kingship and the relationship of the ruler to his subjects from a Christian perspective and the viewpoint of the Established Church. That this was so and could be cause for eyebrow-raising is caught in George Morley, Bishop of Winchester's dedication of his sermon to Charles II, when he wrote that he had been criticised afterwards as 'I medled with matter of State'.

Evidence indicates that the choice of the preacher must have been reached by way of consultations between the king, the Archbishop of Canterbury and the Earl Marshal. But all the clerics would have been capable of delivering what was known as a court sermon. The three crucial sermons are those by Morley in 1661, Francis Turner, Bishop of Ely, in 1685 and Gilbert Burnet, Bishop of Salisbury, in 1689. In them we can see theories of Divine Right gradually recede, although no one actually enunciates the fact.

The Sermons open with Morley's which, like the Coronation itself, was a voyage back in time, with Charles II depicted as a Christ-like figure rebuilding a shattered kingdom, a monarch whose effect on his subjects was something akin to a resurrection.[97] Here Divine Right is accepted as a matter of fact: 'at the coming of Christ there was nothing but Monarchy in the World; so that Monarchy as it was Instituted by God at the Creation, so it seems to be restored by Christ at the Redemption of Mankind, and to be recommended both by the Father and the Son as the best and onely Form of Government for all Nations'.

In the case of James II, Francis Turner had been his chaplain when the king was Duke of York. Preaching to the Supreme Governor of the Church of England who was a member of the Church of Rome was a difficult assignment.[98] Now we hear much less about the divinity of kings and more about the sanctity of the Stuart dynasty: 'And I presume to Style him the very Similitude and Picture of Charles the Martyr.' Even in the face of the 'abominable' Exclusion Bill the succession of the sacred Stuart line had been preserved, so that in Turner's eyes James II fully justified the text he had chosen: 'Then Solomon sate on the Throne of the Lord, as King, instead of David his Father, and prospered, and all Israel obeyed him.' Alas, within only a couple of years that was no longer true.

Sixteen eighty-nine produced a very different kind of sermon in which divinity vanishes merely by the mechanism of omission.[99] Burnet was closely associated with both William and Mary and his sermon rewrites the role of the monarchy in the light of the Declaration of Rights. There is no trace in Burnet of the mysticism found in earlier Stuart Coronation sermons. 'Happy we,' he declared, 'who are delivered from both Extreams; who neither live under the Terror of Despotick Power [i.e. James II], nor are cast loose to the wildness of ungovern'd Multitudes [i.e. the Interregnum] . . .' The role of a king is to render justice to the whole of society, 'not breaking through the Limits of their Power, nor invading the Rights of People; neither inventing new Pretensions of Prerogative, nor stretching those that do belong to them, to the Ruine of their Subjects . . .'. John Evelyn records that it was received with 'infinite appaluse', implying that the congregation in the Abbey must have clapped.

By 1702 there was a realisation that their length was making the Coronation service interminable.[100] 'I am aware,' said John Sharp, Archbishop of York, in hailing Queen Anne as Gloriana returned, 'how much time the following Solemnity will take up, and therefore I mean to give as little Interruption to it as possible . . .' This is a far cry from

George Morley 40 years earlier, who had gone on for an hour and half. It struck the death knell of the great age of the Coronation sermon, one which fully reflected an era in which the accession of each new monarch was viewed still within an apocalyptic light as yet another opportunity for the Heavenly Jerusalem to descend to earth.

Sermons are one means of penetrating what might be described as the 'idea' of these Coronations. Medals are another.[101] They, while the homage was being rendered, were scattered by the Treasurer of the King's Household, accompanied by the Lord Keeper of the Great Seal, at each side of the great theatre. The number struck was strictly limited. In 1685, for instance, there were 100 gold and 800 silver medals for the king and half that number of each for the queen, a figure which was later upped. The medals, like the sermons, reflected how a particular ruler viewed his reign. In 1661 Charles II was depicted by Thomas Simon crowned and wearing the Garter collar while, on the reverse, the Restoration was represented as an act of the Divine Will, for the king, portrayed in robes of state and holding a sceptre, receives the victor's laurels and an imperial crown from an angel. The motto read: 'EUERSO. MISSUS. SUCCURRERE', meaning either 'sent to save a sinking ship' or 'sent to support a fallen age'. This is a vivid image of monarchy by Divine Right with iconographical roots back in the mists of time.

James II saw his accession as a progression from a naval to a regal crown (he had been Lord High Admiral). That is captured in the motto: 'A. MILITARI.AD.REGIAM', meaning 'from a military to a royal crown'. On the reverse a heavenly hand no longer bestows a crown but supports it from beneath so that it hovers over the victor's laurels. Four years later, for the Coronation of his daughter and son-in-law, James is cast as Phaeton struck down from his celestial chariot by Jove's thunderbolt, 'NE.TOTVS.ABSUMATUR', 'that the whole may not be consumed' or 'lest the whole be lost'. Evelyn, an authority on medals, was pretty acerbic about this one: 'which was but dull seing they might have had out of the poet something as apposite' and, as for its quality, 'the sculpture is very meane'.[102] In 1702 the fallen Phaeton made way for Anne cast as Minerva, shield in hand, hurtling Jove's thunderbolt at the Hydra Louis XIV: 'VICEM. GERIT.ILLA. TONANTIS', 'She is the Thunderer's Vice-Regent'.

Everywhere one looks there is more information than ever and a proliferation of interest and activity. The state entry into London may

James II's Coronation medal, 1685

have gone but the procession to the Abbey was still intact and, to some degree, had replaced it as an object of public display for the populace. These late Stuart Coronations had become great Baroque festivals with more stage-management than ever before. In 1685, the moment James II was crowned a succession of signals caused the trumpeters within the Abbey to sound 'a Point of War', the drummer outside beating 'a Charge' as well as everyone in the congregation crying 'God save the King.' Further signals from the roof triggered gun salutes in St James's Park and from the Tower of London as well as from the ships that lay moored there. In this way the news was taken across the metropolis.

What also happens after 1660 is a renaissance in the musical tradition, a whole subject in itself.[103] Everything had to be recreated: the royal musicians, the Gentlemen and Children of the Chapel Royal as well as the Abbey choir. The great innovation was the 24 violins. Evelyn records that at the 1661 Coronation there were 'Anthems & rare musique playing with Lutes, Viols, Trumpets, Organs, Voices, &c'.[104] We know that 'Zadok the Priest' was sung to a setting by Henry Lawes, then aged sixty-five and a survivor from the court of Charles I for whom he had composed masque music. Choirs and instrumentalists were disposed in the Venetian *cori spezzati* manner both on the north and the south sides of the Abbey.[105]

Most is known about 1685, thanks to Sandford. The Gentlemen and Children of the Chapel Royal were disposed in galleries on both sides of the sacrarium. The Abbey choir went into the organ gallery. There was also a large instrumental ensemble, including the 24 violins, and a second organ was imported into the Abbey by the composer Henry Purcell. There were nine anthems on that occasion, culminating in Purcell's 'My heart is inditing' which was 'performed by the whole consort of viols and instruments' with an eight-part choir and eight soloists. Not all of it can have been a success. Purcell's 'I was glad' was nine minutes long, far too lengthy for a procession that only had to walk 70 yards from the west door to the choir screen. One scholar has castigated it for being as unsuitable for its purpose as one could get. It was never used again. In addition to that there was a further innovation, one which has been repeated ever since, the greeting by the scholars of Westminster School singing *Vivat* as the king and queen passed through the choir screen. All of these Coronations were grand musical occasions, even the somewhat muddled affair of William and Mary, which had splendid music by Purcell and John Blow. All the evidence points to the Coronation already being a musical event long before the arrival of Handel.[106]

What is difficult to divine is the behaviour of the congregation through all of this. Pepys, who was intensely musical, wrote that in 1661 there was 'so great a noise that I could make but little of the Musique; and indeed, it was lost to everybody'.[107] That pinpoints the fact that we know nothing about the behaviour of the spectators during this great ceremonial, and perhaps it is unwise to conclude that they sat through it mutely. We already have evidence that they could clap the preacher and it is likely that they were far more boisterous than we would wish to imagine. They must have taken something with them to eat, and Pepys's hasty exit registers the lack of plumbing. He had after all arrived in the Abbey at 4 a.m., and the king did not arrive there until 11 a.m. Queen Anne took care of herself on that score, for there are payments for two close stools for her in the Wardrobe accounts. So much is known, more than ever before, but also much remains unknown and that is the same for the Coronation's finale, the feast.

THE FEAST REVISITED

Music was not confined to the Abbey, for it was a major feature also of the feast. Pepys records as much, with satisfaction as to its variety: 'all sorts; but above all, the 24 violin'.[108] This means that the musicians in the Abbey must have moved across to Westminster Hall. On Sandford's invaluable ground plan the musicians' gallery is on the west side and in the perspective view they can be seen in action, quite close to the royal enclosure. That to-scale plan provides us with a plethora of information about the placing of people, and even goes on to provide ground plans of the actual food, each platter being numbered to match an itemised menu. The huge listing of dishes brings the overall total to 1,445 : 175 for the royal table, 639 for the tables along the west side and 631 for those on the east. Sandford also tells us that the cost was £1,209 15s 7½d.

Food at this feast retained its medieval role as an expression of hierarchy. This was medieval eating mummified, for by the late seventeenth century the great hall of the castle or manor house had long since been abandoned and the various sections of the household ate in different parts of the house. Sandford gives us an account of Charles

II's feast in which he and his brother had three courses (James II had reduced it two in the interests of economy), each of 32 dishes, followed by what was known as the banquet (dessert) which filled twelve great basins. The lords spiritual had 144 dishes, the lords temporal 320 dishes and the table with the Lord Mayor, City worthies, Barons of the Cinque Ports and various legal dignitaries 128 dishes, with a corresponding apportionment of numbers of basins for the banquet. These dishes did not include those which contained vegetables and salad.

The engraving of the feast in action presents us with an astonishing spectacle. Boxes up above each side are crammed with spectators, and a ceremonial procession headed by serjeants-at-arms with gold maces and the three great officers of state, the Lord High Constable, the Lord Great Chamberlain and the Earl Marshal, on horseback, ushers in the first meat course. The food is arranged on the tables in symmetrical patterns in the late-seventeenth-century manner with vertical accents formed by food piled high *en pyramide*, an effect we can see best on the royal table. What is puzzling about the view is the absence of any apparent form of lighting, which must have been omitted by the engraver in the interest of giving the view clarity.

These feasts must have been something of a hurly-burly, for Pepys writes: 'I went from table to table to see the Bishops and all others at

A table plan for the Coronation Banquet in 1685, engraving, 1687

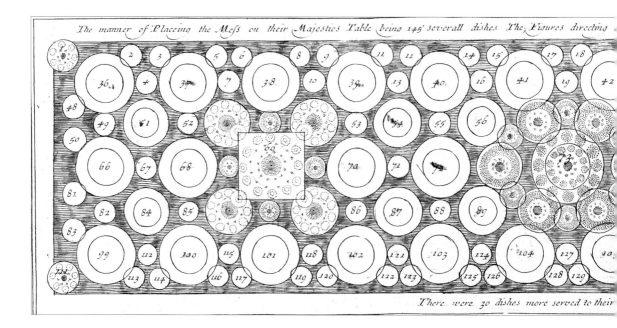

The manner of Placeing the Mess on their Majesties Table being 145 severall dishes The Figures directing

There were 30 dishes more served to their

their dinner . . .', suggesting that those who could get in just wandered around. More than that, he goes on to describe how he cornered someone waiting on Lord Sandwich with the result that the earl 'did give him four rabbits and a pullet; and so I got it, and Mr Creed and I got Mr. Michell to give us some bread and so we at a Stall eat it, as everybody else did what they could get'.[109] That cameo gives a vivid impression of the liveliness of the occasion, with visitors getting what titbits they could from the loaded tables of the great ones.

The climax was the entry of the Champion, always, due to tenure, a Dymock. This, it must be recalled, had not even happened in 1559, so it was reliving the past to the extreme. The moment is caught in the engraving in Sandford. Sir Charles Dymock, attired in armour from the royal armoury, is flanked by the Earl Marshal and the Lord High Constable, both coroneted and clasping their batons of office. Trumpeters above the north door are signalling his arrival. At the head of this procession go serjeants-at-arms bearing maces, two squires carrying the Champion's lance and shield, and York Herald who read the challenge. On the ground we see the gauntlet which has just been flung down. Up the hall this cortège passed, repeating this action thrice. When it reached the royal table a gilt bowl with a cover was brought to the king, who drank to the Champion and passed it to his cupbearer,

1. Pistachio Cream in Glasses.
2. Anchoviz,
3. Custards,   } cold.
4. Collar'd Veal,
5. Lamb-Stones,
6. Cocks-Combs,   } hot.
7. Marrow Patie,
8. Jelly,
9. Sallet,   } cold.
10. Stags Tongues,
11. Sweet-Breads,
12. Patty Pidgeon, } hot.
13. Petty-Toes,
14. Cray Fish,
15. Blumange,   } cold.
16. Bolonia Sausages,
17. Collops and Eggs,
18. Frigase Chick, } hot.
19. Rabbets Ragou,
20. Oysters Pickled,
21. Portugal Eggs, } cold.
22. Dutch Beef,
23. Andolioes,
24. Mushroomes,   } hot.
25. Veal,
26. Hogs Tongues,
27. Cheese-Cakes,   } cold.
28. Ciprus Birds,
29. Tansie,
30. Asparagus,   } hot.
31. A Pudding,
32. Ragou of Oysters,
33. Scallops,   } cold.
34. Salamgundy,
35. Three Dozen Glasses of Lemon Jelly.
36. Five Neats Tongues, cold.
37. Four Dozen of wild Pidgeons, Twelve Larded, hot.
38. A whole Salmon, cold.
39. Eight Pheasants, three Larded, cold.
40. Nine small Pidgeon Pyes, cold.
41. Twenty four Fat Chickens, six Larded, hot.
42. Twelve Crabs, cold.
43. Twenty four Partridges, six Larded, hot.
44. A Dish of Tarts.
45. Soles Marinated, cold.
46. Twenty four Tame Pidgeons, six Larded, hot.
47. Four Fawns, two Larded, hot.
48. Four Pullets la Dobe,
49. Twelve Quails, } hot.
50. Four Partridges hasht,
51. Ten Oyster Pyes, hot.
52. Sallet.
53. Pease.
54. Four Dozen of Puddings, hot.
55. Artichokes.
56. Beef a la Royal, hot.
57. An Oglio, hot.
58. Pease.
59. A Betalia Pye.
60. Artichokes.

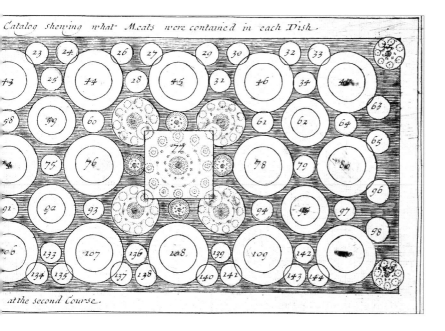

Catalog shewing what Meats were contained in each Dish.

at the second Course.

The Manner of the CHAMPIONS Performing the Ceremony of the CHALLENGE.
A. The Kings Champion. B. The Ld High Constable. C. The Earle Marshall. D. The Champions Gantlet cast down upon the Floor.
E. York Herald proclaiming the Challenge. FF. The Champions two Esquires. G.G. Two Sergeants at Arms. H. The Sergeant Trumpeter. II. Two Trumpe...

The entry of the Champion, 1685, engraving, 1687

who delivered it to the Champion. He then drank a little, bowed and departed.

Then the officers of arms descended with their coronets on their heads and, pausing to make three deep obeisances to the stage, processed the length of the hall, mounting the steps towards the royal enclosure. Garter cried 'Largesse' thrice and then proclaimed the king's style in Latin, French and English. The heralds then descended and, walking backwards 'still keeping their Faces towards the KING', stopped in the middle of the hall and repeated the action, finally performing it yet again at the north end. Then came the second course.

There were still the various rituals consequent upon this or that historic tenure in the form of cups of wine or a particular dish. The Lord of the Manor of Nether Stillington in Kent presented the king with a maple cup, and the Lord of the Manor of Lynton in Essex a charger filled with wafers. One of the most ancient of these rituals was when the Lord Mayor presented the king with a bowl of wine in a gold cup, which was returned to him as his fee.

When did it end? In 1661 Charles II left promptly after the third course. In 1685 we learn that James II and Mary of Modena departed at seven o'clock so exhausted that the great firework display planned for that evening was postponed to the following one 'by reason of the great Fatigue of the Day'. Fireworks had been a feature of 1661, too, and they also suffered delay. Sandford gives a very full account of those in 1685 which the royal party viewed from the roof of Whitehall Palace. Statues of Pater Patriae and Monarchia together with two huge pyramids flanked the sun hovering over the crown imperial with the monogram of the royal couple below it. Was this a hint of the aspirations of James to be also *un roi soleil*? The spectacle lasted three-quarters of an hour and included Neptune, trident in hand, leading in nineteen artificial swans, the first two bearing the king and queen's monograms and the third an admiral's badge. Reflected in the waters of the Thames this was spectacle open to everyman, and that touches something else which happens after 1660, the spread of the festivities across the country.

The coronation and popular rejoicing

In spite of the demise of the state entry, which gave entertainment to the teeming thousands of the metropolis, there was enough left to draw them into the celebrations. There was the procession to the Abbey, if they could get a place, the gun salutes and the great firework display on the river. But the people themselves began to turn the Coronation into a popular festival as never before. Pepys describes going to Axe garden on the night of the Coronation and 'there were three great bonefyres and a great many gallants, men and women; and they laid hold on us and would have us drink the King's health upon our knee, kneeling upon a faggott . . .'. That night Pepys got thoroughly

PATER PATRIÆ

MONARCH

drunk: 'if ever I was foxed it was now'.[110] Sandford similarly records in 1685, 'Bonfires, Ringing of Bells, Royal Healths to Their MAJESTIES, and all other Expressions of an Universal Joy . . .'.

What seems to have been wholly new was the spread of this kind of popular rejoicing to other towns and cities. That must have been prompted by the quite exceptional nature of the Restoration as an event. In 1661 we learn of bell-ringing, pageants, a sermon and music-making at Bruton in Somerset. In Cambridge the city was strewn with herbs and the windows decked with tapestries, pictures and garlands along with Charles II's portrait 'richly adorned'. Salutes were fired and Oliver Cromwell was hanged in effigy. At Melton Mowbray in Leicestershire the local baronet kept open house for 'all persons of quality', while outside his front door an ox was roasted as part of three days of bonfires, bell-ringing, salutes, dancing and music-making. All of this was so joyful 'that after the ox was eaten they accounted him happy that could carry away either one of the ribs of the ox or the least shiver of the bones to treasur up as reliques'. Such merrymaking even percolated north of the border. In Edinburgh the city dignitaries attended a sermon followed by a feast, while a bonfire blazed in the courtyard of Holyroodhouse and, in the city itself, the figure of Bacchus presided over a free-flow of wine.[111]

The city of Bath developed a particular form of pageantry for Coronations. In 1661 400 virgins paraded through the streets, 'most in white Waistcoats and green petticoats', bearing flowers, wreaths and crowns.[112] Celia Fiennes describes the festival as it was staged on the occasion of Queen Anne's Coronation. Maids came attired as Amazons and there was a huge procession of civic worthies, the Lady Mayoress being followed by six maids dressed in white bearing shields and gilt sceptres, two of whom carried a crown bedecked with pearls followed by the royal arms. There was a sermon in the Abbey, followed by a feast in the Guildhall and bonfires, music and dancing.[113] So, by 1702, what had begun as a ritual in Westminster Abbey was well on the way to becoming a day of national rejoicing.

Opposite Detail of the firework display in 1685, engraving, 1687

After the party comes the reckoning. One aspect of this was the long list of perquisites claimed by this or that person or group of persons who had taken part in the ritual. In 1661 the Dean and Chapter claimed the robes, tapestries, carpets, ornaments, canopy and other moveables in the Abbey or their cash equivalent. In 1685 there is a warrant from Lord Arlington to the Yeoman of the Removing Wardrobe to take everything from the Abbey pending the king's decision 'how they shall be Dispos'd of '.[114] In 1702 Anne removed everything, donating to the Abbey instead the great marble altarpiece which had been part of James II's Catholic chapel in Whitehall Palace.[115] The gift was to prove a formidable white elephant.

The claims could be endless. Charles II returned to Whitehall 'where his Majestie for that night did lye in a rich bed provided by the Great Chamberlaine of England the Earl of Lindsey, which bed properly belonged to the great Chamberlaine the next morning, or the value of it in mony'.[116] Sandford gives comparable examples. The Archbishop of Canterbury got his purple velvet chair along with its cushions. And the Officers of the Removing Wardrobe were allowed the royal canopy. Things, however, could get out of hand. In 1661 there was that terrible punch-up between the Barons of the Cinque Ports and the royal footmen, who had tried to tear the canopy with its tinkling bells from them.[117] The fisticuffs broke out during the feast and the barons were dragged the length of the hall. The king was so furious that the footmen were immediately dismissed and imprisoned. Since time immemorial the canopy had always been the perquisite of the barons.

Money was a perennial problem for the Stuarts. The Works side alone of the Coronation cost £1,558 for Charles II, £1,181 for James II, £2,240 for William and Mary and £4,677 for Anne.[118] The total cost of Charles II's Coronation as £31,798 9s 11d of which £12,050 3s 5d appertained to the remaking of the regalia.[119] The real expense came with the Great Wardrobe. In 1661 it ran up a bill of £21,000, but that included the new regalia. In 1685 it was £4,553, in 1689 £9,758 and in 1702 £8,828. The Coronation was not a cheap event, and it is hardly surprising to read that at one meeting of James II's Coronation Committee the Wardrobe personnel were asked 'to consider how low the Prices might be reduced', also what Sir Christopher Wren's bill would be as Surveyor, or, on hearing the cost of the feast, that they promptly reduced it by one course.[120]

One thing has not been touched upon, and it is tangential to this story: the fate of the Scottish Coronation. James VI of Scotland had already been crowned when he came south in 1603. Thirty years later his son had gone north for what has already, in the previous chapter, been referred to as a disastrous Coronation ceremony in which the king mortally offended his Presbyterian subjects. It was a hugely elaborate affair which introduced elements from the English rite and laced it with Laudian high-church visual spectacle and ritual. When Charles II made a bid for the throne in 1650 he underwent a stripped-down Presbyterian Coronation at Scone, the ancient site of Scottish regal inaugurations, in which he was crowned King of Great Britain. Whether James II had any intention of voyaging north to be crowned is unknown, but that event, if it had happened, would have precipitated even more outrage than his father's. Nothing more is heard of the need for a Scottish Coronation.[121]

Thanks to a quite extraordinary sequence of political crises the Coronation underwent what can only be described as a renaissance during the last half of the seventeenth century. What began as a medieval rite was robust enough to respond fully to the demands of each occasion, revealing its amazing vigour and flexibility. By responding to and incorporating into its ceremonial the new concept of a king below and not above the law, its future was to be an assured one. It had, by 1702, become an indispensable rite of passage for anyone who aspired to wear the crown. That fact ensured its survival.

8

Insubstantial Pageants

THE CENTURY AND A QUARTER which runs from the Coronation of George I to that of Victoria is memorable as far as public consciousness is concerned for one thing only, the exclusion of George IV's discarded queen, Caroline, from his Coronation in 1821. The scene was a dramatic one. Escorted by Lord Hood she had made her way to an entrance via Poets' Corner in the north transept of Westminster Abbey. Lord Hood had said to the doorkeeper (most of them were pugilists employed for just such an eventuality): 'I present to you your Queen, do you refuse her admission?' At that point Caroline made a bid to enter, but found her way barred by the doorkeeper who said no ticket, no admission. Lord Hood promptly produced one, to which the response was one ticket, one person. The queen was then asked whether she would enter alone, and Lord Hood inquired whether any preparations had been made to receive her, to which the reply was 'No.' 'Then am I to understand,' said Lord Hood, 'you refuse your Queen admittance to Westminster Abbey?' The doorkeeper merely reiterated his instructions, no ticket, no admission. At this juncture the queen and her party retreated, Caroline being 'a good deal agitated'. As her carriage procession made its way through the crowds lining the processional route outside the Abbey she was greeted with cries of 'Shame, shame.' A fortnight later she was dead.[1]

That incident has coloured our perception of Hanoverian Coronations, a period more important than any other for the transmission of this medieval ceremony to the modern world. If it had not been for the events of 1688/89, the chances are that the rite might eventually have been abandoned. As we shall discover, William IV wanted to get rid of

Opposite George II in his Coronation robes with Westminster Abbey behind, painting, *c.*1727

Admission ticket to the
Coronation of George IV,
1821

it, regarding it as a gigantic irrelevance. As it was, it was not only to be transmitted but given a whole new lease of life as the monarchy changed itself to meet the challenge of a new society. During the century and a quarter of these six Coronations the monarchy was faced by lingering loyalty to the Stuarts, the implications of both the French and Industrial Revolutions, a twenty-year war with France, plus the expansion of the franchise through the great Reform Bill of 1832 to a far wider constituency of people. In addition there were other, ideological, currents, like the rise of antiquarianism and the Romantic movement, which were also to have an impact on the Coronation. But everything stemmed from what was to be a radical recasting of the role of the crown, one which used to be assigned to the reign of Queen Victoria but which modern scholarship rightly attributes to George III.

FROM DIVINITY TO DOMESTICATION[2]

The change of dynasty was an unwelcome necessity. In order to preserve Protestantism, the magnates were reduced to importing a grandson via the female line of James I's daughter, Elizabeth, Queen of Bohemia. Neither George I nor George II were stars in the regal firmament. Indeed, it is amazing how little effort they, in fact, made to project a new image of the monarchy. They were not popular, and the first five years of George I's rule were marked by sporadic urban riots in protest against it. What kept them firmly on the throne was their Protestantism and the coincidence of their arrival with an era of peace and economic prosperity. With the defeat of the Young Pretender in 1745 and the accession of a British-born king in 1760, the position of the new dynasty took an upward turn, only to be threatened first by the loss of the American colonies and then by the French Revolution. George III was a king perfectly happy to play the unassertive role of first citizen, and the twenty-year war with France enabled the monarchy to re-position itself as the focus of national patriotism drawing on a far more complex network of loyalties than ever before.

Simultaneously with the advent of the House of Hanover, we also enter the era of the mass media. For the first time newspapers and journals abounded. More than ever before, political debate was open to a wide section of the educated classes and, of course, the media recorded all royal doings in a way which was unprecedented. By 1821 the importance of the media was such that members of the press were accorded seats at George IV's Coronation which commanded 'an excellent view of all the ceremonies'.[3]

The monarchy had entered the eighteenth century as a greatly weakened institution. In comparison with the French monarchy it was impoverished, and its executive power had been savagely curtailed in 1688/9. All the time, too, there was the perpetual threat of a Stuart restoration. That only receded after 1750 with the collapse of the Jacobite cause, after which the Scots began to integrate themselves more and more into a society which was preoccupied with redefining itself as British. During the eighteenth century we can trace the gradual evolution of the monarchy from a sacerdotal manifestation of kingship to one whose being rested on the exertion of royal benevolence through the patronage of hospitals and other charities. Much of the old structure continued to remain in place. The service for touching for the King's Evil remained in the Book of Common Prayer until 1732. The ritual of the Royal Maundy, far from vanishing, took on new life, although the monarchs ceased to be present (George I was an exception in 1715). Sometime during this period the foot-washing ceased and the occasion was turned into a grand royal almsgiving accompanied by increasingly elaborate music (another feature of Coronations). Although divinity was no longer dwelt upon, regal sanctity remained. The alliance of God and the monarchy was now sealed by the hand of Providence, which was seen to have been instrumental in bringing the House of Hanover to the throne. Both the first two Hanoverians were punctilious in their observation of the Church's holy days, and in George III the country had a committed and pious Anglican. All three realised that their rule depended on the Protestant clergy of all denominations. Britain thus continued her role as the new Israel, and the Coronation ceremony continued to cast the king as an Old Testament ruler. William Talbot, Bishop of Oxford, eulogised George I in his Coronation sermon as a new David. Taking as his text Psalm 118:24–5 ('This is the day which the Lord hath made . . .'), which was said to have been composed by David after his anointing as King of Israel, he went on to celebrate 'this great event' which had averted the accession to the throne of 'one educated in the Maxims of French Tyranny, and the Principles of Popish Superstition . . .'.[4] At George II's, where John Potter, Bishop of Oxford, preached, he exalted the king as a being 'seated on God's throne, and is King for the Lord his God'.[5] All of this was to be heightened from 1727 onwards by Handel's sacred music.

That such views were not confined to the Abbey is caught in 'A Song to a Minuet att a Ball on the Happy Coronation Day of George our King, October the 11th' by one William Cobbett, a royal musician:

> 'Tis he, 'tis he
> That keeps us free,
> And with his mighty strength defies
> The chevalier
> From coming here,
> And quell his traiterous allies.[6]

The attitude of those who brought in George I is revealed in the diary of Mary, Countess Cowper, who had been appointed a Lady of the Bedchamber to the new Princess of Wales. She viewed the Coronation from the steps of the pulpit, as she found her place amongst the peeresses taken: 'it brought Tears in my Eyes, and I hope I shall never forget the Blessing of seeing our holy Religion thus preserved, as well as our Liberties and Properties.'[7]

The 1689 settlement was the foundation stone of eighteenth-century government. It was based on a series of Acts, the Clarendon Code of 1661–5, the Test Acts of 1673 and 1678 and the Toleration Act of 1689. As the eighteenth century wore on, however, these were seen to be more and more repressive, so much so that the laws affecting Roman Catholics were, by tacit agreement, generally ignored. The consequence was there was no call to repeal them. Problems only arose in respect of a statute of William III which laid down that anyone joining the army had to take the attestation oath. Up until 1778 that oath had been taken by Roman Catholics but with any sections offensive to them dropped. But the pressure for more soldiers for the American War of Independence was such that a Catholic Relief Bill was passed. In 1780 Lord George Gordon charged the king with complicity because he had given consent to the Relief Bill. There followed the explosion of violent anti-Catholic demonstrations known as the Gordon Riots. That charge left George III profoundly unhappy and, although he was tolerant to Catholics, he would not budge any further along the road to emancipation. To do so would, in his view, be a violation of his Coronation oath. And that was true, for the oath together with the declaration were seen to be the bulwark upon which the Church of England depended. His reaction to a Bill in favour of Catholic emancipation in 1795 sums up his position as defender of the Protestant faith:

> a sense of religious as well as particular duty made me, from the moment I mounted the throne, consider the Oath that the wisdom of our forefathers had enjoined the Kings of this realm to take at their Coronation, and enforced by the obligation of instantly following it in the course of the ceremony with taking the Sacrament, as so binding a religious obligation on me to maintain the fundamental maxims on which our Constitution is placed, namely the Church of England being the established one, and that those who hold employments in the State must be members of it, and consequently obliged not only to take Oaths against Popery, but to receive the Holy Communion agreable to the rites of the Church of England.[8]

He sought the opinion of the Lord Chief Justice, Lord Kenyon, and the Archbishop of Canterbury. Catholics were affected by the Acts of Supremacy and Uniformity besides the Test Acts and the Bill of Rights. Both Lord Kenyon and the archbishop were unanimous that the king could not repeal any of these 'without a breach of His Coronation Oath, and of the Articles of Union with Scotland'. 'The Coronation Oath was understood at the Revolution to bind the Crown not to

Assent to any Repeal of any of the Existing Laws at the Revolution, or which were then enacted for the Maintenance and defence of the Protestant Religion by Law Established.'[9]

It was only the Lord Chancellor, Lord Loughborough, who demurred, arguing that the oath imposed no restriction on any Bill Parliament might wish to pass. George III, however, was never to change his stance and when Catholic Emancipation was meant to follow the Act of Union with Ireland in 1801, his immovability was such that Pitt was forced to resign as prime minister. Emancipation was not to come until 1829, athough Catholic peers were summoned to the Coronation in 1821.[10]

The Coronation of George I was only a few years on from the Act of Union with Scotland. In 1801 there was a similar one in respect of Ireland. It was not for nothing, therefore, that George I was depicted on his Coronation medal being crowned by Britannia, a figure whose presence becomes more and more all-pervading as the century advances. It was to affect the wording of the Coronation oath. George I's read: 'And will you maintain and preserve inviolably the settlement of the Church of Scotland, and the Doctrine, Worship & Disciplined Government thereof as by Law established within the Kingdoms of England & Ireland, the Dominion of Wales, & Town of Berwick upon Tweed, and Territories thereunto belonging before the Union of the two Kingdoms?'[11]

In George IV's oath 'the people of this kingdom of Great Britain' became 'this united Kingdom of Great Britain and Ireland' and 'the Church of England' the 'Church of England and Ireland'.[12] That creation of a nation of Britons had an effect on the Coronation, as it had now to be built up as a British occasion and the Scots and Irish somehow brought in to be part of it. In 1714 the Earl Marshal of Scotland was bidden to summon the Scottish peers. It was at that Coronation that the Scottish peers first appeared, being assigned places next to their English counterparts. That change is caught most vividly in the petitions which the Court of Claims had to deal with on the Coronation of George III. Virtually all of these were from Scottish aristocrats who had held hereditary roles at the Scottish Coronation which they now wanted transferred south of the border and incorporated into the English rite. The Earl of Errol, Lord High Constable of Scotland, for example, 'Claims a Silver Batton or Staff of 12 ounces weight typped with Gold at each end, with Your Majesty's Arms on one

OPPOSITE
Hanoverian Crowns
Left George II with the Crown of St Edward and the Sovereign's Orb and Sceptre, painting, *c.*1727
Right George I's Crown of State, drawing, 1718
Below left to right Crown of Queen Charlotte, painting, *c.*1761; Crown of Caroline of Ansbach, painting, *c.*1727; a casting of George IV's Imperial State Crown, 1820–21

end, and your petitioner's on the other.' His request was granted and he was to walk on the right hand of the Lord High Constable of England nearest to the sword of state. The Duke of Argyll also petitioned. In 1727 he had 'presented the first Gold Cup His Late Majesty drank out of at Dinner'. This was granted him again along with the right to carry a staff. So, too, was Sir Thomas Brand, Gentleman Usher of the Green Rod or Usher of the Order of the Thistle, permitted to walk with his English equivalent, Black Rod. But on the whole, most claims were put on hold as indeed they were again in 1821.[13] The latter was to be the first Coronation at which the figures of Guyenne and Aquitaine ceased to appear, representing the final abandonment of claims to a French empire.

George IV's response to this newfangled Britishness was innovative, having standard bearers carry flags with the coats of arms of the various domains over which he ruled, Hanover, Ireland, Scotland with, in addition, the Union Flag and the Royal Standard. The Scottish and Irish peerage in the great procession was there as members of the Order of the Thistle or of St Patrick. More interestingly, George IV included members of both the Scottish and the English episcopacy. And into his jewels and robes he introduced the motifs of the English rose, the Scottish thistle and the Irish shamrock.

Even though the Hanoverian heirs were permanently at war with their fathers, it was true to say that for the first time since Charles I there was a royal family. That was a huge novelty. Both Caroline of Ansbach and Charlotte of Mecklenburg-Strelitz were fruitful of progeny. Never had the royal succession been so secure in the male line. That family context guaranteed stability and was emphasised in the Coronation. At George I's, the Prince of Wales was assigned a special place in the proceedings and wore Mary of Modena's crown. In 1727 Caroline's daughters carried their mother's train, and even the Duke of Cumberland, then aged only six, was dressed as a Knight of the Bath and made to walk in the procession. In 1761 Augusta, Princess Dowager of Wales, widow of Frederick, had her train carried by her third and fourth sons. For the Coronation of George IV and at that of his two successors, the royal dukes and duchesses wore diamond coronets. Whatever the failures in the relationships of the various members of the House of Hanover, the public emphasis was always on the united family as fully evidenced in their ready adoption of the new genre of the family group. Moreover, through their exaltation of family life, as

exemplified by George III and Charlotte, they brought a series of attributes which they shared with everyman. The royal family was now projected as an example of marital happiness and of the joys of parenthood in a manner which anticipated Victoria and Albert.

What was even more important was the gradual withdrawal of the monarchy from party politics. That was to secure its future. Both George I and George II had no option but to be partisan because they owed their throne to the Whig magnates and they certainly had no grassroots support from the populace. That shift only began to happen later in the century as George III moved away from politics to an involvement with public and charitable causes. The idea, however, of a monarch above party politics was first aired by Henry St John, Viscount Bolingbroke, in *The Patriot King* (1749), in which the monarch was cast as a figure of virtue who was above party strife and

George IV's Diamond Hat Circlet
Left George IV wearing the Diamond Circlet, 1821, print, 1824, 1839
Top right The Diamond Circlet, 1820
Below Detail of a diamond spray

who could thus regenerate the constitution. Although the book was slightly vague on practicalities its contents were taken up by the circle around George III's father, Frederick, Prince of Wales. It was during the reign of George III that this became a reality, the monarchy became more and more disengaged from party politics, releasing it to become a neutral icon of a nation at war. The king's exemplary life saw the Hanoverians also gain roots for the first time with the populace, and the new splendour with which the crown framed itself began to be viewed as some kind of collective glory. George III and Charlotte indeed established the format which has obtained ever since, that of a combination of public splendour with private probity.

Even though George IV in many ways eroded what had been achieved by his parents through his reckless extravagance and decadent lifestyle, that did not detract from the crown's increasing neutrality. Indeed, nothing at his Coronation in 1821 was to move Sir Walter Scott more than the sight of the great Whig nobility gathered around the king 'giving open testimony that the differences of political opinions are only skin-deep wounds . . . but have no real effect on the wholesome constitution of the country'.[14] By 1821 Coronations had become national events with bonfires and feasting all over the island. This would have been impossible but for the drift into impartiality first by George IV, and even more so with his two successors. Thus by 1838 the monarchy was seen as the embodiment of a far more plural society than in 1714, one which now embraced Roman Catholics and the vastly extended electorate, the result of the 1832 Reform Bill.

The changed perception of the crown was aided by a recasting of paternalism, which in the previous century had been an argument for absolutism, but now, instead, became a vehicle of a very different kind, one in which the ruler was committed to the moral and social improvement of his subjects. This began with George II, was accelerated by George III and even sustained by George IV, who continued to patronise charitable causes and to be a generous donor. William IV and Queen Adelaide assumed a more overt patronage of every kind of philanthropic endeavour, so that by 1838 and the Coronation of Victoria the stage was set for a royal family as the living embodiment of family rectitude. A sermon delivered in the Scottish Church in Covent Garden on that occasion entitled 'Our Queen: Responsibilities and Rewards' unequivocally stated that 'all influence, for good or evil, descends from the higher to the lower. The moral influence of a

Opposite Queen Charlotte in her Coronation robes, 1761, painting, 1761

Below Queen Charlotte's Coronation Chair, 1761

Queen, in a nation where the female character is revered, and the royal looked up to, must necessarily be vast.' And that was to be the monarchy's rock until undermined first by Edward VIII in the 1930s, and secondly by the children of Elizabeth II in the 1980s.[15]

The republican tradition was never more than slender in Britain, so that even Oliver Cromwell in the end was offered a crown in 1657. Republicanism inevitably went underground in 1660, not to resurface until the close of the eighteenth century in the form of clubs of dissenting schoolmasters. The impact of the French Revolution was twofold, for it not only unleashed conservatism but it equally revived the republican spirit. That found its most forthright expression in the second part of Tom Paine's *Rights of Man* (1792) which attacked the cost of the monarchy and the whole hereditary system, an attack which was re-echoed in William Godwin's *Enquiry Concerning Political Justice* (1793) which presented every king as being at heart a despot. These assaults, far from damaging the monarchy, strengthened it, for George III was a model king. In addition, they prompted a serious re-examination of the assumption upon which monarchical government was based, which led to the crown being recast as the bulwark of the democratic system. The republican virtues were no longer a threat, but now numbered among the attributes of the crown. Even though George IV did damage (as *The Times* obituary read, 'Never was there a human being less respected than this late king . . .'), the monarchy continued to climb steadily upwards in public esteem, first under William IV and then under the young Victoria. Placed within a European context this was an astonishing achievement.[16]

FROM ANTIQUARIANISM TO TRADITION

As though these developments were not enough, we must add to them other cultural and ideological currents which were also to be turned to the monarchy's advantage. These were to transform the monarch into the living incarnation of the nation's history or, rather, a selective version of it, one which was capable of being rewritten according to time and circumstance. That this was possible stemmed directly from the old medieval concept of the king's two bodies, that he was two persons, the first a transient human being and the second the living representative of an institution which was immortal. By 1838 this concept had been extended in such a way that it contrived to embrace a whole list of antithetical qualities. A king was royal yet he was also republican, permanent yet transitory, sacred yet mortal. Modern scholars differ as to the exact nature of the royal duality, but no one questions the huge flexibility that it gave the crown, enabling it to respond to virtually any political or social circumstance. So if the monarchy had lost its spiritual power in the eighteenth century it acquired instead a psychological one over its people, one which was often far from rational and certainly inexplicable. That psychological pull is still there in the twenty-first century reflecting a deep and, at the same time, unfathomable public need.[17]

That the monarchy could take on the role of repository and living representative of the country's most sacred beliefs and trusts was only possible when there existed a populace which had some knowledge of its own past. The arrival of the Hanoverians coincided exactly with the refounding of the Society of Antiquaries. Under its aegis this was to be the century which explored and constructed a shared British past which now also embraced ancient buildings and artefacts. Architectural styles were codified for the first time, and there was a celebration of the Gothic past and an apotheosis of Elizabethan England. The Hanoverians, who were brought in to replace the Stuart dynasty, naturally responded to this rediscovery of earlier times, for it enabled them to leapfrog the exiled dynasty and establish an affinity with the medieval kings and queens of England. This began quite modestly with the insertion of Westminster Abbey and St Stephen's Chapel in the background of the state portraits of George I and George II. Caroline of Ansbach, who had an intellectual bent, went much further. Her dressing room at Kensington Palace was hung with the early portraits of the kings of England and also with the rediscovered Holbein portrait drawings recording members of the court of Henry VIII. It was for her that William Kent painted scenes in 1729–30 from the life of Henry V and also designed the amazing grotto in her garden at Richmond. This included a tableau of wax figures drawing a parallel between the prophecies by Merlin of the advent of the Arthurian line in the person of Henry VII and the Tudors, and similar prophecies about the House of Hanover. The Gothicisation of the monarchy, if such a term can be applied, was accelerated by the French Revolution which unleashed a reverence for existing ancient institutions. It was George III who commissioned the American painter, Benjamin West, to paint a series of canvases for the Presence Chamber at Windsor Castle depicting the triumphs of an earlier war against France, that waged by Edward III, the founder of the Order of the Garter. The man likely to have been the originator of that idea was Richard Hurd, Bishop of Worcester, tutor to the future George IV, who had extolled the virtues of medieval chivalry in 1762 in his *Letters on Chivalry and Romance*.[18]

We can follow this regal Gothicisation through numerous architectural projects. George III's unfinished new palace at Kew was in the Gothic style, so were the new state apartments at Windsor Castle by James Wyatt. And, although George IV had a penchant for the arts of pre-Revolutionary France, he, too, dabbled in Gothic. His conservatory at Carlton House was modelled on Henry VII's chapel in Westminister Abbey, and his Coronation (to which I will return in greater detail later in this chapter) was a Tudorbethan pageant on a scale which led that arch-Romantic Sir Walter Scott to record how foreign visitors 'were utterly astonished and delighted to see the revival of feudal dresses and grandeur when the occasion demanded it . . .'.[19]

The temporary architecture superimposed on to Westminster Hall and on to the Abbey is another index of the all-pervading obsession with things Gothic. Robert Huish, in his account of George IV's Coronation, describes the temporary arch erected at the north end of the hall in the following way: 'The whole had the appearance of one of the castles built by the powerful barons of the middle ages . . . It was a sight worthy of a great nation priding itself in the antiquity of its institutions . . .'.[20] Inside the Abbey the architect Sir John Soane had overlaid the interior with a mixture of classical, Tudorbethan and Gothic elements. The two Coronations which followed were also in the Gothic mode, the temporary annexe built at the west end of the Abbey for William IV's being in the style of Henry III, and Gothic detailing was superimposed on to both the altar and the organ.

By that date the Palace of Westminster had gone up in flames, a cataclysmic loss, leaving only the hall which was venerated as a relic of the nation's past. That change of attitude is caught in what was written in 1821 when the various law courts which encumbered the hall were ripped out for the Coronation ceremony. Huish records how the space came as a revelation, how it 'excited the warmest admiration of every individual who entered it, accompanied by a fervent hope that its beauties might not again be obstructed'.[21] The change in status is reflected in an abortive scheme by Soane to create a royal processional way from Windsor Castle to the Abbey, which would symbolise through architecture both ancient and modern the role of the monarch as landowner, leader of society, patron of national fame, force inspiring the empire, head of the Church, historical source of law and authority behind representative government. What Soane did achieve was a new entrance to the House of Lords and the creation of Parliament Square designed to set off what was now regarded as an historic ensemble. For a generation that based its views of the world on the principles of the Picturesque here was a tableau which encapsulated a whole mesh of associations with the British past.[22]

The Hanoverians were drawn not only to the medieval past, but also to the Elizabethan era which was portrayed as the nation's greatest heroic age, one from which the Old English virtues had descended.[23] The glorification of this period was sealed also by its association with Shakespeare, whose rise to prominence as the country's greatest writer was sealed by David Garrick's jubilee at Stratford-upon-Avon in 1769. In the England of Elizabeth regal power and literary excellence were seen as one. We can add to that the antiquarians' exploration of past pageantry epitomised by a landmark publication, John Nichols's celebrated *The Progresses and Public Processions of Queen Elizabeth* (1788–1805). It is difficult not to believe that that publication was one of the major inspirations behind George IV's Coronation, the Privy Councillors being attired, we are told, in white and blue satin trunk hose and cloaks 'after the fashion of Queen Elizabeth's time', and the Gentlemen Pensioners arrayed in costume drawn from a famous historic painting: 'The original picture exhibiting the dress was painted by Vertue [the antiquarian], representing Lord Hunsdon in the dress, and is, I believe, now in Sherborne Castle.'[24] That Sir Walter Scott's glorification of the reign of Elizabeth, *Kenilworth*, appeared in that year, 1821, cannot have been a coincidence.

All this antiquarian digging back into past now began to extend to the history of the rite of Coronation itself. Because to the public it became increasingly an arcane and antiquated ritual which had mysteriously survived the Enlightenment age, curiosity began to be aroused as to its exact origin and purpose. The first signs of that are in 1727, the year of the Coronation of George II, in a publication entitled *A Complete Account of the Ceremonies Observed in the Coronations of the Kings and Queens of England . . .*, which opened with material lifted

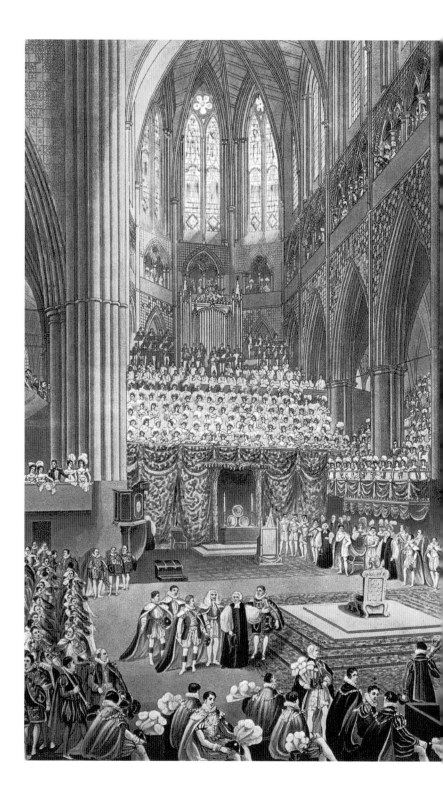

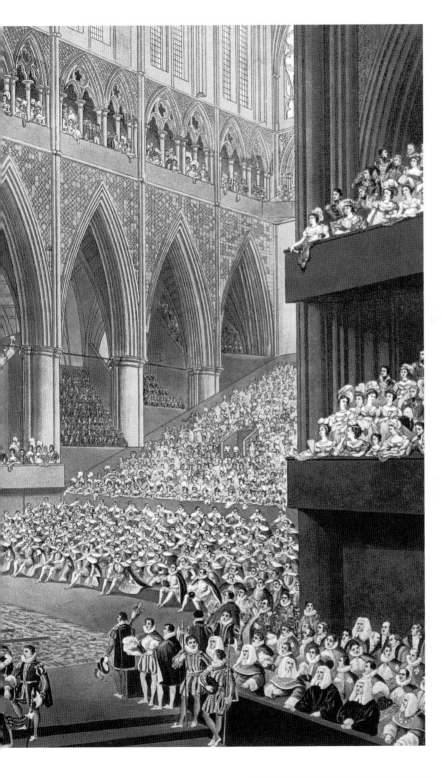

The Recognition at the
Coronation of George IV,
1821, print, 1824, 1839

Re-living the past:
costumes for the
Coronation of George IV
Left to right Pursuivant
and Privy Councillor

from Sandford's account of James II's Coronation, 'the Model of future Coronations', and went on to print accounts of those of Anne and George I. George III's Coronation prompted similar publications,[25] but it was not until George IV's that any real probing back further in time occurred. This time, in addition to the usual reprints describing more recent Coronations, there were books which attempted to study the development of the institution across the centuries. Arthur Taylor's *The Glory of Regality* (1820) and T. C. Banks's *An Historical Account of the Ancient and Modern Forms, Pageantry and Ceremony, of the*

Coronations of the Kings of England (1820) were landmarks publishing material which is still of use to scholars today.[26]

They were the most important contributions amidst a glut of others whose account of both the rite and its meaning could be on the wrong side of fanciful. The Revd Jonas Dennis's *A Key to the Regalia . . .* (1820) might be taken as a typical example of this genre. It opens optimistically enough with the statement: 'It is not a little singular that in an age of extensive information, and research few subjects can be mentioned which appear to be so little understood . . .' Including, I fear we must add, his own. The four swords are here billed as symbolising the four orders of chivalry, the Garter, the Bath, St Patrick and the Thistle, and also, even more surprisingly, the four courts of Chancery, King's Bench, Common Pleas and Exchequer. The origin of the ampulla is garbled into being 'said to have been presented to Henry III. when he was Duke of Lancaster and happened to be in France'.[27] From this it is clear that we are still a few decades from the serious revival of liturgical studies prompted by the Oxford Movement. Nonetheless, these publications do provide evidence for what Huish describes as the 'admiration of the institutions established by our forefathers, and which have been transmitted from sire to son in all their primeval dignity and splendour'.[28]

The early eighteenth century witnessed a reaction against the overbearing ceremonial of the Baroque era and it was not until its close that there were signs of a revival. The first stirrings of that went back to 1757 when a polemicist wrote that what was called for was 'more ceremony, and a greater regard for forms and appearances'. Although George I had revived the Order of the Bath in 1725 as virtually a new institution it was not until the reign of George III that we begin to see any response to that plea for more regal ceremonial. Under his aegis the Order of the Bath was enlarged (1772), the Order of the Garter extended both in 1786 and 1805, and the Order of St Patrick founded to bring Ireland into the chivalrous fold. It is to George III that we owe this revival of medieval chivalry. In 1805 the Garter ceremony was staged with an especial splendour: 'It was his majesty's particular wish, that as many of the old customs should be kept up as possible.'[29] All of this must be set into the wider context of the Romantic movement which, by 1800, had led to a burst of translations or editions of medieval romances, ballads and chronicles, not to mention the spate of castle building which was to reach its height about 1820.

It is this complex of political, social, ideological and cultural currents which we need to keep in our minds as we examine the Coronations which straddle the years 1714 to 1838. They were in fact to ensure the Coronation's survival into the Victorian age.

SIX CORONATIONS: A RITUAL OBSERVED, MISUNDERSTOOD AND MISMANAGED[30]

There were, as I have already written, six Coronations between 1714 and 1838. they were:

20 October 1714	George I
10 October 1727	George II
22 September 1761	George III
19 July 1821	George IV
8 September 1831	William IV
28 June 1838	Victoria

George IV's Coronation should have taken place in 1820, but the return of his estranged queen to England in June of that year led to her trial in the ensuing August. It is striking that the dates chosen for Coronations no longer had to be staged either on a saint's day or on a Sunday. By 1714 the severance from that medieval tradition was complete. Of these occasions three were Coronations of single rulers and three for kings with consorts. As there was no queen for George I, no peeresses walked in the procession or were present at the banquet. That formula was adhered to, except in the case of George IV who had the peeresses present at the banquet.

The cost of these Coronations was as follows:

George I	£7,287
George II	£8,720
George III	£9,430
George IV	£238,000
William IV	£43,159
Victoria	£69,421

The Coronation of George IV leaps out as the most extravagant in history. One hundred thousand pounds had been voted by the government and the rest came from war indemnities from France, appropriate enough, for one of George's aims was to eclipse in magnificence Napoleon's Coronation in 1804. The furnishings of Westminster Hall and the Abbey, excluding what was spent by the Office of Works, cost £16,819. The banquet cost £25,184, £111,810 was spent on jewels and plate and £44,939 on uniforms, costumes, robes and mantles.

Such incredible prodigality outraged public opinion and produced a sharp reaction. William IV actually wished to get rid of the Coronation altogether, but when prevailed upon to go through with one, ensured that it was as pared down as it could be. So he was crowned with George I's old state crown which he did not even have remodelled to fit him, inserting padding instead. It was so cheap an event that 'To accompany the anthem it was thought a single fiddler on a single string would be the cheapest way . . .'[31] The peers wore their parliament robes, and even the ushers in the Abbey were volunteers who paid for their own costumes. It was lampooned as the Penny Coronation, but, it should be remembered, Victoria's and that of her predecessor were staged during a period of acute economic depression.

The physical organisation of the Coronation was the province of the two great hereditary officers, the Lord Great Chamberlain who had control of Westminster Hall and the Earl Marshal whose sphere was the Abbey. The latter's jurisdiction only extended over the area beyond the screen embracing the choir, the transepts, the sacrarium and St Edward's chapel. He was also responsible for the raised walkway along which the procession made its way from the west door to the choir screen, but not otherwise. This arrangement left large areas of the Abbey under the control of the Dean and Chapter, who were quick to turn it to financial advantage.

The Lord Great Chamberlain, the Chief Butler and the Earl Marshal were the only remaining hereditary offices, all the rest having reverted to the crown. That meant they could be disposed of to whom it was thought fit at each Coronation. The Lord High Steward and the Lord High Constable were now both firmly in the giving of the monarch. As the remaining hereditary offices have quite complex histories which take us down to our own day, I will deal with them here.

The office of Lord Great Chamberlain, on the demise of the last Earl of Oxford in whose family it was vested, was, after various contenders for the office, awarded to the son of the last earl's aunt, Lord Willoughby d'Eresby. When the heir-general and heir-male in that line failed, on the death of the Duke of Ancaster in 1779, the office passed to his two daughters, one of whom married the Marquess of Cholmondeley and the other a Mr Burrell. The latter's part-claim to the office was then divided between her two granddaughters who had married Lords Aveland and Carrington respectively. Up until the death of Queen Victoria the role of hereditary Lord Great Chamberlain was exercised by Lord Aveland's son, the Earl of Ancaster. It was a post which was to be contested at the Coronation of Edward VII, but it was again laid down that the co-heirs had to agree amongst themselves about who should occupy the post, which at present is held by the Marquess of Cholmondeley. Although the ceremonies preceding the Coronation in Westminster Hall ceased with William IV and therefore the Lord Great Chamberlain's duties on that day ceased as well, his role in relation to the palace still exists. The present marquess, bearing his white wand of office, still plays a ceremonial role at the state opening of Parliament, and it was he who received the coffin of Queen Elizabeth the Queen Mother at her funeral, standing at the great north door of the hall.

The office of hereditary Chief Butler had no such complications, for it had been filled by the Earls of Arundel since 1243 and they were to officiate in this capacity down to what was to be the last Coronation banquet in 1821. More significant was the post which remains operative to this day, that of Earl Marshal. That post, with its close association with the College of Arms, progressively assumed to itself the role it occupies today of being the key person organising the whole ceremonial. As in the case of the Lord Great Chamberlain, the history is quite a complex one. In 1483 Thomas Howard, 1st Duke of Norfolk, was created Earl Marshal of England. In spite of this, the Howard family did not manage to hold on to the position consistently until 1672. In that year Henry Howard, Earl of Norwich, was created Earl Marshal of England in tail male. He later was to become Duke of Norfolk and henceforth his descendants gradually assumed the primacy which they exercised last in 1953.

However the Dukes of Norfolk were Catholic, and so in the eighteenth century were unable to perform the function, appointing a deputy instead. In 1714 that was the Earl of Suffolk, in 1727 the Earl of Sussex and in 1761 the disastrous Earl of Effingham. In 1824 an Act was passed enabling the Duke of Norfolk to remain Catholic and yet exercise his office, which he and his successors have done ever since.[32]

In this way we can see how the number of hereditary great officers of state eventually dwindled to just two, in effect due to William IV's abolition of the pre-Coronation ceremonial and banquet in Westminster Hall. With those went a whole litany of officers who, over the centuries, owing to their title or their tenure of this or that piece of land, performed a service at the Coronation. An 'Index to the Petitions and Claims of Services and Judgements for James II, George II and George III'[33] provides a useful list, and here are some of them:

> Manor of Scrivelsby: The Champion
>
> Barony of Bedford: Almoner
>
> Manor of Great Wymondley: 'To serve the King with [a] fine cup Silver Gilt, at dinner'
>
> Manor of Bourdelies: Chief Larderer
>
> Manor of Eston: Caterer and Larderer
>
> Manor of Heydon: 'To hold the Bason & Ewer and Towel to the King when he shall wash his Hands before dinner.'
>
> Manor of Addington: 'to find a man to make a Mess of Grout and present the same to the King'.
>
> Manor of Lyston: 'To make Masers for the King and Queen.'
>
> Isle of Man: 'To render two Falcons to the King at his Coronation.'
>
> Manor of Tingreth: Chamberlain to the Queen
>
> Manor of Nether Bilsington: 'To find and present three Maple cups.'
>
> The City of London: 'Mayor to serve the King with a cup of Wine, Mayor and Citizens to perform the Office of Butler in aid of the Chief Butler of England.'
>
> Barons of the Cinque Ports: 'To hold the Canopy over the King and Queen and to dine in the Hall.'

Virtually the only office to survive was that performed by the holder of the Manor of Worksop: 'To find the King a Glove and to support the Kings Right Hand.' As we shall see, this abolition of so much history was greeted with horror by those involved and by the Tories, but there was no going back, even though there were attempts to do so in 1838. This is a period when the Coronation settled into a repetitious formula. George I's was, of necessity, done with all speed, while his son's was not only much more elaborate but performed, as Lord Hervey records, 'with all the pomp and magnificence that could be contrived; the present King differing so much from the last, that all the pageantry and splendour, badges and trappings of royalty, were as pleasing to the son as they were irksome to the father'.[34]

There are no great variations between one Coronation and another, and for practicalities Sandford's account of James II's became the absolute point of reference. The first action of the Privy Council on a new ruler's accession was to turn to the Archbishop of Canterbury for his views about the form of service. In 1727 the council asked Archbishop Wake, who looked at those for James II and Mary II and studied Archbishop Tenison's revisions for Queen Anne and George I. Wake reported to the council that Archbishop Tenison had taken 'great pains to settle this office in a better method than had ever been done before: and indeed he has succeeded so well in it, that in my Opinion a better form cannot be found for the Coronation of His Majestie'.[35] All that had to be added was a formula for the Coronation of a consort, which was lifted from Sandford's account of that of Mary of Modena. With these revisions Wake laid his proposed form of service before the council and, after some hesitation over the investitures (which was solved by looking at a copy of the service for George I in the King's Closet), the format was settled. Out of this emerged a 'Form and Order' of which a hundred copies were printed to be distributed to the necessary participants. Henceforward all that happened at each Coronation was for this text to be revised. It is important to add that the text put down what should happen. Anyone who has participated in the great ceremonials of state will know that there can be quite a discrepancy between what should happen and what actually happens on the day. In 1727 none of the texts, for example, of Handel's anthems actually match those in the printed text.

With the 'Form and Order' to hand it is hardly surprising that the archive of the archbishops of Canterbury at Lambeth Palace should house a whole set of these documents annotated by successive archbishops. In 1761 Thomas Secker made in the main only minor changes to the text of 1727, the most significant revisions being due to the fact that the country was still at war with France and Spain.

George III had stipulated that the template for his Coronation was to be his grandfather's. In 1820 the copy of George III's 'Form and Order', which had belonged to Archbishop Secker, was gone through by Archbishop Manners Sutton to eliminate any mention of the existence of a queen and noting, for example, that the anthem 'The king shall rejoice' was to be omitted and that the litany was to be said, not sung.

The service for the first four Georges is pretty constant, the alterations only becoming radical for William IV and Victoria. The annotated copy of the 'Form and Order' for William IV resembles a battlefield. The anthem 'The king shall rejoice' is dropped altogether, the litany and the creed are to be said, not sung, no oil is to be wiped away from the king's head after his anointing, he was not to be girt with the sword, no armils were to be used and, as regards vestments, he was only to be clothed with a royal robe. Psalm 23 was substituted for the anthem 'Praise be the Lord', the words accompanying the delivery of the Bible were truncated and two more anthems cut, with Handel's Hallelujah Chorus substituted.

What is even more striking is the addition of a whole series of new prayers following the crowning, many of which reflected changes in society on the eve of the passing of the Reform Bill, of which the king was in favour. 'The Lord give you,' so one prayer runs, 'a faithful Senate, wise counsellors and magistrates, loyal nobility, dutiful gentry, pious, learned and useful clergy, an honest, industrious, and obedient commonalty.'[36] Victoria's Coronation followed this pattern, reflecting both efforts towards a new inclusiveness and a keen desire that the rite should not be seen to be an apotheosis of a single human being but rather an action in which the interdependence of king and subjects was enacted in ritual. To achieve this, however, precious little respect was shown for what remained of an ancient liturgical rite, which was cheerfully butchered, producing such absurdities in the case of William IV's Coronation as the Lord's Prayer being said thrice. Indeed, so far had it voyaged that that king could refer to the Coronation as 'the sacred rites attending the administration of the royal oath', bypassing the anointing and investiture which lay at its heart.

In order to grasp just how far things had travelled, here is a list of what happened at the Coronation of Queen Victoria in 1838:

QUEEN VICTORIA'S CORONATION SERVICE

1. The queen enters in procession through the west door of the Abbey from a temporary annexe and is greeted with the anthem 'I was glad . . .'

2. The procession passes down the nave into the choir to the theatre where the queen takes her place in 'Her Chair'.

3. The *recognitio*. The Archbishop of Canterbury accompanied by the Lord Chancellor, the Lord High Constable and the Earl Mashral preceded by Garter King of Arms go in sequence to the east, south, west and north, the queen also turning in each direction. The people cry 'God save Queen Victoria' and the trumpets sound.

4. The first oblation. The bishops who had carried the Bible, chalice and paten place them on the altar and the archbishop and bishops vest themselves in copes. Carpets and cushions are spread on the floor and steps up to the altar. The queen, supported by the bishops of Durham and Bath and Wells and attended by the dean and the great officers of state, descends to offer a pall or altar-cloth of gold together with a gold ingot. They are placed on the altar.

5. The litany. Two bishops in copes read it kneeling at a faldstool in the middle of the east side of the theatre.

6. The opening of the communion service. The sequence runs: Sanctus, Lord's Prayer, collect, the commandments, the epistle and Gospel and the creed.

7. The sermon. The queen sits in a chair to the south side of the altar flanked by the two supporting bishops. The dean and prebendaries stand near the altar on the south and the archbishop on the north side.

8. The oath, This is read and responded to and the queen lays her right hand on the Gospels on the altar and swears the oath and signs it.

9. The anointing. Then the *Veni creator* is sung, followed by 'Zadok the Priest'. The queen is disrobed and then sits in St Edward's chair, which is sited centrally facing the altar. Four Knights of the Garter hold a pall over her while she is anointed by the archbishop with the sign of the cross on her head and palms.

10. The presentation of the spurs and sword. The spurs are presented to the queen and returned to the altar. The lord who carried the sword of state gives it to the Lord Chamberlain who delivers it to be placed in St Edward's chapel. The Lord Chamberlain gives him another sword which he gives to the archbishop who lays it on the altar. Then the

Queen Victoria's sketch of Lord Melbourne bearing the Sword of State, 1838

archbishop, supported by the other bishops, gives it to the queen who holds it and then gives it back to the archbishop who lays it on the altar. The swordbearer redeems it for a sum of money, draws the blade from the scabbard and bears it before the queen for the rest of the ceremony.

11. The investiture. The queen is then attired in 'the Imperial mantle, or Dalmatic Robe' by the dean. The archbishop invests her with the orb, which is returned to the altar, and then with the ring. The Lord of the Manor of Worksop presents the queen with a rich pair of gloves, which she puts on, and then the archbishop invests her with the sceptre with the cross and the rod with the dove.

12. The crowning. The archbishop takes the crown and prays, after which the dean presents it to him and he crowns the queen. The peers put on their coronets, the trumpets sound, there is a gun salute from the Tower and everyone cries 'God save the Queen.' The anthem 'The queen shall rejoice . . .' is sung.

Sketches by Queen Victoria of her Coronation, 1838
Above Being crowned
Right A peer renders homage
Opposite The crowned Queen wearing her dalmatic robes

13. The presentation of the Bible. The dean delivers the Bible to the arch-bishop who presents it to the queen, after which it is returned to the altar.

14. The benediction. The queen is blessed by the archbishop. The Te Deum is sung.

15. The enthronisation. The queen ascends to her throne in the theatre and is lifted into it by the bishops. The great officers of state stand around it and the prayer 'Stand firm, and hold fast . . .' is said.

16. The homage. This is carried out collectively rank by rank, starting with the bishops. Coronets are taken off, the crown is touched and the queen's hand is kissed. Meanwhile the treasurer of the household tosses medals to those present and the anthem 'This is the day which the Lord hath made . . .' is sung.

17. The communion. The service is resumed. The queen, attended by the great officers of state, descends to offer bread and wine and also a purse of gold. She goes to her chair on the south side and takes off her crown. She puts her crown on again after she has communicated. The Gloria is sung, followed by the anthem 'Hallelujah: for the Lord God omnipotent reigneth . . .'.

18. Final prayers. The queen and the officers of state pass through the south door to St Edward's chapel. Any regalia which are to be carried by the lords are delivered back. The queen takes off her 'Imperial mantle' and puts on 'Her Royal Robe of Purple Velvet'. The queen puts on her crown of state and is given the orb and sceptre. The clergy divest. The procession re-forms and returns to the annexe at the west end.[37]

Any study of these documents suggests that those who made the alterations and additions had no or very little idea of the history of the rite. That gave the revisionists the flexibility to do virtually whatever they liked with it. The anointing was contracted to the head, breast and palms and, in the cases of William IV and Victoria, the head and palms only. For consorts it was contracted to the head only. The omission of the breast is likely to have been a reflection of the emergence of Victorian notions of delicacy. All mention of the traditional linen coif and gloves, which used to be put on after the anointing, vanishes. So too, in the case of Victoria, does the centuries-old tradition of the sovereign kissing the bishops after the benediction and before the enthronisation. It has never been restored. And, for the homage, the kiss on the cheek was replaced by one on the royal hand.

It is also clear that several of the vestments ceased to be used, although the history of their progressive abandonment is difficult to trace with any exactitude. In 1714 it is recorded that a dalmatic robe, a supertunica, a girdle, buskins, sandals and the armils were made. But it is one thing for them to be made and quite another for them to be used. No 'Form and Order' ever refers to the use of either buskins or sandals. The formulary for 1714 describes the Dean of Westminster as taking the armils from the altar, putting them around the king's neck and tying them to his arms, and of his being invested with 'the Robe Royal or Purple Robe of State of Cloth of Tissue & lined or furred with Ermin.'[38] In 1727 the 'Form and Order' describes George II as wearing a crimson robe, the supertunica, until it was taken off and the royal robe of tissue put on. In the case of George IV the supertunica and royal robe appear but the armils, although made, were not used. His royal robe, however, was preserved and used subsequently by George V, George VI and the present queen.[39] Victoria's robes also actually survive in the Museum of London. She wore the *colobium sindonis* and the supertunica on arrival at the Abbey, both garments resembling rather a ballgown than a medieval vestment. Her appearance in this guise is recorded in a series of paintings, capturing different moments in the ceremony, as well as in what was to become customary, a Coronation portrait. In the case of George III's by Allan Ramsay, Horace Walpole records that he was 'painted exactly from the very robes which the King wore at his Coronation'.[40] From this picture alone it is clear we have travelled a very long way from the vestments typical of a medieval, Tudor or, indeed, Stuart Coronation. The only vestment, if such it can be designated, of any significance is the royal or imperial robe.

Although the vestments, which had to be made for each Coronation, could be dropped with impunity, the items of insignia demanded to be used, namely, the two sceptres, one topped with a cross and the other with a dove, the spurs, the orb, the ring and the crown of St Edward. To them must be added the state crown which was worn in the return procession and at the banquet. The sceptres and orb remained constant, but new rings were made on each occasion and existing crowns dismantled and reset. The crown of St Edward, indeed, had never been anything other than a frame which was set with hired jewels for each Coronation. The cost of this was enormous.

For George III £375,000 worth of diamonds were bestowed on it, various other items of the regalia and jewels worn by the royal family. For George IV the estimates reached dizzying heights: the imperial crown was estimated to cost £50,000 to £100,000, the hatband which he wore in the procession to the Abbey £8,000, coronets for the royal dukes £4,000, those for the princesses and duchesses £2,000. The drastic economy exercised by William IV led to the jewellers Rundall's offering to produce seven coronets for the royal dukes and duchesses for £50 for the lot, which the firm of Green & Ward undercut by offering to do them for £40. Queen Adelaide went along with wearing Mary of

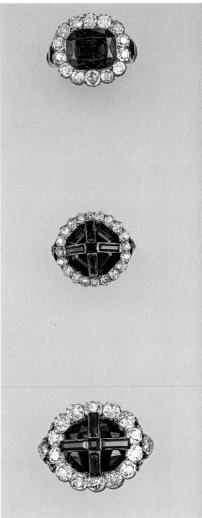

Below left The Imperial State Crown made for Queen Victoria, 1838, hand coloured lithograph, *c.* 1838

Below Sovereign's ring, Consort's ring and Victoria's Coronation ring

Modena's diadem, but refused to wear her crown, having a new one made from jewels taken from those belonging to Queen Charlotte. The final bill for jewels in 1831 was a mere £1,453 19s 8d, far less than the £15,000 originally estimated.

The Coronation of William IV saw a similar economy exercised in respect of the furnishings used in the Abbey, old state chairs being borrowed from St James's Palace and the House of Lords. That was a marked contrast to the superb furniture made for earlier Hanoverian Coronations. Queen Charlotte's Coronation chair can be glimpsed in Ramsay's portrait of her in her robes, a sumptuous rococo piece by the cabinetmakers and upholsterers, William Vile and John Cobb. This and George III's chair are now at Chatsworth. George IV's can be seen at Grimsthorpe Castle, having been claimed by Peter Burrell, Lord Gwydir, in his role as Deputy Lord Great Chamberlain.

Although the Coronation seems to have been progressively less and less understood throughout the eighteenth and into the nineteenth centuries that did not impair an ever-widening fascination for the event. Public interest, aided by the new media, increased almost in inverse proportion to any real comprehension of the rite. This can be followed in the steady upward graph of numbers of seats called for in the Abbey. Those seats fall into two groups, the first, those in the giving of the Earl Marshal and the second, those sold to the public for the benefit of the Dean and Chapter. In the first group there were 2,569 people on seats reduced to 18 inches in width in 1714. Sir Christopher Wren, still Surveyor, was ordered only eight days before the ceremony 'that you take care to make Galleryes and Seats for as many persons as possible on each side of the Choir, and great Theatre and Elsewhere convenient . . .'.[41] In 1727, which was a splendid event, there was a 'Large addition of scaffolding' to accommodate all the foreign visitors. The Works accounts specifically refer to: 'The large addition of scaffolding in Westminster Abbey by making so large accommodation for Foreigners & others, & by placing all the Staircases on the Outside of the said Scaffolds, which before were in the middle of the Seats, very inconvenient & not so secure, together with additional Scaffolds & Extra preparations for the Musick.'[42] The arrangements included four seats 'for those who sold Wine, Coffee &c. in the Abbey'. The total of those seated under royal aegis in 1727 was 1,780, with 140 in the foreigners' box. In George III's case the number was 1,339 and for George IV it leapt up to 4,656.

All of these seats were distributed via the Earl Marshal's office to peers and other officers of state. The number of seats allocated to each person was laid down on each occasion. In 1714 a peer received 6 tickets, a peeress 1, a bishop and Privy Councillor 4, and a Clerk in Council 2. In 1821 the peers received 5, the Privy Councillors 4, the Knights of the Bath 3, the Clerks in Council 2 and each peeress 1 only. These tickets were obtained from the Earl Marshal's office on certain days, the opening times of which were advertised in the newspapers.

From the point of view of the Dean and Chapter the Coronation might be described as a licence to print money. They controlled the area of the Abbey running from the west door to the choir screen, the Jerusalem Chamber with its roof and the exterior churchyard wall. Scaffolds at first only began to be erected along the nave, sometimes in such a way as to give rise to battles with the Earl Marshal as encroachment was made on the width of the processional way. The Coronation

Admission ticket for George III's Coronation, 1761

was a lucrative exercise for the Abbey. In 1714 the takings were £199 10s 6d and in 1727 £380 14s. In the Abbey Muniments there is a document which gives, although the sources are not cited, the history of charging through the ages: a halfpenny for Edward II, a penny for Richard II, twopence for Henry IV, a half groat for Edward IV, rising to a shilling for James I and Charles I.[43] For the Coronations of Charles II and Anne the price escalated to a crown. With the Hanoverians, however, we are on much firmer ground, for the muniment room is crammed with material on this money spinner. In 1727 front seats in the galleries were available at 10 guineas and in 1821 seats could be had for 10, 15 and 20 guineas, with further cheaper seats available at 2 and 3 guineas at the far west end. By that date the choir had petitioned and got a portion of the building known as the vaultings, which they were able to let as their part of the spoils. An advertisement reads: 'The Public are respectfully informed that SINGLE SEATS, or SITTINGS for four, six, or parties of eight may be obtained by an early application at the office, No. 33, corner of Bridge-Street, Westminster.'[44]

For the Coronation of an unpopular king, like George IV, the seats failed to sell. On 18 July 1821 James Wyatt wrote to the dean saying that he had petitioned the Lord Great Chamberlain that 'our Boxes would present an empty appearance to His Majesty', suggesting that all the unsold seats should be offered at six guineas or given away 'rather than the boxes should remain in such a forlorn appearance . . .'.[45]

George III's Coronation offers detailed material on the Abbey's activities. The Dean and Chapter subcontracted the seven arches on the north side and five on the south side of the nave running to the choir screen to a builder for £2,550. On the south side two arches were retained, one of which was the dean's gallery and the other for the use of the twelve prebends. The Chapter also gave permission for the erection of 'Rooms of Entertainment', one on the north side and another on the cloister greensward. An advertisement again expands our picture: 'Seats are to let in WESTMINSTER ABBEY, from the West Door to the Choir. Rooms are built for with drawing, and the best refreshments provided, and every convenience studied that can make it fit for the reception of Ladies and Gentlemen.'[46]

The net result must have been a scene akin to what happens at Ascot today. Robert Huish elaborates on the comforts that were available in 1821: 'Agents attended from some of the most considerable confectioners in town; tables were set out under proper superintendence; and ices, fruit, wine, sandwiches, and "such savoury messes" were to be obtained, of good quality, and upon reasonable terms.[47] Things had certainly moved on from the humble vendors present at late Stuart Coronations.

The escalation in seating in the Abbey was matched by a similar development in respect of Westminster Hall. Although that came to an end in 1831 with William IV's truncation of the Coronation, up until then there was mounting pressure for more and more seating in the hall. In 1727 there was, we are told, 'a very great increase in the number of seats',[48] and in 1761 the galleries for onlookers were increased from two to three, the third 'as it were in the roof'. The final count of onlookers in 1821 was 2,934 people.[49]

Both Hall and Abbey were major medieval buildings sacrificed to these needs, for the damage which could be and indeed was done was considerable. Huish records in the case of George III's Coronation that 'it was the boast of the workmen, that they had broken the noses, and cut off the ears of a whole legion of angels'. By 1821 the atmosphere had changed and the ancient monuments were boarded over for protection.

Every Coronation called for the clearance of Westminster Hall. In 1727 this began with a warrant dated 19 August from the Lord Great Chamberlain asking that all the partitions in the Court of Wards be demolished, along with the shops and the Courts of Justice and Exchequer. It seemed to have occurred to no one that all of these institutions cried out to be housed elsewhere. The space cleared, which was achieved in three days, a second warrant followed laying down a long list of requirements: a box for no less than 50 royal relatives, a platform and steps at the south end upon which the king was to dine enthroned in state, a table for the regalia, a gallery over the north door for trumpeters, kettle-drums and an organ, sheds and cooking ranges outside, rails at the north door to control the crowds, a screen at the foot of the stone stairs, behind which there was to be access to the viewing galleries, accommodation for the peeresses, boxes for the ambassadors, the heralds and the king's Private Musick. Kitchens were to be erected nearby in Cotton Garden.

As in the Abbey the onlookers may have had to endure long hours of waiting but they, too, did not go unprovided for. Although rooms of refreshment and vendors found no place here, what happened to alleviate that lack is vividly described by one John Venning in 1761: 'It was pleasant to see the various stratagems made use of by the company in the galleries to come in for a snack of the good things below. The ladies

Right Triumphal arch
by William Kent in
Westminster Hall for the
Coronation of George II,
1727, engraving, *c.*1727

Opposite Design by William
Oram for the arch erected
in Westminster Hall for the
Coronation of George III,
drawing, 1761

clubbed their handkerchiefs to be tied together to draw up a chicken, or bottle of wine. Some had been so prudent as to bring baskets with them, which were let down like the prisoners' boxes at Ludgate . . .'[50]

The setting for this culinary free-for-all also became progressively more elaborate. Although nothing is known about what was super-imposed over the north door of the hall in 1714, subsequent Coronations overlaid splendid temporary architecture. William Kent designed the arch for George II's Coronation, one which was specifically approved by the king. In 1761 the arch was by the Office of Works architect, William Ouram, and based on the Arch of Titus. More significant was the introduction and development of lighting. In 1727 there were 50 large and 40 smaller chandeliers. In 1761 the lighting was stage-managed to add to the spectacle. The hall was in virtual darkness and, as Queen Charlotte entered, trains of flax were lit and in less than half a minute the hall was 'a blaze of splendor'. The lighting arrangements for George IV were less satisfactory. It was a

very hot day, not helped by 2,000 candles in vast chandeliers and candelabra being lit. As in 1761, the lights were suddenly ignited as the procession entered, but this time the effect was so overpowering that several ladies fainted. Worse followed: 'the superb dresses of the peers and peeresses were spoiled by the profuse globules of melted wax which were continually falling upon them . . . if a lovely female dared to raise her look to discover from what quarter the unwelcome visitation came, she was certain of receiving an additional patch upon her cheeks . . .'[51]

Every Coronation began in Westminster Hall with the assembling of those who were to take part in the ceremony, followed by the arrival of the ecclesiastical procession from the Abbey bearing the regalia, items of which were then distributed to those who would carry them. One document amongst the Abbey's muniments tells us what happened in the Abbey prior to the ecclesiastical procession leaving for the hall on the occasion of George IV's Coronation.[52] It is likely that this was a repetition of what was done on previous occasions. The prebendaries assembled in the high dining room of the deanery, the scholars of Westminster School (who were to greet the monarch with cries of *Vivat*) in the organ room and the various choirs (that of the Abbey and those of the Chapels Royal) in College Hall. There they vested themselves in surplices and copes and the dean delivered the various items of the regalia, including the Bible, to eight senior prebends. That did not always go according to plan, for it is recorded that in 1727 three crowns were carried to Westminster Hall by mistake, the two needed for crowning George II and Caroline and also the state crown which should have been left in St Edward's chapel for the king to wear on his return to the hall.

The copes worn are likely to have been those made for the Coronation of Charles II. That copes were not generally worn by eighteenth-century bishops may be gathered from a letter written by Archbishop Secker to the Dean of Westminster in August 1761, in which he states that he was told that Archbishop Wake had borrowed one from the Abbey to wear at the previous Coronation 'as probably several of his predecessors did', and could they loan him one 'that is decent and not too heavy'.[53] In 1821 there is reference to a cope of flowered purple and gold, four of plain gold, one of embroidered purple and five others which had been lent.[54]

In this manner the procession to Westminster Hall would be ordered, headed by the Westminster Scholars, then the Serjeant of the Vestry followed by the children of the Abbey choir walking two by two, followed by those of the Chapels Royal, and after them the adult members of the Abbey choir and the Gentlemen of the Chapel Royal. The sequence continued with all the members of the Abbey chapter, the king's confessor and the sub-dean, the prebend's verger, the prebends themselves bearing the regalia, the dean's verger and, finally, the dean himself carrying the crown of St Edward.

In this way they entered the Abbey and, as they approached the sacrarium, parted, forming a line up to the high altar which allowed the regalia bearers to place the various pieces on the altar itself. There they remained until the signal was received that they should make their way to the hall. This time the Westminster Scholars peeled off at the organ and took up their places to receive the king. Otherwise the procession was as before, along a raised walkway (to which I will return) to the hall, those prebends not bearing regalia walking in pairs, those with items in single file. On entering the hall they were met by the heralds who conducted them to the enthroned monarch at the far south end. This was a stately progress calling for no less than four separate obeisances at fixed points along the hall, one on entry, a second midway, after which the choirs split forming a lane through which walked the regalia bearers, Garter King of Arms before them. At the foot of the steps to the dais there was a third obeisance, and a fourth as they reached the table on which the items were to be placed.

The dean began by presenting the crown of St Edward to the Lord High Constable, who placed it on the table. Then each prebendary knelt to present an item to the dean, who passed it to the Constable and hence to the table. At the close they all retired again to the far end of the hall.

Thomas Gray, the poet, records in a letter describing the scene in 1761, that the table could be elaborately decorated. There was, he writes, 'in front of the throne . . . a Triomfe of foliage and flowers, resembling nature, placed on the royal table, & rising as high as the canopy itself'.

Everyone who was to walk in the procession had to assemble in the hall and await the entry of the king. The convergence on the place of so many people presented problems of traffic control for aristocrats and officials arriving by coach or sedan chair. Set routes had to be laid down for the delivery of participants, with any lingering of vehicles strictly forbidden. In 1761 the sedan chair porters refused to carry out these orders unless they were paid a large sum. The Privy Council declined and there was almost a strike, which was eventually averted. Peers and peeresses arrived already in their robes, their underdress being in accordance with rules laid down by the Earl Marshal. In 1761 for the peers it was as follows: 'Their Under-Habits of very rich Gold or Silver Brocades white silk Stockings and white Shoes the Swords in Scabbards of Crimson Velvet appended to a Belt of the same and either full bottomed Periwigs or Wigs without bags tied behind with a Ribbon curled and flowing down to the small of the Back.'[55]

No hats were to be worn, although they could be put on at the feast. Peers who were members of an order of chivalry were to wear their collars. The result of all this was to give a visual coherence to the ceremony, one of crimson velvet, furred with ermine according to rank, with glimpses of white, gold and silver beneath.

Control of dress went much further in 1821 than ever before. This was a pageant stage-managed by the king himself as a Tudorbethan spectacle. Prototypes of the 'under habits and dresses' for peers of the realm and other dignitaries were exhibited for the benefit of tailors at the College of Arms on 17 June 1820.[56] A year later there was a similar display and, of course, large numbers of costumes still survive. This venture into theatricality evoked a mixed reponse. The *Annual Register* recorded that 'the splendour and singularity of the costumes produced much amusement among the ladies',[57] but Sir Walter Scott was swept away by it all: 'The whole was so completely harmonised in actual colouring, as well as in association, with general mass of gay and gorgeous and antique dress which floated before the eye.'[58]

On this occasion Scott's pen was to be surpassed by that of the painter Benjamin Robert Haydon, whose description of Westminster Hall at the opening of George IV's Coronation remains unforgettable. The artist dressed for the occasion in a blue velvet coat, ruffles, shoe buckles and a sword, arriving in the Lord Chamberlain's box at 4 a.m. Here is how he viewed the spectacle: 'It combined all the gorgeous splendour of ancient chivalry with the intense heroic interest of modern times – everything that could effect or excite, either in beauty, heroism, genius, grace, elegance or taste; all that was rich in colour, gorgeous in effect, touching in association, English in character or Asiatic in magnificence, was crowded into this golden & enchanted hall!'

And then came the magic moment of the royal entry:

A whisper of mystery turns all eyes to the throne. Suddenly two or three run, others fall back; some talk, direct, hurry, stand still, or disappear. Then three or four of high rank appear from behind the Throne; an interval is left; the crowds scarce breathe! Something rustles, and a being buried in satin, feathers, & diamonds rolls gracefully into his seat. The room rises with a sort

Caroline of Ansbach in her
Coronation robes, painting,
*c.*1727

of feathered, silken thunder! Plumes wave, eyes sparkle, glasses are out, mouths smile, and one man becomes the prime object of attraction to thousands! The way in which the King bowed was monarchic! As he looked towards the peeresses & Foreign Ambassadors, he looked like some gorgeous bird of the East.'[59]

George IV's robe was directly modelled on that of Napoleon, and a tailor had even been sent to Paris to study it. The result was a train so long it called for eight train-bearers The only other royal figure who came close to this bejewelled and befeathered apparition was Caroline of Ansbach. She followed the example set by Mary of Modena by wearing purple, but what set her appearance apart was the cascade of diamonds smothering her petticoat which was 'as fine as the accumulated riches of the City and suburbs could make it'.[60] Her robe was fastened at the shoulders by huge strings of borrowed pearls, her bodice was 'covered with divers large breast Jewels' and her petticoat, which was of cloth of silver, was 'paned up and down with three wide Rows of Lockets of Diamonds and precious stones'.[61] Charles Jervas records this astonishing dress in his portrait of her in the National Portrait Gallery.

Before the procession moved off the king bestowed on those whom he had chosen various items of the regalia. Things inevitably went wrong. In 1727 the dean and his colleagues omitted to bring the chalice and paten. George III's Coronation was a complete shambles. No chairs had been provided for the king and queen to sit on, nor was there a canopy to carry over them. The hurried attempts to improvise and solve these problems left the dean and his colleagues marooned outside the north door for an hour and a half. Then it transpired that the sword of state had also been forgotten and the Lord Mayor's was taken and used in its place. Even the distribution of the regalia was bungled. Thomas Gray records that 'the Bishop of Rochester [who was also Dean of Westminster] would have drop'd the Crown, if it had not been pin'd to the Cushion, & the King was often obliged to call out, & sett matters right'. The heralds were 'stupid', the great officers of state 'knew nothing they were doing . . .'.[62]

All of that done, the great procession could move off. The route lay out of the north door, through New Palace Yard, Parliament Street, Bridge Street and King Street to the west door of the Abbey. Of all the changes that occurred between 1714 and 1838 the procession was to be the most affected. The route was no longer a more or less open space. It was now lined with houses on both sides. In 1738 Westminster Bridge

was built and Bridge Street, George Street and King Street replaced what before had been a maze of alleyways. The unsightly houses which were huddled around the Abbey were demolished and the building itself was repaired by Sir Christopher Wren, to be followed by Hawksmoor's addition of the two west towers which were completed by 1740. Canaletto's panorama of the Abbey with the Knights of the Bath moving in procession records a space which had gained in both clarity and presence.

Georgian medieavalism: Hawksmoor's West Front of Westminster Abbey, painting, 1749

The procession, which was the only part of the event open to more or less anyone, was hugely popular. People viewed it from specially built scaffolds, from the roofs and windows of houses as well as from the pavement. The throng was such in 1727 that a special walkway was constructed 13 feet wide and lifting the procession 18 inches above

The procession back to Westminster Hall at the Coronation of George IV, 1821, lithograph, 1821

ground level. It was railed, and a decision was taken later that it should also be covered in case it rained. Both innovations were adopted for every subsequent Coronation until the procession was dropped in 1831. That what was done in 1727 fell short we can gather from the arrangements in 1761 when the width of the walkway was increased to 15 feet and the level above the ground doubled to 3. That walkway not only wound its way through the streets but also actually into the Abbey itself as far as the choir screen. Inside the abbey its width rose to 24 feet.

On either side of the walkway soldiers were stationed. In 1761 there was 2,800 of them, which obscured the view of the populace, so much so that James Henning describes how 'The mob underneath made a pretty contrast to the rest of the company.' It was to give him 'great pain to see soldiers, both horse and foot, obliged unmercifully to belabour the heads of the mob with their broad swords, bayonets and musquets . . .'.[63] A London mob could be pretty rough, and we read of aristocrats covered in jewels having to be escorted through the rabble to Westminster Hall.

This shows that the army had a repressive connotation which was only to change with the Napoleonic wars. Up until then the army was viewed as a potentially threatening force, there to suppress any dissidents. That changed with the advent of what was in effect the first national army, for it was made up of both volunteer and militia forces. What had been a force for governmental suppression was now transformed into one which was patriotic, the embodiment of a nation's heroism. Only because that happened was it possible to incorporate the military into the carriage procession which replaced the old one on foot from 1831.

All along the route windows and balconies were crammed with onlookers but, in addition, tiers of seats – scaffolds – were built. Horace Walpole records that in 1727 his mother paid 40 guineas for a dining room, a bedchamber and a viewing scaffold. He reckoned that the same facilities in 1761 would cost 250 guineas. The Dean and Chapter leased out St Margaret's churchyard where a scaffold 259 feet long was erected. That exercise brought them in over £950. In addition, for the Coronation of George III, the Jerusalem Chamber with its flat roof and also the stretch of ground before the registrar's house were let for £300 and £125 respectively.

There was great concern by the authorities that these scaffolds should be safe. On 11 September 1727 the Coronation Committee issued an order that all scaffolds should be inspected both for strength and for safety. Any which failed to come up to scratch or encroached upon the processional way were to be demolished. The result of the inspection was that the scaffolds were discovered to be 'so light, that the lives of many of His Majesty's subjects may be endangered thereby'.[64] Each of these scaffolds held between 1,200 to 1,500 seats and the financial pickings made by those who owned property along the route were considerable. In 1761 one little house made £700 and a larger one £1,000. And the opportunity for profit did not end there, for there was money to be made also by the catering trade. In 1761 onlookers were being charged as much as sixpence for a glass of water and a shilling for a humble bread roll.

The procession always excited comment. In 1727 it included all the Knights of the Garter, the Thistle and the Bath in their robes. Lady Mary Wortley Montagu tartly observed: 'The business of every walker was to conceal vanity and gain admiration.'[65] Gray writes in 1761 of the Privy Councillors 'mightily dressed in rich stuffs of gold and colours, with long flowing wigs, some of them comical enough', and that the Knights of the Bath 'with their high plumage, were very ornamental'.[66] 'It was in truth,' wrote Horace Walpole to Lady Ailesbury of the same occasion, 'a brave sight. The sea of heads in Palace Yard, the Guards, horse and foot, the scaffolds, balconies and procession exceeded imagination.'[67]

Gray and Walpole's view of 1761 was not shared by everyone. One newspaper account is scathing, complaining that the overhead awning, 'far from adding to the lustre of the appearance . . . greatly diminished it'. And, as for the procession, it was 'generally less numerous and infinitely less brilliant than was in general expected', going on to

The King's Herb Woman and her Maids, 1821, coloured engraving, 1823

complain of the dearth of diamonds.[68] The sumptuous folio designed to immortalise George IV's procession captures the splendour of these processions, in his case 700 elaborately costumed people parading past like figures resurrected from Gloriana's England with George casting himself as the Faery King as its climax. All this was as dust in 1831 when William IV did away with the procession and everything which happened in Westminster Hall. At the time this was greeted with dismay by the Tory press, but in the long run it was to work to the crown's advantage, for it precipitated a form which still has vigour today, the carriage procession through the streets of London.

One of the most interesting publications in 1761 anticipated this. It is entitled *Thoughts on the Coronation of his Present Majesty King George the Third* . . . 'Our kings,' it complained, 'with their train, have crept to the Temple through obscure Passages; and the Crown has been worn out of Sight of the People.' The old route on foot was both too narrow and too short, the front of the procession entering the west

George IV with his train borne by eight sons of peers, 1821, coloured engraving, 1823

door of the Abbey before the end had even left the hall. The author states that the monarch should go one way to the Abbey and return by another. He lists no less than nine different routes and in particular proposes one which would leave St James's Palace (Buckingham Palace had yet to come), go along Pall Mall, Charing Cross, Whitehall, Parliament Street, King Street, past St Margaret's and into the Abbey. This is a blueprint of what was to happen after 1831.

Whether anyone in 1831 was aware of this anonymous tract is unknown, but the author's wish began to be fulfilled. At 5 a.m. there was a salute in St James's Park, and half an hour later the household troops arrived and a band played. Footguards and two squadrons of Lifeguards lined the route from Parliament Street to the Abbey. At 9 a.m. a carriage procession left the palace, the king and queen leaving an hour later in George III's golden state coach, the first time that it was ever used for a Coronation. All along the route there were stands for the public with places available for as little as 2 guineas. At Charing Cross alone there were scaffolds capable of holding two to three thousand spectators.

That Coronation was staged on the eve of the passing of the Reform Bill. Even more interesting is how the formula was developed in 1838 for Queen Victoria. Lord Melbourne refused any resurrection of the old pageantry, realising the huge potential of displaying the young queen to her new subjects, many of whom now had the vote. Greville writes that the main purpose of the Coronation was 'to amuse and interest them [i.e. the people]'.[69] With Queen Victoria,

Above William IV's Coronation procession (detail), painting

Overleaf The State Coach of George III, 1761, which from the Coronation of William IV became the Coronation Coach

High Constable   Trumpeters   Equerry

The Duchess of Kent's Carriage   *Life Guards*

Ensign and Lieutenant of the Yeomen   *Six of the Queen's Horses, with Rich Trappings*

Life Guards

The Duchess of Gloucester's Carriage

The Queen's State Coach   *The Knight Marshal*   *Capt. - General of the Royal Archers* ↓   *Marshalmen*

Queen Victoria's Coronation procession, 1838, folding engraved panorama, 1838

Buckingham Palace also becomes for the first time part of the scenario. In 1838 the procession came out of Buckingham Palace, along Constitution Hill, Piccadilly, to St James's, Pall Mall, Charing Cross, Whitehall and Parliament Street. All along the route buildings, from the new gentlemen's clubs in Pall Mall to ordinary shops in St James's, were decorated saluting the queen. The procession was far larger than in 1831, opening with the Lifeguards, then the carriages of foreign ambassadors and ministers, two bands of the Household Brigade, a whole suite of carriages bearing members of the royal family and, somewhat oddly, the Queen's Bargemen walking along with 48 of her Watermen. Victoria's own suite ran to a dozen carriages with yet more Lifeguards and military and the queen in what was now described as the Coronation coach.

In Victoria's case we have something utterly unique, her own account of the day: 'It was a fine day, and the crowds of people exceeded what I have ever seen, many as there were the day I went to the City, it was nothing, nothing to the multitudes, the millions of my loyal subjects, who were assembled in every spot to witness the Procession. Their good humour and excessive loyalty was beyond everything, and I really cannot say how proud I feel to be Queen of such a Nation.'[70]

The importance of this innovation cannot be overestimated during a century which was to witness the progressive extension of the franchise and the need for the monarchy to be visible to more and more of its people than ever before.

For those involved in the Coronation the deletion of the old ceremonies curtailed what had become an interminable day. George I arrived at Westminster Hall at about 9 a.m., George II at 8 a.m. and George III at 9 a.m. again. By the time the banquet was over it was dark, a long twelve-hour day, incredibly demanding on all those who took part. Even before the draconian measures of 1831 every effort was made somehow to shorten the ceremony. The sermon was reduced to a bare ten minutes, fifteen at the most, which probably accounts for how little it added to the event. No wonder that in 1902 it was dropped. The homage continued as a contracted affair with each rank rendering it collectively.

With the eighteenth century we enter the era of the diary, the letter and the memoir-writer, with the result that we have more accounts than ever before of what went on in the Abbey or, more often than not, went wrong. The general view, from those utilising these sources, is that the art of ceremonial declined. It is true to say that there are of signs of breakdown, inevitable when gaps of some sixty years could happen between one reign and the next. But in the absence of that kind of material for the earlier periods, how are we to exclude the possibility that much might have been botched at those Coronations, too? There is no way of knowing. But for the Hanoverian Coronations we really have evidence that things did go appallingly awry. In 1727 it was recorded that at the Coronation of George I there had been 'great confusion' because the Gentlemen Pensioners and the Yeomen of the Guard, instead of sticking at their posts, had wandered up into the theatre, getting in the way of those who had a right to be there. Far more interesting is a copy of the 'Form and Order' for George II annotated by Archbishop Wake 'With notes of what was done or omitted at that Coronation', one celebrated for its music by Handel. He records that the anthem which should have greeted the king and queen on entering the Abbey was never sung thanks to 'the Negligence of the Choir of Westminster'. After the anthem trumpets were sounded and another anthem was to be sung but, he notes, 'The Anthem in Confusion: All irregular in the Music.' Even Handel's immortal 'Zadok the Priest' was sung in the wrong place by mistake, replacing the *Veni creator*.[71] This was, of course, glossed over in the published accounts like, for example, that by William Hawkins, Ulster Herald of Arms, published in Dublin, which states that everything was 'conducted with such Exactness and good Order, that I dare venture to say, it has outdone any heretofore . . .'.[72]

George III's Coronation was a disaster area which 'plainly showed all the actors were not perfect in their parts'. A letter by one Catherine Talbot, dated 22 September 1761, describes how the king knew the ceremonial better than the heralds 'and had much patience and good humour in bearing their numerous mistakes, and stupidities, as quickness and attention in setting them right'. Queen Charlotte was observed looking exhausted on account of the weight of her robes and 'half frighted with the state of the Canopy, that being ill put together, and worse held, and likely to fall on her every minute . . .'.[73] Later the queen had the shock of finding the Duke of Newcastle making use of her retiring chamber. James Henning pithily summed it all up: 'The whole was confusion, irregularity, and disorder.'[74] But George III was at least good-humoured enough to take the whole fiasco in his stride. Horace Walpole characteristically records that the king complained to the Deputy Earl Marshal, the Earl of Effingham, who admitted: 'it was true; there had been great neglect in that office, but he had in need taken such care of registering such directions, that the next Coronation would be conducted with the greatest order imaginable'.[75]

For George IV's Coronation everyone who had a part to play was provided with a printed form of their duties, and went through them precisely in the way that they would perform on the day. Even then things went wrong, for when the king retired to St Edward's chapel the peerage left the Abbey before the returning procession, with the consequence that the king walked past tiers of empty seats covered with dirt and litter.

By 1838 seats were being sold to see the rehearsal. But descriptions of early-nineteenth-century Coronations make it clear that, even if those involved did rehearse, the results were far from orderly. The historian Macaulay writes of William IV's truncated affair: 'The Archbishop mumbled, the Bishop of London preached well enough, but not so effectively as the occasion required ... and the King behaved very awkwardly, his bearing making the foolish parts of the ritual appear monstrously ridiculous ...'[76]

When it came to Victoria, Lord Melbourne urged her to go to a rehearsal in the Abbey. Although she wrote: 'I'm very glad I went to the Abbey as I shall know exactly where I am to go', her diary reveals that that was far from the case. The Bishop of Durham, she complains, could 'never tell me what was to take place' and, as for the archbishop, he 'came in and ought to have delivered the Orb to me, but I had already got it, and he (as usual) was so confused and puzzled and knew nothing ...'.[77] Both Disraeli and Greville wrote of the lack of rehearsal, so that in one place it became so bad that two pages were turned over by mistake and the Bishop of Bath and Wells instructed the queen to go through to St Edward's chapel from which she had to be brought back. Nor was she so forgiving to the Archbishop of Canterbury who rammed her Coronation ring on to the wrong finger, which she only managed to remove with a great deal of pain.

Illustrations of George IV's Coronation shows that the arrangements were in the main still those found in Sandford. There could be slight variations. The bishops, for example, did not kiss the king's cheek in 1727, but his hand. This was repeated in 1838 in the interests of modesty. So much of the final impression, however, depended on the personal attributes of the leading player. George III, in the midst of chaos, behaved impeccably. George IV, having cast himself as the Faery King, failed to live up to the part. With his 50-inch waist and layers of velvet, lace and jewels he looked, Lady Palmerston remarked, 'more like the Victim than the Hero of the fete . . . several times he was at the last gasp, but a cheering brought in the shape of a look from L[a]dy C[onyngha]me, and it revived him like Magic or Ether'.[78] Mrs Arbuthnot also noticed this transaction, going on to write: 'Anybody who could have seen his disgusting figure, with a wig the curls of which hung down his back, & quite bending beneath the weight of his robes & his 60 years w[oul]d have been quite sick.'[79] William IV, as we have seen, was just awkward and embarrassed by the whole affair, while the virginal Victoria, a mere slip of a girl, brought tears to Lord Melbourne's eyes.

Whatever the mistakes, the service became an increasingly elaborate musical event. Very little is known about the arrangements in 1714, but the association of George II and Handel in 1727 has gone down as a landmark. The king had, indeed, insisted on having him, and he was appointed organist and composer to the Chapel Royal on

Above George Frederic Handel, painting, 1756

Left A page from the score for the Coronation of 1727

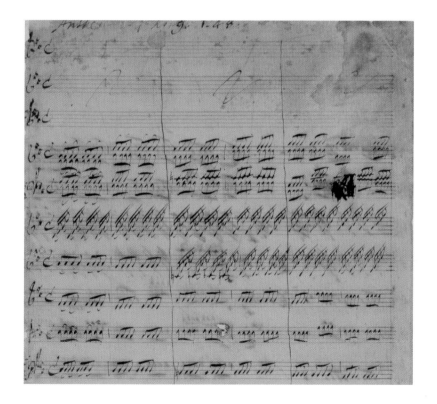

4 August of that year. The numbers of both the musicians and the voices begin to increase. The seating in 1714 includes that for the 'singing mens Gallery next the South East Corner – 24', but George II's Coronation accounts list scaffolds in the choir and those for 'the Private Musick' as having 60 seats 'In the two Arches joyning, westward for the Church Musick' and 120 'seats over to the Alter, and in the side Arches, is for vocall & Instruments of all Musick'. Eighty tickets were assigned to Handel for the music gallery and 38 for the King's Musick. The evidence about the final result is conflicting – we have already described the gaffes – but a lot of the problems arose from the Grinling Gibbons altarpiece which Queen Anne had donated. The problems that this object posed for the musicians were such that William Boyce tried to get the upper part of it dismantled in 1761: 'The First Grand Musical Performance in the Abbey, was at the Coronation of King George the Second, and the late Mr Handel, who composed the Music, often lamented his not having that part of the Altar taken away as He, and all the Musicians concerned, experienced the bad effect it had by that obstruction.'

Other evidence indicates that 1727 was a far from perfect musical event. There was a lack of singers as boys' voices had broken, so that others had to be brought in and a special organ imported to avoid any rows with the Abbey staff.[80]

George III, in fact, agreed to having the offending part of the altar removed for the occasion, for which Boyce composed eight anthems. By 1821 any liturgical sense was beginning to evaporate, and the music for both George IV and William IV was composed by Thomas Attwood, a pupil of Mozart. George IV took an intense and misguided interest in the music, insisting on inserting Handel's Hallelujah Chorus to greet him as he entered the Abbey. To crown even that, 'Rule Britannia' was introduced into the opening of the anthem 'O Lord, grant the King', and the National Anthem prefaced 'I was glad'. William IV had an orchestra of 69 and 118 vocalists, a combination of the choirs of Westminster and both Chapels Royal as well as the choir from St Paul's Cathedral. Their music lecterns were in the form of angel's wings. That escalated even more in 1838 when the intent was to have an orchestra of 400 and female vocalists were introduced for the first time.

In addition to this festival of music, the air was punctuated by peals of bells. In 1821 the Abbey bells rang for an hour at midnight, for

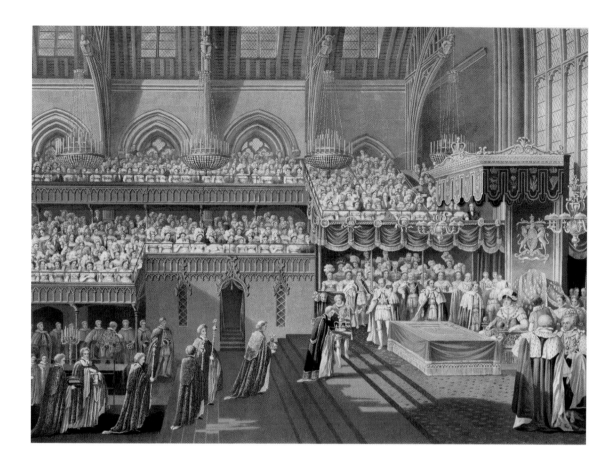

another hour at 4 a.m. or daybreak and then from time to time until the great procession started. The bells rang again at the crowning, during the return to Westminster Hall and for an hour while the king dined.[81] To this we can add the usual signal being given from the Abbey roof at the moment of crowning, which triggered a gun salute in St James's Park.

For those involved in the ceremony the feast was yet to come. That also escalated in terms of numbers to the extent that everybody could no longer be accommodated in the hall. As early as 1727 tables sprang up in the exchequer and by 1821 no less than 47 tables of every shape and size were scattered through the rooms of the old palace. On that occasion there were 1,268 diners and the College of Arms preserves a whole volume dedicated to it, including both menus and plans for every table.[82] Mistakes could, of course, equally be made here. In 1761 no provision had been made for the Barons of the Cinque Ports or for

The Dean and Prebendaries of Westminster Abbey bearing the Regalia to George IV, coloured engraving, 1823

the Lord Mayor of London's party. There was a confrontation with the Lord High Steward, Lord Talbot, resulting in their sitting in the places reserved for the Knights of the Bath, who were reseated where the great officers of state should have sat. What happened to them we are not told. In 1821 the feast also began badly. Lord Anglesea in his role as Lord High Steward was meant to ride the length of the hall with the Lord High Constable and the Deputy Earl Marshal. He was then supposed to dismount and uncover what had been placed on the royal table. Anglesea had lost a leg at the battle of Waterloo and made use of two types of artificial leg, one for riding and the other for walking. Unfortunately he failed to bring the latter and could not get off his horse. This inevitably caused untold mirth amongst those present until his pages hauled him off and somehow propped him up as he uncovered the dishes.

Vast quantities of food and drink were consumed. In 1821 there were 23 temporary kitchens which produced 160 tureens of soup, a similar quantity of fish and roasts, including venison, beef, mutton, veal, vegetables along with gravies in 480 sauce boats. There were also 3,271 cold dishes including ham, pasties, seafood and jellies. In the case of George III's feast, Thomas Gray provides information that the food and decoration could have meaning. There was, he noted, a huge display of good plate and the royal table was adorned with 'a dessert representing Parnassus with abundance of figures of Muses, Arts, etc. designed by Lord Talbot'.[83] Such a tableau signalled that the new reign was to be dedicated to a cultivation of the arts. The trouble with the tableau, however, was not its message but the fact that it was so high that those at the other end of the hall could not see the king and queen.

All the old rituals continued to be gone through, the mess of dilligrout, the various presentations of maple, silver-gilt and gold cups, but the one which always excited the most interest was the arrival of the Champion. By 1821 that was seen through the eyes of people steeped in the gothic novel and the romances of Sir Walter Scott. In 1727 someone had the imagination to place the Champion astride the horse which George II had ridden at the battle of Dettingen. What a contrast to 1821, when the horse was hired from Astley's Circus because the Dymock who should have performed the service was a clergyman and hence was obliged to make the task over to his son. Scott did not think much of the result: 'a little too much the appearance of the maiden-knight to be the challenger of the world on the King's

OPPOSITE
Top The delivery of the first course at the Coronation Banquet of George IV, 1821, engraving, 1823
Bottom The entry of the Lord High Constable, the Acting Earl Marshal and the Lord High Steward, engraving, 1823

behalf'.[84] However, the impact on Haydon was very different: 'The hall doors opened again, & outside in twilight a man in dark shadowed armour against the shining light appeared. He then moved, passed into the darkness under the arch, & Wellington, Howard, & the Champion stood in full view, with doors closed behind them. This was certainly the finest sight of the day'.[85] And with that striking tableau the Champion makes his final exit from the history of the Coronation.

The aftermath of the feast must have resembled a barbarian invasion. In 1761 the king and queen left at 10 p.m., after which the nobility also departed. This is what happened next: '– the hall doors were thrown open according to custom, when the people immediately cleared it of all moveables such as victuals, cloths, plates, dishes &c. and, in short, every thing that could stick to their fingers'.[86]

What happened at the last banquet in 1821 was even worse, the Lord Great Chamberlain just about saving the Coronation plate from being stolen. The people in the galleries descended like a ravening mob and snatched all the food and drink in sight: 'baskets, flower pots, vases, and figures were every where disappearing, and those were followed by glasses, knives and forks, salt spoons, and, finally, the plates and dishes'.[87] The soldiery just about arrived in time to prevent the mob invading the kitchens. At the finish those left were so knocked out that they were laid on the floor and fell asleep. The hall was not cleared until 3 a.m. and some women had to be carried to their coaches.

The Coronation was by no means over, for the festivities in the nineteenth century were spread throughout London and the rest of the country. That was a total *renversement* from 1714, which was certainly no occasion for national rejoicing. The country was split down the middle and on the day of the Coronation in over twenty towns in the south and west of England loyalists holding balls, making bonfires or drinking in celebration of the Protestant succession were assaulted by rioters who broke up such events and sacked the locations. The 1727 Coronation took place during an election, with the consequence that Whigs and Tories held different festivities. The Tory protest against the Hanoverian succession was to continue until it fizzled out in the second half of the century.[88] The change can be pinpointed to the unprecedented celebration of the golden jubilee of George III in October 1810, which had a universal response. The whole nation feasted, lit bonfires, opened some new public amenity or held balls in the local assembly rooms. By the time of George IV's Coronation there were fireworks in Hyde Park, where the trees were illuminated, the Serpentine was lit and there was a boat race. At one end of the lake, over the cascade, there was a transparency depicting the king in a triumphal chariot drawn by milk-white horses. On the bank opposite there was a temple surmounted by an imperial crown.[89] Robert Huish lists events taking place all over the country, and this was to be repeated both for William IV and Victoria. For her, extra rations of beef and porter were distributed in the workhouses and prisons, wine was donated to the voluntary hospitals with which to drink the new queen's health, and in charity schools what was called Coronation Pudding was served and the National Anthem sung.[90]

In a pre-television age the opportunity for those who had not seen the Coronation somehow to vicariously witness it did not go uncapitalised upon in the theatre. In 1761 Horace Walpole wrote to Lady Ailesbury: 'Garrick [at Drury Lane] exhibits the Coronation, and opening the end of the stage, discovers a real bonfire and real mob . . . Rich [at Covent Garden] is going to produce a finer Coronation, nay, than the real one, for there is to be dinner for the Knights of the Bath and the Barons of the Cinque Ports, which Lord Talbot refused them.'[91]

At Drury Lane the Coronation was an afterpiece inserted at the end of a production of Shakespeare's *Henry VIII*, while at Covent Garden both the procession and the feast were put on stage and the Abbey choir was employed in a production which ran for three or four months.

All of this registers the beginning of the spread of the event across a wider and wider spectrum of people as an incipient mass media came into being. The later Coronations prompted prints of the king and queen in their robes and regalia, popular equivalents of the grand state portraits. From George IV onwards prints also appeared which depicted this or that aspect of the event. But in the case of George IV only was there a serious attempt to produce a festival book in the grand tradition. This work, initiated and 'Undertaken by His Majesty's Especial Command' and with a £3,000 royal subsidy, had only one end in view: 'This work will excel any of the kind in the known world; and the folio History of Bonaparte's Coronation, the most important and perfect yet published, will sink into nothing by contrast.'[92] Alas, it was not Napoleon's volume which was to sink but this one!

It began well enough. Sir George Nayler's *The Coronation of His Most Sacred Majesty King George the Fourth* was to be published in parts, the first two appearing in 1823 and 1827 with three more to come. It was to founder on the inability of the artists employed to produce their material on time. After Nayler's death H. G. Bohn purchased the copyright and the plates. He reworked the publication, increasing the number of plates and completing the text. It eventually appeared in 1839 with a further de luxe edition in 1841 in two elephant portfolios. Nothing was to surpass the quality of this publication, with its hand-coloured plates lavishly heightened with gold, in the entire history of the English Coronation.

Money was to be made out of the Coronation not only by the theatre and publishing worlds, but also by those entitled to the perks after the event. In the case of the Abbey there was a long tradition that the furnishings of the theatre and the sacrarium were theirs. If the monarch wanted any item, compensation had to be paid to the chapter. In 1714, for instance, the Dean and Chapter petitioned for compensation as the hangings had been removed. The sale of the scaffolding on that occasion realised £430, out of which everyone had a handout, from the dean's verger who received £20 to the laundress who got £5. In 1727 each prebend was supposed to receive items worth £28 in all. If they were worth less then the amount was to be topped up. The subdean's portion in this division of the spoils was a green velvet chair and both a crimson and a Turkey carpet. After the Coronation of George III the Lord Great Chamberlain had removed the two chairs used for the enthronement 'under a Guard'. Otherwise the furniture was divided into fourteen lots of which this time the subdean did rather better, with a whole suite of furniture in green velvet, two chairs, two stools, four cushions and a tablecloth, together valued at £26 7s 0d. A similar division occurred in 1821, this time of no less than 33 items. Some ink was spilt over the Bible, which had been given to the Bishop of Ely whereas it had been a customary perk of the dean. It was also traditional for the Archbishop of Canterbury to claim his chair, cushion and stool. There were, of course, yet more recriminations and arguments in the aftermath of the Coronation, the worst being the consequence of dismantling the choir in 1821. The row was to rumble on for three years. And then, finally, that great extravaganza was laid to rest.

Where, we may well ask, had the Coronation got by 1838? Currents were, in fact, going in contrary directions. One was positive in that the spectacle had never been more popular and as the monarchy became ever more as well, the Coronation took off across the country in terms of national rejoicing in a manner which would have astonished the Middle Ages. But there was a contrary current, potentially disruptive. This had its origins amongst the educated classes of the Enlightenment who began to dismiss the whole thing as a gigantic irrelevance. 'What is the finest sight in the world?' asked the wicked and waspish Horace Walpole, 'A Coronation. What is delightful to have passed? A Coronation . . .' And then comes the deadly sting: 'I . . . saw the Hall, the dinner, and the Champion, a glorious illuminated chamber, a wretched banquet, and a foolish puppet show . . .'[93]

That view of it as an anachronistic mummery may well have been fairly widespread by the 1820s and 1830s. Lady Palmerston viewed most of what happened in the Abbey as 'Monkish and twaddling and foolish and spun out', thinking it 'rather shocking mixing up the Sacrament and the Gravest Ceremonies of the Church with all the Vanity and the Jokes . . .'[94] Only the necessity of appeasing the Tories ensured a Coronation in the case of William IV, the king wishing to dispense with it altogether. Eventually, and under pressure, he caved in, 'to satisfy the tender consciences of those who thought it necessary'. Even Greville viewed it as 'the greatest of all bores', and the *Gentleman's Magazine* had called for an abridgement of a ceremony which it regarded as 'Compounded of the worst dregs of popery and feudalism'.[95]

The attack was even more severe in 1838. On 28 May Earl Fitzwilliam in the House of Lords argued that 'Coronations were fit only for barbarous, or semi-barbarous ages; for periods when crowns were worn and lost by unruly violence and ferocious contests'. Even more shocking to him was the exposure of a young girl to the staring populace, an act wholly at variance with the demands of feminine delicacy. That outburst had been in response to Lord Londonderry's speech deploring the abrogation of the procession and banquet. His

The Coronation Fair in
Hyde Park for Queen
Victoria's Coronation, 1838,
coloured lithograph, *c.*1838

lordship went on to ask Lord Fitzwilliam whether by this he meant that
there should be no Coronation at all, to which the reply came 'Yes' and
the riposte to that was, no Coronation, no Lord Fitzwilliam. The abandonment of the old time-honoured ceremonials was not only
bemoaned, however, by the Tory peers. It was equally lamented by the
world of commerce, with no less than 500 merchants petitioning for
their revival. Amongst the Tory agitators was the 26-year-old Earl of
Eglinton whose stepfather was Sir Charles Lamb, Deputy Earl Marshal
and Knight Marshal of the Household. The eventual outcome of this
lord's disappointment was the Eglinton Tournament of 1839 in which
the flower of Tory chivalry attempted to relive the Middle Ages.[96]

Even more devastating was Harriet Martineau's revulsion at the Coronation. Once in the Abbey she was disgusted by the sight of the old Regency aristocrats who did not even observe 'the decent differences of dress which, according to middle-class custom, pertain to contrasting periods of life ...'. And here speaks the voice of mid-Victorian respectability, aghast at the sight of 'old hags' with dyed and false hair, their wrinkled and withered flesh festooned with diamonds in manner enough 'to make me sick'. In her eyes the Coronation was some hangover from an age of decadence.

As Harriet Martineau munched her sandwich and looked down at what went on, she concluded it 'was worthy only of the Pharaonic times in Egypt, and those of the Kings in Palestine'. Such a service, and here she really lets go, was: 'offensive to the God of the nineteenth century in the Western world ... I remember remarking to my mother on the impiety of the service ... and I told her when the celebration was over, that this part of it had turned out even worse than I expected ...'[97]

Perhaps it was as well that the nineteen-year-old girl who was crowned on that occasion was to reign over sixty years. By 1902 things were very different.

9

Imperial Epiphanies

IN THE SPRING OF 1936 Cosmo Gordon Lang, Archbishop of Canterbury, gave the new king, Edward VIII, a copy of the service used at his father's Coronation in 1911. Edward had taken part in it, providing one of its most touching scenes as the golden-haired prince kneeling in homage to his father. Alarm bells, however, started to ring when the king first of all hoped that the service could be shortened, and then came the shock: 'indeed he began,' wrote the stunned archbishop, 'by saying he hoped the whole service might not be used'. When Lang went on to explain its importance the king acquiesced, mollified by the promise of chopping out the litany and the sermon.[1]

On 24 June Ramsay MacDonald, Lord President of the Council, met with the Earl Marshal, the Duke of Norfolk, about the Coronation.[2] Apparently there had been some delay in setting up the customary Coronation Committee under the Lord President's chairmanship, and equally and in practical terms the even more important Coronation Executive Committee chaired by the Earl Marshal. As the king was going away (the notorious Nahlin cruise with Wallis Simpson in tow) all the meetings were to be attended by the king's brother, Albert, Duke of York. The Lord President's Coronation Committee met on 7 July, a formidable gathering of eminences which included the likes of Stanley Baldwin and Lloyd George. The challenge they faced was to accommodate the event with the new status accorded so many of the countries of the Empire which now, by dint of the Statute of Westminster (1931), had attained full Dominion status. The overall aim, however, was to remain true to the intent of 1911, to 'harmonise ancient tradition with modern constitutional usage'. At that meeting

Opposite Queen Elizabeth II in her Coronation robes, photograph by Cecil Beaton, 1953

the Executive Committee was set up with the 16th Duke of Norfolk in the chair. Their task was to get on with sorting out a vast range of practicalities from the processional route to the liturgy itself, from the programme of events to the accommodation of several contingents of dominion and colonial troops in the London parks.

Such meetings continued to be held throughout the late summer and into the autumn of 1936 with absolutely no hint that anything might go awry. Then, on 10 December, came the Abdication. When the Executive Committee met twelve days later, on 22 December, no reference was made at all to the change of sovereign, everything immediately being assumed to have been done for the new king, George VI, and his consort, Queen Elizabeth. Fortunately the new king, having been present at many of the previous meetings, must have known more about the Coronation than his exiled brother. The only indication of change is the existence of a volume in the College of Arms archive labelled *The Intended Coronation of Edward VIII*.

Reading between the lines it is clear that he, following William IV, never wanted a Coronation in the first place. And even though he submitted to enduring it, other evidence shows that he was attempting to put into reverse what had been the guiding principle dictating those of both 1902 and 1911, central to which was the importance of exhibiting the monarch to the populace in the new democratic age. For Edward VIII there was to have been no royal progress through London the day after the Coronation, no service of thanksgiving at St Paul's followed by lunch at the Guildhall with the Lord Mayor and other City dignitaries. The latter was to be a dinner at some later unspecified date.

It must have been extraordinary preparing for the Coronation during the summer and autumn of 1936 against the backcloth of the events we know as the Abdication crisis. What is so striking is that everything went ahead as though nothing had happened, and George VI and Queen Elizabeth were crowned on the very day designed for Edward VIII, 12 May 1937. That meant there were only five months in which to alter everything from the Coronation of an unmarried king to one with a consort. Fortunately there was all the information needed to hand in the records of the previous two Coronations. But nonetheless, one senses the urgency, that there must be no delay and that every effort must be made to build up the new king and queen in the eyes of a bewildered public.

Can we, in fact, detect anything about 1937 which reveals the hand of the exiled monarch? Five months would have been time enough to recast the service and adjust the physical appearance of the interior of the Abbey. The photographs reveal that everything there resembled as much as possible 1911, and in that we can surely trace the hand of the Dowager Queen Mary to whom the British monarchy was sacred, so much so that she broke the rule that dowager queens should be absent, by actually attending the Coronation. Only one thing stands out as an anomaly which it would have been surely too late to reverse, the architecture of the annexe. Up until 1937 that had always been in pastiche Gothic, as though the exterior of the Jerusalem Chamber had been multiplied across the façade of the Abbey. But, in 1937, the annexe was stridently of its own time, modernist, resembling more the façade of one of the innumerable Art Deco cinemas which had sprung up during the thirties. In this perhaps we can trace one of Edward VIII's gestures to modernise the monarchy.

That juxtaposition of then and now, of past and present, of tradition and innovation sums up in visual terms the dilemma of the Coronation as it was to develop during the twentieth century. How could a rite which had relevance to feudal England have any validity in the modern era, for, by 1900, the speed of change had brought the railways, the telephone, the motor car, the telegraph, the steamship and trams. By the turn of the nineteenth into the twentieth century society had changed far more rapidly than at any earlier period. The franchise by 1937 now embraced the whole adult population including women, so that the Coronation in no way reflected where power lay in the modern state. In spite of this it was to survive two world wars and the advent of the country being in all but name a republic, and it would be re-enacted four times. It is arguable that no other period is so fascinating in its history, nor reveals so much its extraordinary ability to adapt and change to meet every circumstance. While empires and monarchies crashed throughout Europe and other Coronations vanished, the English Coronation went in exactly the opposite direction. Already in the aftermath of the First World War it was a rare survival. But it did not only survive as some weird antiquarian aberration, indeed it flourished and not only grew in importance as a national event but, in 1953, graduated to becoming a global one. That that happened was due to a whole complex of circumstances which were to render the ceremonial a touchstone of the nation's historic identity, all of which we shall need to explore. But our point of departure must inevitably be some account of what modern historians have designated the crowned republic and its sovereigns.

Already, by the first half of the nineteenth century, as we have seen, the monarchy had managed to accommodate a remarkable array of antithetical qualities. These were still to obtain during the twentieth century and, although political power had gone, apart from personal influence and the role of calling upon someone to form a government, the monarchy sustained a hold on the public which continues to defy rational explanation. The needs it filled were now as often as not psychological rather than spiritual ones, as an embodiment of the country's history and traditions, a focus, above all, of national unity outside of the political arena, a uniting role even more significant in the aftermath of devolution to Scotland and Wales at the close of the century.

The expression the 'Crowned Republic' was coined by Tennyson and was to express exactly the British Constitution as it emerged in the twentieth century. Frank Prochaska in his study of the modern monarchy demonstrates how the institution was to ride the successive tides which threatened it, both through the strong hold which tradition had on the public and by the crown's own extension of its activities into every arena of voluntary service.[3] The latter never faltered throughout the Victorian age. Indeed, it increased. But what did falter was the crown's visibility as the long years of Victoria's cloistered widowhood eroded the public image of the monarchy. All of that, however, went into reverse as the century drew to its close in a series of public spectacles which were to determine the form of the Coronation in the century to come. The first of these was the service of thanksgiving at St Paul's in 1872 for the recovery of the Prince of Wales from typhoid fever. That was followed in 1887 by the Queen's Golden Jubilee and, finally, of even greater significance, her Diamond Jubilee a decade later. The latter established what was to be a leitmotif of the twentieth-century Coronation, vast cavalcades through the streets by representatives of the British Empire. All of these were reponses also to the extension of the franchise from 1867 onwards, the ability of people to travel to the metropolis to witness such occasions, not to mention the vast expansion of the city itself which made it the greatest urban complex in the world.[4]

The Coronation of Edward
VII, 1902, painting, c.1902

The monarchy, however, was not devoid of problems, for the
expansion of the state during the first decade of the twentieth century
into areas hitherto regarded as the province of the private sector
threatened its role as the leader of the voluntarist one. The leftwards
trend of politics, the rise of trade union power and the suffragette
movement all put the monarchy before 1914 on the alert, especially
after the Liberal landslide of 1906. But Edward VII, who succeeded

Victoria in 1901, was the first of a succession of sovereigns who responded exactly to the needs of the times. He restored the monarchy's prestige, delighting in public spectacle and revelling in historical landmarks and associations. The king and those around him, above all his mentor Lord Esher (to whose importance I will come), saw the British monarchy, which by 1900 ruled over a worldwide Empire, as attracting a loyalty which arose above and crossed all class and party boundaries.

Edward VII was an easy-going, colourful, cosmopolitan, accessible man devoid of any snobbery, who opened up the monarchy to the new rich, Jews and City magnates, whose wealth he unashamedly tapped for his charities. In addition, the proliferation of new orders in the honours system met the needs of an ever-expanding meritocratic and professional society. To all this we can add that, by the close of the first decade, it was abundantly clear that the survival of the crown would depend on the attitude of the working classes and on coming to terms with the emergence of a socialist party with an egalitarian agenda.

In the long run philanthropy was to prove of far more importance to the continuation of the monarchy than the Empire, which by the second half of the twentieth century had assumed its attenuated form of the Commonwealth. Following the late Victorian precedent, all great royal celebratory events were turned into fund-raising endeavours. That began in 1897 with Queen Victoria's Diamond Jubilee. In 1901 Edward VII was to appoint a committee to launch a 'Coronation Appeal' in aid of the London voluntary hospitals. This was billed as a gift to the king and, under Esher's aegis, it was opened to contributions from the Empire. The result was the enormous sum of £600,000, which was donated to what was renamed 'The King Edward's Hospital Fund for London'. Every Coronation since has been marked by such an appeal.

Although the the socialist Keir Hardie attacked the Coronation of 1911 as 'an orgy for the display of wealth and senseless spending',[5] the fact was the working classes supported the monarchy and could see its philanthropic work. By that date there were 42 Labour MPs, and we enter an era of severe social unrest which was to continue into the 1920s. George V, who succeeded in 1910, and Queen Mary established the basis upon which the monarchy was to move until the breakdown of the Prince of Wales's marriage in the 1990s, that of private probity with the exercise of public duty leavened from time to time by manifestations of magnificence. The king was seen as dutiful, patriotic, decent and good-humoured. And, although he and his formidable queen disliked socialism and feared revolution, the king's strong determination to democratise the monarchy meant that by 1924, when the first socialist government came to power, he was an unassailable model constitutional and welfare monarch. His silver jubilee in 1935 was a popular triumph.

George VI inherited his father's virtues. He was a slow, reserved, dutiful and thoughtful man, totally devoid of pretension and with a wife who was to prove an admirable foil. The Second World War, which followed quickly on their accession, gave them a powerful identity, where there had been little, as icons of the nation during an heroic struggle. After the war they were faced with a Labour government, but by then the socialist party had been tamed. Even the nationalisation of areas of private endeavour like health provision, which was initially seen as a threat to the voluntarist sector, was accommodated. The monarchy by then was useful to the Labour government, providing a backcloth of seeming continuity during a period of huge social change. The accession of Elizabeth II in 1952 saw little shift in the pattern established by her grandparents. It was not until almost twenty years into the reign that new forces began to demand that the monarchy reconsider its strategy for survival.

That concern by the monarchy for extending its contacts with an ever-widening constituency is also vividly reflected in who now got asked to the Coronation. In 1902 a whole new raft of people appeared, including the chairmen of the recently formed county councils, representatives of non-Anglican religious bodies, the mayors of the London boroughs, the Mayor of Winchester, various deans plus representatives of the legal and medical professions, the new London County Council and a long list of learned and professional societies, nearly all of which had been established in the previous century.[6] This was a deliberate move to incorporate the new professional middle classes. Three hundred seats were also reserved for premiers and governors from various parts of the Empire. And huge attention was accorded to India, its maharajahs, governors, officers and eminent citizens.[7] In November the figure given for those in the Abbey was 5,873, with a breakdown of seats issued by various government departments as follows: the Foreign Office 568, the Admiralty 350, the War Office 350 to 400, the India Office 183 and the Civil Service 235.

A subsequent figure indicates a total of 6,603. Tucked in amongst that number were the occupants of what was called the 'Loose Box' in which sat Edward's women friends.

That rose at the next Coronation to 7,139, and by then the importance of drawing in new sections of a changed society meant the excision for the first time of many who regarded it as their prerogative to come. Numbered amongst those dropped were peers' daughters, widows and eldest sons, along with the sheriffs of Scotland, the chairmen of county councils, provincial mayors and the wives of the representatives of the various societies. At a meeting of the Coronation Committee on 31 October 1910 Sir Schomberg McDonnell, Secretary in the Office of Works, 'raised the question of the representation of the working classes in Westminster Abbey'. The topic was returned to on 23 November and the decision was taken to accord two seats each to representatives of the Trades Congress Parliamentary Committee, the Central Board of the Co-operative Union and the National Conference of Friendly Societies.[8]

The 1911 Coronation was staged simultaneously with the passing of the Parliament Act which neutered the power of the House of Lords and in effect ended the aristocratic age. Although both in 1937 and 1953 lists were drawn up to accord to some degree with shifts in society, no attempt was made to dislodge the hereditary peerage from its place. Viewed in that way the homage became a complete anomaly bearing no relationship to the power structure of twentieth-century Britain. In 1953 there were stirrings on this front when Clement Attlee, the former Labour prime minister, supported by James Chuter Ede and Herbert Morrison, asked at a meeting of the Coronation Committee on 16 February 1953 that the Speaker of the House of Commons do homage after the peers as representing 'the common man'. To the deep unhappiness of Attlee this imaginative idea was dismissed out of hand on the basis that it was now too late to consult members of the Commonwealth, but it was a lost opportunity.[9]

One other role which was to present increasing problems for the monarchy during the twentieth century was that of being Supreme Governor of the Church of England. Indeed, the Coronation was a rite which worked from the premise that the State and the Church of England were coeval. However, by 1900 much had changed. No one any longer was excluded from office on account of their religious beliefs except, of course, the monarch who had, by dint of the 1689

Settlement, to be Protestant. That remained firmly in place throughout the twentieth century, tempered only by some amelioration in the wording of the declaration. Although reading of the declaration, with all its violently anti-Catholic language, had migrated from the Coronation ceremony itself to being the first act of an incoming monarch in his first Parliament, it was still demanded, being fundamental to the country's constitution and its Established Church. Understandably it was greatly resented by the Roman Catholic community.

Edward VII was far from happy about the declaration but had little choice but to make it. Cardinal Bourne objected and the Cabinet agreed with the king that its terms were not in accordance with 'public policy of the present day'. Edward VII, anxious that his successor should not 'have to make such a Declaration in such crude language',

The Coronation of George V, 1911, photograph by Benjamin Stone asked Lord Salisbury to have the law changed, not discarding the declaration but recasting it.[10] That was not achieved until the accession of George V, who refused point-blank to utter such offensive language. After much toing and froing between the prime minister, H. H. Asquith, and the Archbishop of Canterbury, Randall Davidson, a new form of words was devised: 'I . . . declare that I am a faithful Protestant, and that I will, according to the true intent of the enactments which secure the Protestant succession to the Throne of my Realm, uphold and maintain the said enactments to the best of my powers according to law.'[11] These words were to be reused by both George VI and Elizabeth II.[12] A reconsideration of this enactment is bound to be on the agenda for any reappraisal in the twenty-first century.

The commitment of the monarchs is crucial to the continuation of the Coronation rite. Edward VIII was the only one to demur, but all the others recognised the importance in their lives of this ancient ceremonial and its power as an inspiring rite of passage for persons who were to personify the traditions and aspirations of a country and an Empire and, latterly, a Commonwealth. At the outset of our examination of the Coronation in the twentieth century it is crucial to grasp how much it meant to those who underwent the rite. All of them were committed Christians and, for the first time, apart from Victoria, we learn what some of those involved thought of it all.

Although there is no record of Edward VII's inner reactions, we do have those of his wife, the beautiful Queen Alexandra. She wrote in retrospect to her daughter-in-law, Queen Mary, 'nothing in this world comes up to it – having felt and gone through it all myself only 9 short years ago – how beautiful & solemn it was & quite ineffaceable from one's mind for ever – & the heavenly music – adding to it all'.[13] In 1911 Queen Mary was to write to her aunt, the Grand Duchess of Mecklenburg-Strelitz: 'it was an awful ordeal for us both especially as we felt it all so deeply and taking so great a responsibility on our shoulders – To me who love tradition & the past, & who am English from tip to toe, the service was a very real solemn thing & appealed to my feelings more than I can express . . .'[14] George V's diary entry echoes this sentiment. That it somehow had the ability to transform we catch in a letter by Alexander Murray, Master of Elibank. On her arrival at Westminster Abbey Queen Mary looked 'pale and strained. You felt she was a great lady but not a Queen.' However, 'the contrast on her "return" – crowned – was magnetic, as if she had undergone some marvellous transformation'.[15]

George VI and Queen Elizabeth also entered into it with commitment. The evening prior to the Coronation Cosmo Lang, the archbishop, went to Buckingham Palace. He describes what happened: 'they knelt with me; I prayed for them and for their realm and Empire, and I gave them my personal blessing. I was much moved and so were they. Indeed, there were tears in their eyes when we rose from our knees.' And, although George VI's diary entry is overconcerned with what went wrong, he is unequivocal in describing the Coronation as 'the most important ceremony in my life'.[16] These preliminary arrangements were repeated under the aegis of Archbishop Fisher for Elizabeth II and the Duke of Edinburgh in 1953. Indeed, Fisher had compiled for the queen's use *A Little Book of Private Devotions . . .* which covered the days leading up to the event.[17] It is too early to know of the present queen's reactions, if indeed she recorded them, but enough is known to say that both the oath and the anointing were viewed by her as pivotal events in her life, seen as acts of personal dedication to the service of the nation.

The monarchy and the media

The monarchy also owed its survival partly to something else, the media. That alliance only began to break down at the close of the 1960s, but for the period covered by the four Coronations between 1902 and 1953 it was intact. By 1902 there was a proliferation of illustrated magazines as well as mass circulation newspapers. Illustrators and increasingly photographers recorded each action of the event for reproduction, the processes for which became better and better with the advent of the half-tone block. There was also moving film which rapidly developed in technical competence from jerky monochrome to glorious technicolour. By 1937 there was public broadcasting in the form of the BBC, with radio and also television in their infant stages. All of this means that we have unprecedented visual documentation of all four Coronations (matched by a comparable ocean of written and printed archival material). It also means that for the first time the Coronation was no longer some occult ceremonial witnessed by a chosen elite, but progressively one which became a shared experience for the nation.

This was quite slow to develop. The acceptance of the new media always lagged behind its arrival and each development was regarded by those involved in staging a Coronation with deep suspicion, if not actual hostility. On 1 May 1902 there appears an entry in the transactions of the Coronation Executive Committee which reads as follows: 'Consideration of the installation of the Electrophone in the Abbey on the occasion of the Coronation cannot be entertained.'[18] The reaction to photography, then more than half a century old, was slightly less hostile. Even though it was ubiquitous by that date public photographers were only allowed to record the appearance of the Abbey before the event, whereas Edwin Abbey, the official Coronation artist, and the illustrators viewed the whole action from a special platform. The only exception to the photography rule was a pillar of the establishment, Sir Benjamin Stone, dubbed the 'Knight of the Camera'.[19] The external procession, which did not labour under such constraints, was not only photographed but also filmed, but when it was shown at Balmoral after dinner one evening it was recorded that 'very few of the figures were recognisable, and the oscillation of the medium affected the optic nerve most unpleasantly'.[20] Denial of entry to the Abbey did not impede a six-minute fake newsreel being made in France in which a wash-house attendant played Edward VII and a music hall singer Queen Alexandra.[21]

This was, in fact, to be the last Coronation recorded in the grand manner in a publication which emulated George IV's, H. Farnham Burke, Somerset Herald's *The Historical Record of the Coronation of their Most Excellent Majesties King Edward VII. and Queen Alexandra Solemnised in the Abbey Church of Westminster on Saturday the Ninth Day of August in the Year of Our Lord 1902* (1905). This is a folio volume, privately printed, with magnificent colour and black-and-white plates by Byam Shaw recording particular figures, processions and moments such as the Duke of Wellington bearing the Union Standard or a group of maharajahs. But that book was almost irrelevant, for the public could savour the Coronation in a flood of coverage by magazines like the *Illustrated London News* and *The Sphere*. After the event it was recorded *in extenso* in two popular, fully illustrated publications, J. E. C. Bodley's *The Coronation of Edward the Seventh: A Chapter of European and Imperial History* (1903), published 'By His Majesty's gracious command', and W. J. Loftie's *The Coronation Book of Edward VII* (n.d.). Both provide a gloss as to the ideas which motivated the occasion.

Peers caught in a shower, 1953, photograph

No such books exist for 1911, by which time the pressure for admitting the new media was increasing. 'I regard it,' wrote Archbishop Randall Davidson, 'as essential that there should be no photography at the moment of the most solemn parts of the Service', that is the anointing, the crowning and the reception of communion.[22] The photographer admitted was again Sir Benjamin Stone who became known thereafter as the royal photographer and who was allowed to record the *recognitio*, the presentation of the sword and the homage.[23] On 2 March the Earl Marshal and others were deputed 'to examine the question as to the feasibility of admitting a cinematograph operator to Westminster Abbey . . .'. A month later it was deemed 'neither fitting nor feasible'.[24] Photography by 1937 was fully accepted with the usual provisos, not the anointing or communion, and censorship by the Earl Marshal,[25] but when the question of film came up again opinions were divided. Lang, the archbishop, was opposed and so the decision was taken to experiment in the Abbey with what effect the lighting would produce. Could it be done without extra lighting?[26] It was decided that it could, and the archbishop was overruled, although along with the photographers no film was to be shot of the anointing or communion and the Earl Marshal was to have the right of censorship. When it came to this, he only cut out a shot of Queen Mary crying.[27] Television, then in its infancy, transmitted for the first time the exterior procession live.[28] In 1953 the only change in filming was the acceptance of a move from black and white to colour.

By 1937 radio had arrived in most homes. The advent of sound was important in more ways than one for the Abbey was wired up with loudspeakers wherever there were members of the congregation, so, for the very first time in its history, all those who were present at the Coronation actually heard it. A.C. Benson gives an account of 1902: 'The service I could hardly hear at all – except odd provincial and gutteral vowels from the Archbishop – here and there a word – the King was inaudible to me except as a kind of hoarse grunt.[29] The decision to broadcast had its supporter from the outset in Lang, the archbishop, as early as 20 October 1936, two months before the Abdication, but the new king, George VI, was equally keen. Lang wanted the Coronation broadcast as far as the homage but not to go on to include the communion, and that was the arrangement adopted.[30] What was innovative was the king's broadcast to the country and the Commonwealth in the evening, prompted no doubt by the absence of any royal Christmas broadcast in 1936. That formula was to be repeated in 1953. All of this opening up to the media in 1937, however, is a vivid reflection of the desire and, indeed, need to re-establish the continuity and stability of the monarchy in the eyes of the general public after the shock of the Abdication.

By 1953 the importance of the media had been fully taken on board. Geoffrey Fisher, the archbishop, saw that through it the religious aspect of the event could be brought home to the nation, the consecration and dedication of a sovereign to the service of her peoples.[31] Bearing this in mind it is difficult to explain his objection to television. In 1937 that had transmitted the street procession to the small number of owners of a set, but in 1953 the potential to reach out across the country and, indeed, the world was even greater. But at a meeting of the Joint Coronation Committees on 7 July 1952 everyone was against admitting the cameras, headed by the archbishop and the Dean of Westminster, Dr Alan Don. It was 'unfair to expose THE QUEEN and others to this searching method of photography . . .'. At the most they would consider allowing the event to be televised as far as the choir screen.[32]

Jock Colville, the queen's secretary, informed the prime minister, Sir Winston Churchill: 'Whereas film of the ceremony can be cut

appropriately, live television would not only add considerably to the strain on the Queen (who does not herself want TV) but would mean that any mistakes, unintentional incidents or undignified behaviour by spectators would be seen by millions of people.' That decision was endorsed by the Cabinet, only to produce a furore in the press. In October the decision was reconsidered and reversed, Colville only revealing 30 years later that the *renversement* was due to the queen. Overnight the number of licence-holders doubled from one and a half to three million viewers. To that was added a European link-up taking extended coverage through France, West Germany and Holland. In the UK 27 million people watched the Coronation live.[33]

The two films which were made, *A Queen is Crowned* and *Elizabeth the Queen*, were both in colour and both were edited, completed and released on 8 June, just six days after the event. *A Queen is Crowned* is the better of the two and for the first time the largest number of prints

BBC commentators at the 1953 Coronation, photograph

The Coronation as it
appeared on television, 1953

of a Technicolor film was struck, 700. It was dubbed in nine languages
and shown in 54 countries. The script was by Christopher Fry and it
was narrated by Laurence Olivier. On to a reverent account of the
liturgy it embroidered images, words and music of mythic national
status from the 'This England' speech from Shakespeare's *Richard II* to
Holst's 'I vow to thee my country'. The procession of the colonial and
Commonwealth troops was presented in an overtly imperial light.[34]

Twentieth-century Coronations precipitated a deluge of publications unparalleled by any other period. A small avalanche of books,
usually inaccurate, attended that of 1902, for by that date few were alive
who could have remembered Victoria's Coronation, let alone seen it.
Every succeeding Coronation equally produced a flurry explaining the
significance of the event and its history, many aimed at schoolchildren,
for whom it became a public holiday. In these publications we can
trace the transmutation of a medieval initiation ceremony in which
Holy Church sanctified the ruler of the small island state of England
into the crowning of a king-emperor whose domains stretched over a
third of the globe. And it is indeed the Empire which provides us with
the key to what happened to the Coronation in the twentieth century.

The Coronation of 1902 was five years on from the diamond jubilee of 1897 which is recognised as one of the key monuments in what modern historians have designated as 'the invention of tradition'. The public was treated to a rich diet of ceremonial display, speech-making and official processions deployed around a sustained programme of public and semi-public events which included a military tattoo at Windsor, a service in St George's Chapel, a garden party at Osterley culminating in the day of the great procession to St Paul's. Over 50,000 troops drawn from all over the Empire took part in that procession through the London streets, the public being suitably astonished at its exoticism.[35]

But this carefully stage-managed imperial apotheosis, in fact, shielded an insecurity, for Britain during the last decade of the nineteenth century was in isolation. Worse, both Germany and Italy were now carving out for themselves empires in Africa, and Britain's commercial hegemony was under threat from the United States. The jubilee celebration deflected the public from these realities by using the great length of Victoria's reign to focus the nation's attention on Britain's imperial achievement. The fact that that global hegemony was already on the wane was not to deter government from revisiting it at every Coronation including that of 1953.

The reason why the Coronation became the ideal vehicle for imperialism was that the crown was virtually the only central link holding the Empire together. By 1900 it was a jumble of colonies and protectorates and, as the century progressed, became a conglomeration of dominions and, later still, when the Empire gradually dissolved, one also of republics, members of a Commonwealth whose head was Elizabeth II.

Coronations were deliberately transformed into occasions when representatives of this global domain could gather. This was a complete innovation with no historical precedent. Colonial Conferences began in 1887, the year of the Golden Jubilee. Another was convened in 1897, the occasion of the Diamond Jubilee, when it was agreed that one should be held every five years. That meant that one was held in 1902,

A cavalcade of imperial
troops at the Coronation of
George VI, 1937, photograph

the year of Edward VII's Coronation, and another was made to coincide with that of George V in 1911. Every Coronation in the twentieth
century was to occasion a global gathering of premiers and also of
troops and police who were to march in the great processions.[36]

This cultivation of imperial spectacle was completely new. It was only in 1876 that Victoria was proclaimed Empress of India, a title in riposte to that of the new German Emperor. What happened to the Coronation in 1902 reflected what was happening at all the great European courts in the decade before 1914; in Berlin, Vienna and St Petersburg there was an efflorescence of imperial dynastic celebratory pageantry. Both the Coronations of Edward VII and George V need to be set into this European context. Indeed, the European dimension still remained important in 1937 when the other monarchies had vanished, for, as one fervent royalist wrote with an eye towards Hitler and Mussolini, the English Coronation was 'a pageant more splendid than any dictators can put on: beating Rome and Nuremberg hollow at their own bewildering best, and with no obverse side of compulsion or horror'.[37] The 1937 Coronation reminded the world, threatened by the new dictators, of Britain's imperial might and also of her long dedication to the freedom of her peoples. This was ancient pageantry, a mixture of religion, history, nostalgia, mumbo-jumbo and military display in the service of liberty and freedom. Even in 1953 the Coronation was still deployed to demonstrate to the world that even after the deprivations of the Second World War the country and its Commonwealth was still a force to contend with, one which looked to be a block balanced between those of the United States and Europe. In the case of the latter, initial discussions were already underway which were to lead to the European Union, ones from which Britain stood proudly aloof basking in the illusion of a second Elizabethan age.

All of this began with the Coronation of 1902 which was conceived as a monument to imperial reconciliation in the aftermath of the Boer War. The fact that the event had to be cancelled owing to the king's appendicitis made the Coronation when it did happen on 9 August, in Lord Rosebery's eyes, 'something of a family festival of the British Empire'.[38] In spite of the cancellation, many of the events planned went ahead, including the review of the Indian and colonial contingents. Sir Almeric FitzRoy, Clerk to the Council, captures exactly the mood in 1902 in his description of this event: 'the stalwart figures and brilliant uniforms of many of the contingents stimulated the imagination to flights of imperial feeling fully coloured by an oriental glow. The antiquity and mystery of India, its polyglot and multiform peoples, its haunting racial traditions and profound religious idealism, all seemed summed up and expressed in this fugitive pageant, the brevity of which struck me like the glory of a dream.'[39]

Lord Esher wrote of it: 'Such a show of Imperial force – a wonderful object-lesson.'[40] Bodley actually lists who came: Maoris from New Zealand, Dyaks from North Borneo, Singhalese from Ceylon, Nigerians and Hausas from West Africa, Sudanese and Swahilis and, the crowning glory, India: 'To hail the Emperor of India it had sent to England representatives of a vast array of races and castes. There were Tamils from Southern India, Telegus from the East Coast, Mahrattas from the Deccan, Brahmins, Jats and Rajputs from Oudh and Rajputana, Gurkhas from Nepal, Sikhs from the Punjab, Afridis and other Pathans from the wild borderland across the Indus, Hazaras from Afghanistan and Mussulmans of diverse origin and locality.'[41]

On the following day another great fête went ahead, this time at the India Office when the great magnates presented their sword hilts to the Prince of Wales 'as a sign of fealty and submission' to the king-emperor.[42] In 1911 the Coronation was followed by a durbar, and one would have followed 1937 if it had not been interrupted by the war.

J.E.C. Bodley's book fleshes out the Edwardian imperial theme of 1902 describing 'a monarch whose crown . . . had become an emblem of Empire wider than Darius or the early Caesars dreamed of', an event to which came 'British subjects from the ends of the earth'.[43] And, as for the Coronation itself, this was 'the consecration of the imperial idea . . . The usage by an ardent yet practical people of an archaic rite to signalise the modern splendours of their empire, the recognition, by a free democracy, of a hereditary crown, as a symbol of world-wide dominion . . .'[44] To it came the premiers of Canada, Australia, Cape Colony, New Zealand, Natal and Newfoundland, the governors of the eastern colonies, the West Indies, the West African and Mediterranean colonies. In the case of India the viceroy was asked to select five or six ruling chiefs as royal guests. To these were added the ex-viceroys, six governors or past governors as well as fifteen persons of distinction from every province.[45]

Grafting all this on to the Abbey rite did stretch the imagination, and attempts began to be made somehow to integrate the Empire and latterly the Commonwealth in some more tangible way. Ceremonial robes were seen as one means of incorporating the Empire. In a submission concerning the robes for Edward VII, the imperial mantle was to be embroidered with the rose, thistle and shamrock, but, it goes on to suggest: 'As, however, the Empire over which His Majesty rules is far greater and altogether different from what it was at that time (1838), it is humbly suggested that the heraldic emblems of various parts of it be

Opposite George V and Queen Mary in their Coronation robes, photograph, 1911

introduced also, together with the badges used by His Majesty's ancestors who have sat on the throne of England.'[46]

In 1911 the procession in the Abbey included bearers carrying the standards of the Union of South Africa, the Dominion of New Zealand, the Commonwealth of Australia, the Dominion of Canada and the Empire of India. Queen Mary's dress was embroidered not only with emblems of the United Kingdom but also the lotus of India and the Star of Africa, with the oceans linking the Empire swirling around its hem. Variations of this formula were repeated in 1937, when Queen Elizabeth's dress was similarly embroidered and her purple train scattered with emblems of the ten countries of the Empire, and again in 1953 when Sir Norman Hartnell scattered symbolic flowers across the young queen's dress, this time the leek, the thistle, the shamrock and the oak leaf for the United Kingdom and the maple, the mimosa and the fern for Canada, Australia and New Zealand. Nor should the fact be ignored that some of the most glittering jewels in the regalia, like the Koh-i-Noor and Cullinan diamonds, were the prizes of Empire. But all of this was so much froth which in no way faced up to the truth that the Coronation ceremony bore no relation to the existing political reality.

Changes at the most were minimal. Some had to come in 1937 because in 1931 the Statute of Westminster recast countries as dominions in the fullest sense of the word, 'autonomous communities within the British Empire . . . united by a common allegiance to the Crown, and freely associated as members of the British Commonwealth of Nations'. The standards were carried again but, for the first time, there had to be alterations to the wording of the actual rite. One was prompted by religion. An accommodation had to be reached with several of the Commonwealth premiers who were Roman Catholic, so that the king now swore to maintain 'the true profession of the Gospel and to maintain the Protestant Reformed Religion only as established by law in the United Kingdom'. That was a minor adjustment. Others were more important.

At the outset in 1936 it was hoped that something much more might be done as Edward VIII wanted the service cut: 'this may be counterbalanced by the possible addition to the rite of some symbolic ceremony for representatives of the Dominions'.[47] As a result of this a separate committee was set up under the chairmanship of the Duke of York with an executive committee attached to it.[48] Nothing, however,

OPPOSITE
Top Norman Hartnell's design for the Coronation dress of Elizabeth II, 1953, drawing, 1953
Below Detail of the dress embroidered with the flowers of the Commonwealth (*see also page 465*)

Left Standard bearers of the Empire of India and the Dominions leaving the Abbey, 1937, photograph came of all this except the essential revisions to the text. So at the *recognitio* George VI was presented not as 'the undoubted King of this Realm' but as 'King George your undoubted King'. The oath, of course, had to be altered to take in all the multiple kingships: 'Do you solemnly promise and swear to govern the peoples of Great Britain, Ireland, Canada, Australia, New Zealand, the Union of South Africa, of your possessions, and other territories to them belonging or appertaining and of your Empire of India, according to their respective laws and customs?'[49] No symbolic action was introduced into the Coronation for the Commonwealth, whose main event was a lunch given to its parliamentary representatives in Westminster Hall, an arrangement which was repeated in 1953.

By that occasion it was realised that any alterations only opened up a hornet's nest of complex negotiations, far more complicated than in 1937 as the Empire was in dissolution. The royal style was much diminished: 'Elizabeth the Second, by the grace of God of the United Kingdom of Great Britain and Northern Ireland and of Her other Realms and Territories Queen, Head of the Commonwealth, Defender of the Faith'. India had gained its independence and Nehru forbade the high commissioner to bear a standard in the Abbey procession[50] and refused to send any military contingents for the street procession. A young journalist called John Grigg, later Lord Altrincham, stirred things up by suggesting that a large number of the hereditary peers should be dropped and replaced by members of the Commonwealth.[51] In retrospect he was right.

It was also even more transparently obvious that the Coronation ignored the other Christian denominations and also other faiths. It was after all the enthronement of the Supreme Governor of the Church of England. Suggestions were made that the homage should revert to its medieval location in Westminster Hall as a separate event, thus accommodating the new post-imperial order. But none of this got anywhere. And, when it came to the day, the colonial contingents which did come were even larger than in 1937, to 'reflect the growing importance of the Colonial Empire and . . . in accordance with the wishes of the Colonial Office'.[52] In the revision of the liturgy (to which I will come in due course) the armils were correctly reinstated as bracelets which were paid for by the Commonwealth, but that was as near as anyone got to the Commonwealth countries actually figuring in any more concrete manner.

The British public probably had no idea that what they were witnessing was a mirage of a power which had gone. In the procession

Detail of Queen Mary's
Crown, 1911, containing the
Koh-i-Noor and one of the
Cullinan diamonds

marched colonial armed police from Cyprus, the Solomon Islands, Trinidad, the Bahamas, the Windward Islands, North Borneo, Sarawak and Malaya. Then came representatives of the air forces of Hong Kong, Malaya and Aden and armed and naval forces from Barbados, Bermuda, British Guiana, British Honduras, the Leeward Islands, Singapore, Hong Kong, Malta, Gibraltar, Jamaica, Malaya, Fiji, Kenya, Somaliland, East Africa, Northern Rhodesia and West Africa. In their wake came the massed contingents of the Commonwealth and the dominions. To those looking on, including myself, it seemed that Britain still had an Empire and was yet a major power in the post-war world. And that no doubt was what was intended.

Although by 1838 the Coronation was marked by events across the country, those in London never extended much beyond the actual day, closing with the obligatory firework display whose ancestry went back to the late Stuart period. Nineteen hundred and two, in the wake of 1897, changed all that in a quite dramatic way. The Coronation became the climatic moment during a whole fortnight's festivities. The original programme in 1902 was as follows:

23 June	Arrival of guests from abroad. A dinner for visiting royalty at Buckingham Palace
24 June	The king and queen receive special envoys from abroad. A state dinner
25 June	Reception of the colonial premiers. The Prince of Wales gives a dinner for visiting royalty at St James's Palace
26 June	The coronation. A small family dinner
27 June	Procession through London
28 June	Naval review at Spithead. Dinner at Lansdowne House
29 June	Reception at the Wallace Collection. Ambassadors and ministers give dinners for their own representatives
30 June	Gala at the Royal Opera House
1 July	Garden party at Windsor Castle. Lady Lansdowne's reception
2 July	Foreign representatives leave
3 July	Service of thanksgiving at St Paul's Cathedral followed by lunch at the Guildhall
4 July	The king and queen dine at the Foreign Office. Reception of the Indian princes
5 July	The king's coronation dinner to the people[53]

Although the cancellation of the June Coronation meant a contraction of what was planned when staged in August (the foreign suites had gone home), the idea of a sustained series of great fêtes set the pattern for the century. In the history of festivals nothing quite like this had been done in England since medieval Coronations, and for more recent precedents we must look back to the magnificences of Catherine de' Medici at the late Valois court or those staged by Louis XIV at Versailles. Such splendid occasions set out to dazzle the civilised world with the power, richness and glory of both court and country. And as often as not they concealed a cankered reality of decline glossed over with glitter. In spite of this all, four Coronations exalted the British crown in the eyes of both the nation and the world with a display celebrating both its global dominion and the loyalty of all its diverse peoples.

It is worth studying these successive programmes as they are faithful mirrors reflecting shifts in emphasis as the monarchy extended its basis for support. In 1911 there were notable innovations, including a gala at the Haymarket Theatre in addition to that at the Opera House, a minor one not to be repeated (Queen Mary's aunt, the Grand Duchess of Mecklenburg-Strelitz was to write in horror at the possibility that *Der Rosenkavalier* might be chosen).[54] More significant were a drive through the East End of London and the king entertaining a hundred thousand children at Crystal Palace. And here, for the first time also, comes the prime minister's dinner for the king and queen.

The programme for 1937 is an even more remarkable index reflecting what almost seems like panic after the Abdication. The escalation here is on such a scale that again it is worth listing, just to grasp the enormity of what had been grafted on to a right that had begun its life as a liturgical ceremony. In 1937 the monarchy went into overdrive to recapture the confidence of the nation:

---

4 May   Reception by the Marquess and Marchioness of
          Londonderry for visitors from overseas
5 and 6 May   Courts
7 May   The king attends the Empire Parliamentary
          Association's luncheon in Westminster Hall.
          Government reception at Lancaster House for
          overseas visitors

9 May	State visits of envoys and deputations start
10 May	State banquet
11 May	Reception by the king and queen of representatives of the dominions. Presentation of addresses. Luncheon for them and the premiers. The Duke and Duchess of Gloucester host a dinner
12 May	The Coronation. Broadcast by the king. Ships of the Home Fleet moor in the Thames
13 May	Drive through north London. State banquet
14 May	Presentation by the king of Coronation medals to the overseas contingents. First Plenary Session of the Imperial Conference. Court ball
15 May	Foreign envoys and deputations take leave of the king and queen. The Duke and Duchess of Sutherland's garden party for overseas visitors.
18 May	The king and queen attend a ball given by the Duke and Duchess of Sutherland at Hampden House
19 May	The king and queen drive to the Guildhall for luncheon. Empire Service of Youth in Westminster Abbey. The king and queen go to Portsmouth
20 May	The king and queen inspect the fleet
21 May	The king visits four flagships. The king and queen return to London
22 May	The queen receives the contingents of St John's Ambulance in Hyde Park. Queen Mary and the Princess Royal drive through part of north London
24 May	Empire Day. The king and queen attend a service of thanksgiving at St Paul's Cathedral
26 May	Queen Mary's birthday. A court ball
27 May	The king and queen attend the opening of the Royal Tournament and an evening reception given by the London County Council[55]

And this was not the end of it for there were public royal events throughout June followed in July by state visits to Scotland, Wales and Northern Ireland.

It is difficult to relate any of this to what happened in previous centuries, for the Coronation had as it were been hijacked for other purposes, ones necessary to the monarchy's survival in the democratic age. By 1953 anything which remotely reflected events which would have been part of the old London aristocratic Season finally vanished. There was still a court ball but the only other ball was at the Hurlingham Club hosted by the Royal Empire Society, Victoria League and Overseas League, a very far cry from the world of Lady Londonderry or the Duke and Duchess of Sutherland. In contrast the drives are multiplied, not only through the East End but also through both north and south London. And the visits to Scotland, Wales and Northern Ireland are upgraded from being almost afterthoughts to being punctuation marks through the long series of metropolitan events.

All of this presupposes a London very different from that of 1838. Although the city was never to have Baron Haussmann creating great ceremonial routes, the first decade and a half of the twentieth century gave voice to a desire that Westminster should become a capital worthy of the British Empire.[56] Thus the complex so familiar today came into being. The east front of Buckingham Palace, a somewhat colourless essay by Sir Aston Webb, was built in three months during the summer of 1913 replacing that by Edward Blore. Both had a balcony, and from 1902 onwards the finale of the actual day of Coronation was always a balcony appearance by members of the royal family. This was inaugurated by Edward VII and Queen Alexandra. By 1937 the palace was floodlit, a crowd of some fifty thousand milled around and the balcony appearances had multiplied to four. In 1953 there were five, the first being to view a fly-past of two to three hundred planes in a group choreographed to form the letters ER.

Aston Webb was also responsible for the circus before the palace framing Sir Thomas Brock's celebration of Queen Victoria, for Admiralty Arch, and for transforming the Mall into the major ceremonial thoroughfare that it had never been. That led on to Trafalgar Square and thence to Whitehall, Parliament Street and the Abbey. Other new streets which were to play their part in Coronation processions were Northumberland Avenue, constructed in 1876 and leading down to the Victoria Embankment, made in 1864 to 1870, and affording another approach to Parliament Square. Together these spaces, plus Horseguards Parade, provided what were in effect the Theatre of the Monarchy. But what about those processions?

Overleaf Watching the fly-past from the balcony of Buckingham Palace, 1953, photograph

From the moment the decision was reached that the precedent for the Coronation of 1902 was less that of 1838 and more that of the Diamond Jubilee of 1897, it was inevitable that there had to be a spectacular procession through the London streets. This, in effect, meant reviving the old state entry from the Tower to the Palace of Westminster which had last taken place in 1661. That was obviously the historical justification for it, but Sir Almeric FitzRoy records as early as December 1901 that the king took 'a long time to convince himself that the Procession through the streets . . . should precede the event . . .'[57] The initial concept would have fitted neatly with FitzRoy's and the king's private secretary, Sir Francis Knollys's desire 'for reconciling innovation with usage'. But that was not to be, for the king changed his mind and opted for a procession through the London streets after the Coronation. No one records why he changed his mind, although perhaps it was a realisation that in the medieval progress the king entered as not quite fully king.

Such a procession inevitably had to be invented, as the Earl Marshal recognised, 'out of the raw material supplied by the departments representing the Army, Navy, Indian, and Colonial interest: a task of no small difficulty'.[58] Nothing went right with it as long as it remained in the hands of Lord Esher's *bêtes noires*, the heralds, but once removed from them and put into those of guards officers 'seasoned to discipline and precision of movement', the result was 'order out of chaos'.[59] The king reversed the proposals for the route to and from the Abbey, opting for a short one there and a long one back: 'The foregoing Programme is mainly in accordance with the Procession of 1897.'[60] In 1902 triumphal arches erected by members of the Empire straddled the route, the Canadian arch bearing the message: 'Canada, Britain's granary in war and peace'.

Each Coronation was to bring a reconsideration of the route. In 1937, reflecting the need to establish the new king and queen in the public eye, the route back was of an extraordinary length: Bridge Street, Victoria Embankment, Northumberland Avenue (where 40,000 schoolchildren were massed), Trafalgar Square, Cockspur Street, Pall Mall East, Lower Regent Street, Piccadilly Circus, Regent Street, Oxford Circus, Marble Arch, East Carriage Road in Hyde Park and Constitution Hill, three and half miles in all. That was not repeated in 1953. Instead, the route to the Abbey was lengthened under the aegis of the Duke of Edinburgh to include Northumberland Avenue, Victoria

Embankment (where I stood among the schoolchildren) and Bridge Street.

What has not been mentioned is the conscious archaism of continuing with carriage processions. There is no trace in any of the voluminous minutes pertaining to these Coronations of anyone questioning why, in a mechanised age, the mode of transportation should not be the motor car. That decision to continue with horse-drawn carriages must to some degree have been conditioned by the use of what was universally recognised as the Coronation coach. It also met that perpetual criterion of those who put together Coronations, of 'reconciling innovation with usage', even though in 1953 it meant borrowing carriages from the film studios at Elstree.

George V and Queen Mary's state drive through London, 1911, photograph

Overleaf The Coronation procession in the Mall, 1953

Taking all these incrustations into consideration, the twentieth-century Coronation seems very distant from any of its predecessors. It also proliferated across the country on each occasion in a manner which calls for a separate study. In 1902, for example, there was the king's dinner for half a million 'of the humbler classes'. In Sheffield 10,000 were feasted and in Liverpool 130,000 schoolchildren were given refreshments.[61] There was also a special form of church service.[62] This type of event became the norm for every Coronation, with street parties, firework displays, municipal banquets, garden parties, tree-planting and every form of commemoration, not to mention a glut of souvenir mugs and other ephemera. And that, of course, reflected another aspect of the twentieth century, consumerism. Arguments, indeed, would be advanced in favour of royal pageantry and cere-monial in the second half of the century based on the premise that it encouraged tourism and was a boon to the commercial sector.

Above Coronation souvenirs, 1953, photograph by Cartier Bresson, 1953
Below Coronation mug, designed by Eric Ravilious 1937

Right Coronation street
party, 1953, photograph

Opposite Coronation fireworks, 1953, photograph

All in all, the Coronation had become a massive secular festival in
a century during which organised religion went into sharp decline. But
no one could demur from the fact that all of this could not happen
without that ancient liturgical rite at its heart.

THE PRACTICALITIES OF PAGEANTRY

The four twentieth-century Coronations were:[63]

Edward VII	9 August 1902
George V	22 June 1911
George VI	12 May 1937
Elizabeth II	2 June 1953

What we know of their respective cost is as follows: Edward VII £193,000; George V £185,000; George VI £454,000 and Elizabeth II £912,000. Those are the bare bones but we need to prise out the motives, the changes and particular circumstances which framed each of these great state events. Imperial epiphanies they may have been, secular festivals, as we have seen, they most certainly were, but each had at its core an ancient religious rite which it could not also escape responding to with a very different set of imperatives. But such ceremonies call for both an administrative structure and a physical setting, and it is to a consideration of those we must now turn our attention.

In 1902 a structure was created which was to be repeated with variations for all its successors. The Privy Council set up a Coronation Committee which in turn set up a Coronation Executive Committee chaired by the Earl Marshal, the Duke of Norfolk, and including the Archbishop of Canterbury along with both household and government officials who were to deal with the practicalities. Twentieth-century Coronations were the province by hereditary right of two Dukes of Norfolk, the 15th and 16th. Henry, 15th Duke of Norfolk, was involved in staging the funerals of Gladstone and Queen Victoria and also the Coronations of 1902 and 1911. Neither Edward VII nor George V seems to have had much faith in his organisational skills, the former asking Lord Esher whether he would take over 'stage-managing' the Coronation (which he refused) and the latter commenting that the duke was 'a charming, honourable, straightforward little gentleman, no better in the world. But as a man of business he is absolutely impossible.'[64] We, perhaps, get a reflection of that when, in 1910, there was an

Design for the Abbey
Annexe, 1937, drawing

attempt to dislodge the Earl Marshal together with the heralds and erect a 'direction of state ceremonies', but it failed. His successor, Bernard, however, was to become a master of majestic ceremonial, something perhaps he owed to his military career as a soldier in the Sussex Regiment. Under his direction no nonsense was put up with from anyone either in 1937 or, more particularly, in 1953 which was subject to the camera's merciless eye. To him more than anyone else was owed the ever increasing precision of the secular ceremonial.[65]

As in the case of all previous Coronations, everything went according to precedent. Each demanded that an annexe to the Abbey be built. In 1902 it was designed by a Mr Nutt of Windsor Castle, under the aegis of Lord Esher, to look as though it was an extension of the Jerusalem Chamber across the Abbey's west front. It was in the Perpendicular style and adorned with figures of the six Edwards who had preceded the present one. Inside there was an octagonal entrance hall and an antechamber hung with tapestries borrowed from Blenheim Palace, depicting Marlborough's victories, along with figures in armour from the Tower of London.[66] The formula was repeated in 1911 and then, in 1937, came the modernistic pavilion adorned with

heraldic beasts carrying the arms of the United Kingdom and the
dominions. Within, it was festooned with tapestries from the collection of the dukes of Buccleuch. The royal beasts similarly appeared in
1953 in a pavilion of which it was written, 'No attempt was made to create a Gothic structure. The purpose of the design was rather to link
contemporary design with the design of the Abbey . . .'[67] What went up
looked like a pavilion from the Festival of Britain two years before, an
event which set contemporary style for the 1950s.

Much had happened to Westminster Abbey since 1838. In the first
place, its status had been lifted. Under Dean Stanley (1864–81) it had
acquired the place which it occupies today, in his words 'the centre of
national life in a truly liberal spirit'. But it had had to transfer the
majority of its estates and financial assets to the Ecclesiastical
Commissioners and by the closing decades of Victoria's reign was in
financial difficulties. The dean and canons had now only limited financial resources and a fabric which was in radical decay, forever calling
for restoration. Whatever the financial woes of the Abbey, there was no
question in 1902 of returning to the palmy days of selling off parts of
the Abbey for a handsome profit at the Coronation.[68]

A decision was made then to reduce the congregation to 6,000,
both on grounds of safety and, more interestingly, in the interest of
achieving a 'spectacular effect'.[69] The serried ranks of seating above the
high altar, which had for so long accommodated Members of
Parliament, vanished thanks to a report by the Abbey's Surveyor of the
Fabric. 'It beggared imagination,' Sir Almeric FitzRoy wrote, 'to think
of the occupants of this stand being shot down like a living cascade
upon the King and the Archbishops and great Officers of State . . .'[70]
The dean and chapter were inevitably 'pained' by this, and an accommodation was reached by offering them seats. But this was the end of
turning the Abbey at each Coronation into the equivalent of a theatre
ranged around with boxes for hire and refreshment rooms to hand.
Nor, after the event, was there any more a division of the spoils either
to the dean and chapter, or, for that matter, to the great officers of state.

At all four Coronations the Abbey was made over to the Earl
Marshal and then, at some stage, handed to the officers of the King's
Works to build the annexe and install the theatre and the seating. Since
1838 the Abbey had undergone significant restorations and, with the
rise of architectural history, the often cavalier treatment of the historic
fabric now had to go into reverse and every care be taken lest some

irreparable damage was done. In 1953, for example, statuary, wall tablets, the choir stalls and organ screen were all wrapped in felt and boarded over. Felt was laid over the floors. The often brutal treatment of the building to which it had been subject at earlier periods ceased.

Hand in hand with the revision of the actual liturgy (to which I will come) there was a strong historicising impulse behind the internal appearance of the Abbey. Looking at the visual evidence of Edward VII's Coronation, its counterpart can be found in the sumptuous illustrative and highly romantic productions of Shakespeare's plays by Sir Herbert Beerbohm Tree at His Majesty's Theatre between 1888 and 1914. These were re-creations of the historic past on the grand scale. The Coronations of 1902, 1911 and 1937 all conform to this mould, with that of 1953 only making minor concessions to a more contemporary taste in the choice of fabrics and the design of the furniture. But the overwhelming concern was with tradition, realised by the use of fabrics and furniture in period styles. In 1911, for example, the chairs used were modelled on the famous 'King James I' X-frame chairs at Knole together with 'Charles II' ones, again copied from those at Knole, while the peers and peeresses sat on 'Chippendale'. In 1937 Queen Mary, with her strong feeling for history, exerted her personal influence on the furnishings which all looked back to 1911. In terms of colour, blue and gold prevailed on all four occasions, a foil to the many figures in crimson and scarlet involved in the ritual.

That the relationship to theatre was realised at the time we catch in a phrase recorded in the minutes of the Executive Coronation Committee in connexion with the decision to have no tiers of seats over the high altar in 1902 'in order to improve the scenic effect'.[71] All the visual records of these Coronations show a concern with spectacle, including the massing of an array of historic plate on the altar and elsewhere in the sacarium. In 1902 plate was taken from the Chapel Royal at St James's, Marlborough House and the Tower to boost the display.[72]

That desire to create an historic and timeless scene lifted from the pages of history did not impede the adoption of technical advance. Up until 1937 the structure and seating within the Abbey was in wood (hence the fear of fire), but for George VI tubular steel was used for the first time, 400 tons of it in addition to 72,000 cubic feet of wood. On that occasion three to four hundred men were employed in its construction.[73] In 1953 the number of men went down, just 200, while the count of materials went up: 1,350,000 feet of tubular scaffolding and 132,000 cubic feet of timber. Even more important was the arrival of electricity within the Abbey. That made its first spectacular appearance in 1902 when, at the moment of crowning, suddenly the lights were turned on for the very first time. The trumpets sounded, the bells rang and gun salutes were fired. This must have been a stunning *coup de théâtre*. That not everything was satisfactory we gather from complaints after the event. In 1902 the pile of the carpet was so thick that peeresses' heels got stuck in it and in 1937 the peers had difficulty dragging their robes over it while, in the sacrarium, the carpet had been laid the wrong way round so that the queen had to enlist the aid of the Archbishop of Canterbury in order to move. There were also significant changes to the layout of the theatre and the sacrarium. The theatre now only accommodated thrones, the king and queen going on first entry to two faldstools to the south of the sacrarium. The chairs of estate recorded in the arrangement we see in the engravings in Sandford placed immediately below the thrones vanish. Even more striking was the final elimination of any elevation of the theatre. That space, which in the Middle Ages had been so high that it was possible for an armed knight on horseback to pass beneath it and later was able to accommodate a room for refreshment, had gradually descended over the centuries to ground level until, finally, in 1911, the order was reversed and there was a step up into the sacrarium.[74] In 1937 and 1953 both the theatre and the sacrarium were reduced to a flat level area. In the light of the effort to restore as much as possible of the medieval rite in terms of ritual, it is surprising that no one thought to restore also its *mise-en-scène*. But then, perhaps, the new arrangement mirrored more exactly what twentieth-century Coronations were about, no longer the creation of priest-kings who ascended in glory but the sanctification and dedication of one human being as the representative of a nation.

There was an enormous interest in dress and also in the royal regalia, which continued on an ever-upward curve through a century that saw the emergence of the couturier and the fashion industry. It started with what was to be worn by the king and queen. Queen Alexandra set her own style, defying tradition by wearing a petunia velvet dress made in Paris and having her train borne not by maids of honour but by page boys, much to her daughter-in-law's dismay. She also had her own crown made, into which she put the Koh-i-Noor diamond, and she festooned herself with pearls and diamonds. Her

OVERLEAF
The fate of George IV's Diamond Hat Circlet. Queen Alexandra wearing it as a tiara in 1905 (*left*) and Queen Mary wearing it in 1911 (*right*) Queen Elizabeth II wearing it to the Abbey in 1953

464   CORONATION

canopy bearers she commanded wear white and gold, a scheme followed by Queen Mary who reverted to female train bearers. Crowns came and went or were adjusted or commissioned according to circumstance. Edward VII could not be crowned with the crown of St Edward because he was ill and could not sustain the weight of it. New crowns had to be made for both Queen Mary and Queen Elizabeth, while a new state crown was necessary for George VI as the existing one was over a century old. He paid for it from his own personal account. George V had George IV's mantle presented to him, which he wore at his Coronation and which has been used at every one since. By 1953 we enter the age of the couturier: Norman Hartnell designed not only the queen's dresses and robes but those of her attendants and other female members of the royal family. The result was a coherence of composition necessary for the television age.

The peers and peeresses on each occasion were bidden to appear in their robes, although in 1902 it was stated that they could appear wearing ones used at earlier Coronations. Peeresses' dresses were to be white, later amended to include 'slightly cream coloured, with lace, embroidery, or brocade'. Models of peeresses' robes were put on display at the Earl Marshal's London residence, and an initial banning of tiaras was rescinded, although it was to present a perennial problem to those involved, navigating the insertion of their coronets behind them at the moment of the queen's crowning.[75] Both in 1902 and in 1911 peeresses still had also to wear feathers and veils, an obligatory element in full court dress which was only abandoned in 1937.

More interesting than this was the quite remarkable fascination the public had with ecclesiastical dress, so much so that the illustrated magazines would include spreads in which the various church dignitaries stood arrayed in their copes. Indeed what is noteworthy is the burgeoning of ecclesiastical dress which could only have occurred in the aftermath of the Tractarian Movement. The sets of copes for the various Coronations are still in use at Westminster Abbey. They open with those made for Edward VII's Coronation, brick-red velvet with a pattern of imperial crowns and Tudor roses, with the orphreys adorned with an E.[76] These were used again in 1911, but new ones in green and gold were made for 1937 and in blue for 1953.[77]

Copes had been in continuous use since the Reformation, but although no one seems to have protested at the adoption of processional crosses and croziers, the reintroduction of mitres for the bishops raised hackles in a manner which was to rumble on down to 1953, when they were finally worn for the first time. In 1902 Edward VII had no objection but Frederick Temple, Archbishop of Canterbury, an old High Churchman, would have none of it, turning down almost with revulsion the offer of the gift of a bejewelled mitre to wear on the occasion. He firmly directed the bishops to wear black velvet caps together with rochets with sleeves. In response to this directive Percy Dearmer, the pillar of Anglican liturgical art, designed a new square cap based on the one worn by Archbishop Cranmer in his portrait in the National Portrait Gallery. And, indeed, several of the bishops wore just that.[78]

To the decor and costumes we must add what became a hugely significant part of the Coronation in the twentieth century, the music. This was due to the musical renaissance which began with Sir Hubert Parry and went on through Sir Edward Elgar to Sir William Walton. Each Coronation occasioned new commissions for music, much of which was so successful that it has been assumed into the repertory of patriotism. Such was Parry's setting of 'I was glad' for 1902, which incorporated the *Vivats* of the Westminster schoolboys. J. S. Shedlock before the event wrote: 'I am inclined to think that the anthem which Sir Hubert Parry has written for this will make a great effect, and make everyone who knows what music is think of it as a great, noble, and novel setting of the words.'[79] It has been used at every Coronation since.

Each time, the music was placed in the hands of the Abbey's Master of Music working in collaboration with the Master of the King's Musick. The resources at their disposal were formidable, always making use of a full orchestra and the Abbey choir, plus a second, even larger, choir. In 1902 the orchestra numbered 80 and the choir 400. And, as with every thing else, there was a strong historicist impulse, which in this case would be typical of an era in which the whole history of early English church music was opening up. So the 1902 Coronation not only included new works by Parry, Stanford and Sir Frederick Bridge, but also pieces by Victorian composers like S. S. Wesley, Sir Arthur Sullivan and Sir John Stainer, together with items from the more distant past by Tallis, Gibbons and Purcell, as well as the inevitable Handel 'Zadok the Priest'. The musical arrangements fully accorded with the desire that each Coronation should marry tradition with innovation. In achieving this the musical side of the event has been eminently successful, but then music presents fewer problems than the words and shape of liturgy.

The 1937 Coronation offers a perfect example of what those involved set out to achieve. The music was chosen by the future Sir Ernest Bullock, the organist of Westminster Abbey, and Sir Walford Davies, Master of the King's Musick. As was written at the time, 'their choice shows that musical scholarship has moved far in the last thirty years or so'. 'Our plan,' they wrote, 'was to include representatives of English Church Music from Tudor times to the present', hence the works by Tallis and Byrd.[80] But there was a formidable array of new pieces by Arnold Bax, Arthur Bliss, Granville Bantock, William Walton and Vaughan Williams. These included 'Crown Imperial', the first of the two great Walton marches; the second, 'Orb and Sceptre', was composed for 1953.

Everything was planned down to the last detail, even the entry marches for the various members of the royal family. In 1937 the little princesses entered to Grieg and Queen Mary to Edward German's Coronation march, while the new king and queen progressed up the nave to the strains of Walton's superb 'Crown Imperial'.

These were festivals of patriotic music on the grand scale lasting the length of the average opera, events which called for careful rehearsal and immaculate timing. There were nine new pieces for 1953, including a Te Deum by Walton, but what catches the eye is the list of what was played before and after. Before included the chaconne from Purcell's 'King Arthur', Walton's 'Crown Imperial', Holst's 'Jupiter', Elgar's 'Pomp and Circumstance March No. 2', Vaughan Williams's arrangement of 'Greensleeves', Elgar's 'Nimrod' from his *Enigma Variations* as well as Walton's 'Orb and Sceptre'. After came Elgar's 'Pomp and Circumstance March No. 1', Bax's 'Coronation March' and Elgar's 'Pomp and Circumstance March No. 4'. We see here the creation of a national musical mythology which entwines the crown with nostalgia and pride in an heroic past, with pride in the splendour of an imperial present.

There was one significant musical innovation in 1953. Vaughan Williams arranged the music for the hymn 'All people that on earth do dwell' so that it could sung by the whole congregation gathered in the Abbey. Ironically, this involvement of those present in the service was certainly the most revolutionary departure of all in musical terms and perhaps in liturgical ones, too. Up until 1953 those assembled were virtually passive onlookers apart from the *recognitio* and acclamation. Now, for the very first time, they were called upon to take part in the action, a departure fully in accord with the new democratic age. Once again we see an indicator for the future.

The history of the Coronation proper during the twentieth century is one of the restoration of a rite. By 1838 it had become a jumble far removed from the ceremony laid down in the fourteenth-century *Liber Regalis*. But Victoria's Coronation had taken place before the effect of the Oxford Movement on Anglican liturgical practice had got underway.[81] That was to precipitate the revival of liturgical studies as the Church of England sought to validate its claim to be the true continuation of the pre-Reformation Church. The first publication to include early texts of Coronation recensions was William Maskell's *Monumenta Ritualia Ecclesiae Anglicanae* (1846). Although the author was to convert to Rome in 1850, this work was the first major landmark in the study of the evolution of the liturgy reflecting exactly the Oxford Movement's stress on tradition, apostolic succession, authority and liturgical reform based firmly on ancient practice. Here, for the first time, were texts of the Coronation from the Middle Ages printed and presented as evidence of an uncorrupted and pure tradition in which it was presented as a uniquely English synthesis of Church–State relations. But Queen Victoria had a very long reign, and so it was not until the close of the century that both the golden and diamond jubilees triggered a backward glance to the Coronation of 1838, together with an increasing awareness that a new one would soon be in the offing.[82]

Coronation studies generally surface before and during the anticipated end of one reign and the beginning of another. The turning point here came a decade before, in 1890, with the foundation of the Henry Bradshaw Society, whose purpose was the editing of rare liturgical texts. One of its earliest volumes was by Christopher Wordsworth, then rector of a Dorset parish and a prebendary of Lincoln, who published the manuscript texts of the Coronation of Charles I in 1892. As the century drew to its close the Society published also an edition of the *Liber Regalis* (1896–7), the *Coronation Book of Charles V* (1899) and *Three Coronation Orders* (1900). The last was a curious amalgam of the Coronation of William and Mary, a fourteenth-century Anglo-French version of the Coronation order and one of the Anglo-Saxon texts. In the preface the editor, J. Wickham Legg, wrote:

when the Henry Bradshaw Society was founded in 1890, it was thought the Coronation and consecration of our English sovereigns, an act so important . . . from the civil, as well as from the religious, point of view, might well be illustrated by the new Society; and a series of English Coronation Orders was spoken of. Beyond a haphazard assignation of services to individual sovereigns, very little seemed to have been done in the way of classification, or investigation into the liturgical principles on which these services were constituted.[83]

The society continued this work throughout the twentieth century, making available for the first time all the major recensions. Wickham Legg was also to edit in 1902, the year of Edward VII's Coronation, *The Coronation Order of James I* as a separate publication.

There were two Wickham Leggs, father and son, who loom large in any account of the history of the English Coronation.[84] John Wickham Legg, who was to be such a major pioneer of English Coronation studies, began his career as a medical doctor who, in 1887, abandoned that profession in order to pursue his passion for liturgy, becoming a founding member and, later, chairman of the Henry Bradshaw Society. In 1894 he produced an article entitled 'The Sacring of the English Kings' in the *Archaeological Journal*, and four years later another on the Coronation of Queens for the Church History Society. His son, Leopold George Wickham Legg, inherited his father's passion for Coronations and, in 1900, published what remains by far the most accessible and comprehensive collection of texts and documents on the subject, *English Coronation Records*. In this work all the various texts are sorted into a series of recensions and, even more usefully, translated into English. It is to be regretted that no one since has attempted to revise or replace this work, bringing to bear on it all the advances in liturgical and other scholarship during the twentieth century.

This uncovering of the past was to set the agenda for the coming century, for it immediately became apparent just how much the rite had changed. That awareness was signalled by another important article, H. A. Wilson's 'The English Coronation Orders' in the *Journal of Theological Studies* for 1900–1. Wilson was the first one to castigate both Sancroft and Compton for the butchery of what he and others who studied the Coronation believed to be a uniquely English rite. He was animated by the same conviction as the Leggs, that here was a ritual which was the foundation stone of English liberties, both in the secular as well as the religious sphere. In this patriotic and insular view they were abetted in the year of Edward VII's Coronation by publications like F. C. Eeles's *The English Coronation Service* (1902).

Catholic hackles were already aroused by the Declaration, and it was almost inevitable that an attack on this interpetation would come. It came in ferocious form at the hand of the eminent Jesuit liturgical scholar, Herbert Henry Thurston, who pointed out the disjunction caused by what had been done in 1685 and 1689 and that no Coronation since had fully restored the rite's ancient ritual and meaning. More, he went on to demonstrate in no uncertain terms that this was not an insular phenomenon but one with continental origins.[85] The great German scholar who was to flesh this out even more was Percy Schramm, who dedicated his life to a study of the subject as a European phenomenon, and whose still magisterial book, *The English Coronation*, appeared in English translation in 1937, the year of George VI's Coronation.

This voyage into the past was inevitably to have huge repercussions on twentieth-century Coronations. It is unnecessary to pursue this work by academics throughout the century (in the main focused on the oath and not the anointing). What is important is that those involved in revising the various Coronation services had at their disposal for the very first time not only published texts, but even more, liturgical scholars able to pronounce on correct sequence and structure. That, indeed, has been the central thrust of all four Coronations, an attempt to re-establish a true order bringing out more fully the inner meaning of the ritual. As far as the general public and the majority of those in the Abbey were concerned, these constant tinkerings probably went virtually unnoticed. What also emerged from this burst of scholarship is that the Coronation has always accommodated both continuity and change, showing an ability to respond to every political, social and cultural current.

Everything so far points to 1902 as setting the template for the century.[86] The last Coronation had been virtually seventy years ago and could hardly be viewed as anything arising much above archaeology. We get the greatest insight into the principles guiding Edward VII's Coronation from the memoirs of the Clerk in Council, Sir Almeric FitzRoy. He and Sir Francis Knollys, the king's private secretary, were household officials in the daily orbit of the king, people who could quietly guide things in whatever direction they thought fit. In an entry dated 15 June 1901 FitzRoy writes that the king and those around him showed signs of being 'reckless of precedent', and then follows a passage which perceptively sums up the quintessence of the evolution of the Coronation: 'though precedent . . . is liable to change, there should be a method in the modifications introduced, and with a view to historic continuity the changes that are made should seem to grow out of altered conditions, and not be loosely grafted on them. In course of conversation opportunities suggested themselves for reconciling innovation with usage, and investing the King's ideas with the prestige of tradition . . .'[87]

We have already examined the growth of secular spectacle and the ideas that motivated it. We now need to consider the actual liturgical rite. Just as the secular ceremonial lay within the competence of the Earl Marshal, the religious pertained by right to the archbishops of Canterbury. And in this instance there was not the continuity of two dukes but of four very different archbishops: Frederick Temple, Randall Davidson, Cosmo Gordon Lang and Geoffrey Fisher. As we shall see, Temple was virtually neutralised by the influence of Davidson in 1902 who, with his two successors, had definite visions as to what the Coronation meant. And all three were also acutely aware that they were occupying the archiepiscopal throne during a period of continuous decline on the part of the Church of England. As the Coronation took off as a mega national event with blanket media coverage, each saw it as a vehicle whereby to bring spirituality back to the people. It was a quest which ended in failure.

We should not, of course, discount the influence of the royal family on what happened in the Abbey. It is clear that Edward VII had very firm views which had to be got round. In the case of George V and VI the views would have been those of Queen Mary. That she must have been the dominant force in 1937 we can gather from her diary entry for 24 January 1937: 'Bertie, E & I, Cromer & Wig (Sir Clive Wigram) had a long confabulation about Coronation arrangements . . . A good many points were decided on . . .'[88] Queen Mary was still around in 1953, although she died shortly before the event. Her voice would have been an overwhelmingly conservative one. Both Elizabeth II and the Duke of Edinburgh were young and inexperienced in 1953. The duke chaired the Coronation Committee and was anxious to modernise, asking Geoffrey Fisher, the Archbishop, 'how some features relevant to the world today could be introduced'.[89] (*The Times* on 5 May 1952 had written a leader on the subject.) He got nowhere, for the forces of conservatism headed by the two previous queen consorts and the Earl Marshal, the 16th Duke of Norfolk, were too strong for him. But when the queen demanded that some recognition be granted her husband, a blessing was somewhat oddly placed between the offertory and the prayer for the Church Militant. In the actual Coronation rite 'usage' certainly won over 'innovation'.

The household officials and courtiers, too, were overwhelmingly cautious and conservative, often forgetting that the monarchy's strength lay in the fact that it could 'invent' tradition, something which it only began to rediscover in the last decades of the twentieth century. Without doubt the most innovative Coronation was that of 1902. All the others were clones of what happened then. The fact that it was so original a piece of 'invented tradition' was quickly forgotten as it became the sacred icon upon which all that followed had to be modelled.

The two key figures in the Coronation of 1902 were Reginald Brett, 2nd Viscount Esher, and Randall Davidson, Bishop of Winchester. Esher was a repressed homosexual and aesthete whose work as Secretary of the Office of Works from 1895 to 1902 brought him into contact with the royal family.[90] In this capacity he became responsible for a series of public events: the diamond jubilee, Gladstone's funeral, the opening of the Victoria & Albert Museum, Queen Victoria's funeral and the 1902 Coronation. Just how important Esher was in 1902 is revealed by the fact that, as we have already seen, the king actually asked Esher to 'stage-manage' the Coronation. He refused as the Earl Marshal, the Duke of Norfolk, would have been 'horribly hurt'. But he then goes on to write 'So I shall help, but nothing more.'[91]

Modern historians have generally accorded Esher the role of reformer of royal ceremonial, the man who set the British monarchy on the path to immaculate pageantry. The argument runs that by the close of the nineteenth century ceremonial had decayed. The great hereditary officers no longer knew their roles, coffins were carried back to front and marching columns could concertina. Esher himself blamed the heralds, who were also cast as the culprits by Sir Arthur Ellis, Comptroller of the Lord Chamberlain's Department. In his view the heralds were 'ghastly cads, not a gentleman among them and Cath[olic] hangers on of the Duke of Norfolk'.[92] There may be a great deal of truth in the belief that the execution of ceremonial had from time to time gone wrong, but that assumes some kind of lost golden age of ritual. All through the history of the Coronation we have had, in fact, frequent glimpses of things going awry. It can be argued that it is wrong to project back in time the immaculate choreography of the late twentieth century, essentially the result of modern technology and of the demands of the watching eye of both film and television. The fact that things did go wrong in the past was also less important, only noticed by the likes of Horace Walpole. Immaculate pageantry only became important when it was scrutinised by the whole world as it was happening. But there is no doubt that ceremonial and its performance did gradually improve through the century.

Esher's letters and journals from 1901 and into 1902 are peppered with phrases which indicate his involvement, such as 'Then we [i.e. Esher and the king] talked a good deal about the Coronation, and I told him all the ancient customs, of which he is profoundly ignorant', or 'settled a lot of small Coronation details'.[93] During the run-up Esher was promoted to another position but the king insisted on his seeing through the Coronation, and after the event he was effusive in his gratitude. Seen in this light Esher's presence must account for the attempt to resolve some of the outstanding sores caused by the truncation of the Westminster Hall ceremonial. Many of these came to the surface with the traditional Court of Claims, which excited so much interest that its proceedings were published.[94] The result of their transactions signalled a number of palliatives. The return of the Barons of the Cinque Ports, who no longer carried a canopy but were now allowed to walk in the procession into the Abbey as far as the choir screen, where they acted as recipients of the banners borne by the grandees of the realm.[95] The Champion, the Dymock of the day, also returned and rode in both public processions bearing the standard of England.

The Barons of the Cinque Ports and the Dymock family were not the only people who were aggrieved by what had happened in 1821 and 1838; so were the Dean and Chapter of Westminster. It had been their task to carry the regalia from the Abbey to Westminster Hall. There was no going back to that, but a procession of a different kind was devised to replace it. This went from the Jerusalem Chamber via the cloisters, St Faith's chapel and the ambulatory to the high altar. As the Bishop of Bath and Wells wrote on 22 May: 'This is a reduced form of the Dean's Procession which used to go from the High Altar to Westminster Hall . . .'.[96]

Two imperatives were uppermost in the minds of those who put together the rite for 1902, the first was the king's desire that the service should be shortened, and the second that something should be done in response to the discoveries of liturgical scholarship. Those destined to play leading roles in the event were in a sad state of health. Frederick Temple, Archbishop of Canterbury, was a pre-Tractarian High Churchman, simple and austere, a man who stuck to the letter of the Book of Common Prayer. He was eighty, with both his eyesight and his physical strength in serious decline. One of the reasons that the king wanted the service cut was that he doubted whether Temple would be able to get through it. To meet his failing eyesight scrolls in large letters bearing the texts he needed to utter were made, but as these were never firmly held mistakes occurred.[97] Nor was G. G. Bradley, the Dean of Westminster, in any better condition and the general view was that all he could do was just about manage to sit through it.

Although these men were meant to play leading roles on the great day it was Randall Davidson, Temple's successor, who was to have the greatest influence and voice in the Coronation Committee as appointed by the Privy Council. Davidson had been Dean of Windsor and was a great favourite of Queen Victoria, and of her successor, when he became also Clerk of the Closet. As the only cleric on the all-important Coronation Executive Committee his voice was paramount and he, in addition, had private access to the king whom he was anxious to please. Davidson also wanted to meet the challenge of the scholars, but he knew that any changes should not be so radical as to seem to invalidate the late Stuart and Hanoverian Coronations.

The revision took the usual form of the Coronation Committee entrusting the archbishop with revising the service. Temple, hopelessly at sea, turned at once to Davidson. Following the Hanoverian archbishops, his point of departure was inevitably what had happened in 1831 and 1838, to which was added the charge of the king to keep it short, a view which caused Lord Salisbury to tartly express 'his surprise that any of it was left'.[98] Now what is so striking is the fact that Davidson did not turn to either of the Wickham Leggs but to Joseph Armitage Robinson, formerly Norrisian Professor of Divinity at Cambridge, but, in 1901, a new canon at Westminster Abbey. Robinson was a patristic scholar rather than a liturgist, but nonetheless he set about restoring the rite to what it had been before the butchering of 1685 and 1689. But he viewed it in a particular way as a rite, in his eyes, based on the form of an episcopal consecration. He enunciated this

476   CORONATION

view of it in the sermon he delivered in the Abbey on Easter Monday 1902: 'The Coronation is a veritable consecration.' This, he went on to say, was a solemn enactment in which the king dedicated himself, under God's protection, to his people.[99] The result of this was a far better service. The first oblation, with its offering of a pall (an altar-cloth) together with a pound of gold, was dropped along with many of the anthems typical of the Hanoverian period. The litany and the address on the delivery of the Bible were abridged and, to balance these changes, older features were restored: the blessing of the oils, the triple anointing and the blessing of the royal regalia. The communion service was given an introit to replace the Sanctus which, most inappropriately, had long been used in its place. In addition, a proper collect was composed for the communion service based on the tenth-century Pontifical of Egbert.

There was a mistaken belief that the sermon was the prerogative of the Bishop of London, founded only on the fact that he had preached in 1831 and 1838. The Bishop of London was, in fact, asked, but his sermon was never delivered as the king's delicate health meant further truncations when the Coronation actually happened on 9 August. This time the *recognitio* was reduced to a single presentation, and not only the sermon was dropped but the litany also, while the Te Deum, instead of following the benediction, was moved to the very end of the service as the royal procession left the sacrarium. The sermon was to reappear in an abbreviated form in 1911 (as a palliative to the Archbishop of York) but was dropped in 1937 and 1953, resulting in a radical diminution of the ministry of the Word, an integral part of any Christian liturgy.

Not everything was plain sailing. The archbishop, who wrongly believed that the triple anointing was a post-1689 innovation, wanted a single one on the grounds that 'That and that alone is Biblical and the Biblical is best for Englishmen.' Davidson, who was closer to the king than Temple, got this overruled.[100] The blessing of the oil was billed as reviving an ancient rite, but the grounds for what was actually done were extremely shaky ones. The authority on this was Archdeacon Christopher Wordsworth of Westminster Abbey, who, on 19 May, wrote to Armitage Robinson giving him the whole history or what little was, in fact, known. The last account they had of this rite was the formula used by Laud in 1626. From that occasion it was somewhat surprisingly concluded that it was traditional for the oil to be blessed

OPPOSITE
Top George VI receives the homage of the peers, 1937, photograph
Below left and right George VI and Queen Elizabeth leave the Abbey, 1937, photograph

The anointing of Queen
Alexandra, 1911, painting,
c.1911

by a bishop who was also a canon of Westminster. The result was that
the oil in 1902 was blessed by Canon James Welldon, formerly Bishop
of Calcutta. It was made up by the Royal Apothecary and was a mixture of sesame oil and olive oil perfumed with roses, orange flowers,
jasmine, cinnamon and flowers of benzoin together with musk, civet
and ambergris. This also provided enough for George V and Queen
Mary. Both for George VI and for Elizabeth II the oil was blessed semi-
privately in the chapel of St Edward.[101]

What happened in 1902, which was never to be repeated, was the
king's apparent insistence that the queen should be crowned by the
Archbishop of York, William Maclagan. There was absolutely no
historical precedent for this and it evoked a horrified reaction on the
part of Leopold Wickham Legg.[102] In 1911, when this was looked back
upon, it was concluded that it had come about because Temple had no
idea that this was other than the norm. The fact that the king went
along with it was driven on by the knowledge that Temple was so frail

and tottery that it was doubtful whether he would get through anointing and crowning the king, let alone the queen.[103] It was a proposal which the Court of Claims went along with but, at the same time, it recognised that York had no right to it. The pragmatic decision of the king, if such it was, is vindicated by the fact that when it came to the homage Temple had to try three times to kneel, and when he eventually achieved it he could not get up again and had to be lifted from the ground by those in proximity.

What are we to conclude about 1902? On the whole, Davidson achieved his aims, as did the courtiers. Temple, whose papers reveal that he, too, had someone devilling for him, was not completely obliterated. But he knew little history and belonged to an era before the birth of modern liturgical scholarship and, as a consequence, was outflanked. Just how much, is reflected in the fact that Davidson, who was on the Coronation Executive Committee, went through the changes to the service before even the archbishop had formally delivered his own text. Lord Halifax summed up the dilemma well in a letter to Davidson in April 1901: 'What a pity Archbp Benson and Arthur Stanley are not respectively Canterbury and Westminster when the Coronation takes place. They would have been interested in all the historical and religious traditions and associations and would have seen all was as it should be. Now, the present Archbishop is useless, and the dean of Westminster more useless still.'[104]

Not everyone was happy with 1902. J. Wickham Legg was most certainly not. He vented his sour grapes in his edition of the Coronation of James I published that year, in that he had several swipes at those who had put together the 'maimed rites' of the 1902 service. Seeing the success of the Archbishop of York in infringing the prerogatives of the see of Canterbury, he wrote with a degree of sarcasm, 'the time perhaps may be thought to have come when the claim of Westminster may be disputed; and the Dean and Chapter of St Paul's may be successful hereafter if they attempt to carry away the Coronation to their own church'. He then goes on to lament the loss of the great medievalist, Bishop Stubbs, who would have been 'deeply vexed at the marred rites which the officials of our time have thought good enough for the Coronation of Edward VII and at the indifference to historical considerations displayed by those whose duty, it may be thought, was to maintain and defend them'.[105]

But let the learned Jesuit Herbert Thurston have the last word in this academic mud-slinging. In referring to the publications of the Henry Bradshaw Society he expresses his thanks for them, but then goes on to write that 'the net results of all that has been written seems to me profoundly disappointing'.

In spite of all this, what happened for better or worse in 1902 was to set the pattern for its three successors. The service in 1911 was prepared by Claude Jenkins, the Lambeth Palace librarian, under the supervision of Armitage Robinson who, by that date, had graduated to being Dean of Westminster. Jenkins, who was ordained in 1903, specialised in patristic studies and was also an eccentric antiquarian. He became librarian at Lambeth in 1910 and held the post until 1952, and was still around when Elizabeth II was crowned the year after.[106] It was then that he recorded what happened in 1911. Dean Robinson had told him that 'We must not remove all the date markings of the centuries.'[107] In other words any Coronation service should be a cumulative document. Once again we come back to that complex marriage of innovation and tradition.

By 1911 Davidson, like Armitage Robinson, had also advanced and was now Archbishop of Canterbury. This time he turned for advice to the liturgist, F. E. Brightman, fellow of Magdalen College, Oxford from 1902–32. Brightman lamented that Cranmer had not written the Coronation rite and went on to give a number of suggestions, virtually all of which were in relation to the rubrics. Davidson was particularly concerned over the nonsense of investing the king with the orb and then immediately taking it away. Brightman's advice was to leave things as they were or, if they had to be changed, to remove the orb altogether.[108]

The actual changes in 1911 were, in fact, few. At the crowning a briefer and more ancient form of words was restored to replace the bombastic prose of 1689, and the introit to the communion service was changed to what had been the gradual in the medieval rite: 'Let my prayers come into thy presence as the incense . . .' (Psalm 141: 2) and a proper preface was restored. More interesting than any of this is the letter Davidson wrote to the king after the event on 22 June describing what he considered the rite was about:

> If our 'Coronation Service' means anything, it means the promise of that [i.e. God's] help, a promise accompanied by the knowledge on the King's part that his people are in almost

every English-speaking home praying for him and expecting that their prayers will be answered, and that GOD will indeed grant them as their head a 'consecrated' man, not in any pedantic or over-wrought sense of the word – but a man who deliberately means, by the help of God, to lead a life of 'service', a life of straightforward devotion to some of the most important duties on Earth, a life of manly purity and justice and truth.[109]

In the letter he also writes that his thoughts were very much with the Parliament Act both at the anointing and during the girding with the sword. In that he had no luck for, as Almeric FitzRoy wrote, the Parliament Act was 'in effect a sentence of death on the oldest legislative Chamber in the world'.[110] That death sentence was passed. All they could console themselves with was the 'splendour of the pageantry and the well-ordered movement of the great ceremonial' and that, yes, 1911 was much better than 1902.[111]

Armitage Robinson died in 1933 and his role in relation to the Coronation was replaced by Edward Ratcliff, Professor of Divinity at Cambridge, who was responsible for what happened in 1937 and in 1953. On each occasion there were further tinkerings. In 1937 the litany was moved yet again, this time to accompany the entrance procession of the dean and canons, and there it stayed in 1953. More important was the transposition of the oath to its logical medieval place immediately after the *recognitio*, and equally the restoration of the ancient sequence in the anointing, working upwards from hand to head.

Cosmo Gordon Lang was a born thespian whose voice dominated every committee meeting and who also dominated all eight rehearsals. Lang's agenda was that the Coronation should be made the occasion to bring home to the peoples of the Commonwealth the real and spiritual significance of the event via the medium of radio. He was also successful in involving other denominations, seven representatives of the Free Churches and four of the Church of Scotland walking in the Abbey procession, anticipating the ecumenism which was to follow after 1945. The aim for Lang was to establish the king, in Walter Bagehot's phrase, as the 'head of our morality'.[112] The nearest we get to what the Coronation meant in 1937 comes from the pen of Cyril Garbett, Archbishop of York from 1942 to 1955, who describes the coronation in the following words in his book *The Claims of the Church of*

England, published in 1947, two years after the war:

It is the Archbishop who presents the King to the people for their acclamation; it is he who anoints the King, who hands the Sword to him, who delivers the Orb with the cross shining upon it, who places in his hand the Sceptre and receiving the Crown from the Altar sets it on the King's head. All through the service the Archbishop blessing and exhorting the King is also

The Queen takes the Oath, 1953, photograph

The Queen at the anointing, 1953, photograph

hallowing the State. And throughout the rite the King is seeking the help of God for his great office, now kneeling previous to the anointing while the Holy Spirit is invoked, afterwards for the Archbishop's blessing, later to make his oblation, and finally to receive Holy Communion.[113]

Hallowing the state seems a very far cry from what Coronations had previously been about, but such an adjustment accorded well with a parliamentary democracy.

Geoffrey Fisher in 1953 was equally vocal as to the role of the monarchy and the Coronation in the scheme of things. In a series of

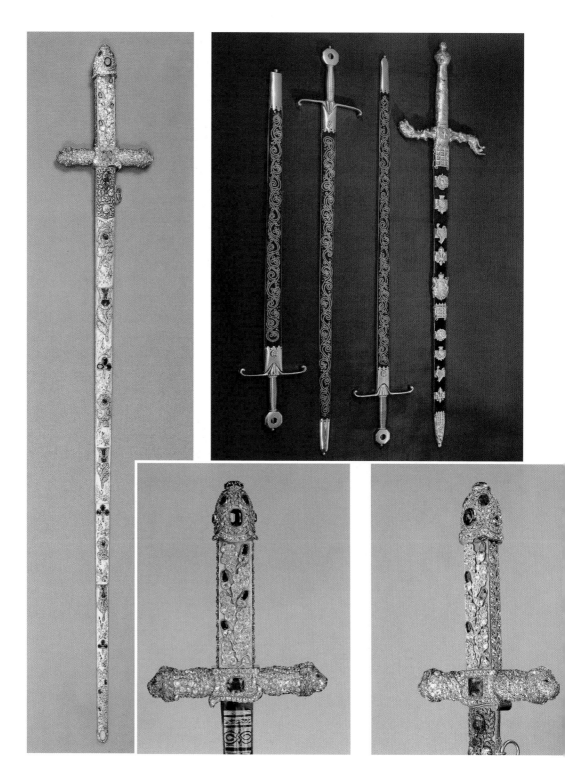

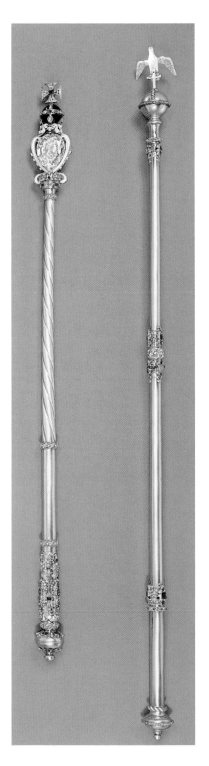

OPPOSITE
The Coronation Swords.
Top left and details below
The jewelled Sword of State.
Top right The curtana or
Sword of Mercy, *c.*1610–50;
The Sword of Spiritual
Justice, *c.*1610–50;
The Sword of Temporal
Justice, *c.*1610–50;
The Sword of State, 1678

Left The Sovereign's Sceptre,
1660–61, and the Sovereign's
Sceptre with the Dove, 1661;
Right Detail of the
Sovereign's Sceptre with
Cullinan Diamond I added,
1910–11

sermons leading up to the event he defined the monarchy, now devoid of secular power, as being somehow released to take up an enhanced leadership role: 'the possibility of a spiritual power far more exalted and far more searching in its demands: the power to lead, to inspire, to unite, by the Sovereign's personal character, personal conviction, personal example'.

The role of the queen was to uphold 'the pillars of a true society' which was based on 'domestic fidelity' and 'united homes'. Through the anointing, he argued, the queen was brought into God's presence in a relationship which was based on self-denial, the burdens of her office reflected in the weight of the crown upon her head. Reading these in retrospect it is difficult not to conclude that Fisher was not a little over the top as the sword was cast as 'power of the crown', the bread and wine 'all the labours of men and the fruits of their labours' and the altar-cloth and the gold 'all the skills and crafts, the enterprise and invention, the arts and culture by which men adorn the art of living and make it beautiful'.[114] By 1953 the Coronation service, through these interpretations laid upon it by successive archbishops, had succeeded in turning itself into a legitimisation of temporal power and the institutions of what had become a liberal society.

In accord with post-1945 committee-speak, a committee was set up by the archbishop to consider the text. On it were Leopold Wickham Legg who had seen that of 1902, Claude Jenkins who had been involved in that of 1911, E. C. Ratcliff, Ely Professor of Divinity at Cambridge, who had acted in a similar capacity in 1937, Norman Sykes, Dixie Professor of Ecclesiastical History, also at Cambridge, and Dr Alan Don, Dean of Westminster.[115] The results were neatly summed up by Fisher on 10 February 1953 after he had seen the queen: 'In not a few instances there has been a return in the words of the rite to the strength and simplicity of earlier forms abandoned in the last two centuries. . . .'[116] Or perhaps we get closer in Claude Jenkins's comment: 'I managed to get back some of the old last time and we are getting back some more of it now. But we must not disturb people more than is necessary and we may be quite content to leave something for our successors.'[117]

So in 1953 the regalia procession was again moved, this time to the very beginning of the service. The presentation of the Bible, an awkward legacy of 1689, was shifted to follow the oath where it was equally badly placed, the sovereign only minutes before having sworn the oath on it. But in liturgical terms it fulfilled the sequence which demanded that the Word precede the Sacrament. This was turned into a solitary ecumenical gesture, for it was presented to the queen by the Moderator of the Church of Scotland. But his presence posed more problems than it solved, for he had no reason to be part of a ceremony

I solemnly promise and swear to govern the Peoples of the United Kingdom of Great Britain and Northern Ireland, Canada, Australia, New Zealand and the Union of South Africa, Pakistan and Ceylon, and of my Possessions and the other Territories to any of them belonging or pertaining, according to their respective laws and customs.

I will to my power cause Law and Justice, in Mercy, to be executed in all my judgements.

I will to the utmost of my power maintain the Laws of God and the true profession of the Gospel. I will to the utmost of my power maintain in the United Kingdom the Protestant Reformed Religion established by law. And I will maintain and preserve inviolably the settlement of the Church of England, and the doctrine, worship, discipline, and government thereof, as by law established in England. And I will preserve unto the Bishops and Clergy of England, and to the Churches there committed to their charge, all such rights and privileges as by law do or shall appertain to them or any of them.

The things which I have here before promised, I will perform and keep.

So help me God.

The Coronation Oath, 1953

installing the Supreme Governor of the Church of England. In addition, the introit to the communion service was again changed, this time to 'Behold, O God our defender . . .' (Psalm 84: 9–10), which was the one used in the medieval rite. And, in turn, the 1911 introit was restored to its medieval role as the gradual. More importantly, the centuries-old muddle about the armils was at long last put in order. They were reinstated as a pair of bracelets which became part of the investiture, and what had, wrongly, been called the armils was firmly called the royal stole. There was also an attempt to sort out the giving of the orb along with a number of other minor details.

As 1953 will be the point of departure for those compiling the next Coronation it is important to record what the sequence was:

1. The preparation. Processions into the Abbey, during one of which the litany was sung.

2. The entrance into the church. The queen entered and was received with an anthem from Psalm 122, prayed and went to her chair in the sacrarium. The lords bearing the regalia presented the items to the archbishop who, in turn, handed them to the dean who placed them on the altar.

3. The *recognitio*. The archbishop presented the queen to the four compass points. The people cried 'God save Queen Elizabeth'.

4. The oath. The queen took the Coronation oath, to govern justly, and to 'maintain in the United Kingdom the Protestant Reformed Religion established by law'.

5. The presentation of the Bible. This was done by the Moderator of the Church of Scotland, the Bible being 'the most valuable thing that this world affords'.

6. The beginning of the communion service. This used the 1662 text and included the introit, collect for purity, one for the Queen, unique to this occasion, the epistle, gradual, Gospel and Nicene Creed.

7. The anointing. The *Veni creator*, a prayer over the ampulla, the anthem 'Zadok the Priest'; the queen moved to St Edward's chair and the archbishop anointed her on the palms, breast and head: 'be anointed, blessed and consecrated Queen over the People'. The monarch was then blessed.

Queen Elizabeth II
enthroned, 1953, photograph

8. The investiture. Presentation of the spurs, then the sword, with a prayer for the execution of justice, which the queen returned to the altar and which was redeemed by a peer and bare-bladed carried before her. Then were put on the armils, the robe and stole, the orb, the ring, the sceptre and the rod, all with injunctions. The crown was blessed and the archbishop crowned the queen, at which the people shouted 'God save the Queen' and the peers and peeresses put on their coronets, trumpets sounded and salutes were fired. The archbishop prayed that God might grant the queen a crown of glory, and a series of blessings followed. An anthem was sung: 'Be strong and of good courage'.

9. The enthronisation. The queen was lifted into her throne by bishops and peers. The archbishop bade her to 'hold fast' and prayed that God would establish her in her throne.

10. The homage. First the archbishops and bishops, then the Duke of

Edinburgh and then the peerage in sequence. During this, anthems were sung and drums and trumpets led to those assembled shouting: 'God save Queen Elizabeth. Long live Queen Elizabeth. May the Queen live for ever.'

11. The communion service. This opened with the congregational hymn, 'All people that on earth do dwell', and concluded with the archbishop's blessing, after which the Te Deum was sung.

12. The recession. Processions out of the Abbey in sequence. It closed with the singing of the National Anthem.

―――――――――――――――――――――――――

Just how far we have travelled is revealed in what those who practised the new discipline of sociology made of it. It 'was the ceremonial occasion for the affirmation of the moral values by which the society lives. It was an act of national communion.'[118]

But perhaps we ought to accord the last word to the two celebrated diarists who were present on the occasion, but who were certainly no intellectuals, Sir Henry or 'Chips' Channon as he was known and Cecil Beaton, who was the official royal photographer. 'The ceremonial,' Beaton wrote, 'seemed to be as fresh and inspiring as some great play or musical event that was being enacted upon a spontaneous impulse of genius.'[119] 'What a day for England,' wrote Channon, 'and the traditional forces of the world. Shall we ever see the like again?'[120] That question remains to be answered.

Coda: pageantry made perfect, or almost so

Channon also wrote: 'it was all finer, and better organised than last time', for he had been present, too, in 1937. The gradual journey towards immaculate ceremonial is easily traced; it was the result of the increasing professionalism expected of anything in the twentieth century and made possible by the arrival of ever more technical means whereby to achieve perfection.

It did not start like that. Indeed, Almeric FitzRoy's view was that if the Coronation of Edward VII had actually taken place on the original date it would have been a fiasco. Esher was equally concerned at the lack of rehearsals, writing on 1 June 1902: 'they are dreadfully behind

Opposite The Duke of Edinburgh renders homage, 1953, photograph

with the rehearsals; I only trust they will not bungle'.[121] The postponement, in fact, ensured many more rehearsals, with the consequence
that when it was staged over a month later there was 'the utmost order
and dignity'.[122] In FitzRoy's view it was at the anointing of the queen
that 'the ceremonial reached its highest pitch of beauty', adding that
'when the group dissolved it seemed like the passing of a dream that
might have haunted the imagination of a Vathek or De Quincy'.[123]

I have already touched on the decrepit archbishop unable to read
his lines and even less able to get up from his knees once on them. But
we get a further insight as to what else went wrong from a memorandum written by George Wyndham Kennion, Bishop of Bath and Wells,
one of the two bishops on constant attendance on the king, and who
had the task of having to learn by rote the entire service in his role as
the king's prompt. All, he relates, went well until it came to the actual
crowning, 'when, though I suppose it ought not to get out, the
Archbishop who could not see well, put on the Crown the wrong way
to the front, and, endeavouring to alter it, made it worse, and I had to
take hold of it with the hand . . . and help to put it straight on his head
. . .'.[124] Fortunately the sudden blaze of electric light, acclamations, gun
salutes and bells covered up the gaffe. Later Kennion recalls he just
managed to prevent Temple dropping the consecrated bread. No wonder all the way through the king kept muttering, 'I am very anxious
about the Archbishop.'

In 1911 'There were hardly any hitches', or so Lang reported to his
mother.[125] Amongst the Davidson Papers that sense of greater organisation is evident in a list of exact timings: 11.06 procession starts; 11.11
the procession enters the west door; 11.16 it arrives at the high altar;
11.20 the queen arrives in the sacrarium; 11.26 the king arrives there;
11.27 the *recognitio*; 11.31 the close of the *recognitio*; 12.30 the crowning;
1.26 the peace.[126]

Nineteen thirty-seven was another matter, as the king's own diary
records. Trouble began when the dean tried to put on the *colobium sindonis* inside out and the king had to firmly resist him. When it came to
the oath neither of the supporting bishops could find the place so that
the archbishop stepped in and, George VI writes, 'held his book down
for them to read, but horror of horrors his thumb covered the words
of the oath'. On that occasion the Lord Great Chamberlain was so
shaky that the king had to vest himself, added to which, as he left the
chair of St Edward, one of the bishops stepped on his train, pulling

Crown, 1838 and replicated
1937, with the 'Black Prince's
Ruby' and the Cullinan
Diamond II at the front

him. 'I had to tell him to get off it pretty sharply as I nearly fell down.'[127] By then there were telephone links to aid them and there were no less than eight rehearsals. So it is hardly surprising that we come across one author writing 'as a people we are, if not artists, at any rate not bad at pageantry'.

In 1953 the rehearsals were almost on a daily basis from 14 May onwards, with what can be described as a dress rehearsal on 1 June. The queen herself came to four of these. Fisher notes in his diary that there were some mistakes, the queen omitting one curtsy and Fisher himself starting to present the queen with the armils before the sword had been redeemed. But what made him absolutely furious was the replacement by the dean of the small basin used at rehearsals with a weighty alms dish he could hardly carry at the offertory. But the then dean, Dr Alan Don, captures just how near perfect the 1953 Coronation was:

> For the next two hours or more everything passed off without any hitch worth mentioning. The Queen did her part with great recollectedness and simplicity, and without any outward trace of nervousness or self-consciousness. The Mistress of the Robes and the Maids of Honour were dignified and graceful, and moved with notable precision. The supporting Bishops – Durham, aged under fifty and looking venerable as a septuagenarian, and Bath and Wells, not good looking but full of solicitude for the Queen – performed their evolutions with conspicuous skill. The Archbishop of Canterbury (who has it in his power to make or mar a Coronation) rose to the occasion nobly. His voice was clear, his articulation unaffected, and his mastery of detail complete.[128]

The Abbey's sacrist, Jocelyn Perkins, who had also been present in both 1911 and 1937, reckoned that it was 'out and away the most impressive of the three'.[129] The likelihood is that this judgement would also qualify it to be the most impressive ever staged in the Coronation's thousand and more years history.

EPILOGUE

2005

Fifty years on from 2 June 1953 I found myself standing *en tableau*, wearing what is known as one's 'scarlet and black', as a member of the College of the Abbey Church of St Peter at Westminster to welcome the queen on the fiftieth anniversary of her Coronation. Beyond the west door the dean and subdean, appropriately wearing the 1953 copes, greeted the queen who, I recall, was in pale yellow. The state trumpeters were stationed on the choir screen and, as she entered the church, a fanfare was sounded, after which we all saluted her in unison, welcoming her to this her Coronation church. Then a great procession formed and there followed a service whose theme was that of sharing the queen's own ideals of self-dedication as epitomised in that ceremony of half a century ago. It was a grand yet oddly modest and moving event which went off like clockwork, with lots of trumpeting in the hymns and fine choral singing. After the blessing and the National Anthem, which we all sang with fervour, we processed back down the nave again and this time out through the west door into the light of day. As the queen stepped out we all applauded, at which she lit up and smiled. What a different memory, I thought, from that rainy Embankment all those years ago.

Looking back through this book the reader may well be left, along with its author, thinking, what happens next? Even as far back as 1911 Archbishop Davidson wrote to his opposite number in the north: 'The usings of Feudal times don't fit well into a Democratic age!'[1] By the time the next Coronation happens the interval separating it from the last one is likely to be as long or even longer than the decades which separated the Coronation of 1838 from that of 1902. What such a huge lapse of time certainly signals is innovation, but of what kind and how will it be married to ancient usage? The question is an intriguing one to which some, we are told, are already giving thought.

The decisions made will certainly be affected by everything that has happened to the monarchy since 1953.[2] It managed successfully to hold its own as a welfare monarchy in a welfare state until the 1960s when a new generation began to attack it on the grounds of cost and stuffiness. Kingsley Martin's *The Crown and the Establishment* (1962) cast the monarchy as blatant institutionalised privilege. But when the silver jubilee came in the middle of the impoverished and strife-ridden 1970s it was a huge success, precipitating an upward curve in popularity which reached an apogee in the marriage of the Prince of Wales. Against that, however, has to be set the breakdown of the alliance of the crown and the media as the latter, from the late 1960s onwards, became more and more intrusive, sometimes to the point of vindictiveness. But part of that the younger generation of the royal family brought upon themselves, living out what at times cannot be categorised as other than a shoddy saga culminating in the break-up of the Waleses' marriage and Princess Diana's death.

Republicanism, which had seen no real resurgence since 1870–1, began to rear its head. These were crisis years, and it was only from 1997 onwards that the slow climb back began, reaching another peak in the queen mother's funeral and the queen's golden jubilee in 2002. In response to its critics the monarchy redoubled its charitable endeavour, set out to embrace new communities and cut its running expenses. As it stood at the opening of the twenty-first century its bedrock remained dedication to public service and voluntarism. Both roles grew rather than diminished in importance in the face of the increasing power and politicisation of every aspect of government and daily life. The monarchy, standing outside the political system, has the unique power of reaching out wherever it wants in society irrespective of class, education, religion, ethnic origin or any other social or political characteristic. In addition, with devolution, the monarchy came to occupy a position within the country analogous to what it had once held in respect of the Empire, as a major link holding the whole entity together. Now, when the Prince of Wales visits Scotland, he advertises himself as Duke of Rothesay. More will have happened by the time of the next Coronation, and its relevance and success will depend on its ability to express all of this through a ceremonial and liturgy which is at once true to the past and yet contemporary.

In many ways it will mean putting into action what I have already signalled in the previous chapter. The shortcomings as well as the virtues of the service became ever more apparent as the twentieth century unfolded. The circumstances of all four Coronations, however, inevitably propelled those involved to conservatism, although in 1953 that was less excusable. So much since has changed and would have to be come to terms with. The role of the hereditary peers has been abolished, although the reform of the House of Lords is *in medias res* with a rump of them remaining. But they may well not be there by the time of the next Coronation to render homage. The life peers will certainly need to be accommodated and perhaps Attlee's idea that the Speaker should render homage as the 'common man' was not such a bad one after all, although the option lies open to move the homage, which is a purely secular action, back into Westminster Hall where it was often performed in the Middle Ages. Indeed the revival of the use of Westminster Hall may well provide a solution to many of the problems thrown up by what is now a multi-faith and multi-cultural society. There is no reason why the next sovereign, after anointing and crowning, should not, for example, process back to the hall to be blessed or saluted by the representatives of other faiths.

In respect of the latter much has changed, as there is a far greater ecumenical spirit among the various Christian denominations and the open and liberal tradition of the Abbey, epitomised by its Commonwealth Day service, may well mean that certainly places if not roles could be assigned within the action of the main rite to representatives of the various denominations, if not to those of wholly other faiths. In the case of the communion service the liturgy of the Church of England has changed substantially since 1953 when the old Book of Common Prayer was still firmly in place. Although Common Worship (2000) incorporates the whole of it, few Anglican churches now use the old communion service, preferring the far better structured new ones which restore the role of the laity. Although the Prince of Wales is an earnest supporter of the old Prayer Book it would be difficult, in a democratic age, not to have far more participation by the congregation in the way of hymns, joint prayers (the litany was originally a communal prayer) and readings. At present the communion service falls short on the ministry of the Word, and the sermon, however brief, should certainly be restored. No modern eucharistic celebration confines those who communicate to so few, nullifying its essence as a shared sacrament.[3]

In the case of the anointing, perhaps Archbishop Temple was right that it should revert to the biblical precedent of a single one to the head. This is the most solemn part of the whole service, the moment of the dedication of a single human being to represent and give service to the nation. The continuation of the Coronation depends on the acceptance of the notion that one person can be set aside in this way and undergo such an initiatory rite, one which, in the medieval period, verged closely on a Christian sacrament. What is undeniable is that all societies demand rites of passage and ceremonial of some kind, combinations of words, gestures and music often enhanced by an architectural setting, all resonant of a collective past. Looked at dispassionately it would be very easy to ditch the Coronation, ceremony but it would be very difficult, once gone, to put it back. Everything in its history, however, has revealed it to be extraordinarily flexible and adaptable to present circumstance.

The fruits of technological advance could, indeed, enhance the service. Participation beyond the confines of the Abbey's walls could be achieved. With screens and modern visual links there is no reason why the *recognitio* and other parts of the service could not be actions in which people gathered in the public squares of the great urban centres of the country could take part. That would brilliantly reflect today's society.

There remains, however, one central dilemma. The Coronation still expresses the constitution of the state as it was shaped by the Parliament of 1559, in which the monarch was accorded the title of Supreme Governor of the Church of England. For centuries membership of Church and State was coeval, and that survives to this day in the fact that, however much the Church of England now governs its own affairs, it still is subject to the will of a Parliament which now includes Roman Catholics and members of other denominations together with those of non-Christian faiths. The 1559 settlement was reinforced by the 1689 Act of Settlement which, in the aftermath of the Catholic James II, made it mandatory that the wearer of the British crown be Protestant and a communicant member of the Church of England. To unravel this would precipitate a major constitutional crisis. Somehow or other a way would have to be found for the new monarch to reaffirm his traditional role, should he so wish to do, and, at the same time, acknowledge the existence of other faiths.

Perhaps I should end this book with the words of the liturgist E.C. Ratcliff in his edition of the 1953 service:

> The tradition of the English Coronation is not rigid and immutable like that of the Byzantine Imperial ceremony; without losing its individuality, it can adapt itself, or its parts, to new conditions with such signal success that we may not inaptly say of it, Plus ça change, plus c'est la même chose. Borrowing from biblical, Frankish, Roman, Byzantine, German and French sources, arranging and re-arranging these diverse elements from period to period, and adding to them from its own native inspiration, it has presented them, and still presents them to us in a remarkable unity, which is distinctively English in aspect. The Coronation Service is a mirror, as no other institution can be, in which our nation has been formed, and in which we ourselves are living to-day. It reflects the persistent English intertwining of sacred and secular, of civil and ecclesiastical. It reflects particularly the historic English conception of the mutual relations of Sovereign, Church and People, and of all three to God, Whose blessing and protection it invokes. In a word, the English Coronation Service symbolises national continuity considered sub specie Christianitatis.[4]

Long may that remain so.

NOTES

CHAPTER ONE

1 *Vita Oswaldi Archiepiscopi Eboracensis*, in *The Historians of the Church of York and its Archbishops*, ed. James Raine (RS, 1879), I, pp. 436–8. For discussions of Edgar's coronation see H. G. Richardson and G. O. Sayles, *The Governance of Mediaeval England from the Conquest to Magna Carta* (Edinburgh: Edinburgh University Press, 1964), Appendix 1; Eric John, *Orbis Britanniae and Other Studies* (Leicester: Leicester University Press, 1966), pp. 276–89; Adrienne Jones, 'The Significance of the Royal Coronation of Edgar in 973', *Journal of Ecclesiastical History*, 33 (1982), pp. 375–90; Chistopher Brooke, *The Saxon and Norman Kings* (London: B. T. Batsford, *London*, 1963), pp. 44–6; Janet L. Nelson, 'Inauguration Rituals', in Janet L. Nelson, *Politics and Ritual in Early Medieval Europe* (London: Hambledon, 1986), pp. 283–307; *Crown Jewels*, I, pp. 72–6.

2 Schramm, *English Coronation*, pp. 179ff. This difference is powerfully demonstrated in Richard A. Jackson, *Vive le Roi! A History of the French Coronation from Charles V to Charles X* (Chapel Hill and London: University of North Carolina Press, 1984), esp. pp. 219–20.

3 E. Fortes, 'Of Installation Ceremonies', *Proceedings of the Royal Anthropological Institute for 1967* (1968), pp. 5–20.

4 See Schramm, *English Coronation*, pp. 115ff.; *Crown Jewels*, pp. 55ff.

5 On chrism and holy oil see L. Duchesne, *Christian Worship: Its Origin and Evolution*, trans. M. L. McClure, 5th edn (London: SPCK, 1919), pp. 331ff.

6 On this see Janet L. Nelson, 'National Synods, Kingship as Office, and Royal Anointing: An Early Medieval Syndrome', in Nelson, *Politics and Ritual*, pp. 239–57; same author's 'Symbolism in Context: Rulers' Inauguration Rituals in Byzantium and the West in the Early Middle Ages,' in *ibid.*, pp. 259–81; Marc Bloch, *The Royal Touch: Sacred Monarchy and Scrofula in France and England*, trans. J. E. Anderson (London: Routledge & Kegan Paul, 1973), pp. 36–41; *Crown Jewels*, I, pp. 7–9.

7 Quoted in Nelson, 'National Synods', *op. cit.*, pp. 239–57.

8 Michael J. Enright, *Iona, Tara and Soissons. The Origin of the Royal Anointing Ritual* (Berlin and New York: Walter de Gruyter, 1985).

9 *Ibid.*, pp. 7–8; also in Legg, *English Coronation Records*, pp. 1–2.

10 Nelson, 'Symbolism in Context', *Crown Jewels*, I, pp. 12ff.

11 Janet L. Nelson, 'The Lord's Anointed and the People's Choice: Carolingian Royal Ritual', in *Rituals of Royalty Power and Ceremonial in Traditional Societies*, ed. David Cannadine and Simon Price (Cambridge: Cambridge University Press, 1987), pp. 137–80; *Crown Jewels*, I, pp. 19–20.

12 F. E. Brightman, 'Byzantine Imperial Coronations', *Journal of Theological Studies*, 2 (1901), pp. 359–92: E. F. Twining, *European Regalia* (London: B. T. Batsford, 1967), pp. 11–17; Averil Cameron, 'The Construction of Court Ritual: The Byzantine Book of Ceremonies', in *Rituals of Royalty*, ed. Cannadine and Price, pp. 106–36; *Crown Jewels*, I, pp. 1–5.

13 William A. Chaney, *The Cult of Kingship in Anglo-Saxon England: The Transition from Paganism to Christianity* (Manchester: Manchester University Press, 1970).

14 Twining, *European Regalia*, pp. 21–2, 32ff., 171–4; *Crown Jewels*, I, pp. 26–8.

15 For the early ordines generally see C. A. Bouman, *Sacring and Crowning: The Development of the Latin Ritual for the Anointing of Kings and the Coronation of the Emperor before the Eleventh Century*, Bijdragen van het Instituut voor Middeleeuwse Geschiedenis der Rijks-Universiteit te Utrecht (Groningen, Djakarta: J. B. Wolters 1957). For England the two founding studies are Percy Ernst Schramm 'Ordines-Studien III: Die Krönung in England', *Archiv für Urkundenforschung*, 15 (1938), pp. 305–88, and *English Coronation*. See also P. L. Ward, 'The Coronation

Ceremony in Medieval England', *Speculum*, 14 (1939), pp. 160–8.

16 For texts of the First Recension: Legg, *English Coronation Records*, pp. 3–13; *The Leofric Missal*, ed. F. E. Warren (Oxford: Clarendon Press, 1883), pp. 230–32; *Two Anglo-Saxon Pontificals (the Egbert and Sidney Sussex Pontificals)*, ed. H. M. J. Banting (HBS, 1989 (for 1985–6)), pp. xxff.; *The Pontifical of Egbert, Archbishop of York, A.D. 732–766*, ed. W. Greenwell (Surtees Society, XXVII, 1853), pp. 100–5. *Pontificale Lanaletense*, ed. G. H. Doble (HBS, LXXIV, 1937), pp. 41–65. For further commentary and discussion: Schramm, *English Coronation*, pp. 18–23; Bouman, *Sacring and Crowning*, pp. 9–15; Janet L. Nelson, 'The Earliest Surviving Royal *Ordo*: Some Liturgical and Historical Aspects', in *Authority and Power, Studies in Medieval Law and Government Presented to Walter Ullmann on his Seventieth Birthday*, ed. Brian Tierney and Peter Linehan (Cambridge: Cambridge University Press, 1980), pp. 29–48; also in Nelson, *Politics and Ritual*, pp. 341–60; *Crown Jewels*, I, pp. 57–64; O'Meara, *Monarchy and Consent*, pp. 67–9.

17 *The Anglo-Saxon Chronicle*, trans. and ed. Dorothy Whitelock (London: Eyre and Spottiswoode, 1965), p. 35. The anointing of the young King Alfred by Pope Leo IV in Rome in 855 is recognised now to be a later insertion, *ibid.*, p. 43. See Janet L. Nelson, 'The Problem of King Alfred's Royal Anointing', in Nelson, *Politics and Ritual*, pp. 309–27.

18 *William of Malmesbury's Chronicle of the Kings of England*, trans. J. A. Giles (London: Henry G. Bohn, 1847), pp. 131–2.

19 *VCH., Surrey*, ed. H. E. Malden, III (1911), p. 487.

20 *Memorials of St Dunstan, Archbishop of Canterbury*, ed. W. Stubbs (RS, 1874), pp. 32–3.

21 For the texts of the Second Recension see: Legg, *English Coronation Records*, pp. 14–29; *The Claudius Pontifical*, ed. D. H. Turner (HBS, XCVII, 1971 (for 1964)), pp. xxix–xxxiii, xxxviii–xlvii; A. Taylor, *The Glory of Regality* (London; Payne and Fosse, 1820), pp. 395–405; *The Benedictional of Archbishop Robert*, ed. H. A. Wilson (HBS, XXIV, 1903), pp. 140–8. For discussions see: J. Armitage Robinson, 'The Coronation Order in the Tenth Century', *Journal of Theological Studies*, 19 (1918), pp. 56–72; Schramm, *English Coronation*, pp. 28–30; Paul L. Ward, 'An Early Version of the Anglo-Saxon Coronation Ceremony', *English Historical Review*, 17 (1942), pp. 345–61; Jones, 'The Significance of the Royal

Consecration of Edgar in 973', Janet L. Nelson, 'Ritual and Reality in the Early Medieval *Ordines*', in Nelson, *Politics and Ritual*, pp. 329–39; same author's 'The Second English *Ordo*', in *ibid.*, pp. 361–74; *Crown Jewels*, I, pp. 64–9; O'Meara, *Monarchy and Consent*, pp. 75–9.

22 Nelson, 'Ritual and Reality', p. 337.

23 Janet L. Nelson, 'Early Medieval Rites of Queen-making and the Shaping of Medieval Queenship', in Janet L. Nelson, *Rulers and Ruling Families in Early Medieval Europe* (Aldershot: Ashgate, *c*.1999). pp. 301–15.

24 *Crown Jewels*, I, pp. 28–33.

25 *Anglo-Saxon Chronicle*, p. 107. The story that Archbishop Æthelnoth refused to consecrate Canute's illegitimate son Harold 'Harefoot' in 1035 is apocryphal: see *Encomium Emmae Reginae*, ed. Alistair Campbell (CS, 3rd series, LXXII, 1949), pp. lxiii–lxiv, 39.

26 For Harold's coronation see *Crown Jewels*, I, pp. 79–81; for the orb, *ibid.*, pp. 322–24; *English Romanesque Art 1066–1200*, Arts Council Exhibition, Hayward Gallery, 1984 (London: Arts Council in association with Weidenfeld & Nicolson, *c*.1984), p. 301 (no. 328).

CHAPTER TWO

1 For the coronation of William I see David C. Douglas, *William the Conqueror* (London: Eyre & Spottiswoode, 1964), pp. 247ff.; Janet L. Nelson, 'The Rites of the Conqueror', in Janet L. Nelson, *Politics and Ritual in Early Medieval Europe* (London: Hambledon Press, 1986), pp. 375–401; *Crown Jewels*, I, pp. 81–5, 92–5; *The Carmen de Hastingae Proelio of Guy of Amiens*, ed. C. Morton and Hope Muntz (Oxford: Clarendon, 1972), pp. liv–lix, 51–3; Elisabeth M. C. van Houts, 'Latin Poetry and the Anglo-Norman Court 1066–1135: The *Carmen de Hastingae*', *Journal of Medieval History*, 15(1) (1989), pp. 39–57.

2 Krijnie Ciggaar, 'Byzantine Marginalia to the Norman Conquest', *Anglo-Norman Studies*, 9 (1986), pp. 57–9.

3 On the Romanesque Abbey see J. T. Micklethwaite, 'Further Notes on the Abbey Buildings at Westminster', *Archaeological Journal*, 2nd series 51(1) (1894), pp. 1–27; J. Armitage Robinson, 'The Church of Edward the Confessor at Westminster', *Archaeologia*, 80(1) (1910), pp. 81–100; H. F. Westlake, *Westminster Abbey* (London: Philip Allan & Co., 1923), pp. 1–25; R. Allen Brown H. M. Colvin and A. J.

Taylor, *The History of the King's Works: The Middle Ages* (London: HMSO, 1963), I, pp. 14–17; R. D. H. Gem, 'The Romanesque Rebuilding of Westminster Abbey', *Anglo-Norman Studies*, 3 (1980–1), pp. 33–60.

4 See Ernst Kantorowicz, *Laudes Regiae* (Berkeley: University of California Press, 1958), pp. 13ff., 53ff.; Nelson, 'Rites of the Conqueror', pp. 399–401; H. E. J. Cowdrey, 'The Anglo-Norman Laudes Regiae', *Viator*, 12 (1981), pp. 37–78.

5 Quoted in Nelson, 'Rites of the Conqueror', p. 385.

6 *The Anglo-Saxon Chronicle*, ed. Dorothy Whitelock (London: Eyre & Spottiswoode, 1965), p. 145.

7 For these various coronations see *Chronicles of the Reigns of Stephen, Henry II and Richard I*, ed. R. Howlett (RS 1889), IV, pp. 46, 81; Frank Barlow, *William Rufus* (London: Methuen 1983), pp. 53, 57–8; W. L. Warren, *Henry II* (London: Eyre Methuen, 1973), p. 14; C. Warren Hollister, *Henry I*, Yale U. P., 2001), pp. 102–14. The most important overall study is by Raymonde Forville, 'Le sacre des rois anglo-normands et le serment du sacre (XIe–XIIe siècle)', in *Proceedings of the First Battle Conference on Anglo-Norman Studies* (Woodbridge: Boydell Press, 1978), I, pp. 49–62.

8 On the Third Recension see Wickham Legg, *English Coronation Records*, pp. 30–42; *The Pontifical of Magdalen College*, ed. H. A. Wilson (HBS, XXXIX, 1910), pp. 89–97; Paul L. Ward, 'The Coronation Ceremony in Medieval England', *Speculum*, 14 (1959), pp. 160–8; *The Claudius Pontifical*, ed. D. H. Turner (HBS, XCIII, 1971 (for 1964)), pp. xxxviii–xliii, 115–22; *Crown Jewels*, I, pp. 88–92.

9 For what follows see Fritz Kern, *Kingship and Law in the Middle Ages* (Oxford: Basil Blackwell, 1939), pp. 27–61; Norman F. Cantor, *Church, Kingship, and Lay Investiture in England 1089–1135* (Princeton: Princeton University Press, 1958), pp. 131 ff., 174 ff.; *Crown Jewels*, I, pp. 85–88.

10 Quoted in Cantor, *Church, Kingship and Lay Investiture*, p. 191.

11 On which see Janet L. Nelson, 'Early Medieval Rites of Queen-making and the Shaping of Medieval Queenship', in Janet Nelson, *Rulers and Ruling Families in Early Medieval Europe* (Aldershot: Ashgate (c.1999), pp. 301–15.

12 E. W. Brayley and J. Britton, *The History of the Ancient Palace of Westminster* (London, 1836), pp. 7–22; W. R. Lethaby, 'The Palace of Westminster in the Eleventh and Twelfth Centuries', *Archaeologia*, 60/1 (1906), pp. 131–48; Brown, Colvin and Taylor, *King's Works:*

The Middle Ages, I, pp. 45–7, 491–3; Christopher Wilson, 'Rulers, Artificers and Shoppers: Richard II's Remodelling of Westminster Hall, 1393–99', in *The Regal Image of Richard II in the Wilton Diptych*, ed. Dillian Gordon, Lisa Monnas and Caroline Elam (London: Harvey Miller, 1997), pp. 33–4.

13 On the Abbey during this period see Edward Carpenter, ed., *A House of Kings* (London: Westminster Abbey Bookshop, 1966), pp. 1–24; *The Life of King Edward who Rests at Westminster Attributed to a Monk of Sainty-Bertin*, ed. and trans. Frank Barlow (Oxford: Clarendon Press, 1992), pp. 155–63; Emma Mason, *Westminster Abbey and its People 1050–c.1215* (Woodbridge: Boydell Press, 1996), pp. 269–305.

14 I have synthesised here the conclusions of the most complete study of the complex evidence by Ronald Lightbown in *Crown Jewels*, I, pp. 257–343.

15 On royal robes see Michael Moore, 'The King's New Clothes: Royal and Episcopal Regalia in the Frankish Empire', in *Robes and Honor: The Medieval World of Investiture*, ed. Stewart Gordon (London: Palgrave, 2001), pp. 95 ff.

16 W. H. St John Hope, 'On the Funeral Effigies of the Kings and Queens of England . . .', *Archaeologia*, 60(2) (1907), pp. 523, 524, 525, 529, 530–1, 536.

17 On swords and spurs see Edith M. R. Ditmas, 'The Curtana or Sword of Mercy', *Journal of the British Archaeological Association*, 3rd series, 29 (1966), pp. 122–33; *Crown Jewels*, I, pp. 28–31, 315–17.

18 On the role of the Archbishop of Canterbury see Wickham Legg, *Coronation Records*, pp. 43–5; Warren, *Henry II*, pp. 500–5.

19 Quoted *Roger of Wendover's Flowers of History*, trans. J. A. Giles (London: Bohn, 1849), II, p. 181.

20 On the oath in this period see Forville, 'Le sacre des rois anglo-normands . . .'; H. G. Richardson and G. O. Sayles, *The Governance of Medieval England from the Conquest to Magna Carta* (Edinburgh: Edinburgh University Press, 1964), pp. 136–5.

21 Hollister, *Henry I*, pp. 109–12.

22 *Roger of Wendover*, II, p. 182 and note 24 for Richard I.

23 *Crown Jewels*, I, pp. 95–9.

24 Quoted from the translation in Wickham Legg, *English Coronation Records*, pp. 50–3.

25 For the coronation of Richard I see *Chronicles and Memorials of the Reign of Richard I*, ed. W. Stubbs (RS XXVI, 1864), I, pp. 142–3; *Chronicles of the Reigns of Stephen, Henry II and Richard I*, pp. 294–7; J. H.

Round, 'The Coronation of Richard I', in his *The Commune of London and Other Studies* (London: Constable & Co., 1899), pp. 201–6; Wickham Legg, *English Coronation Records*, pp. 46–53; *Crown Jewels*, I, pp. 99–102.

26 John Gillingham, *Richard I* (New Haven and London: Yale University Press, 1999), pp. 107–8.

27 *Ibid.*, p. 141.

28 *Six Old English Chronicles*, ed. J. A. Giles (London, 1872), pp. 243–5.

29 Richard Barber, *The Knight and Chivalry*, revised edn (Woodbridge: Boydell Press, 1995), p. 277.

CHAPTER THREE

1 There is a huge literature on the building and architecture of Westminster Abbey. From the viewpoint of this chapter by far the most important book is Paul Binski's *Westminster Abbey and the Plantagenets: Kingship and the Representation of Power 1200–1400* (New Haven and London: Yale University Press for Paul Mellon Centre for Studies in British Art, 1995) I have also used R. Allen Brown H. M. Colvin and A. J. Taylor, *The History of the King's Works, I, The Middle Ages* (London: HMSO, 1963), pp. 130–57; *Crown Jewels*, I, pp. 111–15.

2 Binski, *Westminster Abbey*, pp. 52–89.

3 *Crown Jewels*, I, pp. 114–15.

4 Richard Foster, *Patterns of Thought. The Hidden Meaning of the Great Pavement of Westminster Abbey* (London: Jonathan Cape, 1991), pp. 8–27.

5 This is based on the latest account of the chair, Paul Binski, 'A "Sign of Victory": The Coronation Chair, its Manufacture, Setting and Symbolism', in *The Stone of Destiny: Artefact and Icon*, ed. Richard Welander, David J. Breeze and Thomas Owen Clancy, Society of Antiquaries of Scotland, Monograph Series, XXII, pp. 207–22. There is an extensive literature on the Stone, tangential to the history of the English coronation, but relevant to its status before its appropriation by Edward I. See also J. Hunter, 'King Edward's Spoliations in Scotland in AD 1296 – The Coronation Stone – Original and Unpublished Evidence', *Archaeological Journal*, 13 (1856), pp. 245–55; William F. Skene, *The Coronation Stone* (Edinburgh: Edmonston & Douglas, 1869); James Hilton, 'The Coronation Stone at Westminster Abbey', *Archaeological Journal*, 2nd series, 54(4) (1897), pp. 201–24; Legg, *English Coronation Records*, pp. 77–8; R. W. Symonds, 'New Light on the Coronation Chair',

Connoisseur, 133 (1954), pp. 80–1; S. Rees Jones, 'The Coronation Chair', *Studies in Conservation*, 1 (1952–4), pp. 103–13; Binski, *Westminster Abbey*, pp. 135 ff.; *Crown Jewels*, I, pp. 144–7.

6 Quoted in Binski, *Westminster Abbey*, p. 138. For the argument for its use prior to 1399 see G. W. S. Barrow, 'Observations on the Coronation Stone of Scotland', *Scottish Historical Review*, 76(1) (1997), pp. 115–21.

7 On which see E. W. Brayley and J. Britton, *The History of the Ancient Palace . . . at Westminster* (London, 1836), pp. 45 ff.; Brown, Colvin and Taylor, *The History of the King's Works*, I, pp. 491–3.

8 Paul Binski, *The Painted Chamber at Westminster* (Society of Antiquaries, Occasional Papers (New Series), IX, 1986).

9 The best discussion of this tangled and opaque subject is in *Crown Jewels*, I, pp. 107–11, 115–19 and chapter 3. See also M. R. Holmes, 'The Crowns of England', *Archaeologia*, 86 (1937), pp. 73–90; same author's 'New Light on St. Edward's Crown', *Archaeologia*, 97 (1959), pp. 213–23.

10 Quoted in Binski, *Westminster Abbey*, p. 50.

11 For the spoon see C. J. Jackson, 'The Spoon and its History, its Form, Material and Development, more particularly in England', *Archaeologia*, 53(1) (1892), pp. 118–19; the definitive account is in *Crown Jewels*, II, pp. 295–303.

12 Quoted in Holmes, 'The Crowns of England', p. 77.

13 The major study of the Fourth Recension complete with edited texts remains unpublished: John Bruckmann, 'English Coronations 1216–1308: The Edition of the Coronation Ordines', PhD Thesis, University of Toronto, 1964. For published texts of the Fourth Recension see Legg, *English Coronation Records*, pp. 81–130 (the *Liber Regalis*); also *Liber Regalis* (Roxburghe Club, 1870); W. Maskell, *Monumenta Ritualia Ecclesiae Anglicanae* (London: William Pickering, 1847), III, pp. 1–81; *Missale ad usum Ecclesiae Westmonasteriensis*, ed. J. Wickham Legg (HBS, XII, 1896–7), ii. For commentary and studies see Schramm, *English Coronation*, pp. 74–9; H. G. Richardson and G. O. Sayles, 'Early Coronation Records', *BIHR*, 13 (1935–6), pp. 129–45; John Bruckmann, 'English Coronations 1216–1308', MA Dissertation, University of Toronto, 1958, pp. 129–34; H. G. Richardson, 'The Coronation in Medieval England: The Evolution of the Office and the Oath', *Traditio*, 16 (1960), pp. 136–50; Andrew Hughes, 'The Origin and Descent of the Fourth Recension of

the English Coronation', in *Coronations*, ed. Bak, pp. 197–216; O'Meara, *Monarchy and Consent*, pp. 102–5.

14 Hope Emily Allen, 'A Thirteenth-Century Coronation Rubric', *Church Quarterly Review*, 95 (1923), pp. 335–41; see Bruckmann, 'English Coronations', PhD, pp. 394ff.

15 Jacques Le Goff, 'A Coronation Program for the Age of Saint Louis: The Ordo of 1250', in *Coronations*, ed. Bak, pp. 46–57.

16 Marc Bloch, *The Royal Touch: Sacred Monarchy and Scrofula in England and France* (London: Routledge & Kegan Paul, 1973).

17 Quoted in *ibid.*, p. 57.

18 Printed in *Three Coronation Orders*, ed. J. Wickham Legg (HBS, XIX, 1900, pp. 121–4).

19 The text for *Liber Regalis* is printed in Legg, *English Coronation Records*, pp. 81–130 with a useful English translation. See also F. Idoate, 'Un ceremonial de coronacion de los reyes de Inglaterra', *Hispania Sacra*, 6 (1953), pp. 151–80. For the dating of the *Liber Regalis* see Paul Binski, 'The Liber Regalis: Its Date and European Context', in *The Regal Image of Richard II and the Wilton Diptych*, ed. Dillian Gordon, Lisa Monnas and Caroline Elam (London: Harvey Miller, 1997), pp. 232–3.

20 *Crown Jewels*, I, pp. 148–51.

21 Generally see Bertie Wilkinson, *Constitutional History of Medieval England 1216–1399*, III, *The Development of the Constitution 1216–1399* (London: Longmans, Green & Co., 1958), pp. 72–84.

22 For what follows on the coronation oath see Bertie Wilkinson, 'The Coronation Oath of Edward II', in *Historical Essays in Honour of James Tait*, ed. J. G. Edwards, V. H. Galbraith and E. F. Jacob (privately printed: Manchester, 1933), pp. 405–16; Schramm, *English Coronation*, pp. 179–211; H. G. Richardson, 'The English Coronation Oath', *TRHS*, 4th series, 23 (1941), pp. 129–58; Bertie Wilkinson, 'The Coronation of Oath of Edward II and the Statute of York', *Speculum*, 19 (1944), pp. 445–69; Ernst Kantorowicz, 'Inalienability: A Note on the Canonical Practice and the English Coronation Oath in the Thirteenth Century', *Speculum*, 29 (1954), pp. 488–502; Bertie Wilkinson, 'Notes on the Coronation Records of the Fourteenth Century', *EHR*, 70 (1955), pp. 581–600; Robert S. Hoyt, 'The Coronation Oath of 1308', *EHR*, 70 (1955), pp. 581–600; Robert S. Hoyt, 'The Coronation Oath of 1308', *EHR*, 81 (1956), pp. 353–83; Richardson, 'The Coronation in Medieval England',

pp. 161–74; Bruckmann, '*English Coronation*', MA Dissertation 135 ff.; Bruckmann, 'English Coronations', Ph.D Thesis, pp. 93–131.

23 Wilkinson, 'Notes on the Coronation Records of the Fourteenth Century', pp. 591–8; same author's *Constitutional History*, III, pp. 96–8.

24 The text of the letter is in Legg, *English Coronation Records*, pp. 66–8.

25 See Bloch, *The Royal Touch*, pp. 113–14; Bruckmann, 'English Coronations', Ph.D Thesis, pp. 59–72.

26 For this see D. A. Carpenter, 'The Burial of King Henry III, the Regalia and Royal Ideology', in D. A. Carpenter, *The Reign of Henry III* (London: Hambledon Press, 1996), pp. 427–36.

27 Brown, Colvin and Taylor, *The History of the King's Works*, II, p. 1044 no. 40.

28 Binski, *Westminster Abbey*, p. 132.

29 *Crown Jewels*, I, p. 119.

30 *Ibid.*, I, p. 142.

31 For the pavement see Foster, *Patterns of Thought*.

32 Andrew Hughes, 'Antiphons and Acclamations: The Politics of Music in the Coronation Service of Edward II, 1308', *Journal of Musicology*, 6 (1988), pp. 150–68.

33 Brown, Colvin and Taylor, *The History of the King's Works*, I, pp. 504–7; Crown *Jewels*, I, pp. 128–9, 134.

34 *Crown Jewels*, I, pp. 141–2.

35 Brown, Colvin and Taylor, *The History of the King's Works*, I, pp. 504–7.

36 Michael Prestwich, *Edward I* (London: Methuen, 1988), pp. 88–91.

37 For the text and translation see Legg, *English Coronation Records*, pp. 57–65.

38 For rights and services see Arthur Taylor, *The Glory of Regality* (London, 1820), Book III; J. H. Round, *The King's Sergeants and Officers of State with their Coronation Services* (London, 1911); Richardson, 'The Coronation in Medieval England', pp. 131–6; *Crown Jewels*, I, pp. 120–8. For services in 1308 see Thomas Rymer, *Foedera* (The Hague, 1745), I, ii, p. 112; for 1327 see Richardson and Sayles, 'Early Coronation Records', pp. 1–9.

39 Thomas Ross, 'Coronation Services of the Barons of the Cinque Ports', *Sussex Archaeological Collections*, 15 (1863), pp. 118–210; K. M. E. Murray, *The Constitutional History of the Cinque Ports* (Manchester: Manchester University Press 1935), pp 19–21; *A Calendar of the White and Black Books of the Cinque Ports 1432–1955*, ed. Felix Hull (London: HMSO, 1966), pp. xxxiii–xxxv.

40 H. G. Richardson and G. O. Sayles, 'Early Coronation Records', *BIHR*, 16 (1938–9), 39, p. 45.

41 Taylor, *Glory of Regality*, pp. 135–8; *Crown Jewels*, I, pp. 126–8.

42 *Annales Paulini in Chronicles of the Reigns of Edward I and Edward II*, ed. W. Stubbs (RS, XXVI, 1882), I, pp. 259–62.

43 *Ibid.*.

44 All of these are reproduced and discussed in O'Meara, *Monarchy and Consent*.

45 For a discussion of these see Binski, *Westminster Abbey*, pp. 126–30.

46 *Age of Chivalry: Art in Plantagenet England 1200–1400*, ed. Jonathan Alexander and Paul Binski, Royal Academy Exhibition Catalogue, 1987, p. 201 (no. 11); O'Meara, *Monarchy and Consent*, pp. 104–5.

47 O'Meara, *Monarchy and Consent*, pp. 39–44.

48 See p. 106.

CHAPTER FOUR

1 *Political Works of James I*, ed. C. H. McIlwain (Cambridge, Mass.: Harvard University Press, 1918), p. 12.

2 David Starkey, 'Representation through Intimacy: A Study of the Symbolism of monarchy and Court office in Early Modern England', in *The Tudor Monarchy*, ed. John Guy (London: Arnold, 1997).

3 Quoted in Marc Bloch, *The Royal Touch: Sacred Monarchy and Scrofula in England and* France (London: Routledge & Kegan Paul, 1973), p. 65.

4 *Ibid.*, pp. 64–7.

5 Raymond Craufurd, 'The Blessing of Cramp-rings. A Chapter in the History of the Treatment of Epilepsy', in *Studies in the History and Method of Science*, ed. Charles Singer (Oxford, Clarendon: 1917), pp. 165–87; Bloch, *The Royal Touch*, chap. 2.

6 Quoted in Bloch, *The Royal Touch*, p. 106.

7 On the Holy Oil of St Thomas see Wickham Legg, *English Coronation Records*, pp. 169–76; Walter Ullmann, 'Thomas Becket's Miraculous Oil', *Journal of Theological Studies*, new series, 8(1) (1957), pp. 129–33; J. W. McKenna, 'The Coronation Oil of the Yorkist Kings', *EHR*, 82 (1967), pp. 102–4; T. A. Sandquist, 'The Holy Oil of St. Thomas of Canterbury, in *Essays in Medieval History Presented to Bertie Wilkinson*, ed. T. A. Sandquist and M. R. Powicke (Toronto: University of Toronto Press, 1969), pp. 330–44; *The Coronation of Richard III: The Extant Documents*, ed. Anne F. Sutton and P. W. Hammond (Gloucester; Alan Sutton, and New York, St. Martin's Press, 1983), pp. 240–1; *Crown Jewels*, I, pp. 171–5.

8 For the cult of 'St' Henry VI see Sydney Anglo, *Spectacle, Pageantry and Early Tudor Policy* (Oxford: Clarendon Press, 1969), pp. 37–43; same author's *Images of Tudor Kingship* (London: Seaby, 1992), pp.61–73.

9 *Liber Regie Capelle*, ed. Walter Ullmann (HBS, XCII, 1961 for 1959), p. 18.

10 Legg, *English Coronation Records*, pp. 191–2. See also *Crown Jewels*, I, p. 269 and also for a second list *c*.1443 by the monk John Flete.

11 Printed in Ricardi de Cirencestria, *Speculum Historiale de Gestis Regum Angliae*, ed. J. E. B. Mayor (XXX, ii, 1969), pp. 26–39; see Patricia J. Eberle, 'Richard II and the Literary Arts', in *Richard II. The Art of Kingship*, ed. Anthony Goodman and James Gillespie (Oxford: Clarendon Press, 1999), pp. 239–40.

12 Michael J. Bennett, 'Richard II and the Wider Realm', in *Richard II*, ed. Goodman and Gillespie, pp. 187–204; Nigel E. Saul, 'Richard II's Ideas of Kingship', in *The Regal Image of Richard II in the Wilton Diptych*, ed. Dillian Gordon, Lisa Monnas and Caroline Elam (London: Harvey Miller, 1997), pp. 27–32.

13 Paul Binski, *Westminster Abbey and the Plantagenets* (New Haven, London: Yale University Press, 1995), p. 199.

14 *The Westminster Chronicle 1381–1394*, ed. L. C. Hector and Barbara F. Harvey (Oxford: Clarendon Press, 1982), pp. 415–17.

15 *Ibid.*

16 The best discussion of this is Dale E. Hoak, 'The Iconography of the Crown Imperial', in *Tudor Political Culture*, Dale E. Hoak (Cambridge: Cambridge University Press, 1995), pp. 54–103; see also Philip Grierson, 'The Origins of the English Sovereign and the Symbolism of the Crown', *British Numismatic Journal*, 33 (1964), pp. 118–34; see also Lord Twining, *European Regalia* (London: B. T. Batsford, 1967), pp. 46–7; *Crown Jewels*, I, p. 177.

17 Twining, *European Regalia*, pp. 208–10; *Crown Jewels*, I, pp. 322–8; *Coronation of Richard III*, p. 235.

18 *Crown Jewels*, II, pp. 317–23.

19 On swords see *Coronation of Richard III*, pp. 236–8, 243–4; *Crown Jewels*, I, pp. 179–82.

20 *Chronicon Adae de Usk, A.D. 1377–1421*, ed. and trans. E. M. Thompson (London: Henry Frowde, 1904), p. 187.

21 *Political Poems and Songs Relating to English History . . .*, ed. Thomas Wright (London, 1851), p. 146.

22 Legg, *English Coronation Records*, p. 195.

23 For all of these see *Crown Jewels*, I, pp. 318–22.

24 I list here the material on the coronations used throughout this chapter:

RICHARD II

SOURCES: *Munimenta Gildhalae Londoniensis*, ed. H. T. Riley, II, Part II, *Liber Custumarum*, pp. 456–87; T. Walsingham, *Historia Anglica*, ed. H. T. Riley (RS, 1863), I, pp. 331–8; *The Anonimalle Chronicle 1333 to 1381*, ed. V. H. Galbraith (Manchester University Press, 1927), pp. 107–15; Thomas Rymer, *Foedera* (The Hague, 1740–5), III, ii, pp. 62–3; Legg, *English Coronation Records*, pp. 131–68.

STUDIES: Sandquist, 'English Coronations', chapter 2; *Crown Jewels*, I, pp. 161–7; Nigel E. Saul, *Richard II* (New Haven, London: Yale University Press, 1997), pp. 24; Joel Francis Burden, 'Rituals of Royalty: Prescription, Politics and Practice in English Coronation and Royal Funeral Rituals *c.*1327–*c.*1485', unpublished Ph. D. Thesis, University of York, Centre for Medieval Studies, 1999, pp. 164–94.

HENRY IV

SOURCES: *Chronica Monasterii S. Albani*, ed. H. T. Riley (London: RS, 1866), pp. 291–7; *The Chronicle of Froissart*, trans Lord Berners (London, 1903), VI, pp. 379–83; *Chronicon Adae de Usk*, pp. 184–91; Robert Fabyan, *The New Chronicles of England and France*, ed. Henry Ellis (London, 1811), pp. 564–5.

STUDIES: Sandquist, 'English Coronations', chap. 3; *The Coronation of Richard III*, pp. 92–9; *Crown Jewels*, I, pp. 168–71.

HENRY V

STUDIES: Sandquist, 'English Coronations', chap. 4; Christopher Allmand, *Henry V* (London: Methuen, 1992), pp. 63–5.

CATHERINE OF VALOIS

SOURCES: *William Gregory's Chronicle of London* in *The Historical Collections of a London Citizen*, ed. James Gairdner (CS, 1876), pp. 138–40.

STUDIES: Burden, 'Rituals of Royalty', pp. 195–220.

HENRY VI

SOURCES: *William Gregory's Chronicle of London*, pp. 164–70; Fabyan, *New Chronicles*, pp. 599–601; C. Marson, 'The Ritual in November 1429, when the Boy-King Henry VI was Crowned', *The Antiquary*, 48 (1912), pp. 220–3.

STUDIES: Sandquist, 'English Coronations', chap. 5; Bertram Wolfe, *Henry VI*, (London: Eyre Methuen, 1981), pp. 48–64. *The Coronation of Richard III*, pp. 91–2. Crown *Jewels*, I, pp. 191–2.

EDWARD IV

SOURCES: Fabyan, *New Chronicles*, p. 640.

STUDIES: Sandquist, 'English Coronations', chap. 6; *The Coronation of Richard III*, pp. 91–2; *Crown Jewels*, I, pp. 91–2.

RICHARD III

SOURCES: The Little Device was prepared for this coronation, but went on to be the basis of that of Henry VII and of Henry VIII. The text is printed in William Jerdan, *Rutland Papers* (CS, XXI, 1842), pp. 1–24; Legg, *English Coronation Records*, pp. 219–39; *The Coronation of Richard III*, pp. 213–27. Otherwise see *Hall's Chronicle*, . . . (London, 1809), pp. 375–7; *Grafton's Chronicle* . . . (London, 1809), pp. 113–15; Legg, *English Coronation Records*, pp. 193–7.

STUDIES: Sandquist, 'English Coronations', chap. 7; *The Coronation of Richard III*; *Crown Jewels*, I, pp. 195–8.

ELIZABETH WOODVILLE

SOURCES: George Smith, *The Coronation of Elizabeth Wydeville* (London: Ellis, 1935).

STUDIES: *Crown Jewels*, I, pp. 192–4.

HENRY VII

SOURCES: Legg, *English Coronation Records*, pp. 198–218; *Materials for a History of the Reign of Henry VII*, ed. W. Campbell (London: RS. 60, 1873–7), I, p. 97.

STUDIES: Sydney Anglo, 'The Foundation of the Tudor Dynasty: The Coronation and Marriage of Henry VII', *Guildhall Miscellany*, 2 (1960), pp. 3–11; same author's *Spectacle*, pp. 10–16.

ELIZABETH OF YORK

SOURCES: John Leland, *Collectanea* (London, 1774), IV, pp. 216–33; *Materials for a History*, I, pp. 253–4.

STUDIES: Anglo, *Spectacle*, pp. 49–51; *Crown Jewels*, I, pp. 198–201.

HENRY VIII

SOURCES: CA MS I 7, fols. 21–8; J. S. Brewer, *Letters and Papers, Foreign and Domestic of the Reign of Henry VIII* (London: HMSO, 1920), I, pp. 37–43; *Hall's Chronicle*, pp. 507–9; see also Stephen Hawes, 'A Ioyfull medytacyon to all Englonde of the coronacyon of our moust naturall souerayne lord kinge Henry the eyght' in *The Minor Poems*, ed.

Florence W. Gluck and Alice B. Morgan (Early
English Text Society, 1974), pp. 85–91.

STUDIES: *Crown Jewels*, I, pp. 201–02; S. J. Loach, 'The
Function of Ceremonial in the Reign of Henry VIII',
Past and Present, no. 142 (1994), pp. 45–55.

ANNE BOLEYN

SOURCES: Brewer, *Letters and Papers of Henry VIII*,
1533, nos. 561–5, 583, 601; *The Noble and Triumphant
Coronation of Queen Anne . . .*, in E. Arber, *An
English Garner* (London: Constable & Co., 1845), II,
pp. 41–60; *Hall's Chronicle*, pp. 798–805; Charles
Wriothesley, *A Chronicle of England*, ed. W. D.
Hamilton (CS, 1875), I, pp. 17–22; Henry Ellis, 'Copy
of a Letter from Archbishop Cranmer . . .',
Archaeologia, 18 (1817), pp. 77–82; Anglo, *Spectacle*,
p. 249 note 1 for a list of manuscript accounts.

STUDIES: Anglo, *Spectacle*, pp. 247–61; *Crown Jewels*, I,
pp. 202–6. See also H. M. Colvin, John Summerson,
Martin Biddle, J. R. Hale and Marcus Merriman, *The
History of the King's Works*, IV, *1485–1660*, Part II
ed. H. M. Colvin (London: HMSO, 1982), pp. 290–91;
E. W. Ives, *Anne Boleyn* (Oxford: Basil Blackwell,
1986), pp. 214–28.

25 *The Chronicle of Froissart*, VI, pp. 378–80.
26 See Sandquist, 'English Coronations', chap. 3.
27 *Chronicon Adae de Usk*, pp. 184–6.
28 See above chapter 3.
29 C. A. J. Armstrong, 'The Inauguration Ceremonies
of the Yorkist Kings and their Title to the Throne',
TRHS, 4th series, 30 (1948), pp. 51–73; see also May
McKisack, 'London and the Succession to the Crown
during the Middle Ages', in *Studies in Medieval
History Presented to Frederick Maurice Powicke*,
ed. R. W. Hunt, W. A. Pantin and R. W. Southern
(Oxford: Clarendon Press, 1948), pp. 76–89.
30 See *The Coronation of Richard III*, pp. 13 ff.
31 *Three Books of Polydore Vergil's English History*,
ed. Henry Ellis (CS, 1844), p. 266.
32 Francis Sheppard, *London: A History* (Oxford: Oxford
University Press, 1998), pp. 98–100.
33 See texts cited in note 24. See also Caroline M.
Barron, 'Richard II and London', in *Richard II*, ed.
Goodman and Gillespie, p. 150.
34 For this and much of what follows see Gordon
Kipling, *Enter the King: Theatre, Liturgy, and Ritual in
the Medieval Civic Triumph* (Oxford: Clarendon
Press, 1998).
35 Ralph Giesey, 'Inaugural Aspects of French Royal
Ceremonial', in *Coronations*, ed. Bak, pp. 35–45.
36 Ernst Kantorowicz, 'The "King's Advent" and the

Enigmatic Panels in the Doors of Santa Sabina', *Art
Bulletin*, 26 (1944), pp. 20–31.

37 *Matthew Paris's English History*, trans. J. A. Giles
(London: Bohn, 1852), pp. 8–9.
38 *Chronicles of Edward I and Edward II*, ed. W. Stubbs
(London: RS 76, 1882), p. 152.
39 Gordon Kipling, 'Richard II's "Sumptuous Pageants"
and the Idea of the Civic Triumph', in *Pageantry and
the Shakespearean Theater*, ed. David M. Bergeron
(Athens: University of Georgia Press, 1985),
pp. 83–103.
40 For Margaret of Anjou's entry see Fabyan, *New
Chronicles*, pp. 617–18; *William Gregory's Chronicle
of London*, p. 186; Carleton Brown, 'Lydgate's Verses
on Queen Margaret's Entry into London', *Modern
Language Review*, 7 (1912), pp. 225–34; Brian Crow,
'Lydgate's 1445 Pageant for Margaret of Anjou',
English Language Notes, 19 (1981), pp. 120–4.
41 See below.
42 For Henry VI's entry see Fabyan, *New Chronicles*,
pp. 603–6; Richard H. Osberg, 'The Lambeth
Palace Library Manuscript Account of Henry VI's
1432 London Entry', *Medieval Studies*, 52 (1990),
pp. 255–67; Laurence M. Bryant, 'Configurations of
the Community in Late Medieval Spectacles: Paris
and London During the Dual Monarchy', in *City
and Spectacle in Medieval Europe*, ed. Barbara A.
Hananwalt and Kathryn L. Reyerson, Medieval
Studies at Minnesota, VI (Minneapolis: University
of Minnesota, 1994), pp. 3–33. See also Anglo,
Spectacle, p. 284 for a detailed list of sources.
43 *York Civic Records*, ed. Angelo Raine (printed for the
Yorkshire Archaeological Society, 1939), I, pp. 1505–9.
See also Anglo, *Spectacle*, pp. 22–8.
44 F. Grose and T. Astle, *The Antiquarian Repertory*
(London, 1804–9), I, p. 296.
45 For Elizabeth of York's entry see Leland, *Collectanea*,
pp. 218–22.
46 For Anne Boleyn's entry see sources cited in note
24.
47 Anglo, *Spectacle*, p. 57.
48 Ives, *Anne Boleyn*, pp. 273–85; Gordon Kipling, '"He
that saw it would not believe it": Anne Boleyn's Royal
Entry into London', in *Civic Ritual and Drama in
Medieval and Renaissance Europe*, ed Alexandra F.
Johnston and Wim Huskin. Ludus: Medieval and
Early Renaissance Theatre and Drama, II
(Amsterdam: Rodofi (1997), pp. 39–70.
49 Fabyan, *New Chronicles*, p. 617.
50 See Bryant, 'Configurations', p. 19.

51 Quoted Sandquist, 'English Coronations', p. 221.

52 *Hall's Chronicle*, p. 508.

53 *Ibid.*

54 See note 24 under Richard III for sources.

55 For the Wardrobe see *The Coronation of Richard III*, pp. 47–57; Janet Arnold, *Queen Elizabeth's Wardrobe Unlock'd* (Leeds: W. S. Maney & Sons, 1988), pp. 163–5.

56 *The Coronation of Richard III*, pp. 99 ff.

57 Legg, *English Coronation Records*, pp. 198–218.

58 The *Forma et Modus* is printed in *The Manner of the Coronation of King Charles the First of England*, ed. Christopher Wordsworth (HBS II, 1892), pp. 65–72; Legg, *English Coronation Records*, pp. 172–90; Harold Arthur, Viscount Dillon, 'On an MS. Collection of Ordinances of Chivalry of the Fifteenth Century', *Archaeologia*, 57 (1900), pp. 47–55. See also *Crown Jewels*, I, pp. 177–9.

59 Quoted Anglo, *Spectacle*, p. 15.

60 Leland, *Collectanea*, IV, p. 259.

61 Anthony Wagner, Nicolas Barker and Ann Page, *Medieval Pageant: Writhe's Garter Book* (Roxburghe Club, 1993).

62 For what follows see Sir Anthony Wagner, *Heralds of England: A History of the Office and College of Arms* (London: HMSO, 1967), chap 1 to 3.

63 The *Processus* is printed in Legg, *English Coronation Records*, pp. 131–68.

64 *Hall's Chronicle*, p. 798.

65 For the various offices see *The Coronation of Richard III*, pp. 245–53.

66 Leland, *Collectanea*, IV, p. 223.

67 For the Abbey during this period see Edward Carpenter, ed., *A House of Kings* (London: Westminster Abbey Bookshop, 1966), pp. 76–80, 87–100.

68 'The Abbey before the Dissolution of the Monasteries', *Westminster Abbey Chorister* (Winter, 2002–3), pp. 31–4.

69 For Westminster Hall see Christopher Wilson, 'Rulers, Artificers and Shoppers: Richard II's Remodelling of Westminster Hall, 1393–99', in *The Regal Image*, pp. 33–59; see also R. Allen Brown, H. M. Colvin and A. J. Taylor, *The History of the King's Works* (London: HMSO, 1963), I, pp. 527–33.

70 *Ibid.*, pp. 543–5.

71 Scott L. Waugh, *England in the Reign of Edward III* (Cambridge: Cambridge University Press, 1991), pp. 119 ff.

72 Wagner, *Heralds of England*, pp. 35, 76; Anthony Wagner and J. C. Sainty, 'The Origin of the Introduction of Peers in the House of Lords', *Archaeologia*, 101 (1967), pp. 119–50.

73 Leland, *Collectanea*, IV, p. 223.

74 *Hall's Chronicle*, p. 803.

75 For the text of the Little Device see under Richard III in note 24.

76 Wagner, *Heralds of England*, p. 138 note to plates X–XII.

77 Richard Barber, *The Knight and Chivalry*, revd edn (Woodbridge: Boydell Press, 1995), pp. 35 ff.

78 See J. L. Nevinson, 'The Robes of the Order of the Bath', *Connoisseur*, 134 (1954), pp. 153–9.

79 Fionn Pilbrow, 'The Knights of the Bath: Dubbing to Knighthood in Lancastrian and Yorkist England', in *Heraldry, Pageantry and Social Display in Medieval England*, ed. Peter Cox and Maurice Keen (Woodbridge: Boydell Press, 2002), pp. 195–218. Many of the documents for the Knights of the Bath are gathered in John Anstis, *Observations Introductory to an Historical Essay, upon the Knighthood of the Bath* (London, 1725); see also Sir Nicholas Harris Nicolas, *History of the Orders of Knighthood of the British Empire III, Order of the Bath* (London, 1842), pp. 1–38.

80 The reader is referred to note 24 for the bibliography used for this section.

81 *Liber Regie Capelle*, pp. 22 ff.

82 *William Gregory's Chronicle of London*, pp. 169–70.

83 *Crown Jewels*, I, pp. 334–41.

84 Roy Strong, *Feast: A History of Grand Eating* (London: Jonathan Cape, 2002), chap. 3.

85 For references see note 24.

86 *Hall's Chronicle*, pp. 510–11.

87 *Ibid.*, p. 511.

88 *Ibid.*, p. 512.

89 Walsingham, *Historia Anglica*, p. 155.

CHAPTER FIVE

1 E. Arber, *An English Garner* Constable & Co.: (London: 1845), II, p. 47.

2 *Ibid.*, p. 53.

3 G. R. Elton, ed., *The Tudor Constitution: Documents and Commentary* (Cambridge: Cambridge University Press, 1960), p. 344.

4 R. Koebner, ' "The Imperial Crown of this Realm". Henry VIII, Constantine the Great, and Polydore Vergil', *BIHR*, 26 (1953), pp. 29–52.

5 For the new dating of this oath see Dale Hoak, 'The Iconography of the Crown Imperial', in *Tudor*

Political Culture, ed. Dale Hoak, (Cambridge: Cambridge University Press, 1995), p. 55 note 3.

6 Legg, *English Coronation Records*, pp. 240–1; Schramm, *English Coronation*, pp. 216–17; Walter Ullmann, '"This Realm of England is an Empire"', *Journal of Ecclesiastical History*, 30 (1979), pp. 175–203.

7 For what follows see John N. King, *Tudor Royal Iconography* (Princeton: Princeton University Press, 1989).

8 BL Additional MS 9069, fol. 30v.

9 For what follows see A. J. Collins, *Jewels and Plate of Queen Elizabeth I* (London: British Museum, 1955), pp. 63–80, 264–68; Lord Twining, *A History of the Crown Jewels of Europe* (London: B. T. Batsford, 1960), pp. 139–40; *Crown Jewels*, I, pp. 292 ff.

10 Twining, *Crown Jewels of Europe*, pp. 141–2.

11 Janet Arnold, 'The "Coronation" Portrait of Queen Elizabeth I', *Burlington Magazine*, 120 (1978), pp. 727–41; same author's *Queen Elizabeth's Wardrobe Unlock'd* (Leeds: W. S. Maney & Sons, 1988), pp. 52–7.

12 Arnold, *Queen Elizabeth's Wardrobe Unlock'd*, p. 255.

13 *CSP Venetian 1558–80*, p. 12.

14 For Westminster Hall and Palace see H. M. Colvin, John Summerson, Martin Biddle, J. R. Hale and Marcus Merriman, *The History of the King's Works*, IV, *1485–1660* (London: HMSO, 1982), Part II, pp. 286–300.

15 For the Abbey during this period see Edward Carpenter, ed. *A House of Kings* (London; Westminster Abbey Bookshop, 1966), pp. 107–30; see especially the essays in, C. S. Knighton and Richard Mortimer, eds, *Westminster Abbey Reformed 1540–1640* (Aldershot: Ashgate, 2003).

16 Legg, *English Coronation Records*, pp. 242–4.

17 See C. S. Knighton, 'Westminster Abbey from Reformation to Revolution', in *Westminster Abbey Reformed*, ed. Knighton and Mortimer, pp. 1–15.

18 The most important study of the Tudor coronations is Dale Hoak, 'The Coronation of Edward VI, Mary I, and Elizabeth I and the Transformation of the Tudor Monarchy', in *Westminster Abbey Reformed*, ed. Knighton and Mortimer, pp. 114–51. What follows in this chapter is deeply indebted to this major contribution.

19 *Acts of the Privy Council 1547–50*, ed. R. Dasent (London: Stationery Office 1890–), p. 29.

20 For the coronation of Edward VI see:
SOURCES: Society of Antiquaries MS 123; Corpus Christi College, Cambridge MS 105/18 printed from a copy in the Library of Ely Cathedral in Edward C.

Ratcliff, *The English Coronation Service* (London: Skeffington & Son, 1936), pp. 111–15; College of Arms MS I. 7 fols. 28–44v and MS I. 8 fols. 68–97v; Gilbert Burnet; *Acts of the Privy Council*, pp. 9–10, 29–33, 48, 72, 104; also partly printed in *Bishop Burnet's History of the Reformation* (London, 1820), II, ii, pp. 130–4; BL Additional MS 9069 fols. 14–43; BL Additional MS 3026; BL Additional MS 71009, fols. 51–6; Charles Wriothesley, *A Chronicle of England during the Reigns of the Tudors* (CS, 1875–7), I, pp. 182–3; *The Chronicle and Political Papers of King Edward VI*, ed. W. K. Jordan (London: George Allen & Unwin, 1966) John Leland, *Collectanea* (London, 1774), IV, pp. 322–33; *Literary Remains of King Edward the Sixth*, ed. J. G. Nichols (reprinted New York: Burt Franklin, 1964), pp. ccxcii ff. which prints College of Arms MSS I. 7 and I. 8.

STUDIES: Schramm, *English Coronation*, pp. 96 ff., 139–40; Jasper Ridley, *Thomas Cranmer* (Oxford: Clarendon Press, 1962), pp. 246–57; Sydney Anglo, 'The Coronation of Edward VI and Society of Antiquaries Manuscript 123', *Antiquaries Journal*, 78 (1998), pp. 452–7; Jennifer Loach, *Edward VI* (New Haven, London: Yale University Press, 1999), chap. p. 4; *Crown Jewels*, I, pp. 207–9, 213–18.

21 *Miscellaneous Writings of Thomas Cranmer*, ed. J. E. Cox (Parker Society, 1846), pp. 126–7.

22 Lord Twining, *European Regalia* (London: B. T. Batsford, 1967), pp. 87 ff.; same author's *Crown Jewels of Europe*, chap. 9.

23 Twining, *European Regalia*, pp. 113 ff.; same author's *Crown Jewels of Europe*, chap. 12.

24 Margaret Aston, *The King's Bedpost* (Cambridge: Cambridge University Press, 1993), pp. 26 ff.

25 For Mary's coronation see:
SOURCES: College of Arms MS I 7, fols. 65–77; MS I 18, fols. 112–35, 143–5; *Acts of the Privy Council 1552–54*, pp. 335, 339; *CSP Spanish 1553*, pp. 231, 238–41, 259–60, 262–3; *The Chronicle of Queen Jane . . .*, ed. J. G. Nichols (CS, 1851), p. 30; *The Diary of Henry Machyn*, ed. J. G. Nichols (CS, 1848), pp. 45–6; J. R. Planche, *Regal Records or, A Chronicle of the Coronations of the Queens Regnant of England* (London, 1838), pp. 1–32; *Ambassades de Messieurs de Noailles en Angleterre*, ed. Verot (Leiden, 1763), II, pp. 199–203; Antonio de Guaras, *The Accession of Queen Mary* (London: Laurence & Bullen, 1892), pp. 117–23 printing an Italian account, *Coronatione de la serenissima Maria d'Inghilterra il primo d'Ottobre MD. LIII.* (Rome, 1553); *CSP Spanish, 1553*,

pp. 220, 231; John Anstis, *Observations Introductory to an Historical Essay, upon the Knighthood of the Bath* (London, 1725), nos. LXVII–LXVIII.

STUDIES: Carolly Erickson, *Bloody Mary* (London: J. M. Dent & Sons, 1978), pp. 317–24; David Loades, *Mary Tudor. A Life* (Oxford: Basil Blackwell, 1989), pp. 205 ff.; *Crown Jewels*, I, pp. 218–20.

26 For the coronation of Elizabeth I see:

SOURCES: CA MS WY. fol. 198; Bodleian Ashmole 863 and PRO SP 15/19 no. 9 fols. 17–19; BL Egerton MS 3320 fols. 12v–22; *Acts of the Privy Council 1558–70*, pp. 10, 19, 42; *The Diary of Henry Machyn*, pp. 186–7; John Nichols, *The Progresses . . . of Queen Elizabeth* (London, 1823), I, pp. 61–2 for an anonymous English account; *CSP Venetian 1558–80*, pp. 11–19 and the amended translation in G. Lockhart Ross, 'Il Schifanoya's Account of the Coronation of Queen Elizabeth', *EHR*, 23 (1908), pp. 533–4; all the sources are printed in G. G. Bayne cited below.

STUDIES: G. C. Bayne, 'The Coronation of Queen Elizabeth', *EHR*, 22 (1907), pp. 650–73; H. A. Wilson, 'The Coronation of Queen Elizabeth', *EHR*, 23 (1908), pp. 87–91; G. C. Bayne, 'The Coronation of Queen Elizabeth', *EHR*, 24 (1909), pp. 322–3; A. F. Pollard, 'The Coronation of Queen Elizabeth I', *EHR*, 25 (1910), pp. 125–6; A. L. Rowse, 'The Coronation of Queen Elizabeth', *History Today*, 3 (1953), pp. 301–10; W. P. Haugaard, 'The Coronation of Elizabeth I', *Journal of Ecclesiastical History*, 19 (1968), pp. 161–70; Richard C. McCoy, '"Thou Idol Ceremony": Elizabeth I, The Henriad, and the Rites of the English Monarchy', in *Urban Life in the Renaissance*, ed. Susan Zimmerman and Ronald F. E. Weissman (Newark: University of Delaware Press, 1989), pp. 240–51; same author's '"The Wonderfull Spectacle": The Civic Progress of Elizabeth I and the Troublesome Coronation', in *Coronations*, ed. Bak, pp. 217–27; *Crown Jewels*, I, pp. 224–26.

27 For Elizabeth's religious preferences see Roger Bowers, 'The Chapel Royal, the First Edwardian Prayer Book and Elizabeth's Settlement of Religion, 1559', *Historical Journal*, 43(2) (2000), pp. 317–44.

28 Peter J. French, *John Dee: The World of an Elizabethan Magus* (London: Routledge & Kegan Paul, 1972), p. 6.

29 *The Diary of Henry Machyn*, p. 49.

30 Carpenter, *House of Kings*, p. 128.

31 *CSP Venetian, 1558–80*, pp. 11–12.

32 CA MS I 18 fol. 96 printed in *Literary Remains of King Edward the Sixth*, p. cclxxix–ccxci.

33 PRO E 429/4; E 429/3 and LC2/4 (3)

34 CA MS M6, fols. 35–48.

35 R. Malcolm Smuts, 'Public Ceremony and Royal Charisma: the English Royal Entry in London', in *The First Modern Society: Essays in English History in Honour of Lawrence Stone*, ed. A. L. Beier, D. N. Cannadine and J. M. Rosenheim (Cambridge: Cambridge University Press, 1989), pp. 65–82.

36 John Topham, 'An Historical and Descriptive Account of the Ancient Painting Preserved at Cowdray in Sussex . . .', *Archaeologia*, 8 (1787), pp. 406–22.

37 For Edward VI's entry see:

SOURCES: Leland, *Collectanea*, IV, pp. 310–22; *Literary Remains of King Edward the Sixth*, pp. cclxxviii ff.; *CSP Spanish 1547–49*, pp. 46–8.

STUDIES: R. Withington, *English Pageantry: An Historical Outline* (Cambridge, Mass.: Harvard University Press, 1918), I, pp. 185–7; S. Anglo, *Spectacle, Pageantry and Early Tudor Policy* (Oxford: Clarendon Press, 1969), pp. 281–94; *Crown Jewels*, I, pp. 210–13.

38 *CSP Spanish 1547–49*, pp. 46–8.

39 For the entry of Mary see:

SOURCES: City of London Repertories XLII, pt I, fols 74v–75; John Stowe, *Annales* (London, 1631 edn), pp. 616–17; *Two London Chronicles*, ed. C. L. Kingsford, *Camden Miscellany*, 12 (1910), pp. 29–30; Guaras, *Accession of Queen Mary*, p. 117; *Ambassades de Messieurs de Noailles*, pp. 196–9; *Diary of Henry Machyn*, pp. 43, 45; *The Chronicle of Queen Jane*, pp. 27–9.

STUDIES: Anglo, *Spectacle*, pp. 318–22.

40 J. A. Kingdon, *Richard Grafton* (London, 1901), p. 76.

41 For Elizabeth I's entry see:

SOURCES: BL Egerton MS 3320 fols. 1–11v; CAMS M 6 fols. 35–48, 87–97; *The Diary of Henry Machyn*, pp. 186–7; *CSP Venetian 1558–80*, pp. 11–15; Nichols, *Progresses*, I, pp. 38–58; Arber, *English Garner*, IV, pp. 217–47; *The Quenes Maiesties Passage through the Citie of London to Westminster the Day before her Coronation*, ed. James Osborn (New Haven, London: Yale University Press, 1963); *The Quene's Majestie's Passage*, ed. Arthur Kinney, in *Elizabethan Backgrounds* (Hamden, Conn.: Archon Books, 1975), pp. 7–38.

STUDIES: Withington, *English Pageantry*, I, pp. 199–203; Anglo, *Spectacle*, pp. 344–9; David M. Bergeron, *English Civic Pageantry 1558–1642* (London: Edward Arnold 1971), pp. 11–23; Richard L. DeMolen, 'Richard Mulcaster and Elizabethan

Pageantry', *Studies in English Literature*, 14 (1974), pp.
209–21; David M. Bergeron, 'Elizabeth's Coronation
Entry (1559): New Manuscript Evidence', *English
Literary Renaissance*, 8 (1978), pp. 3–8; Jean Wilson,
Entertainments for Elizabeth I (Woodbridge: D. S.
Brewer, 1980), pp. 5–7; Mark Breitenberg, '"... the
hole matter opened": Iconic Representation and
Interpretation in "The Quenes Majesties Passage"',
Criticism, 28 (1986), pp. 1–25; McCoy, '"Thou Idol
Ceremony"', pp. 49–51; Roy Strong, 'The 1559 Entry
Pageants of Elizabeth I', in Roy Strong, *The Tudor and
Stuart Monarchy*, II, *Elizabethan* (Woodbridge:
Boydell & Brewer Press, 1995), pp. 33–54; *Crown
Jewels*, I, pp. 222–4; Judith M. Richards, 'Love and a
Female Monarch: The Case of Elizabeth Tudor',
Journal of British Studies, 38(2) 1999, pp. 133–59; D. E.
Hoak, 'A Tudor Debora? The Coronation of Elizabeth
I, Parliament and the Problem of Female Rule', in
John Foxe and his World, ed. C. Highley and J. N. King
(Aldershot: Ashgate, 2002), pp. 73–88.

42 *The Quene's Majestie's Passage*, ed. Kinney, p. 15.

43 *Ibid.*, p. 23.

44 *Ibid.*, p. 26.

45 David H. Horne, ed., *The Life and Minor Works of
George Peele* (New Haven, London: Yale University
Press, 1952), p. 232.

46 For what follows see Frances A. Yates, *Astrea: The
Imperial Theme in the Sixteenth Century* (London:
Routledge & Kegan Paul, 1975), pp. 29–87; Koebner,
'"The Imperial Crown of this Realm"', pp. 48–52.

47 Roy Strong, *Gloriana: The Portraits of Queen Elizabeth
I* (London: Thames & Hudson, 1987), pp. 101–7,
131–3.

48 McCoy, '"Thou Idol Ceremony"', pp. 251 ff.

CHAPTER SIX

1 *Crown Jewels*, I, p. 244.

2 Peter Heylyn, *Aerius Redivivus: or The History of the
Presbyterians* (London, 1670), pp. 461–2.

3 David Norbrook, 'Levelling Poetry: George Wither
and the English Revolution 1642–49', *English Literary
Renaissance*, 21 (1991), pp. 217–56.

4 Quoted in *ibid.*, p. 218 note 5.

5 For James I's theoretical stance see *The Political Works
of James I*, ed. C. H. McIlwain (Cambridge, Mass.;
Harvard University Press, 1918), introduction.

6 *Ibid.*, pp. xxxiii, xxxv, xxxix.

7 Quoted in *Crown Jewels*, I, p. 229.

8 *The Coronation Order of King James I*, ed. J. Wickham

Legg (London: F. E. Robinson & Co., 1902), p. lxxix.

9 *Crown Jewels*, I, p. 244. Peter Heylyn, Thomas Fuller
and Joseph Mead, the biblical scholar, all testify that
this passage was used.

10 H. Ellis, *Original Letters, Illustrative of English History
...* (London, 1825), III, pp. 219–20.

11 Thomas Fuller, *The Church History of Britain*,
ed. J. S. Brewer (Oxford, 1845), VI, p. 32; *Coronation
Order of King James I*, p. xcv.

12 *Coronation Order of King James I*, pp. 11–12.

13 Quoted in *Crown Jewels*, I, p. 230.

14 *Political Works of James I*, p. 55.

15 David J. Sturdy, 'English Coronation Sermons in
the Seventeenth Century', in *Herrscherweihe und
Königskrönung im Frühneuzeitlichen Europa*,
ed. H. Duchhardt (Franz Steiner Verlag: Wiesbaden,
1983), pp. 69–81.

16 Thomas Bilson, *A Sermon Preached at Westminster
before the King and Queenes Maiesties, at their
Coronations on Saint James his Day, Being the 28 of
July 1603* (1603); Richard Senhouse, *Four Sermons
Preached at Court upon Severall Occasions by the
Late Reverend and Learned Divine, Doctor Senhouse,
L. Bishop of Carlisle* (1627).

17 Bilson, *Sermon*, p.3.

18 *Ibid.*, p. 37.

19 *Political Works of James I*, p. 226.

20 *Ibid.*, p. 69.

21 *Ibid.*

22 Sir William S. Holdsworth, *A History of English Law*
(London: Methuen & Co., 1923), III, p. 464.

23 *CSP Venetian 1625–26*, p. 51.

24 *The Manner of the Coronation of King Charles the First
of England*, ed. Christopher Wordsworth (HBS 1892),
pp. xlvii–xlviii.

25 *Ibid.*, pp. lvii–lxv. For a discussion of this see
Schramm, *English Coronation*, pp. 218–19.

26 Henry Wharton, *The History of the Troubles and Tryal
of ... William Laud* (London, 1695), p. 319.

27 Quoted and discussed in Sharon Achinstein, 'Milton
and King Charles', in *The Royal Image: Representations
of Charles I*, ed. Thomas N. Corns (Cambridge:
Cambridge University Press, 1999), pp. 156–7. See
C. C. Weston and Janelle Greenberg, *The Grand
Controversy over Legal Sovereignty in Stuart England*
(Cambridge: Cambridge University Press, 1981),
pp. 62–65; Glenn Burgess, *Absolute Monarchy and
the Stuart Constitution* (Newhaven and London: Yale
University Press, 1996), pp. 145 note, 153, 216–17.

28 Edmund Lodge, *Illustrations ...* (London, 1791), III,

29 Arthur Wilson, *History of Great Britain, Being the Life and Reign of King James the First* (London, 1653), p. 12. For a discussion of this see R. Malcolm Smuts, 'Public Ceremony and Royal Charisma: The English Royal Entry into London', in *The First Modern Society: Essays in English History in Honour of Lawrence Stone*, ed. A. L. Beier, D. N. Cannadine and J. M. Rosenheim (Cambridge: Cambridge University Press, 1989), pp. 82–9.

30 Gilbert Dugdale, *The Time Triumphant . . .* (1604) reprinted in J. Nichols, *The Progresses . . . of King James the First* (London, 1828), I, p. 416.

31 Jonathan Goldberg, *James I and the Politics of Literature* (Baltimore: Johns Hopkins University Press, 1983), pp. 30–55.

32 J. Richards, 'The Kingship of Charles I before 1640', *Past and Present*, 113 (1982), pp. 70–96; Kevin Sharpe, *The Personal Rule of Charles I* (New Haven and London: Yale University Press, 1992), pp. 217–19.

33 See David Lowenstein, 'The King among the Radicals', in *The Royal Image*, ed. Corns, pp. 108 ff.

34 Elizabeth Skerpan Wheeler, 'Eikon Basilike and the Rhetoric of Self-representation', in *The Royal Image*, ed. Corns, pp. 122–40.

35 *CSP Venetian 1603–1607*, pp. 24–8.

36 *Ibid.*, pp. 43–4.

37 For this see Kevin Sharpe, *Sir Robert Cotton 1586–1631: History and Politics in Early Modern England* (Oxford: Oxford University Press, 1979), chap. I.

38 John Selden, *Titles of Honor*, 3rd edn (London, 1672), pp. 107 ff.

39 Sharpe, *Cotton*, p. 25 note 53.

40 Thomas Milles, *The Catalogue of Honor* (London, 1614), p. 59.

41 *Coronation Order of King James I*, pp. 20, 25, 26, 28, 29, 31, 33.

42 *Manner of the Coronation of King Charles the First*, pp. vii ff.

43 Quoted in *ibid.*, p. xlvii.

44 Wharton, *Troubles*, pp. 26–7.

45 Francis Wormald, 'The So-called Coronation-Book of the Kings of England', in *Essays in Honor of Georg Swarzenski*, ed. O. Goetz (Chicago: Henry Regnery & Co., 1951), pp. 233–7.

46 *Cambridge*, St John's College, Cambridge, MS. L 12, p. 12.

47 Fuller, *Church History*, VI,

48 As quoted in *Crown Jewels*, I, p. 346.

49 CA, Coronations, Anstis. fols., 215–24.

50 Wharton, *Troubles*, p. 28.

51 PRO SP 16/19 nos. 5, 109.

52 Edward Carpenter, ed., *A House of Kings* (London: Westminster Abbey Bookshop, 1966), p. 144.

53 *Coronation Order of King James I*, p. lxix.

54 On which see *ibid.*, pp lv–lvi; *Manner of the Coronation of King Charles the First*, pp. xxi–xxiii, Appendix 5; Legg, *English Coronation Records*, p. 246 where the prayer of consecration of the holy oil is printed.

55 CA, Coronations, Anstis, fols. 215–24. It breaks off in the middle.

56 Wharton, *Troubles*, p. 28.

57 I list here the sources I have used for the two coronations:

JAMES I

SOURCES: 'Lambeth Palace MS 1075 A brief aswell out of the rites of the Coronation called Liber Regalis as allso other bookes of good recorde in Coronation Order', pp. 1–50; 'The Coronation of King James and Queene Anne his wife July 1603', PRO SP 14/2; BL Sloane MS 1494 fols. 89 ff: printed in *Coronation Order of King James I*, pp. 65–79; BL Additional MS 6284 printed in Nichols, *Progresses*, I, pp. 231–4; Bodleian Ashmole 863 printed in *Manner of the Coronation of King Charles the First*, pp. 106–37; account 'delivered to his Majesty by the Lord Archbishop of Canterbury', in Milles, *Catalogue of Honor*, pp. 167–9; *The Ceremonies, Form of Prayer, and Services used in Westminster-Abbey at the Coronation of King James the First and Queen Ann his Consort* (London, 1685); account of Humphrey Repington in *Coronation Order of King James II*, pp. lxxvii–lxx; account of a Roman, Giovanni degli Effetti, printed in ibid. pp. xlviii–lxxiv; account at a remove by Giovanni Carlo Scaramelli, Venetian Secretary, *CSP Venetian 1603–1607*, pp. 74 ff.; also partly in *Coronation Order of King James I*, pp. lxxv–lxxvi; account of the ambassador the Duke of Württemberg in W. B. Rye, 'The Coronation of King James I, 1603', *The Antiquary*, 22 (1890), pp. 18–23; account probably from a French ambassadorial source in Pierre-Victor Palma-Cayet, *Chronique Septenaire* (Paris, 1605), pp. 252–3 printed in translation in *Crown Jewels*, I, pp. 235–6; see also HMC Hatfield, XV, pp. 40, 43, 49, 52, 169.

STUDIES: *Coronation Order of King James I*, introduction; *Crown Jewels*, I, pp. 228–36; Roy Strong, 'How James I was Crowned', *Country Life*, 22 May 2003, pp. 106–9.

CHARLES I

SOURCES: St John's College, Cambridge, MS L. 15

printed in *Manner of the Coronation of King Charles I the First*, pp. 1–62; Laud's annotated copy used during the service, St John's College, Cambridge, MS L12; Coronatio Regis Caroli 2 Februarij Ao: 1625 in PRO SP 16/20 no. 13; Forme of Coronation. Things necessarie to be prepared before the day of Coronation PRO SP 16/19 no. 114; A Collection out of the Book called Liber Regalis remaining in the Treasurie of the Church of Westminster Touching the Crowning of the King and Queene together . . . PRO SP 16/19 no. 111; The Abreviament of the Ordre how the King of England shall behave himself in his coronation, and the Ordre of the Quene, crowned together, and what services all other person shall doe att the same PRO SP 16/19 no. 113; BL Harleian MS 5222 printed in Legg, *English Coronation Records*, pp. 245–71; CA WY, fols. 175–7; CA, Coronations, Anstis, fols. 204, 205, 206, 209; CA, Coronation of Charles I, pp. 1–24 (transcript of St John's College, Cambridge MS L15); account of John Bradshaw, Windsor Herald in *Manner of the Coronation of King Charles the First*, pp. liii–lvi.

STUDIES: Ronald Lightbown, 'The King's Regalia, Insignia and Jewellery', in *The Late King's Goods*, ed. Arthur MacGregor (Oxford: Oxford University Press, 1989), pp. 257–5; *Crown Jewels*, I, pp. 236–45.

58 *CSP Domestic 1603–1610*, p. 10, no. 90.

59 PRO SP 14/19.

60 Fuller, *Church History*, V, p. 263.

61 *CSP Domestic 1625–26*, pp. 229, 238, 384.

62 *The Life of Edward Lord Herbert of Cherbury Written by Himself* (London, 1791), p. 54; Roy Strong, *The English Icon. Elizabethan and Jacobean Portraiture* (London: Paul Mellon Foundation, 1969, p. 245 (226).

63 *Ibid.*, p. 244 (218).

64 George Scharf, *A Descriptive and Historical Catalogue of the Collection of Pictures at Woburn Abbey* (1890), pp. 117–18 (170).

65 CA, Coronations, Anstis., fols. 144–65v; *CSP Domestic 1603–10*, pp. 10, 19, 22, 24; *CSP Domestic 1625–26*, pp. 232–33.

66 PRO SP 14/19.

67 CA, Coronations, Anstis, fol. 210.

68 H. M. Colvin, John Summerson, Martin Biddle, J. R. Hale and Marcus Merriman, *The History of the King's Works*, IV, *1485–1660* (London: HMSO, 1982), part II p. 300.

69 Ellis, *Original Letters*, III, pp. 213–19.

70 *Crown Jewels*, I, pp. 235–6.

71 *Manner of the Coronation of King Charles the First*,

pp. xxvi–xxx; H. R. Trevor-Roper, *Archbishop Laud 1573–1645* (London: Macmillan & Co., 1962), pp. 140–1; Sharpe, *Personal Rule*, pp. 780–1.

72 For Henrietta Maria see *CSP Venetian 1625–26*, pp. 276, 311; *CSP Domestic 1625–26*, pp. 225, 246; *The Letters of John Chamberlain*, ed. N. E. McClure (Philadelphia, 1939), II, p. 627.

73 *Medallic Illustrations of the History of Great Britain and Ireland to the Death of George II* (London: British Museum, 1911), plate XIV no. 11; plate XX (i).

74 Dom Anselm Hughes, 'Music of the Coronation over a Thousand Years', *Proceedings of the Royal Musical Association*, 79 (1952–3), pp. 81–5, 93.

75 Gail Kern Paster, 'The Idea of London in Masque and Pageant', in *Pageantry in the Shakespearean Theater*, ed. David Bergeron (Athens: University of Georgia Press, 1985).

76 Nichols, *Progresses . . . James* I, I, p. 366.

77 *Ben Jonson*, ed. C. H. Herford, P. and E. Simpson (Oxford: Clarendon, 1941), VII, p. 90.

78 Quoted in David Bergeron, *English Civic Pageantry 1558–1642* (London: Edward Arnold, 1971), p. 73.

79 *Letters of John Chamberlain*, I; *CSP Venetian 1603–1607*, pp. 62–5, 67–8.

80 For James I's entry into London see Nichols, *Progresses*, I, pp. 329–401; *Coronation Order of King James I*, pp. 59–62; *The Dramatic Works of Thomas Dekker*, ed. Fredson Bowers (Cambridge: Cambridge University Press. 1964), II, pp. 229–303; *Ben Jonson*, VII, pp. 81–109; Glynne Wickham, 'Contributions de Ben Jonson et Dekker au fêtes du couronnement de Jacques Ier', in *Les Fêtes de la Renaissance* (Paris: CNRS, 1956), I, pp. 279–83; Per Palme, 'Ut Architectura Poesis', *Acta Universitatis Upsaliensis, Figura*, new series 1, pp. 95–107; David M. Bergeron, 'Harrison, Jonson and Dekker: The Magnificent Entertainment for King James (1604)', *Journal of the Warburg and Courtauld Institutes*, 31 (1968), pp. 445–8; same author, *English Civic Pageantry*, pp. 71–88; Graham Parry, *The Golden Age Restor'd: The Culture of the Stuart Court, 1603–42* (Manchester: University Press Manchester, 1981), pp. 1–20; Goldberg, *James I*, chap. 1; Richard Dutton, ed., *Jacobean Civic Pageants*, Ryburn Renaissance Texts and Studies (Keele: Keele University Press, 1995), pp. 19–25.

81 A. M. Hind, *Engraving in England in the Sixteenth and Seventeenth Centuries*, Part II, *The Reign of James* I (Cambridge: Cambridge University Press, 1955), pp. 17–29.

82 Nichols, *Progresses . . . of James I*, I, p. 338.

83 *Ben Jonson*, VII, p. 91.

84 Nichols, *Progresses . . . of James I*, I. For Charles I's distaste for the City see Smuts, 'Public Ceremony and Royal Charisma', pp. 89–93.

85 *CSP Venetian 1625–26*, pp. 294, 464; Bergeron, *English Civic Pageantry*, pp. 121, 254–5, 262–3.

86 For the destruction see A. J. Collins, *Jewels and Plate of Queen Elizabeth I* (London: British Museum, 1955), pp. 190–1; Lord Twining, *A History of the Crown Jewels of Europe* (London: B. T. Batsford, 1960), pp. 149–50; *Crown Jewels*, I, pp. 345–6.

87 *The Inventories and Valuations of the King's Goods*, ed. O. Millar (Walpole Society, XLIII, 1972), p. 51. For a detailed discussion: Valerie Cumming, '"Great Vanity and Excess in Apparell"', in *The Late King's Goods*, ed. MacGregor, pp. 324–27; both Anne of Denmark's and Charles I's coronation robes were sold, *ibid.*, pp. 337–9, 344.

88 *Crown Jewels*, II, pp. 335–49.

89 *The Inventories*, ed. Millar, pp. 49–50.

90 *Ibid.*, pp. 49–50.

91 St John's College, Cambridge MS, L 12, p. 6.

92 Fuller, *Church History*, Brewer, VI, p.31.

CHAPTER SEVEN

1 Lois G. Schwoerer, *The Declaration of Rights, 1689* (Baltimore: Johns Hopkins University Press, 1981), chap. 1; same author's 'The Glorious Revolution as Spectacle: A New Perspective', in *England's Rise to Greatness 1660–1763*, ed. Stephen B. Baxter (Berkeley: University of California Press, 1983), pp. 109–49.

2 Carolyn A. Edie, 'The Popular Idea of Monarchy on the Eve of the Stuart Restoration', *Huntington Library Quarterly*, 29 (1976), pp. 343–73.

3 See Gerard Reedy, 'Mystical Politics: The Imagery of Charles II's Coronation', in *Studies in Change and Revolution. Aspects of English Intellectual History 1640–1800*, ed. Paul J. Korshin (Menston: Scolar Press, 1972), pp. 19–42.

4 *The Diary of Samuel Pepys*, ed. Robert Latham and William Matthews (London: HarperCollins, 1995), II, p. 86.

5 George Morley, *A Sermon Preached at the Magnificent Coronation of the Most High and Mighty King Charles the IId . . .* (London, 1661), dedication.

6 John Evelyn, *A Panegyric to Charles II*, ed. Geoffrey Keynes (Augustan Reprint Society, xxxviii, 1951), p. 4.

7 Marc Bloch, *The Royal Touch: Sacred Monarchy and Scrofula in England and France* (London: Routledge & Kegan Paul, 1973), pp. 219–23.

8 Sir William S. Holdsworth, *A History of English Law* (London: Methuen & Co., 1938), X, pp. 430–2.

9 For the background see Lois G. Schwoerer, 'Propaganda in the Revolution of 1688–89', *American Historical Review*, 82(2) (1977), pp. 843–74.

10 See Schwoerer, *The Declaration of Rights*, esp. chaps. 9, 10, 11 and 16; David Ogg, *England in the Reigns of James II and William III* (Oxford: Clarendon Press, 1957), pp. 235–6; Howard Nenner, 'The Later Stuart Age', in *The Varieties of British Political Thought, 1500–1800*, ed. J. G. A. Pocock (Cambridge: Cambridge University Press, 1993), pp. 180–208.

11 See J. G. A. Pocock, *The Ancient Constitution and the Feudal Law: A Study of English Historical Thought in the Seventeenth Century*, a reissue with a retrospect (Cambridge: Cambridge University Press. 1987), esp. pp.229–39.

12 On the oath see Lois G. Schwoerer, 'The Coronation of William and Mary, April 11, 1689,' in *The Revolutions of 1688/9*, ed. Lois G. Schwoerer (Cambridge: Cambridge University Press, 1991), pp. 118 ff. For the committee's debates see Architell Grey, *Debates of the House of Commons, from the Year 1667 to the Year 1694* (London, 1769), IX, pp. 1908–98.

13 *The Statutes of the Realm* (1820), VII, p. 748 and V, p. 784 for 25. Car.II.c.2. The text of Anne's Oath is given in J. R. Planche, *Regal Records . . .* (London, 1838), pp. 118–19.

14 See *New Oxford DNB*. For the importance of his role in the coronation see *Crown Jewels*, I, pp. 355–7.

15 Walker's transcript is in CA, Coronations, Anstis fols. 395–6.

16 *Ibid.*, fols. 361–84.

17 *Ibid.*, fols. 352–7.

18 I quote from the MS copy in the College of Arms. See note 54 for full citation.

19 PRO LC 5/60 fol. 87.

20 *The Diurnal of Thomas Rugg 1659–61*, ed. William L. Sachse (CS, 3rd series, XCI, 1961), p. 178.

21 See also the memorandum of 26 October 1660 by Walker, *CSP Domestic 1660–61*, p. 323.

22 PRO A 03/1188.

23 Generally on this see *Crown Jewels*, I, pp. 365–8.

24 Walker, *Preparations*, fol. 2.

25 Ibid., fols. 53 ff. This MS includes two sets of

drawings, one in colour and the other in monochrome.

26 BL Stowe MS 580 fol. 15v.

27 For all this see CA, *Coronations*, Anstis fols. 397–9.

28 *Ibid.*, fols. 352–7.

29 *CSP Venetian 1659–61*, p. 148.

30 See the entries for the individual items in *Crown Jewels*, II.

31 Sara Stevenson and Duncan Thompson, *John Michael Wright: The King's Painter*, Exhibition catalogue, Scottish National Portrait Gallery (1982), pp. 80–2 (no. 28).

32 *The Diary of John Evelyn*, ed. E. S. de Beer (Oxford: Clarendon, 1959).

33 See *Crown Jewels*, I, pp. 397–9 for the new regalia and the individual catalogue entries in volume II.

34 See Thomas P. Slaughter, *Ideology and Politics on the Eve of the Restoration: Newcastle's Advice to Charles II* (Philadelphia: American Philosophical Society, 1984), pp. 44–5.

35 *Memoirs of Sir John Reresby*, ed. Andrew Browning (Glasgow: Jackson, Son & Co., 1936), p. 38.

36 For the 1661 entry see:

SOURCES: John Ogilby, *The Relation of His Majesties Entertainment Passing through the City of London to His Coronation . . .* (London, 1661); same author's *The Entertainment of His Most Excellent Majestie Charles II, in his Passage through the City of London to his Coronation . . .* (London, 1662) (with engravings); this has been the subject of a reprint with an introduction by Ronald Knowles, Medieval & Renaissance Texts & Studies, XLIII, Renaissance Triumphs and Magnificences, new series, III (Binghampton, NY, 1988); John Ogilby *The Kings Coronation: Being an Exact Account of the Cavalcade with a Description of the Triumphal Arches, and Speeches Prepared by the City of London for His Late Majesty Charles the Second . . .* (London, 1685); Anon., *The Cities Loyalty Display'd* (1661).

STUDIES: R. Withington, *English Pageantry* (Cambridge, Mass.: Harvard University Press, 1918), I, pp. 343–7; Eric Halfpenny, '"The Citie's Loyalty Display'd": A Literary and Documentary Causerie of Charles II's Coronation Entertainment', *Guildhall Miscellany*, 10 (1959). This prints the City's financial accounts; Roy Strong, 'A Note on Charles II's Coronation Entry', *Coat of Arms*, 6 (42) (1960), pp.43–7; Reedy, 'Mystical Politics', *passim*; *Crown Jewels*, I, pp. 358–65.

37 For Ogilby see *New Oxford DNB*.

38 He petitioned probably in March, *CSP Domestic 1660–61*, p. 553.

39 *Ibid.*, p. 606.

40 On whom see Howard Colvin, *A Biographical Dictionary of British Architects 1600–1840* (New Haven and London: Yale University Press, 1995 edn.), pp. 396–8.

41 Pepys, *Diary*, II, p. 73.

42 Evelyn, *Diary*, II.

43 *CSP Venetian 1661–62*, p. 115.

44 Quoted in Ogilby, *Entertainment*, Knowles' introduction, p. 17.

45 Quoted Halfpenny, '"The Citie's Loyalty . . ."', p. 24.

46 Rugg, *Diurnal*, p. 176.

47 CA, Walker, *Preparations*, fol. 22.

48 Pepys, *Diary*, II, p. 83.

49 CA, Walker, *Preparations*, fol. 21.

50 Ogilby, *Entertainment* (1662), p. 1.

51 *Ibid.*, pp. 1–2.

52 For which see Eric Halfpenny, 'The "Entertainment" of Charles II', *Music and Letters*, 38 (1957), pp. 32–44.

53 Lawrence Eachard, *The History of England* (London, 1718), III, p. 734.

54 From 1661 onwards the sources, both manuscript and printed, for coronations multiply alarmingly. From now on no list is comprehensive.

CHARLES II

PRO A03/1188 and LC 5/60, both Wardrobe accounts; *CSP Domestic 1660–61*, pp. 412, 423, 424, 466, 500, 528, 570, 575; Rugg, *Diurnal*, pp. 176–9; CA, Sir Edward Walker, THE PREPARATIONS FOR His Majesties Coronation. TOGEATHER WITH the Installation of Knights of ye Garter. The Makeing of Knights of the Bath. Creations of Noblemen. His Ma ties Royall Proceeding through London. AND His Ma ties Coronation at Westminster the 23rd of Aprill 1661; this was printed as *A Circumstantial Account of the Preparations for the Coronation of His Majesty King Charles the Second . . .* (London, 1820), Elias Ashmole, 'A Brief Narrative of His Majesties Solemn Coronation . . .', in Ogilby, *Entertainment* (1662), pp. 165–92; Legg, *English Coronation Records*, pp. 276–86; *Crown Jewels*, I, pp. 365–91.

JAMES II

Francis Sandford, *The History of the Coronation of the Most High, Most Mighty and Most Excellent Monarch James II . . .* (London, 1687); CA, Coronation of James II and William and Mary, fols.

5–14v; Form of the Coronation of James II in St John's College, Cambridge MS 31, fols. 7 ff., printed in Legg, *English Coronation Records*, pp. 287–316; *The Manner of the Coronation of King Charles the First of England*, ed. Christopher Wordsworth (HBS, 1892), pp. xxx–xxxix; *Crown Jewels*, I, pp. 392–404; Henry Everett, 'The English Coronation Rite: From the Middle Ages to the Stuarts', in *Coronations Past and Present*, ed. Paul Bradshaw (Cambridge: Grove Books, 1997), pp. 5–21.

WILLIAM III AND MARY II

CA, Coronation of James II and William and Mary, fols 27–57; WA 51123–32; CA. L 19 Coronations, Charles II, James II; William and Mary printed in *Three Coronation Orders*, ed. J. Wickham Legg (HBS, XIX, 1900), pp. 10–36 along with appendices printing material from the Wardrobe and other sources; Legg, *English Coronation Records*, pp. 317–42 (from CA L 19) *An Account of the Ceremonial at the Coronation of Their Most Excellent Majesties King William and Queen Mary: The Eleventh Day of this Instant April, 1689* (London, 1689); *The Form of the Proceeding to the Coronation of Their Majesties King William and Queen Mary, The Eleventh Day of this Instant, Aprill, 1689*; Evelyn, *Diary*, IV, pp. 632–3; Legg, *Coronation Documents*, pp. 317–24; Schwoerer, 'The Coronation of William and Mary'; *Crown Jewels*, I, pp. 426–46.

ANNE

PRO AO1/2316/133 Wardrobe accounts; CA, Coronations, Anstis unpaginated; WA 51133–44; *The Form of the Proceeding to the Royal Coronation of Her Most Excellent Majesty Queen Anne, The Twenty Third Day of this instant April, 1702*; full text of the service in Planche, *Regal Records*, pp. 95–161; *The Journeys of Celia Fiennes*, ed. Christopher Morris (London: Cresset Press, 1947), pp. 296–304; David Green, *Queen Anne 1665–1714* (History Book Club, 1970), pp. 95–6; *Crown Jewels*, I, pp. 446–63.

55 Sandford, *History*, p. 4.

56 *Memoirs of Mary, Queen of England (1689–1693)*, ed. R. Doebner (Leipzig, 1886), p. 12.

57 Schwoerer, 'The Coronation of William and Mary', p. 115.

58 *CSP Venetian 1659–61*, pp. 201, 220.

59 Sandford, *History*, pp. 1–2.

60 PRO 1/2366/133.

61 *Three Coronation Orders*, p. 108

62 *CSP Domestic 1660–61*, pp. 584–6.

63 Sandford, *History*, pp. 4, 129–35.

64 Evelyn, *Diary*, II.

65 Rugg, *Diurnal*, pp. 165–9 gives a lively narrative; John Anstis, *Observations Introductory to an Historical Essay, upon the Knighthood of the Bath* (London, 1725), pp. 81–5 (no. LXXXIV).

66 PRO Works 36.

67 Pepys, *Diary*, II, p. 84.

68 CA, Coronations, Anstis fol. 32.

69 WAM 51117.

70 WAM 51147.

71 WAM 51137. See also Frank B. Zimmerman, *Henry Purcell 1659–1695* (London: Macmillan, 1967), pp. 123–8; Walker, *Preparations*, fol. 3.

72 *An Account* (1689) . . ., p. 3.

73 *The Journeys of Celia Fiennes*, p. 302.

74 CA, Coronations of James II and William and Mary, fol. 9.

75 WAM 51140.

76 Pepys, *Diary*, II, p. 84.

77 PRO LC5/60.

78 *Three Coronation Orders*, pp. 78–87. For the various royal throne chairs see Hugh Roberts, 'Royal Thrones 1760–1840', *Furniture History Society*, 25 (1989), pp. 85; Adam Bowett, 'George I's Coronation Throne', *Apollo* (January 2005), pp. 42–7.

79 PRO AO1/2366/133.

80 *The Journeys of Celia Fiennes*, p. 300.

81 Rugg, *Diurnal*, p. 178.

82 H. M. Colvin, J. Mordaunt Crook, Kerry Downes and John Newman, *The History of the King's Works*, V, *1660–1782* (London: HMSO, 1976) p. 454.

83 Pepys, *Diary*, II, p. 85.

84 Walker, *Preparations*, fol. 47v.

85 WAM 5666.

86 *Three Coronation Orders*, p. 93.

87 WAM 51157.

88 *The Journeys of Celia Fiennes*, p. 301.

89 Anthony Harvey and Richard Mortimer eds, *The Funeral Effigies of Westminster Abbey* (Woodbridge: Boydell Press, 1994), pp. 94–108.

90 *The Journeys of Celia Fiennes*, p. 301.

91 The prayers dropped are listed in *The Coronation of Charles the First*, pp. xxxviii note 1.

92 *Three Coronation Orders*, p. xvii.

93 Evelyn, *Diary*, IV, pp. 437–8.

94 *Three Coronation Orders*, p. 27.

95 H. W. Henfry, 'Oliver Cromwell's Sceptre', *Journal of the British Archaeological Association* 31 (1875), pp. 306–9.

96 On the sermons see David J. Sturdy, 'English Coronation Sermons in the Seventeenth Century', in *Herrscherweihe und Königskrönung im frühneuzeitlichen Europa*, ed. H. Duchhardt (Wiesbaden; Franz Steiner Verlag, 1983), pp. 69–81; also Carolyn Edie, 'The Public Face of Royal Ritual: Sermons, Medals, and Civic Ceremony in Later Stuart Coronations', *Huntingdton Library Quarterly*, 53 (1990), pp. 31–6.

97 Morley, *A Sermon Preached at the Magnificent Coronation of the Most High and Mighty King Charles the IId* . . .

98 Francis Turner, *A Sermon Preached before Their Majesties K. James II. and Q. Mary at their Coronation in Westminster-Abbey, April 23, 1685* (London, 1685).

99 Gilbert Burnet, *A Sermon Preached at the Coronation of William III and Mary II* . . . (London, 1689).

100 John Sharp, *A Sermon Preach'd at the Coronation of Queen Anne* . . . (London, 1708 edn).

101 For these see Edie, 'The Public Face of Royal Ritual', *passim*; *Medallic Illustrations of the History of Great Britain and Ireland* . . . (London: British Museum, 1909–11), plate XLV no. 7 (Charles II), LXIII nos. 5–6 (James II), no. 7 (Mary of Modena), plate LXXIII no. 2 (William and Mary), plate CXV nos. 4–6 (Anne).

102 Evelyn, *Diary*, IV, pp. 632–3.

103 Dom Anselm Hughes, 'Music of the Coronation over a Thousand Years', *Proceedings of the Royal Musical Association*, 79 (1952–3), pp. 93–4.

104 Evelyn, *Diary*, II.

105 Also see Robert King, *Henry Purcell* (London: Thames & Hudson, 1994), pp. 23–5.

106 *Ibid.*, pp. 117–18. Bruce Wood, 'A Coronation Anthem – Lost and Found', *Musical Times*, 108 (1977), pp. 466–8.

107 Pepys, *Diary*, II, p. 84.

108 *Ibid.*, II, p. 86.

109 *Ibid.*, II, pp. 85–6.

110 *Ibid.*, II, p. 87.

111 Rugg, *Diurnal*, pp. 179–80.

112 Withington, *English Pageantry*, I, p. 244.

113 *The Journeys of Celia Fiennes*, pp. 21–2.

114 WAM 51122.

115 WAM 51162.

116 Rugg, *Diurnal*, p. 178.

117 Pepys, *Diary*, II, p. 86.

118 Colvin, Crook, Downe and Necoman, *The History of the King's Works*, V, p. 454.

119 *Crown Jewels*, I, pp. 389–91.

120 Sandford, *History*, p. 8.

121 John, Marquess of Bute, *Scottish Coronations* (Alexander Gardner, 1902), pp. 63–214.

CHAPTER EIGHT

1 CA. Coronations 1820, 1821, Ceremonials & c., Church Services. The most recent account is in Flora Fraser, *The Unruly Queen: The Life of Queen Caroline* (London: Macmillan, 1996), pp. 456–7.

2 For what follows see Linda Colley, 'The Apotheosis of George III: Loyalty, Royalty and the British Nation 1760–1820', *Past and Present*, 102 (1984), pp. 94–124; Simon Schama, 'The Domestication of Majesty: Royal Family Portraiture 1500–1800', *Journal of Interdisciplinary History*, 17 (1986), pp. 155–83; Linda Colley, *Britons: Forging the Nation 1707–1837* (New Haven and London: Yale University Press, 1992); Matthew Charles Kilburn, 'Royalty and Public in Britain 1714–1789', unpublished D.Phil. Thesis, Oxford University, 1997, chaps 1 and 2; Marilyn Morris, *The British Monarchy and the French Revolution* (New Haven and London: Yale University Press, 1998).

3 WAM 51292.

4 William Talbot, Bishop of Oxford, *A Sermon Preach'd at the Coronation of King George* (London: W. Wilkins for John Churchill, 1714).

5 John Potter, Bishop of Oxford, *A Sermon Preach'd at the Coronation of King George II. and Queen Caroline* . . . (London: C. Ackers for R. Knaplick, 1727).

6 G. A. Thewlis, 'Coronation of George I: A Bodleian Song', *Musical Times*, 78 (1937), p. 311.

7 *Diary of Mary Countess Cowper . . . 1714–1720* (London: John Murray, 1864), p. 4.

8 D. G. Barnes, *George III and William Pitt, 1783–1806* (Stanford, Calif.: Stanford University Press, 1939), pp. 377–8.

9 *Ibid.*, p. 343.

10 On this see Barnes, *George III and William Pitt*, pp. 348–51, 377–8, 434; *The Later Correspondence of George III*, ed. A. Aspinall (Cambridge: Cambridge University Press, 1963), II, pp. 317–21; Christopher Hibbert, *George III: A Personal History* (London: Viking, 1999), pp. 216–18 312–13, 345.

11 *Crown Jewels*, I, p. 470.

12 LP 1083.

13 PRO C 195/8, pp. 1–36.

14 J. G. Lockhart, *Memoirs of the Life of Sir Walter Scott*

(Edinburgh: Adam & Charles Black, 1878), II, p. 455.

15 Frank Prochaska, *The Royal Bounty: The Making of a Welfare Monarchy* (New Haven and London: Yale University Press, 1995).

16 John Cannon, 'The Survival of the British Monarchy', *TRHS* 5th series, 36 (1986), pp. 143–64.

17 Morris, *British Monarchy*, pp. 1–12.

18 Roy Strong, *Painting the Past: The Victorian Painter and the British Past* (London: Pimlico, 2004), pp. 11–15.

19 Lockhart, *Memoirs*, II, p. 456.

20 Robert Huish, *An Authentic History of the Coronation of His Majesty King George the Fourth . . .* (London: J. Robins & Co., 1821), p. 105.

21 *Ibid.*, p. 87.

22 Sean Sawyer, 'Sir John Soane's Symbolic Westminster: The Apotheosis of George IV', *Architectural History*, 39 (1996), pp. 54–6.

23 Michael Dobson and Nicola J. Watson, *England's Elizabeth* (Oxford: Oxford University Press, 2002), pp. 116 ff.

24 Huish, *History*, p. 129.

25 *The Entire Ceremonies of the Coronations of His Majesty King Charles II. and of Her Majesty Queen Mary, Consort to James II* (London: W. Owen, 1761); *An Account of the Ceremonies Observed in the Coronations of the Kings and Queens of England* (London, 1760); *A Particular Account of the Solemnities Used at the Coronation of His Sacred Majesty King George II . . .* (London: W. Bristow, 1761).

26 Arthur Taylor, *The Glory of Regality: An Historical Treatise of the Anointing and Crowning of the Kings and Queens of England* (London, 1820); T. C. Banks, *An Historical Account of the Ancient and Modern Forms, Pageantry and Ceremony, of the Coronations of the Kings of England* (London, 1820); T. Mantell, *Coronation Ceremonies and Customs Relative to the Barons of the Cinque Ports . . .* (Dover: G. Ledger, 1820); *The Round Table: The Order and Solemnities of Crowning the King . . .* (London: W. Goodhugh, 1820); *Historical and Descriptive Account of the Ceremonies Performed at the Inauguration of the Kings of England* (London: H. K. S. Causton, 1820). For a study of this development see David J. Sturdy, '"Continuity" versus "Change": Historians and English Coronations of the Medieval and Early Modern Periods', in *Coronations*, ed. Bak, pp. 228 ff.

27 The Revd. Jonas Dennis, *A Key to the Regalia . . .* (London: John Hatchard & Son, 1820).

28 Huish, *History*, p. 11. For the background of this chivalrous revival see Mark Girouard, *The Return to Camelot: Chivalry and the English Gentleman* (New Haven and London: Yale University Press, 1981), pp. 19 ff., 42, 56 ff.

29 See Colley, 'The Apotheosis of George III'.

30 What is written in this part of the chapter draws on the following sources. Where there are quotes I have given a full reference to a particular text for the sake of clarity. For the Works side see H. M. Colvin, J. Mordaunt Crook, Kerry Downes and John Newman, *The History of the King's Works*, V, *1660–1782* (London: HMSO, 1976), p. 454.

GEORGE I
CA, Coronations of William & Mary & George I & II, Anstis, Coronations I; Coronation of James II and William and Mary (includes George I); WAM 51146, 51170, 56760, 56570, 47699, CA 53. *The Form of Proceeding to the Royal Coronation of His Most Excellent Majesty King George . . . on Wednesday the 20th Day of this Instant October, 1714*; William Talbot, Bishop of Oxford, *A Sermon Preached at the Coronation of King George . . .* (London: W. Wilkins for John Churchill, 1714); *Diary of Mary Countess Cowper . . . 1714–1720*, p. 4; *Crown Jewels*, I, pp. 463–72.

GEORGE II
PRO Works 21/13/1; 21/1; CA, Anstis, Coronations I; Coronations of William & Mary and George I & II; Coronation Misc. William III to George III; Coronation of James II and William and Mary (includes George II); WAM 60017 (Clarke collection), 51174–81. 5660–1, 51165, 5117A–C, 51173; LP 1079B; LP 1080, 1081A, 1081B: John Potter, *A Sermon Preach'd at the Coronation of King George II and Queen Caroline . . .* (London: C. Ackers for R. Knaplick, 1727); *The Autobiography . . . of Mrs Delany*, ed. Lady Llanover (London, 1862), I, pp. 136, 137–40; Donald Burrows, 'Handel and the 1727 Coronation', *Musical Times*, 108 (1977), pp. 469–73; *Crown Jewels*, I, pp.472–85.

GEORGE III
LP 1082; 1719, fol. 35–43 (letter of Catherine Talbot); PRO 21/13/8; 21/1; C 195/8; C 195/8/40; CA, Coronation of George III (3 vols.), Coronations Misc: William III to George III; WAM 64624–5, 51240, 51338, 51339, 51395, 51398, 51399, 51402, 5643, 5645, 5647, 5649, 54621, 5655, 5651, 61781, 61782, 51185, 51186, 51187, 51188, 51191, 51193, 51195, 51197, 51198,

51200, 51201, 51204, 51209, 51212, 51221, 51222, 51225, 51235; *The Form of Proceeding to the Royal Coronation of Their Most Excellent Majesties George III. and Queen Charlotte* (London: William Bowyer, 1761); *Orders to be Observed on Tuesday the 22nd of September, Being the Day appointed for their Majesties Coronation . . .* (1761); John Hume, Bishop of Oxford, *A Sermon Preached at the Coronation of King George III. and Queen Charlotte . . .* (Charles Bathurst, 1761); *Thoughts on the Coronation of his Present Majesty King George the Third . . .* (London: F. Noble, 1761); *The Public Ledger*, 28 September 1761; Letter of James Henning in *Annual Register, 1761*, 7th edn (1800), pp. 229–35; *Companion for the Coronation: Being the Order of the Grand Procession . . .* [(n.d.)]; Richard Thompson, *A Faithful Account of the Procession and Ceremonies Observed in the Coronation (George III)* (London, 1821); *The Correspondence of Thomas Gray*, ed. Paget Toynbee and L. Whibley (Oxford: Clarendon, 1935), pp. 752–7; *Horace Walpole's Correspondence*, ed. W. S. Lewis and George L. Cam (Oxford: Oxford University Press, 1960), pp. 534–7; *ibid.*, XXXVIII, Part II (Oxford: Oxford University Press, 1974), pp. 90 note 30, 109, 121–3, 126–7, 133 and note 27; Joseph Taylor, *Relics of Royalty or Remarks, Anecdotes & Conversations of His Late Majesty George the Third . . .* (London, 1820), pp. 104–33; J. Heneage Jesse, *Memoirs of the Life and Reign of King George the Third* (London, 1867), I, pp. 103–11; *The Diaries of a Duchess: Extracts from the Diaries of the First Duchess of Northumberland (1716–1776)*, ed. James Grieg (London: Hodder & Stoughton, 1926), pp. 36–7; W. T. Passingham, *A History of the Coronation* (London: Sampson Low, 1937), pp. 226–42; *Crown Jewels*, I, pp. 485–503.

GEORGE IV
PRO Works 21/13/8; 21/15/1; C 195/8; WAM 51244, 51246, 51247, 51248, 51253, 51256, 51257, 51258, 5259A–N, 51261, 51262, 51264A–C, 51265, 51266B, 51269, 51271, 5284A–B, 51288, 51289, 51292, 51293, 51297, 51299, 51300, 51303, 51308, 56775, 56768, 56770, 51528B, 51439, 66504, 66511, 66512, 66523, 66528, 66537, 66539, 66542, 57063, 51318, 51319–25, 5133, 51385, 51409, 51411, 51412–19, 5140, 51421A–B, 51422, 51423, 51424, 51425–6, 56766; LP 1312 (Coronation Service); CA Coronation 1820, 1821. Ceremonial &c. Church Service; Coronation Banquet 1821; Coronation of George IV (series of vols. III to XVII); Sir George Nayler, *The Coronation of His Most Sacred Majesty King George the Fourth* (London, 1839 edn); Robert Huish, William Cobbett, *History of the Regency and Reign of King George the Fourth* (London, 1830), chap. 8 (no. 456); *The Letters of King George IV 1812–1830*, ed. A. A. Aspinall (Cambridge: Cambridge University Press, 1958), II, pp. 322, 323–4, 329, 442–3, 444–6, 448; *The Croker Papers*, ed. Louis J. Jennings (London: John Murray, 1865), I, pp. 195–7; J. G. Lockhart, *Memoirs of the Life of Sir Walter Scott* (Edinburgh: Adam and Charles Black, 1878), II, pp. 453–6; Emma Sophia, Countess Brownlow, *The Eve of Victorianism: Reminiscences of the Years 1802 to 1834* (London: John Murray, 1940), pp. 116–23; *The Journal of Mrs Arbuthnot 1820–32*, ed. F. Bamford and the Duke of Wellington (London: Macmillan, 1950), I, pp. 106–9; *The Letters of Lady Palmerston*, ed. Tresham Lever (London: John Murray, 1957), pp. 86–8; *The Diary of Benjamin Robert Haydon*, ed W. B. Pope (Cambridge, Mass.: Harvard University Press, 1960), II, pp. 348–51, Legg, *English Coronation Records*, pp. 343–62, *Crown Jewels*, I, pp. 503–27; *London – World City 1800–1840*, ed. Celina Fox, Exhibition catalogue (New Haven and London: Yale University Press, 1992), pp. 254–5 (38), 250–4 (37 a–g) (35), 249–50 (36); Valerie Cumming, 'Pantomine and Pageantry: The Coronation of George IV' in *ibid.*, pp. 39–50; Steven Parissien, *George IV: The Grand Entertainment* (London: John Murray, 2001), pp. 303–15.

WILLIAM IV
CA, Coronation of K. Will. IV and Q. Adelaide (9 volumes); WAM 60017, 51446, 51476A–B, 56779*, 66547, 66553: Coronation 1831; 51462 (ground plan of the annexe); *The Ceremonies to be Observed at the Royal Coronation of Their Most Excellent Majesties King William the Fourth and Queen Adelaide . . .* ([nd.]); *The Form and Order of . . . the Coronation of their Majesties King William IV. and Queen Adelaide . . .* (London: George Eyre & Andrew Strachan, 1831); Charles Blomfield, Bishop of London, *A Sermon Preached at the Coronation of their most Excellent Majesties King William IV. and Queen Adelaide . . .* (London: B. Fellowes 1831); William Maskell, *Monumenta Ritualia Ecclesiae Anglicanae* (London: W. Pickering, 1847), III, p. 108; *The Ladies' Pocket Magazine*, 1831, pp. 11–13; *The Greville Memoirs 1814–1860*, ed. Lytton Strachey and Roger Fulford (London: Macmillan, 1938), II, pp. 100, 166–7, 176, 180–1, 183, 187, 188–9, 194, 196–7; *Correspondence of Mr. Joseph Jekyll*, ed. Algernon Bourke (London: John Murray, 1894), pp. 116, 273, 275; W. Gore Allen, *King William IV* (London: Cresset Press,

1960), pp. 129–33; Philip Ziegler, *King William IV* (London: Collins, 1971), pp. 192–3; *Crown Jewels*, I, pp. 527–40.

VICTORIA

CA, Coronation of Queen Victoria (10 volumes); PRO Works 21/9/12. WAM Coronation 1838 (volume presented by Sir George Smart); Coronation of Queen Victoria (3 volumes); *The Sun*, 7 July 1838; *The Times*, 29 June 1838; *The Mirror*, 32 (901–2); *The Letters of Queen Victoria . . . 1837 and 1861*, ed. A. C. Benson and Viscount Esher (London: John Murray, 1907), I, pp. 145, 153–9; *Harriet Martineau's Autobiography* (London: Smith, Elder & Co., 1877), II, pp. 121–9; Dormer Creston, *The Youthful Queen Victoria* (London: Macmillan, 1952), pp. 325–38; *Crown Jewels*, I, pp. 541–53.

31 *Correspondence of Mr. Joseph Jekyll*, p. 275.

32 For this I draw on GEC *Complete Peerage*, II, Appendix D.

33 PRO C 1958/8/41.

34 John, Lord Hervey, *Some Materials towards Memoirs of the Reign of King George II*, ed. Romney Sedgwick (London, 1931), p. 66.

35 See note 30 s.v. George II.

36 *The Form and Order of . . . the Coronation of their Majesties King William IV. and Queen Adelaide . . .*, pp. 42–3.

37 Legg, *Coronation Records*, pp. 363–82.

38 *A Formulary of that Part of the Solemnity which is performed in the Collegiate Church of St Peter Westminster at the Coronation of his Majesty King George 20th October 1714*.

39 *Crown Jewels*, I, p. 553.

40 Oliver Millar, *The Later Georgian Pictures in the Collection of Her Majesty the Queen* (London: Phaidon, 1969), I, pp. 93–5.

41 WAM 51153.

42 PRO Works 21/1.

43 WAM 60017 (Clarke Collection).

44 *Ibid.*

45 WAM 51297.

46 CA, Coronation of George III 1761, fol. 184v.

47 Huish, *History*, p. 214.

48 PRO Works 21/1.

49 Huish, *History*, p. 105.

50 *Annual Register, 1761*, 7th edn (1800), pp. 229–35.

51 Huish, *History*, p. 100.

52 WAM 51154.

53 WAM 64625.

54 WAM 513300.

55 CA, Coronations, Misc. William III to George II, item 39.

56 A design for one of the costumes is in CA, Coronation of George IV, 15, fol 18.

57 *Annual Register, 1821*, pp. 348, 352.

58 Lockhart, *Memoirs*, II, p. 455.

59 *The Diary of Benjamin Robert Haydon*, ed. W. B. Pope (Cambridge, Mass.: Harvard University Press, 1960), II, pp. 348–50.

60 Hervey, *Some Materials*, i, p. 66.

61 CA, Coronations Misc. William III to George III, item 5.

62 *Correspondence of Thomas Gray*, p. 755.

63 *Annual Register, 1761*,

64 PRO Works 21/13/1.

65 *The Letters and Works of Lady Mary Wortley Montagu . . .* I, p. 393.

66 *Correspondence of Thomas Gray*, II, p. 753.

67 *Horace Walpole's Correspondence . . .*, XXX VIII, Part II, pp. 126–7.

68 Cutting in CA, Coronation of George III 1761 I, p. 185.

69 Greville, *Memoirs*, II, Part I, p. 109.

70 *The Letters of Queen Victoria . . . 1837 to 1861*, I, p. 154.

71 LP 1079B.

72 LP 1081B; William Hawkins, *The Ceremonial of the Coronation of King George II. And of His Royal Consort Queen Caroline . . .* (Dublin, 1727).

73 LP 1719, fols. 35–43.

74 *Annual Register, 1761*.

75 *Horace Walpole's Correspondence*, V, pp. 534–7.

76 Quoted in Allen, *King William IV*, p. 131.

77 *The Letters of Queen Victoria*, I, p. 156.

78 *The Letters of Lady Palmerston*, pp. 86–7.

79 *The Journal of Mrs Arbuthnot 1820–32*, I, p. 108.

80 J. S. Shedlock, 'Coronation Music', *Proceedings of the Royal Musical Association*, 28th series (1901–2), pp. 141–60; Donald Burrows, 'Handel and the 1727 Coronation', *Musical Times*, pp. 469–73.

81 WAM 51438.

82 CA, Coronation Banquet 1821.

83 *Correspondence of Thomas Gray*, II, p. 755.

84 Lockhart, *Memoirs*, II, p. 455.

85 Haydon, *Diary*, II, p. 350.

86 *Annual Register, 1761*.

87 Huish, *History*, p. 2.

88 Paul Kleber Monod, *Jacobitism and the English People 1688–1788* (Cambridge: Cambridge University Press, 1982), pp. 173–4.

89 CA, Coronation 1820, 1821. Ceremonial, & c. Church Service.

90 For this development see Colley, *Britons*, p. 222; Prochaska, *Royal Bounty*, pp. 76–7.

91 Walpole, *Correspondence*, XXXVIII, p. 133.

92 Newspaper cutting in CA.

93 Walpole, *Correspondence*, pp. 534–7.

94 Palmerston, *Letters*, pp. 87–88.

95 Greville, *Memoirs*, II, p. 167; *Gentleman's Magazine*, 1 September 1831.

96 *Hansard*, 43 (1838), p. 350; see also Ian Anstruther, *The Knight and the Umbrella* (London: Geoffrey Bles, 1963), chap. I; Girouard, *Return to Camelot*, pp. 88 ff.

97 *Harriet Martineau's Autobiography*, II, pp. 123, 127–8.

CHAPTER NINE

1 G. Lockhart, *Cosmo Gordon Lang* (London: Hodder & Stoughton, 1949), p. 408.

2 See note 63 for the sources. In the main CA, Coronation of King George VI and Queen Elizabeth 12 May 1937, 12, Intended Coronation of Edward VIII.

3 This section owes much to John Cannon, 'The Survival of the British Monarchy', *TRHS*, 5th series, 36 (1986), pp. 143–64; Frank Prochaska, *Royal Bounty: The Making of a Welfare Monarchy* (New Haven and London: Yale University Press, 1991), pp. 16 ff. and the same author's *The Republic of Britain, 1760–2000* (London: Allen Lane, 2000).

4 For which see the important article by David Cannadine, 'The Context, Performance and Meaning of Ritual: The British Monarchy and the "Invention of Tradition", c. 1820–1977', in *The Invention of Tradition*, ed. Eric Hobsbawm and Terence Ranger (Cambridge: Cambridge University Press, 1983), pp. 101–64.

5 Quoted Prochaska, *Royal Bounty*, p. 147.

6 CA, Coronation of Their Majesties King Edward VII and Queen Alexandra 1902, 15, Executive Committee Minutes 20 October, 12 November 1901 and 1 May 1902.

7 *Ibid.*, 4, Privy Council.

8 CA, Coronation of George V and Queen Mary 1911, 8, Executive Committee Minutes 31 October and 21 November 1910.

9 CA, Coronation of Elizabeth II, 2, Minutes of Coronation Committee 16 February 1953; Minutes of the Subcommittee, 20 February 1953.

10 See Philip Magnus, *King Edward the Seventh* (London: John Murray, 1964), pp. 29–93. See also Sir Almeric FitzRoy, *Memoirs* (London: Hutchinson & Co., 1926), I, pp. 55–6.

11 G. K. A. Randall, *Randall Davidson, Archbishop of Canterbury* (Oxford: Oxford University Press, 1935), I, pp. 612–17.

12 John W. Wheeler-Bennett, *King George VI: His Life and Reign* (London: Macmillan & Sons, 1958), p. 308 note a.

13 James Pope-Hennessy, *Queen Mary* (London: Unwin paperbacks, 1987), p. 435.

14 *Ibid.*, p. 439.

15 Quoted Kenneth Rose, *George V* (London: Macmillan, 1983), p. 103.

16 Wheeler-Bennett, *King George VI*, pp. 310, 312.

17 Geoffrey Fisher, *For the Queen: A Little Book of Private Devotions in Preparation for Her Majesty's Coronation* (n.d.). Copies are in Lambeth Palace Library.

18 CA, Coronation . . . 1902, 15, Minutes of the Executive Committee 1 May.

19 *The Sphere*, 16th, Augst 1902.

20 FitzRoy, *Memoirs*, I, p. 105.

21 Jeffrey Richards, 'The Coronation of Queen Elizabeth II and Film', *Court Historian*, 9 (2004), pp. 69–70.

22 LP, Davidson Papers, 280, fols. 206–7.

23 *Ibid.*, fol. 315.

24 CA, Coronation of . . . 1911, 8, Executive Committee Minutes 2 March, 11 April.

25 CA, Intended Coronation of Edward VIII, item 186.

26 *Ibid.*,

27 LP. Fisher Papers, 123, fol. 4.

28 Humphrey Jennings and Charles Madge, *May the Twelfth: Mass-observation Day Surveys 1937 . . .* (London: Faber & Faber, 1937), p. 14.

29 David Newcome, *An Edwardian Excursion: From the Diaries of A. C. Benson 1898–1904* (London: John Murray, 1981), pp. 64–75.

30 CA, Intended Coronation of Edward VIII, item 186.

31 LP, Fisher Papers, 123, fol. 6; William Purcell, *Fisher of Lambeth: A Portrait from Life* (London: Hodder & Stoughton, 1969), p. 238.

32 CA, Coronation of Elizabeth II, 9, pp. 8–9.

33 Ben Pimlott, *The Queen: A Biography of Elizabeth II* (London: HarperCollins, 1996), pp. 205–7.

34 Richards, 'The Coronation of Elizabeth II', pp. 72–4; James Chapman, 'Cinema, Monarchy and the Making of Heritage: A Queen is Crowned (1953)', in *British Historical Cinema*, ed. Claire Monk and

Amy Sargeant (London, 2002), pp. 82–91.

35 Denis Judd, 'Queen Victoria's Diamond Jubilee, 1897', in Denis Judd, *Empire: The British Imperial Experience from 1765 to the Present* (London: HarperCollins, 1996), pp. 130–53.

36 P. J. Marshall, 'Imperial Britain', in *The Cambridge Illustrated History of the British Empire*, ed. P. J. Marshall (Cambridge: Cambridge University Press, 1996), pp. 318–27; Denis Judd, 'The Imperial Conference of 1911', in Judd, *Empire*, pp. 214–25.

37 G. Dennis, *Coronation Commentary* (London: William Heinemann, 1937), p. 306.

38 Edward C. Ratcliff, *The Coronation Service of Her Majesty Queen Elizabeth II . . .* (London: SPCK and Cambridge: Cambridge University Press, 1953), p. 18.

39 FitzRoy, *Memoirs*, I, p. 43.

40 *Journals and Letters of Reginald, Viscount Esher*, I, *1870–1903*, ed. Maurice V. Brett (London: Nicholson and Watson, 1934–8), p. 337.

41 J. E. C. Bodley, *The Coronation of Edward the Seventh: A Chapter of European and Imperial History* (London: Methuen & Co., 1903), p. 223.

42 FitzRoy, *Memoirs*, I, p. 94.

43 Bodley, *Coronation*, p. 4.

44 *Ibid.*, p. 201.

45 CA, Coronation of . . . 1902, 15, Executive Committee Minutes 30 July 1901.

46 Ibid., 6, fol. 43.

47 CA, Intended Coronation of Edward VIII, item 58.

48 *Ibid.*, item 59.

49 Wheeler-Bennett, *King George VI*, p. 307.

50 CA, Coronation of Elizabeth II, 9, Minutes of the Joint Committee, 20 October 1952; Edward Carpenter, *Archbishop Fisher: His Life and Times* (Norwich: Canterbury Press, 1991), pp. 249–51.

51 J. Grigg, 'The Queen's Opportunity', *National and English Review*, 139 (834) (August 1952), p. 83.

52 CA, Coronation of Elizabeth II, 9, Minutes of the Joint Coronation Committee 20 October 1952.

53 CA, Coronation of . . . 1902, 1, fol. 34 'Copy of Notes by Sir Francis Knollys of the Meeting of the Subcommittee at Marlborough House 26th Day March 1902' in which the programme is listed. See also CA, Coronation of . . . 1911, 8, where the 1902 programme precedes the 1911 one after the Minutes of the Executive Committee 12 January 1911.

54 Pope-Hennessy, *Queen Mary*, p. 237.

55 CA, Coronation of . . . 1937, 13, p. 41.

56 For what follows see Simon Bradley and Nikolaus Pevsner, *The Buildings of England, London, VI,*

Westminster (Becches: The Penguin Collectors Society for the Buildings Boons Trust, 2001), pp. 73 ff. and under the relevant streets and buildings.

57 FitzRoy, *Memoirs*, I, p. 65.

58 *Ibid.*, I, p. 79.

59 *Ibid.*, I, p. 96.

60 CA, Coronation of . . . 1902, 15, Minutes of the Executive Committee 19 March 1902.

61 W. J. Loftie, *The Coronation Book of Edward VII* (London: Cassell & Co., [n.d.]), pp. 117–28, 144–59.

62 *Forms of Prayer with Thanksgiving to Almighty God . . . for General Use on Thursday, the 22nd Day of June, 1911 . . .* (London: Novello & Co. and Eyre & Spottiswoode [1911]).

63 For no other period is there so much archival and printed material. I would not claim, therefore, that what is cited below is in any sense exhaustive. Also many of the archives duplicate each other with the same sets of minutes. In the case of the Works Accounts I have worked through the majority of them as listed in *Crown Jewels*, II, pp. 535–6. If the study of twentieth-century coronations suffers from anything it suffers from a superfluity of material.

EDWARD VII

SOURCES: CA, Coronation of Their Majesties King Edward VII and Queen Alexandra 1902, 21 vols.; H. Farnham Burke, *The Historical Record of the Coronation of Their Most Excellent Majesties King Edward VII. and Queen Alexandra Solemnised in the Abbey Church of Westminster on Saturday the Ninth Day of August in the Year of Our Lord 1902* (London: privately printed, Harrison & Sons, 1905); *The Ceremonies Observed at the Royal Coronation of Their Most Excellent Majesties King Edward the Seventh and Queen Alexandra in the Abbey Church of Westminster on Saturday, the 9th day of August MDCCCCII; The Form and Order of . . . The Coronation of Their Majesties King Edward VII and Queen Alexandra . . . on the 26th Day of June 1902* (Cambridge: Cambridge University Press, [1902]) (several versions of this, including one with the music); G. Woods Wollaston, *Coronation of Edward VII: The Court of Claims* (London: Harrison & Sons, 1903); W. J. Loftie, *The Coronation Book of Edward VII* (London: Cassell & Co., [1902]).

SECONDARY: Newcome, *Edwardian Excursion: From the Diaries of A. C. Benson 1898–1904*, pp. 64–75;

G. K. A. Bell, *Randall Davidson, Archbishop of Canterbury* (Oxford: Oxford University Press, 1935), I, pp. 367–72; Peter Hinchliff, 'Frederick Temple, Randall Davidson and the Coronation of Edward VII', *Journal of Ecclesiastical History*, 48(1) (1997), pp. 71–99; *Crown Jewels*, I, pp. 553–71; Peter Evans, *Lord Esher: A Political Biography* (London: Hart-Davis, MacGibbon, 1973), pp. 81–3.

GEORGE V
SOURCES: CA, Coronation of George V and Queen Mary 1911, 4 vols.; LP, Davidson Papers, 280; WAM 58490–58521; WAM 58300–58489 (J. Armitage Robinson Papers); H. Farnham Burke, *The Historical Record of the Coronation of Their Majesties King George the Fifth and Queen Mary, 1911* (London: McCorquodale & Co. [1911]); *The Ceremonies to be Observed at the Royal Coronation of Their Majesties King George the Fifth and Queen Mary . . . 22nd June MDCCCCXI*; *The Form and Order . . . of the Coronation of Their Majesties King George V and Queen Mary* (London: Eyre & Spottiswoode, 1911).
SECONDARY: Kenneth Rose, *George V*, pp. 102–5; Pope-Hennessy, *Queen Mary*, pp. 421 ff.; *Crown Jewels*, I, pp. 571–85; Lockhart, *Cosmo Gordon Lang*, p. 240.

EDWARD VIII
CA, Intended Coronation of Edward VIII (vol XII of 1937 coronation).

GEORGE VI
SOURCES: CA, Coronation of George VI and Queen Elizabeth May 12 1937, twelve vols.; WAM 586559 (account by Howard M. Nixon); *The Form and Order . . . of the Coronation of Their Majesties King George VI and Queen Elizabeth*, official souvenir programme (1937); Ben Pimlott, *The Queen: A Biography of Queen Elizabeth II*, pp. 45–6 (the present queen's account of her father's coronation); *The Preparation of Westminster Abbey for the Royal Coronation of Their Most Excellent Majesties King George VI and Queen Elizabeth* (London: John Mowlem & Co., 1937); *Crown and Empire: The Coronation of King George VI May 12, 1937* (London: The Times Publishing Co. 1937); Gordon Beckles, *Coronation Souvenir Book 1937* (London: Daily Express Publications, 1937); *Chips: The Diaries of Sir Henry Channon*, ed. Robert Rhodes James (London: Weidenfeld & Nicolson, 1967), pp. 123–6.
SECONDARY: Wheeler-Bennett, *King George VI*, pp. 293–314; Lockhart, *Cosmo Gordon Lang*,

pp. 408–23; Jennings and Madge, *May the Twelfth. Mass-Observation Day-Surveys 1937 . . .*; Sarah Bradford, *George VI* (London: Fontana, 1991), pp. 270–85; Pope-Hennessy, *Queen Mary*, pp. 583 ff.

ELIZABETH II
SOURCES: CA, Coronation of Elizabeth II (10 vols; WAM 63189 (account by the dean, Dr Alan Don), 63364 (account of the anointing oil by Jocelyn Perkins), 63476 (volume of ceremonial detail); also in WAM a volume with plans and elevations of what was erected by the Ministry of Works; LP, Fisher Papers, 123; LP, Miscellaneous Papers of Claude Jenkins 1901–52; Ratcliff, *The Coronation Service of Queen Elizabeth II . . .*; *The Form and Order of . . . the Coronation of Her Majesty Queen Elizabeth II . . .* (London: Eyre & Spottiswoode, 1953); G. F. Fisher, *I Here Present Unto You . . . Addresses interpreting the Coronation of Her Majesty Queen Elizabeth II* (London: SPCK, 1953); *The Coronation of Her Majesty Queen Elizabeth II 2nd June 1953 and Celebrations in Connection Therewith . . .* (record by the Ministry of Works); James Laver, *The Place of Crowning, its History, Arrangement, and Preparation for the Coronation of Her Majesty Queen Elizabeth II* (London: John Mowlem & Co., 1953); *The Music and Musicians at the Coronation Service of Her Majesty Queen Elizabeth II in Westminster Abbey, Tuesday, June 2, 1953*; *Chips*, pp. 475–77; Cecil Beaton, *The Strenuous Years: Diaries 1948–55* (London: Weidenfeld & Nicolson, 1973), pp. 136–41.
SECONDARY: *Crown Jewels*, I, pp. 605–23; Philip Ziegler, *Crown and People* (London: Collins, 1978), pp. 97–126; William Purcell, *Fisher of Lambeth, A Portrait from Life* (London, 1969), pp. 238–42; Carpenter, *Archbishop Fisher*, pp. 245–67; Anthony Taylor, *'Down with the Crown': British Anti-monarchism and Debates about Royalty since 1790* (London: Reacktion Books, 1999), pp. 225 ff.; Elizabeth Longford, *Elizabeth R.* (London: Weidenfeld & Nicolson, 1983), pp. 157–64; Sarah Bradford, *Elizabeth: A Biography of Her Majesty the Queen* (London: Heinemann, 1996), chap. 7.

64 Rose, *George V*, p. 73.
65 For biographies of both see *New Oxford DNB*.
66 Pictures are in the *Illustrated London News*, 14 and 16 August 1902.
67 *The Coronation of Her Majesty Queen Elizabeth II . . .*, para. 13.

68 Carpenter *A House of Kings*, chaps. 17–19.
69 FitzRoy, *Memoirs*, I, p. 62.
70 *Ibid.*, I, p. 86.
71 CA, Coronation of . . . 1902, Minutes of the Executive Committee 16 July 1901.
72 *Ibid.*, Miscellaneous and Index, p. 81.
73 Laver, *The Place of Crowning* . . .
74 Photographs of the interior of the abbey in 1911 are reproduced in Jocelyn Perkins, *The Crowning of the Sovereign of Great Britain and the Dominions Overseas* (London: Methuen & Co., 1937).
75 CA, Coronation of . . . 1902 (6 Costume).
76 *Westminster Gazette*, 30 April 1902.
77 Laurence Tanner, 'Abbey Coronation Vestments', *Guardian*, 14 May 1937.
78 Hinchliff, 'Frederick Temple . . .', pp. 89, 96.
79 J. S. Shedlock, 'Coronation Music', *Proceedings of the Royal Musical Association*, 28th series (1901–2), pp. 148–60; see also 'Notes on the Coronation Music 2nd', *Musical Times*, 6 (1902), pp. 387–8.
80 Preface to *The Form and Order . . . with music.*
81 The best discussion of what happened in the twentieth century is in Paul Bradshaw, 'Coronations: The Eighteenth to the Twentieth Century', in *Coronations Past and Present*, ed. Paul Bradshaw (Cambridge: Grove Books, 1997), pp. 22–31.
82 The most comprehensive treatment of what follows is D. J. Sturdy, '"Continuity" vesus "Change": Historians and English Coronations of the Medieval and Early Modern Periods', in *Coronations*, ed. Bak, pp. 228–45.
83 *Three Coronation Orders*, ed. J. Wickham Legg (HBS, 1900), p. viii.
84 For the Leggs see the *New Oxford DNB.*
85 Herbert Henry Charles Thurston, S.J., *The Coronation Ceremonial: Its True History and Meaning* (London: Catholic Truth Society, 1902).
86 For an account of this see Hinchliff, 'Frederick Temple . . .'
87 FitzRoy, *Memoirs*, I, p. 52.
88 Pope-Hennessy, *Queen Mary*, pp. 584–5.
89 LP, Fisher Papers, 123, fol. 4.
90 For Esher see James Lees-Milne *The Enigmatic Edwardian: The Life of Reginald, 2nd Viscount Esher* (London: Sidgwick & Jackson, 1986); Fraser, *Lord Esher. A Political Biography.*
91 Esher, *Letters and Journals*, I, p. 333.
92 Quoted in Lees-Milne, *The Enigmatic Edwardian*, p. 133.
93 Esher, *Journals and Letters*, I, pp. 322, 325, 341, 343.
94 Wollaston, *Coronation of Edward VII.*
95 Sir Wollaston Knocker, *The Coronation of their Majesties King Edward VII and Queen Alexandra. The Report of the Proceedings of the Barons of the Cinque Ports* . . . (Dover: Richard Times, 1902).
96 CA, Coronation of . . . 1902, 16; FitzRoy, *Memoirs*, I, p. 81.
97 CA, Coronation of . . . 1902, 2, fol. 6.
98 FitzRoy, *Memoirs*, I, p. 54.
99 T. F. Taylor, *J. Armitage Robinson* (Cambridge: James Clarke & Co., 1991), pp. 49–51.
100 Hinchliff, 'Frederick Temple . . .', pp. 85, 93.
101 WAM 58370.
102 L. G. Wickham Legg, 'On the Right of the Archbishop of York to Crown the Queen Consort', *Transactions of St Paul's Ecclesiological Society*, 5 (1902), pp. 77–84.
103 LP, Davidson Papers, 280, fol. 11, letter of Arthur Bigge to Davidson 15 October 1910.
104 Hinchliff, 'Frederick Temple . . .', p. 77.
105 *The Coronation Order of King James I*, ed. J. Wickham Legg (London: F. E. Robinson, 1902), pp. xlvi–xlvii, liii note 1.
106 For Claude Jenkins see *New Oxford DNB.*
107 LP, Miscellaneous Papers of Claude Jenkins, fols. 61–6.
108 LP, Davidson Papers, 280, fols. 47–52, 107.
109 *Ibid.*, fols. 250–2.
110 FitzRoy, *Memoirs*, II, p. 443.
111 *Ibid.*, II, p. 450.
112 Lockhart, *Cosmo Gordon Lang*, pp. 408–22.
113 Cyril Garbett, *The Claims of the Church of England* (London: Hodder & Stoughton, 1947), pp. 189–90.
114 Fisher, *I Here Present Unto You* . . . .
115 LP, Fisher Papers, 123, fol. 6.
116 *Ibid.*, Minute of 10 February 1953.
117 LP, Miscellaneous Papers of Claude Jenkins, fols. 61–6.
118 Edward Shils and Michael Young, 'The Meaning of the Coronation', in Edward Shils, *Center and Periphery: Essays in Macrosociology* (Chicago: University of Chicago Press, 1975), pp. 135–52; and a denunciation of this by N. Birnhaum, 'Monarchs and Sociologists: A Reply to Professor Shils and Mr Young', *Sociological Review*, 3 (1953), pp. 5–23.
119 Beaton, *The Strenuous Years*, p. 141.
120 *Chips*, p. 477.
121 Esher, *Journals and Letters*, I, p. 330.
122 FitzRoy, *Memoirs*, I, p. 98.

123 Ibid., I, pp. 99–100.
124 WAM 58429.
125 Lockhart, *Cosmo Gordon Lang*, p. 240.
126 LP, Davidson Papers, 280, fol. 353.
127 Wheeler-Bennett, *King George VI*, p. 313.
128 WAM 63189.
129 *Ibid.*

EPILOGUE

1 LP, Lang Papers, 189, fol. 264, Letter of 10 December 1910.

2 For which see, for example, Frank Prochaska, *The Republic of Britain 1760 to 2000* (London: Allen Lane, 2000), pp. 205 ff.
3 The only consideration of this so far is Colin Buchanan, 'The Next Coronation', in *Coronations Past and Present*, ed. Paul Bradshaw (Cambridge: Grove Books, 1997), pp. 34–44.
4 E. C. Ratcliff, *The Coronation Service of Her Majesty Queen Elizabeth II* (London: SPCK and Cambridge: Cambridge University Press, 1953), p. 23.

BIBLIOGRAPHY

ABBREVIATIONS

BIHR – *Bulletin of the Institute of Historical Research*
BL – British Library
CA – College of Arms
Coronations ed. Bak – Janos Bak, ed., *Coronations: Medieval and Early Modern Monarchic Ritual*
Crown Jewels – Claude Blair, *The Crown Jewels: The History of the Coronation Regalia in the Jewel House of the Tower of London*
CS – Camden Society
CSP – *Calendar of State Papers*
EHR – *English Historical Review*
English Coronation Records – J. Wickham Legg, *English Coronation Records*
HBS – Henry Bradshaw Society
LP – Lambeth Palace Library
O' Meara, *Monarchy and Consent* – Carra Ferguson O'Meara, *Monarchy and Consent: The Coronation Book of Charles V of France*
PRO – Public Record Office
RS – Rolls Series
Schramn, *English Coronation* – Percy Ernst Schramm, *The English Coronation, A History of*
SP – State Papers
TRHS – *Transactions of the Royal Historical Society*
VCH – *Victoria County History*
WAM – Westminster Abbey Muniments

MANUSCRIPT SOURCES

The following archives have been consulted and I indicate here the repositories I have used. The details of each manuscript source are given in the footnotes.

British Library
College of Arms
Lambeth Palace Library
Public Record Office
  State Papers
St John's College, Cambridge
Westminster Abbey Muniments

PRINTED SOURCES

An Account of the Ceremonial at the Coronation of Their Most Excellent Majesties King William and Queen Mary. The Eleventh Day of this Instant April, 1689 (London, 1689)

An Account of the Ceremonies Observed at the Coronation of Our Most Gracious Sovereign George III and his Royal Consort Queen Charlotte . . . (London: G. Kearsly, [1761])

Acts of the Privy Council, ed. J. R. Dasent (London: Stationery Office, 1890–)

Adam of Usk, *Chronicon Adae de Usk, A.D. 1377–1421*, ed. and trans. E. M. Thompson (London: Henry Frowde, 1904)

The Anglo-Saxon Chronicle, ed. Dorothy Whitelock (London: Eyre and Spottiswoode, 1965)

Annales Paulini in Chronicles of the Reigns of Edward I and Edward II, ed. W. Stubbs (RS, 1882), I, pp. 253–370

Annual Register, 1761, 7th edn (1800), pp. 229–35

The Anonimalle Chronicle 1333 to 1381, ed. V. H. Galbraith (Manchester: Manchester University Press, 1927)

Anstis, John, *Observations Introductory to an Historical Essay, upon the Knighthood of the Bath* (London, 1725)

Arber, E., *An English Garner* (London: Constable & Co., 1845)

Arbuthnot, Mrs, *The Journal of Mrs Arbuthnot 1820–32*, ed. F. Bamford and the Duke of Wellington (London: Macmillan, 1950)

Banks, T. C., *An Historical and Critical Enquiry into the Nature of the Kingly Office . . .* (London: Sherwood, Neely and Jones, 1814)

Bilson, Thomas, *A Sermon Preached at Westminster before the King and Queenes Maiesties, at their Coronations on Saint James his Day, Being the 28 of July 1603* (London, 1603)

Blomfield, Charles James, Bishop of London, *A Sermon Preached at the Coronation of Her Most*

Excellent Majesty Queen Victoria . . . (London: B. Fellowes, 1838)

——, *A Sermon Preached at the Coronation of Their Most Excellent Majesties King William IV and Queen Adelaide . . .* (London: B. Fellowes, 1831)

Brewer, J. S., *Letters and Papers, Foreign and Domestic of the Reign of Henry VIII* (London: HMSO, 1920)

Burnet, Gilbert, *A Sermon Preached at the Coronation of William III and Mary II . . .* (London, 1689)

Calendar of State Papers, Domestic

Calendar of State Papers, Spanish

Calendar of State Papers, Venetian

The Carmen de Hastingae Proelio of Guy of Amiens, ed. C. Morton and Hope Muntz (Oxford: Clarendon, 1972)

The Ceremonial of the Coronation of His Most Sacred Majesty King George II. And of His Royal Consort Queen Caroline . . . (Dublin, 1727)

The Ceremonies, Form of Prayer, and Services used in Westminster-Abbey at the Coronation of King James the First and Queen Ann his Consort (London, 1685)

The Ceremonies to be Observed at a service to be held . . . (London: Harrison & Co., 1911)

The Ceremonies to be Observed at the Royal Coronation of Their Most Excellent Majesties King George the Fourth and Queen Adelaide . . . ([n.d.])

Chamberlain, John, *The Letters of John Chamberlain*, ed. N. E. McClure (Philadelphia: American Philosophical Society, 1939)

Chronica Monasterii S. Albani, ed. H. T. Riley (RS, 1866)

The Chronicle of Queen Jane . . ., ed. J. G. Nichols (CS, LXVIII, 1851)

Chronicles and Memorials of the Reign of Richard I, ed. W. Stubbs (RS, 1864)

Chronicles of the Reigns of Stephen, Henry II and Richard I, ed. R. Howlett (RS, 1889)

The Claudius Pontifical, ed. D. H. Turner (HBS, XCIII, 1971 (for 1964)

Cobbett, William, *History of the Regency and Reign of King George the Fourth* (London, 1830)

A Complete Account of the Ceremonies observed in the Coronations of the Kings and Queens of England . . ., 3rd edn ([London], 1727)

The Coronation of Her Majesty Queen Elizabeth II, Approved souvenir programme ([1953])

The Coronation of Richard III: The Extant Documents, ed. Anne F. Sutton and P. W. Hammond

(Gloucester: Alan Sutton and New York: St Martin's Press, 1983)

The Coronation of Their Majesties King George VI and Queen Elizabeth: Official Souvenir Programme ([1937])

The Country Life Picture Book of the Coronation (London: Country Life, 1953)

Dekker, Thomas, *The Dramatic Works of Thomas Dekker*, ed. Fredson Bowers (Cambridge: Cambridge University Press, 1964)

Delany, Mrs, *The Autobiography . . . of Mrs Delany*, ed. Lady Llanover (London, 1862)

Dennis, Revd Jonas, *A Key to the Regalia . . .* (London: John Hatchard & Son, 1820)

Dillon, Harold Arthur, Viscount, 'On an MS. Collection of Ordinances of Chivalry of the Fifteenth Century' (contains a version of the *Forma et Modus*), *Archaeologia*, 57 (1900), pp. 47–55

Drayton, Michael, *A Paean Triumphall . . .* (1604). Reprinted in John Nichols, *The Progresses, Processions and Magnificent Festivities of King James the First* (London, 1828), I, pp. 402–7

Drummond, Robert, Bishop of Salisbury, *A Sermon Preached at the Coronation of King George III. and Queen Charlotte . . .* (London: Charles Bathurst, 1761)

Dugdale, Gilbert, *The Time Triumphant . . .* (1604). Reprinted in Nichols, *Progresses*, I, pp. 408–19.

Eachard, Lawrence, *The History of England* (London, 1718)

Edward VI, *The Literary Remains of King Edward the Sixth*, ed. J. G. Nichols (reprinted New York: Burt Franklin, 1964)

Ellis, Henry, 'Copy of a Letter from Archbishop Cranmer . . .', *Archaeologia*, 18 (1817), pp. 77–82

——, *Original Letters, Illustrative of English History . . .* (London, 1825)

Encomium Emmae Reginae, ed. Alastair Campbell (CS, 3rd series, LXXXII, 1949)

The Entire Ceremonies of the Coronations of His Majesty King Charles II. and of Her Majesty Queen Mary, Consort to James II (London: W. Owen, 1761)

Esher, Viscount, *Journals and Letters of Reginald, Viscount Esher, I, 1870–1903*, ed. Maurice V. Brett (London: Nicholson and Watson, 1934–8)

Evelyn, John, *The Diary of John Evelyn*, ed. E. S. de Beer (Oxford: Clarendon, 1951)

——, *A Panegyric to Charles II*, ed. Geoffrey Keynes (Augustan Reprint Society, XXVIII, 1951)

Fabyan, Robert, *The New Chronicles of England and France*, ed. Henry Ellis (London: 1811)

Fiennes, Celia, *The Journeys of Celia Fiennes*, ed. Christopher Morris (London: Cresset Press, 1947)

The Form and Order of . . . the Coronation of Her Majesty Queen Elizabeth II . . . (Oxford: Oxford University Press, [1953])

The Form and Order of . . . the Coronation of Their Majesties King Edward VII. and Queen Alexandra . . . (London: Novello & Co., 1902)

The Form and Order . . . of the Coronation of Their Majesties King George V and Queen Mary . . . ([1911])

The Form and Order of the Coronation of Their Majesties King George VI and Queen Elizabeth (Oxford: Oxford University Press, 1937)

The Form and Order of . . . the Coronation of their Majesties King George VI and Queen Elizabeth . . . (with the music) (London: Novello & Co., 1937)

The Form and Order of the Service that Is to be Performed . . . in the Coronation of Their Majesties, King George II. and Queen Caroline . . . (London, 1727)

The Form and Order of . . . the Coronation of their Majesties King William IV. and Queen Adelaide . . . (London: George Eyre and Andrew Strachan, 1831)

The Form of the Proceeding to the Royal Coronation of Her Most Excellent Majesty Queen Anne, The Twenty-Third Day of this Instant April, 1702

The Form of Proceeding to the Royal Coronation of His Most Excellent Majesty King George [I] . . . on Wednesday the 20th Day of this Instant October, 1714

The Form of the Proceeding to the Royal Coronation of Their Most Excellent Majesties King George III. and Queen Charlotte . . . On Tuesday the 22d Day of September 1761 (London: William Bowyer, 1761)

The Form of Proceeding of the Royal Coronation of Their Majesties King George II. and Queen Caroline . . . (London, 1727)

The Forms of Prayer with Thanksgiving to Almighty God . . . for General Use on Thursday, the 22nd Day of June, 1911 . . . (London: Novello & Co. and Eyre & Spottiswoode, [1911])

Froissart, Jean, *The Chronicle of Froissart*, trans. Sir

John Bourchier, Lord Berners (London: David Nutt, 1903)

Fuller, Thomas, *The Church History of Britain*, ed. J. S. Brewer (Oxford, 1845)

Grafton's Chronicle . . . (London, 1809)

Gray, Thomas, *The Correspondence of Thomas Gray*, ed. Paget Toynbee and L. Whibley (Oxford: Clarendon, 1935)

——, *The Letters of Thomas Gray*, ed. Duncan C. Tovey (London: G. F. Bell & Sons, 1913)

Gregory, William, *William Gregory's Chronicle of London* in *The Historical Collections of a London Citizen*, ed. James Gairdner (CS, 1876)

Greville, C., *The Greville Memoirs 1814–1860*, ed. Lytton Strachey and Roger Fulford (London: Macmillan, 1938)

Grey, Architell, *Debates of the House of Commons, from the Year 1667 to the Year 1694* (London, 1769)

Guaras, Antonio de, *The Accession of Queen Mary* (London: Lawrence and Bullen, 1892)

Hall's Chronicle . . . (London, 1809)

Hawes, Stephen, *The Minor Poems*, ed. Florence W. Gluck and Alice B. Morgan (Early English Text Society, 1974)

Heaton-Armstrong, Sir John (Chester Herald), *The Coronation of Her Majesty Queen Elizabeth II in Westminster Abbey on 2nd June 1953*

Materials for the Reign of Henry VII, ed. W. Campbell (RS, 1873–7)

Cherbury, Lord Herbert of, *The Life of Edward Lord Herbert of Cherbury Written by Himself* (London, 1791)

Hervey, John, Lord, *Some Materials Towards Memoirs of the Reign of King George II*, ed. Romney Sedgwick (London, 1931)

Heylyn, Peter, *Aerius Redivivus: or The History of the Presbyterians* (London, 1670), Historical Manuscripts Commission, Hatfield

Historical and Descriptive Account of the Ceremonies Performed at the Inauguration of the Kings of England (London: H. K. S. Causton, 1820)

Huish, Robert, *An Authentic History of the Coronation of His Majesty King George the Fourth . . .* (London: J. Robins & Co., 1821)

Hull, Felix, ed., *A Calendar of the White and Black Books of the Cinque Ports 1432–1955* (London: HMSO, 1966)

Ideote, F., 'Un ceremonial de coronacion de los reyes

de Inglaterra', *Hispania Sacra*, 6 (1953), pp. 151–80

The Inventories and Valuations of the King's Goods, ed. O. Millar (Walpole Society, XLIII, 1972)

James I, *The Political Works of James I*, ed. C. H. McIlwain (Cambridge, Mass.: Harvard University Press, 1918)

Jekyll, Joseph, *Correspondence of Mr. Joseph Jekyll*, ed. Algernon Bourke (London: John Murray, 1894)

Jerdan, William, *Rutland Papers* (CS, XXI, 1842)

Jesse, J. Heneage, *Memoirs of the Life and Reign of King George the Third* (London, 1867)

Jonson, Ben, *Works*, ed. C. H. Herford and P. and E. Simpson (Oxford, 1941)

Kinney, Arthur, 'The Queenes Maiestie's Passage', in *Elizabethan Backgrounds* (Hamden, Conn.: Archon Books, 1975), pp. 7–39

Legg, J. Wickham, ed., *The Coronation Order of King James I* (? London: F. E. Robinson & Co., 1902)

——, *English Coronation Records* (London: Archibald Constable & Co., 1901)

——, *Three Coronation Orders* (HBS, XIX, 1900)

Leland, John, *Collectanea* (London, 1774)

Leofric, *The Leofric Missal*, ed. F. E. Warren (Oxford: Clarendon Press, 1883)

The Letters of George IV 1812–1830, ed. A. A. Aspinall (Cambridge: Cambridge University Press, 1938)

Letters and Papers, Foreign and Domestic, of the Reign of Henry VIII (London: The National Archives, 1862–1932)

Liber Regalis (Roxburghe Club, 1870)

Liber Regie Capelle, ed. Walter Ullmann (HBS, XCII, 1961 for 1959)

The Life of King Edward who Rests at Westminster Attributed to a Monk of Saint-Bertin, ed. and trans. Frank Barlow (Oxford: Clarendon Press, 1992)

Lockhart, J. G., *Memoirs of the Life of Sir Walter Scott* (Edinburgh: Adam and Charles Black, 1878)

Machyn, Henry, *The Diary of Henry Machyn*, ed. J. G. Nichols (CS, 1848)

The Manner of the Coronation of King Charles the First of England, ed. Christopher Wordsworth (HBS, II, 1892)

Martineau, Harriet, *Harriet Martineau's Autobiography* (London: Smith, Elder & Co., 1877)

Mary, Queen, *Memoirs of Mary, Queen of England (1689–1693)*, ed. R. Doebner (Leipzig, 1886)

Memorials of St Dunstan, Archbishop of Canterbury, ed. W. Stubbs (RS, 1874)

Milles, Thomas, *The Catalogue of Honor* (London, 1614)

Montagu, Lady Mary Wortley, *The Letters and Works of Lady Mary Wortley Montagu . . .* (London: George Bell & Sons 1898)

Morley, George, *A Sermon Preached at the Magnificent Coronation of the Most High and Mighty King Charles the IId . . .* (London, 1661)

Munimenta Gildhalae Londoniensis, II, ii, *Liber Custumarum*, ed. H. T. Riley (RS, 1860)

The Music with the form and order of the service to be performed at the coronation of the Most Excellent Majesty Queen Elizabeth II in the Abbey Church of Westminster on Tuesday of 2nd day of June, 1953 . . . (London: Novello & Co., 1953)

Nichols, John, *The Progresses, Processions and Magnificent Festivities of King James the First* (London, 1828)

——, *The Progresses . . . of Queen Elizabeth* (London, 1823)

Noailles, Messieurs de, *Ambassades de Messieurs de Noailles en Angleterre*, ed. Veroh (Leiden, 1763)

Northumberland, Duchess of, *The Diaries of a Duchess: Extracts from the Diaries of the First Duchess of Northumberland (1716–1776)*, ed. James Grieg (London: Hodder & Stoughton, 1926)

Ogilby, John, *The Entertainment of His Most Excellent Majestie Charles II, in his Passage through the City of London to his Coronation . . .* (London, 1662)

——, *The Entertainment of His Most Excellent Majestie Charles II . . .*, Facsimile, intro. Ronald Knowles, Medieval & Renaissance Texts & Studies, 43; Renaissance Triumphs and Magnificences, new series, III (Binghampton, NY, 1988)

——, *The Kings Coronation: Being an Exact Account of the Cavalcade with a Description of the Triumphal Arches, and Speeches prepared by the City of London for his Late Majesty Charles the Second . . .* (London, 1685)

——, The Relation of His Majesties Entertainment Passing through the City of London to His Coronation: with a Description of the Triumphal Arches, and Solemnity (London, 1661)

Orders to be Observed on Tuesday the 22d of September, Being the Day Appointed for Their Majesties Coronation . . . (London, 1761)

Orders to be Observed on Wednesday the 11th of October, Being the Day Appointed for Their

Majesties Coronation [George II and Queen Caroline] (London, 1727)

Palmerston, Lady, *The Letters of Lady Palmerston*, ed. Tresham Lever (London: John Murray, 1957)

A Particular Account of the Solemnities used at the Coronation of His Sacred Majesty King George II . . . (London: W. Bristow, 1761)

Pepys, Samuel, *The Diary of Samuel Pepys*, ed. Robert Latham and William Matthews (London: HarperCollins, 1995)

Planche, J. R., *Regal Records or, A Chronicle of the Coronations of the Queens Regnant of England* (London, 1838)

Political Poems and Songs Relating to English History . . ., ed. Thomas Wright (London, 1851)

The Pontifical of Egbert, Archbishop of York, A.D. 732–766 (Surtees Society, XXVII, 1853)

The Pontifical of Magdalene College, ed. H. A. Wilson (HBS, XXXIX, 1910)

Pontificale Lanaletense, ed. G. H. Doble (HBS, LXXIV, 1937)

Potter, John, Bishop of Oxford, *A Sermon Preach'd at the Coronation of King George II. and Queen Caroline . . .* (London: C. Ackers for R. Knaplick, 1727)

Prynne, William, *Signal Loyalty and Devotion to Gods True Saints and Pious Christians under the Gospel (Especially in this Our Island) towards Their Christian Kings and Emperors, etc.* (London, 1660)

The Public Ledger, 28 September 1761

Reresby, Sir John, *The Memoirs of Sir John Reresby*, ed. Andrew Browning (Glasgow: Jackson, Son & Co., 1936)

Ricardi de Cirencestria, *Speculum Historiale de Gestis Regum Angliae*, ed. John E. B. Mayor (London: II, 1869)

Roger of Wendover, *Roger of Wendover's Flowers of History*, trans. J. A. Giles (London: Bohn, 1849)

The Round Table: The Order and Solemnities of Crowning the King . . . (London: W. Goodleigh, 1820)

Rugg, Thomas, *The Diurnal of Thomas Rugg 1659–61*, ed. William L. Sachse (CS, 3rd series, XCI, 1961)

Rymer, Thomas, *Foedera* (The Hague, 1740–5)

Salvetti, Giovanni Antiminelli, 'La Forma del Banchetto del Re nella Sala grande di Westminster il 23 Aprile Giorno della Coronazione di S. Maesta', *Nozze*, 8 June 1896

Sandford, Francis, *The History of the Coronation of the Most High, Most Mighty and Most Excellent Monarch James II . . .* (London, 1687)

Selden, John, *Titles of Honor*, 3rd edn (London, 1672)

Senhouse, Richard, *Four Sermons Preached at Court Upon Severall Occasions by the Late Reverend and Learned Divine, Doctor Senhouse, L. Bishop of Carlisle* (London, 1627)

Sharp, John, *A Sermon Preach'd at the Coronation of Queen Anne . . .* (London, 1708 edn)

Six Old English Chronicles, ed. J. A. Giles (London, 1872)

Smith, George, *The Coronation of Elizabeth Wydeville* (London: Ellis, 1935)

The Statutes of the Realm (1820)

Stowe, John, *Annales* (London, 1631 edn)

Talbot, William, Bishop of Oxford, *A Sermon Preach'd at the Coronation of King George [I] . . .* (London: W. Wilkins for John Churchill, 1714)

Thoughts on the Coronation of his Present Majesty King George the Third (London: F. Noble, 1761)

Three Books of Polydore Vergil's English History, ed. Henry Ellis (CS, 1844)

Turner, Francis, *A Sermon Preached before Their Majesties K. James II. and Q. Mary at their Coronation in Westminster-Abby, April 23. 1685* (London, 1685)

Two Anglo-Saxon Pontificals (the Egbert and Sidney Sussex Pontificals), ed. H. M. Banting (HBS, 1989 for 1985–7)

'Two London Chronicles', ed. C. L. Kingsford, *Camden Miscellany*, 12 (1910), pp. 29–30

Victoria, Queen, *The Letters of Queen Victoria . . . 1837 to 1861*, ed. A. C. Benson and Viscount Esher (London: John Murray, 1907)

Vita Oswaldi Archiepiscopi Eboracensis, 3, ed. James Raine in *The Historians of the Church of York and its Archbishops*, I (RS, 71, 1879)

Walker, Sir Edward, *A Circumstantial Account of the Preparations for the Coronation of His Majesty King Charles the Second . . .* (London, 1820)

Walpole, Horace, *Horace Walpole's Correspondence*, ed. W. S. Lewis et al. (Oxford: Oxford University Press)

Walsingham, T., *Historia Anglica*, ed. H. T. Riley (RS, 1863)

The Westminster Chronicle 1381–1394, ed. L. C. Hector

and Barbara F. Harvey (Oxford: Clarendon Press, 1982)

Wharton, Henry, *The History of the Troubles and Tryal of . . . William Laud* (London, 1695)

Wilson, Arthur, *History of Great Britain, Being the Life and Reign of King James the First* (London, 1653)

Wriothesley, Charles, *A Chronicle of England during the Reigns of the Tudors*, ed. W. D. Hamilton (CS, 1875–7)

York Civic Records, ed. Angelo Raine (printed for the Yorkshire Archaeological Society, 1939), I

SECONDARY WORKS

Achinstein, Sharon, 'Milton and King Charles,' in Corns, ed., *The Royal Image*, pp. 141–61

Allen, Hope Emily, 'A Thirteenth-Century Coronation Rubric', *Church Quarterly Review*, 95 (1923), pp. 335–41

Allen, W. Gore, *King William IV* (London: Cresset Press, 1960)

Allmand, Christopher, *Henry V* (London: Methuen, 1992)

Anglo, Sydney, *Spectacle, Pageantry and Early Tudor Policy* (Oxford: Clarendon Press, 1969)

——, 'The Coronation of Edward VI and Society of Antiquaries Manuscript 123', *Antiquaries Journal*, 78 (1998), pp. 452–7

——, 'The Foundation of the Tudor Dynasty: The Coronation and Marriage of Henry VII', *Guildhall Miscellany*, 2 (1969), pp. 3–11

Anstruther, Ian, *The Knight and the Umbrella* (London: Geoffrey Bles, 1963)

Armstrong, C. A. J., 'The Inauguration Ceremonies of the Yorkist Kings and Their Title to the Throne', *TRHS*, 4th series, 30 (1948), pp. 51–73

Arnold, Janet, *Queen Elizabeth's Wardrobe Unlock'd* (Leeds: W. S. Maney & Sons, 1988)

Aspinall, A.. ed., *The Later Correspondence of George III* (Cambridge: Cambridge University Press, 1963)

Aston, Margaret, *The King's Bedpost* (Cambridge: Cambridge University Press, 1993)

Bak, Janos, ed., *Coronations: Medieval and Early Modern Monarchic Ritual* (San Francisco: University of California Press, 1990)

——, 'Coronation Studies – Past, Present, and Future', in *Coronations*, pp. 1–15

Barber, Richard, *The Knight and Chivalry*, rev. edn (Woodbridge: Boydell Press, 1995)

Barlow, Frank, *William Rufus* (London: Methuen, 1983)

Barnes, D. G., *George III and William Pitt, 1783–1806* (Stanford, Calif.: Stanford University Press, 1939)

Barrow, G. W. S., 'Observations on the Coronation Stone of Scotland', *Scottish Historical Review*, 76(1) (1997), pp. 115–21

Bayne, G. C., 'The Coronation of Queen Elizabeth', *EHR*, 22 (1907), pp. 650–73

——, 'The Coronation of Queen Elizabeth', *EHR*, 24 (1909), pp. 322–3

Beaton, Cecil, *The Strenuous Years: Cecil Beaton's Diaries, 1948–55* (London: Weidenfeld & Nicolson, 1973)

Beckles, Gordon, *Coronation Souvenir Book 1937* (London: Daily Express, 1937)

Bell, G. K. A., *Randall Davidson, Archbishop of Canterbury* (Oxford: Oxford University Press, 1935)

Bennett, Michael J., 'Richard II and the Wider Realm', in *Richard II*, ed. Goodman and Gillespie, pp. 187–204

Bergeron, David, 'Elizabeth's Coronation Entry (1559): New Manuscript Evidence', *English Literary Renaissance*, 8 (1978), pp. 3–8

——, *English Civic Pageantry 1558–1642* (London: Edward Arnold, 1971)

——, 'Harrison, Jonson and Dekker: The Magnificent Entertainment for King James (1604)', *Journal of the Warburg and Courtauld Institutes*, 31 (1968), pp. 445–8

——, ed., *Pageantry in the Shakespearean Theater* (Athens: University of Georgia Press, 1985)

Binski, Paul, *The Painted Chamber at Westminster* (Society of Antiquaries, Occasional Paper (New Series) IX, 1986)

——, '"A Sign of Victory". The Coronation Chair, its Manufacture, Setting and Symbolism', in Richard Welander, David J. Breeze and Thomas Owen Clancy, eds., *The Stone of Destiny: Artefact and Icon* (Society of Antiquaries of Scotland, XXII, 2003), pp. 207–22

——, *Westminster Abbey and the Plantagenets: Kingship and the Representation of Power 1200–1400*

(New Haven, London: Yale University Press for The Paul Centre for Studies in British Art, 1995)

Birnhaum, N., 'Monarchs and Sociologists: A Reply to Professor Shils and Mr Young', *Sociological Review*, 3 (1953), pp. 5–23

Blair, Claude, *The Crown Jewels. The History of the Coronation Regalia in the Jewel House of the Tower of London* (London: HMSO, 1998)

Bloch, Marc, *The Royal Touch: Sacred Monarchy and Scrofula in England and France* (London: Routledge & Kegan Paul, 1973)

Blumler, J. G., Brown, J. R., Ewbank, A. J. and Rossiter, T. J., 'Attitudes to Monarchy: Their Structure and Development During a Ceremonial Occasion', *Political Studies*, 19 (1971), pp. 149–71

Bodley, J. E. C., *The Coronation of King Edward the Seventh: A Chapter in European and Imperial History* (London: Methuen & Co., 1903)

Bonne, Jean-Claude, 'The Manuscript of the Ordo of 1250 and its Illuminations', in *Coronations*, ed. Bak, pp. 58–71

Bouman, C. A., *Sacring and Crowning: The Development of the Latin Ritual for the Anointing of Kings and the Coronation of an Emperor before the Eleventh Century* (Groningen: Bijdragen van Het Instituut voor Middeleeuwse Geschiedenis der Rijks-Universiteit te Utrecht, 1957)

Bowers, Roger, 'The Chapel Royal, the First Edwardian Prayer Book and Elizabeth's Settlement of Religion, 1559', *Historical Journal*, 43(2) (2000), pp. 317–44

Bradford, Sarah, *George VI* (London: Fontana, 1991)

Bradshaw, Paul, 'Coronations from the Eighteenth to the Twentieth Century', in *Coronations Past and Present*, ed. Bradshaw, pp. 22–31

——, ed., *Coronations Past and Present* (Cambridge: Grove Books, 1997)

——, 'On Revising the Coronation Service', *Theology*, 96 (1993), pp. 300–97

Brightman, F. E., 'Byzantine Imperial Coronations', *Journal of Theological Studies*, 2 (1901), pp. 359–92

Brown, Carleton, 'Lydgate's Verses on Queen Margaret's Entry into London', *Modern Language Review*, 7 (1912), pp. 225–34

Brown, R. Allen, Colvin, H. M. and Taylor, A. J., *The History of the King's Works*: I and II *The Middle Ages* (London: HMSO, 1963)

Bruckmann, John, 'English Coronations 1216–1308', MA Dissertation, University of Toronto (1958)

——, 'English Coronations, 1216–1308: The Edition of the Coronation Ordines', Ph.D Thesis, University of Toronto, 1964

——, 'The Ordines of the Third Recension of the Medieval English Coronation Order', in *Essays in Medieval History Presented to Bertie Wilkinson*, ed. T. A. Sandquist and M. R. Powicke (Toronto: University of Toronto Press, 1969)

Bryant, Laurence M., 'Configurations of the Community in Late Medieval Spectacles: Paris and London During the Dual Monarchy', in *City and Spectacle in Medieval Europe*, ed. Barbara A. Hanawalt and Kathryn L. Reyerson, Medieval Studies at Minnesota VI (Minneapolis: University of Minnesota Press, 1994), pp. 3–33

——, 'The Medieval Entry Ceremony at Paris', in *Coronations*, ed. Bak, pp. 88–118

Buchanan, Colin, 'The Next Coronation', in *Coronations Past and Present*, ed. Bradshaw, pp. 34–44

Burden, Joel Francis, 'Rituals of Royalty: Prescription, Politics and Practice in English Coronation and Royal Funeral Rituals *c*.1327–1485', unpublished Ph.D Thesis, University of York, Centre for Medieval Studies, 1999

Burgess, Glenn, *Absolute Monarchy and the Stuart Constitution* (New Haven and London: Yale University Press, 1996)

Burke, H. Farnham, *The Historical Record of the Coronation of Their Majesties King George the Fifth and Queen Mary 1911* (London: McCorquodale & Co. [1911])

Burnet, Gilbert, *Bishop Burnet's History of the Reformation* (London, 1820)

Burrows, Donald, 'Handel and the 1727 Coronation', *Musical Times*, 108 (1977), pp. 469–73

Bute, John, Marquess of, *Scottish Coronations* (London: Alexander Gardner, 1902)

Cameron, Avril, 'The Construction of Court Ritual: the Byzantine Book of Ceremonies', in *Rituals of Royalty*, ed. Cannadine and Price, pp. 106–36

Cannadine, David, 'The Context, Performance and Meaning of Ritual: The British Monarchy and the "Invention of Tradition", *c*.1820–1977', in *The Invention of Tradition*, ed. Eric Hobsbawm and Terence Ranger (Cambridge: Cambridge University Press, 1983), pp. 101–64

——, 'Splendor out of Court: Royal Spectacle and Pageantry in Modern Britain, *c.*1820–1977', in *Rites of Power*, ed. Wilentz, pp. 206–43

——, and Price, Simon, eds, *Rituals of Royalty: Power and Ceremonial in Traditional Societies* (Cambridge: Cambridge University Press, 1987)

Cannon, John, 'The Survival of the British Monarchy', *TRHS*, 5th series, 36 (1986), pp. 143–64

Cantor, Norman F., *Church, Kingship, and Lay Investiture in England 1089–1135* (Princeton: Princeton University Press, 1958)

Carpenter, D. A., 'The Burial of King Henry III, the Regalia and Royal Ideology', in D. A. Carpenter, *The Reign of Henry III* (London: Hambledon Press, 1996), pp. 427–59

Carpenter, Edward, *Archbishop Fisher – His Life and Times* (Norwich: Canterbury Press, 1991)

——, ed., *A House of Kings* (London: Westminster Abbey Bookshop, 1966)

Chambers, E. K., *The Medieval Stage* (Oxford: Oxford University Press, 1903)

Chaney, William A., *The Cult of Kingship in Anglo-Saxon England: The Transition from Paganism to Christianity* (Manchester: Manchester University Press, 1970)

Chapman, James, 'Cinema, Monarchy and the Making of Heritage: A Queen is Crowned (1953)', in *British Historical Cinema: the history, heritage and costume film*, ed. Claire Monk and Amy Sargeant (London: Routledge, 2002), pp. 82–91

Charlot, Monica, *Victoria. The Young Queen* (Oxford: Blackwell, 1991), pp. 115–27

Ciggaar, Krijnie, 'Byzantine Marginalia to the Norman Conquest', *Anglo-Norman Studies*, 9 (1986), pp. 43–69

Colley, Linda, *Britons: Forging the Nation 1707–1837* (New Haven and London: Yale University Press, 1992)

——, 'The Apotheosis of George III: Loyalty, Royalty, and the British Nation 1760–1820', *Past and Present*, 102 (1984), pp. 94–129

Collins, A. J., *Jewels and Plate of Queen Elizabeth I* (London: British Museum, 1955)

Colvin, H. M., Crook, J. Mordaunt, Downes, Kerry and Newman John, *The History of the King's Works*, V, *1660–1782* (London: HMSO, 1976)

Colvin, H. M., Ransome, D. R. and Summerson, John, *The History of the King's Works*, III, *1485–1660*, Part I (London: HMSO, 1976)

Colvin, H. M., Summerson, John, Biddle, Martin, Hale, J. R. and Merriman, Marcus, *The History of the King's Works*, IV, *1485–1660*, Part II (London: HMSO, 1982)

Colvin, Howard, *A Biographical Dictionary of British Architects 1600–1840* (New Haven and London: Yale University Press, 1995)

Corns, Thomas N., ed., *The Royal Image: Representation of Charles I* (Cambridge: Cambridge University Press, 1999)

——, 'Duke, Prince and King', in *The Royal Image*, ed. Corns, pp. 1–25

Cowdrey, H. E. J., 'The Anglo-Norman Regiae', *Viator*, 12 (1981), pp. 37–78

Craufurd, Raymond, 'The Blessing of Cramp-rings: A Chapter in the History of the Treatment of epilepsy', in *Studies in the History of Method of Science*, ed. Charles Singer (Oxford: Clarendon Press, 1917), pp. 165–87

Creston, Dormer, *The Youthful Queen Victoria* (London: Macmillan, 1952)

Crow, Brian, 'Lydgate's 1445 Pageant for Margaret of Anjou', *English Language Notes*, 19 (1981), pp. 170–4

Crown and Empire: The Coronation of King George VI May 12, 1937 (London: The Times Publishing Co., 1937)

Cumming, Valerie, '"Great Vanity and Excesse in Apparell". Some Clothing and Furs of Tudor and Stuart Royalty', in *The Late King's Goods*, ed. MacGregor pp. 322–50

——, 'Pantomine and Pageantry: The Coronation of George IV', in *London – World City 1800–1840*, ed. Celina Fox, exhibition catalogue (New Haven and London: Yale University Press, 1992), pp. 39–50

DeMolen, Richard L., 'Richard Mulcaster and Elizabethan Pageantry', *Studies in English Literature*, 14 (1974), pp. 209–21

Dillon, Harold Arthur, Viscount, 'A MS. Collection of Ordinances of Chivalry of the Fifteenth Century', *Archaeologia*, 57 (1900), pp. 47–55

Ditmas, Edith M. R., 'The Curtana or Sword of Mercy', *Journal of the British Archaeological Association*, 3rd series, 29 (1966), pp. 122–33

Dobson, Michael and Watson, Nicola J., *England's Elizabeth* (Oxford: Oxford University Press, 2002)

Douglas, David C., *William the Conqueror* (London: Eyre & Spottiswoode, 1964)

Duchesne, L., *Christian Worship. Its Origin and Evolution*, 5th edn (London: SPCK, 1956)

Dutton, Richard, ed., *Jacobean Civic Pageants*, Ryburn Renaissance Texts and Studies (Keele: Keele University Press, 1995)

Eberle, Patricia J., 'Richard II and the Literary Arts', in *Richard II*, ed. Goodman and Gillespie, pp. 231–53

Edie, Carolyn A., 'The Popular Idea of Monarchy on the Eve of the Stuart Restoration', *Huntington Library Quarterly*, 29 (1976), pp. 343–73

——, 'The Public Face of Royal Ritual: Sermons, Medals and Civic Ceremony in Later Stuart Coronations', *Huntington Library Quarterly*, 53 (1990), pp. 311–65

English Romanesque Art 1066–1200, Arts Council Exhibition Catalogue, Hayward Gallery, 1984

Enright, Michael J., *Iona, Tara and Soissons: The Origin of the Royal Anointing Ritual* (Berlin, New York: Walter de Gruyter, 1985)

Erickson, Carolly, *Bloody Mary* (London: J. M. Dent & Sons, 1978)

Everett, Henry, 'The English Coronation Rite: From the Middle Ages to the Stuarts', in *Coronations Past and Present*, ed. Bradshaw, pp. 5–21

'Exhibitions in Coronation Year', *Archives*, 10 (1953), pp. 70–3

Fisher, Geoffrey, *I Here Present to . . . Six Addresses Interpreting the Coronation of Her Majesty Queen Elizabeth II* (London: SPCK, 1953)

——, *For the Queen: A Little Book of Private Devotions in Preparation for Her Majesty's Coronation* ([1953])

FitzRoy, Sir Almeric, *Memoirs* (London: Hutchinson & Co., [1926])

Fortes, E., 'Of Installation Ceremonies', *Proceedings of the Royal Anthropological Society for 1967* (1968), pp. 5–20

Forville, Raymonde, 'Le Sacre des rois anglo-normands et le serment du sacre . . . XIe–XIIe siècle', in *Proceedings of the First Battle Conference on Anglo-Norman Studies* (Woodbridge: Boydell Press, 1978), I, pp. 49–62

Fraser, Flora, *The Unruly Queen: The Life of Queen Caroline* (London: Macmillan, 1996)

Fraser, Peter, *Lord Esher, A Political Biography* (London: Hart-Davies, MacGibbon, 1973)

Fuller, Thomas, *The Church History of Britain*, ed. J. S. Brewer (Oxford: Oxford University Press 1845)

Garbett, Cyril, *The Claims of the Church of England* (London: Hodder & Stoughton, 1947)

Gem, R. D. H., 'The Romanesque Rebuilding of Westminster Abbey', *Anglo-Norman Studies*, 3 (1980–1), pp. 53–60

Giesey, Ralph, 'Inaugural Aspects of French Royal Ceremonials', in *Coronations*, ed. Bak, pp. 35–45

——, 'Models of Rulership in French Royal Ceremonial', in *Rites of Power*, ed. Wilentz, pp. 41–64

Gieysztor, Alexander, 'Gesture in the Coronation Ceremonies of Medieval Poland', in *Coronations*, ed. Bak, pp. 152–64

Gillingham, John, *Richard I* (New Haven and London: Yale University Press, 1999)

Girouard, Mark, *The Return to Camelot: Chivalry and the English Gentleman* (New Haven and London: Yale University Press, 1981)

Goldberg, Jonathan, *James I and the Politics of Literature* (Baltimore: Johns Hopkins University Press, 1983)

Goodman, Anthony and James Gillespie, *Richard II: The Art of Kingship* (Oxford: Clarendon Press, 1999)

Gordon, Dillian, Monnas, Lisa and Elam, Caroline, *The Regal Image of Richard II and the Wilton Diptych* (London: Harvey Miller, 1997)

Green, David, *Queen Anne 1665–1714* (London: History Book Club, 1970)

Grierson, Philip, 'The Origins of the English Sovereign and the Symbolism of the Crown', *British Numismatic Journal*, 33 (1964), pp. 118–34

Grigg, J., 'The Queen's Opportunity', *National and English Review*, 139/834 (August, 1952), p. 83

Grose, F., and Astle, T., *The Antiquarian Repertory* (London, 1804–9)

Guaras, Antonio de, *The Accession of Queen Mary* (London: Laurence and Bullen, 1892)

Halfpenny, Eric, '"The Citie's Loyalty Display'd": A Literary and Documentary Causerie of Charles II's Coronation Entertainment', *Guildhall Miscellany*, 10 (1959), pp. 19–35

——, 'The "Entertainment" of Charles II', *Music and Letters*, 38 (1957), pp. 32–44

Hammon, Canon, *How and Why Our King Will Be Crowned* (London: Skeffington & Son, 1902)

Harvey, Anthony and Mortimer, Richard, eds, *The Funeral Effigies of Westminster Abbey* (Woodbridge: Boydell Press, 1994)

Haugaard, W. P., 'The Coronation of Elizabeth I', *Journal of Ecclesiastical History*, 19 (1968), pp. 161–70

Henfry, H. W., 'Oliver Cromwell's Sceptre', *Journal of the British Archaeological Association*, 31 (1875), pp. 306–9

Hibbert, Christopher, *George III. A Personal History* (London: Viking, 1999)

Hilton, James, 'The Coronation Stone at Westminster Abbey', *Archaeological Journal*, 54, 2nd series, 4 (1897), pp. 201–24

Hinchliff, 'Frederick Temple, Randall Davidson and the Coronation of Edward VIII', *Journal of Ecclesiastical History*, 48/117, pp. 71–99

Hind, A. M., *Engraving in England in the Sixteenth and Seventeenth Centuries*, Part II, *The Reign of James I* (Cambridge: Cambridge University Press, 1955)

Hoak, Dale, 'The Coronation of Edward VI, Mary I, and Elizabeth I and the Transformation of the Tudor Monarchy', in *Westminster Abbey Reformed*, pp. 114–51

——, 'The Iconography of the Crown Imperial', in *Tudor Political Culture*, ed. D. E. Hoak (Cambridge: Cambridge University Press, 1995), pp. 54–103

——, 'A Tudor Debora? The Coronation of Elizabeth I, Parliament and the Problem of Female Rule', in *John Foxe and his World*, ed. C. Highley and J. N. King (Aldershot: Ashgate, 2002), pp. 73–88

Holdsworth, William S., *A History of English Law* (London: Methuen & Co., III, 1923, X, 1938)

Hollister, C. Warren, *Henry I* (New Haven and London: Yale University Press, 2001)

Holmes, M. R., 'The Crowns of England', *Archaeologia*, 86 (1937), pp. 73–90

——, 'New Light on St. Edward's Crown', *Archaeologia*, 97 (1959), pp. 213–23

Hope, W. H. St John, 'The Funeral, Monument and Chantry Chapel of King Henry the Fifth', *Archaeologia*, 65, (1930), pp. 129–86

——, 'On the Funeral Effigies of the Kings and Queens of England . . .' *Archaeologia*, 60(2) (1907)

Hoyt, Robert S., 'The Coronation Oath of 1308', *EHR*, 81 (1956), pp. 353–83

Hughes, Andrew, 'Antiphons and Acclamations. The Politics of Music in the Coronation Service of Edward II, 1308', *Journal of Musicology*, 6 (1988), pp. 150–68

——, 'The Origins and Descent of the Fourth Recension of the English Coronation', in *Coronations*, ed. Bak, pp. 197–216

Hughes, Dom Anselm, 'Music of the Coronation over a Thousand Years', *Proceedings of the Royal Musical Association*, 79 (1952–3), pp. 81–5, 93

Hunter, J., 'King Edward's Spoliations in Scotland in AD 1296 – The Coronation Stone – Original and Unpublished Evidence', *Archaeological Journal*, 13 (1856), pp. 245–55

Ideote, F. 'Un ceremonial de coronacion de los reyes de Inglaterra', *Hispania Sacra*, 6 (1953), pp. 151–80

Jackson, C. J., 'The Spoon and its History, its Form, Material and Development, More Particularly in England', *Archaeologia*, 53(1) (1892), pp. 118–19

Jackson, Richard A., *Vive le Roi! A History of the French Coronation from Charles V to Charles X* (Chapel Hill and London: University of North Carolina Press, 1984)

James, Robert Rhodes, *Chips. The Diaries of Sir Henry Channon* (London: Weidenfeld & Nicolson, 1967)

Jennings, Humphrey and Madge, Charles, eds, *May the Twelfth. Mass-Observation Day-Surveys 1937 . . .* (London: Faber & Faber, 1937)

John, Eric, *Orbis Britanniae and Other Studies* (Leicester: Leicester University Press, 1966)

Jones, Adrienne, 'The Significance of the Royal Consecration of Edgar in 973', *Journal of Ecclesiastical History*, 33 (1982), pp. 375–90

Josten, C. H., *Elias Ashmole (1617–1692)* (Oxford: Oxford University Press, 1966)

Judd, Denis, *Empire: The British Imperial Experience from 1765 to the Present* (London: HarperCollins, 1996)

Kantorowicz, Ernst, 'Inalienability: A Note on the Canonical Practice and the English Coronation Oath in the Thirteenth Century', *Speculum*, 29 (1954), pp. 488–502

——, 'The "King's Advent" and the Enigmatic Panels

in the Doors of Santa Sabina', *Art Bulletin*, 26 (1944), pp. 207–31

——, *Laudes Regiae* (Berkeley: University of California Press, 1958)

Kern, Fritz, *Kingship and Law in the Middle Ages* (Oxford: Basil Blackwell, 1939)

Kilburn, Matthew Charles, 'Royalty and Public in Britain: 1714–1789', Unpublished D.Phil., Oxford University, 1997

King, John N, *Tudor Royal Iconography* (Princeton: Princeton University Press, 1989)

King, Robert, *Henry Purcell* (London: Thames & Hudson, 1994)

Kingdon, J. A., *Richard Grafton* (London, 1901)

King-Hall, Stephen, *The Crowning of the King and Queen* (London: Evans Bros., 1937)

'The King's Protestant Declaration', *Contemporary Review*, April 1901

Kipling, Gordon, *Enter the King: Theatre, Liturgy, and Ritual in the Medieval Civic Triumph* (Oxford: Clarendon Press, 1998)

——, '"He that saw it would not believe it": Anne Boleyn's Royal Entry into London', in *Civic Ritual and Drama in Medieval and Renaissance Europe*, ed. Alexandra F. Johnston and Wim Huskin, Ludus: Medieval and Early Renaissance Theatre and Drama, II (Amsterdam: Rodopi, 1997), pp. 39–70

——, 'Richard II's "Sumptuous Pageants" and the Idea of the Civic Triumph', in *Pageantry in the Shakespearean Theater*, ed. Bergeron, pp. 83–103

Knighton, C. S., 'Westminster Abbey from Reformation to Revolution', in *Westminster Abbey Reformed*, pp. 1–15

Knocker, Sir Wollaston, *The Coronation of their Majesties Edward VII. and Queen Alexandra 1902: The Report of the Proceedings of the Barons of the Cinque Ports . . .* (Dover: Richard Turner, 1902)

Koebner, Richard, ' "The Imperial Crown of this Realm": Henry VIII, Constantine the Great, and Polydore Vergil', *BIHR*, 26 (1953), pp. 29–52

Laird, Dorothy, *Queen Elizabeth the Queen Mother* (London: Coronet Books, 1966)

Lees-Milne, James, *The Enigmatic Edwardian: The Life of Reginald, 2nd Viscount Esher* (London: Sidgwick & Jackson, 1986)

Legg, J. Wickham, 'On the Right of the Archbishop of York to Crown the Queen-Consort', *Transactions of St Paul's Ecclesiological Society*, 5 (1902), pp. 77–84

——, 'On an Inventory of the Vestry in Westminster Abbey, Taken in 1388', *Archaeologia*, 52 (1890), pp. 195–286

Le Goff, Jacques, 'A Coronation Program for the Age of Saint Louis', in *Coronations*, ed. Bak, pp. 46–57

——, Palazzo, Eric, Bonne, Jean-Claude and Colette, Marie-Noel, *Le Sacre royal à l'époque de Saint Louis d'après le manuscrit 1246 de la BNF* (Paris: Gallimard, 2001)

Le Hardy, William, *The Coronation Book* (London: Hardy & Beckett, 1937)

Lethaby, W. R., 'The Palace of Westminster in the Eleventh and Twelfth Centuries', *Archaeologia*, 60/1 (1906), pp. 131–48

——, *Westminster Abbey and the Antiquities of the Coronation* (London: Duckworth & Co., 1911)

Lightbown, Ronald, 'The King's Regalia, Insignia and Jewellery', in *The Late King's Goods*, ed. MacGregor, pp. 257–75

Loach, Jennifer, *Edward VI* (New Haven, London: Yale University Press, 1999)

Loades, David, *Mary Tudor: A Life* (Oxford: Basil Blackwell, 1989)

Lockhart, J. G., *Cosmo Gordon Lang* (London: Hodder & Stoughton, 1949)

Loftie, W. J., *The Coronation Book of Edward VII* (London: Cassell & Co. [n.d.])

London – World City 1800–1840, ed. Celina Fox, exhibition catalogue (New Haven and London: Yale University Press, 1992)

Longford, Elizabeth, *Elizabeth R* (London: Weidenfeld & Nicolson, 1983)

Lowenstein, David, 'The King among the Radicals', in *The Royal Image*, ed. Corns, pp. 96–121

MacGregor, Arthur, ed., *The Late King's Goods* (Oxford: Oxford University Press, 1989)

Macleane, Douglas, *The Great Solemnity of the Coronation of the Kings and Queens of England . . .* (London: F. E. Robinson & Co., 1902)

Magnus, Philip, *King Edward the Seventh* (London: John Murray, 1964)

Marshall, P. J., 'Imperial Britain', in *The Cambridge Illustrated History of the British Empire*, ed. P. J. Marshall (Cambridge: Cambridge University Press, 1996), pp. 318–37

Marson, C., 'The Ritual in November 1429, when the

Boy-King Henry VI Was Crowned', *The Antiquary*, 48 (1912), pp. 220–3

Mason, Emma, *Westminster Abbey and its People, c.1050–1216* (Woodbridge: Boydell Press, 1996)

McCoy, Richard C., '"Thou Idol Ceremony": Elizabeth I, The Henriad, and the Rites of the Monarchy', in *Urban Life in the Renaissance*, ed. Susan Zimmerman and Ronald F. E. Weissman (Newark: University of Delaware Press, 1989), pp. 240–66

——, '"The Wonderfull Spectacle". The Civic Progress of Elizabeth I and the Troublesome Coronation', in *Coronations*, ed. Bak, pp. 217–27

McKenna, J. W., 'The Coronation Oil of the Yorkist Kings', *EHR*, 82 (1967), pp. 102–4

McKisack, M., 'London and the Succession to the Crown during the Middle Ages', in *Studies in Medieval History Presented to Frederick Maurice Powicke*, ed. R. W. Hunt, W. A. Pantin and R. W. Southern (Oxford: Clarendon Press, 1948), pp. 76–89

Medallic Illustrations of the History of Great Britain and Ireland to the Death of George II (London: British Museum, 1911)

Millar, Oliver, *The Later Georgian Pictures in the Collection of Her Majesty the Queen* (London: Phaidon, 1969)

Mitchell, Shelagh, 'Richard II: Kingship and the Cult of Saints', in *The Regal Image*, ed. Gordon, Monnas and Elam, pp. 115–24

Monod, Paul Kleber, *Jacobitism and the English People 1688–1788* (Cambridge: Cambridge University Press, 1982)

Moore, Michael, 'The King's New Clothes: Royal and Episcopal Regalia in the Frankish Empire', in *Robes and Honor: The Medieval World of Investiture*, ed. Stewart Gordon (Basingstoke: Palgrave, 2001)

Morris, Marilyn, *The British Monarchy and the French Revolution* (New Haven and London: Yale University Press, 1998)

Murray, K. M. E., *The Constitutional History of the Cinque Ports* (Manchester: Manchester University Press, 1935)

Murray, Robert H., *The King's Crowning* (London: John Murray, 1936)

Nelson, Janet, 'The Earliest Surviving Royal Ordo: Some Liturgical and Historical Aspects', in *Authority and Power: Studies on Medieval Law and Government Presented to Walter Ullmann on his Seventieth Birthday*, ed. Brian Tierney and Peter Linehan (Cambridge: Cambridge University Press, 1980), pp. 29–48; also in Nelson, *Politics and Ritual*, pp. 341–60

——, 'Early Medieval Rites of Queen-making and the Shaping of Medieval Queenship' in Janet Nelson, *Rulers and Ruling Families in Early Medieval Europe* (Aldershot: Ashgate, c.1999), pp. 301–15

——, 'Hincmar of Reims on King-making: The Evidence of the Annals of St. Bertin 861–882', in *Coronations*, ed. Bak, pp. 16–34

——, 'Inauguration Rituals', in Nelson, *Politics and Ritual*, pp. 283–307

——, 'The Lord's Anointed and the People's Choice: Carolingian Royal Ritual', in *Rituals of Royalty*, ed. Cannadine and Price, pp. 137–80

——, 'National Synods, Kingship as Office, and Royal Anointing: An Early Medieval Syndrome', in Nelson, *Politics and Ritual*, pp. 239–57

——, *Politics and Ritual in Early Medieval Europe* (London: Hambledon Press, 1986)

——, 'The Problem of King Alfred's Anointing', in Nelson, *Politics and Ritual*, pp. 309–27

——, 'The Rites of the Conqueror', in Nelson, *Politics and Ritual*, pp. 375–401

——, 'The Second English Ordo', in Nelson, *Politics and Ritual*, pp. 361–74

——, 'Ritual and Reality in the Early Medieval Ordines', in Nelson, *Politics and Ritual*, pp. 329–39

——, 'Symbols in Context: Rulers' Inauguration Rituals in Byzantium and the West in the Early Middle Ages', in Nelson, *Politics and Ritual*, pp. 259–81

Nevinson, J. L., 'The Robes of the Order of the Bath', *Connoisseur*, 134 (1954), pp. 153–9

Newcome, David., ed., *Edwardian Excursion: From the Diaries of A. C. Benson 1898–1904* (John Murray, London, 1981)

Nicolas, Sir Nicholas Harris, *History of the Orders of Knighthood of the British Empire*, III, *Order of the Bath* (London, 1842), pp. 1–38

Norbrook, David, 'Levelling Poetry: George Wither and the English Revolution, 1642–1649', *English Literary Renaissance*, 21 (1991), pp. 217–56

'Notes on the Coronation Music', *Musical Times*, 1 June 1902, pp. 387–8

Ogg, David, *England in the Reigns of James II and William III* (Oxford: Clarendon Press, 1957)

O'Meara, Carra Ferguson, *Monarchy and Consent: The Coronation Book of Charles V of France* (London; Harvey Miller, 2001)

Osberg, Richard H., 'The Lambeth Palace Library Manuscript Account of Henry VI's 1432 London Entry', *Medieval Studies*, 52 (1990), pp. 255–67

Ottley, H. Bickersteth, *The Sacring of the King* (London: Simpkin, Marshall, Hamilton, Kent & Co., 1902)

Palme, Per, 'Ut Architectura Poesis', *Acta Universitatis Upsaliensis, Figura*, new series, 1 pp. 95–107

Parissien, Steven, *George IV: The Grand Entertainment* (London: John Murray, 2001)

Parry, Graham, *The Golden Age Restor'd: The Culture of the Stuart Court, 1603–42* (Manchester: Manchester University Press, 1981), pp. 1–20

Paster, Gail Kern, 'The Idea of London in Masque and Pageant', in *Pageantry in the Shakespearean Theater*, ed. Bergeron, pp. 83–103

Perkins, Jocelyn, *The Crowning of the Sovereign of Great Britain and the Dominions Overseas* (London: Methuen & Co., 1917)

Pilbrow, Fionn, 'The Knights of the Bath: Dubbing to Knighthood in Lancastrian and Yorkist England', in *Heraldry, Pageantry and Social Display in Medieval England*, ed. Peter Cox and Maurice Keen (Woodbridge: Boydell Press, 2002), pp. 195–218

Pimlott, Ben, *The Queen: A Biography of Elizabeth II* (London: HarperCollins, 1996 edn)

Pocock, J. G. A., *The Ancient Constitution and the Feudal Law: A Study of English Historical Thought in the Seventeenth Century*, reissued with a retrospect (Cambridge: Cambridge University Press, 1987)

Pollard, A. F., 'The Coronation of Queen Elizabeth', *EHR*, 25 (1910), pp. 125–6

Ponsonby, Sir Frederick, *Recollections of Three Reigns* (London: Eyre & Spottiswoode, 1951)

Pope-Hennessy, James, *Queen Mary* (London: Unwin Paperbacks, 1987)

Prestwich, Michael, *Edward I* (London: Methuen, 1988)

Prochaska, Frank, *The Republic of Britain 1760–2000* (London: Allen Lane, 2000)

——, *Royal Bounty: The Making of A Welfare Monarchy* (New Haven and London: Yale University Press, 1995)

Ratcliff, Edward C., *The Coronation Service of Her Majesty Queen Elizabeth II* (London: SPCK, 1953)

——, *The English Coronation Service* (London: Skeffington & Son, 1936)

Redmond, Joad, 'Popular Representations of Charles I', in *The Royal Image*, ed. Corns, pp. 47–73

Reedy, Gerard, 'Mystical Politics: The Imagery of Charles II's Coronation', in *Studies in Change and Revolution: Aspects of English Intellectual History 1640–1800*, ed. Paul J. Porshin (Menston: Scolar Press, 1972), pp. 19–42

Rees Jones, S., 'The Coronation Chair', *Studies in Conservation*, 1 (1952–4), pp. 103–13

Richards, J., 'The Kingship of Charles I before 1640', *Past and Present*, 113 (1982), pp. 70–96

Richards, Jeffrey, 'The Coronation of Queen Elizabeth II and Film', *Court Historian*, 9(1) (2004), pp. 69–79

Richards, Judith M., 'Love and a Female Monarch: The Case of Elizabeth Tudor', *Journal of British Studies*, 38(2) (1999), pp. 133–59

Richardson, H. G., 'The Coronation in Medieval England: The Evolution of the Office and the Oath', *Traditio*, 16 (1960), pp. 111–202

——, 'The Coronation of Edward I', *BIHR*, 15 (1937–8), pp. 94–9

——, 'The English Coronation Oath', *Speculum*, 24 (1949), pp. 44–75

——, 'The English Coronation Oath', *TRHS*, 4th series, 23 (1941), pp. 129–58

——, and Sayles, G. O., 'Early Coronation Records', *BIHR*, 13 (1935–6), pp. 129–45; 14 (1936–7), pp. 1–9

——, and Sayles, G. O., 'Early Coronation Records: The Coronation of Edward II', *BIHR*, 16 (1938–9), pp. 1–45

——, and Sayles, G. O., *The Governance of Medieval England from the Conquest to Magna Carta* (Edinburgh: Edinburgh University Press, 1964)

Roberts, Hugh, 'Royal Thrones 1760–1840', *Furniture History Society*, 25 (1989), pp. 60–85

Robinson, J. Armitage, 'The Church of Edward the Confessor at Westminster', *Archaeologia*, 52(1) (1910), pp. 81–100

——, 'The Coronation Order in the Tenth Century', *Journal of Theological Studies*, 19 (1918), pp. 56–72

Rose, Kenneth, *George V* (London: Macmillan, 1983)

Rose, R. and Kavanagh D., 'The Monarchy in Contemporary British Culture', *Comparative Politics*, 8 (1976), pp. 548–76

Ross, G. Lockhart, 'Il Schifanoya's Account of the Coronation of Queen Elizabeth', *EHR*, 23 (1908), pp. 533–4

Ross, Thomas, 'Coronation Services of the Barons of the Cinque Ports', *Sussex Archaeological Collections*, 15 (1863), pp. 178–210

Round, J. H., 'The Coronation of Richard I', in J. H. Round, *The Commune of London and Other Studies* (London: Constable & Co., 1899), pp. 201–6

——, *The King's Serjeants and Officers of State with their Coronation Services* (London, 1911)

Rowse, A. L., 'The Coronation of Queen Elizabeth', *History Today*, 3 (1953), pp. 301–10

Rye, W. B., 'The Coronation of King James I', *The Antiquary*, 22 (1890), pp. 18–23

Sandquist, T. A., 'English Coronations, 1377–1483', Ph.D Thesis, University of Toronto, 1962

——, 'The Holy Oil of St. Thomas of Canterbury', in *Essays in Medieval History Presented to Bertie Wilkinson*, ed. T. A. Sandquist and M. R. Powicke (Toronto: University of Toronto Press, 1969), pp. 330–44

Saul, Nigel E., *Richard II* (New Haven, London: Yale University Press, 1997)

——, 'Richard II's Ideas of Kingship', in *The Regal Image*, ed. Gordon, Monnas and Elam, pp. 27–32

Sawyer, Sean, 'Sir John Soane's Symbolic Westminster', *Architectural History*, 39 (1996), pp. 54–76

Schama, Simon, 'The Domestication of Majesty: Royal Family Portraiture 1500–1850', *Journal of Interdisciplinary History*, 17 (1986), pp. 155–83

Schramm, Percy Ernst, *A History of The English Coronation* (Oxford: Clarendon Press, 1937)

——, 'Ordines-Studien III: Die Krönung in England', *Archiv für Urkundenforschung*, 15 (1938), pp. 305–88

Schwoerer, Lois G., 'The Coronation of William and Mary, April 11, 1689', in *The Revolutions of 1688/9*, ed. Lois G. Schwoerer (Cambridge: Cambridge University Press, 1991)

——, *The Declaration of Rights, 1689* (Baltimore: Johns Hopkins University Press, 1981)

——, 'The Glorious Revolution as Spectacle: A New Perspective', in *England's Rise to Greatness, 1660–1763*, ed. Stephen P. Baxter (Berkeley: University of California Press, 1983), pp. 109–49

——, 'Propaganda in the Revolution of 1688–89', *American Historical Review*, 82(2) (1977), pp. 843–74

Sharpe, Kevin, *Sir Robert Cotton 1586–1631: History and Politics in Early Modern England* (Oxford: Oxford University Press, 1979)

Shears, W. S., *The King: The Story and Splendour of the British Monarchy* (London: Hutchinson & Co., 1937)

——, *The Personal Rule of Charles I* (New Haven and London: Yale University Press, 1992)

Shedlock, J. S. 'Coronation Music', *Proceedings of the Royal Musical Association*, 28th series (1901–2), pp. 141–60

Sheppard, Francis, *London: A History* (Oxford: Oxford University Press, 1998)

Shils, Edward and Young, Michael, 'The Meaning of the Coronation', in Edward Shils, *Center and Periphery. Essays in Macrosociology* (Chicago: University of Chicago Press, 1975), pp. 135–52

Slaughter, Thomas P., *Ideology and Politics on the Eve of the Restoration: Newcastle's Advice to Charles II* (Philadelphia: American Philosophical Society, 1984)

Smuts, R. Malcolm, 'Public Ceremony and Royal Charisma: The English Royal Entry into London', in *The First Modern Society: Essays in English History in Honour of Lawrence Stone*, ed. A. L. Beier, D. N. Cannadine and J. M. Rosenheim (Cambridge: Cambridge University Press, 1989), pp. 65–82

Starkey, David, 'Representation through Intimacy: A study of the Symbolism of Monarchy and Court Office in Early Modern England', in *The Tudor Monarchy*, ed. John Guy (London: Arnold, 1997)

Stevenson, Sara and Thompson, Duncan, *John Michael Wright: The King's Painter*, Exhibition Catalogue, Scottish National Portrait Gallery, 1982

Strong, Roy, *The English Icon: Elizabethan and Jacobean Portraiture* (London: Paul Mellon Foundation, 1969)

——, *Feast: A History of Grand Eating* (London: Jonathan Cape, 2002)

——, 'The 1559 Entry Pageants of Elizabeth I', in Roy Strong, *The Tudor and Stuart Monarchy* (Woodbridge: Boydell & Brewer, 1995), pp. 33–54

——, *Painting the Past: The Victorian Painter and British History* (London: Pimlico, 2004)

Sturdy, David J., ' "Continuity" versus "Change": Historians and English Coronations of the Medieval and Early Modern Periods', in *Coronations*, ed. Bak, pp. 228–45

——, 'English Coronation Sermons in the Seventeenth Century', in *Herrscherweihe und Königskrönung im frühneuzeitlichen Europa*, ed. H. Duchhardt (Wiesbaden: Franz Steiner Verlag, 1983), pp. 69–81

Symonds, M., 'New Light on the Coronation Chair', *Connoisseur*, 133 (1954), pp. 80–1

Tanner, Laurence, 'Abbey Coronation Vestments', *Guardian*, 14 May 1937

——, 'Westminster Abbey and the Coronation Service', *History*, new series, 21 (1936), pp. 289–301

Taylor, Arthur, *The Glory of Regality* (London, 1820)

Taylor, T. F., *J. Armitage Robinson* (Cambridge: James Clarke & Co., 1991)

Thewlis, G. A., 'Coronation of George I: A Bodleian Song', *Musical Times*, 78 (1937), pp. 310–11

Thurley, Simon, *The Royal Palaces of Tudor England* (New Haven and London: Yale University Press, 1993)

Thurston, Herbert Henry Charles, *The Coronation Ceremonial: Its True History and Meaning* (London: Catholic Truth Society, 1902)

Topham, John, 'An Historical and Descriptive Account of the Ancient Painting Preserved at Cowdray in Sussex . . .', *Archaeologia*, 8 (1787), pp. 406–22

Trevor-Roper, Hugh, *Archbishop Laud 1573–1645* (London: Macmillan & Co., 1962)

Tuting, W. C., *King Edward the Eighth: Why and How He Will Be Crowned* (London: Skeffington & Son, [1936])

——, *King George the Sixth: Why and How He Will Be crowned* (London: Skeffington & Son, [1937])

Twining, Lord, *European Regalia* (London: B. T. Batsford, 1967)

——, *A History of the Crown Jewels of Europe* (London: B. T. Batsford, 1960)

Ullmann, Walter, ' "This Realm of England is an Empire" ', *Journal of Ecclesiastical History*, 30 (1979), pp. 175–203

——, 'Thomas Becket's Miraculous Oil', *Journal of Theological Studies*, new series, 8(1) (1957), pp. 129–33

Vestergaard, Elisabeth, 'A Note on Viking Age Inaugurations', in *Coronations*, ed. Bak, pp. 119–24

Victoria County History, Surrey, ed. H. E. Malden, III (1911)

Wagner, Sir Anthony, *Heralds of England: A History of the Office and College of Arms* (London: HMSO, 1967)

——, and Sainty, J. C., 'The Origin of the Introduction of Peers in the House of Lords', *Archaeologia*, 101 (1967), pp. 119–50

——, Barker, Nicolas and Page, Ann, *Medieval Pageant: Writhe's Garter Book* (London: Roxburghe Club, 1993)

Ward, Paul L., 'The Coronation Ceremony in Medieval England', *Speculum*, 14, pp. 160–8

——, 'An Early Version of the Anglo-Saxon Coronation Ceremony', *EHR*, LVII (1942), pp. 345–61

Wardle, Patricia, 'The King's Embroiderer: Edmund Harrison (1590–1667)', *Textile History*, 26/2 (1995), pp. 139–84

Warnicke, Retha M., *The Rise and Fall of Anne Boleyn* (Cambridge: Cambridge University Press, 1989)

Warren, W. L., *Henry II* (London: Eyre Methuen, 1973)

Waugh, Scott L., *England in the Reign of Edward III* (Cambridge: Cambridge University Press, 1991)

Westlake, H. F., *Westminster Abbey* (London: Philip Allan & Co., 1923)

Westminster Abbey Reformed 1540–40, ed. C. S. Knighton and Richard Mortimer (Aldershot: Ashgate, 2003)

Westminster Gazette, 30 April 1902 (on coronation copes)

Weston, C. C. and Greenberg, Janelle, *The Grand Controversy over Legal Sovereignty in Stuart England* (Cambridge: Cambridge University Press, 1981)

Wheeler, Elizabeth Skerpan, 'Eikon Basilike and the Rhetoric of Self-representation', in *The Royal Image*, ed. Corns, pp. 122–40

Wheeler-Bennett, John W., *King George VI: His Life and Reign* (London: Macmillan & Co., 1958)

Wickham, Glynne, 'Contributions de Ben Jonson et Dekker aux fêtes du Couronnement de Jacques Ier', in *Les Fêtes de la Renaissance*, I, ed. Jean Jacquot (Paris: CNRS, 1956), I, pp. 279–83

Wilentz, Sean, ed., *Rites of Power: Symbolism, Ritual, and Politics Since the Middle Ages* (Philadelphia: University of Pennsylvania Press, 1985)

Wilkinson, Bertie, *Constitutional History of Medieval England 1216–1399*, III, *The Development of the Constitution 1216–1399* (London: Longmans, Green & Co., 1958)

——, 'The Coronation Oath of Edward II', in *Historical Essays in Honour of James Tait*, ed. J. G. Edwards, V. H. Galbraith and E. F. Jacob (Privately printed: Manchester, 1933), pp. 405–16

——, 'Notes on the Coronation Records of the Fourteenth Century', *EHR* 70 (1955), pp. 581–600

——, 'The Coronation Oath of Edward II and the Statute of York', *Speculum*, 19 (1944), pp. 445–69

Wilson, Christopher, 'Rulers, Artificers and Shoppers: Richard II's Remodelling of Westminster Hall, 1393–99', in *The Regal Image*, ed. Gordon, Monnas and Elam, pp. 33–59

Wilson, H. A., 'The Coronation of Queen Elizabeth', *EHR*, 23 (1908), pp. 87–91

Withington, Robert, *English Pageantry: An Historical Outline* (Cambridge, Mass.: Harvard University Press, 1918–20)

Wolfe, Bertram, *Henry VI* (London: Eyre Methuen, 1981)

Wood, Bruce, 'A Coronation Anthem – Lost and Found' *Musical Times*, 103 (1977)

Woodham-Smith, Cecil, *Queen Victoria* (London: Hamish Hamilton 1972), pp. 155–60

Wormald, 'The So-called Coronation Oath-Books of the Kings of England', in *Essays in Honor of Georg Swarzenski*, ed. O. Goetz, (Chicago: Henry Regnery Co., 1951), pp. 233–7

Yates, Frances A., *Astraea: The Imperial Theme in the Sixteenth Century* (London: Routledge & Kegan Paul, London, 1975)

The Year that Made the Day, BBC (London: [1953])

Ziegler, Philip, *Crown and People* (London: Collins, 1978)

——, *King William IV* (London: Collins, 1971)

Zimmerman, Franklin B., *Henry Purcell 1659–1695* (London: Macmillan, 1967)

INDEX

Stone of Scone, 73, 75–6
Stoop, Dirk, 304
Stow, John, 195; *Annales*, 206
Streeter, Robert, 328
Strigul, William Marshal, Earl of, 65
Stuart dynasty: and concept of
    monarchy, 234, 236, 278, 309; and
    coronation oath, 238–41; coronation
    liturgy and ceremonies, 248, 336–9;
    and public spectacle, 264–5; touching
    for scrofula, 280–1, 309; deposed, 282;
    money problems, 351; threat of
    restoration, 355
Stubbs, William, Bishop of Oxford, 479
Sturdy, D.J., 237, 339
Suffolk, Henry Howard, 16th Earl of, 375
Sullivan, Sir Arthur, 467
Supremacy, Act of (1534), 175
Sussex, Talbot Yelverton, 15th Earl of, 376
sword: in investiture, 5, 125, 167; in
    coronation regalia, 56–8, 125, 247; and
    knighthood, 58; and Reformation
    symbolism, 187; in Charles I's
    coronation, 250; in James II's
    coronation, 268
Sykes, Norman, 486
Sylvester I, Pope, 11

Talbot, Catherine, 407
Talbot (of Hensol), Charles, Baron, 413,
    415
Talbot, William, Bishop of Oxford, 356
Tallis, Thomas, 467–8
Tancred, King of Sicily, 68
Taylor, Arthur: *The Glory of Regality*, 370
television, 433–5
Temple, Frederick, Archbishop of
    Canterbury, 467, 472, 475, 478–9, 492,
    500
Tension, Thomas, Archbishop of
    Canterbury, 377
Tennyson, Alfred, 1st Baron, 424
Test Acts (1673 and 1678), 356
Thirlby, Thomas, Bishop of Westminster,
    196
Thomas, St: holy oil, 116–18, 167
Thorney, island of, 39
*Thoughts on the Coronation of his Present
    Majesty King George the Third*, 400
Three Coronation Orders, 469
throne: introduced by Vikings, 22; Henry
    III's, 157; *see also* coronation chair
Thurston, Herbert Henry, 471, 480
Toleration Act (1689), 356

Tomkins, Thomas, 260
touching (for King's Evil), 82, 113, 115,
    243, 280–2, 355
tournaments: as coronation festivities,
    101, 176–9
Tower of London: King's Armoury, 145;
    monarchs escorted to, 213–14; crown
    jewels kept in, 298; *see also* Princes in
    the Tower
Tractarian Movement, 466
Tree, Sir Herbert Beerbohm, 462
Tudor dynasty: and proposed
    canonisation of Henry VI, 118;
    imperialism, 184–5, 187–8;
    coronations, 198–9
Tunstall, Cuthbert, 122
Turner, Francis, Bishop of Ely, 340

Udall, Nicholas, 141, 183
Unam Sanctam (papal bull, 1302), 82
unction: and anointing of kings, 9, 46,
    63, 94, 116–17; history of, 9–14, 17, 26;
    administered to William the
    Conqueror, 40, 42; and coronation
    spoon, 79; and mystical kingship, 112;
    under Protestant Tudors, 201–2; in
    Stuart coronations, 249; *see also*
    anointing; oil
Uniformity, Act of (1549), 225
Union, Act of (Ireland, 1801), 359
Union, Act of (Scotland, 1707), 324, 359
Unxerunt Salomonem (anthem), 5, 28, 87,
    100, 260
Upton, Nicholas, 150
Urban VI, Pope, 121

Vaughan Williams, Ralph, 468
Venning, John, 387
Vergil, Polydore, 133
Vertue, George, 367
vestments *see* robes and vestments
Victoria, Queen of Great Britain: family
    life, 361, 363; moral influence, 363–4;
    public esteem for, 364; coronation,
    372, 409, 469; cost, 372, 374; coronation
    service, 378–82; robes, 382; procession,
    401, 406; personal account of
    coronation, 406; rehearses coronation,
    408; nationwide celebrations, 415;
    Jubilees (1887 and 1897), 424, 426, 437;
    withdrawal in widowhood, 424;
    proclaimed Empress of India, 439; and
    Buckingham Palace circus, 449;
    funeral, 458, 473

vigils: coronation, 76; processions,
    133–40, 197, 214; knightly, 163; omitted,
    167
Vikings, 22
Vile, William, 384
Virginia: as colony, 228
voidee, 134
Vyner, Sir Robert, 297

Wake, William, Archbishop of
    Canterbury, 377, 390, 407
Walker, Sir Edward, 288–90, 302–3, 319,
    329
Walpole, Horace, 382, 398, 407, 415, 417,
    474
Walsingham, Thomas of, 76, 126, 181
Walter of Durham, 75
Walter, Hubert, Archbishop of
    Canterbury, 61
Walter of Sudbury: *De Primis Regalibus
    Ornamentis Regni Angliae*, 119
Walter of Wenlock, Abbot of
    Westminster, 82
Walton, Sir William, 467–8
Wamba, Visigothic ruler of Spain, 14
Ware, Richard de, Abbot of Westminster,
    98
Warenne, William de, Earl, 102
Wars of the Roses, 112–13, 133
Warwick, Richard Beauchamp, Earl of,
    122, 154
Webb, Sir Aston, 449
Weelkes, Thomas, 260
Welldon, James, Canon of Westminster,
    478
Wesley, S.S., 467
West, Benjamin, 365
Westminster: as royal enclosure, 50; as
    administrative centre, 76, 194–5;
    Henry III rebuilds, 76, 91; awarded
    city status by Henry VIII, 196; Gothic
    architecture, 194
Westminster Abbey: Edward the
    Confessor builds, 30, 36, 39, 71; as
    coronation setting, 33, 126, 152–4, 194,
    255, 318–19; William the Conqueror
    crowned in, 39–42; Henry III rebuilds,
    42, 71–2, 80, 91; royal associations,
    51–3, 71; cult and shrine of Edward the
    Confessor, 53, 194–5; receives payment
    in goods for coronation, 88; stage and
    thrones, 95–6, 98, 255–6, 319, 322–3;
    Cosmati pavement, 98; Henry V
    chapel, 118; abbot's role, 152;

Westminster Abbey – *cont.*
appearance, 154–8; Henry VII's
chapel, 154; rebuilding under Richard
II and Edward IV, 154–6; processions,
166, 342, 349, 367, 390–1, 394–400, 452,
474; changing status under Tudors,
196–7; at Elizabeth I's coronation,
209–11; internal arrangements,
318–19, 322–9, 343–4, 387–90, 423,
462–3; spectators, 322–3, 384–7; lack
of toilet facilities, 343; donations and
perquisites to, 350, 416; as background
to state portraits of royals, 365;
Gothicisation, 366; earnings from
coronation, 386, 398; refreshments and
catering, 387–8; bells, 410–11; choir
dismantled, 416; and access of mass
media, 432–5; annexe built for
modern coronations, 459–60;
restorations in 19th century, 460, 462;
status raised, 460; electricity installed,
463; Master of Music, 467; *see also*
coronation
Westminster Great Hall: built by
Normans, 50–1; transformed for
coronation, 100, 327; as festival venue,
154–8; processions, 166; as assembly
point for coronation, 329, 499
Westminster Missal *see* Lytlington Missal
Westminster Palace: Henry III rebuilds,
76, 91; as royal residence, 76; destroyed
by fires, 195, 366; replaced as royal
residence by Whitehall Palace, 195;
tapestries, 327; redesigned by Soane,
367
Westminster School: scholars sing *Vivat*,
343, 390–1, 467

Westminster, Statute of (1931), 421, 442
Weston, Hugh, Dean of Westminster, 197
Whigs: and revised coronation oath
(1689), 286–7
Whitehall: development, 195, 197
Whitgift, John, Archbishop of
Canterbury, 244
Wigram, Sir Clive, 472
William I ('the Conqueror'), King of
England: accession and coronation in
Westminster Abbey, 35–43, 59; and lay
investiture of clerics, 45; nominates
successor, 60; and coronation oath,
284; coronation procession, 332
William II ('Rufus'), King of England:
coronation, 43; builds Great Hall at
Westminster, 50; sword, 58; in
succession to throne, 60; injustices, 62;
proclaimed King, 314
William III (of Orange), King of
England, Scotland and Ireland:
accession, 275, 278, 283; declines to
touch, 280, 282; invited to invade, 283;
and revised coronation oath, 289;
makes no state entry into London,
309; coronation, 311, 336, 338;
Protestantism, 311; coronation
sermon, 339–40; music, 343;
coronation costs, 351; and attestation
oath, 357
William IV, King of Great Britain:
patronage of philanthopy, 103, 363;
wishes to abolish coronation, 103,
353–4, 374, 417; public esteem for, 364;
coronation, 366, 372, 374; abolishes
pre-coronation ceremonies, 375–6;
coronation service, 378; economies,

383–4, 387, 400; conduct of
coronation, 408–9; music, 410;
nationwide celebrations, 415
William of Sudbury, 56
Willoughby d'Eresby, Peregrine Bertie,
18th Baron (*later* Marquess of
Lindsey), 375
Wilson, Arthur, 241
Wilson, H.A.: 'The English Coronation
Orders', 470
Winchester: Edward the Confessor
crowned at, 30
Winchester, William Paulet, 1st Marquess
of (1557), 206
Windsor Castle: proposed processional
way to Westminster, 367
Wither, George, 233
Wolsey, Cardinal Thomas: fall, 127, 195
women: enfranchised, 423
Worcester, Edward Somerset, 4th Earl of,
241
Wordsworth, Christopher, 469, 477
Worksop: Manor of, 315, 376
Wren, Sir Christopher, 313, 324, 329, 351,
384, 395
Wright, John Michael, 296
Wriothesley, Sir Thomas, 148
Writhe, John, 146, 163
Wyatt, James, 366, 386

Yevele, Henry, 156
York, archbishops of: forbidden to
perform coronation, 60
York (city): receives Henry VII, 139
York Place, London, 195

Zadok the Priest, 5, 9, 17, 25, 28, 342

The Open Pall.

A

The Second Sword.

N

The Supertunica of Cloath of Gold.
B

The Surcoat of Crimson Sattin.
E

ye Armilla.
C

The Colobium Sindonis.
D

A Buskin.
F

A Sandall.
G

The Sword of Justice to the Spiritualtie, born on the Right hand.

W. Sherwin fe.